# The Diaries of
# GEORGE WASHINGTON

## Volume V

### July 1786–December 1789

D1035161

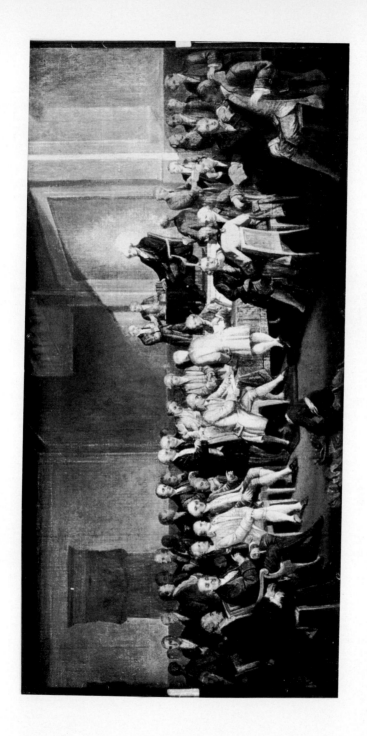

ASSISTANT EDITORS

Beverly H. Runge, Frederick Hall Schmidt,
Philander D. Chase, and Christine Hughes

George H. Reese, CONSULTING EDITOR

Joan Paterson Kerr, PICTURE EDITOR

# THE DIARIES OF
# GEORGE
# WASHINGTON

VOLUME V

July 1786–December 1789

DONALD JACKSON AND DOROTHY TWOHIG

*EDITORS*

UNIVERSITY PRESS OF VIRGINIA

CHARLOTTESVILLE

This edition has been prepared by the staff of
*The Papers of George Washington,*
sponsored by
The Mount Vernon Ladies' Association of the Union
and the University of Virginia
with the support of
the National Endowment for the Humanities
and
the National Historical Publications and Records
Commission.

THE UNIVERSITY PRESS OF VIRGINIA

Copyright © 1979 by the Rector and Visitors
of the University of Virginia

First published 1979

*Frontispiece:* "The Constitutional Convention of 1787" by Thomas Rossiter.
(Independence National Historical Park Collection)

Library of Congress Cataloging in Publication Data  (Revised)

Washington, George, Pres. U.S., 1732–1799.
The diaries of George Washington.

Includes bibliographies and indexes.
1. Washington, George, Pres. U.S., 1732–1799.
2. Presidents—United States—Biography.    I. Jackson,
Donald Dean, 1919–      II. Twohig, Dorothy.    III. Title.
E312.8 1976   973.4'1'0924 [B]   75–41365
ISBN 0–8139–0801–9   (v. 5)

Printed in the United States of America

# Contents

# Illustrations

## Illustrations

# Acknowledgments

The editors wish to take this opportunity to acknowledge several new obligations incurred since the publication of Volume I of *The Diaries of George Washington*. The editors wish to acknowledge in particular the contribution of Jessie Shelar, research assistant on *The Papers of George Washington*, whose services have been of inestimable value in the preparation of these volumes. In addition they are indebted to Jeffrey D. Delahorne and Joanne Schehl, members of the staff of *The Papers of George Washington*, who have performed with distinction countless tasks relating to the preparation of the manuscript for publication, and to John C. Van Horne of *The Papers of Benjamin Latrobe*, who, while a graduate student at the University of Virginia, was of great assistance to the editors in the annotation of the 1769 diary.

# Editorial Procedures and Symbols

Transcription of the diaries has remained as faithful as possible to the original manuscript. Because of the nature of GW's diary entries, absolute consistency in punctuation has been virtually impossible. Where feasible, the punctuation has generally been retained as written. However, in cases where sentences are separated by dashes, a common device in the eighteenth century, the dash has been changed to a period and following word capitalized. Dashes which appear after periods have been dropped. Periods have been inserted at points which are clearly the ends of sentences. In many of the diaries, particularly those dealing with planting and the weather, entries consist of phrases separated by dashes rather than sentences. Generally if the phrase appears to stand alone, a period has been substituted for the dash.

Spelling of all words is retained as it appears in the manuscript. Errors in spelling of geographic locations and proper names have been corrected in notes or in brackets only if the spelling in the text makes the word incomprehensible. Washington occasionally, especially in the diaries, placed above an incorrectly written word a symbol sometimes resembling a tilde, sometimes an infinity sign, to indicate an error in orthography. When this device is used the editors have silently corrected the word.

The ampersand has been retained. The thorn has been transcribed as "th." The symbol for per has been written out. When a tilde is used to indicate either a double letter or missing letters, the correction has been made silently or the word has been transcribed as an abbreviation. Capitalization is retained as it appears in the manuscript; if the writer's intention is not clear, modern usage is followed.

Contractions and abbreviations are retained as written; a period is inserted after abbreviations. When an apostrophe has been used in contractions it is retained. Superscripts have been lowered, and if the word is an abbreviation a period has been added. When the meaning of an abbreviation is not obvious, it has been expanded in square brackets: H[unting] C[reek]; so[uther]ly.

Other editorial insertions or corrections in the text also appear in square brackets. Missing dates are supplied in square brackets in diary entries. Angle brackets ($<$   $>$) are used to indicate mutilated material. If it is clear from the context what word or words are missing, or missing material has been filled in from other sources, the words are inserted between the angle brackets.

A space left blank by Washington in the manuscript of the diaries is indicated by a square bracketed gap in the text. In cases where Washington has crossed out words or phrases, the deletions have not been noted. If a deletion contains substantive material it appears in a footnote. Words inadvertently repeated or repeated at the bottom of a page of manuscript have been dropped.

If the intended location of marginal notations is clear, they have been inserted in the proper place without comment; otherwise, insertions appear in footnotes.

In cases where the date is repeated for several entries on the same day, the repetitive date has been omitted and the succeeding entries have been paragraphed.

Because Washington used the blank pages of the *Virginia Almanack* or occasionally small notebooks to keep his diaries, lack of space sometimes forced him to make entries and memoranda out of order in the volume. The correct position of such entries is often open to question, and the editors have not always agreed with earlier editors of the diaries on this matter. Such divergence of opinion, however, has not been annotated.

Bibliographical references are cited by one or two words, usually the author's last name, in small capitals. If two or more works by authors with the same surname have been used, numbers are assigned: HARRISON [2]. Full publication information is included in the bibliography for each volume. The symbols used to identify repositories in the footnotes precede the bibliography.

Surveying notes and dated memoranda kept in diary form have not been included in this edition of Washington's diaries, although the information contained in them has often been used in annotation.

Individuals and places mentioned for the first time in this volume have been identified in the footnotes; those which have been identified in the first four volumes may be located by consulting the indexes of those volumes. A cumulative index will be included in the last volume of the *Diaries*.

# The Diaries of
# GEORGE WASHINGTON

## Volume V

### July 1786–December 1789

# Visitors and Planting

## July–December 1786

### July 1786

Saturday 1st.    Mercury at 66 in the Morning–72 at Noon and 72 at Night.

Calm all day–cool & pleasant in the Morning–but warm afterwards.

Rid to the Ferry, Dogue run, and Muddy hole Plantations. Finished (about Noon) crossing the cut in which Barrys Houses stand & went to crossing in the one adjoining next the woods. The hoes by this Evening will have got over all the forward Corn. At Muddy hole the Corn was got over with the Hoes this afternoon, but the Plows were not able to accomplish it. Compleated Hoeing Corn in the Neck this afternoon and also plowing it the second time.

Preparing to begin my harvest generally, on Monday, & made the arrangemts. accordingly.

Planted 4 of the Ramnus Tree (an ever green) one on each side of the Garden gates–a peg with 2 Notches drove down by them (Pegs No. 1 being by the Pyramidical Cyprues). Also planted 24 of the Philirea latitolio (an ever green shrub) in the shrubberies by Pegs No. 3 and 48 of the Cytise–a Tree produced in a cold climate of quick growth by pegs No. 4. All these plants were given to me by Mr. Michaux.

Walking into my Orchard grass this evening, I found the seed very ripe, and shedding at a small touch, tho' the stalk and under part appeared quite green (head brown). Immediately set to cutting the heads with reap hooks, with such hands as I could pick up, lest by delaying it till Monday the greater part might be lost.

Doctr. La Moyeur who went from this on Wednesday last to Alexandria returnd this afternoon and Major Gibbes went away after breakfast.

His rhamnus tree is *Rhamnus alaternus,* an evergreen buckthorn. PHILIREA LATITOLIO: *Phillyrea latifolia,* a small shrub native to southern Europe and Asia Minor. CYTISE: *Cytisus anagroides,* golden chain or bean tree.

Sunday 2d.    Mercury at 68 in the Morning 78 at Noon and 76 at Night.

Clear with but little [wind], and that at South; very warm.

About Noon I set out for the intended meeting (to be held to morrow) at the Seneca falls. Dined at Colo. Gilpins, where meeting with Colo. Fitzgerald we proceeded all three of us to Mr. Bryan Fairfax's, and lodged.

Monday 3d.   After a very early breakfast (about Sun rise) we left Mr. Fairfax's, and arriving at the head of the Seneca falls (where a vessel was to have met us) was detained till near ten o'clock before one arrived to put us over to our place of rendezvous at Mr. Goldsboroughs. Met Governor Johnson here; Govr. Lee was prevented by the situation of Mrs. Lee, from attending. A Colo. Francis Deakins, appointed on the part of Maryland, to lay out the road which was to be opened between the Eastern & western waters at the expence of that state & Virginia, also attended, and made a verbal report of his, & Colo. Nevilles surveys to effect this purpose; the result of which was, that they had agreed that the best rout for the said road was from the Mouth of Savage river, through the glades to cheat river, a little below the Dunker bottom; and from thence to the Monongahela (as they conceived the Navigation of Cheat river thro the laurel hill very difficult) below the Tygers valley; distance about 50 Miles. He was of opinion that besides the difficulties in the No. branch between the Mouths of savage & stony rivers that little or nothing would be short[e]ned in the road from the bearing, or trending off, of the North branch between these two places. To these matters however he did not speak with precision, or certainty, as his assistant who had his field notes & Surveys, had not returned.
A heavy shower of rain, a good deal of wind, and much thunder and lightning just abt., and after dark. A house, to appearance about 3 miles off, was consumed by fire, occasioned as was supposed by lightning; but whether it was a dwelling house or Barn we did not hear—nor could we discover to whom it belonged.
The day was very warm, and with out wind, till the gust arose.

OUR PLACE OF RENDEZVOUS: On the following day James Rumsey paid Monica Goldsborough "nine Shillings Virginia currency in full for nine breakfasts and dinners for both at the meeting of the President & directors" of the Potomac Company (*American Clipper*, 2 [Dec. 1935], 191).
Francis Deakins (1739–1804), Montgomery County, Md., surveyor and land speculator, was the eldest son of William Deakins, Sr., and Tabitha Marbury Hoye Deakins of Prince George's County. He had served for several years in the Maryland state militia during the Revolution, attaining the rank of lieutenant colonel.

Tuesday 4th.   The Directors determined to prosecute their first plan for opening the Navigation of the River in the bed of it, &

as streight as it was practicable, and ordered the Manager to proceed accordingly; & to remove the hands from the works at the
great falls to the Seneca & other parts of the river—as it was their
wish, having but 3 years from the commencemt. of the Act to perfect the Navigation above the falls. Mr. Rumsey having signified
his disinclination to serve the Company any longer for the pay and
emoluments which had been allowed him, and the Directors not
inclining to encrease them, they parted and Mr. Stuart (the first
assistant) was appointed in his place. Mr. Smith the other assistant
had his wages raised to £200 Maryld. Curry. pr. Ann.

These matters being settled, Govr. Johnson returned home.
Colo. Fitzgerald proceeded on to Berkeley & Frederick, and Colo.
Gilpin and myself resolved to send our horses to the Great falls
and go by water to that place ourselves; and were happy to find
that the passage on the Virginia side of *all* the Islands, was vastly
the best; and might be made easy and good at little expence—
There being in short only 3 places where there was any difficulty,
& these not great. Shallow water in a low state of the river, is all
that is to be feared.

After dining with Mr. Rumsey at the Great falls Colo. Gilpin
and myself set out in order to reach our respective homes, but a
gust of wind & rain, with much lightning, compelled me to take
shelter, about dark at his house, where I was detained all night.

This day was also exceedingly warm, there being but little
wind.

OPENING: In MS this reads "openting."
     Mr. Smith is James Smith (*Va. Journal,* 4 Dec. 1788).

Wednesday 5th.     I set out about sun rising, & taking my harvest
fields at Muddy hole & the ferry in my way, got home to breakfast.

Found that my harvest had commenced as I directed, at Muddy
hole & in the Neck on Monday last—with 6 Cradlers at the first—
to wit, Isaac, Cowper Tom, Ben overseer Will, Adam, & Dogue
run Jack who tho' newly entered, made a very good hand; and
gave hopes of being an excellent Cradler. That Joe (Postilian)
had taken the place of Sambo at the Ferry since Monday last, &
the harvest there proceeded under the cutting of Caesar, Boatswain, & him. That in the Neck 6 cradles were constantly employed, & sometimes 7—viz. James, (who having cut himself in the
meadow could not work constantly) —Davy, Overseer who having
other matters to attend to, could not stick to it; Sambo, Essex,
George (black smith) Will, Ned; and Tom Davis who had never
cut before, and made rather an awkward hand of it. Tom Nokes
was also there, but he cut only now & then, at other times shock-

ing, repairing rakes &ca. That the gangs at Dogue Run & Muddy hole were united, & were assisted by Anthony, Myrtilla & Dolshy from the home house—That besides Tom Davis Ben from the Mill had gone into the Neck and that Sall brass (when not washing) & Majr. Washingtons Tom were assisting the ferry people— That Cowpers Jack & Da[v]y with some small boys & girls (wch. had never been taken out before) were assisting the Farmer in making Hay after two white men who had been hired to cut grass. And found that the State of the Mercury in the thermometer had, during my absence, been as follow—viz.

|              | Morng. | Noon | Night |
|--------------|--------|------|-------|
| Sunday 2d.   | 68     | 78   | 76    |
| Monday 3d.   | 72     | 79   | 79    |
| Tuesday 4    | 78     | 81   | 81    |
| Wednesdy. 5  | 78     | 75   | 72    |

This day (Wednesday) clouded about Noon and before dinner began to rain, tho not much & rained again at, and in the Night but not a great deal.

The slaves named here can all be found in the entry for 18 Feb. 1786 of the *Diaries*. They were often shifted temporarily from one farm to another for special tasks. THE FARMER: James Bloxham.

Thursday 6th.    Mercury at 71 in the Morning—77 at Noon and 76 at N.
Morning hazy, with thunder & rain in the afternoon.
Rid to Muddy hole and into the Neck; found that the Rye at the first had been cut down yesterday and that the wheat was entered upon and that the grain being wet this Morning, it could not either be shocked, or bound. The rakers were therefore employed in succouring the drilled Corn at Muddy hole. The Rye at the Ferry was also cut down yesterday about dinner time. The plows at this place 3 in number having finished crossing the Corn on the hill had begun to cross that cut below, adjoining the drilled Corn. In the Neck, after the Plows had finished crossing the river cut, in the great field, 6 plows went into the drilled Corn (on Tuesday) and were running a single furrow on each side of it, the Peas, Potatoes, & Cabbage by way of giving them a hill.

Friday 7th.    Mercury at 72 in the Morning—80 at Noon and 75 at Night.
Clear in the forenoon but very sultry, with wind, thunder, lightning & rain in the afternoon. Rid to all the Plantations; The

Plows at Muddy hole (where 3 were at work) had finished the East cut of Corn, and had begun to plow that cut by the bars, adjoining the drilled Corn the 3d. time. Those at Morris's, four in number, had got about half over the Eastermost cut, next the overseers House and the Farmer was stacking the grass which had been in cocks some time in the meadow adjoining it.

Brought in the remainder of the clover Hay, & seed at Muddy [hole] to the stack at the barn there.

Washington Custis being sick I sent for Doctr. Craik to visit him, and a sick child in the Neck. He arrived before dinner, & after going into the Neck & returning, stayed all night.

Mr. Shaw went up to Alexandria to day on my business in the waggon also to bring sundries down.

Saturday 8th.   Mercury at 74 in the Morning—78 at Noon and 77 at Night.

Clear & warm, with very little Wind till about 2 oclock, when a black & extensive cloud arose to the westward out of which much wind issued with considerable thunder & lightning and a smart shower of Rain.

Rid to the Ferry, Muddy hole & Neck Plantations. Finished cutting the Rye about noon at the latter, and set into the wheat adjoining, immediately after. Should have finished cutting & securing in shocks the wheat at Muddy hole this afternoon had it not been for the interruption given by the rain.

The Rye at all the Plantations had been much beat down & tangled previous to the cutting any of it, and much loss will be sustained from this cause in addition to the defection in the head; but neither this grain nor the wheat have been so much layed by the late winds & rains, as might have been expected. Of the latter indeed, tho much was threatned, not a great deal fell.

Sunday 9th.   Mercury at 76 in the Morning 79 at Noon and 78 at Night.

Clear, calm & warm all day. Doctr. Stuart, Mrs. Stuart, and Betcy & Patcy Custis came here to breakfast and Doctr. Craik to dinner—the last of whom went away in the evening.

Monday 10th.   Mercury at [      ] in the Morning—82 at Noon and 82 at Night.

Very warm all day, and calm till the evening, when a breeze from the Southward sprung up. More appearances of rain in the morning than the evening, but none fell.

Rid to the Neck, Muddy hole & Dogue Plantations. Began harvest at the latter this morning with the people belonging to the place; the Muddy hole hands finished theres by breakfast, after wch. (about half after eleven) the two gangs united again. In the Neck the Plows on Saturday finished running the furrows on each side the drilled Corn, by way of hilling it; and to day began to break, or plow the intermediate spaces.

John Knowles, who was absent all last week came here to work again this Morning in good Season.

Doctr. Stuart, Mrs. Stuart & the two girls Betcy & Patcy Custis returned after breakfast.

John Knowles came to work for GW as a common laborer in May 1786 for £5 a month and a daily pint of rum (see entry for 18 May 1786). In 1789 GW contracted with him for one year to be a bricklayer and his wife, Rachael, to be a household servant. In return they were to receive £30, a house, and a garden spot (articles of agreement between Knowles and GW, 7 July 1789, DLC:GW).

Tuesday 11th.    Mercury at 77 in the Morning—83 at Noon and 82 at Night.

Clear, with the wind at So. Wt. and pretty fresh.

Rid to the Ferry, Dogue run, & Muddy hole Plantations and to the Mill. At the first, the Plows had just finished plowing the drilled Corn & Potatoes by the Fish House—at the second got into stacks all the wheat in the Meadow by the Overseers House.

Finished cutting the remainder of the wheat in the great Field in the Neck on the Creek.

Doctr. Craik came here to breakfast and returned after it to Alexandria.

Wednesday 12th.    Mercury at 79 in the Morning—[    ] at Noon and [    ] at Night.

Wind pretty fresh from the So. West all day. About Noon a cloud arose in the west, from whence proceeded a shower of rain and severe lightning and loud thunder.

Visited all my Plantations and the Mill to day. Finished the wheat harvest at the Ferry about Noon. Gave the People employed in it the remainder of the day for them selves, but ordered Boatswain & Joe (cradlers) and the hands from the home House to go into the Neck tomorrow and the other Cradler (Caesar) with 2 or 3 rakers to go to Dogue run (being most convenient) having before ordered Isaac, & Cooper Tom (cradlers) — the house people and 3 rakers from Muddy hole gang, to go into the Neck to

morrow morning, supposing the People belonging to the Plantation, with the aid above mentioned, would be able to compleat
the Harvest at Dogue run in the course of tomorrow.

On my return home found Mr. Man Page of Mansfield Mr.
Frans. Corbin, and Doctr. Stuart here. And after Dinner Mr.
Lawe. Washington & his son Lawe, came in. Doctr. Stuart re-
turned in the evening.

Perceived as I rode thro my drilled corn at Muddy hole to day,
that the alternate rows of early corn was Tassling and shooting.

MAN PAGE: Mann Page, Jr. (c.1749–1803), of Mannsfield, near Fredericksburg
in Spotsylvania County, was the eldest son of Mann Page (c.1718–1781), of
Rosewell, Gloucester County, and his second wife, Anne Corbin Tayloe, the
daughter of John Tayloe (1687–1747) and Elizabeth Gwyn (Gwynn,
Gwynne) Lyde Tayloe of Mount Airy, Richmond County (PAGE, 61, 63;
MEADE [1], 2:181). Mann Page, Jr., was a member of the House of Burgesses
in 1775, the Continental Congress in 1777, and a lieutenant colonel with
the Spotsylvania militia during the Revolution (CROZIER [2], 35, 523). In
1776 he married his cousin Mary Tayloe (b. 1759), daughter of John Tayloe
II (1721–1779) and Rebecca Plater Tayloe of Mount Airy (PAGE, 73).

Francis Corbin (1759–1821), of Middlesex and Caroline counties, was a
cousin of Mann Page, Jr., and a son of Richard and Elizabeth Tayloe Corbin
of Laneville, King and Queen County. He went to England in 1773 where
he attended the Canterbury School and Cambridge University, and entered
the Inner Temple in Jan. 1777. At the close of the Revolution, he returned
to Virginia. He represented Middlesex County in the House of Delegates
from 1784 to 1794. A staunch supporter of the Constitution, Corbin was an
influential member of the Virginia Ratifying Convention of 1788 (*Va. Mag.,*
29 [1921], 522, 30 [1922], 315–16; NEILL, 137n).

Thursday 13th.   Mercury at 72 in the Morning–[    ] at Noon
and [    ] at Night.
   Cloudy all day, with the Wind pretty fresh from the Eastward.
   Finished the wheat harvest at Dogue run about Sundown.
   Doctr. Craik came here to Dinner & returned afterwards.
   In the Night there fell rain.

Friday 14th.   Mercury at [    ] in the Morning–[    ] at Noon
and [    ] at Night.
   Cloudy more or less all day, with the wind pretty fresh from the
So. West.
   After Breakfast I rid to all my Plantations. Found the Plows in
the Neck after compleatly, that is, after having broke the ground
between the furrows that had been run on each side the Corn for
the purpose of hilling it, had got into the Middle cut to do the
like there, in the Drilled corn. Perceived the Irish Potatoes were

coming into blossom at this place and that after the rain on Wednesday, whilst the wheat was too wet to bind, the harvest People had pulled a little of the flax at this place also. The Plows at Dogue run finished plowing the Cut they were in next the overseers House, & had begun to plow the drilled corn, on the East side of the field; leaving every other row untouched & turning the mould from the corn in these rows; by wch. the middle between the rows where the cabbages, Potatoes, Peas &ca. grow would be ridged—intending these ridges to be reduced at the last Plowing, & the rows of corn to form them. At the same place the hands had begun to hoe corn in the cut including Barrys houses, beginning next Wades old dwelling. Some of the People belonging to this plantation had come to Muddy hole for Rye, which they were threshing there for their horses. Muddy hole [people] were hoeing a small corner of Corn which was not finished before Harvest. At the ferry the Plows finished about two oclock crossing the cut on the flat, and would begin to plow the drilled wht. by the Mea[do]w. The rest of the People were preparing a yard to tread out wheat.

After breakfast Mr. Page & Mr. Corbin, accompanied by Majr. Washington, went up to Abingdon (taking Alexandria in their way) and before breakfast Mr. Lawe. Washington & his son went up by water to the latter place—they all returned again in the Evening, when a Mr. Hatfield of England came in.

MR. HATFIELD OF ENGLAND: probably either Joseph Hadfield, merchant of Manchester, Eng., who had visited Mount Vernon in 1785, or one of the other partners in the family firm. By 1788 Joseph Hadfield was established temporarily in Baltimore. He was a partner in the "house of John Hadfield Thomas Hadfield and Joseph Hadfield" (Fairfax County Deeds, Book R, 239, Vi Microfilm).

Saturday 15th.    Mercury at 77 in the Morning—85 at Noon and 83 at Night.

Clear, calm, and very warm all day.

After breakfast the Company all going away, I rid to all the Plantations except that at the Ferry. Compleated my wheat harvest in the Neck about Noon—which made a finish of the whole; after wch. I directed my people, engaged therein, to pull flax till dinner, & take the remainder of the day to themselves. Much Wheat has been left in all the fields this year occasioned 1st. by the frequent rains and winds which preceeded, and happened during harvest (which had laid down and tangled it in some degree) — 2d. by beginning my harvest too late and 3d. by the manner of cutting and gathering it into shocks. It is unlucky, that from several causes, I was prevented trying by experiment, this year, how early wheat or Rye might be cut without injury to the grain; but satisfied I am that, this may be done with safety as soon as it is out of its milky state—at any rate, that the loss by shrinkage in the beginning of a harvest from this cause, is not equal to the loss by shattering at the latter end of it or to the hazard of its being entangled, or laid down by winds and rain, which every year is the case in a greater, or lesser degree when harvest is long, & the grain ripe. For these reasons the following method may, I think, be attempted with success in future; and it will be found that many advantages will flow from it.

    1st. To make every Plantation, or farm, take care of its own grain witht. uniting their hands.

    2d. To encrease the number of cradlers at each; to such a number *only,* as will give two rakers to each, and leave a sufficiency besides to gather, and put the wheat into shocks and, generally speaking, with Negro labourers, the following distribution may be found to come as near the mark in wheat made in corn ground, as any—viz.—for every two Cradlers to allow 4 rakers, 1 Shocker, and two carriers—for the last of which boys and girls are competent.

    3d. To give the Cradlers a start of two days of the rakers & shockers; letting them begin to cut as soon as the milk leaves the grain, and before it becomes hard & flinty—leaving the grain this time in the swarth, for the straw to cure, before it is raked, bound & put into shocks.

    4th. To order, & see that the Cradlers cut slow, & lay their grain regular & well; after it is cut low & clean; which will be found more advantages than to hurry over the gr[oun]d in order to put an end to harvest, as is usual. By beginning early time will be allowed for these, especially as wheat cut in this state yields much easier, and pleasanter to the stroke, & can be laid much better than when the straw gets dry & harsh.

    5th. By giving this start to the cradlers, the straw (as hath been observed before) will be sufficiently cured to bind and shock and it must be seen that the Rakers also do their work clean and well, which is more likely to be the case without particular attention, than when one half their time they are scampering after the cutters to keep up; and the other half are standing whilst the cradlers are whetting their Scythes, drinking, or talking.

    6th. Each raker must take a swarth & not two go in one that the authors of bad work may be more easily detected. By this mode of proceeding the raking & binding will be done with more ease, regularity and dispatch, because it becomes a sober settled work—there being no pretext for hurrying at one time, and standing at another—but

7th. By this means, I am persuaded that the number of rakers which usually follow cradlers, would, by the middle of harvest, or by the time the grain is in condition to shock as it comes from the Cradle be fully up with them and then might go on together if it should be conceived best.

Admitting that the grain can be cut with safety as soon as it comes out of the Milky state, the advantages here described, added to the superior quality of the straw for fodder, and indeed for every other purpose, greatly over ballances any inconveniencies which may result from the practice, & which must lay chiefly, if not wholly, in these: 1st. The hazard of a heavy beating rain, which may settle the swarth among the stubble so as to make it bad to rake, & difficult perhaps to get up clean and 2d. lighter rains and Dews which may interrupt the binding, the straw not drying so soon in swarth as it does standing—nor can it be meddled with so early in the morning generally—But as neither rain nor dews will hurt the grain (on the contrary, will make it thresh easier, and do very little injury to the straw) and as there is allways work enough on the Plantations to employ the hands in (such as succouring & hoeing of Corn, pulling flax, weeding of vines, Pease, &ca. &ca.) supposing the interruptions above mentioned to happen no labour need be lost because as each harvest will be managed by the hands belonging to the farm or Plantation they can without inconvenience (having their tools always at hand) shift from one kind of work to another without preparation or fitting themselves for it.

Sunday 16th.    Mercury at 78 in the Morning—86 at Noon and 84 at Night.

Very little wind at any time in the day but very hot.

Doctr. Craik came here in the forenoon—dined, and returned afterwards.

Monday 17th.    Mercury at 78 in the Morning—85 at Noon and 79 at Night.

Exceedingly warm all day with but little wind. Afternoon a cloud arose out of which we had only a sprinkling of Rain—the body of the cloud passing above, i.e. to the Northward of this place.

Rid to the Plantations in the Neck—Muddy hole, Dogue run & Ferry. At the first began to cut the ripest of the Oats, but thinking them in general too green quitted after breakfast and set all hands to pulling flax the doing of which was compleated about Sun down. At Muddy hole the People were employed in clearing a yard to tread wheat in, and in getting in wheat & Rye. Of the latter 6 Shocks (got in by the Dogue run hands) yielded 11½ bushels of clean Rye and 4 other Shocks brought in by the hands of the Plantation & threshed by them 5 Bl. of clean rye was produced. Dogue run people cut their Oats in the upper meadow and the Ferry were employed as yesterday about their Wheat.

Tuesday 18th.     Mercury at 77 in the Morning—87 at Noon and 84 at Night.

A heavy forenoon with much appearances of rain but none fell —very hot afterwards when the sun at intervals came out—a breeze from the So. West all day.

Rid to all the Plantations, except that at the Ferry. Began to cut the Meadow at the Neck plantation to day and to clean & prepare the yard for treading wheat there. Finished hilling with the Plows, all the Corn at Muddy hole which was planted in the usual way & ordered the plows to turn the ground in the drilled corn, designed for Turnips, & to plow it deep & well. Dogue run people (in part) cleaning & preparing their wheat yard and getting the Oats to it. Finished a Hay rick at the House which contained all the Hay that was made at the upper Meadow at Dogue run and all that came off the Ferry Meadow.

Wednesday 19th.     Mercury at 82 in the morning—89 at Noon and 81 at Night.

Clear until about 2 Oclock when a cloud arose to the Westward out of which proceeded a powerful rain.

Rid to all the Plantations to day. At that in the Neck, the Scythemen having cut (yesterday) the upper part of the Meadow, & to the cross fence; returned to the Oat field to day at the old orchard point, which they cut down; but did not shock, the straw being too green for it. At the same place, the Plows finished the middle cut of the drilled corn, & plowed, in the same cut, the intervals between the corn rows which were designed for Turnips. The Plows at Muddy hole began yesterday afternoon to give the middle cut (next to, & adjoining, the drilled corn) another plowing from the road to the woods back. 4 other shocks of rye at this place from another part of the field, yielded about the same quantity of clean grain that the first did—viz.—five bushels; from which, their being 177 shocks in the field, it may be computed that not more than 220 or 225 will be obtained.

On my return home I found Mr. Calvert of Maryland and his son, Colo. Bland, Mr. Geo. Digges, Mr. Foster & Lund Washington here—all of whom dined. The 3 first stayed the evening the other three returned.

MR. CALVERT OF MARYLAND AND HIS SON: The son accompanying Benedict Calvert to Mount Vernon is probably one of his two eldest boys, Edward Henry Calvert (1766–1846) or George Calvert (1768–1838).

Theodorick Bland (1742–1790), of Prince George County, was the son of Theodorick and Frances Bolling Bland of Cawsons on the Appomattox River. After receiving a M.D. degree at the University of Edinburgh in 1763, Bland returned to Virginia to practice medicine. He served as a colonel in the Continental Army 1776–79, and as a delegate to the Continental Congress 1780–83. In 1786 he was elected to the Virginia House of Delegates where he served until 1788.

Ralph Foster (Forster) was George Digges's brother-in-law. His wife, Theresa (Tracy) Digges Foster (Forster), had died in Oct. 1784 (*Va. Journal*, 14 Oct. 1784).

Thursday 20th.    Mercury at 78 in the Morning—86 at Noon and 80 at Night.

Very warm all day—about 4 Oclock a Cloud arose out of which proceeded a shower of rain—after which it cleared, but towards sun down it overcast, and rained moderately for several hours.

Before the rain the Flax in the Neck was thrown into shocks as was part of the oats. Another part was set on end (as much as could be of it) and the third part was caught on the ground in the sheaf by the rain.

Finished cutting the Meadow in the Neck this afternoon; & had begun to plow the ground designed for Turnips there, but the Rain put a stop to it. The plows then went into the Corn adjoining thereto in the cut next the Barn.

Mr. Calvert & Son was prevented recrossing the river this afternoon by the rain.

Friday 21st.    Mercury at 76 in the Morning—80 at Noon—and 80 at Night.

A little cloudy in the Morning but clear afterwards and not so warm as it had been.

Mr. Calvert & Son went away very early in the Morning. After breakfast Colo. Bland and my self road to my Plantations at Muddy hole and in the Neck. At the first found the grd. was too wet for Plowing and that 4 other shocks of rye from another part of the field had been threshed, which yielded rather better than 7½ bushels of clean grain. At the other I examined the shocks of Flax wch. seemed to be tolerably dry, & in good order—but I directed the Overseer to keep an attentive watch upon them, and the Oats; & open & dry them if they appeared to need it; and to get both as soon as he could to the Barn.

Having finished cutting the meadows in the Neck, the farmer & two or three hands remained there to make the Hay, whilst Six cutters came over & cut down the orchard grass at the House which had been stripped of the head (for the seed) on or about the first instant. It may be remarked of this grass, and it adds to the value of it, that it does not turn brown at the bottom, after it heads, nor does the stubble appear dry when it is cut, as that of Timothy. Consequently the aftermath is more valuable, and the Second growth quicker. Whether this effect is natural to the grass, or has been produced by having had the seed taken from it, is not *altogether* certain, but the first is much more probable; because Timothy would, before it should have approached the same state of maturity, have been quite brown & rusty at bottom, which was not the case with the Orchd. Grass when the seed was taken from it, nor at any time since and is an evidence that it will wait longer after it is fit for the Scythe than timothy without injury. It also appeared by some that had been mixed with, and grown near to the clover wch. was cut about the 7th. or 8th. of June that it vegetates much quicker after cutting, that [than] Timothy does.

Saturday 22d.    Mercury at 74 in the Morning—82 at Noon and 80 at Night.

Clear all day with the Wind at South, but not very fresh.

An Overseer of mine (at the ferry) informed me that the chintz bug was discovered in his Corn and that he apprehended if the weather should turn dry, they would encrease, and destroy it. He also informed me that the fly was discovered about the shocks of wheat in his field.

At home all day with Colo. Bland.

OVERSEER OF MINE: Hezekiah Fairfax.

CHINTZ BUG: GW had discovered the chinch bug in his corn the previous year (see 15 Aug. 1785). The Hessian fly (*Phytophaga destructor*), the larvae of which sucked the juices from green wheat and ate the leaves, was a more serious problem. This fly, which first appeared on Long Island, was called the Hessian fly in the mistaken belief that Hessian soldiers had brought it to this continent. In some areas, wheat had been abandoned

that to be at Dogue run yesterday. The rows of Corn wch. were intermixed with Irish Potatoes, along the fence wch. divides the wheat field (or stubble) from it were perceived to be much better, & more uniform than any other part of the field, but whether it has been occasioned by dunging, or otherwise, I could get no distinct acct. Some of the Negros ascribed it to this cause & it is more probable than that the Potatoes should have been the cause of it. Sowed about five acres of Turnips in br[oa]d cast, in the Neck in that grd. which originally was prepared for the Saintfoin & other Seeds. These seeds were sowed after a plowing which the ground had just received, and were harrowed in with a heavy harrow which raked the grass very much into heaps (the ground tho' frequently plowed before, having got very grassy). Two hands at this place began yesterday to cut the drilled Oats, which they would about accomplish to morrow. This Oats (24 rows) I ordered to be secured & threshed by itself. 5 plows only were at work here the Waggon & two Ox Carts being employed in getting in the grain. All hands except those at plow were engaged in this business, in stacking the wheat, and threshing of Rye. At Muddy hole, except the three people at the Plows, and those employed in drawing in & stacking the Wheat at the Barn, all hands had begun to weed the drilled corn and the Plants between the rows. The Oats at this place had been cut two or 3 days, & the Wheat would be all drawn in & stacked to day. The Dogue run people did not finish the cut they were in yesterday till noon this day when they entered the one adjoining. The Ferry People wd. nearly get the wheat at that Plantation into Stack to day.

Doctr. Craik was sent for to visit Carpenter James & Cowper Jack. He also prescribed for a Child Nat, over the Creek who was brought here.

Wednesday 26th.    Mercury at 70 in the Morning—at Noon 80 and 80 at Night. Calm, Clear & pleasant all day.

Mr. Herbert, Colo. Ramsay, Colo. Allison and Mr. Hunter dined here and returned in the afternoon.

One Edwd. Moystan who formerly lived with Mr. Robt. Morris as a Steward, & now keeps the City Tavern in Philadelphia came here to consult me on the Propriety of his taking the Coffee Ho[use] in Alexandria, i.e., on the prospect of its answering his purposes for keeping Tavern.

Having fixed a roller to the tale of my drill plow, and a bush harrow between it & the barrel, I sent it by G. A. Washington to Muddy hole and had the intervals betwn. the corn which had been left for the purpose sowed with Turnips in drills and with which it was done very well.

The coffeehouse in Alexandria apparently did not answer Moyston's purposes, for he was still in Philadelphia in April 1787 when he wrote GW to urge that he and his acquaintances stay in his City Tavern in Philadelphia while attending the Constitutional Convention (Edward Moyston to GW, 4 April 1787, DLC:GW). Moyston had become the proprietor of the City Tavern in Philadelphia on Second Street above Walnut in 1779 (*Pa. Mag.,* 46 [1922], 75, n.162). The Alexandria Inn and Coffeehouse, which had been managed by Henry Lyles until his death in April 1786, was being advertised for rent in the summer of 1786 (*Va. Journal,* 27 July 1786).

**Thursday 27th.**    Mercury at 74 in the morning—84 at Noon and 80 at Night.

Clear in the forenoon and pretty warm—Cloudy afterwards with great appearances of a settled rain little of which fell. What did was chiefly light and more a mist making little impression in the Earth.

Rid to Muddy hole, Dogue run & Ferry Plantations, and to the Mill. Found the Wheat all got in and stacked at the first and last mentioned places and that the Plows had finished plowing the drilled corn on thursday evening last and were plowing the Cut on the Hill. The rest of the hands at this place, & cart were employed in getting in Rye. The drilled Oats between the corn at Muddy hole, being threshed & cleaned measured 18 bushls.

In the evening Mr. Thos. Fairfax (son of Bryan Fairfax Esqr. now Parson) came in and stayed all Night.

Thomas Fairfax (1762–1846), the eldest son of Bryan and Elizabeth Cary Fairfax, had returned recently from England where he had visited his uncle and aunt George William and Sarah Cary Fairfax at Bath. Bryan Fairfax was ordained a deacon in 1786 (KILMER, 39, 43).

**Friday 28th.**    Mercury at 75 in the Morning—74 at Noon and 72 at Night.

Day very lowering & some times light Rains or Mists, but not to wet the ground. Wind at No. Et.

Mr. Fairfax went away after breakfast.

At home all day.

**Saturday 29th.**    Mercury at 68 in the morning—74 at Noon and 71 at Night.

Wind Northwardly and pleasant—The Morning cloudy, but clear about Noon, and a little warm. Accompanied by Colo. Humphrys I rid to Muddy hole & Neck Plantations. The Drilled oats at the latter, between the Corn, being threshed out & cleaned, measured 54 B.—There being 24 Rows of these, each (allowing for the divisions between the Cuts and the bouting rows at the ends) about 1075 yards long amounts to 25,800 yards running measure—or 160 yds. sqr. which is better than 5¼ acres. The quantity to the Acre therefore, cannot exceed 10 Bushels, which is less, it is presumed, than the same kind of Land would have produced in broadcast. It is to be remarked however that the abundant wet which had fallen from the middle of May, or thereabouts, till Harvest had in most of the low places destroyed the grain either wholly, or in part—by which the quantity growing was reduced but this would also have happened in any square piece of ground as there is scarce any that is not subject to the same accident.

Sunday 30th.    Mercury at 67 in the Morning—78 at Noon and 70 at Night.

Morning a little cloudy, the day upon the whole cool & pleasant with the wind at East.

Monday 31st.    Mercury at 67 in the Morning—73 at Noon and 70 at Night.

Morning lowering, with small sprinklings of rain, but too light to wet any thing. About one Oclock it cleared—Wind pretty fresh from the No. East & clear afterwards.

Mr. Willm. Craik who came here to dinner, afterwards went away for Alexandria on his journey to Hampshire [County].

Accompanied by Colo. Humphreys, rid to the Plantations at the Ferry and Dogue run. At the first, the plowing of the cut upon the hill was finished and the plows in the drilled corn by the fish house. The Hoes were at work in the other drilled corn. At Dogue run the Hoes had just finished the Cut they had been in; and the Plows the drilled corn; into which the Hoes had entered on the East side next the Swamp. The Plows would now cease till the Horses could be a little refreshed & get out wheat for sowing.

# August 1786

Tuesday 1st.    Mercury at 67 in the Morning—69 at Noon and 66 at Night.

Morning heavy & sometimes mizzling but clear afterwards, till Night when the clouds assembled and rained the whole Night, sometimes very fast—Wind at East.

Two of Samuel Washington's children, possibly Harriot and her brother, Lawrence Augustine. (Dumbarton House)

Mrs. Fendall, Harriot Washington, and Lucy Lee (a child) — Colo. Fitzgerald, Colo. Simms, Captn. Conway, Messrs. Saml. and Thos. Hanson & Mr. Charles Lee came here to dinner—all of whom, except the 3 first named, went away after it.

Harriot Washington (1776–1822), the daughter of Samuel and Anne Steptoe Washington, was GW's niece.

Lucy Grymes Lee (1786–1860) was an infant, the third child of Henry and Matilda Lee. When Henry Lee went to New York as a delegate to the Continental Congress and took his wife and two older children north with him, it was thought best, because of Mrs. Lee's poor health, to leave the baby in Alexandria in the care of her grandmother, Elizabeth Steptoe Lee Fendall.

Wednesday 2d.    Mercury at 65 in the Morning—70 at Noon and 70 at N.

Much rain had fallen in the Night. The day was variable, but generally cloudy with fine rain about 10 or 11 Oclock which lasted more than an hour—after which the Sun came out but for a short duration.

Rid to Muddy hole, but proceeded no further as, at the time I was there the appearances of a wet day were greatest.

Thursday 3d.    Mercury at 72 in the Morning—75 at Noon and 76 at Night.

A good deal of rain fell last Night. The day for the most part was cloudy and Warm, altho' the wind blew pretty fresh from the East. In the afternoon there was again the appearance of much rain but none fell here.

Rid to the Plantations at the Ferry, Dogue run, and Muddy hole. At the first fd. the drilled corn had been wed with the Hoes and the People were cleansing the Meadow ditches & that the Plows had done with the Corn till seeding with wheat. I set them to plowing that part of the New Ground which had been gone over with the Colter plow with a view of sowing Turnips therein.

Turned the two old draft Oxen at Home house, one of the old cows from ditto, and [      ] steers & cows from Dogue run into the Meadows at that place. At the same time put my Rams into the same place & 25 ewe Lambs on the Clover at Muddy hole where I ordered the work horses to be put.

My Overseer returned from a Mr. Reynolds in Calvert Cty. Maryland with 1 Ram & 15 ewe Lambs of the English breed of sheep wch. I ordered to be turned into the same place.

In the Evening Richd. Sprig Esqr. of Annapolis & another Mr. Sprig came in and stayed all night.

MY OVERSEER: John Fairfax.
During GW's long absence from his farm during the war, his flock of sheep was greatly diminished. In May 1786 GW wrote William Fitzhugh, Jr., to say that if any of his neighbors raised lambs for sale he would "gladly buy one or two hundred Ewe lambs, and allow a good price for them" (15 May 1786, MdBJ). Such a large number of ewe lambs proved not to be available, but Fitzhugh's fellow Calvert County, Md., resident, Edward Reynolds, said he could spare 15 or 20 ewes at $2.00 each. GW agreed to buy these (Fitzhugh to GW, 26 May 1786, and GW to Fitzhugh, 5 June 1786, DLC:GW).

Friday 4th.     Mercury at 72 in the Morning—77 at Noon and 74 at Night.

The appearances of rain yesterday afternoon fell very heavily about Ravensworth and that part of the County occasioning greater freshes in Accatinck, Pohick & Hunting C[ree]k than had been known for many years & it is thought a good deal of damage to the Crops of Corn & other grain on the grd.

Rid to the Plantations in the Neck, Muddy hole and Dogue run and dined afterwards at Mr. Lund Washingtons with Mrs. Washington Colo. Humphreys & Mrs. Fendal, and Major Washington (who had first been to Alexa. on business) and his wife. Some showers this Aftern.

At the Neck plantation the Plows had, on Monday last finished plowing the drilled corn East cut and would this day have compleated all the other corn except the cut on the River in wch. wheat will be first sowed.

George Washington, John Fitzgerald, and George Gilpin, as officers of the Potomac Company, approved this receipted bill for supplies at the 5 August 1786 meeting. (Mount Vernon Ladies' Association of the Union)

Saturday 5th.    Mercury at 71 in the Morning—at Noon 79 and 79 at Night.

Clear and very warm all day. Went to Alexandria to a meeting of the Directors of the Potomac Compa. in order to prepare the Accts., and a Report for the Genl. Meeting of the Co. on Monday next. Neither of the Maryland Gentn. attended. Dined at Wises Tavn.

Finished weeding the drilled Corn at Muddy hole this day.

MARYLAND GENTN: Thomas Johnson, Jr., and Thomas Sim Lee, the two Maryland directors of the Potomac Company.

John Wise's tavern on Royal Street in Alexandria was used frequently by groups as a meeting place. GW attended a number of annual general meetings of the Potomac Company here.

Sunday 6th.    Mercury at 75 in the Morng.—84 at Noon and 79 at Night.

Clear and tolerably pleasant.

At home all day without company.

Monday 7th.    Mercury at 72 in the Morning—78 at Noon and 77 at Night.

Went to Alexandria to the Genl. Meeting of the Potomack Co. Colo. Humphreys accompanied me. A sufficient number of shares being present to constitute the Meeting the Accts. of the Directors were exhibited and a Genl. report made but for want of the Secretarys Books which were locked up, and he absent the Orders and other proceedings referred to in that report could not be exhibited.

SECRETARYS BOOKS: The secretary was John Potts, Jr.

Tuesday 8th.    Mercury at 72 in the Morning—79 at Noon and 75 at Night.

Wind Southerly and day warm, especially the forepart of it. In the Evening there were appearances of a settled rain, enough of which fell to make the eves of the House run but it was of short continuance.

Rid by Muddy hole Plantation to my meadow in the Mill swamp; and leveled from the old dam, just below Wades Houses, to the head of the Old race by the stooping red oak; stepping 27½ yds. or as near as I could judge 5 Rods between each stake, which are drove in as follows. 1 at the Water edge where I begun, and levl. with the Surface thereof; two in the old race (appearances of which still remain) and a fourth by a parcel of small

Persimon bushes after having just passed the Bars leading into the Meadows. The others at the distance above mentioned from each other to the stooping red oak.

| No. | | | feet | I. | qrs. | | feet | I. | qrs. |
|---|---|---|---|---|---|---|---|---|---|
| 1. | Stake in, & levl. with the water | | | | | | | | |
| 2. | 5 Rod | rise | 1 | 0 | 2 | | | | |
| 3. | 5 Do. | do. | | 10 | | | | | |
| 4. | 5 Do. | do. | | 10 | 3 | by Bars. | | | |
| 5. | 5 Do. | do. | 1 | 5 | 1 | | | | |
| 6. | 5 Do. | | | | | Fall | 1 | 0 | 3 |
| 7. | 5 Do. | | | | | Do. | | 5 | 3 |
| 8. | 5 Do. | rise | | 10 | | | | | |
| 9. | 5 Do. | | | | | Fall | | | 1 |
| 10. | 5 Do. | rise | | | 1 | | | | |
| 11. | 5 Do. | rise | | 6 | | | | | |
| 12. | 5 Do. | | | | | Fall | | 9 | |
| 13. | 5 Do. | | | | | | | 2 | 3 |
| 14. | 5 Do. | rise | | 4 | 3 | | | | |
| 15. | 5 Do. | rise | | 2 | 1 | | | | |
| 16. | 5 Do. | | | | | Fall | | 4 | |
| 17. | 5 Do. | | | | | Fall | | 2 | 2 |
| 18. | 5 Do. | rise | | 10 | 1 | | | | |
| 19. | 5 Do. | | | | | Fall | 2 | 3 | |
| 20. | 24 yds. | rise | | 1 | 2 | | | | |
| | 7 ditto into Ditch } | rise | | 2 | | | | | |
| | Total Rise | | 7 | 3 | 2 | Fall | 5 | 4 | |
| | difference | | | | | | 1 | 11 | 2 |
| | | | 7 | 3 | 2 | | 7 | 3 | 2 |

By this it appears that the ground from the level of the Water at the old dam by Wades Houses to the race by the Stooping red oak, is higher by two feet (wanting half an Inch) than the bottom of the race in its present filled up state, is, and that the ditch, or old race must be considerably sunk – the old dam considerably raised, and strengthned in order to throw the water into the New ditch – or a dam made higher up the run so as to gain a greater fall which of the three, may be most eligable as it will, without any great additional expence drain a good deal more of the Swamp. But if it should be thought more eligable – deepning the race and raising the dam will carry of the water from the Meadow below but then it may Drown the land above.

William Fitzhugh of Chatham, in a painting attributed to Cephas Thompson. (Washington and Lee University, Washington-Custis-Lee Collection)

At Muddy hole the hands finished hoeing the drilled Corn, on Saturday last and on Monday & this day were employed in getting out Wheat.

In the evening Mr. Fitzhugh of Chatham and Mr. Robt. Randolph came here from Ravensworth.

William Fitzhugh (1741–1809), of Chatham, owned Ravensworth in Fairfax County. He was married to Robert Randolph's sister Anne. Robert Randolph (1760–1825), of Fauquier County, was a son of Peter and Mary Bolling Randolph of Chatsworth, Henrico County. During the Revolution Robert served as a lieutenant in the 3d Continental Dragoons and was wounded and taken prisoner at Tappan, N.Y., in Sept. 1778 (WMQ, 1st ser., 7 [1898–99], 124; HEITMAN [2], 458).

Wednesday 9th.    Mercury at 74 in the Morning—81 at Noon and 79 at Night.

Wind Southerly—Morning a little lowering but clear afterwards till about 3 oclock when a cloud in the So. West produced a pretty heavy shower of rain attended with a good deal of wind in a short space. In the Night it again rained.

Began to sow Wheat at the Ferry and in the Neck yesterday—at the first in the cut on the flat adjoining the drilled Corn and at the other in the cut on the river.

Finished cleaning two stacks of wheat which had been tread out at Muddy hole. Each measured 24 bushels of light wheat weighing only [      ] lbs. pr. Bushel.

Thursday 10th.    Mercury at 73 in the Morng.—74 at Noon and 70 at Night.

Wind at No. Et. with mists and very light showers till towards noon when the Sun came out. Warm till towards the afternoon when it grew cooler & pleasanter.

Rid to Muddy hole, Dogue run, and ferry Plantations—at the first of which Wheat Seeding will commence tomorrow. At the second things are not in order for it & at the third the sowing has been stopped by the heavy rain which fell yesterday.

Mr. Fitzhugh and Mr. Randolph went away after Breakfast.

Friday 11th.    Mercury at 68 in the Morning—76 at Noon and 74 at Night.

Clear & pleasant with the wind at So. West.

Rid to Muddy hole and Dogue run Plantations. At the first, Sowing wheat begun this Morning. At the latter I agreed with one James Lawson who was to provide another hand to ditch for me in my mill swamp upon the following terms—viz.—to allow them every day they work—each 1 lb. of salt or 1½ of fresh meat pr. day—1¼ lb. of brown bread, 1 pint of spirits and a bottle of Milk —the bread to be baked at the House, & their Meat to be Cooked by Morris's wife—and to allow them 16 d. pr. rod for ditches of 4 feet wide at top, 1 foot wide at bottom, and 2 feet deep; with 12 or 15 Inches footing and 2/. for ditches of 6 feet wide at top, 2 feet at bottom, and two ft. deep with equal footing.

On my return home found Mr. John Barnes and Doctr. Craik here—the last of whom returned to Alexandria. The other stayed all night.

GW and James Lawson of Fairfax County signed an agreement on 14 Aug. in which GW hired the latter on a temporary basis as a ditcher. In November Lawson agreed to a year's service at a salary of £31 10s. Virginia currency. Patrick Sheriden was probably the hand Lawson provided, as GW also engaged him in November, at eight dollars per month (agreements with Lawson, 14 Aug. and 18 Nov. 1786, DLC:GW). GW discharged Sheriden in Dec. 1786, and Lawson left Mount Vernon because of ill health in Sept. 1787 prior to the termination of his contract (see entry for 18 Dec. 1786; GW to Thomas Nelson, Jr., 3 Aug. 1788, DLC:GW).

Saturday 12th.    Mercury at 72 in the Morning—79 at Noon and 74 at Night.

Warm, with a tolerably bri[s]k Southerly wind all day.

Mr. Barnes went away before Breakfast.

After which I rid to my Meadow in order to mark out a middle ditch, and to try how much the water within the Meadow is above

the water in the run below where the two courses of it unite, below the old Mill Seat, and which is found to be nearly 3 feet; esti-
mating between the Surfaces of the two. It also appears that the
Meadow, just by where a breach is made in the dam, is as low as
any part in it reckoning from the Surface of the water (from the
bottom of the bed of the run would undou[b]tedly be deeper) and
that from this place to the Surface of the run at a turn of it by a
spreading spanish bush the rise is about 14 Inches.

Thomas McCarty left this yesterday—it being found that he was
unfit for a Household Steward.

Richard Burnet took his place on the wages of Thirty pounds
pr. ann.

Richard Burnet, whose tenure at Mount Vernon began in 1783, was a
"House keeper," or steward. He lived in Benjamin Dulany's family before
coming into GW's employ (Lund Washington to GW, 12 Mar. 1783,
ViMtV). Lund described him as "clever in his Way, he is a very good
Natured Peacable inoffensive well behaved man, and so far as we have
been able to judge, will answer the purpose for which he was got, he
certainly is a good cook, he appears to be careful active & Industrious, with
respect to preservg., Pickling &c.—he is at no loss, but does these things very
Ready & Well" (Lund Washington to GW, 1 Oct. 1783, ViMtV). He seems
to have left Mount Vernon briefly early in 1786 and returned in May (see
entry for 29 May 1786). He is probably the same man who worked as butler
or house steward at Mount Vernon from 1786 until 1789 under the name of
Richard Burnet Walker (LEDGER B, 234). Walker may have been married
to John Alton's daughter Ann.

Sunday 13th.    Mercury at 69 in the Morning—70 at Noon and
69 at Night.

Day lowering with the wind at East—now and then a little
sprinkle of rain but not enough to wet the roots of any thing.

Mr. Shaw quitted this family to day.

Colo. Humphreys, Geo. Washington & wife went to Church at
Alexandria to day & dined with Mr. Fendall. The first remained
there all Night.

William Shaw resigned to go to the West Indies (see entries for 2 July 1785
and 25 Aug. 1786).

Monday 14th.    Mercury at 72 in the Morng.—73 at Noon and 70
at Night.

Day clear, and the wind fresh from the No. West, from Morn
till eve.

Went by way of Muddy hole & Dogue run plantations to the
Meadow, in my Mill Swamp, to set the Ditche[r]s to work, only
one of whom appeared. About Noon he began on the side ditch,

East of the meadow. After doing this, and levelling part of the ground (with a Rafter level) along which the Ditch was to be cut I intended to have run a course or two of Fencing at Muddy hole but Meeting with Genl. Duplessis in the road who intended to Mt. Vernon but had lost his way I returned home with him where Colo. Humphreys had just arrived before us.

Thomas Antoine Mauduit du Plessis (1753–1791), born in Hennebont, France, came to America in 1777 and served in the Continental Army before France officially joined the war, distinguishing himself at Brandywine, Germantown, Red Bank, and Monmouth. In 1780 he became senior adjutant of the artillery park with Rochambeau's army. Mauduit returned to France after the war, but remained only temporarily. Writing to GW from New York on 20 July 1786, he reported that he had bought a large tract of land in Georgia and was looking forward to becoming an American citizen (DLC:GW). On 15 Aug. 1786, the day after Mauduit arrived at Mount Vernon, GW wrote to Theodorick Bland: "Nothing but cultivation is wanting. Our lot has certainly destined a good country for our inheritance. We begin already to attract the notice of foreigners of distinction. A French general officer whose name is Du Plessis is now at Mount Vernon on his way to Georgia, with a design to settle there as a farmer" (DLC:GW). In 1787, however, Mauduit returned to French service and was sent to Santo Domingo to command a regiment at Port-au-Prince, where he was killed in 1791 during the insurrection on the island.

Tuesday 15th.    Mercury at 64 in the Morning—70 at Noon and 65 at Night.

Cool, & for the most part of the day lowering, with but little wind.

At home all day. Doctr. Stuart & Mr. Keith, deputed by the Potomack Co. to present its thanks to the President & directors thereof came for that purpose, dined here & returned in the Afternoon.

James Keith (1734–1824), the son of Rev. James and Mary Isham Randolph Keith, was a Hampshire County burgess 1761–62 and later served as clerk of Frederick County, Va., 1762–1824. After the Revolution Keith moved to Alexandria where he practiced law. In 1784 he served as mayor of the city.

Wednesday 16th.    Mercury at 66 in the Morning—71 at Noon and 70 at Night.

Cloudy and lowering for the greater part of the day and in the night a good deal of rain fell—wind at So. West.

Colonels Fitzgerald and Lyles Mr. Brailsford (an English Gentleman) and Mr. Perrin came here to dinner & returned afterwards. In the afternoon a Major Freeman who looks after my concerns west of the Alligany Mountains came in and stayed all night.

Thursday 17th.    Mercury at 68 in the Morning—74 at Noon and 70 at Night.

Drizling morning with the Wind at So. West—Cloudy and misting at times all day.

About breakfast time my Baggage which had been left at Gilbert Simpsons arrived here.

Settled Accts. with Major Freeman and engaged him to continue his agency till he should remove from his present residency to Kentucke & then to put all my Bonds into the hands of Lawyer Smith to bring suits on.

At home all day—understood that the River cut in the Neck had been sowed with Wht.

Friday 18th.    Mercury at 70 in the Morning—74 at Noon and 72 at Night.

Misty morning, with light showers of rain through the day— wind at No. East.

Rid to the plantations at the Ferry, Dogue run, & Muddy hole, and to the Mill—The hands at each place working on the Public roads. At Dogue Run the Plows & Hoes began to put in wheat on Wednesday last.

The ditcher at the Meadow wd. by noon have compleated about 6 rod of the 6 feet ditch which would be about 1 rod and half pr. day.

A Mr. Jno. Dance, recommended by Genl. Mifflin, & Willing Morris & Swanwick came here to offer his services to me as a Manager but not wanting such a person he returned after Dinner.

WORKING ON THE PUBLIC ROADS: The public roads in Virginia were maintained by a system which had originated in England in the sixteenth century, and had changed little for over 200 years. Basically, the plan required that all tithables (males 16 years of age or over) were to be required to work on the public roads for a certain number of days each year, or to provide someone to work in their place. In Virginia the system was first administered at the parish level as it was in England, but soon came under the jurisdiction of the county courts. The greater use of roads into the back country after the Revolution had increased the difficulty of keeping up the roads, and in 1785 the Virginia legislature had passed new legislation designed to help solve the problems of the bad road conditions (see HENING, 12:75–80, 174–80).

JNO. DANCE: possibly the John Dance listed in the Pennsylvania census of 1800 from Bucks County. Thomas Mifflin was at this time speaker of the Pennsylvania legislature and Thomas Willing was president of the Bank of North America. Willing and Robert Morris, mercantile partners since 1757, added John Swanwick (1740–1798), of Philadelphia, to their firm in 1783. Swanwick had been a clerk in that countinghouse and a cashier in the office of finance under Morris during the Revolution.

Saturday 19th.    Mercury at 69 in the Morning—72 at Noon and 70 at Night.

Wind Easterly, misting, & lowering in the forenoon but clear afterwards.

General Duplessis left this by 5 Oclock in the Morning.

After breakfast I accompanied Colo. Humphreys by water to Alexandria and dined with him at Captn. Conways to whom he had been previously engaged. The Tools & Baggage of Mr. Rawlins's workmen were carried to Alexandria in my Boat to day.

Sunday 20th.    Mercury at 69 to day, Morng.—at 74 at Noon and 70 at Night.

Very little Wind at any period of the day—lowering for the most part and in the Morning a little misty.

Monday 21st.    Mercury at 69 in the Morning—79 at Noon and 76 at Night.

Clear and warm with but little [wind].

Rid to the Plantations at Dogue Run Muddy hole & Ferry. At the 2d. the Hoes & Plows had just finished putting in wheat in the middle cut, which took [       ] bushels to sow it; after which they were ordered to thin the drilled Turnips & to weed the Carrots.

Tuesday 22d.    Mercury at 72 in the Morning—85 at Noon and 82 at Night.

Very warm with little or no wind & that Southerly.

In the evening clouds with appearances of much rain but not a great deal fell at any of my Plantations—more at Dogue run than elsewhere.

Finished sowing the middle cut in the large field in the Neck; to do which took [       ] bushls. of grain, as it did [       ] bushels to seed the river side cut.

Mrs. Jenifer came here to Dinner yesterday and Mr. Wm. Craik & his Sister (Miss Craik) came in the afternoon. Doctr. Craik came in before breakfast, after which he, his son & daughter went away.

Wednesday 23d.    Mercury at 72 in the morning—86 at Noon and 84 at Night.

Quite calm and exceedingly Sultry. Very clear.

Rid to my Plantations at Muddy hole, dogue run and Ferry—also to the Mill.

Colo. Humphreys went away to day to take the stage at Alexandria for the No. Ward.

Mr. & Mrs. Fendall — Mr. Charles Lee Miss Flora & Miss Nancy Lee — Miss Countee & Hariot Washington came here to Dinner — all of whom went away after it, except the 4 last named.

Having wed the Carrots & thinned the Turnips at Muddy hole I directed the People to sow some wheat in the cut adjoining the middle one which had been put into brine.

MISS COUNTEE: probably a member of the Contee family in Prince George's or Charles County, Md.

Thursday 24th.    Mercury at 76 in the Morning — 77 at Noon and 70 at Night.

Wind pretty fresh from the Northward all day with appearances of rain in the forenoon. In the afternoon there were slight showers, but scarcely more than would make the eves of the House run.

Mr. Shaw came down before dinner and stayed all night.

At home all day myself.

Friday 25th.    Mercury at 68 in the Morning — 70 at Noon and 69 at Night.

Lowering all day with slight showers about 1 Oclock; with distant thunder in the evening there were still greater appearances of a settled rain.

Mr. Shaw went to Alexandria after breakfast in order to proceed to the Northward to embark at Philadelphia for the West Inds.

I rid to Muddy hole and Dogue run Plantations. At the first I marked out lines for a new partition of my fields and directed the best plowman at it to break up about 10 Acres of Pasture land which had produced Wheat the year of 1785, to try how it would yield (upon a single plowing) wheat next, sowed this fall.

At Dogue run Meadow (Mill Swamp) I marked the middle ditch for the hired men to work on, while the season was proper.

Mr. Rawlins from Baltim[or]e and Mr. Tharpe came here before dinner to measure the Work which had been done for me & to receive payment.

Saturday 26th.    Mercury at 68 in the Morning — 77 at Noon And 73 at Night.

A great deal of rain, in many hard showers fell in the course of last night. Morning cloudy, but clear after wards and warm.

Rid to the Neck, Muddy hole, and Ferry plantations. At the two first (as also at Dogue run Plantation) the Plows & Hoes were stopped by the earth being surcharged with water. At the ferry, the cut of Corn on the Hill having discharged the water more freely the People were putting in wheat there.

On my return home found Mr. Geo. Fitzhugh (son of Colo. Wm. Fitzhugh of Maryland) here. They dined, and returned to Alexandria afterwards as did the Miss Lees & Miss Countee this Morng.

George Lee Mason Fitzhugh (1748–1836) was the son of Col. William Fitzhugh of Maryland by his first wife, Martha Lee Turberville Fitzhugh.

**Sunday 27.** Mercury at 67 in the Morning—70 at Noon and 69 at Night.

Weather clear and very pleasant the wind being pretty fresh from the No. West point.

At home all day alone.

**Monday 28th.** Mercury at 64 in the Morning—72 at Noon and 70 at Night.

The forenoon clear, but lowering afterwards, with a slight sprinkling of rain about dusk. Wind at No. Et. all day.

Just after we had breakfasted, & my horse was at the door for me to ride, Colonel and Mrs. Rogers came in. When they sat down to breakfast which was prepared for them, I commenced my ride for

Lt. Col. Nicholas Rogers of Baltimore, by John W. Jarvis. (Maryland Historical Society, Baltimore)

Muddy hole, Dogue run & Ferry Plantations also to my meadow on Dogue run and the Mill.

At Muddy hole and the ferry a plow at each begun this day to break ground, for the purpose of Sowing Wheat, or rye, or both as shall be thought best.

The Ditchers (for one was added to James Lawson to day) began the middle ditch in the meadow at the Mill this morning.

And my Carpenters began to take up the forebay at my Mill this Morning also.

Began to level the unfinished part of the lawn in front of my House.

Nicholas Rogers (1753–1822), the son of Nicholas Rogers III, was a prominent Baltimore merchant. After graduating from the University of Glasgow in 1774, Nicholas traveled in Europe until the Revolution began, at which time he volunteered as aide-de-camp to Maj. Gen. Tronson du Coudray and Baron de Kalb, attaining the rank of lieutenant colonel. In 1780 he returned to Baltimore where he managed his estate, Druid Hill, and was active in politics. Three years later he married his cousin Eleanor Buchanan (1757–1812), the daughter of Lloyd Buchanan who died in 1761 (*Md. Hist. Mag.*, 44 [1949], 192–95).

Tuesday 29th.    Mercury at 69 in the Morning—81 at Noon and 80 at Night.

Lowering Morning with drops of Rain. Clear afterwards till the afternoon, when a cloud arose in the No. West quarter and extending very wide emitted after dark a great deal of rain with much thunder and lightning—Wind very brisk from the So. West all day. In the evening it shifted more to the westward.

Plowed up the Cowpens on the left of the road in order to sow Turneps but was prevented by the rain—spreading stable dung on the poorest parts of my clover at home.

Thatching the Haystacks at the same place.

Taken with an Ague about 7 Oclock this Morning which being succeeded by a smart fever confined me to the House till evening. Had a slight fit of both on Sunday last but was not confined by them.

Colonel and Mrs. Rogers left this about 10 Oclock for George Town, on their way to Baltimore.

Lund Washington called in to inform me that Mr. William Triplet would be here to morrow to converse with me on the subject of renting Mrs. Frenchs Lands in this Neck now in the occupation of one Robinson.

RENTING MRS. FRENCHS LANDS: Rather than taking a lump sum for relinquishing her life interest in the land, Penelope Manley French insisted that GW pay her an annual rental for the use of the land during her lifetime (see entries for 9, 16 Sept. and 16 Oct. 1786). ONE ROBINSON: John Robertson was the tenant on Mrs. French's land. William Triplett, a relative of Mrs. French's by marriage, was acting for her in her negotiations with GW.

**Wednesday 30th.** Mercury at 69 in the Morning—68 at Noon and 62 at Night.

More rain fell last Night and this forenoon—Wind at East.

Prevented riding in the Morning by the weather. About Noon Mr. Willm. Triplet & Mr. L. Washington came in and after a great deal of conversation respecting the Renting of Mrs. French's Land, and the purchase of Manley's it ended in postponement till Friday for further consideration.

**Thursday 31st.** Mercury at 60 in the Morning—63 at Noon and 62 at Night.

More rain last Night & this forenoon—with heavy weather all day. Wind Easterly.

Siezed with an ague before Six Oclock this morning after having laboured under a fever all night.

Sent for Doctr. Craik who arrived just as we were setting down to dinner; who, when he thought my fever sufficiently abated, gave me a cathartick and directed the Bark to be applied in the Morning.

BARK: Quinine derived from the bark of various species of the cinchona tree was ground into a powder and taken to reduce fevers.

## September 1786

**Friday 1st.** Mercury at 62 in the Morning—68 at Noon and 65 at Night.

A heavy dull Morning, with little wind—close and warm all day—at least till abt. 2 oclock when the wind sprung up from the Eastward.

Doctr. Craik went away after Breakfast. About 10 oclock I set out for Mr. Triplets—called upon Lund Washington. Mrs. French required more time for consideration before she could determine to give a lease for her life—but he agreed to sell me Manleys Land on the following terms—viz.—

I to pay Three pounds pr. Acre, and to pass my bond therefor, payable on demand with an interest of 5 pr. Ct. pr. Ann. till discharged—The money not to be called for Only as the Children come of age, or may require it—When the interest becomes due my Bond to be given for the same in order that the sum may be accumulating for their benefit instead of paying the cash.

In returning home I passed by my Meadow at the Mill—Dogue run & Muddy hole plantations. Found that the rains had been so constant & heavy that an entire stop had put to the sowing of Wheat among the Corn and to my ditching in the middle of the meadow at the mill but that the grds. which I had ordered to be broke up at the Ferry and Muddy hole and in the Neck was advancing very well.

Took 8 dozes of the red bark to day.

Saturday 2d.    Mercury at 66 in the Morning—72 at Noon and 70 at Night.

Foggy morning, but clear & warm afterwards with the wind at So. West.

Kept close to the House to day, being my fit day in course least any exposure might bring it on. Happily missed it.

Sowed Turnep Seed on the Cowpen ground which had been just plowed—harrowed them in, at the home house adjoining the clover.

Doctr. Craik came here in the afternoon & stayed all Night.

MY FIT DAY IN COURSE: That is, it was the day the intermittent ague which had struck him at two-day intervals was again due.

Sunday 3d.    Mercury at 70 in the morning—82 at Noon and 80 at Night.

Very thick fog in the Morning but clear afterwards and warm with the wind at South.

Majr. Washington & Mr. Lear went to Pohick church, dined at Colo. McCartys and returned afterwards.

I rid by the Ferry to the Mill and back by way of exercise.

Doctr. Craik returned after he had breakfasted to Alexandria.

Monday 4th.    Mercury at 74 in the Morning—86 at Noon and 82 at Night.

Clear and very warm with scarcely a breath of wind all day & that from the Southward.

Majr. Washington went up to Alexandria on my business & did not return till Night.

I rid to Muddy hole & Dogue run Plantations and to the Mill and meadow. At Muddy hole the overseer began this morning to sow wheat again among Corn, but the ground was full wet and heavy for it. At Dogue run the People were repairing my outer Fences.

Too much wet in the meadow to work on the middle ditch. The ditchers proposed doing it to morrow if the waters contind. to subside.

**Tuesday 5th.** Mercury at 76 in the Morning—86 at Noon and 80 at Night.

Very warm, with but little wind and that Southerly.

Rid to the Neck and muddy hole Plantations. At the first though unnoticed at the time the cut adjoining the drilled corn had been sowed with Wheat ever since Tuesday last and this day (having taken the seed from it 14½ Bushls.) the Flax was spread but not well the weeds not being sufficiently Cut & taken off to let it lye well on the Earth. At Muddy hole finished all the wheat Sowing in Corn ground I intended—viz. 19 Bushels in the cut adjoining the drilled Corn, & 14 in the other East of it—the remainder of this latter cut being designed for Rye. Mr. Wm. Peake dined here.

William Peake (died c.1794), a son of GW's former neighbor, Humphrey Peake, probably lived on his father's old farm. GW bought wheat from him on at least one occasion (LEDGER B, 228).

**Wednesday 6th.** Mercury at 76 in the Morning—76 at Noon and 72 at Night.

Variable day—wind, what there was of it, Southerly in the forenoon & warm, tho' cloudy—No. Westerly afterwards and cool, with sprinkling of Rain & great appearances of more but none fell.

Rid to my Plantations at the Ferry, Dogue run & Muddy hole —also to the Mill & the meadow where the Ditchers were at work. At the two first, the People were Sowing Wheat again in Corn ground. At Dogue run two acres of turf had been plowed up agreeably to my farmers orders to Sow Wheat on. This was done yesterday & the day before. The Lands—plowed in the same way tho' not so well turfed, some of it being Wheat Stubble of the last year and the remainder in Wheat the year before—I directed to be immediately Sowed; The latter with Wheat, and the former with Rye and thereafter the plowing of every day to [be] Sowed & harrowed in before Night, that no rain might intervene between the plowing & Sowing. Timothy Seeds were ordered to be sowed therewith, & after the grain was harrowed in to be brushed in with a bush harrow. These directions applied to the Ferry, Muddy hole, & Neck the first & last having rye to sow & the other both Wheat & Rye. Note – The Rye at the Ferry to be sowed in this way, is on Wht. land of the last year and not on Stubble of the last year as mentioned above.

Mr. Rozer – a Mr. Hall & a Mr. Matthews from the Eastern Shore dined here and returned in the afternoon – after which Mr. & Mrs. Fendall came in on their [way to] Esquire Lee's of Maryland (who is very ill) & stayed all night.

Mr. Rozer is probably either Henry Rozer (Rozier, born c.1725) of Notley Hall, Prince George's County, Md., or one of his sons.

ESQUIRE LEE'S: Richard Lee (c.1707–1787) of Blenheim in Charles County, Md., was usually known as Squire Lee. He was the son of Philip Lee, a member of the influential Virginia family, who had gone to Maryland to live about 1700. Richard Lee had been president of the Maryland council and naval officer for one of the Potomac districts of Maryland for many years before the Revolution. However, his Loyalist sympathies had led to his retirement from public life. Philip Richard Fendall's first wife, Sarah Lettice Lee Fendall, was Richard Lee's daughter, and Fendall himself was probably a nephew. Although Richard Lee's tombstone incorrectly gives his death as 1789, he died on 26 Jan. 1787 after "a series of complicated illness" (*Md. Gaz.*, 15 Feb. 1787). Squire Richard Lee of Blenheim is frequently confused with his cousin, Squire Richard Lee (1726–1795) of Lee Hall, who was naval officer for the South Potomac District of Virginia.

**Thursday 7th.**   Mercury at 64 in the Morning – 71 at Noon and 67 at Night.

Cool morning with the wind pretty fresh from the westward in the Morning and from the Eastward in the Evening.

Mr. & Mrs. Fendall crossed the [river] early.

I rid to the Plantations at Muddy hole Dogue run and Ferry. At the first Wheat had, this day, been sowed up to the Land in whch. the Plow was at work & harrowed in. The part next the hedge row (being the first plowed) had receivd a heavy rain since it was plowed which occasioned it not to harrow well but as the greater part of it was a slipe of Cowpens it is more than probable, nevertheless, that the best Wheat will grow there. The People making a fence round that field.

At Dogue run the hands had been employed in putting in abt. 1½ bushls. of the Cape Wheat raised below my Stables. This was put into a well cowpened piece of ground (now in Corn) adjoining the meadow – the grass & weeds of which I had cut up & carried off the ground before the Seed was sowed.

Getting out Rye at the Ferry to sow the Newly broken up grd.

Began to Paper the yellow room this day – Majr. Washington &

Thos. Green the undertakers—by the directions I received with the Paper from England.

A SLIPE OF COWPENS: Slipe, a term used frequently by GW, simply denotes an area or a quantity. One method of fertilizing was to pen cattle in a field, moving the pens systematically and periodically. A note in Jefferson's farm book indicates the number of cattle which, when "folded," would satisfactorily fertilize a given area of crop land (BETTS [1], 82).

Friday 8th.    Mercury at 60 in the morning—69 at Noon and 64 at Night.

Wind Easterly all day and cool, with a rawness in the Air.

Rid into the Neck, and called at Muddy hole. Found at the former that the last years cut of Wheat surrounding the Meadow would be nearly broke up for Rye by the evening and that that part of it South of the meadow adjoining the gate had been sowed with 2½ bushels of Rye which was nearly harrowed in and that the rest of the hands were employed in hoeing the drilled Turneps & in weeding & hilling the Cabbages between the Corn rows.

Saturday 9th.    Mercury at 62 in the Morning—72 at Noon and 68 at N.

A brisk North Easterly wind all day, with great appearances of rain but none fell.

Rid to the Plantations at Muddy hole, Dogue run, and Ferry; & went also to the Mill. At the latter, rye & grass Seed (Timothy) would be sowed on all the Land that is plowed. Sowing Rye on the plowed wheat stubble in the same manner at Muddy hole.

The ground at the Ferry being stiff, breaking up in pretty large & heavy clods, and the Seed harrowed in with my lightest harrow, was not well covered & left the ground very rough & lumpy with hollows between the furrows that would prevent the grain from being well covered and the Timothy seed still worse.

On my return home from riding, found Mr. William Triplett here, who delivered me the Papers respecting Manleys Land for which I had agreed with him and who informed me that Mrs. French had consented to rent me her Dower Land & Slaves in this Neck during her life, and to assign Robinsons Lease to me on the same terms Robinson holds—viz.—£136 pr. Ann. to be paid to her clear of all expences. I am not to move the Negroes out of the County and a clause is to be inserted in the lease that in case of my death and they should by my successor be maltreated in any respect that a forfeiture of the lease shall be incurred.

About 5 Oclock the Widow Randolph of Wilton, with her 3

Sons & a daughter, a Miss Harrison (daughter to Colo. Charles Harrison) and Captn. Singleton came in and about an hour afterwards Mr. Fendall & Mrs. Fendall arrived.

PAPERS RESPECTING MANLEYS LAND: William Triplett was possibly a half-brother of Harrison Manley and was one of the executors of Manley's estate. The deed for the 142-acre tract of land was signed 22 Sept. 1786 (deed of Manley's executors to GW, Fairfax County Deeds, Book Q-1, 295–97, Vi Microfilm).

WIDOW RANDOLPH: Anne Harrison Randolph had by her husband, William Randolph, five sons, one of whom died young, and three daughters. Her brother, Charles Harrison (c.1744–1794), colonel of the 1st Continental Artillery 1777–83, married Mary Claiborne Herbert and by her had six children, three of whom were daughters. Anthony Singleton (d. 1795) served as a captain in the 1st Continental Artillery and about 1788 married Lucy Harrison Randolph, widow of Peyton Randolph of Wilton and niece of Charles Harrison.

Sunday 10th.    Mercury at 62 in the Morning—67 at Noon and 63 at Night.
    Wind variable—sometimes at No. West & then at East—weather lowering all day and at times especially after noon dripping.
    Mr. & Mrs. Fendall went away after breakfast & Colo. Gilpin came in dined & returned in the afternoon.

Monday 11th.    Mercury at 62 in the Morning—66 at Noon and 64 at Night.
    Rain fell in the Night. Morning drizzling with the Wind at North tho' little of it.
    Rid to Muddy hole, Dogue run & Ferry Plantations, and to my Ditchers at the Meadow. At the last mentioned Plantation my people would have about finished this afternoon sowing the cut of Corn on the Hill with Wheat.
    Colo. Simms came here and dined on his way to Port Tobacco Court, & crossed the River afterwards.

Tuesday 12th.    Mercury at 61 in the Morning—70 at Noon and 68 at Night.
    A good deal of rain fell in the course of the Night and early this Morning. About 8 Oclock the clouds began to dispel and the Wind blowing fresh from the No. Wt. the weather cleared, the Sun came out and the day was pleasant & drying and towards evening cool.
    Mrs. Randolph, Miss Harrison, Mrs. G. Washington, Captn.

Singleton, & Mr. Lear went to Alexandria after breakfast & returned before dinner.

I rid to the Plantations at Muddy hole and in the Neck. Began
at the former to gather the tops & blades of the early corn in drills.

Wednesday 13th.    Mercury at 53 in the morning—64 at Noon
and 60 at Night.

Wind at No. West, raw and cold all day, but especially in the
morning.

Mrs. Randolph & her Children, Miss Harrison & Captn. Singleton left this after breakfast.

I rid to the Plantations at the Ferry, Dogue run & Muddy hole
also to the Mill.

At the first, the people having finished sowing the cut on the
hill with Wheat, were chopping this grain in in the drilled corn
by the fish house among the Potatoes, which they did by shifting
the tops of the vines from side to side as they hoed. At the other,
or second place, the hands continued hoeing & plowing in Wheat
in the Corn ground, tho' it was wet & heavy. At the last Will
(plowman) finished in the afternoon the 10 Acre piece of Wheat
he began the 28th. Ulto. by which it appears he was 15 days accomplishing it; and had not plowed quite ¾ of an Acre a day
altho' the ground, except in one or two small spots which had
been made wet & heavy by the Rains, was in as good order for
plowing as were to be wished—better & much easier than if the
weather had proved dry & the ground consequently hard.

My Corn being out, or nearly so, I was obliged to have midlings
& ship stuff mixed for bread for my white Servants and the latter
& rye for my Negroes till the New Corn is ripe enough to pull.

Thursday 14th.    Mercury at 49 in the Morning—60 at Noon and
56 at Night.

Wind pretty fresh again today and cool.

At home all day repeating dozes of Bark of which I took 4 with
an interval of 2 hours between. After dinner Messrs. Thos. and
Elliot Lee came in, as did Doctr. Craik by desire, on a visit to
Betty—who had been struck with the palsey. The whole stayed
all Night.

Finished sowing Wheat and Timothy seed on the 10 acre piece
of wheat at Muddy hole this day.

And also finished that cut with rye adjoining the Meadow in
the Neck it taking including the 2½ Bushels sowed in the piece

between the gate and the meadow [    ] Bushels. On the small piece (sowed with 2½ Bushels) by mistake a bushel of Timothy seed nearly if [not] quite clean was sowed which was at least 6 times as much as ought to have been sown.

MESSRS. THOS. AND ELLIOT LEE: probably Thomas Ludwell Lee (d. 1807) and William Aylett Lee, sons of Thomas Ludwell Lee (1730–1778). BETTY: There were three slaves named Betty at this time. This is probably the dower slave, a seamstress, who worked at the Home House plantation.

Friday 15th.    Mercury at 54 in the Morning—66 at Noon and 64 at Night.

Clear, calm, and very pleasant.

After breakfast the two Mr. Lees and Doctr. Craik went away. I rid to Muddy hole & Neck Plantations. Treading out Wheat & rye at both retarded fodder getting at the first, & wheat Sowing at the other.

Sent my Boat to Alexandria for Molasses & Coffee which had been sent to me from Surinam by a Mr. Branden of that place.

SENT MY BOAT TO ALEXANDRIA: GW wished to breed Royal Gift, the jackass he had received from Spain in late 1785. Hearing that South America was noted for its jennies, GW, through William Lyles & Co. of Alexandria, got in touch with Samuel Branden, a merchant in Surinam (Netherlands Guiana), and asked him to purchase for him "one of the largest & best she asses that can be obtained in your country fit to breed from." Unsure how much such an animal would cost, GW had 25 barrels of superfine flour placed on board one of Lyles's ships bound for Surinam. If Branden could not procure an ass for him, GW asked that he send instead two hogsheads of molasses and some coffee. Branden sent GW an ass, and molasses and coffee as well, in exchange for the flour (GW to Branden, 10 Feb., 20 Nov. 1786, DLC: GW).

Saturday 16th.    Mercury at 58 in the Morning—69 at Noon And 66 at Night.

Morning a little lowering, but clear & pleasant afterwards, with but little wind.

Rid to Mr. Willm. Tripletts in expectation of meeting Mrs. French, in order to get the lease from her & Deed from Mr. Triplett executed but his indisposition & confinement in bed prevented the latter and the nonattendance of Mrs. French & a misunderstanding with respect to the rent, she conceiving it was to be £150 pr. Ann. & I £136 only, put an end to the negotiation of the former.

I visited my Mill, Ditchers and the Plantations at the Ferry, Dogue run, and Muddy hole. At the last, the fodder (top & blade) of the drilled corn was gathered & the Sowing of the Rye kept up with the plow. At the first the same was done with the rye in the newly plowed field and the people had begun (on thursday) to sow Wht. in the drilled Corn by the meadow.

On my return home found the Attorney General (Randolph) his Lady & two Children; and Mr. Charles Lee here. The last returned to Alexandria after Dinner under promise to come down to dinner to morrow, and that he would ask Mr. Herbert Colo. Fitzgerald & others to dine here also.

ATTORNEY GENERAL: Edmund Randolph married Elizabeth Nicholas in 1776 and their two children mentioned here were Peyton Randolph (1781–1828) and Susan Randolph (b. 1782). The Randolphs' third child, John Jennings Randolph (b. 1785), died in the summer of 1786. Shortly after his son's death, Randolph took his family from Richmond to Annapolis where he headed the Virginia delegation to the convention meeting to establish a uniform system of commercial regulations. Randolph's purpose in stopping at Mount Vernon on his return to Richmond after the close of the conference was no doubt in part to give GW an accounting of the proceedings in Annapolis.

Sunday 17th.    Mercury at 59 in the Morning–68 at Noon and 65 at Night.

Wind fresh at East all day & very lowering. About 5 Oclock it began to rain and continued to do so incessantly the whole Night.

Colo. Fitzgerald Mr. Herbert, Colo. Simm & Mr. Chs. Lee, & a Mr. Snow (living with Mr. Porter) came down to dinner and were detained by the rain all night.

Gideon Snow entered the employ of the Alexandria firm of Porter & Ingraham in 1786. According to some accounts, he had been Eleanor Parke and George Washington Parke Custis's first tutor (CUSTIS, 39).

Monday 18th.    Mercury at 62 in the Morning–70 at Noon and 71 at Night.

Morning very rainy till about 9 Oclock altho the wind had got to No. Wt.

Mr. Randolph, Lady & family and all the Gentlemen from Alexandria left this as soon as the weather cleared–the first on his return to Richmond.

Rid to my Plantations at Muddy hole, Dogue run, & Ferry. Plows, & sowing Wheat and other grain, stopped at all the places.

In the Neck one of the Womn. & 2 girls began to gather Pease on Friday last. Nearly half on the vines appearing to be ripe.

Getting in the Fodder or rather spreading it at Muddy hole being wet that it might dry.

Tuesday 19th.    Mercury at 64 in the Morning—71 at Noon and 70 at Night.

Wind at No. West, clear and pleasant.

Rid to Muddy hole and into the Neck—No plowing in corn ground but renewed it at Muddy hole & in the Neck for Rye in the wheat stubble. Began to get fodder in the Neck and at Morris' from the drilled Corn.

Wednesday 20th.    Mercury at 65 in the Morning—73 at Noon and 70 at Night.

Clear warm & pleasant all day—Wind Southerly.

Rid to the Ferry, Muddy hole, & Dogue run. At the first the People had begun yesterday, & were at it to day, sowing wheat in the drilled Corn by the meadow—The ground especially in places too wet—At the next cutting down tops & securing the first cut fodder. At the latter all except 3 plows which were breaking up more of the lay land were getting fodder—it being too wet to sow wheat in corn ground.

My Farmer sowed this day the lay land which had been broken up at this place by his own directions—part of which at the east end adjoining the Corn had been plowed [      ] days. The other part at the West end also adjoining the Corn had been plowed [      ] days. The first cont[ai]ns about [      ] acres; the 2d. about [      ]. This wheat was put in in the following manner—viz.— sowed on the first plowing, which tho' the ground was well enough broke the sod was not properly turned. In the roughest & heaviest part the Seedsman was followed by a heavy harrow the same way as the ground was plowed in the lighter part by two light harrows, side by side (fastened together) and the whole cross harrowed with the light double harrow to smooth & fill the hollows. Alongside this, I set two plows as above to break up about [      ] acres more of the lay and directed it to be sowed as fast as the Lands were finished, & to receive the same harrowings to try (the Land being nearly of the same quality) wch. method will succeed best.

MY FARMER: James Bloxham.

Thursday 21st.    Mercury at 65 in the Morning—76 at Noon and 74 at Night.

But little wind, and Southerly, clear & warm.

Rid to the Plantations in the Neck, Muddy hole, Dogue run, and Ferry—also to the ditchers.

At the first, the flax which was put out to Dew rot was turned yesterday and the Fodder which the people begun to get yesterday was discontinued to day in order to get out Oats. At the second finished sowing Rye on the Wheat Stubble—put in 15 Bushels on abt. 13 Acres—securing the Fodder which had been cut & pulled at this place—at the 3d. gathering Fodder & plowing the lay land and at the last threshing out Rye & putting in rye in the lay land.

Friday 22d.    Mercury at 69 in the Morning—78 at Noon and 76 at Night.

Calm & very warm in the forenoon with appearances of Rain in the afternoon a little of which only fell.

Went to Mr. Tripletts in my way to Alexandria, and got his conveyance before Evidences of Manleys land—after which in the same manner in Town, obtained the signatures to the Deed of Mr. & Mrs. Sanford who were necessarily made parties thereto. Did business with Colo. Simm & others and returned home in the evening.

Edward Sanford, an Alexandria silversmith, was married to Harrison Manley's widow, Margaret. GW acquired from the Sanfords, for £426 Virginia currency, approximately 142 acres of land, part of the old Spencer-Washington patent (Fairfax County Deeds, Book Q-1, 295–97, Vi Microfilm).

Saturday 23d.    Mercury at 64 in the Morning—70 at Noon and 68 at Night.

A very heavy fog in the Morning, which was dispersed by a Northerly wind which cooled the air a good deal.

Rid to all the Plantations between breakfast and Dinnr. getting fodder at all, & securing it, excepting the Ferry where the People had just finished sowing the drilled Corn by the Meadow which compleated all the Corn ground and all the wheat sowing at this place. Interrupted at the River Plantation in getting Fodder in order to clean Rye & Oats for the House.

In the Afternoon Mr. Josh. Jones, Mr. Tucker & Lady, Doctr. Stuart, Mrs. Stuart, Betcy & Patcy Custis came in and stayed all Night. My Nephews George & Lawrence (whom I had sent Horses for) came down before dinner.

Finished sowing wheat upon the Lay land at Dogue run in the manner proposed. On this [      ] Bushels was sowed. On that part of the other which had been first plowed [      ] Bushels was sowed and on the west side [      ] Bushels.

Joseph Jones (1727–1805), of King George County, Va., the son of James and Hester Jones, had a long, exemplary career in public service. He was a delegate to the House of Burgesses from King George County before the

Revolution, a member of the Continental Congress 1778–79 and 1780–83, and a judge of the general court 1778–79 and 1789–1805.

St. George Tucker (1752–1827), son of Henry and Anne Butterfield Tucker, left his native Bermuda in 1771 for Virginia where he had a long and distinguished legal career. Tucker and his first wife, Frances Bland Randolph Tucker (1752–1788), daughter of Theodorick and Frances Bolling Bland and widow of John Randolph of Matoax, Chesterfield County, traveled to Annapolis in Sept. 1786 where Tucker attended the meeting on commerce.

Sunday 24th.   Mercury at 55 in the Morning—59 at Noon and 57 at Night.

Wind at No. West & weather clear & cool—Lund & Lawe. Washn. dined here.

The Company mentioned above remained here all day & Night. In the afternoon Colo. Bassett, & his Son Burwell arrived—with servants and horses.

Monday 25th.   Mercury at 50 in the Morning—66 at Noon and 64 at Night. The Morning and day through was very pleasant, turning warm—the wind getting to the Southward.

Sent Mr. Tucker & his Lady to Colchester. Doctr. Stuart, Mrs. Stuart & family together with Nelly Custis went up to Abingdon. In the afternoon the Revd. Mr. Bryn. Fairfax came in and stayed all Night.

Began to day with my Waggon Horses at their leizure moments, to plow alternate Lands, at Dogue run, in the Lay Land adjoining the Wheat sowed in it to try the difference in Barley (if to be had) or Oats next spring between fall & spring plowing.

Tuesday 26th.   Mercury at 58 in the Morning—72 at Noon and 68 at Night.

Day clear & very pleasant, with the wind at South; towards evening however it began to lower.

Mr. & Mrs. Lund Washington dined here & returned in the afternoon.

At home all this day as I was yesterday. Mr. Bryan Fairfax went away after breakfast.

Wednesday 27th.   Mercury at 66 in the Morning—80 at Noon and 78 at Night.

Clear, calm, and warm all day.

Colo. Bassett his Son & George Washington took a ride to Alexandria. I rid into the Neck, by Muddy hole, to measure a piece of ground intended for Corn another year & to new model my fields.

[ 44 ]

Took up the flax that had been spread to rot at the latter place. Engaged at every plantation in gathering fodder. No plow going but at the ferry for Rye.

Put my Rams to the Ewes this day.

Thursday 28th.    Mercury at 69 in the Morning—81 at Noon and 79 at Night.

Calm, clear and warm; all day. Accompanied by Colo. Bassett, I rid to the Plantations at Muddy hole, Dogue run and Ferry. Employed in getting & securing Fodder at all of them.

Only one Ditcher at work in my Mill swamp—the other left it (at least discontinued work) on Tuesday last.

Friday 29th.    Mercury at 67 in the Morning—82 at Noon and 80 at Night.

Clear calm, and warm from Morn to evening.

Colo. Bassett and Mrs. Washington made a mornings visit at Mr. Lund Washington's.

I rid by Muddy hole Plantation into the Neck. Employed at both in gathering & securing Fodder.

The Flax which I thought had been taken up on Wednesday last was still on the ground. Directed it to be critically examined and taken up this afternoon if it should be found sufficiently rotted.

The Alexandria Academy, built in 1786. From a drawing in Mary G. Powell's *History of Old Alexandria,* Richmond, 1928. (Alexandria Library)

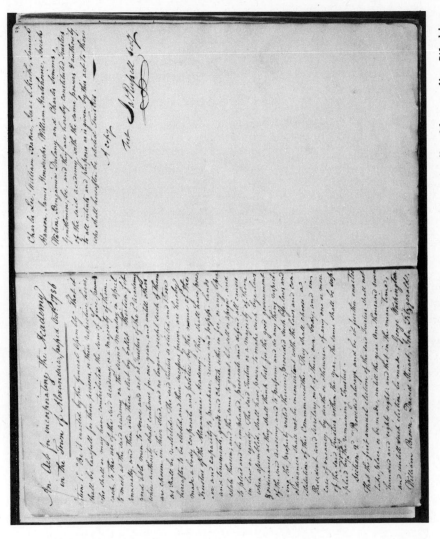

Page from the minute book of the Alexandria Academy for 14 April 1786, recording Washington's appointment as one of the original trustees. (Alexandria-Washington Lodge No. 22, A.F. & A.M., Alexandria, Va.)

After dinner Majr. Washington and his wife set off for Fredericksburgh—intending as far as Belmont on Occoquan this afternoon.

Saturday 30th.    Mercury at 67 in the Morning—78 at Noon and 75 at Night. Calm, clear and pleasant all the forenoon. In the afternoon a light breeze from the Eastward.

Rid to the Mill, Meadow, and Plantations at the Ferry, Dogue run, and Muddy hole. Gathering and securing fodder at all of them. At the last the whole would be gathered, but not secured this evening.

Mr. Burwell Bassett Junr. left this after Breakfast.

Mr. McQuir came here to Dinner & to invite me to the Accadamical commencement in Alexandria on Thursday next.

ACCADAMICAL COMMENCEMENT: "On Friday the 6th instant was held in the Alexandria Academy, an Examination of the Classical School, under the Care of the Rev. William M'Whir" (*Va. Journal*, 19 Oct. 1786).

# October 1786

[Sunday 1st.]    Mercury at 68 in the Morning—78 at Noon and 76 at Night.

The day clear and warm. Took an early Dinner and set out for Abingdon on my way to the Great Falls to meet the Directors of the Potomack Co.

Left Doctr. Craik at Mt. Vernon who came in a few minutes before I set off.

Monday 2d.    Mercury at 67 in the Morning—78 at Noon and 75 at Night.

Morning lowering but clear warm, & pleasant afterwds.

Set out before Six Oclock, & arrived at the Great Falls abt. half after nine. Found Colo. Gilpin there & soon after Govrs. Johnson & Lee, and Colo. Fitzgerald & Mr. Potts arrived when the board proceeded to enquire in to the charges exhibited by Mr. James Rumsey the late against Mr. Richardson Stuart the present Manager of the Companys business. The examination of the Witnesses employed the board until dark when the members dispersed for Lodgings. I went to Mr. Fairfax's.

Tuesday 3d.    Mercury at 67 in the Morng.—79 at Noon—74 at Night.

Morning somewhat lowerg. with thunder lightning and rain in the evening.

Returned to the Falls by appointment at 7 Oclock to Breakfast: we proceeded immediately afterwards to a consideration of the evidence, and to decide upon each article of charge: a record of which was made & upon the whole appeared (the charges) malignant, envious, & trifling. After this the board settled many accts. and adjourned till 8 oclock next Morning.

Wednesday 4th.    Mercury at 68 in the morning—78 at Noon and 72 at Night.

Morning clear, and it continued so till near 3 Oclock when it began to rain and continued with little or no intermission untill past 6 Oclock.

The Board having agreed to a Petition to be offered to the assemblies of Virga. and Maryland for prolonging the time allowed by Law for improving the Navigation of the river above the Great Falls—Directed the Manager respecting the Winter Work for the hands and having settled and regulated every other matter which came before them broke up about three oclock—when in company with Colos. Fitzgerald & Gilpin, & Mr. Potts I set off home. With much difficulty on acct. of the rising of the Water by the rain of last Night we crossed Difficult run and through a constant rain till I had reached Cameron. I got home a little before 8 oclock where I found my Brother Jno. Auge. Washington.

A PETITION . . . TO THE ASSEMBLIES: Frequent rains and high water in the summer and fall of 1785 and the summer of 1786 had prevented much work from being done on the bed of the Potomac River. The Potomac Company petition, signed by GW, requested an extension of the three years originally allowed until Nov. 1790 or "such other time as your Honors shall deem reasonable for making and improving the Navigation between Great Falls and Fort Cumberland." Both the Maryland and Virginia legislatures promptly complied with the request (BACON-FOSTER, 78–79, 80).

Thursday 5th.    Mercury at 70 in the Morng.—72 at Noon and 68 at Night.

A good deal of Rain fell in the Night; & a great deal in the course of this day (with the Wind from the So. East & sometimes very high) which occasioned very high tides, and high freshes. At home all day.

Friday 6th.    Mercury at 62 in the morning—60 at Noon and 57 at Night.

## October 1786

Morning clear, except scattering clouds—Winds high from the westward.

In the afternoon (having first dined) rid with my Brother to Mr. Lund Washington's and returned. Found the waters had been exceeding high.

Saturday 7th.    Mercury at 52 in the Morning—58 at Night [Noon] and 56 at Night.

Morning clear and tolerably pleasant—wind still westerly and pretty fresh—No frost though one was expected from appearances.

Immediately after breakfast my Brother left this, when I rid to all my Plantations. Found my People securing fodder in the Neck, Dogue run and Ferry—at the last of which the drilled corn by the meadow was untouched. At Muddy hole the fodder had all been secured on Monday last and some of the Wild Pea vine (such as came from the Eastn. shore) had been pulled. The hands on Tuesday went to assist the Dogue run people to get in their fodder —a suspension of all wch. business was had on Wednesday afternoon & all day thursday. In the Neck, the first gathering of 6 rows of drilled pease measured 4¾ bushels and the first gathering of the next 6 rows planted in rows also, but 18 Inches a part in the rows yielded 6½ bushels.

Sunday 8th.    Mercury at 56 in the Morning—60 at Night [Noon] and 57 at Night. A brisk southerly wind all day & pleasant.

Mr. Rumney, Mr. Powell, and a Mr. Patterson an English Gentn. dined here & returned in the afternoon.

Monday 9th.    Mercury at 56 in the Morning—66 at Noon and 60 at Night.

Clear warm & pleasant, with but little wind.

Rid to all the Plantations & to the Ditchers in my Mill swamp. Finished securing Fodder at the River Quarter & would nearly do so at Dogue run—at the Ferry, gathering the Fodder of the Drilled Corn by the Meadow—Pulling pease in the Neck with the small hands. Allowed all my People to go to the races in Alexandria on one of three days as best comported with their respective businesses—leaving careful persons on the Plantations.

Tuesday 10th.    Mercury at 59 in the Morning—74 at Noon and 72 at Night.

In company with Major Washington (who with his wife returned yesterday evening from Fredericksburgh) and Mr. Lear went up to Alexandria to see the Jockey club purse run for (which was won by Mr. Snickers). Dined by invitation with the Members of it and returned home in the evening.

William Snickers (b. 1759), son of Edward and Elizabeth Taliaferro Snickers of Frederick County, won 100 guineas at the Alexandria Jockey Club Purse with his horse Paul Jones. In 1793 Snickers married Frances Washington (b. 1775), daughter of Warner Washington, Jr. (1751–1829) and Mary Whiting Washington (MCILHANY, 107, 111; *Va. Journal,* 12 Oct. 1786).

Wednesday 11th.    Mercury at 60 in the Morning—74 at Noon and 73 at Night.

This day as yesterday, was clear, calm, and warm.

Majr. Washington, his wife, and Nelly & Washington Custis went up to the race at Alexa. All but the Major returned to Dinner with Betcy & Patcy Custis along with them.

I rid to all the Plantations, found most of my People had gone to the races. Those remaining in the Neck were cleaning rye which had been tread out the day before & preparing to continue their wheat sowing tomorrow.

Thursday 12th.    Mercury at 60 in the Morning—74 at Noon and 72 at Night.

Clear, calm, and warm all day, or rather till noon when a breeze from the Southward came up.

Rid to all the Plantations. Began in the Neck to sow wheat in the middle cut of drilled Corn. Ferry people all gone to the race and those at home at Dogue run all idle—Overseer being gone to the Race.

In the afternoon Doctr. Stuart and his wife Mr. Fitzhugh of Chatham, Mr. Presley Thornton Mr. Townshend Dade, and Mr. Stith came here, and stayed all Night.

Presley Thornton (1760–1807), of Northumberland County, was the son of Presley Thornton (1721–1769) and Charlotte Belson Thornton. The younger Thornton left with his mother for England in the early 1770s and served with the British army on the Continent during the Revolution. Thornton returned to Virginia immediately after the war and restored his citizenship by taking the required oaths of allegiance. In 1799 he served as a captain in the 8th United States Infantry and an aide to Charles Cotesworth Pinckney. About 1800 Thornton sold his Northumberland estate and moved to Genesee, N.Y., where he died (GW to James McHenry, 4 Feb. 1799, and GW to Thornton, 12 Aug. 1799, DLC:GW; WMQ, 1st ser., 5 [1896–97], 198–99).

Townshend Dade who appears on this day may be David Stuart's brother-in-law Townshend Dade (b. 1743). He had been married to Stuart's sister Jane Stuart (1751–1774).

Mr. Stith was possibly John Stith (1755–1808), son of Buckner Stith (1722–

1791) and brother of Col. Robert Stith of Chotank. John Stith married Ann (Nancy) Washington, daughter of Lawrence Washington (b. 1728) of Chotank and Elizabeth Dade Washington. Stith served as a captain with several different Virginia regiments during the Revolution.

Friday 13th.    Mercury at 64 in the Morning—76 at Noon and 74 at Night.

Clear Calm, and very warm all day. At Night it began to Thunder & lighten—accompanied in the course of it with frequent & hard Showers.

All the company except Mrs. Stuart went away directly after breakfast. She with Betcy & Patcy Custis did not leave this till after dinner.

Rid to the Ferry, Dogue run, & Muddy hole Plantations and to the Mill and Ditchers. Finished securing the Fodder at the Ferry. Tread out a stack of Wheat at Dogue run in order to renew my sowing of this grain at that place. Tried here and in the Neck to plow before sowing, then sow and harrow in, but it would not answer in the Corn ground. The grass occasioned the Earth to be drawn in heaps. Began to pull the early Corn at Muddy hole.

Saturday 14th.    Mercury at 62 in the Morning—70 at Noon and 68 at Night.

Morning cloudy but clear afterwards with the Wind at So. West & warm.

Rid to all the Plantations. In the Neck, found the rain of last Night had wet the Corn ground so much that there was no plowing in Wheat. Ordered them to shift to the Wheat Stubble (where they had formerly been) and Plow for Rye. Finding at the same place that part of the first sowed rye had either not come up, or had been destroyed by some insect, I directed that part of the first cut—North of the Meadow, to be sowed over again; and to be harrowed in by the double harrow—if sufficient to cover the grain. At Muddy hole gathering the early Corn & husking it. At Dogue run Sowing Wheat—the ground, in places rather too wet. At the Ferry just finished plowing, sowing & harrowing the ground allotted for Rye at the Ferry and securing the fodder. Directed, as the fly appeared to be getting into the Wheat more or less at all the Plantations, that that at the Ferry should be immediately tread out & sent to the Mill.

Sunday 15th.    Mercury 65 at Morn—76 at Noon and 74 at Night.

Clear, warm, & pleasant all day.

Accompanied by Majr. Washington his wife Mr. Lear & the two

Childn. Nelly & Washington Custis went to Pohick Church & returned to Dinner. Fell in with on the Road, Colo. Jno. Mercer, his Lady & child coming here and their nurse.

Col. John Francis and Sophia Sprigg Mercer of Maryland had a son, Richard, born 19 Nov. 1785. He died before reaching maturity (GARNETT [2], 52–53).

Monday 16th.    Mercury at 64 in the Morning – 72 at Noon and 72 at Night.

A Watery Sun in the morning and Clouds in the afternoon but no rain fell till towards day in the Night.

Colo. Mercer &ca. crossed the River after breakfast on their way to Annapolis.

Majr. Washington & myself went up to Alexandria, & dined at Lomax's. Got the Deed from Manley's Exrs. acknowledged to me in open Court & for the 2d. time agreed with Mr. Wm. Triplett for the use of Mrs. French's Plantation for wch. during Robinsons term and Interest in it, I am, for the Land & Negroes, to pay £136 & 150£ afterwards during her life.

Returned home in the Evening.

For further information on the complicated French-Dulany land transactions, see GW to David Stuart, 12 Dec. 1790, PHi: Dreer Collection; GW to William Triplett, 25 Sept. 1786, DLC:GW; Fairfax County Deeds, Book P-1, 311–16, 318–20, and Book Q-1, 392–96, Vi Microfilm).

Tuesday 17th.    Mercury at 68 in the Morning – 64 at Noon and 59 at Night.

Wind Southerly and raining till about 9 Oclock when it chopped round to the No. Wt. – blew hard & cleared.

At home all day. Began to set a brick kiln.

Wednesday 18th.    Mercury at 48 in the Morning – 56 at Noon and 55 at Night.

Clear and cool, wind pretty fresh from the No. West.

Rid by Muddy hole and Dogue run Plantations to Mr. Tripletts. 3 plows and most of the hands from the first had gone to the latter to assist in sowing Wheat in Corn ground.

Having met Mrs. French at Mr. Tripletts, I concluded the bargain with her for her Plantation & Negroes in my Neck and had a Lease executed for the same and sent word to a Mr. Robertson the present tenant to come to me to see if I cd. not engage him to quit it, and coming accordingly some propositions were made to him of which he was to consider till saturday night or Monday Morning & then give an answer.

Monsr. Ouster, French Consul at Williamsburgh & Mr. Lacaze two French Gentlemen dined here & returned to Alexa. in the evening.

Martin Oster, who came to Philadelphia from France in 1778 as an officer in the French consular service, held the post of vice-consul of Philadelphia 1781–83 and of Norfolk and Williamsburg from 1783 until his recall in 1792. He was traveling to several port cities at the time of this visit to Mount Vernon (NASATIR AND MONELL, 196, 566–67). Mr. Lacaze was a French merchant active in the Franco-American trade during the 1780s.

[Thursday] 19th. October 1786.    Mercury at 46 in the Morning —55 at Noon and 52 at Night.

A large white frost this Morning—the air cool, but calm & pleasant afterwards.

Rid to my Plantations in the Neck and at Muddy hole & from thence to Colo. McCartys to Dinner where I met Mrs. Washington & Fanny Washington.

On our return home found Mr. John Dawson and Mr. Theodk. Lee here.

In the Neck my People were sowing Wheat; but the ground was much too wet for it—but it was either to be put in in this condition or put off altogether. The former I chose. The resowing of Rye (directed on Saturday last) had been suspended, & was now put off altogether to see whether the part which appeared so thin would come to any thing—Sowing Rye on the New plowed Wheat stubble and had it harrowed and cross harrowed which put the ground in much finer order than the single harrowing had done the first. This Rye had both the harrowing after it was sowed as the lay land at Dogue run was managed. At Muddy hole the Overseer & two or three of the weak hands (the rest being at Dogue run) were gathering the Wild (or Magity bay) Pea a tedious operatn.

John Dawson (1762–1814), of Spotsylvania County, was the son of Rev. Musgrave and Mary Waugh Dawson. He represented Spotsylvania County in the House of Delegates 1786–89, was a member of the Continental Congress in 1788 and 1789, and served in the United States Congress from 1797 to 1814.

Theodorick Lee (1766–1849) was the fourth son of Henry Lee of Leesylvania, and younger brother of Light Horse Harry Lee and Charles Lee.

Friday 20th.    Mercury at 50 in the Morning—60 at Noon and 56 at Night.

Calm clear & pleasant in the Morning—lowering afterwards with the Wind Southe[r]ly.

Rid (after Mr. Dawson & Mr. Lee went away) first to the Ferry plantation, and thence to Dogue run through the Plantation lately rented of Mrs. French which I find less injured by Gullies than I expected.

At the Ferry the people were getting out the wheat and at Dogue run upon the point of finishing sowing the last cut of common corn (about the Houses) —after which I directed them to sow part of the drilled Corn.

In the afternoon Geo. Dunnington, a Tenant of mine in Charles County, Maryland, came in to give an acct. of the situation of the place on which he lives and of the attempts to take part of the Land away by one Strumat.

It ought to have been mentioned on Thursday that the early Corn drilled, in alternate rows, at Muddy hole had been measured; that of it there was only 19 Barrls. of sound corn—3 Barrls. of faulty Corn (fit only for Hogs) and 2 Barrls. of the Common Corn which had got intermixed—In all from these Alternate rows, 24 Barrls. Much rotten & bad corn was found in this early kind & proves as well from the experiment of this year as the last, that it does not do in this climate or soil.

George Dunnington lived on the land in Maryland which GW had obtained from Daniel Jenifer Adams (see 22 Jan. 1775 and 12 Sept. 1785). In 1790 Dunnington was the head of a household of 10 whites and 15 slaves in Charles County (HEADS OF FAMILIES, MD., 49). ONE STRUMAT: Capt. John Stromatt in 1790 was the head of a household of 8 whites and 8 slaves in Charles County (HEADS OF FAMILIES, MD., 54).

Saturday 21st.     Mercury at 50 in the Morning—58 at Noon and 55 at Night.

Wind at No. Et. all day with various appearances—sometimes threatning Rain—at other times promising to be fair.

Colo. Richard Henry Lee with his daughter Nancy, who came here yesterday to dinner, going away after breakfast, I rid into the Neck, and to Muddy hole & Dogue run Plantations. At the first the People had finished sowing Wheat about Noon yesterday; & to day were picking up the fallen Corn and gathering the residue of the Pease. The Plows were preparing the Wheat Stubble for rye, & sowing it. At Dogue run the Plows had got into the drilled Corn, the stalk of which were cut down & entirely taken of the ground. The ground with this plowing seemed to be in perfect tilth, & in good order. I was about to harrow it after sowing & plowing, but my Farmer advised the contrary & I desisted.

NANCY: Anne Lee (1770–1804) was the eldest daughter of Richard Henry Lee and his second wife, Anne Gaskins Pinckard Lee.

Anne (Nancy) Lee, daughter of
Richard Henry Lee. (The Society of the Lees of Virginia)

Sunday 22d.    Mercury at 48 in the Morning—59 at Noon and 56
at Night.

Clear and pleasant with but little wind.

The Honble. Wm. Drayton and Mr. Walter Izard came here to
dinner and stayed all Night. Mr. Rumney, Mr. Hunter, Mr. Wilson & Mr. Porter also came here to dinner all of whom except the
first went away after it.

William Drayton (1732–1790), of Charleston, S.C., was the son of Thomas
Drayton, prominent in political circles in that colony. Before the Revolution
Drayton practiced law in South Carolina and was chief justice of East Florida.
He spent part of the war in England. After his return to South Carolina in
1780, Drayton served as judge of the admiralty court, associate justice of the
state supreme court, and in 1789 became the first judge of the United States
court for the district of South Carolina.

Drayton began corresponding with GW on 23 Nov. 1785 when he informed
GW that the South Carolina Society for Promoting and Improving Agriculture and Other Rural Concerns had elected him its first honorary member
(DLC:GW). At the time of this visit to Mount Vernon, Drayton and Izard
were en route to South Carolina from New York.

Walter Izard (c.1750–1788) was a son of Ralph Izard (1717–1761), of
Berkeley County, S.C., and cousin of Ralph Izard (1742–1804), the revolutionary diplomat. During the Revolution Walter Izard served as a volunteer
in the Continental Army. In 1779 he married Mary Fenwick, the second
daughter of Edward Fenwick.

James Monroe, painted c.1786 by an un-known artist. (Virginia State Library)

James Madison, a pastel by James Sharp-les. (Independence National Historical Park Collection)

**Monday 23d.**   Mercury at 48 in the Morning—60 at Noon and 58 at Night.

Calm clear and pleasant all day.

Mr. Rumney went away directly after breakfast and Mrs. Wash-ington with Nelly and Washington Custis for Abingdon about the same time.

I remained at home all day. In the evening Colo. Monroe, his Lady and Mr. Maddison came in.

James Monroe (1758–1831) had served as a delegate from Virginia to the Continental Congress since 1783 but had recently resigned because no dele-gate was eligible to serve more than three out of six years. Writing from New York on 7 Oct. 1786, Monroe had suggested to James Madison, who was in Philadelphia on personal business after attending the convention in Annapo-lis, that they travel to Virginia together and stop over at Mount Vernon to visit GW (MADISON, 9:121–22, 143). Monroe and his wife, Elizabeth Kortright Monroe (d. 1830), were on their way to Fredericksburg, Va., where they in-tended to reside in a house belonging to Monroe's uncle, Joseph Jones. Madi-son was going to Richmond for the fall session of the General Assembly.

**Tuesday 24th.**   Mercury at 53 in the Morning—68 at Noon and 66 at Night.

Clear, calm, and extremely pleasant all day.

Mr. Drayton and Mr. Izard set out after breakfast on their rout to South Carolina.

I remained at home all day, being prevented from going up to Abingdon to Meet Mrs. Washington according to promise by the above company.

Entered into articles of agreement and bonds for the performance of the Covenants with John Robertson for the Plantation I lately leased of Mrs. French, and on which he lives.

Sent up to Abingdon for a young Bull of extraordinary make for which I had exchangd and given a young heifer of the same age.

John Robertson agreed to give up the use of the land and slaves on or before 1 Jan. 1787, and in the meantime GW could "employ the labourers on the said Plantation in such works as may have a tendency to prepare for his crops & Inclosures designed for the next year, when they are not necessarily engaged in finishing the present crop, and taking care of the stock and other Interests" of Robertson. Robertson could have use of a tenant house, now occupied by Peter Pool, rent free for 1787, and for an additional year for payment of rent. GW was to pay Robertson for the wheat actually sown this year and Robertson would in turn pay Pool for the wheat planted on the tenement Pool relinquished to Robertson (agreement between GW and Robertson, 24 Oct. 1786, DLC:GW).

Wednesday 25th.    Mercury at 53 in the Morng.—67 at Noon and 66 at Night.

An exceedingly heavy fog till 10 Oclock—after which it became clear warm & pleasant.

Mr. Maddison and Colo. Monroe & his Lady set out after breakfast for Fredericksburgh.

I called at the Ferry, Dogue run, & Muddy hole plantations on my way to Mr. Fendalls where I met Mrs. Washington, dined, & returned home in the evening bringing Betcy & Patcy Custis with the other two home with us. Found all the Wheat at the Ferry tred out but not quite cleaned or carried to the Mill. At Muddy hole the 4 rows of Irish Potatoes had been dugged. Out of one which appeared to be best set (though they were all much missing) 2¼ bushels were obtained and from the other 3 rows 4½ Bushels were gathered—In all 6¾ Bushels. This at best is a poor encrease—but would have been very bad if the rows had been nearly compleated but this they were not—the flat places having none on them.

Thursday 26th.    Mercury at 56 in the Morning—70 at Noon and 68 at Night.

Calm, clear, and very pleasant day throughout.

Immediately after breakfast I rid into the Neck, and to Muddy hole & Dogue run Plantations. At the first finished sowing and plowing in all the Rye, but had not compleated the harrowing & Hoeing of it. This comprehended the 3d. cut of Wheat and the furthest cut of drilled corn except 52 rows which were left for Oats in the Spring & this sowing having advanced 18 rows into the Corn which had Peas between I directed the same number of Pea rows in the middle cut to be sowed with Wheat to bring them even. This would be set about tomorrow. Ordered three plows from this place to Dogue run to assist in putting in the Wheat & rye there wch. was more backward than at any other place in sowing. At Muddy hole the people had recommenced sowing rye in the Corn ground which had been left for this purpose. The Pease of the 6 rows in the Neck which had been drilled or sowed thick, yielded 15 bushels after they were cleaned (besides the green ones) and the next 6 rows of the same kind, dropped 18 inches in the row, measured (besides the green ones) 16 Bushels. The whole field therefore (if Pease had been planted between all the Corn rows) would have yielded at this rate, 410 bushels there being 159 of them and it is to be observed that many of the rows if not all of them were greatly missing occasioned by too early planting and the frequent rains which drowned them in all low and cold places. Ordered a piece of ground to be prepared in the Neck on which to transplant Turneps for the purpose of saving seed.

Colo. and Mrs. McCarty & Colo. Ball and his Lady came here to dinner & returned afterwards and abt. Sun down Mr. Mayo & his wife & Miss D'Hart in a Post Chaise & 4 came in.

John Mayo (1760–1818), the son of John and Mary Tabb Mayo of Richmond, represented Henrico County in the House of Delegates in 1785–86, 1793, and 1796. Mayo married Abigail De Hart (1761–1843), the daughter of John De Hart (1728–1795) and Sarah Dagworthy De Hart of Elizabethtown, N.J. (MAYO, xiii, 143–44). Before her marriage to John Mayo, Abigail De Hart had made one or more shadow silhouettes of GW (GW to William Gordon, 8 Mar. 1785, DLC:GW; EISEN, 2:590). MISS D'HART: probably a sister of Abigail's.

Friday 27th.    Mercury at 56 in the Morning—58 at Noon and 56 at Night.

Cloudy in the Morning, with the wind very fresh at N. W. About 10 oclock it cleared but continued to blow fresh, and grew colder.

Rid to the Plantations at the Ferry, Dogue run, and Muddy hole and examined the Land I lately bought from the Exr. of

Manley more attentively. Find some of it in very good condition and other parts much gullied and worn and that there is more & better meadow ground on it than I expected.

Saturday 28th.     Mercury at 46 in the Morning—62 at Noon and 60 at Night.

Clear and pleasant all day with but little wind and that from So. West.

Mr. Mayo, his wife and Miss D'Hart went away after breakfast.

Rid to the Plantations in the Neck, Muddy hole, and Dogue Run. At the first compleated sowing Wheat yesterday and finished covering Rye with the Hoes & Harrows the same day—Gathering for plantation use some of the drilled Corn at Muddy hole & plowed a poor ½ acre to Cowpen on—Taking up the Irish Potatoes at Dogue run out of the way of the Wheat sowing.

Found Mrs. Stuart and her two youngest children here on my return home.

Mrs. Stuart's two youngest children were Ann Calvert (Nancy) Stuart (b. 1784) and Sarah (Sally) Stuart (born c.1786).

Sunday 29th.     Mercury at 54 in the Morning—60 at Noon and 58 at Night.

Lowering at times through the day—very little wind and that South—very smoaky all day.

Gov. William Smallwood of Maryland, by Charles Willson Peale, 1823. (State House, Annapolis, Maryland Commission on Artistic Property)

About noon Mrs. Stuart and one of her youngest Children left this for Mr. Lund Washingtons. At the same time I crossed the river with intention to view & Survey my land in Charles County Maryland. Went to and lodged at Govr. Smallwoods about 14 Miles from the Ferry.

William Smallwood (1732–1792) came from a distinguished Charles County, Md., family. In 1761 he represented Charles County in the Maryland legislature, joined the Maryland nonimportation association in 1769, and became a delegate to the Maryland Convention of 1775. During the Revolution he attained the rank of major general. He was elected to Congress in 1785 but before assuming office was chosen to succeed William Paca as governor of Maryland. After serving three one-year terms, Smallwood retired in 1788 to his home in southern Maryland.

Monday 30th.    Mercury at 49 in the Morning—52 at Noon and 50 at Night.

Raining all the forenoon with the Wind at No. Et.—Misting & very cloudy all the latter part of the day altho the Wind had shifted to the No. Wt.

About One Oclock accompanied by the Governor, I set out to take a view of my land which lay 12 Miles from his House—after doing which and finding it rather better than I expected we returned to the Governrs. having from the badness of the Weather & wetness of the ground given over the idea of Surveying.

This land lyes full level enough. The cleared part has been lively & good but much abused and a good deal worked. The wood part, of wch. there is a good deal, is tolerably full of rail timber and Wood (chiefly spanish Oak & black Jack) but the soil is thin and of a mean quality tho very capable of improvement from the Nature of it & levelness. Govr. Smallwood thinks the whole is worth and would sell for 35 or 40. Shillings Maryland Curry. pr. Acre and seems to have an inclination to buy it himself and that his Manager (one Franklin) is that way inclined also. Being informed by my Tenant (on this Land) George Dunnington of a vacancy containg. 20 or 30 acres within, or adjoining to my lines the Governor promised to obtain a warrant for it on my behalf and a Mr. Stromat who had obtained Warrants for sevel. vacancies one of which being within my Tract sent me word by the above Geo. Dunnington that I might have the latter (more than 100 acres) upon condition of my paying a proportionate part of the expence he had been at to obtain them, which I consented to do & sent him word so by Dunnington.

AN INCLINATION TO BUY IT: GW wrote Smallwood on 6 Oct. 1787: "When I had the pleasure of being at your house last fall, you gave me reason to believe that you would become the purchaser of my land adjoining yours, in Charles County—And if I recollect rightly, was to have written to me on that subject from Annapolis" (NjP) . GW expressed his continued interest in selling the land to Smallwood, but apparently nothing ever came of it, for GW still owned the land when he died. A VACANCY: There were several strips of unclaimed, or waste, land bordering on, or intruding into, GW's land. Both GW and John Stromatt, whose land marched with GW's, obtained a warrant to survey the land for their own use. For the ensuing dispute and final settlement, see GW to William Craik, 19 and 27 Mar. 1789 and 8 Feb. 1790, DLC:GW. ONE FRANKLIN: George Augustine Washington mentions an F. P. Franklin as "Govr. Smallwoods agent" in 1788 (LEDGER B, 270) . He may have meant Francis B. Franklin who lived in the area in 1790 and owned 29 slaves (HEADS OF FAMILIES, MD., 49) .

Tuesday 31st.    Mercury at 41 in the Morning—42 at Noon and 42 at Night.

Wind pretty fresh at No. West in the Morning but cloudy which it continued to be through the day with Mists in the afternoon and rain at Night, the wind getting round to No. Et.

After breakfast I left Govr. Smallwoods & got home to dinner. Attempted to cross at the Widow Chapmans in order to pay Colo. Mason a visit but could not get over.

Constantia Pearson Chapman (c.1714–c.1791) was the daughter of Capt. Simon Pearson (d. c.1733) of Stafford County, Va., and the widow of Nathaniel Chapman of Charles County, Md.

# November [1786]

Wednesday 1st.    Mercury at 38 in the Morning—41 at Noon and 41 at Night.

Cloudy all the forenoon, with a light sprinkle of rain—Wind at No. West, & afternoon clear.

Rid to all the Plantations, & to the Ditchers. Found, in the Neck that the People had begun to take up the Irish Potatoes, and during the rain had been cleaning rye & thrashing out the Pease and yesterday, & part of this day, were setting out (the summer) Turnips for Seed—at Muddy hole Sowing rye and at Dogue run that 3 pecks of the black spelt had been sowed yesterday in the drilled Corn next the Swamp, where the turnips and cabbages had been planted at the North end. On Saturday last one plow had begun a winter fallow for Oats; adjoining the rye at the Ferry; & the other people were clearing the Bryers & Shrubs out of the way of it. The Ditchers had nearly compleated the middle ditch on

Saturday, but the rain on Monday obliged them to shift to the upper ditch.

On my return found Mrs. Stuart.

Thursday 2d.    Mercury at 35 in the Morning—49 at Noon and 47 at Night.

A very large white frost—the ground froze and Ice. Morning calm, wind afterwards variable and evening cool.

Rid to the Ferry, Dogue run & Muddy hole Plantations. From the latter the Potatoes and Pease were brought home; of the former there were [      ] Bushels; and of the latter [      ] Bushels [      ] whereof were of the large kind (had from the Revd. Mr. Stuart). The Potatoes at Dogue run, from the rows planted in the drilled corn, measured 38½ Bushels. At this place the Plows were at work for Rye crossing the Corn rows; on which plowing I mean to sow the grain and then harrow & cross harrow the ground as had been done before with both Wheat & rye. At the ferry getting out Rye. Directed one or two plows more to assist in breaking up the ground at this place if the plowers could do it well. Left this to the Overseer to determine.

Levelled round to the Road at a Stake by the bridge near Manleys, & begun to do the same on the other side of Muddy hole swamp from the plank bridge.

Mr. Lund Washington and his wife dined here and returned in the evening.

Friday 3d.    Mercury at 49 in the Morning—56 at Noon and 56 at Night.

Cloudy with small showers at intervals, till after noon, when the weather cleared & became warm and pleasant. Wind Southerly all day.

At home writing Letters.

Saturday 4th.    Mercury at 43 in the Morning—54 at Noon and 54 at Night.

Morning mild, clear, and pleasant with the wind Southerly in the afternoon.

Rid to all the Plantations. In the Neck, finished gathering and Measuring the Irish Potatoes, wch. turned out as follow—viz.—In the Cut next the Barn 100 Bushels—There being 10 rows, every alternate one had a sprinkling of dung; 4 of which produced 52 bushels—the other being of another kind of Potatoe, produced not more than 1 Bushel, the 5 undunged rows yielded 48 Bushels.

The Middle cut turned out 50 Bushels & the Easternmost cut 25 Bushels only. As the number & length of the Rows were the same in these as the first the differe. in the quantity is to be ascribed to the difference of Land and to that part of the first cut in wch. the Potatoes grew having been dunged formerly over and above the sprinkling it got at Seed time. It is to be noted however that the last mentioned cuts were more missing than the first; and the whole more or less so. At Muddy hole compleated sowing the rye and at Dogue run only began this day to sow—the ground being too wet before. At the Ferry 2 plows employed in fallowing.

On my return home found Colo. Pinkney his Lady & 4 Childn., Mrs. Middleton her Child nurse &ca. here—also Mr. Robt. and Mr. Lawe. Washington and Mr. Thompson. The 3 last went away after dinner—the others stayed all Night.

Charles Cotesworth Pinckney (1746–1825), the son of Charles and Elizabeth Lucas Pinckney of South Carolina, had a distinguished career in the public service of his state and country as a soldier, statesman, and diplomat. Pinckney's first wife, Sarah Middleton Pinckney, was the daughter of Henry Middleton (1717–1784). Sarah died in 1784, and on 23 June 1786 Pinckney married Mary Stead, the daughter of Benjamin Stead. The children GW mentioned here were Pinckney's by his first wife. Mrs. Middleton probably referred to Mary Izard Middleton, the daughter of Walter Izard of Cedar Grove, S.C., and the wife of Arthur Middleton (1742–1787), who was the brother of Sarah Pinckney. At this time Pinckney and his entourage were returning from a trip north.

Sunday 5th.    Mercury at 44 in the Morning—54 at Noon and 54 at Night.

The forenoon variable—sometimes threatning and then promising—but clear, fine and agreeable in the afternoon. Wind southerly all day.

Colo. Pickney &ca. set out after breakfast.

At home all day writing.

Monday 6th.    Mercury at 43 in the Morning—58 at Noon and 57 at Night.

But very little wind and that southerly. Clear & remarkably pleasant all day.

After breakfast Mrs. Stuart & all her Children except Washington Custis went away.

I rid to the Plantations at the Ferry, Dogue run & Muddy hole —Making a farm pen at the latter.

On my return home found Colo. Lewis Morris and his Brother Major Jacob Morris here, who dined and returned to Alexandria afterwards where Mrs. Lewis Morris & her Mother Mrs. Elliot were on their way to Charleston.

Lewis and Jacob Morris (1755–1844) were sons of Lewis Morris (1726–1798) and Mary Walton Morris of Morrisania, Westchester County, N.Y., and nephews of Gouverneur Morris. Both brothers served during the Revolution in the New York militia before becoming aides-de-camp. Jacob was aide to Charles Lee 1776–78 and Nathanael Greene 1781–82, and Lewis was aide to John Sullivan 1776–79 and to Greene from 1779 to the end of the war. In 1783 Lewis married Ann Elliott, the daughter of William and Sabina Elliott (d. 1793) of Accabee on the Ashley River near Charleston, S.C.

Tuesday 7th.   Mercury at 53 in the Morning–60 at Noon and 59 at Night.

Clear mild & very pleast. all day–Calm in the forenoon & a light Southerly breeze after Noon.

Rid to all the Plantations to day. In the Neck the people had just finished gathering and measuring the Pease which in all amounted to only 80 Bushels. They were, in places, very much missing to which this short quantity is principally to be ascribed. Some had not ripened and were destroyed by the frost & left on the Vines. Ordered the three plows belonging to Muddy hole to go to Dogue run to assist in getting in the rye while the weather continued good.

My old Farmer thinking the Nights had got too long tho' the weather as yet has been mild to keep the Cattle in open pens on the naked ground, I ordered the whole not to be penned till proper shelters were made for them.

Wednesday 8th.   Mercury at 54 in the Morning–58 at Noon and 58 at Night.

Very mild, with but little Wd. and that Southerly–Lowering more or less all day with great appearances now & then of rain but none fell. In the evening the clouds dispelled.

Rid to the Ferry & Dogue run Plantations. At the first, the wheat & rye having been all Tread & threshed out, there was in the whole of the former [     ] Bushels; and of the latter [     ] Bushels. The people were employed in digging the Irish Potatoes near the Fish House. At the latter 9 plows & 2 harrows employed in getting in rye–the rest of the People getting off the Corn & Stalks of the only unsowed Corn ground at this Plantation.

The Farmer having carrd. the level & staked it for conducting the Water on the South side of Muddy hole swamp below the fork by Manleys old House and Cornelius McDermot Roe having done the same on the No. Side from the plank bridge on Muddy hole (where the farmer also began) I tried with a water level across in several places within Manleys field and found that the farmer was higher on his side than the other by between 13 and 16 Inches. But this will make no essential difference in a ditch for the water 18 Inches deep.

Thursday 9th.    Mercury at 48 in the Morning—54 at Noon and 52 at Night.

Morning heavy, about Noon it began to rain, & continued to do so all the Afternoon moderately.

Rid to the River, Muddy hole, and Dogue run Plantations. At the first the People were employed in removing the Potatoes from thence to the Mansion House—at the 2d. in gathering Corn except the 3 plow people who were at Work at Morris's—at the 3d. they were employed as yesterday.

Friday 10th.    Mercury at 53 in the Morning—[      ] at Noon and [      ] at Night.

Morning a little lowering—more favourable at Noon but raining afterwards. But little wind in the forepart of the day and that Southerly. Towards evening it got to the Eastward and in the Night Westerly & cleared.

With Mrs. Washington and all the family, I went to Alexanda. and dined with Doctr. Craik. Returned in the Evening.

DINED WITH DOCTR. CRAIK: James Craik seems to have moved with his family from Maryland to Alexandria, probably during the summer or early fall of 1786.

Saturday 11th.    Mercury at 41 in the Morning—45 at Noon and 42 at Night.

Morning clear and cool, with the wind pretty fresh from the No. Wt. By noon it became calm & very pleasant.

Rid to the Mill, and to Dogue run & Muddy hole plantations. At the first named Plantation finished plowing for Rye in the Morning, but there remained of it 8 or 10 acres to sow & harrow in. By Night the ground from which the Corn & Stalks had been taken off would be plowed (4 or 5 acres of it) for to lay down in Spelts provided for me by Colo. Deakins.

Having received a letter from Baltimore, announcing the arrival of three Asses (a male and two females) from the Marquis de la Fayette for me together with some Pheasants and Patridges from France, I sent my Overseer Jno. Fairfax and a servant to bring the former.

Received from the Ferry Plantation 48½ bushels of a fine red (Irish) Potatoe, which were planted in the rows of drill corn by the fish house. This with [    ] bushels of the white kind, which were planted in the missing places—of which after all replanting, there were many—is what came of that piece of drilled ground.

The common Corn in the alternate rows of Drilled, at Muddy hole, turned out 28 Barrels wch. is 7 Barrels more than the other rows did of the early Corn. In the Neck the disproportion between these is much greater.

Sunday 12th.    Mercury at 41 in the Morning—48 at Noon and 48 at Night.

Morning clear, wind fresh from the Southward—lowering after wards till Noon when it began to rain & continued to do so moderately all the afternoon.

Monday 13th.    Mercury at 39 in the morning—47 at Noon and 46 at Night.

Morning clear and cool, the Wind being fresh at No. West. Towards the afternoon the wind veered round (backed) to the Southward and in the evening lulled.

Rid to all the Plantations—getting up Hogs for feeding at all. Finished sowing and harrowing in Rye at Dogue run & began to gather Corn in the Neck and at the Ferry for lofting.

Agreed to let the Widow Alton have the House used for a School by my Mill if the School should be discontinued and

Told James Bloxham, my Farmer, who was about to write to England for his Wife & family, and who proposed the measure that he might write to one Caleb Hall a Neighbour of his in Gloucestershire (who had expressed a desire to come to this Country, and who he said was a compleat Wheel Wright, Waggon builder, and Plow & Hurdle maker) that I wd. give him 25 Guineas a year for his Services (if he paid his own passage to this Country) the first year, and if I found he answered my purposes, & we liked each other, that I might give him 30 guineas the next yr. and held out encouragemt. if he chose to work for himself, that I would provide him with some place to live at—Whilst with me that he should be found in Provisions, Washing & lodging.

WIDOW ALTON: Mrs. Elizabeth Alton was the widow of GW's old servant John Alton, who had died the previous year (see entry for 4 Dec. 1785).

James Bloxham noted, in a letter of 12 Nov. 1786 to his former employer William Peacey, that he had sent for his wife and two daughters to join him at Mount Vernon, while his two sons were to remain in England to obtain an education. Bloxham's former neighbor, Caleb Hall, eventually decided against emigrating (Peacey to GW, 2 Feb. 1787, DLC:GW; GW to Peacey, 16 Nov. 1786, PHi, and 7 Jan. 1788, ViMtV).

Tuesday 14th.    Mercury at 41 in the Morning—50 at Noon and 50 at Night.

Lowering in the Morning with appearances of rain. About Noon the Clouds broke; and the afternoon became clear mild & exceedingly pleasant.

Rid to Muddy hole, Dogue run, & Ferry Plantations. At the latter compleated all my fall Sowing of winter grain, by putting into the Corn ground wch. had been prepared for the purpose, 6½ bushels of the Common Spelts. This ground after the Corn, & stalks were taken off, was plowed—the grain then Sowed, & harrowed & cross harrowed. The Soil is strong, but being very grassy, the Spelts with all this working were not put in very well —some places not being broke, & by means of the grass choaking the harrow, drawn, it is to be feared, in heaps—abt. 5 Acres of it.

Beat about one Bushel of the Wild Crab into pummice, and sowed it in the hop Inclosure—lower end, in 19 rows, one foot apart.

Wednesday 15th.    Mercury at 46 in the Morning—58 at Noon and 54 at Night.

Wind Southerly but not very fresh in the forepart of the day. About Noon it came out very powerfully at No. West and towds. Night turned cold.

Rid to Muddy hole and Dogue run Plantations. The hands at these places & the ferry at work on the public Roads.

Attempted to level to day, but the wind was too high to admit it.

Thursday 16.    Mercury at 36 in the Morning—48 at Noon and 47 at Night.

Morning windy clear, and cold; before Noon it moderated and became mild & pleasant and before Night it got to the Southwd. and lowered a little.

Mr. & Mrs. Fendall came from Maryland here to Breakfast—as did Mr. Willm. Craik—after which they all went away.

Rid into the Neck, and to Muddy hole plantations. At the first having measured the remainder of the Middle cut of drilled Corn it was found to turn out 85 Barls.—the further, or Eastermost cut of drilled Corn in the same field turned out miserably bad—there being only 6 barrl. of the early Corn & 18 of the other or common corn. Here the difference against the early or Eastern is found greater than at Muddy hole and decidely in both in favor of the common Corn of the Country.

On my return home, found Mons. Campoint sent by the Marqs. de la Fayette with the Jack and two She Asses which he had procured for me in the Island of Malta and which had arrived at Baltimore with the Chinese Pheasants &ca. had with my Overseer &ca. got there before me. These Asses are in good order and appear to be very fine. The Jack is two years old and the She Asses one three & the other two. The Pheasants and Patridges will come round by Water.

ON MY RETURN HOME: During his visit to Mount Vernon in 1784, Lafayette had apparently offered to obtain breeding stock from Malta. Because GW was unsure that his Spanish jacks were coming, he asked Lafayette to obtain "a male & female, or *one* of former & *two* of the latter" from the governor of Malta or some other person (GW to Lafayette, 15 Feb., 1 Sept. 1785, DLC:GW). When they arrived, accompanied by caretaker Jacques Campion, GW was delighted. He wrote to Lafayette on 19 Nov. 1786: "On thursday last I received in very good order . . . the most valuable things you could have sent me" (DLC:GW). He named the jack Knight of Malta. GW expected to pay for the animals, but Lafayette clearly intended them as a gift (GW to Lafayette, 25 Mar., 15 Aug. 1787, DLC:GW).

Friday 17th.    Mercury at 38 in the Morning—44 at Noon and 45 at Night.

Cloudy with drops of rain now and then in the forenoon—more promising afterwards with the wind fresh from the Southward all day.

At home writing all day. Finished the ditch along the side of my Mill Meadow intended to conduct the water in common heights of the run.

Saturday 18th.    Mercury at 43 in the Morning—43 at Noon and 40 at Night.

Wind Easterly all day and very cloudy and like for snow—sometimes drops of it for the first this year.

Rid to the Ferry, Dogue run & Muddy hole Plantations—gathering & husking Corn at all. Also rid to the Ditche[r]s who had begun to scour a ditch in the Mill Meadow. One of them, James Lawson went up to Town to day. Yesterday they entered upon standing wages.

Monsr. Campion accompanied by Mr. Lear went to Alexandria & returned in the Evening.

Sunday 19th.    Mercury at 34 in the Morning—38 at Noon and 32 at Night.

Ground lightly covered with Snow this Morning. Continued cloudy all day and Snowing a little, at times, but the ground was never more than an inch thick. At home all day.

Monday 20th.    Mercury at 36 in the Morning—40 at Noon and 34 at Night.

A thick fog & Mist all day with little or no wind. After dark the Clouds dispelled and Stars appeared.

At home all day.

Tuesday 21st.    Mercury at 36 in the Morning—40 at Night [Noon] and 38 at Night.

Flying clouds with the Wind pretty fresh from the No. Wt. in the Morning and cold. Pleasanter afterwards and clear Wind moderating about Noon and by night was calm.

Rid to the Ferry, Dogue run, and Muddy hole Plantn.—gathering and husking Corn at all of them.

Sent George Washington to Town on business.

Colo. Darke dined here.

William Darke (1736–1801), of Berkeley County, during the Revolution attained the rank of lieutenant colonel in the 4th Virginia Regiment, and in the early 1790s he was made a brigadier general as a reward for his frontier service under Maj. Gen. Arthur St. Clair. Often during the 1790s Darke represented Berkeley County in the General Assembly.

Wednesday 22.    Mercury at 34 in the Morning—32 at Noon and 30 at Night.

Two inches or more snow fell in the Night—more [or] less fell all day—but little Wind and that Southerly.

At home all day.

Thursday 23d.    Mercury at 32 in the Morning—36 at Noon and 36 at Night.

Very cold in the forenoon and not very agreeable at any time of the day—Wind at No. West.

Rid to the Plantations at Muddy hole & Dogue run. At the first raking up dung—at the other gathering and husking of Corn.

Set James Lawson and his comrade, Patrick Sheriden, to running a level ditch 2 feet wide at top, 1 at Bottom, and a spit deep, from the bridge over Muddy hole by the corner of the fence till it should come to the road by the other bridge and branch.

On my return home found Colo. (or Judge) Harrison of Maryland here as also Mr. William Craik.

SPIT: the depth of the blade of a spade.

Friday 24th.    Mercury at 31 in the Morning—41 at Noon and 36 at Night.

Very clear, and pretty cold in the Morning Wind being at No. West but not hard. About Noon it moderated, and at Night was calm.

After breakfast Judge Harrison and Mr. Craik returned to Maryland. I rid to the Ditchers and thence to the Ferry Plantation —Grubbing at the latter and getting up wild hogs.

Major Washington went into the Neck, and to Muddy hole. At the first he measured 86½ Barrels of Corn—gathered from the drilled cut of Corn nearest the Barn and at Muddy hole he Measured 67 Barrls. which was gathered out of the Middle Cut besides 14 Barls. of Short Corn givn. Hogs.

Saturday 25th.    Mercury at 36 in the Morning—42 at Noon and 40 at Night.

Mild and but little wind, which was Southerly—lowering all day. In the Night the Wind came out from the No. Wt. and it froze hard.

Rid to Alexandria to place the Papers respecting the Administration of Colo. Thos. Colvills Estate in the hands of Mr. Keith to adjust & settle them & to do some other Business.

Bought the time of a Dutch family consisting of a Man by profession a Ditcher, Mower, &ca., a Woman his wife a Spinner, washer, Milker and their child—names.

Daniel Overdunk

Margarett Overdunk

Anna Overdunk

Dined at Colo. Hooes and returned home in the evening.

GW had secured the services of the Overdoncks, a German family—probably redemptioners—through the agency of Philip Marsteller, an Alexandria merchant. Today GW sent a barge to Alexandria to transport them to Mount Vernon and requested Marsteller "to impress upon them in strong terms the propriety of diligent attention to their duty" (GW to Marsteller, 27 Nov. 1786, and Marsteller to GW, 27 Nov. 1786, DLC:GW; LEDGER B, 245).

Sunday 26th.    Mercury at 32 in the Morning—43 at Noon and 40 at Night. Wind at No. West in the fore noon, but not hard;

about Noon it died away, and in the evening was quite calm. Ground pretty hard frozen in the Morning.

The following Gentlemen dined here.

Colonels Hooe & Henley—Dr. Craik, Mr. Porter, Mr. Swift, Mr. Jackson, Mr. Jenkes, Mr. Thompson, Mr. Lowry, Mr. Abenethy, Mr. [    ] Mr. Peran, Captns. Sullivan and [    ] Lund Washington all of whom went away in the Evening.

Mr. Jackson may be John Jackson who was licensed as a merchant to retail goods in Fairfax County in 1787 (SPROUSE [2], 2:7). MR. JENKES: either John, Joseph, or Crawford Jenckes, partners in the firm of Jenckes, Winsor & Co. In 1787 their store was located at the foot of King Street in Alexandria (*Va. Journal,* 19 April 1787; Alexandria City Hustings Courts, Book D, 227–43, Vi Microfilm).

Mr. Thompson is probably Jonah Thompson, an Alexandria merchant. In 1784 he had a store on Fairfax Street, where he sold imported goods (*Va. Journal,* 11 Nov. 1784; MOORE [1], 74).

James Abernathy, a close friend of Thomas Porter, was probably a young merchant in Alexandria (SPROUSE [2], 2:16; Porter to Benjamin Lincoln, Jr., 11 July 1787, MHi: Benjamin Lincoln Papers).

Capt. Giles Sullivan of the ship *Union* had brought with him from Ireland a letter and gift for GW from Richard Harrison, of the Alexandria firm of Hooe & Harrison (Harrison to GW, 10 July 1786, DLC:GW).

Monday 27th.    Mercury at 38 in the Morning—48 at Noon and 44 at Night.

Wind Southerly, and moderately all day. Sometimes there were great appearances of rain at other times it looked promising. Evening clear but a circle and bur both rd. the Moon.

Rev. Jedediah Morse, by Samuel F. B. Morse. (Yale University Art Gallery, bequest of Josephine K. Colgate)

Rid to the Ferry, Dogue run and Muddy hole Plantations—also to the Mill and to the Ditchers—about the Corn at all the places— Measd. 68 Barls. at Dogue run.

The Revd. Mr. Keith, and the Revd. Mr. Morse dined here & returned to Alexandria in the Evening.

Received my Chinese Pheasents &ca. from Baltimore by the Packet—viz.—

A Cock & Hen } of the Gold Pheast.

A Cock & Hen } of the Silver Pheat.

A Cock & 2 Hens } of the French Pheat.

and one French Patridge. The other French Patridge died in coming round from Baltimore.

The German Man, his wife and Child came home last Night by water from Alexanda.

Jedidiah Morse (1761–1826) was born in Woodstock, Conn., the son of Jedidiah and Sarah Child Morse. While studying theology at Yale in the early 1780s, Morse expanded an early interest in geography and in 1784 published the first school textbook on the subject, *Geography Made Easy*, a forerunner of his more ambitious later works. The day after his ordination in the Congregational Church on 9 Nov. 1786, Morse left his position as tutor at Yale and at this time was on his way to become pastor of a church in Midway, Ga. Morse and a fellow classmate, Abiel Holmes, exchanged posts temporarily so that Holmes could visit New England and Morse could learn more about the geography of the South. By Aug. 1787 Morse had returned to Yale to embark on a career in the ministry (MORSE [1], 26–28).

MY CHINESE PHEASENTS: The birds, from the royal aviary of France, were a gift from Lafayette. Charles Willson Peale wrote from Philadelphia that if any of the birds should die he would like to obtain the bodies for display. GW replied on 9 Jan. 1787: "I cannot say that I shall be happy to have it in my power to comply with your request by sending you the bodies of my Pheasants; but I am afraid it will not be long before they will compose a part of your Museum" (sold by American Art Association, 17 Mar. 1931, Item 260). In February GW sent Peale the body of a golden pheasant packed in wool, and said he would like to free the others but feared they would be taken by hawks. In acknowledging receipt of the Chinese pheasant on 27 Feb. 1787, Peale admitted that until receiving the specimen he thought the birds he had seen in Chinese paintings were only "works of fancy" (DLC:GW).

Tuesday 28th.    Mercury at 36 in the Morning—29 at Noon and 27 at N.

Wind fresh all day from the No. West, and North, with clouds and appearances of Snow. Towards evening it cleared, and was very cold all day.

A Hound bitch which like most of my other hounds appearing to be going Mad and had been shut up getting out, my Servant Will in attempting to get her in again was snapped at by her at the arm. The Teeth penetrated through his Coat and Shirt and contused the Flesh but he says did not penetrate the skin nor draw any blood. This happened on Monday forenoon. The part affected appeared to swell a little to day.

Rid to the Plantations at Dogue run, Muddy hole, and in the Neck. Set my Dutchman to ditching within the fence at the Ferry where the water level of the branch was traced out.

Wednesday 29th.    Mercury at 17 in the Morning—23 at Noon and 22 at Night.

Wind Northerly and rather fresh in the forenoon and about So. Et. afterwards—very raw and cold all day with appears. of Snow. Towards Night a mixture of it and hail fell but not enough to cover the ground.

Rid to the Plantations at the Ferry, Dogue run, and Muddy hole and to the Ditchers.

At the first G. Washington measured 72 Barrls. of Corn from the cut on the flat (exclusive of the drilled corn) which with 9 used for the Hogs and 6 for the Negroes makes 87 out of that Cut.

At the same time John Fairfax my Overseer 76 Barrls. in the Neck from the Cut next the Barn.

Gathering, husking, and securing Corn at all the Plantations.

Mr. Campion (who brought the Asses and Pheasants here from the Marqs. de la fayette) for Alexa. to proceed in the Stage for Baltimore. Gave him 30 Louis dores for his trouble.

LOUIS DORES: A louis d'ore was a French gold coin first struck in 1640 and issued until the French Revolution. In 1717 its legal value in England was fixed at 17s. In his ledger, GW entered the amount given Campion as "30 Guineas & 28s.," or "£42" (LEDGER B, 238).

Thursday 30th.    Mercury at 26 in the Morning—[    ] at Noon and [    ] at Night.

Morning cloudy but Mild—Wind westerly all day. About 9 or 10 Oclock the clouds dispersed and the day turned out very fine and pleasant. Thawing considerably—the frost having stopped the Plow at the Ferry Plantation.

Surveying my New purchases of Manley's and French Land, in order to lay the whole of into proper inclosures.

Geo. Washington went up to Abingdon in my Chariot to bring his wife and Nelly Custis home who went thither on Monday last.

Jno. Fairfax measured 42 Barrls. of corn at Muddy hole gathered out of the Eastermost (& furthest) cut in the field.

Mr. Lear left this for the Western Parts of Pensylva. in the Neighbourhood of Pittsburgh on my business.

Tobias Lear's journey to Pennsylvania was precipitated by news from GW's Pennsylvania lawyer, Thomas Smith, that GW had won his suit of ejectment in the Pennsylvania court against the settlers trespassing on the Millers Run tract in Washington County (see entries for 14, 20, and 22 Sept. 1784). Smith urged GW to appoint an agent in the area to take possession of the lands as soon as the settlers left (Smith to GW, 7 Nov. 1786, DLC:GW). Lear's primary objective on the trip was undoubtedly to persuade Presley Neville, John Cannon, or George McCarmick to act as an agent. GW also needed local information as to the highest prices he could expect to get for these lands and the smaller Washington's Bottom tract in Fayette County. GW gave Lear additional commissions: at Bath he was to inquire into the condition of a small tract of land owned by GW in the area; at Col. John Stephenson's on the road from Fort Cumberland to Pittsburgh, he was to try to collect money owed GW; at Pittsburgh he was to request Gen. Richard Butler's help in acquiring an Indian vocabulary requested by Catherine the Great; he was to ascertain the condition of GW's small tenement on Braddock's Road; and at Winchester he was to attempt to collect money owed GW by the estate of Maj. Gen. Charles Lee (instructions for Lear, 30 Nov. 1786, CSmH). Lear carried with him letters, dated 27 Nov., from GW to Neville, Butler, and McCarmick; to Thomas Freeman, Cannon, and Stephenson dated 28 Nov.; and a blank power of attorney to be given to the person who accepted the job of agent for the Millers Run land (DLC:GW).

# December 1786

**Friday 1st.** Mercury at 36 in the Morning—[      ] at Noon and [      ] at Night.

Wind Southerly and pretty fresh—clear and pleasant all day.

Employed as yesterday, running round the Lands of Manley and French.

Geo. Washington and his wife returned home in the Evening.

Received 50 Bushels of Buck Wheat from Colo. Leven Powell of Loudoun.

Leven (Levin) Powell (1737–1810), a Loudoun County merchant, was a major in the Virginia militia 1775–76 and a lieutenant colonel of the 16th Regiment of the Continental line 1777–78. Powell served as a Virginia delegate in the late 1780s and early 1790s as well as a United States congressman 1799–1801. For a discussion of GW's experiments with buckwheat, see the entry for 2 Aug. 1762.

**Saturday 2d.** Mercury at 35 in the Morning—46 at Noon and 45 at Night.

Wind at No. West very early in the Morning—after which it turned calm and then came out pretty brisk from Southward.

Finished running round the Fields of Manleys and French's and rid afterwards to Dogue run and Muddy hole plantations.

Measured at the latter 19 Barrls. of long Corn & 6 of Short which with the 42 Measured there on Thursday last makes 67 out of that cut and 201 Barrls. in all made at the Plantation this year.

Sunday 3d.    Mercury at 38 in the morning—46 at Noon and 42 at Night.

Clear and very pleasant in the Morning with a light air from the Westward. Continued fine till towds. evening when the Sky looked gloomy in the horizon of the Suns setting and a great circle appeared round the Moon at Night.

At home all day alone.

Monday 4th.    Mercury at 31 in the Morning—36 at Noon and 32 at Night.

Began to Snow an hour or two before day, and continued steadily at it quite through it—by Night it was about 6 Inches deep—the Wind at No. East.

No stirring out to day. Doctr. Craik who had been sent for to a laying in Woman at the river Plantation came here after dark and stayed all Night.

Tuesday 5th.    Mercury at 30 in the Morning—34 at Noon and 31 at Night.

Morning clear and cold. Wind (which had blown all Night) continued hard at No. West till near Sun down when it lulled, but rose again after dark.

Doctr. Craik went away after Breakfast. I remained at home all day writing.

Wednesday 6th.    Mercury at 16 in the Morning—30 at Noon and 31 at Night.

Morning calm and foggy—Wind Southerly afterwards, and towards evening rather brisk. River froze quite across in the Morning, but broke before Noon by the Wind; and by Night the Ice remained on the flats only.

Writing in the forenoon prevented my riding out to day also.

Major Washington measured 41½ barrls. of Corn at Dogue run to day.

# December 1786

Thursday 7th.    Mercury at 36 in the Morning—40 at Noon and 36 at Night.

Wind Southerly all day and Weather lowering. In the afternoon it began to rain slowly, & continued to do so I believe through the Night.

Rid to the Ferry, Dogue run & Muddy hole Plantations—also to the Mill, & to the Ditchers—Grubbing at the first place and beating out & cleaning, for house use, Corn at the latter. Gathering in, and husking this at Dogue run.

The Wheat made, and disposition of it at the Ferry is as follow

| Made | How disposed of | |
|---|---|---|
| Bushels 245⅓ | Sowed | 95 Bls. |
| | Sent to D. Run | 20 |
| | Ditto to the Mill | 130⅓ |
| | | 245⅓ |

Acct. of Rye made at the same place and disposition of it.

| Made | Disposed of | Bls. |
|---|---|---|
| Bushels 139 | Sowed | 25 |
| | Do. sent to D. run | 28½ |
| | Do. to Home Ho[use] | 26 |
| | Do. to Muddy hole | 19½ |
| | Given to the Horses | 25 |
| | Overseers Share | 15 |
| | | 139 |

At Muddy hole 2 Stacks of Rye of equal size with three remaining have been got out, and disposed of as follows

| To Dogue run | 52½ Bushls. |
|---|---|
| Sowed | 28 |
| Given to the Horses | 24½ |
| | 105 |

Friday 8th.    Mercury at 38 in the Morning—34 at Noon and 34 at Night.

Wind Southerly all day & with the rain that fell last Night, and at intervals to day occasioned much Water in and on the Earth. Towds. Night a mixture of snow and fine hail began (from the No. West) & continued through the night.

Rid to where the Ditchers were at work and to the Ferry Plantation.

Saturday 9th.    Mercury at 34 in the Morning—26 at Noon and 26 at Night.

A sharp hail, and hard wind all day from the No. West—very cold & disagreeable.

Received the Accts. of Wheat sown at Dogue run—159 Bushels.

Sunday 10th.    Mercury at 30 in the Morning—31 at Noon and 24 at Night.

Wind fresh all day from the No. Wt. & Cold. The clouds dispersed in the Night—Morning & day clear excepting a few flying Clouds and freezing hard.

Monday 11th.    Mercury at 14 in the Morning—26 at Noon and 24 at Night.

Wind at No. West all day and Cold—very little, or no thawing though clear. The River was entirely closed this Morning and the Ice so hard as not to be opened or broke by the Wind or tide.

At home all day.

My Ditchers not being able to level & thereby to carry on the Ditch they were about I shifted them to the Wood on the hither side Muddy hole branch wch. had been levelled by my Farmer.

In the Afternoon a Mr. Anstey (Commissioner from England for ascertaining the claims of the refugees) with a Mr. Woodorf (supposed to be his Secretary) came in and stayed all Night.

John Anstey (d. 1819), the son of Christopher Anstey (1724–1805) and Ann Calvert Anstey of Bath, Eng., was a barrister of Lincoln's Inn and a commissioner for auditing public accounts, as well as a poet who used the pseudonym John Surrebutter. In 1785 Anstey was made a member of the Commission for Enquiring into the Losses, Services, and Claims of the American Loyalists. After stopping at Mount Vernon, Anstey left for Charleston, eventually touring much of America before returning to England in Sept. 1788 to render a final report on the Loyalists' claims (George William Fairfax to GW, 25 Jan. 1786, and GW to Edmund Randolph, 12 Dec. 1786, DLC:GW).

Tuesday 12th.    Mercury at 13 in the Morning—28 at Noon and 26 at Night.

Wind Southerly, but cold not withstanding with great appearances every now and then through the day of Snow. At other times the Sun seemed to prevail.

Mr. Anstey & his companion going away about 11 Oclock I rid to the Ditchers and to Dogue run Plantation, also to Muddy hole —little doing at either.

Geo. Washington went to the Ferry Plantation & Measured the corn which was drilled. In the small piece by the fish house, containing rather under 2 acres, the yield was 9 Barrls. 1 bushl. & an half and in the other piece adjoining the Meadow containing 16¼ acres the yield was 29 Barrls. It is to be observed of both; that they were late planted, which was apparently of considerable disadvantage to them and of the latter, that it was of the Eastern rare ripe Corn which had yielded so unproductively both at Muddy hole & in the Neck.

RARE RIPE CORN: any early ripening variety. GW sent a shipment of rare-ripe seed corn to William Pearce 27 July 1794, saying, "it will be fine for the wet grounds which cannot be planted early, next Spring" (DLC:GW).

Wednesday 13th.    Mercury at 27 in the Morning—37 at Noon and 35 at Night.

Wind Southerly—air temperate but heavily charged with Snow or rain all the forenoon. In the afternoon it began to rain and continued to do so pretty steadily through the greater part of the Night. It cleared however before day.

Rid to the Ferry, Dogue run, and Muddy hole Plantations and to the Ditchers. At the first the People had begun to gather Corn in the cut on the Hill. At Dogue run the hands were also employed in gathering & husking of Corn. At Muddy hole a yard was clearing out to tread Rye.

Thursday 14th.    Mercury at 37 in the Morning—59 at Noon and 49 at Night.

Clear, calm, warm, and exceedingly pleasant over head—but wet under foot occasioned by the Thaw. Towards night the river began to open by the breaking of the Ice.

Rid to the Neck, and all the other Plantations; and to the Ditchers. At Muddy hole the hands were employed in threshing Wheat —at all the others gathering Corn as usual.

Doctr. La Moyeur came in just as we were going to dinner.

Friday 15th.    Mercury at 36 in the Morning—37 at Noon and 34 at Night.

Morning a little Rainy, it having begun to fall (though not fast or much) sometime in the Night. Before Noon it ceased Raing. and the evening became clear with the Wind (tho' not fresh) at North West.

Mr. Bushrod Washington, his Wife and Miss Polly Blackburne came here whilst we were at Dinner.

The River in the Ferry way became entirely free from Ice this Morning, and my Boat & hands which had been froze up on the Maryland side since Saturday last returned.

At home all day.

Saturday 16th. Mercury at 28 in the Morning—47 at Noon and 41 at Night.

Last Nights frost pretty hard. Day clear, calm, and pleasant for the Season—thawing after the Sun got up a little.

Rid to the Plantations at the Ferry, dogue run and Muddy hole —Gathering and husking corn at the two first—Treading out a Stack of Rye at the latter.

Received the following acct. of the Corn measured in the Neck by Jno. Fairfax, to day—viz. 42 Barrels from the riverside cut which makes the whole crop stand thus at that Plantation

| Drilled Corn | |
|---|---|
| Cut nearest the Barn | 86½ |
| Middle cut | 85 |
| Easternmost ditto | 24 |
| Common Planting | 195½ |
| Cut next the Barn | 76 |
| Middle do. | 74 |
| River side cut | 42 |
| Total | 387½ |

The Oats made at, and recd. from that Plantation this year are

| Of those drilled between the rows of drilled Corn | 55 |
|---|---|
| From the point 29 Acres | 275 |
| Total | 330 |

The Wheat sowed here this year, is—

| | Bush. |
|---|---|
| In the field on the River | 126 |
| In part of the Middle cut Timberlanding field | 30 |
| In all | 156 |
| Rye Ditto in field No. 1 | 50 |
| Eastn. most cut of No. 2 | 19 |
| Sowed in all | 69 |

| Besides the Rye sowed as mentioned on the other side, there has been | Bush. |
|---|---|
| used by the Negroes | 25 |
| Ditto by the Horses | 65 |
| Sent to Dogue run | 19 |
| brought from other side | 69 |
| | 178 |

Sunday 17th.    Mercury at 36 in the Morning—41 at Noon and 40 at Night.

Perfectly calm all day—lowering with great appearances of Snow or rain till the afternoon when the clouds broke and the Sun set Clear.

In the afternoon a Mr. Brown Son of Mr. Jno. Brown of Providence came in and stayed all Night.

John Brown (1736–1803), of Providence, R.I., the son of James and Hope Power Brown, was one of Rhode Island's leading merchants. The voyage of John Brown's ship the *General Washington* in 1787 marked the beginning of the Rhode Island trade with the East Indies and China. James Brown (1761–1834) was John and Sarah Brown's eldest son, and the only one to survive to manhood. This younger Brown attended Rhode Island College, now Brown University, but graduated in 1780 from Harvard.

Monday 18th.    Mercury at 42 in the Morning—52 at Noon and 42 at Night.

Clear, warm, and perfectly calm & pleasant all day.

George Washington went up to town on my business.

I rid to the Plantations at the Ferry—Dogue run and Muddy hole—Gathering & husking Corn at the two first & cleaning Rye at the latter.

Rid also to the place where James Lawson ought to have been at Work, but he was not there. Patrick Sheriden his companion, was discharged on friday evening last.

Doctr. Craik who had visited Negroe Ben in the Neck came here last Night.

Ben, a dower slave and laborer at River Farm, was about 57 years old.

Tuesday 19th.    Mercury at 36 in the Morning—45 at Noon and 40 at Night.

Quite calm all day, with slow rain, which contributed much to the dissolution of the Snow.

At home all day.

Doctr. Craik went away after Breakfast.

Killed 41 Hogs from the different Plantations—weights as follow

| | | |
|---|---|---|
| Ferry | 19 | 3034 |
| Dogue run | 6 | 936 |
| Muddy hole | 6 | 798 |
| River Plan. | 10 | 1466 |
| | | 6234 |

Wednesday 20th.    Mercury at 31 in the Morning—41 at Noon and 36 at Night.

A little Snow fell in the night scarcely half an inch thick. Weather cleared in the Night. Day fair, and tolerably [warm] for the Season tho' the wind was pretty fresh from the No. West.

Mr. Bushrod Washington and Wife & Miss Blackburn went up to Alexandria after breakfast as did Doctr. La Moyeur. George Washington went up there also on my business; after having measured the remaindr. of the Corn at the Ferry plantation on the Hill, which with 6 Barrels brought home, and four given to the Hogs

| | |
|---|---|
| amounted in that cut to | 49 Barls. |
| On the Flat comn. plantg. | 87 |
| Drilled Corn by Meadow | 29 |
| Do. by Fish House | 9 |
| Total made this yr. | 174 |

Rid to the Plantations at the Ferry, Dogue run & Muddy hole. James Lawson the Ditcher not at Work to day nor has he been seen since Sunday.

Killed the following Hogs to day

| | | |
|---|---|---|
| From Rivr. Plann. | 12 | 1876 |
| Muddy hole | 11 | 1366 |
| | | 3242 |
| Killed Yesterday | | 6234 |
| | | 9476 |
| Supplied Ths. Green with | | 300 |
| Remains | | 9176 |

Thursday 21st.    Mercury at 31 in the Morning—45 at Noon and 45 at Night. Morning clear, calm, and very pleasant. Afternoon it lowered—but seemed to clear up again towards night.

Mr. Brown went away after Breakfast.

I rid to the Plantations at the Ferry, Dogue run and Muddy hole. Just finished securing the Corn at the Ferry which was measured yesterday—still gathering this at Dogue run and threshing at Muddy hole.

James Lawson (the Ditcher) returned to his work to day.

Bushrod Washington and his Wife returned from Alexandria to day—got in before dinner. Mr. Potts came soon after dinner and Mr. Richardson Stuart at Night.

A plate from *La Nouvelle Maison Rustique,* Paris, 1798. (Mount Vernon Ladies' Association of the Union)

Friday 22d.    Mercury 34 at Morning—49 at Night [Noon] and 46 at Night.

Morning Cloudy, but clear calm & pleasant afterwards—ground hard froze in the morning but thawed afterwards where there was no Snow.

Rid to the Neck, Muddy hole, Dogue run & Ferry Plantations—getting Wheat into the Barn at the first—threshing it at the 2d. about finishing gathering Corn at the 3d. and cutting down Corn stalks for the Farm pen at the last.

Doctr. Craik for whom I had sent to visit the sick people in the Neck came across from there after Sun down.

Doctr. La Moyeur came in about the sametime from Alexandria.

My Farmer brought home for the purpose of Stall feeding 3 Steers from Dogue run—Viz. the two old draught Steers wch. went from the House, & one that was on the Wheat field at Dogue run all last Winter & Spring—the latter to be slaughtered tomorrow.

Doctr. Craik who visited my Sick people in the Neck came here to night as did Doctr. La Moyeur.

Saturday 23d.    Mercury at 49 in the Morning—39 at Noon and 30 at Night.

Morning very cloudy—about 8 Oclock began to rain and continued to do so, more or less, through the day—in the forepart of which it was Southerly. Afterwards it got to the Northward blew hard & turned very cold by night when there fell a mixture of snow and rain, and was exceedingly disagr[eeable].

Doctr. Craik went away after breakfast—Mr. Bushrod Washington & his wife were prevented doing it by the Weather.

I remained at home all day. Finished gathering & husking of Corn at Dogue run, yesterday; but the weather to day prevented the measuring & lofting it.

Ordered the Overseer at the Ferry and my Negroe Overseers, to kill of the Hogs up fatting, each as follow.

|  |  | weight |
|---|---|---|
| Ferry. Hezh. Fairfax | 2 | 279 |
| River Plantation | 2 | 247 |
| Dogue run Ditto | 2 | 256 |
| Muddy hole Do. | 2 | 143 |
| Head Carpr. Isaac f[ro]m do. | 1 | 84 |
|  |  | 1009 |

Sunday 24th.    Mercury at 24 in the Morning—30 at Noon and 26 at Night. Wind very high from the No. West all day, & cold—also clear. Ground which was uncovered in places yesterday was slightly covered this Morning (not an Inch deep) and no thawing except on the Sun sides of Houses out of the Wind.

At home all day.

B. Washington & his wife left this.

Monday 25th.    Mercury at 26 in the Morning—38 at Noon and 36 at Night.

Clear and pleasant with the Wind at South. River froze across in the Morning but open afterwards.

At home all day.

Miss Allan—Betcy, Patcy and Nelly Custis came here to dinner.

Tuesday 26th.    Mercury at 29 in the Morning 48 at Noon and 36 at Night.

The Wind shifting last Night to the No. West, it grew colder but this day was pleasant notwithstanding and clear.

Doctr. La Moyeur went to Alexandria to day and Colo. Lee (late of Congress) came here to Dinner as did Mr. Lund Washington.

Wednesday 27th.    Mercury at 28 in the Morning—49 at Noon and 42 at Night.

Quite calm and pleasant, with little or no wind, and that from the Southward—clear.

After Breakfast Colo. Lee set out for Richmond.

Mr. Lear returned from his journey into the Western Country about 4 Oclock to day having been absent 28 days.

Miss Allan returned to Abingdon to day and Doctr. La Moyeur came back from Alexandria.

At home all day.

Thursday 28th.    Mercury at 28 in the Morning—55 at Noon and 50 at Night.

Calm, clear, warm, and very pleasant all day; towards evening it began to lower a little in the So. Western horizon—A very white frost in the Morning.

At home all day.

Friday 29th.    Mercury at 30 in the Morning—55 at Noon and 51 at Night.

Clear, calm, warm, and exceeding pleasant all day.

The hollidays being over, and the People all at work, I rid to the Ferry—Dogue run, and Muddy hole Plantations—also to the Ditchers (who were at Work). At the first Plantation cutting stalks and getting farm pen in order—at the next (Dogue run) measured the remainder of the Corn.

|  |  |  | Barls. |
|---|---|---|---|
| viz. |  |  | 106 |
| 27th. Novr. was measured |  |  | 68 |
| 6 Decr.      Do.     Do. |  |  | 41½ |
| Given to Hogs    25    Neg[roe]s    15 |  |  | 40 |
| At the Plantation |  | Total | 255½ |

My whole Crop of Corn will stand

| Neck Plantation | 387½ Barls. |
|---|---|
| Dogue run | 255½ |
| Muddy hole | 201 |
| Ferry | 174 |
| Total | 1018 |

Mrs. Peake and Miss Eaglin dined here to day and returned afterwards.

**Saturday 30th.**    Mercury at 28 in the Morning—36 at Noon and 30 at Night.

An exceeding heavy close fog all day without Wind.

Staked out the fields at the Ferry Plantation to day, according to the late modification of them. Visited the Ditchers and rid to Dogue run where the People had just finished securing the corn measured yesterday and were going to grub a piece of ground for the Muddy hole plows to work on East of the Branch in Field No. 1. The Muddy hole hds. began to succour, or take the sprouts from the stumps in the New ground to prepare it for Hoeing for corn.

Killed the following Hogs

| | | |
|---|---|---|
| Neck Plantn. | 25 Hogs | 2861 |
| Dogue Run Do. | 5 Do. | 571 |
| Ferry Do. | 8 | 867 |
| From this quantity | | 4299 |
| Thoms. Bishop has had | 400 | |
| Thos. Green—2d. parcel | 200 | |
| Richd. B. Walker | 300 | |
| Overseer Morris | 45 | |
| Ditto    Davy | 55 | |
| Ditto    Will | 157 | |
| Ditto    Isaac | 116 | |
| | 1273 | |

|  |  |  |
|---|---|---|
| In addn. to the former | | |
| Killed the 19th. & 20th. | | 9476 |
| Ditto at the Plantns. for Overrs. | | 1009 |
| Ditto for forward Bacon | | |
| from Neck 6 Hogs | 905 | |
| Mill      3 Do. | 460 | |
| | | 1365 |
| Total amt.       120 Hogs | | 16149 |
| Delivered to sundries pr. ⎫ the foregoing acct.    ⎭ | | 2282 |
| For family consumpn. | | 13867 |

Besides the above, there are 4 Hogs yet at the ferry Plantn. to Kill—from which the overseer [will receive] the Balle. due to him.

The Snow was mostly gone especially off Grass land. Wheat Fields still were partly covered.

Sunday 31st.    Mercury at 31 in the Morning—60 at Noon and 55 at Night.

Clear and remarkably pleasant—Wind Southerly all day but not fresh.

At home all day.

# At the Constitutional Convention

## 1787

### [January 1787]

[Monday 1st.]    Mercury at 55 in the Morning—67 at Noon and 58 at Night.

But little wind and that southerly—very warm. Morning foggey —flying vapour rather than a standing fog.

Went to the Plantation of Jno. Robinson to have his Stock of Horses & Cattle appraised to me. Colo. McCarty on my part and Mr. Lund Washington on his valued them—as follow

| | £ | s | d |
|---|---|---|---|
| A Black (or dark brown) Mare about 14 hands high—no white but a long switch tail and supposed to be 9 years old. With a sorrel horsecolt of last spring—a long narrow blaze—a little white on the upper lip and 2 White hind feet | 9 | 0 | 0 |
| A Bla. Mare. No white except a few gray hairs on her nose abt. 13½ hands high 6 yrs. old. A bla. horse colt—last Spring no white but a small snip on the nose | 6 | 0 | 0 |
| A Sorrel Mare blazed face off hind foot white abt. 14 hands high 7 years old. A Sorrel Mare colt. 1 year old—blaze in the face. A Sorrel horse Colt of this Spring blaze in the face white rd. the hoofs both hers | 11 | 10 | 0 |
| A Sorrel Stallion—a blaze face—2 hind feet & off fore foot white—13½ hds. high & 6 years old | 5 | 0 | 0 |
| A Sorrel horse with a kd. of blaze & snip in one 2 hind feet white—Thin & badly made. 13½ hds. high and 7 years old | 4 | 10 | 0 |

[ 87 ]

| | | | |
|---|---|---|---|
| A Dark bay horse (Stallion) one hind foot near one white—4 next Spg. 13½ hands high. | 5 | 10 | 0 |
| A Sorrel two years old horse Colt—long Star & white Nose | 3 | 0 | 0 |
| 11. in all amountg. to | £44 | .10 | — |

### Cattle

| | | | |
|---|---|---|---|
| 1 Brindle Bull. 3 yrs. next Sprg. | 4 | 0 | 0 |
| 1 Red }  Oxen<br>1 Brindle & pied | 12 | 0 | — |
| 1 Brindle & White Steer unbroke | 4 | — | |
| 1 Bla. Cow—White Belly—& red Yearlg. Bull Calf | 4 | — | |
| 1 Bla. Cow & bla. Bull Calf | 4 | — | |
| 1 Brindle Cow & brind. B. Calf | 4 | — | |
| 1 Red Cow & pied bull Calf | 4 | — | |
| 1 Brindle Cow with white belly & red calf with wh. belly | 4 | — | |
| 1 Brindle hiefer with calf | 2 | 10 | — |
| 15 head in all amt. | £42 | . 10 | |
| 11 horses as above | 44 | . 10 | |
| Total | £87 | . | |

For the payment of the Sum on the other side viz. £87 I passed my Certificate payable to Mrs. French.

Besides the above 20 bushls. of Wheat sowed on the Plantation, and putting it in, was valued by the aforementioned Gentlemen at 7/6 pr. Bushel; for [    ] Bushels I am to pay Thos. Pool.

It being wet where James Lawson was ditching, I ordered him to quit & go to that part where he had left off the [    ] of Decr. last & to continue that ditch up to the road by the bridge.

Began to Plow in Field No. 1 at Dogue run to day 4 plows for Barley &ca. & to prepare the fencing for field No. 4. at the same place.

Also begun with the Muddy hole people to Hoe the ground on the right of the road (going out) at the Home House for Corn.

Colo. McCarty and Mr. Lund Washington came home with me to dinner. Found the wife of the latter & Colo. White and a Mr. West the two last of whom stayed all Night. The rest went away in the evening.

JNO. ROBINSON: John Robertson. HORSES & CATTLE APPRAISED TO ME: GW's agreement with Robertson on 24 Oct. 1786 had specified that GW would buy Robertson's horses and cattle at an appraised price and pay the sum to Mrs. French. Robertson in turn would be exonerated from part of the rent owed to her (DLC:GW). THOS. POOL: GW may mean Peter Pool, who had relinquished his tenant house to Robertson (see entry for 24 Oct. 1786). Both Thomas and Peter Pool appear in the 1785 Virginia tax census in the same Fairfax County tax list (HEADS OF FAMILIES, VA., 85). GW's opinion of the Pool family, which in 1794 was living on land near his mill, was that "a more worthless set are no where to be found" (GW to William Pearce, 14 Dec. 1794, DLC:GW).

Anthony Walton White (1750–1803), of New Jersey, often called Walton White, was the son of Anthony and Elizabeth Morris White, daughter of Gov. Lewis Morris of New Jersey. White was privately educated and before the Revolution assisted his father in the management of the family's considerable estates. During the Revolution he served as a lieutenant colonel and colonel in various New Jersey regiments. From 1788 to 1793 White resided in New York and attempted to recoup his finances, depleted by wartime expenditures and unsuccessful business ventures, through applications for a government post (White to GW, 1 May and 22 Sept. 1789, DLC:GW). In 1793 he returned to New Jersey.

**Tuesday 2d.** Mercury at 46 in the Morning—63 at Noon and 59 at Night.

A Moist, vapoury morning but clear till afternoon when it lowered & looked much like rain. The ground quite uncovered and the frost entirely out of it.

Colo. Walton White and Mr. West went away before breakfast. I rid to the Ferry—Frenchs & Dogue run Plantations. Set the Muddy hole Ploughs 3 to work, to prepare a small piece of ground East of the Branch in field No. 1 for Barley & grass Seeds.

**Wednesday 3d.** Mercury at 53 in the Morning—61 at Noon and 60 at Night.

Moist, warm, and giving all day; with little or no wind. At times it dripped a little of rain and at other times was foggy.

Rid to Alexandria to a meeting of the board of Directors of the Potomack Co. Did the business which occasioned the Meeting. Dined at Lomax's & returned home in the evening.

Dug the 10 Rows of Carrots wch. I had sowed between the Rows of drilled Corn at Muddy hole Plantation which turned out as follow—viz.—the first and most Northerly row yielded 3 Bushls. and the next to this 2½ Bushels—the other 8 were measured together and amounted to 14 Bushels—The tops ends and fibres being first taken from the whole. It is to be noted, that these Carrots came up exceedingly thin, whether owing to the Seeds being burried too deep, or to any other cause is not certain – They were even much thinner than the Potatoes in the same field – That the two rows first named were transplanted, the tip ends of the Roots being first taken off; which, or some thing else occasioned them to fork, & branch improperly – that the first of these rows i.e. the one which produced 3 bushels had no sprinkling of dung at the time of Planting – the second (yielding 2½ bushels) had and so alternately though the whole ten rows. The 8 rows not transplanted produced very fair Carrots the medium size of which might be [     ] inches in length and [     ] in circumference about midway the length of them. The greater part of these Carrots too grew in more indifferent land apparently than the Potatoes did tho part of the latter being low was drowned. Notwithstanding this I think there were more plants upon the whole of Potatoes than Carrots in the rows. Hence it appears that in the same kind of Land the latter yields more bushels to the acre than the former – for of Potatoes, 4 rows nearly of the same length as those with Carrots, produced only 6¾ Bush. and the best set one of the 4, two and a ¼ Bushels. The average of which is not quite a bushel and three pecks Whereas the average of the 10 rows of Carrots is nearly 2 Bushels – which of these is most valuable by the Bushel – in feeding or for any farm uses must be determined by experience or the accounts of others. One great advantage seems to attend Carrots and that is that they may remain without any detriment in the ground till this time for those now spoken off appear to have received no damage during the last severe frost. How much longer they woud. have remained unhurt in the ground I can not say.

Thursday 4th.    Mercury at 57 in the Morning – 67 at Noon and 64 at Night.

Exceedingly pleasant all day, being clear, calm and warm. Ground much dried. About dusk the wind sprung up from the South west and blew very fresh till near day.

Rid to the Ferry, Dogue run, & Muddy hole Plantations and to the Ditchers – also to Frenchs. At the last 3 Men had begun to get rails – at the Ferry the People were grubbing and cleaning up the Swamp below the Meadow and at Dogue run I set them to filling up gullies where the Plows were at work.

Friday 5th.    Mercury at 54 in the Morning – 51 at Noon and 46 at Night.

Day clear. In the Morning it was calm but by 8 oclock the wind Sprung up at No. Wt. & encreased till it came to blow hard & continued to do so till Night and some time within it. It grew colder but was not disagreeably cold.

A Mr. Smith — Boat builder came here to build me a fishing Boat for which I am to allow him 8/. a foot and a pint of rum pr. day.

Rid to the Plantations, all. In the Neck began with 8 plows to plow the cut which had been in drilled Corn next the Barn — crossing the old farrows at this plowing.

MR. SMITH: On 17 Mar. GW settled his account with Simon Smith "for buildg. & repai[rin]g boats" (LEDGER B, 242).

Saturday 6th.   Mercury at 35 in the Morning — 49 at Noon and 45 at Night.

The wind pretty fresh all day from the Southward — weather tolerably clear & pleasant — ground not froze.

Brought [    ] Bullocks from the Mill Meadow to Stall feed. At home all day.

Mrs. Stuart, Miss Allan, and the two youngest Children of the former came here just before dinner.

The Muddy hole Plows finished plowing the ground they were in at Dogue run and began to plow No. 2 at home.

Purchased, and had brought home from Alexandria 10 Bushels of red Clover Seed — a bushel of which was weighed 68½ lbs.

Sunday 7th.   Mercury 32 at Morn 46 at Noon and 43 at Night.
   Wind Southerly and pretty brisk all day — clear and warm.
   At home.

Monday 8th.   Mercury at 45 in the Morning — 48 at Noon and 46 at Night.

Heavy & lowering all day & sometimes sprinkling. Abt. 4 Oclock it set in to a fine & constant rain which continued through the Night. But little Wind all day & tht. southerly till the evening whn. it got to the No. Et.

Rid to all the Plantations. Finished cleaning and grubbing the New Meadow at the Ferry. Old Will & the Women at Fren[ch's] were grubbing and clearing away for the Plows in the field (No. 1) on the Road. At Dogue run they were plowing & filling gullies — In the Neck clearing the ground from Corn Stalks before the Plows and the Muddy hole people employed as usual in the New ground front of the home house.

OLD WILL: Will was one of the 24 slaves belonging to Mrs. French who were leased to GW along with the land (deed of Penelope French to GW, Fairfax County Deeds, Book Q-1, 392–96, Vi Microfilm).

[ 91 ]

Tuesday 9th.    Mercury at 38 in the Morning—39 at Noon and 38 at Night.

Wet Morning with the Wind tho' light at No. Et. Cloudy and Mizzling all day.

Two Millwrights who came to my Mill yesterday began to work to day on a new Cog wheel to the grist Mill.

Kept within doors by the badness of the weather.

Took an acct. of my grass seeds on hand—which are as follows

| | |
|---|---|
| 10  Bushl. Clover a 68½ | 685 lbs. |
| Expected from Phil. | 300 |
| | 985 |

20  Bushels orchard Grass
16½  Ditto Timothy
1  Ditto New river
6  Quarts Pumpkin Seeds
½  Bushl. Magity bay Pease
½  Ditto Spg. Barley Mr. Lee
½  ditto Wheat of the Cape of
    Good hope.

NB—The above Clover Seed at 10 lbs. to the Acre will sow 98½ acr.—at 12 lbs., 82 acres—at 14 lb. 70 lbs.—& at 16 lbs. the largest quantity bestowed on an acre. 61½ acres.

The Orchard grass at a bus. to the acre will sow 20 acres.

The Timothy Seed at a quart to the Acre will sow 528 acres at 3 pints 352 acres and at 2 Quarts to the Acre, 264 acres.

At home all day.

TWO MILLWRIGHTS: Some time in late March or early April of this year these two artisans were paid a total of £12 12s. by GW "for repairs done my mill" (LEDGER B, 245).

New River grass is probably not a variety; GW often used localities as a means of designating plants for which he had no other name. The New River joins the Gauley to form the Kanawha, an affluent of the Ohio, and GW may have collected the grass seed on his western trip of 1784. In the entry for 14 May 1788 he says it appears to be a "course kind of grass."

Wedneday 10th.    Mercury at 33 in the Morning—38 at Noon and 37 at Night.

Raining in the Morning, and lowering, & sometimes mizzling the rest of the day with the wind at No. Et.

Mrs. Stuart & her Children and Miss Allan went away after breakfast.

Just before Dinner Mr. Brindley Manager of the Susquehanna Works & his Son in law came on their way to South Carolina.

Washington's "beloved Brother," John Augustine Washington. (Alexandria-Washington Lodge No. 22, A.F. & A.M., Alexandria, Va.)

About the sametime I recd. by express the acct. of the sudden death (by a fit of the Gout in the head) of my beloved Brother Colo. Jno. Auge. Washington.

At home all day.

Thursday 11th.    Mercury at 31 in the Morning – 32 at Noon and 30 at Night.

Cloudy all day with the Wind at No. East. The greatest part of the day it was spitting Snow, but so thin and lighty, as never to whiten the ground.

Sent Mr. Lear to Alexandria to receive money and do other business for me.

Rid to the Plantations at the Ferry, French's and Dogue run and to the Ditchers. At the first the labourers had begun to grub & clean up the 19 acre field on the hill part of No. 1.

Friday 12th.    Mercury at 24 in the Morning – 27 at Noon and 22 at Night.

Wind at No. Wt. with flying clouds and very cold.

At home all day, writing letters, & doing other matters previous to Majr. Geo. Washingtons setting of for New Kent for which place he set out after dinner, in order to receive & bring up some Negroes which his Wife's Father Colo. Bassett had given him.

A notation in the Mount Vernon store book for this date says that the white workers are to have a bottle of rum per day "on acct. of the Cyder's being out" (ViMtV).

Saturday 13th.    Mercury at 17 in the Morning—32 at Noon and 30 at Night.

Wind at No. West in the Morning but at South East in the Evening—forenoon clear, but lowering afterwards but not very much—rather raw and cold.

Rid to the Ferry, French's, and Dogue Run & Muddy hole Plantations; also to the Mill & the Ditchers—Nothing remarkable at any of them.

About 8 Oclock in the evening Doctr. Stuart on his return from the General Assembly at Richmond & Mr. Anstey came in.

Sunday 14th.    Mercury at 34 in the Morning—51 at Noon and 46 at Night.

Day clear and pleasant the Wind being Southerly.

Doctr. Stuart stayed and dined as did Mr. Anstey after which both went away—the 1st. to his own home and the other to Alexandria.

At home all day.

Monday 15th.    Mercury at 42 in the Morning—52 at Noon and 50 at Night. Rain last Night with the wind fresh from the So. Wt. which continued so through the day. Very lowering all day & now and then a sprinkling with rain but not enough to drive people from work. The Sun set clear and the Western horison indicated fair weather.

Rid to all the Plantations & to the Ditchers. In the Neck set the best plowman (Nat) to marking field No. 3 into 5 feet rows for Corn, Potatoes, Pease &ca. and finding the plowing in No. 2 wet & heavy I directed the plows to list after Nat every alternate row as soon as he had got sufficiently ahead and in the meantime while No. 2 (which was in Corn last year) remained so wet to endeavour to plow the New field about to be taken in for Corn next year. Plowing and other work going on as usual at the other places. Began to Maul Rails for French's & to fit up two plows for plowing there.

James Lawson just finished the Ditch through the Woods from the Road to the fence where the Dutchman began & began below Manleys Ho[use] opposite to work up till he meets the Dutchman.

Ascertained how many of the following Sorts of Seeds there are in a lb. Troy—The weight of a bushel of each & how much an acre will take of each sort to sow it.

See table on next page.

Tuesday 16th.    Mercury at 35 in the Morning—55 at Noon and 52 at Night.

The forenoon a little lowering, but the afternoon clear and remarkably pleasant—little or no Wind all day.

Rid to the Plantations at the Ferry, French's, Dogue run and Muddy hole—also to the Ditchers. The same kind of work going on as usual at all of them.

On my return home found Mr. Porter and Mr. Ingraham here, who dined and stayed all night.

Nathaniel Ingraham was a business partner of Thomas Porter of Alexandria.

Wednesday 17th.    Mercury at 33 in the Morning—54 at Noon and 45 at Night.

Clear, with the Wind very brisk all day from the So. West— moderate but not very warm.

At home all day. Just as we had dined Messrs. Richd. & Theodk. Lee came in, and after Sundown Colo. Carrington from Congress, and Major Swan from Boston arrived, all of whom stayed the Night.

Maj. James Swan (1754–1830), who was twice wounded at Bunker Hill, subsequently held several civil offices in Massachusetts during the Revolution. In 1785, at the request of Henry Knox, GW wrote Swan letters of introduction for a trip by Swan to France where he developed a career in commerce and international finance (GW to Knox, 28 Feb. 1785, MHi: Knox Papers; PRICE [2], 2:834–37).

Thursday 18th.    Mercury at 34 in the Morning—55 at Noon and 47 at Night.

The Morning was exceedingly pleasant & perfectly calm. The Wind afterwards rose in the So. Wt. quarter & shifted to the westward. The ground was froze this Morning tho' not very deep.

All the Gentlemen (messrs. Porter & Ingraham who had stayed two Nights with the others) went away after Breakfast.

I rid to all the Plantations. The plows began on Tuesday to break up the New field for Corn in the Neck on Tuesday last. Worked there yesterday and would do so to day also; after which, as the ground they had left, appeared to be a good deal dried by yesterdays Wind I directed them to return to it to morrow. Finished except two lands which were left untouched, plowing the

| Sorts of Seeds | Numbr. of Grains | | Propn. of Chaff in ea. | Weight of a bush of ea. seed | Seeds for an Acre | | | |
|---|---|---|---|---|---|---|---|---|
| | | | | | at 4 Inchs. sqr. | | at 12 Inch sqr. | |
| | in the lb. | in the Bush | | | lbs. | galls. | lbs. | galls. |
| Red Clover | 71,000 | 4,863,500 | 1/30 | 68½ | 5 4/8 | 0 5/8 | | |
| Timothy | 298,000 | 13,410,000 | 1/13 | 45 | 1 2/8 | 0 2/8 | | |
| New Rivr. Grass | 844,800 | 8,448,000 | 1/14 | 10 | 0 4/8 | 0 3/8 | | |
| Orchd. grass | 387,800 | 4,459,700 | 1/6 | 11½ | 1 | 0 7/8 | | |
| Eastn. Shore Pea | 14,400 | 964,800 | 1/30 | 67 | | | 3 | 3/64 |
| Bla: eye Pease | 2,300 | 140,300 | 1/32 | 61 | | | 18 7/8 | 2½ |
| Crouder do. | 1,600 | 97,600 | 1/34 | 61 | | | 27 2/8 | 3 7/8 |
| Barley | 8,925 | 455,685 | 1/37 | 51 | 44 | 7 | | |

Lay land at Dogue run, and began to list the field (alternate rows) intended for Corn at that place and began plowing with 2 plows at French's for Oats & Barley. Set another (makg. 3 plows) to work at the Ferry Plantation to day. The Muddy hole people went from the New ground in front of the Ho[me] Ho[use] to the Plantation to work, to grub & clear the stumps & bushes before the Plows at that place.

Friday 19th.    Mercury at 27 in the Morning—37 at Noon and 27 at Night.

Wind at No. Et. in the Morning, with appearances of a change of Weather. About Noon it was calm, clear, and very pleast. but towards sundown the wind Sprung up again at No. Et.—the clouds gathered fast, and indicated rain speedily.

Went to French's and marked of the fields (as they are to be divided in future) by stakes.

Saturday 20th.    Mercury at 32 in the Morning 45 at Noon and 43 at Night.

About 8 Oclock in the evening of yesterday it began a slow, & very moderate rain which continued it is supposed through the Night. In the morning it was very heavy with great appearances of a repetition of rain but none fell. Towards noon the Sun shone & the afternoon was clear & very pleasant. Wind at So. Et. all day but not much of it.

Rid to the Ferry, French's, Dogue run, & Muddy hole plantations—as also to the Ditchers and to the Mill. Employed as yesterday at all of them.

Mr. Lund Washington dined here.

Sunday 21st.    Mercury at 37 in the Morning—42 at Noon and 42 at Night.

A very heavy thick fog till 10 Oclock—Cloudy & lowering Most part of the day afterwds. though the sun made feeble efforts to shine. Evening clr.—but little wind and that at No. Et.

Major Swan (of Boston) & Mr. Hunter of Alexandria came here to dinner & stayed all nig[ht].

Monday 22d.    Mercury at 37 in the Morning—37 at Noon and 36 at Night.

Wind still at No. Et. Morning very heavy, which, about 10 Oclock turned to a thick mist and in the Afternoon to rain.

Major Swan & Mr. Hunter set off for Fredericksburgh before Breakfast.

At home all day.

Tuesday 23d.    Mercury at 32 in the Morning—34 at Noon and 32 at Night.

Heavy & thick—always misting & sometimes raining. A good deal of the latter fell in the night. Wind—tho' not much of it at No. Et.

At home alone all day.

Wednesday 24th.    Mercury at 46 in the Morning—49 at Noon and 48 at Night.

Raining more or less all day. In the Morning there were some appearances of the weather clearing, but it soon thickened and set in to raining, slowly till towards sundown, when the clouds again broke to the Westward. In the Night the wind blew fresh from the So. West & Continued to come from that quarter all day but very moderately.

At home all day.

Thursday 25th.    Mercury at 35 in the Morning—42 at Noon and 39 at Night.

Lowering morning, with some appearances of the weathers breaking in the forenoon but it soon thickened again and before 3 began a fine snow which soon turned to rain which it continued to do thru the whole, or greater part of the Night. Wind at So. West.

Rid to the Ditchers & Mill and to the Ferry, French's Dogue run, & Muddy hole Plantations. At work as usual at the Ferry and Frenchs—at Dogue run repairing & altering the Meadow fence & filling up gullies before the Plows. The Muddy hole Hoe People had returned to the New ground in front of the house and were breaking it up as heretofore. They came to this work on Monday Morning.

On my return home found Mr. Madison here and after Dinner Mr. Griffith came in both of Whom stayed all night.

Friday 26th.    Mercury at 36 in the Morning—46 at Noon and 46 at Night.

In the Morning early it rained—about 9 Oclock the weather seemed disposed to break but sooned thickened again and rained more or less from abt. Noon till Night when the weather again seemed inclined to clear. Wind tho' not much of it, was at So. Wt. in the Morning & more Westerly in the afternoon.

Mr. Madison & Mr. Griffith going away after breakfast (the former to attend Congress) I rid as yesterday to all the Plan[tation]s.

The Ditchers abt. Noon this day finished the level ditch as far as was intended on both sides the Swamp at French's Plantation and then began to dig a 4 feet ditch at top, & a foot (intending it for a dble. ditch) deep, on the dividing line between this & the Ferry Plantation immediately after.

Saturday 27th.    Mercury at 36 in the Morning—40 at Noon and 36 at Night.

A good deal of Rain falling in the Night, the ground was very wet; after 9 oclock it became clear with little or no Wind till towards Sundown, when it came out pretty brisk from the No. West.

Rid to all the Plantations and to the Ditchers whom I found had made a mistake and instead of working on the line dividing the Plantations were on one which divides the fields 2 & 3. Shifted them to the right place about 1 Oclock.

Sunday 28th.    Mercury at 26 in the Morning—36 at Noon and 32 at Night.

Wind Westerly all day, and not much unlike Snow—Grd. froze in the Morning.

Colo. Henry Lee, his Lady, Miss Lee and Mr. Fendall came here to dinner—the last of whom went away afterwards (crossing the river for Maryland).

Miss Lee is undoubtedly Mrs. Matilda Lee's sister Flora Lee.

Monday 29th.    Mercury at 30 in the Morning—30 at Noon and 30 at Night.

Wind cold & raw from the So. West. About Sun rise it began to snow & continued to do so for 3 or 4 hours when it turned to rain, and rained thro' the day. The Wind was Southerly but raw & cold; ground hard frozen.

Rid in the Morning before breakfast to Muddy hole Plantation in order to set the Ditcher (Danl. Overdonck) to work, but the ground was so hard froze & the weather setting in so stormy he could not proceed and returned.

[ 99 ]

Tuesday 30th.    Mercury at 32 in the Morning—38 at Noon and 32 at Night.

Foggy and warm with very little or no Wind the greater part of the day. In the evening it became clear.

Rid to the Ferry, & French's Plantation, and intended to have gone further but getting wet in passing a Mirey place at French's I returned home to get on dry cloaths.

Sent Danl. Overdonck to Muddy hole again who with a fellow Charles belonging to the place began a ditch 3 feet wide at top, one at bottom, and [      ] Inches deep.

Set the Plows to work again at French's where the women & boys had begun to fence.

Wednesday 31st.    Mercury at 32 in the Morng.—48 at Noon and 40 at Night.

Wind at No. West and pretty fresh early in the Morning, but decreased as the Sun rose and became quite calm & a little lowering towards Night.

Accompanied by Colo. Lee I rode to the Ferry, Frenchs Dogue run and Muddy hole Plantations and also to my Mill & the Ditches. At Dogue run the Women were altering the Meadow fences and at Muddy hole finding the Ditch too small I ordered it to be made 4 feet wide. Being in a Sandy soil the ditching here was perfectly dry, but where James Lawson & Boston were ditching at French's in Clayey ground it was very wet and disagreeable.

Mr. Fendall returned from Maryld. to dinner.

# February [1787]

[Thursday 1st.]    Mercury at 32 in the Morning—46 at Noon and 46 at Night.

Wind (tho' not much of it) variable and weather lowering but with changeable appearances.

Mr. Fendall, Colo. Lee & his Lady, & Miss Lee went away after breakfast.

I rid to the Ferry & French's Plantations. At the first the women were cleaning up field No. 1 below the Hill.

Friday 2d.    Mercury at 30 in the Morning—36 at Noon and 36 at Night.

Very cloudy most part or all the day. Wind at No. Wt. in the Morning and So. Wt. afterwards and cold and raw.

Majr. G. Washington & Mr. Jno. Dandridge came here to dinner yesterday. Rid to all the Plantations to day and to the Ditchers. At the River Plantn. began to sow 3 pints of Timothy seed (mixed in a bushel of Ashes) to the Acre on Tuesday last, on the Snow—but it melted so fast that not more than 2 Acres were sown before the ground getting uncovered put a stop to the Sowing. Began at the same place to plow the Homestead for Barley or Oats, or both, as Seeds could be obtained. A horse failing at French's yesterday one of the plows was stopped about 12 Oclock.

Yesterday Morning the Dogue run (Men 3 of them) began to get rails to fence in the Largest piece of Tobo. ground at Frenches for Corn.

The Mill wrights finished the repairs at my Mill last Night.

John Dandridge (d. 1799) was the son of Martha Washington's brother Bartholomew Dandridge by his second wife, Mary Burbidge Dandridge. Young Dandridge lived in New Kent County where he practiced law.

Saturday 3d. Mercury at 30 in the Morning—36 at Noon and 36 at Night.

About 8 Oclock in the evening of yesterday it began to Snow & continued to do so moderately thro the Night & till about 10 Oclock this day when after getting to be about 6 Inches deep it cleared. Wind, what little there was of it being Southerly the whole time.

Rid to the Plantations at the Ferry, French's Dogue run and Muddy hole; also to the Mill and to the Ditchers.

Sunday 4th. Mercury at 24 in the Morning—30 at Noon and 34 at Night.

In the Night; or early this Morning, the Wind shifted to the No. West blew very hard and turned cold.

At home all day. About two Oclock Doctr. Stuart came in.

Monday 5th. Mercury at 18 in the morning—30 at Noon and 30 at Night.

Ground very hard froze. Wind at So. Et.; raw & cold with great appearances of a change in the weather.

After breakfast Doctr. La Moyeur went up to Alexandria and Doctr. Stuart and Mr. Jno. Dandridge to Abingdon.

I rid to the Plantations at the Ferry, Frenchs Dogue run & Muddy hole. At the Ferry the Overseer had begun to sow Timothy seed mixed with Sand in the Rye field on the Snow—but the Sand being too wet & clammy to do it regular I ordered him to desist till the Sand could be dried. Three gallons of Timothy Seed mixed with ashes was Sown on Rye in the Neck on Saturday—adjoining what was sown there on the last Snow. Heaping the dung in the Farm pens at Muddy hole.

THE OVERSEER: Hezekiah Fairfax.

Tuesday 6th.    Mercury at 34 in the Morning—50 at Noon and 48 at Night.

Last evening & Night being Soft no frost to day—little or no Wind. Clear and exceedingly pleasant. Snow tho' there was a good deal in the Morning had quite disappeared by Night.

Mr. Willm. Craik who came here to dinner yesterday went away after breakfast. I rid to all the Plantations and to Simpsons with my Nephew G. A. Washington to advise him (as he was going to settle a plantation there) abt. his fencing. Sowed [     ] gallons of Timothy Seed mixed in ashes on the Rye in the Neck. Began to put up a New fence through the wood at the Ferry plantation to day—The Dogue run people putting up the rails that wer mauled by them a round frenchs Tobacco grd.—French's People also fencing and getting New rails.

About Sun down Messrs. Bushrod & Corbin Washington came in on their return from Berkeley County.

SIMPSONS: a plantation in Clifton's Neck and part of GW's 1760 purchase from William Clifton. The land had originally been leased by Clifton to Gilbert Simpson, and after Simpson's death in 1773 the lease was inherited by his son Gilbert Simpson, Jr. In Nov. 1786 Simpson agreed to sell his lease to GW (agreement between Gilbert Simpson, Jr., and GW, 21 Nov. 1786, DLC:GW).

Wednesday 7th.    Mercury at 36 in the Morning—30 at Noon and 32 at Night.

A good deal of rain fell in the Night. About Sun rise it began to Snow and continued to do so, more or less all day.

Continued at home.

Thursday 8th.    Mercury at 27 in the Morning—30 at Noon and 30 at Night.

The Wind which had been at No. Et. all day yesterday still continued there. In the Night and early this Morning it Rained after which it hailed and then Snowed.

At home all day.

Friday 9th.    Mercury at 32 in the Morning—42 at Noon and 38 at Night.

Clear, with the wind at No. Wt.; but neither hard, nor cold.

Mr. Bushrod Washington and his Brother Corbin went away after breakfast and Geo. Washington went up to Alexandria. Doctr. La Moyeur left this but meeting with some accident to his Chaise returned again.

I rid to the Plantations at the Ferry, French's, Dogue run, & Muddy hole and to the Mill & Ditchers. At the first the people were cutting down Corn stalks—at the latter heaping the dung of the Farm yards and at the other two fencing.

In the evening Doctr. Craik returned with Majr. Washington.

Saturday 10th.    Mercury at 30 in the Morning—38 at Noon and 36 at Night.

Clear but raw and cold the Wind being pretty fresh all day from the So. Et. In the Night it blew very hard.

After breakfast Doctr. La Moyeur again set out & soon after Docter Craik went away.

I went into the Neck to run the outer lines of my land there bounded by Mr. Mason and Mr. Alexander and to ascertain lines for the fences of the Plantation let Major Geo. Washington.

Meeting with Mr. Edwd. Williams I bought his lease for 20 pds. and some other priviledges wch. I agreed to allow him.

BOUNDED BY MR. MASON: This land, consisting of four tracts totaling 676 acres, had formerly been owned by Col. George Mason. He had transferred it to his son Thomson Mason by deeds of 1781 and 1786 (Fairfax County Deeds, Book Q-1, 249–54). The younger Mason began building his home, Hollin Hall, on the property at about this time, and he and his wife, Sarah McCarty Chichester Mason, and their children moved into the new house in Dec. 1788 (COPELAND, 237–38).

PLANTATION LET MAJOR GEO. WASHINGTON: Although George Augustine Washington and his wife, Fanny, had made their home at Mount Vernon since their marriage, in a statement to George on 25 Oct. 1786 GW wrote that "to make that situation more stable and pleasing . . . it is my present intention to give you, at my death, my landed property in the neck; containing by estimation, between two and three thousand acres . . . And under this expectation and prospect, that you may, moreover, when it prefectly suits your inclination and convenience, be preparing for, and building thereon by degrees." GW stressed that he did not intend this as a hint for the young couple to prepare another home. "To point you to a settlement which you might make at leisure, and with convenience, was all I had in view. More than once I have informed you that in proportion as age and its concomitants encrease upon me, I shall stand in need of some person in whose industry and integrity I can confide, for assistance." GW added that "no other married couple could give, or probably would receive the same satisfaction by living in it [the Mount Vernon family] that you do" and that with George's help he would be able "to manage my concerns without having recourse to a Steward, which comports neither with my interest nor inclination to employ" (GW to George Augustine Washington, 25 Oct. 1786, WRITINGS, 29:28–31). Young Washington stayed on as manager at Mount Vernon until his death in 1793. It was he who managed the estate during GW's absence at the Constitutional Convention and during the early years of the presidency.

Edward Williams had a lease on some of William Clifton's land in the neck when GW purchased it in 1760 (see entry for 5 Dec. 1772). In 1782 Williams had 12 whites and no slaves in his household, and in 1785 he still had 10 whites (HEADS OF FAMILIES, VA., 17, 86). In 1786 one Edward Williams was exempted by the Fairfax County court from paying any further taxes (SPROUSE [2], 2:15).

**Sunday 11th.** Mercury at 31 in the Morng.–33 at Noon and 33 at Night.

Began to rain at or before day and kept very steadily at it— sometimes hard, till abt. 2 Oclock when the Sun came out for a short duration–little or no Wind & that Southerly.

**Monday 12th.** Mercury at 36 in the Morning–42 at Noon and 40 at Night.

The Sun rose clear, and the Morning was tolerably free from clouds but it soon over cast, and all the latter part of the day had great appearances of Snow or rain.

Rid to the Plantations at The Ferry, French's, Dogue run and Muddy hole–Plowing at the Ferry in the New Meadw. and at French's in field No. [    ] intended for Turnips Potatoes &ca. Field No. 5 in which they had been plowing for Oats & Barley being too wet. Three Plows from Muddy hole went to work at this place about Noon. Neither the Dogue run, nor Neck Plows were at Work to day.

Mr. Lear went to an Assembly at Alexandria to be held this evening and Mr. John Dandridge came from Abingdon here to Dinner.

**Tuesday 13th.** Mercury at 38 in the Morning–48 at Noon and 45 at Night.

Moderate and pleasant with Sun and Clouds alternately–Wind Southerly.

Rid to all the Plantations. Plows at Work–those of Muddy hole at work at Frenchs.

Ferry people came to work in the New ground front of the Mansion house on Friday the 9th.

**Wednesday 14th.** Mercury at 36 in the Morng.–36 at Noon and 36 at Night.

Thick and heavy clouds in the Morning and wind at No. Et. About 8 Oclock A. M. it began to rain and kept steadily at it all day—at times raining very fast.

Rid immediately, after breakfast to French's Plantation to see a sick man and intended to have gone to others but was driven back by the rain.

Thursday 15th.　Mercury at 40 in the Morning—56 at Noon and 48 at Night.

Clear, wind at So. Wt. in the Morning which blew fresh by Noon—after which it came out at No. Wt. blew hard and turned cold.

Rid to the Plantations at The Ferry, French's Dogue run and Muddy hole—also to the Mill and ditchers—Plowing at all except Muddy hole—the plows of that being at Fr[enc]hs—where No. 5 being too wet they were plowing in No. 2—at the other two places, plowing the ground intended for Meadow.

Friday 16th.　Mercury at 28 in the Morning 52 at Noon and 50 at Night. Very clear and pleasant in the Morning with little or no Wind. About 9 Oclock it Sprung up at No. Wt. and seemed inclined to blow hard—but before Noon it died away and came out afterwards at So. Wt.

Mr. Dandridge went away after an early breakfast and G. A. Washington set out for Berkley.

I rid to all the Plantations. Plowing at all except at Muddy hole the plows of wch. at Frenchs—In the Neck the men employed in getting Posts for railing. The Plows at that place had just got into the Orchard—the Women heaping dung.

Bath (a Negro Man from the Neck) joined the Dutch man Danl. Overdonck in ditching, yesterday.

Mr. & Mrs. Lund Washington dined here to day.

Saturday 17th.　Mercury at 32 in the Morng.—48 at Noon and 42 at Night.

Wind Southerly and warm all day. Towards night it lowered.

Went into the Neck to Mark some lines for fences. Finished this Evening plowing the orchard for Barley.

Received, before I had done a message acquainting me that Colo. Wadsworth and a Mr. Chaloner were here which brought me home.

Jeremiah Wadsworth (1743–1804), of Hartford, Conn., was an active advocate of independence and for several years served as commissary general for

Jeremiah Wadsworth. (New-York Historical Society)

the Continental Army. Of his service GW wrote: "I only wish his successor may feed the Army as well as he has done" (GW to Samuel Huntington, 24 Nov. 1779, DLC:GW). After the war Wadsworth became an active member of the Cincinnati. Now a member of the Continental Congress while also engaging in various business enterprises, he was visiting Mount Vernon to discuss his hopes for a new and stronger national government (PLATT, 199).

Mr. Chaloner was John Chaloner, formerly an assistant commissary of purchases during the Revolution, and now a partner in the Philadelphia firm of Chaloner and White. Chaloner had been the Philadelphia agent for John Barker Church and his wartime partner Jeremiah Wadsworth, and he was at this time engaged in settling the tangled business affairs of their now defunct company (HAMILTON [2], 3:12, 432, n.1, 634, n.4).

Sunday 18th.    Mercury at [    ] in the Morning–[    ] at Noon and [    ] at N.

Clear, Warm, and very pleasant all day, with very little wind. Towards dusk it began to lower again.

After dinner Colo. Wadsworth & Mr. Chaloner returned to Alexandria.

Monday 19th.    Mercury at 36 in the Morning–60 at Noon and 56 at N.

A very thick fog till nine or 10 Oclock when it dispelled, became clear & exceedingly pleasant.

Rid to all the Plantations. In the Neck heaping dung with the

Women ar[oun]d the Barn. Began after the Fog dispelled to plow for Oats in the Easternmost cut of drilled Corn (Timber landing field) intending to sow and harrow close at the heels of the Ploughs. At the other Plantations (Muddy hole plows at Frenchs) Plowing as before. The Muddy hole People finished hoeing thr. side of the New ground in front of the house.

Tuesday 20th.    Mercury at 40 in the Morning—35 at Noon and 30 at Night.

The Wind in the Night sprung up at No. West and blew very hard all day and till within Night. Ground froze this Morn.

Went with Mrs. Washington to Mr. Fendalls to make a visit to Colo. and Mrs. Lee. Dined and returned home in the Evening. Found Doctr. Craik here.

Wednesday 21st.    Mercury at 24 in the Morning—45 at Noon and 36 at Night.

Morning clear, but cold; ground hard froze—wind fresh all day from West.

Doctr. Craik went away before breakfast—after wch. I rode to Muddy hole and Neck Plantations. Began to Sow Oats at the latter in the ground which the Plows went into on Monday abt. Noon, & finished yesterdy. about dinner time. They were not more than half (at the East end) harrowed; in the way the plow went yesterday and this forenoon it was too hard to do it. Ordered it to be done this afternoon tho' the ground has not thawed much. Part of the ground about the place where the water had been drained from broke up in large flakes—whether because wet, or because the frost was in it when plowed yesterday I know not, but does not appear as if it would be made fine by harrowing & cross harrowing. The ground adjoining this (intended for Barley) which they were plowing to day, broke up in large flakes owing to the frost not being sufficiently out of it. Quaere will these large lumps or flakes crumble & fall to pieces by the sun & Rain when the frost is out?

Thursday 22d.    Mercury at 30 in the morng.—55 at Noon and 48 at Night.

Day pleasant, with the Wind at South till the evening when it began to lower. The Wind had shifted to the No. Et. & the Moon & Stars looked dim.

Rid to Muddy hole Dogue run & Frenchs Plantation.

At the first about a fence on the New ditch which was begun

yesterday. At the second, the Plows having done all they could in the newly inclosed Meadows for the Washes & wet places went over into the Mill Meadow & had begun to plow the Island where the hay stacks are (containing by stepping abt. 4¼ acres) which would be done today when they wd. get into the piece above East side the Mill race which was in Wheat last year and which by stepping contains about 5¾ acres. At the last, i.e. Frenchs Plantation the plows having finished plowing the Cut along the Road were beginning to plow the Corn ground next adjoining between that & Manleys old Houses but finding it too Wet to sow immediately with Oats and that by lying (as one plowing only was intended) it might get hard again before it was dry enough to sow I directed the Plows to continue there no longer than this day and to morrow to go into No. 1 and plow that part of it which was intended for Barley and which would receive before it was seeded two plowings. Staked off a ditch along the ferry road.

On my return home found Mr. Bryan Fairfax, his wife & daughter here.

Bryan Fairfax and his first wife, Elizabeth Cary Fairfax (1738–1788), had two daughters, the younger of whom, Elizabeth, appears here with her parents (KILMER, 39–42, 90–100).

**Friday 23d.**   Mercury at 27 in the Morning—33 at Noon and 30 at Night.

The Wind which shifted last Night to No. Et. brought Snow which by day break was abt. 2 Inches deep. It continued Snowing with the wind in the same quarter till 12 Oclock this day when the Sun appeared, tho it did not perfectly clear.

At home all day. In the Evening Mr. Griffith came in and stayed all night.

**Saturday 24th.**   Mercury at 30 in the Morning—44 at Noon and 36 at Night.

Cloudy, heavy morning—wind Southerly tho not fresh—Red horison at the Suns rising & lowering all day.

After breakfast Mr. Fairfax, his wife & daughter and Mr. Griffith went away.

I rode to the Plantations at the Ferry, French's, Dogue run, & Muddy hole. Plowing at Frenchs and Dogue run. Finished the Ditch at Muddy hole which divides fields No. 2 & 3. Would this afternoon finish plowing the other piece about 5¾ acres of Wheat Stubble on the East of the Mill race for Barley. This would have been done yesterday but there was no plowing any where.

Looked at the Dogue run Wheat. That which was sowed on lay land seemed to be well set in the ground—the Roots but little turned out with the frost. The early sown wheat in the Corn ground also looked tolerably well; but in places the roots were turned out of the ground, and in spots was injured by Water lying, or remaining on them too long. The latter sown Wheat cut but a very indifferent appearance—little being to be seen & that which was, seemed (the Root) to be entirely thrown out, except on the highest parts of the ridges. What alterations, or whether any for the better will take place must be determined here-after.

Rev. David Griffith was going to Nomini Hall with a letter of introduction from GW to Robert Carter (24 Feb. 1787, PHi: Dreer Collection).

Sunday 25th.    Mercury at 32 in the Morning—50 at Noon and 44 at Night.
Dull heavy morning, with the Wind what little there is of it at No. Et. The Moon last Night had a dim circle round it—also a bur and the Stars when they did appear were dim also. About Noon it became quite calm—this afternoon was clear & exceedingly pleasant.

Monday 26th.    Mercury at 33 in the Morning—44 at Noon and 32 at Night.
Red Sky at Sunrising—Wind Southerly in the fore Noon and at East in the afternoon. Morning heavy and damp with great appearances of rain. About Noon the clouds broke and the Sun appeared after which it clouded and looked very much like rain.
Rid to all the Plantations—to the Mill, and to the Ditchers. In the Neck, the ground which had been sowed the 21st. instt. with Oats, and which (though I sent 15 bushels of seed for it) was sown with 12 (on about 8 acres) was this day cross harrowed with the light harrows—the part I mean which was not cross harrowed on Thursday last and sowed with quarts of Timothy seed previous to the last harrowing. Finished at the same place plowing in the Middle cut adjoining the Wheat, and went about 11 Oclock into field No. 9 to breaking up—The other People grubbing, cutting, & filling up Gullies in the same field. At Muddy (except the Plows, which were at French's) the People were making the New fence. At Dogue run the Plows began to Plow in the No. end of the field west of the Mill race for Oats—all the other hands filling gullies before them the 2 Men who were Mauling. At Frenchs the Plows &ca. were employed as on Saturday. At the Ferry Caesar was beginning to lay out the list for Corn. The other two were plowing in

the ground intended for the New Meadow. The Women were fencing.

Began to Ditch along the Ferry road from where the New fence East of the Plantation comes to it towards the Mill—The Dutchman, Charles Bath & Cupid employed abt. it.

G. A. Washington returned this Evening from Berkeley.

Tuesday 27th.    Mercury at 44 in the Morning—52 at Noon and 44 at Night.

Morning early, cloudy, with the Wind Southerly. Before Noon it became clear—warm, and very pleasant, after which the wind came out at No. Wt. blew pretty fresh turned cloudy, & grew colder, but not disagreeably so, or likely to freeze.

Rid to the Plantations at the Ferry, Frenches, Dogue run and Muddy hole. Set the Plows at the first to crossing the Winter fallow, in order to sow Oats. The Plows and hands at the other Plantations, all working as yesterday.

Wednesday 28th.    Mercury at 40 in the Morning—54 at Noon and 44 at Night.

Morning clear—ground not froze—Wind westerly, but not very fresh. Afterwards it shifted more to the No. West and blew hard but did not freeze.

Rid to all the Plantations. In the Neck began to cross the Plowing in the homestead (orchard inclosure) in order to sow Oats; but the grd. in places having been tolerably well turfed, and stiff and not having had time since the plowing thereof for the grass to rot the last furrows were only cut in two, and remained exceedingly rough. Finding this would not answer I ordered the Plows to discontinue crossing and a heavy harrow to go over the ground the way the Ploughs run last to see if that, and harrowing after the Seed was sown, & cross harrowing, would be sufficient for the Oats. Began to cross the So. Et. quarter of the plowing at the ferry, to prepare it for Oats; intending to Sow the No. Et. quarter without crossing. At French's finished plowing all the ground between the Wheat and the Creek about 10 Oclock; and got into that pt. which was in Wheat last year immediately afterwards. At the Ferry spread some dung which had been carted out on the plowed ground which would be with in the New Meadow No. Wt. Corner of it.

On my return home, found young Doctr. Craik and his two Sisters Mariamne and Nancy here. The first returned after dinner— the girls remained.

## March, 1787

Thursday First.    Mercury at 40 in the Morning—56 at Noon and 46 at Night.

Morning very pleasant with little or no wind—but it soon Sprung up at No. West and blew fresh and though it grew cooler was not cold.

Rid to all the Plantations. The operation of harrowing which was begun yesterday in the Neck was going on; but as it did not appear to me that it would prepare the ground sufficiently for Oats I desired my farmer to go over and give me his Sentiments thereon. Had the Posts, which were morticed at this place counted —of which there were 184 of the long kind, & 116 of the Short. The New fence at Muddy hole being at a st[an]d for want of rails—the old fence round field No. 2 was righted up to keep creatures out of it and the Women went to Threshing rye in the Barn. Began to Sow Oats at Dogue run where the plows had been preparing the ground. The parts that were wet & heavy I ordered to be harrowed before sowing, & to receive the same workings after it, as the other part should. Began to Sow Oats at the Ferry on that part of the field which had been cross plowed. Harrowed after sowing.

Began to spread Ashes on the poorest part of the Lawn, in front of the House. The first levelled, and sown part of it, was the part on which it was laid.

Ordered Robin from Dogue run & Paschal from French's to join James Lawson in the work of Ditching to morrow.

Observed the difference between plowing with a broad furrow and narrow ones and the propriety of a narrow one where one only is to be given, as now in the case of Oats. My Farmer in field No. 1, at Frenchs East side of it began with the Narrow furrow and the ground seen as fitting again for the Oats as that which had been before plowed with a broad furrow. Where the Land is to be a second and a third time plowed broad furrows answer better because it rids over more gr[oun]d.

PASCHAL: one of the slaves leased from Mrs. French.

[Friday] 2d.    Mercury at 31 in the Morning—50 at Noon and 44 at Night.

Morning very clear and pleasant—ground a little frozen. About 8 Oclock the wind sprung up at No. Wt. & blew rather cool. Before Noon it died away and became warm and pleast.—after which it began to lower and towards Night looked very hazy & portentious of a change.

Rid into the Neck with my Compass to ascertain if practicable the outer boundary of My land (had of Clifton). Could not do it effectually but was inclined to think that the place fixed on below Simpsons house was nearly right and I run a straight line accordingly; and fixed Stakes for my fencing thereon as also between Colo. Mason & myself—leaving 20 odd feet for a road.

Began to sow Oats in the Neck to day of the kind had from Mr. Young as the first sowed there also was.

Ordered yesterday; every thing to be turned of the Wheat at all the Plantations—Those in the Neck to be put upon the Rye and those at Dogue run to be turned into the great Meadow.

Ms reads "Saturday." MR. YOUNG: may be either Notley Young (c.1736–1802), of Prince George's County, Md., one of the original proprietors of the Federal City, or the Mr. Young who rented Traveller's Rest in King George County from Col. Burgess Ball. William Deakins, Jr., of Georgetown in Jan. 1787 had contracted for 100 bushels of seed oats for GW from Notley Young, and, at about the same time, Alexander Spotswood had purchased for GW 150 bushels of oats from Mr. Young at Traveller's Rest (Deakins to GW, 31 Jan. 1787 and Spotswood to GW, 13 Jan. 1787, DLC:GW; LEDGER B, 242).

Saturday 3d.    Mercury at 31 in the Morning—42 at Noon and 40 at Night.

Very rainy Morning and till towards Noon—when it ceased, but no sun appeared all day. Wind, tho' very little of it, was at No. Et.

The Revd. Mr. Weems, and yg. Doctr. Craik who came here yesterday in the afternoon left this about Noon for Port Tobo.

Doctr. Stuart came here in the evening.

Mason Locke Weems (1759–1825), born in Anne Arundel County, Md., spent part of his youth in England, where in 1784 he was ordained a priest of the Anglican church, returning to Maryland to be rector (1784–89) of All Hallows Parish at South River in Anne Arundel County. Writing to GW in 1792 Weems recalled he had been "introduced to your Excellency by Doctor [James] Craik [Jr.] . . . some Years ago at M. Vernon" (6 July 1792, PHi: Gratz Collection). In 1785 Weems married Frances Ewell (1775–1843), a cousin of Dr. Craik and daughter of Col. Jesse Ewell of Bel Air, Prince William County, where the Weemses later made their home. Weems supported his wife and their ten children by traveling the east coast promoting and selling popular books, preaching in various sanctuaries (including Pohick Church), and writing moral essays and biographies of American heroes, including one of the earliest biographies of GW, which was published in 1800 (HAYDEN, 339; see WEEMS).

Sunday 4th.    Mercury at 32 in the Morning—44 at Noon and 42 at Night.

In the Morning early it was pleasand with the Wind at So. Afterwards it shifted to the No. Wt. and became variable with appearances all the evening of Snow or rain.

Mr. William Fitzhugh (Son to the Colo.) came here before dinner.

Monday 5th.    Mercury at 34 in the Morning—42 at Noon and 38 at Night.

Cloudy morning with the Wind at No. West, but neither fresh nor cold. Cloudy all day with appears. of rain or Snow.

Doctr. Stuart and Mr. Fitzhugh went away after breakfast.

I rid to the Ferry, French's Dogue run and Muddy hole Plantations. Began at French's to Sow Oats, & to harrow them in and at Dogue run to Cut & Maul rails with the two Jacks for the string of fencing through the Woods to inclose the Meadows.

The Rain which fell on friday Night and the forenoon of Saturday was more considerable than I had conceived by the wetness of the ground and other appearances.

The Ferry plows had desisted from putting in Oats but I ordered them to go at it this afternoon again.

James Lawson with his Party consisting of Boatswain Paschal & Robin just began on friday evening to ditch f[ro]m the Plank bridge towards the other Party but the Rain on Saturday prevented a full commencement of the work till this Morning—when in the two Parties 8 Ditchers were at work.

Whilst we were at dinnr. a Mr. Custis of the Eastern shr. came in—dined and stayed all Night.

MR. CUSTIS: Although Martha Washington had married a Custis before marrying GW, this "Mr. Custis of the Eastern sh[o]r[e]," where that family proliferated, may have come not on family business but to sell GW oats. Later this week GW paid for 125 bushels of oats bought "of an E[aster]n Shore man" (LEDGER B, 242).

Tuesday 6th.    Mercury at 32 in the Morning—54 at Noon and 48 at Night. Wind at No. West tho' not very fresh but raw and Cold; the Sun seldom appearing.

Rid to all the Plantations; No appearance of the first sowed Oats coming up in the Neck—Women, there, putting up a fence by Williams's house—at all the other places working as yesterday.

On my return home found Colo. Ball here and soon after dinner Mr. G. W. Lewis Son to Mr. Fielding Lewis of Frederick came in.

G. W. LEWIS: George Warner Lewis, third child of Fielding Lewis, Jr., and Ann Alexander Lewis who were living in Frederick County (now in Clarke County) at this time.

Wednesday 7th.    Mercury at 36 in the Morning—63 at Noon and 54 at Night.

Cloudy with the wind brisk at So. Et. in the Morning, and varying more westerly afterwards and blowing fresh all day—Clear after 8 Oclock.

Mr. G. W. Lewis went away after breakfast. Colo. Ball rid with me to the Plantations at the Ferry, Frenchs, Dogue run, & Muddy hole—Sowing Oats at the 3 first as also grass seeds—At the Ferry & Dogue Run of no other kind than Timothy, 3 pints, mixed with a bushel of Sand to the acre—at the other (French's) sowing Clover Orchd. Grass and Timothy mixed in the following proportions, 5 pints of Clover, one Gallon Orchd. grass, and 1 quart of Timothy Seeds Which is the allowance for an acre. More would be given of the Orchd. Grass but I had it not to afford. Plowed the last yrs. Wheat Stubble in field No. 1 and began abt. breakfast time to Plow the Corn in the back part of the field—West of the Wheat which was sown by Robinson. Began to thresh the Clover seed at Muddy hole yesterday—very tedious.

Thursday 8th.    Mercury at 34 in the Morning—48 at Noon and 42 at Night.

Grey Morning with some appearances of falling Weather—the wind however at No. West; about 9 Oclock it shifted to the No. East and blew raw and cold; before Noon it died away, and was very pleasant but towards evening it sprung up again at No. Et. and looked threatning again.

Colo. Ball went away immediately after breakfast.

I rid to all the Plantations. In the Neck, removed from the Homestead, or orchard Inclosure where Oats were sowing, to the Middle cut of drilled Corn (plowed for that purpose) and began to sow Poland Oats with Orchard, & Timothy grass Seeds—a gallon of the first, and a quart of the latter to the Acre. Finished sowing the Corn grd. at frenchs below the Tobo. grd. in which the house stands; both with Oats and grass Seeds. Of the first it took 20 bushels of the sort had from Mr. Young—of the latter abt. [     ] lbs. of Clover [     ] gallons of Orchd. grass, and [     ] quarts of Timothy Seed.

No appearance of the 1st. sowed Oats in the Neck coming up.

Finished the Ditch along the Ferry road, East of Muddy hole

branch and began on the west side—Danl. Overdonck and the 3 with him at the Plank bridge and James Lawson with his 3 at the Forks of the Road—each party working towards each other. This was begun late in the afternoon of yesterday.

My Corn house, with Robinsons Corn in it at French's was burned down in the Night, either by carelessness or design. The latter seems most likely, but whom to suspect was not known.

POLAND OATS: producing on dry, warm lands a very large and plump grain (YOUNG, 79).

Friday 9th.    Mercury at 36 in the Morng.—44 at Noon and 42 at Night.

A good deal of Rain fell last Night—wind at South all day. Abt. 9 Oclock it ceased raining; and about Noon the Sun came out, and it was very pleasant; but it clouded and lowered much afterwards.

At home all day.

Saturday 10th.    Mercury at 44 in the Morning—62 at Noon and 59 at Night.

A clear and pleasant Morning with the Wind at So. after wch. it shifted to the No. Wt. and blew fresh but not cold. Towards evening it became calm and exceeding pleasant. A violent [wind] in the Night with storms of rain.

Rid to all the Plantations. Found that much rain had fallen and that the sowing of Oats was stopped at every place on acct. of the wetness of the ground—but that the Plows at Dogue run were at work in that intended for them. In the Neck they were breaking up No. 9 for Corn—at the Ferry they were listing the Stoney field part of No. 1 for Do. and at Frenchs were breaking up No. 2 for Turnips, Pease &ca. At Muddy hole the Overseer and Women were threshing & getting out the clover Seed.

No appearances of the first Sowed Oats in the Neck coming up.

Sunday 11th.    Mercury at 40 in the Morning—58 at Noon and 50 at Night.

Calm, clear and remarkably pleasant all day till about Sun down when the wd. sprung up fresh from the So. Et. and the Sky became Muddy.

Doctr. Craik came here to dinner to day. Mrs. Jenifer came here to dinner yesterday.

Mrs. Jenifer is probably Sarah Craik Jenifer, Dr. Craik's daughter.

Monday 12th.    Mercury at 36 in the Morng.—60 at Noon and 58 at N.

Morning a little Cloudy with the wind at South—much the same all day. Towds. Night the wind freshened and in the Night blew a storm.

Rid to all the Plantations—Plowing, and Sowing Oats and grass Seeds at all except at Muddy hole—threshing clover Seed there.

No appearance of the first Sowed Oats rising yet.

Majr. Washington went up to town on my business.

Tuesday 13th.    Mercury at [    ] in the Morning—68 at Noon and 64 at Night.

The Southerly Storm of last Night was very violent—blowing down some of my fencing and the tops of my Hay & wheat Stacks. Much rain also fell by which the ground was made very wet and the Runs filled with water. Till about 8 Oclock this morning it continued to rain fast after which it cleared with a fresh Southerly Wind which continued till afternoon when it shifted to the No. West and blew hard.

Rid to the Ferry, French's and Dogue run Plantations. No sowing at any—Plows picking the driest spots to plow in. At the Ferry they were listing for Corn in Stoney field & at Frenchs breaking up field No. 2.

Wednesday 14th.    Mercury at 42 in the Morning—60 at Noon and 58 at Night.

Remarkably fine and pleasant all day with little or no wind.

Rid to all the Plantations—began to sow Oats as usual. The first sowed ones in the Neck were beginning to come up. At that place Nat finished on Monday last laying off field No. 3 for Corn. At Dogue run finished filling gullies & grubbing before the Plows in the long field West of the Mill race.

Thursday 15th.    Mercury at 42 in the Morning—[    ] at Noon and [    ] at N.

Clear and pleasant with [wind] at South. Towards sundown the horison looked a little thick in the West.

Went out with my Compass in order to Mark the ground at Muddy hole intended for experiments, into half Acre lotts, and two other places adjoining all on field No. 2—into 10 Acre lotts— Also to mark the lines which divide field No. 1 from No. 2 & 3 and the fields 6 & 7 at Dogue run.

Plowing and Sowing as usual. In the Neck the Middle cut in

field No. 2 wd. be finished sowing this evening with 24 bushels of the Poland Oats; and 12 quarts of Timothy Seed—qty. about 17 Acres.

The Ditchers finished the ditch along the Ferry road this afternoon.

Friday 16th.    Mercury at 40 in the Morning—64 at Noon and 60 at Night.

Clear, warm, and very pleasant all day with but little Wind and that Southerly.

Rid to all the Plantations, to the Mill and to the Ditchers. The last began to ditch on both sides the New Meadow at the ferry—Plowing and sowing as usual at all the other places.

Mrs. Jenifer and the two Miss Craiks went away yesterday and Mr. Porter who came here last Night left it before breakfast this Morning.

Mr. Griffith came in the evening and stayed all Night.

Saturday 17th.    Mercury at 40 in the Morning—52 at Noon and 48 at Night.

Morning tolerably clear but lowering all day afterwards and sometimes misting with the wind at No. Et.

Mr. Griffith went away after breakfast.

I rid to Muddy hole, Dogue run, French's, and Ferry Plantations. At French's the Plows began yesterday after noon to plow in that cut of field No. 5 by Manleys houses. At the Ferry, in ground which had been sown with Oats on Wednesday last, I measured, by stepping, on the line formerly dividing this plantation from French's two Ac[re]s on the most Southerly of wch. I had sowed two bushels, and on the next, one bushel of Oats, in addition to what was in the ground before; and wch. was, as near as could be estimated, two bushels to ea. acre. These two, with the grd. on each side, were as nearly of an equallity as possibly could be in every respect; and perfectly level. It was done as an experiment to try what quantity of Seed was best for an Acre. The one and two bushels added, would give 3 on one Acre and 4 on the other. On the right & left of these the grd. would have only two Bushls. thereabouts to the acre. These two acres on acct. of harrowing in the additional Oats will have had one harrowing more than the other. In all other respects the management, as well as the soil, was precisely the same and will be a fair trial. The same experiment was this day made also in the Neck, in field No. 2; which had been sown & harrowed on thursday last, with abt. a bushel and half of Oats to the acre—the addition making 3½ and 2½ to the Acre. This ground likewise lyes perfectly level, and as near as possible of a quality. The acre which has 3½ bushls. is the most westerly of the two. These will also have had by means of the additional quantity of Seed, an additional harrowing. These two acres as well as those at the ferry are marked of by stakes—in order that they may be Cut and threshed separately at harvest.

Sunday 18th.    Mercury at 44 in the Morning—62 at Noon and 63 at Night.

A thick fog in the early part of the Morning and lowering till towards Noon—Clear afterwards till evening when the Sun set in a bank—Wind at So. Et. till Night when it appeared to be at So. West. The day was warm & pleasant. Wind fresh in the Night.

A Mr. Black from New York, Mr. Hunter, Mr. Porter, Mr. Monshur, Mr. Murray, & Mr. Clanagan of Alexandria dined here & returned in the Evening.

MR. BLACK: may be John Blagge, who sailed as a supercargo between New York and Alexandria. MR. CLANAGAN: probably John McClanaghan (McClenahan), who settled as a merchant in Alexandria and later married Ann (Nancy) McCarty, youngest daughter of Col. Daniel McCarty of Mount Air (O'BRIEN, 121; Fairfax County Deeds, Q-1, 226, Vi Microfilm).

Monday 19th.    Mercury at 58 in the Morning—63 at Noon and 63 at Night.

Morning lowering, and the Wind fresh from South. The same kind of Weather through the day, with drops of rain now and then.

Rid to the Ferry, Frenchs, Dogue run & Muddy hole Plantations; and to the Ditchers. Plowing and Sowing Oats as usual at the 3 first and at all of them the first sowed Oats were coming up. The ground is in gd. order for plowing, but in some places where it had been plowed for some time it had become rather too closely settled by the rains wch. had fallen since, for the harrow to do as good work as were to be wished.

The early Wheat is beginning to spring fast, and looks as well as can be expected from the ground. The lay land Wheat, both at Dogue run & Muddy hole, looks promising, and stands sufficiently thick on the ground. The latter sowed Wheat at Dogue run begins to show something better; but is thin, and very backward, as the Rye at this place also is.

Set the Ditchers this Morning to continue the Ditch wch. runs through the New Meadow at the Ferry into Muddy hole branch and to cleanse the old ditch in the said New Meadow.

Tuesday 20th.   Mercury at 58 in the Morning—62 at Noon and 56 at Night.

A Very thick fog all the Morning—lowering afterwds. with but little Wind. A little rain last N.

Rid to the Plantations at the Ferry, Frenchs, and Dogue run. Had the hands from the latter and Muddy hole brot. to Frenchs to put up the fence along the Road, that that by Grays house might be removed out of the way of the plows.

Mr. Martin Cockburn, for the purpose of taking the list of taxable property; and Mr. Potts & Mr. Roger West for the purpose of taking the privy examination of Fanny Washington came here —dined and returned in the afternoon.

Roger West (c.1755–1801) was the only son of Col. John West of West Grove. He was a justice of the peace for Fairfax County c. 1787–99, and represented Fairfax County in the House of Delegates from 1788 to 1789, 1791–92, and 1797–99.

PRIVY EXAMINATION: When real property in which a married woman had a right was to be sold, a privy (i.e., private) examination of the woman, made by at least two justices of the peace, was provided for by law in order to determine whether or not her agreement to the sale was by her own free will. This examination, made by John Potts, Jr., and Roger West of the Fairfax County court, may relate to a piece of land sold by Fanny and her husband George Augustine Washington, the sale of which was entered into the Spotsylvania County court on 3 April 1787 (CROZIER [2], 405).

Wednesday 21st.   Mercury at 48 in the Morning—64 at Noon and 60 at Night.

Heavy, lowering Morning; with but little wind from the So. Et. Calm all day with Clouds and Sun shine alternately through the whole of it. When the Sun was out, it was very warm—Vegetation advancing very quick. The grass had come on surprisingly & the blossoms of the early fruits were putting forth as were the leaves of the early trees, and the buds of all.

Rid to all the Plantations. In the Neck the Oats in the Homestead or Orchard Inclosure would be all in by noon except just the Orchard part of it—that is the part on which the Trees grow. And the Plows finished breaking field No. 9 except the small Neck next the wood which they entered upon about breakfast time. At Dogue run the plows by dinner time would have finished breaking up the field West of the Mill race except two or 3 wet spots, wch., together would not amount to an Acre. At Frenchs the field No. 1 would be finished this Evening, except abt. 5 Acres designed for Barley which had been plowed and a small slipe adjoining the Wheat, which by mistake the plowing was omitted. This, the Barley ground, and the ground in Wheat, may together, make about 15 acres, wch. will leave about 40 Acres that are sowed in Oats.

The Oats every where, according to the time they were sowed are coming up very well and to appearance sufficiently thick.

In the field No. 1, at Frenchs, which according to the above estimation contains 40 acrs. in Oats 87 Bushels of them were sowed therein, and the following grass—mixed together—viz. 26 gallons and 1 Quart of Red Clover Seed (of that had from Alexandria) 42 gallns. of Orchard grass seeds, and 9½ gallons of Timothy Seed.

Directed the Toll (⅛th.) to be taken from 10 Bushels of Corn and the residue to be ground at my Mill and the quantity of Meal it yielded to be reported to me—wch. is as follow—viz.—

 11 Bushl. & 1 peck of unbolted Meal and
 10 Bushls. 1 peck & 4 quarts when the husks were
  bolted from the Meal.

So that there will be more meal when bolted in Measure than there is of the Corn before the Toll is taken from it. [      ] And [      ]

It appeared by another trial that a peck of unbolted Meal midlingly heaped will yield more than a peck of Meal when bolted or sifted.

Thursday 22d.    Mercury at 44 in the Morning—58 at Noon and 44 at N.

Clear all day, with the wind pretty fresh from the Southward. Towards Night and in the Night, it encreased; and grew colder.

Rid to the Plantations at the Ferry, Frenchs, & Dogue run. Began to sow Oats in Field No. 5 at Frenchs—in the West cut East side thereof with the Oats from George Town (the common kind). At Dogue run the Plows would finish breaking up field No. 1 as follow—the land next the lay wht. quite across the field from the Meadow fence to the Swamp being untouched either in the fall or Winter and which was now coming up very thick with the White clover principally was turned for the first time. The land next to this was untouched having been flush plowed in the fall. The 3d. land was in grass the same as the first and plowed in like manner. The 4th land had been plowed in the fall in half furrows, by my farmers directions—that is, a furrow was turned upon an equal breadth of unbroke ground quite through the land and was then, that is the unbroke part, split and turned with the plow.

My ditchers having cleansed the ditch in the Middle of the New Meadow returned to the side ditches again.

WHITE CLOVER: *Trifolium repens,* white clover or sometimes white Dutch clover.

Friday 23d.    Mercury at 44 in the Morning—46 at Noon And 38 at N.

The Wind shifted from the Southward to the No. West in the Night and blew violently hard, which it continued to do all day turning cold & very disagreeable.

Rid to all the Plantations. Finished about 9 Oclock breaking up all the ground in field No. 9 in the Neck.

The Muddy hole force all at French's putting up the fence along the road as all the Dogue run hands were except the plowers —One of which was cross plowing a piece of ground (abt. an acre) in the Meadow, to receive 3 bushels of Oats sent me by Genl. Spotswood. Two were breaking up as much of the ground between the two Meadows (which they had been obliged to leave on acct. of the wet) as they now could do for water and the 4th was harrowing in Oats. At Frenchs the wind had blown down the fence between Fields No. 1 & 4. From this place Gray moved this day. At the Ferry all the Oats would be Sowed this day in field No. 2 the quantity 55½ Bushels Whereof 45½ bush. were of the Poland sort & 10 bushls. of those from Mr. Young's. The cross harrowing of these could not be given to day, as the wind blew too hard to sow the grass Seeds, which preceeded the 2d. harrowing.

Saturday 24th.    Mercury at 28 in the Morning—[      ] at Noon and [      ] at Night.

The Wind still violent at No. Wt.—ground frozen and so dried & baked with the Wind as not to be in condition for plowing or harrowing in the Morning. Ice almost through the day which was very cold for the season and exceedingly disagreeable.

Rid to the Ferry, French's, and Dogue run Plantations—The Plows at the first listg. of Field No. 3 below the hill. Attempted with the harrow to level and smooth the grd. intended for a New Meadow at this place—righted all the Fencing at Frenchs which had been blown down with the Wind—compleated the New Fence on the ditch by the road up to the plank bridge and as the ground could not be harrowed there, nor the unbroke ground plowed, the plows went to crossing that which had been plowed some time ago

Two types of Virginia fences, drawn by Samuel Vaughan in his 1787 journal.
(Collection of the descendants of Samuel Vaughan)

in the east cut of the same field No. 5 West part. The Harrow
being also stopped at Dogue run all the plows united and finished
breaking up the grd. between the two Meadws. adjoining the
Overseers Ho[use] except the lowest part thereof where the water
drains.

A Captn. Rice came here in the evening with Mr. Lear who
went up to Alexandria to day.

Captain Rice of the brig *Polly*, recently arrived in Alexandria from the West
Indies, was preparing to sail for New England ports (*Va. Journal,* 8 Mar.
1787).

Sunday 25th.    Mercury at 32 in the Morning—48 at Noon and
49 at Night.

Very severe frost last Night—More Ice than yesterday morning
—Wind still at No. West but not so fresh as yesterday and weather
clear.

Mr. Snow from Alexandria came down and dined and returned
in the Afternoon with Captn. Rice—immediately after which a
Mr. Martin—an English Gentleman came in and a few minutes
afterwards Mr. Arthur Lee, both of whom stayed all Night.

Arthur Lee had been appointed to the Board of Treasury in 1785; he served
until the new government went into effect.

Monday 26th.    Mercury at 36 in the Morning—58 at Noon And
54 at Night.

Morning clear and pleasant Wind Southerly but not much of it.

At home all day. The English Gentleman went away after
breakfast and Mr. Lee after

Colo. Gilpin—Doctr. Stuart, Mrs. Stuart and Betcy & Patcy
Custis came here to Dinner. The first went away after it.

Finished sowing Oats in the Neck on Saturday last, in the Homestead, or Orchard Inclosure; Which took 57 bushels; Whereof 15

bushels of the first sown were of those from Mr. Young, the others from the Eastern shore which had been culled from the wild garlick. Had the harrows brot. from hence. The light double ones were carried to French's and the heavy one to Dogue run. Plowed the last years Turnip patch up at this place for Barley (about 5 Acres) on Saturday last and began to lay off field No. 9 for Corn.

At Dogue run about an acre was sown in my Meadow—part of which had been cowpened and part had had dung carried on it, with 3 Bushels of Oats sent me by General Spotswood and after harrowing these in, with abt. half a bushel of New River grass seeds. The ground in which these Oats were sown, had been plowed, cross-plowed, & twice harrowed before Sowing, and twice harrowed afterwards; once for the Oats, & once for the Seed. Removed the Ditchers into field No. 5 at French's to ditch for a fence. The Plows at this place were also removed into the West cut in the same field from whence they were taken when the ground was frozen but finding after trying some time that the ground had got very hard by the late drying & baking winds I shifted them back & continued cross plowing.

Tuesday 27th.    Mercury at 44 in the Morning—50 at Noon and 49 at Night.

Very smoky, and lowering all day with but little wind & that from the Southward.

Rid to the Ferry, French's Dogue run & Muddy hole Plantations. At the first began yesterday, & would finish to day, harrowing Timothy Seed on the Rye which had been omitted in the Fall; and on the Snow during winter. Ordered a part of it to be cross harrowed in order to raise more loose earth for the covering of it. Began at this place also to Harrow & others ways to prepare the New Meadow for the Sowing of Oats & grass Seeds in it. Sowing Oats and fencing at French's and threshing Clover Seed at Muddy hole.

Doctr. Stuart, Mrs. Stuart and the two girls went home after dinner.

Had a descriptive list taken of all my Horses and Cattle in the Neck today.

Wednesday 28th.    Mercury at 48 in the Morning—52 at Noon and 54 at Night.

A heavy fog in the Morning—a pretty brisk shower of Rain for about an hour at Noon and clear warm and pleasant Afternoon.

Rid into the Neck and was [prevented] from going to the other places by the Rain. The cold winds and frost last Week had turned the Oats yellow and in some places had bitten the blades. Rid over my Wheat at this place and found it more indifferent than I expected—indeed scarce any on the ground, especially in the cut on the River; and the whole so weedy that I do not expect it will be worth reaping. Examined the clover also on this place, in field No. [    ] and found this likewise very thin and indifferent, except at the point where it had been sown with flax. Whether the goodness of this was owing to the ground being stronger—better prepared—or by being sown with the flax—I know not; but the difference was very apparent. The clover was also much better where the Mud had been spread last Spring, than it was any where else except at the point; & the white Clover was coming up very thick on it. In the other parts of the field the Clover was not only very thin but looked weak and sickly. Began to set the posts and rails for a ditch fence on the line between Mr. Mason & myself in the Neck and began to list, or rather to renew the listing, in field No. 3 at this place.

Thursday 29th.     Mercury at 38 in the Morning—56 at Noon And 50 at Night.

Raining before day with the Wind fresh and cold from the No. West. About 8 Oclock it began to Snow, and continued to do so by intervals till 11 or 12 but not enough at any time to cover the ground. The afternn. was clear and tolerably pleasant the wind what remained of it having shifted round to the So. West.

Rid to the Plantations at the Ferry, Frenchs, Dogue run & Muddy hole. At the first, finding the harrow to make tolerable good Work in the New Meadow I directed it to continue on, till the ground, with the assistance of the hoes in the places which had been unbroke, were the wettest & most grassy—should be properly prepared for sowing the Oats, and grass seeds. The Ditchers would have finished the side ditches to this Meadow to day and were ordered to open a ditch between the fields No. 2 & 3 at Frenchs. The rain having put the ground about Manleys old House in better order for plowing the Plows, after the rain Let up proceeded to finish this part of field No. 5. At Dogue run the Sowing of Oats &ca. going on as usual—At Muddy hole the clover seed was all threshed out, but not cleaned. Ordered 50 bushels of dung to be carried upon the half acre squares of No. 2 & 4 (counting from the ditch fence) and on that part adjoining the Wheat, in order to sow Oats thereon.

Friday 30th.    Mercury at 39 in the Morning—48 at Noon and 44 at Night.

A Frost this Morning, notwithstanding the Wind appeared to have been Southwardly all Night. Abt. 8 oclock, or Sooner the wd. shifted to No. Wt.—blew fresh—turned cold & spit Snow. Towards the afternoon it veered round more to the Southward again, but continued cool.

Rid to Muddy hole, Dogue run, French's, and the Ferry. The dung ordered to be spread yesterday at the first having been laid on, the cross plowing of the ground was set about. The Square No. 2, the South half of it, was very Sandy, and did not require a 2d. plowing, but that all might have equal culture, this and the other half, as well as the square No. 4, was plowed; this last was much stiffer soil than No. 2 and the North end a good deal stiffer than the South half of it—Cutting down Corn Stalks at Dogue run with the Women. Finished about Noon, Plowing that part of field No. 5 at Frenches round Manleys old houses, & went to cross plowing again in the other part of the same field from whence they had shifted—Preparing the New Meadow with the Hoes & Harrows at the Ferry.

Mrs. Lund Washington & Captn. Walter Brooke dined here.

Saturday 31st.    Mercury at 34 in the Morning—58 at Noon and 54 at N.

The ground was frozen this Morning. The Wind however had got Southerly and the day except flying clouds was for the most part clear. The evening was warm and pleasant.

Rid to all the plantations. In the Neck 105 Pannels of Post and rail fencing which was begun there on Wednesday was compleated —Plows listing & women threshing. At Muddy hole, the Clover seed being cleaned, measured 3 bushls. and 3 quarts—Sowed the Squares No. 2 & 4 at this place with Oats in the following manner —viz.—the East half of No. 2 with half a Bushel of Oats from George Town and the west half with a Bushel of the Poland Oats —The east half of No. 4 with half bushel of the Poland Oats and the West half with a bushel of the George Town Oats. The objects, and design of this experiment, was to ascertn. 3 things—1st. which of these two kinds of Oats were best the George Town (which was a good kind of the common Oat)—2d. Whether 2 or 4 bushels to the Acre was best and 3d. the difference between ground dunged at the rate of 5 load, or 200 bushels to the Acre and ground undunged. It is to be observed however that though these two squares appears to be of equal quality, or rather strength yet the So. half of each, which had no dung was the lightest and much the greater mixture of Sand in them. Brought another of the Muddy hole plows home from French's, & set it to laying off the 20 acre cut designed (if Carrot Seed can be obtained) for Carrots, Potatoes, Peas, & Turnips between the Corn which will be drilled in Rows 10 feet a part. Women Threshing wheat at this place. Employed at Dogue run as yesterday. At Frenchs harrowing in the Oats about Manleys old houses—as also cross plowing the square next the Road in the other cut and about 2 Oclock began to cross plow about half of the other part next the water ditch, east end of it adjoining the Cabins. At the Ferry the west side of the New Meadow—above the *Water* ditch was compleated and Sowed both with Oats & Timothy Seed. The ground appeared to be in very good order by the frequent harrowings it had received.

# April 1787

Sunday. first.    Mercury at 36 in the Morning—54 at Noon and 50 at Night.

Wind at No. West in the Morning and Southerly afterwards but not very fresh at any time of the day—Weather clear.

At home all day.

Mr. Hunter, Mr. Rumney, Mr. Porter, Doctr. Craik and a Captain Nixon dined here—all of whom except Mr. Hunter went away after it. In the evening, one Young who lives on Colo. Balls place, a Farmer, came here to see, he says, my drill plow & stayed all Night.

CAPTAIN NIXON: On 8 Mar. 1787 John Rumney's Alexandria firm advertised: "Just arrived, The ship Friendship, Capt. Wilson Nixon, from Whitehaven, with an assortment of European goods" (*Va. Journal*). ONE YOUNG: possibly the Mr. Young living at Traveller's Rest in King George County. See entry for 2 Mar. 1787.

Monday 2d.    Mercury at 37 in the Morning—56 at Noon and 47 at Night.

Morning Mild, calm, & smoaky till abt. 8 oclock when the wind came out at No. Wt. and blew fresh all day. Weather clear.

Mr. Hunter and Young went away before breakfast and after it I rid to Muddy-hole Dogue run—Frenchs and the Ferry Plantations. At the first began to sow Clover seed at the rate of 6 pints to the acre on the lay Wheat & Timothy; but the wind was so high that the Seed could only be sown at times when it lulled.

This Seed was harrowed in, & where the ground was hard which was pretty generally the case, the harrow run two or 3 times in the same place; this tore out of the ground *some* of the Wheat & Timothy; but not in the proportion it was supposed the rest would be benifitted by the Working. Ordered a pretty heavy roller to follow the harrow to Morrow, & to keep close to it afterwards in order to press the loose earth round the roots of the Wheat, and more effectually to cover the clover seed. The work at Dogue run—Frenchs & Ferry going on as on Saturday. Ordered 2 Carts in the Neck to carry dung on the last years Turnps. and to be immediately spread that it might receive 2d. plowing for Barley.

Tuesday. 3d.    Mercury at 38 in the Morning—50 at Noon and 52 at Night.

Ground froze, and Ice half an Inch thick with a small, white frost. Morning tho' cool, pleasant, being calm and clear.

Scarcely a Morning since the high wind the 23d. of March that has not produced frost in a greater or less degree.

Rid to all the Plantations. In the Neck finished listing field No. 3. Ordered the Plows to do the same in field No. 9 with 3 furrows *only* the others having 5 furrows. Sowing Clover & harrowing and rolling it on the lay wheat at Muddy hole. Finished Sowing the long field, West of the Mill race, at Dogue run with Oats and Timothy Seed; of the first it took [     ] bushels and of the latter [     ] quarts. The quantity of ground may be about 75 Acres. At French's began to Sow Barley.

Began to Fish to day.

Brought the Ditchers to the home house to finish the New road and to compleat the sunk fence in front of the Lawn. Ordered Cupid from the Ferry to return home.

Wednesday. 4th.    Mercury at 44 in the Morning—73 at Noon and 70 at Night.

Wind Southerly, and weather clear, & very warm all day and appearances of dry weather.

Rid to the Fishing Landing and to the Plantations at the Ferry, Frenchs, Dogue run, and Muddy hole. Finished harrowing in all the Oats that were sown in field No. 5 at Frenchs. To sow this field it took 117½ Bushels. The quantity of Land sowed with them is about 40 Acres. The Plows after having cross plowed the grd. for Barley in this field went to breaking up No. 2. but I ordered the 3 belonging to Dogue run to return home at Night and leave the two belonging to the Plantation to continue this work. At Dogue run, The upper piece which was in Wheat, in the Meadow, East of the race, was sowed with Oats from Mattawoman, [      ] bushls. and Timothy [      ] Quarts. Finished sowing, harrowing, and Rolling the Clover which had been sown on the lay wheat at Muddy hole—to do which it took 60 pints of Seed—the ground ten acres.

Thursday. 5th.    Mercury at 54 in the Morning—80 at Noon and 76 at Night.

Wind Southerly in the Morning, variable afterwards, often times at No. Wt. and pretty fresh but clear and very warm all day —very smoaky and hazy with the Sun red and other indications of a drought.

Rid to the Fishing landing, and to the Plantations at the Ferry, Frenchs, Dogue run and Muddy hole. At the first, sowing Oats and grass Seeds on the No. Et. Corner of the New Meadow. At Frenchs finished covering the Barley which was sown on ten acres in field No. 5—quantity 19 Bushels. This ground had been twice plowed and 4 times harrowed after the Barley was sown—as thus —first half the quantity of Seed sown and harrowed—then the other half sown and harrowed; both as the Plows run and then twice cross harrowed. N.B. the half sowings was to cause the ground to be more regularly sown. At Dogue run the Harrows began to Cover Oats in field No. 1 next the road & the Branch by Manleys; and the 3 plows were listing in Field No. 4. At Muddy hole began to Sow, harrow, & roll the Clover & orchard grass Seeds on the Rye by the Barn which I directed to be sown in the following proportion to the Acre—viz.—a gallon of orchard grass Seeds and Six pints of Clover Seed. N.B. all the Clover Seed Sown at this place was raised on it.

In the afternoon a Mr. Beall of Williamsburgh came in & stayed all Night.

Samuel Beall, of Williamsburg, was a merchant in the West Indies trade (KIDD, 58; MASON [1], 399, 462, 470).

Friday 6th.    Mercury at 44 in the Morning—54 at Noon and 45 at Night.

In the Night it turned cool and continued so all day with the Wind at No. East and appearances of rain in the forenn. but much less afterwards.

Mr. Beall went away after breakfast.

Rid to all the Plantations and to the Fishing landing at the

Ferry. Listing, and laying off Corn at Muddy hole, the latter in the South part of field No. 2—the other every eighth row in the No. part for Carrotts. The grd. in field No. 1 at Dogue run preparing for, and sowing with Oats, works very fine and well with the Harrows. Rolling the Barley at Frenchs and Sowing Flax Seed and Clover in the grd. about the huts at that place, on the Et. side the partition fence between the two Plantations. Rolling the ground in the New meadw. at the Ferry, which had been sown with Oats & Timothy and preparing the wettest part of the rest.

Finished Sowing the Flax seed and Clover in the ground mentioned above, this afternoon. Of the first it took 9 bushls. and of the latter 44 Quarts. This Ground has been plowed, & cross plowed, and well harrowed; 3 or 4 times, as occasion required; and will be rolled to morrow—after the roller has passed over the Barley. The qty. abt. 6½ acres.

Sent the other Plow belonging to Muddy hole, home this evening, from French's.

Saturday 7th.    Mercury at 52 in the Morning—58 at Noon and 52 at Night.

Wind Easterly in the Morning & cool; but shifting afterwards more Southerly and dying away till the evening it grew warmer. The appearances of rain vanished.

Rid to the Fishing landing and the Plantations at the Ferry, French's, Dogue run, and Muddy hole. At French's the rolling of the Barley, and the Flax seed & Oats would be compleated by Night and the grd. round the Barn which had been originally intended for Barley was sown upon the first plowing with Oats and grass seeds as the other parts of the field had been. The qty. of grd. being about 5 acres recd. 9 bushls. of Oats and [     ] gallns. of Orchard grass Seed, [     ] pints of red clover, and [     ] pints of Timothy. At Muddy hole plowed the 1st. & 3d. square for Barley; as I had done the 2d. & 4th. before for Oats. These two Squares were, that is the North half of them, manured each with 50 bushels of dung, precisely as those for Oats had been.

In my Botanical garden in the Section immediately adjoining to, & west of the Salt House I sowed first 3 rows of the Kentucke clover 15 inches a part and next to these 9 rows of the guinea grass in rows the same distance apart.

Colo. Henry Lee, and his Brother Mr. Richd. Lee came here to dinner and proceeded to Alexandria afterwards.

Sent up to day for my Nephews George & Lawe. Washington who came down whilst we were at Dinner.

Sunday 8th.    Mercury at 46 in the Morning—58 at Noon and 56 at Night.

Wind Southerly, and Morning a little lowering—About 11 Ock. it began to rain moderately, and continued to do so 15 or 20 Minutes when it ceased and cleared. About Sun down a slight cloud arose in the So. Wt. quarter from whence proceeded a pretty heavy shower for a few minutes which seemed to discharge a good deal of rain for the time.

Mrs. Stuart and her daughters Betcy & Patcy Custis came here to dinner and stayed all Night.

At home all day.

Monday 9th.    Mercury at 56 in the Morning—68 at Noon and 68 at Night.

Clear all day with the Wind variable from So. Wt. to No. Wt. and very high.

Mrs. Stuart went away after breakfast leaving Betcy and Patcy Custis.

At home all day.

Tuesday 10th.    Mercury at 48 in the Morning—74 at Noon and 72 at Night.

Clear, calm, and warm all day. The appearances of fruit is very great from the innumerable blossoms with which every Tree is loaded.

Rid to all the Plantations, spreading as much dung as I could spare, & find time to carry out on the poorest part of the last years Turnip field in the Neck, I ordered it to be cross plowed for sowing Barley and Clover. The first sowed Oats at this place do not look well the blade appearing yellow and singed at the ends by the frost nor have they made much progress in their growth. At Muddy hole, Sowed the 1st. and 3d. half Acre squares (plowed friday last) with three kinds of Barley, in the following manner, viz.—Each being divided from No. to South in three exactly equal parts by which each part was half dunged as mentioned on friday —the Eastermost 1/3 of each was sowed with 8 qts. of the Barley had from Phila. (originally from Rhode Island) and which my Farmer thought very good. The middle third of each was sowed with the same quantity of the naked Barley—had from Colo. Henry Lee and the Westermost 1/3 with a Barley 8 Quarts also, sent me by Genl. Spotswood under the denomination of Bear and which in appearance was very much like the Rhode Island, or Philadelphia Barley just mentioned. This ground had been twice

Plowed, and after the Seed had been sowed was harrowed & Cross harrowed. At Dogue run chopped, and made fine a piece of grd. in the meadow wch. had been plowed, in order to sow in drills the New River grass Seed. At French's finished Sowing the last Oats— viz. a slipe between the Wheat and road—with 2 Bushels together with grass Seeds in the mixture & proportion given to the other ground and began to Sow the same on the Wheat and to harrow it in.

Mrs. Fanny Washington was delivered of a boy this Morning.

Examined the Seed Potatoes which I had buried for preservation in my Garden—and found them all rotten. The Wet had got to them—whether from the nature of the Soil or improper mode of covering them (though the ground was ridged over them) I know not—but the mode does not appear to be efficacious.

Recd. from Mr. Jno. Lawson, Negro Neptune, on trial as a Brick layer.

Miss Sally Ramsay came down this evening with Mr. Lear, who went up to Alexandria on my business.

BEAR [BARLEY]: a kind of common barley, *Hordeum vulgare*, called "bere or big barley." After Spotswood had promised the seed, GW asked him 23 Jan. 1787 whether it was a spring or winter barley and at what time it should be sown (DLC:GW). DELIVERED OF A BOY: Fanny Washington's first child, George Fayette Washington, lived only two weeks (see entry for 25 April 1787). John Lawson (1754–1823), of Dumfries, had agreed to sell his newly acquired slave, Neptune, to GW. Upon the slave's arrival at Mount Vernon, GW wrote Lawson that Neptune, "although he does not profess to be a workman, yet as he has some little knowledge of Bricklaying, seems willing to learn, and is with a man who understands the business, I will keep him." Unfortunately, however, GW learned also that Neptune was unhappy at being sold so far from his wife. GW informed Lawson that he was "unwilling to hurt the feelings of anyone. I shall therefore if agreeable to you keep him a while to see if I can reconcile him to the separation (seeing her now and then) in which case I will purchase him, if not I will send him back." A short time later Neptune ran away and returned to Lawson's plantation. Lawson offered to hire him to GW by the month, an offer Neptune himself agreed to (Lawson to GW, 17 Mar., 2, 18, and 25 April 1787, and GW to Lawson, 10 April 1787, DLC:GW).

Wednesday 11th.   Mercury at 54 in the Morning—76 at Noon and 74 at Night.

Calm, clear, and Warm all day—Wind, what little there was of it, Southerly.

Rid to all the Plantations. In the Neck, cross plowing, as directed, for Barley. At Muddy hole finished harrowing in grass Seeds on the Rye by the Barn—viz.—a bushel of clean red clover

Seed, and 13 gallons of Orchard grass seed—qty. of Land abt. 13 acres. The Barley was sowed as directed; harrowed in, and compleated as mentioned yesterday. Ordered the 6th. half acre to be deep plowed for to receive the Jerusalem Artichoke plants. At Dogue run, began to Sow in drills, in the Meadow, by the Gate (the rows 18 Inches asunder) the new River grass, had from Colo. Chs. Carter, at least what remained of it. The Women at this place were hoeing the wet part of the grd. between the meadows which the plows could not touch. Ordered them as soon as this was done, to go to the Ferry, and Assist in getting the grd. in the New Meadow in order for Oats and Timothy. At Frenchs the Farmer was sowing grass Seeds on the Wheat & was harrowing & rolling it in. The qu[anti]ty to the acre the same as had been given to the Oat Land in the same field. The double harrows do this work better than the heavier single harrow by raising more mould wch. the roller presses down again benifitting both the grain wch. is growing and the Seed wch. is Sown.

JERUSALEM ARTICHOKE: *Helianthus tuberosus,* a potatolike tuber in the sunflower family. Roots for this first planting came from Benjamin Grymes, of Chotank, who sent him five bushels. GW thought this would be sufficient to plant one acre as an experiment. Thomas Jefferson told Tristram Dalton, 2 May 1817 (DLC: Jefferson Papers), that he found this crop better as a winter feed for cattle than carrots or potatoes, maintaining that it far exceeded the potato in output, and could remain in the ground throughout the winter without injury.

Thursday 12th.     Mercury at 60 in the Morning—74 at Noon and 74 at N.

Clear and Warm, wind fresh all day from the Southward. The Sun set in a bank.

Rid to all the Plantatns. The Women from Dogue run had joined those at the Ferry and were working in the New Meadow—preparing it for Oats and Timothy. At French's, the Roller w[oul]d about got over the Wheat which had been sown with grass Seeds and harrowed. At Dogue run I set my Farmer to sowing grass Seeds—Viz. Orchard red Clover, and Timothy; in the proportion the grd. adjoining (in Oats) received—viz.—4 quarts of the first—3 of the 2d. and one of the latter on the lay Wheat. The ground in places being hard, I directed the harrow to go twice over it—the last, crossing the first. Finished yesterday, sowing in drills, the ground allotted, with the New river grass seeds. At Muddy hole directed the 6th. Square which was deep plowed yesterday, to be harrowed and cross harrowed, and then, with the

Plow to be laid off into 4 feet Squares or chequers to receive the Jerusalem Artichoke. In the Neck, finished cross plowing the ground for Barley about Sundown yesterday.

Cut my Ram lambs at the several Quarters to day & at the home house.

Friday 13th.    Mercury at 62 in the Morng.—74 at Noon and 74 at N.

A Fresh Southerly wind all day with some appearances of rain. Warm.

Rid to the Plantations at Muddy hole, Dogue run, French's and the Ferry—and to the Fishing Landing. At Muddy hole the artichokes were planted as directed yesterday but upon recollection the method does not seem to be proper, because the cross in which they were planted (being the bottom of the furrows) must be unbroke earth and the bed not so compendious and light as it might have been in a hill. In each of these checks or crosses, one Root, when it was large and looked well was put and two where they were small. None was cut, but this it seems might have been done, as with Potatoes—leaving an eye to each cutting. About 1½ bushels planted the Square, or half acre. Near half a bushel was left for replanting. At Dogue run, finished Sowing the Winter fallow by the Ferry road with Pold. Oats and grass Seeds. Of the first it took [      ] bushls. and of the latter [      ] gallons of Orchard grass, [      ] pints of Clover, and [      ] quarts of Timothy. From here the harrows went into the Meadow by the house & began to cover Oats in the fork thereof wch. were sowed on the plowing the ground had received about the [      ] of [      ]. The ground in No. 1, by the road, by the harrowing in the Oats with the heavy harrow once; & sometimes where it was hard or grassy, twice, and the crossing, to put in the grass Seeds was got light, smooth, & in very good order. The Barley at this place was begun to be sowed on a second plowing of the ground by the Bars near the house in the Meadow this afternoon and the lay Wheat which had been harrowed, and cross harrowed got rolled this evening. Making the trunnel fence at French's in the line that divides this Plantation from the Ferry. The Barley here was perceived to be coming up thick and well. At the ferry, breaking, and rending as fine as the case would admit, the ground in the New Meadow— Sowed 7½ bushls. of Barley in the Turnip ground wch. had been plowed & cross plowed and harrowed it in with the dble. harrow.

Mr. Benja. Grymes (of the Eagles Nest) came here this Evening and Stayed all Night.

TRUNNEL: treenail. The parts of the fence were fastened together with tree-nails, small wooden pegs. Benjamin Fitzhugh Grymes (died c.1803), son of Benjamin Grymes of Smithfield and Elizabeth Fitzhugh Grymes of Eagle's Nest, in the Chotank area of King George County, had served as a lieutenant and later captain in the Revolution.

**Saturday 14th.    Mercury at 62 in the Morning—74 at Noon and 68 at Night.**

Cloudy in the Morning with a few drops of rain, but the Wind getting to No. Wt. it soon cleared, and blew pretty fresh all day. Towds. Night it grew cool.

Mr. Grymes went up to Alexandria after breakfast, returned to dinner, and crossed the river afterwards.

Rid to all the Plantations. In the Neck Sowed on the Barley which was put in yesterday a bushel (lacking a quart) of the Clover seed which was saved at Muddy hole—harrowed and rolled it in. Began yesterday afternoon to make or rectify the fence around field No. 3. Directed the Plows which were laying off in field No. 9, to lay off what is east of the branch which runs through the field, 4 feet each way; that it may be planted with a single stalk of Corn in a hill. Rid over the rye at this place, and was surprised to see how much it had amended; the two Eastermost cuts (except in a few places which appeared to have been injured by the wet) looked very Promising, and nearly thick enough, and the Westermost cut in wch. hardly any was to be perceived all winter, and till very lately, discovered a good deal.

At Muddy hole laying off, & listing for Corn.

At Dogue run, besides sowing Oats as mentioned yesterday, and grass Seeds in the same proportion as in field No. 1, the Island (abt. 4 Acres) in the Mill meadow was cross plowing, and sowing with Barley. Rid over the rye at this place, which was exceedingly bad; in great part of the field not any; whe[ther] this was altogether owing to late sowing, or to that and harrowing the grd. too level when sowed, is questionable. The forward Wheat at this place where the ground is tolerably good, looks well; and the latter wheat seems to be coming on beyond expectation. The Cape Wheat is forwarder than the common wheat and has a broader blade. The spelts, black and common, look very indifferent[l]y.

At French's the Flax was coming up—Work here going on as yesterday.

At the Ferry the same.

THE SPELTS: *Triticum spelta,* a species of grain similar to wheat.

Sunday 15th.    Mercury at 36 in the Morning—[      ] at Noon
and [      ] at N.
Clear, with the Wind fresh and Cool from the No. West all day.


Monday 16th.    Mercury at [      ] in the Morning—[      ] at
Noon and [      ] at N.
Morning Cold with the wind (tho not fresh) still at No. Wt.
calm afterwards—frost.
Went up to Alexandria to the Election of Delegates to represent
the County in General Assembly—when Colo. Mason and Doctr.
Stuart were chosen.
Returned in the Evening, accompanied by Colo. Mason—his
two Sons William and George—& his Son in Law Colo. Cooke.
Ordered my Overseers in the Neck, and at Muddy hole, to
begin (with the drill plows) to plant Corn.

COLO. COOKE: John Travers Cook (Cooke). George Mason's son William
Mason (1757–1818) had served as a captain in the militia during the Revolution. He lived at Mattawoman in Charles County, Md., part of a large
estate which he inherited from his maternal grandmother, Sarah Edgar
Eilbeck.


Tuesday 17th.    Mercury at [      ] in the Morning—[      ] at
Noon and [      ] at Night.
Calm and very smoaky, but not warm. Towards night it seemed
to lower and put on appearances of rain but cleared after dark
again.
Colo. Mason and his Sons, & Colo. Cook, going away about 11
Oclock I rid to the Plantations at Muddy hole—Dogue run,
Frenchs and the Ferry. At the first they had begun to harrow the
List and plant Corn with the drill plow—but the land having been
thrown into a 3 furrow list and from being hard and dry not well
broke, I ordered both to desist and to make the 3 furrows 5 that
the ground might be better prepared.
At Dogue run the Island in the Mill Meadow had been sown
with Barley and grass (Timothy only) and each harrowed in after
the ground had been cross plowed. From hence the Plows went
in to the other Meadow to cross plow the ground on the West side
of it for Barley—beginning next the piece which had been sowed
with the 3 bushels of Oats from Generl. Spotswoods. The ground
in the fork, within this Meadow between the Meadow and Swamp
was sown both with Oats & the mixture of Clover Orchd. grass &
Timothy seed as usual & the harrowing of them in (on the first

plowing) compleated. To do this it required [    ] bushels of Oats & grass seeds in proportion. From hence they went to the plowed ground between the upper and lower part of this Meadow.

At Frenchs; Fencing as usual.

At the Ferry; they were so near finishing chopping over, and compleating the ground in the New Meadow for Oats and Timothy, that I ordered the Dogue-run hands home. This tedeous job would be about compleated to morrow; though the ground would not be in such good order as were to be wished, as it was next to impossible to get the grassy clods wch. were hoed up, in the lowest part of it perfectly reduced. However, by the assistance of the harrows and roller, it will be laid tolerably smooth and fine; and dry.

Wednesday 18th.    Mercury at [    ] in the Morning—[    ] at Noon and [    ] at Night.

Wind at So. West in the forenoon and at No. Et. afterwards— Cloudy all the forenoon with slow rain; but not much more of it than would lay the dust. About 2 Oclock the Sun came out after which it clouded agn.

Mr. Jonathan Williams of Nantz—Nephew of Doctr. Franklins came here yesterday, dined, and returned to Alexandria in order to proceed on in the Stage for Richmond.

Rid to all the Plantations. In the Neck; they finished fencing of field No. 3. and began to plant Corn with the drill plow on Monday afternoon in it, preceeded by two harrows a heavier and a lighter which were directed to go as often on the list as would make the ground fine. Ordered to day, a hand to follow the drill to cover any Corn that the small harrow at the tale of it should miss doing. These workings would put the Corn in very effectually and well.

At Muddy hole began to sow Carrot Seeds betwn. the rows intended for Corn. Rubbed the Seeds, so as to separate them well; then mixed a pint (thus prepared) in half a bushel of dry sand incorporating them well and sprinkling it along the list which was previously harrowed once, twice, or more, to render it sufficiently fine—lastly followed a light bush to cover the Seed. This method if it answers is expeditious but the plants if too thick will be to be thinned either by the hoe or with the hand. Ordered two plows from French's after they were done with the Barley at Dogue run to come to this place to assist in preparing the ground &ca.

At Dogue run; Sowing Barley, Oats, and grass Seeds in the

home meadow as yesterday. Women putting up the New fence but ordered them to chop in Oats in the low parts wch. had been hoed, and where the Plows & harrows could not make good work.

At Frenchs; about the Fencing—The Barley and Flax at this place were up thick and well.

At the Ferry; finished all the work of the New Meadow—both the Oats and grass being Sowed—harrowed and rolled in.

In the Afternoon, Mr. Wil. Craik and his Sisters Jenifer & Nancy came in and stayed all Night.

Adjoining the rows of Guinea grass in my botanical gardn. (sowed the 7th. instt.) I sowed 12 rows more. Next to these, and compleating the Section are 19 rows of the Birding grass sent me by Mr. Sprigg of Annapolis.

Jonathan Williams (1750–1815), grandson of Benjamin Franklin's sister Anne, served in the Revolution as an American commercial agent in Nantes, France. In 1785 he returned to America and became a merchant in Philadelphia. Because of his interest and expertise in theoretical engineering he was appointed (1801) by Thomas Jefferson the first superintendent of the United States Military Academy at West Point.

Thursday 19th.    Mercury at [      ] in the Morning—[      ] at Noon And [      ] at Night.

The Wind shifting to No. Wt. in the Night it blew fresh and cold. This morning there was a small white frost and a black one wch. was so severe as to stop brick laying till the sun had removed the effect of it. The leaves of the clover in the lawn were quite stiff & there was Ice full half an inch thick. Before noon the Wind got to the Southward but blew moderately. The air nevertheless continued cool.

Mr. Craik and his Sisters went away after breakfast.

I rid to the Plantations at Muddy hole, Dogue run, Frenchs, and the Ferry and to the fishing landing.

At Muddy hole, finished sowing Carrot seed in drills—viz.— Every eighth row of exactly 20 acres of Corn; drilled in rows 5 feet a part. These were sowed in the manner, and in grd. prepared as mentioned yesterday, in two equal parts; The Northernmost of which was sowed with the large orange Carrot Seed (sent to me unaccompanied by a letter, or intimation from whom it came). The other half was sown with Carrot seed saved in my garden, and to be relied on. Of the first it took a quart, and about a gill to sow the Northern 10 Acres; of the latter it is presumed the same quantity sufficed—No. acct. of the qty. rendered. The 8th. square, or half acre which had been plowed the 11th. inst. for the Sweet

Potatoes, was, the West half of it, hilled this day (by order yester-day) to plant, whilst the other half was to have been planted in drills 4 feet a part between the rows; and 8 inches between the cuttings or sets in the rows to try the difference; but the frost last night induced me to postpone this planting. Two plows, according to order, came to work here to day. Recommenced planting of Corn with the drill plow at this place, this afternoon. The harrow was ordered to preceed it once, or as many times as the ground, from the clodiness, or grasiness of it, should appear to need it, to prepare the ground for the drill.

At Dogue run, putting in Barley, Oats, and grass Seeds as yester-day. The Women were hoeing the low part between the two meadows—that is breaking the clods and pulverising the ground to fit it for the Seed. Sowed the remainder of the New river grass seeds in broad cast (yesterday just before the rain fell) adjoining that wch. had been sowed in drills the 11th. inst. at this place.

At Frenchs, fencing on the ditch between fields No. 2 & 3, with trunnels.

At the Ferry, the plows had just finished listing the So. cut of field No. 1 below the hill and the Women were employed in mak-ing the trunnel fence on the ditch along the road.

A good many Herrings were caught last Night and this after-noon, at my fishery—but few this forenoon.

The field crop not previously annotated is *Ipomea batatas,* sweet potato.

Friday 20th.   Mercury at [      ] in the Morng.—[      ] at Noon And [      ] at Night.

Morning cold, with the Wind at No. West at which point it con-tinued most part, if not all of the day. The fruit much injured with yesterdays frost—as it is to be feared that the grain, by this and the drought, also is—the Wheat appearing to turn yellow and the Oats in Week land to be dying; and neither, any more than the grass to grow.

Rid to all the Plantations.

In the Neck, the grd. being rather hard, and in places rough— two harrows could not prepare it sufficiently to keep the drill plow constantly at work. I therefore ordered the plowman who attended it to make good the work of covering the corn, which the little harrow at the tail of it might leave unfinished and this he is well able to do, because where the ground is difficult to prepare he can outgo the harrows, and here it is assistance is wanting. When the ground is light and the harrows prepare it sufficiently there is no

Dr. Arthur Lee of Virginia, by John Trumbull. (Yale University Art Gallery)

occasion of the hoe to follow. This supercedes the necessity of the special hand ordered for this Service on Wednesday last. Where the grd. is naturally light, or well pulverized the drill plow plants with great dispatch regularity and to good effect. Where it is rough and hard manual labour as in the common mode must be applied. Muddy hole-Cross plowed deep the east half of the 10th. half acre, or Square, for the purpose of sowing Carrots in Broadcast. Before plowing the Northern half of this piece was manured with 25 bushels of Dung and after plowing, it was harrowed, to be ready for sowing in the Morning. Finished laying off Corn ground at this place about breakfast time.

At Dogue run, Finished Sowing Oats, wch. compleated my seeding of this grain (except a little at the Mansion house with which to sow grass Seeds). The whole quantity of Oats Sowed at this Plantation amounts to 215 bushls. Whereof 59 were Poland, in field No. 1; the rest were, 50 from York River, 52 from Mattawoming, 29 from Mr. Young's, 13½ from George Town, and 12 from the Eastern Shore. The quantity of Barley sowed here amounted to 22 Bushels. With the Oats and Barley which were sown in field No. 1, and the inclosure of the Meadow near the Overseers house, was sown 4 bushls. and a galln. of red clover Seed —5½ bushls. of Orchard grass Seeds and 1 bushl. and 3 Gal. of Timothy seed. The other Oats in the Mill Meadow, & long field adjoining, had only Timothy seed mixed—of which there was sown in them 3 bushels & 6 gallns.

At French's and the Ferry the People were putting up fences.

On my return home I found Mr. Arthur Lee, the Revd. Mr. West, Mr. McQuir, Mr. Porter and Mr. Triplet here—All of whom went away after dinner except Mr. Lee and Mr. Porter.

Rev. William West (c.1739–1791), originally of Fairfax County, was ordained an Anglican minister in 1761 in England. Upon his return to America he obtained a position in Maryland, for which GW recommended him as being "of a good Family," and "a neighbour of mine . . . one of those few of whom every body speaks well" (GW to Gov. Horatio Sharpe, 26 Mar. 1762, CSmH). In 1779 West became rector of St. Paul's Parish, Baltimore, and in 1790 he was chosen president of the convention of Maryland Episcopalian clergy (RIGHTMYER, 144, 218). West may have visited Mount Vernon in his capacity as the executor of the estate of his deceased brother Capt. John West, Jr., who had been a coexecutor with GW of the Colvill estate (see entry for 26 Feb. 1767; GW to John Rumney, 24 Jan. 1788, DLC:GW).

Saturday 21st.     Mercury at [     ] in the Morning—[     ] at Noon and [     ] at Night.

Wind at No. Wt. all day, and at times fresh & cool. Towards Sundown the Wind increased, seemed to be getting to the Eastward—with appearances of Rain.

Mr. Porter going away before breakfast and Mr. Lee directly after it, I rid to the Plantations at Muddy hole, Dogue run, Frenchs, and the Ferry—and to the fishing landing.

At Muddy hole, in the ground which was cross plowed, & harrowed yesterday, (which did not make it very fine) I sowed 2½ pints of Carrot seeds; which weighed 1 lb. lacking an ounce, and which is at the rate of 4 lbs. to the acre, the qty. directed in Youngs Annals of Agriculture. Harrowed them in with a light bush. Half the Seed was mixed in half a bushel of Sand and sown and then the other half in the like quantity, and sown over it a second time, to spread them more regularly. These Seeds were a mixture of the large Orange, and others, & from my garden. The goodness uncertn.

At Dogue run directed a small spot of low ground, in the swamp, between the two Meadows, to be hoed up, and made fine on which to sow part of the Birding grass which was sent to me by Mr. Sprig; and which he wrote me delighted in low, moist land. Three plows were listing and a heavy harrow running after them, to see if the ground could, without a second plowing, be sufficiently pulverized to plant Corn in with the drill plow.

At Frenchs, and the Ferry, fencing as yesterday.

No great hand made of fishing—few were caught in the fore-noon of this day & only about 30,000 last Night.

Sunday 22d.    Mercury at [      ] in the Morning—[      ] at Noon And [      ] at Night.

Clear and cold, with the wind hard all day at No. Wt.—Ice of considerable thickness in the Morning.

Doctr. Craik returned here this forenoon from Maryland—Dined and proceeded afterwards to Alexandria.

At home all day.

Monday 23d.    Mercury at [      ] in the Morning—[      ] at Noon and [      ] at Night.

Wind at No. Wt. all day, but not so cold as yesterday. Clear with every appearance of a continued drought, the atmosphere being very thick (smoaky) with a red looking Sun.

Rid to all the Plantations.

In the Neck began with James Lawson, Danl. Overdonck, Boatswain, Charles, Bath, Robin and Pascal to dig a ditch to the Post & rail fence erected on the line between Colo. Mason and me. The ditch to be 5 feet at top, 18 Inches at bottom, and two feet deep and to be faced with sod. Lawson, Boatswain, Robin & Paskall beginning at the So. and Danl., Charles, and Bath at the No. end —working towards each other. Drilling Corn going on but slow, because the harrows cannot prepare the ground fast enough for the Drill. Davy, and Ned, Ben, Essex & Robin; and two Women, began to put up the Posts and rails through the woods. Barley coming up at this place. Oats look very thin, and indifferently here, especially in some parts of the Orchard Inclosure. Cutting down Corn Stalks in field No. 2.

At Muddy hole. Planting Corn with the drill plow after the harrow—3 plows listing the intermediate rows, between the Corn. Overseer and Women cutting down Corn Stalks—Carting out dung on field No. 1.

At Morris's (that is Dogue run) —One plow is laying off—2 are listing and one Team harrowing, to prepare the lists for Corn. Sowed abt. a Quart of Birding grass (sent me by Mr. Sprigg) partly on the ground prepared on Saturday and partly on a little Spot near the Spring (which had been sown with Barley). The first was sown with Oats. Overseer & Womn. making up fences round the Mill Meadow.

At French's raising a trunnel fence on the ditch between fields No. 2 & 3 and a harrow employed in crossing the ground which was first plowed in the first. The Barley at this place is come up well, & looks well and the Oats tolerable, considering the dryness of the ground. The Flax also is up thick, and looks well.

At the Ferry 3 plows Are listing the other hands cutting down Corn Stalks.

But poor success in fishing to day.

Sowed in drills in the Inclosure behind the Stables (called the Vineyard) on the West side of it the Seeds of the honey locust. Part of these were sown on Saturday and part to day—part remains yet to be sown. The rows were about 15 Inches a part and the Seeds an inch or two a sunder in them.

Tuesday 24th.    Mercury at [      ] in the Morning—[      ] at Noon And [      ] at Night.

Calm, clear, and very warm.

Rid to the Fishing landing and to the Ferry, French's, Dogue run, and Muddy hole Plantations.

Caught many fish at the first this evening.

At the Ferry, clearing the Wheat field of the Corn Stalks and listing as yesterday with 3 plows.

At French's still about the same fence & harrowing as yesterday.

At Dogue run, laying the worm of the New fence through the Woods. Sowed the remains of my Carrot Seed, between the rows intended for Corn, first ploughing the list a second time (as the first) and then harrowing it 4 times with the heavy harrow, after wch. the Seed (mixed in sand) was sown. The first row (west side next the huts) with a little Seed from Miss Balendine. The next (Carrot) rows, all to 50 yds. from the So. end, at which a stake is driven are of the early Car[ro]t and the others 6 in number besides the part are the large red Carrot. Directed a bush to be passed over the Seeds thus Sown. Of the last kind there was near a Quart Sown.

At Muddy hole, preparing for, & planting Corn with the drill, as yesterday—also cutting down Corn Stalks & Cartg. out Dung.

Majr. G. Washington's Child which had been sick since Sunday, & appearing to be very ill occasioned the sending for the Revd. Mr. Massey to Christen it who arriving about 5 Oclk. performed the Ceremony and stayed the evening.

Wednesday 25th.    Mercury at [      ] in the Morning—[      ] at Noon and [      ] at Night.

The Morning lowering with the Wind—at times great appearances or rain, at other times the clouds looked thin and the Sun shone—but about half after five it began to rain, and continued to do so pretty fast and steadily for about half an hour preceeded by thunder & lightning which continued through the Rain frequent & sharp.

The Majors child dying betwn. 7 & 8 Oclock A.M. Mr. Massey stayed to bury it. About 10 Oclock Doctr. & Mrs. Stuart arrived & as were setting down to dinner Doctr. Craik came in from Maryland—all of whom went away after it.

A good many fish caught before the rain.

Thursday 26th.   Mercury at [      ] in the Morning—[      ] at Noon and [      ] at N.

Cloudy and soft all day with appearances of more rain.

Rid to all the Plantations. In the Neck the People were putting up the fence between fields No. 4 and No. 9—the last of which would be listed by Night when two plows would go to Crossing the list of No. 9 and the rest to preparing No. 3 for Corn by relisting the grd. that had got hard by laying. The harrows and drill plow working as usual. The Overseer & other Men putting up the Posts & rails through the Woods. The ditchers did about 2 rods each of the five foot ditch they began on Monday & sodded it.

At Muddy hole, the Corn Stalks would be cut down and piled this evening & the people would next be employed about the New ground in front of the Mansion house—In hoeing up the old list of last year wch. never was planted. The plows at work as usual.

At Dogue-run, the last sowed Barley, and the Clover wch. was first sown, were coming. The New river grass which was sown broad with Oats and that wch. was sown in drills was also coming up. Began here with 3 pair of dble. harrows and one single one to harrow Clover, orchard grass, & Timothy as a Mixture, & that part of the Wheat & rye which falls within field No. 1. The Women were raising & securing the fence about the Meadow near the Overseers House.

At French's Two plows were, as before, at Work at Muddy hole; & a harrow at Dogue Run. The Overseer, Women and boys grubbing & cleaning the sides of the Meadow by Manley's house.

At the Ferry, the 3 plows were listing, and the Women & other hands after having picked up & piled the Corn Stalks came to their side (South) of the New ground in front of the Mansion house.

Receiving an Express between 4 & 5 O'clock this afternoon informing me of the extreme illness of my Mother and Sister Lewis,

I resolved to set out for Fredericksburgh by daylight in the Morning and spent the evening in writing some letters on business respecting the Meeting of the Cincinnati, to the Secretary General of the Society, Genl. Knox.

A Captn. McCannon came here this evening and got 40 Diplomas signed for the Delaware line.

FRENCH'S: The farm GW refers to as French's contained not only the land acquired from Mrs. French and the Dulanys but the smaller Manley tract which divided the two sections of the French land. The overseer of French's plantation was Will, one of the slaves GW had leased from Mrs. French (see entry for 8 Jan. 1787).

Mrs. Mary Washington had a cancer of the breast, but, despite her weakness and bad health, she lived until 25 Aug. 1789. CAPTN. MCCANNON: Capt. William McCammon served as a second lieutenant in the Flying Camp during the latter part of 1776.

Friday 27th.    Mercury at [      ] in the Morning–[      ] at Noon and [      ] at Night.

Wind Northerly, cool, and pleasant all day.

About sun rise I commenced my Journey as intended. Bated at Dumfries, and reached Fredericksburgh before two Oclock and found both my Mother & Sister better than I expected–the latter out of danger as is supposed, but the extreme low State in wch. the former was left little hope of her recovery as she was exceedingly reduced and much debilitated by age and the disorder. Dined and lodged at my Sisters.

Saturday 28th.    Dined at Mrs. Lewis's and Drank Tea at Judge Mercers; Genl. Weedon, Colo. Chs. Carter, Judge Mercer, and Mr. Jno. Lewis and his wife dined with me at my Sisters.

Of John Lewis's five wives, this wife is probably his third, Elizabeth Jones, daughter of Gabriel Jones of the Shenandoah Valley.

Sunday 29th.    Dined at Colo. Charles Carters and drank Tea at Mr. John Lewis's.

Monday 30th.    Set out about Sun rise on my return home. Halted at Dumfries, for about an hour where I breakfasted. Reached home about 6 Oclock in a sml. shower, which did not continue (and that not hard) for more than 15 Minutes.

On my return, recd. the following report of the Weather and business of the plantations–viz.–

|              |        | M. | N. | Night |
|--------------|--------|----|----|-------|
| Friday 27th. | Mercy. | 50 | 63 | 58    |
| Saturday 28. | Do.    | 51 | 72 | 58    |
| Sunday 29    | Do.    | 58 | 74 |       |
| Monday. 30.  | Do.    | 58 | 74 |       |

27th. In the morning the Wind was at No. Wt.—at Noon So. W. and at Night calm.

Many Fish caught to day—no demand for them.

At the Ferry, the plows were listing, and the People grubbing in the New ground. Drill plow sent for to begin Corn planting, preceeded by the harrow.

At French's, the People were grubbing and cleaning along the sides of the Meadow—two plows at Muddy hole and a harrow at Dogue run.

At Dogue run, The Women were hoeing the enclosed Tobacco ground for Corn—1 Plow listing, and 4 harrows putting in grass Seeds at the rate of [     ] gallns. of Orchard Grass, [     ] quarts of red Clover, and [     ] qts. of Timothy to the Acre on the Wheat and rye in field No. 1.

At Muddy hole, Planted half an acre of the Sweet Potatoes one half of which (containing 1240 hills) were in Hills, the other half was in rows 4 feet apart—The cuttings about 6 inches apart in the Rows; which were marked by the Plow. To plant the hills (with 2 or 3 cuttings in each) it took 11½ Bushl.; a bushl. of wch. was had from Marshalls Neg[roe]s, and the remaining half bushl. was of those brot. from York River. Those in drills (14 in number) took a bushel and a peck—the Bushel had from Marshalls People and the Peck fm. my old Negro fellow Jupiter.

Finished planting the Seed of the honey locust, began on the [     ] instt.

Breaking the remainder of the Turnip patch at the home house for Oats and grass Seeds.

28th. Wind at So. W. in the forenoon—So. afterwards till it grew calm.

Much fish caught and no demand for them; Salting them up.

At the Ferry commenced Corn planting with the drill plow; first running the harrow on the list, to smooth & pulverise the ground, 3, 4, and sometimes oftener, before the drill and this not enabling the small harrow at the end, to cover well, on acct. of the grassiness of the grd. particularly wire grass. A hand followed with a hoe to make the work good.

At French's the hands employed as yesterday.

At Dogue Run, nearly so, except that a plow was re-listing for Parsnips which were intended to commence where the Carrots ended, and to occupy every 8th. Row in like manner as they did. Finished sowing Grass Seeds on the wheat and rye in field No. 1 —quantity of which amounted to 32 gallons of Orchard grass; 12 gallons of red clover and [     ] gallons of Timothy Seed. This ground was harrowed and cross harrowed and the roller was following them. The grd. where the rye was and which had been harrowed in the fall was very hard, run together, and much baked.

At Muddy hole, finished planting Corn with the drill about 1 Oclock, and sent it to Dogue run. All the plows now, 6 in number went to compleating the intermediate lists. Hands at the New grd. in front of the H[ome] House.

In the Neck, 3 plows listing in Field No. 3—two harrows following them—and the drill plow following the Harrows. In field No. 9 two Plows were crossing to prepare for Plantg. Corn. Women staking and ridering fence of the said field.

PARSNIPS: *Pastinaca sativa,* attempted here as a field crop to produce livestock feed. In June, when GW was in Philadelphia to participate in the Constitutional Convention, he wrote manager George Augustine Washington that he was sorry to learn the parsnips and carrots were doing poorly (10 June 1787, DLC:GW). There are additional references to the parsnip in farm records of 1798.

29th.    Wind at So.—& warm all day.
30th.    A brisk Southerly Wind all day, with appearances of rain; some of which, abt. 6 oclock, fell for abt. 15 Minutes.

But few fish caught to day.

At the Ferry drilling Corn as on Saturday but run the harrow oftener—6 times at least, before the drill which made it do better work. One plow listing—the hands in the New grd.

At Frenchs, employed as on Saturday.

At Dogue run, The Harrows having finished puttg. in grass Seeds, the one from French's returned home, and those belonging to the place went to preparing by listing Corn grd. whilst the drill plow preceeded by the harrow began to plant. Women hoeing New ground. Roller going.

At Muddy hole, the Plows were breaking up the Corn field, and the other hands listing the New grd. at the home house.

At the River Plantation began to Plant Corn in field No. 9.

Hoeing up the old road through the Turnip fld. at home, and otherwise preparing the grd. for the intended seed by crossing plowing it.

# [May 1787]

Tuesday—May first.    Mercury at [      ] in the Morng.—[      ]
at Noon and [      ] at Night.

Wind Southerly with appearances in the forenoon of rain but
the Wind shifting to the No. Wt. it cleared.

Notwithstanding my fatiegue I rid to all the Plantations to day.
The Ditchers in the Neck had compleated about 500 yards of the
5 feet ditch—or in other words about 2 rods each pr. day.

The Drill plow would about finish the 2d. cut of No. 3 by
Noon. The Barley by the Barn is either not all come up, or was
irregularly sown. The clover among it is up in places thick. The
first planted Corn is coming up & destroyed by the Birds as fast as
it appears. Harrowing in Timothy Seed on the middle cut of
Rye. This must have been much too long delayed as the Rye was
almost on the point of putting forth its ear—but being thin did
not appear to be much, if any injured by the harrowing and
trampling.

At Muddy hole, the Plows and hands employed as yesterday.
No appearance of the first planted Corn at this place coming up.

At Dogue run Parsnips all but the two last rows of them, west
of the road leading from the gate to the Houses were sown in the
same manner, and with the same preparation of the grd. as the
Carrots had been. In other respects all things were going on as
yesterday.

At French's—the same as yesterday; except that a harrow was
crossing the plowing in No. 2.

Wednesday 2d.    Mercury at [      ] in the Morning—[      ] at
Noon and [      ] at Night.

Cooler than yesterday, and clear Wind being at No. West.

Rid to the Fishing landing where few fish were caught and to
the Ferry, French's & Dogue run Plantations—also to the Carpenters.

At the Ferry, the Work going on as yesterday except that the
drill plow having finished the No. end (beyond a sml. branch)
was stopped till the harrow could make head before it. In the
meanwhile the Plow man went to crossing in the other part of
the field which was intended for Corn in the common way, 5
feet, a Plow was listing in Stony field part of No. 1—Women &ca.
working in the New grd.

At French's, the same work going on as yesterday.

At Dogue run the same. The drill plow about Noon had got on the East side of the road leading up to the Houses.

The Oats every where in strong and moist land seem to thrive; but appear at a std. elsewhere. The Barley at French's look well. And the Cape wheat at Dogue run is forwarder than the common Wheat; but not more branched—perhaps less so, and of a paler green. It was, as has been observed before, more eaten by the Sheep and other Stock that had been fed upon the field than any of the other—whether owing to any peculiar taste or to its being generally forwarder cannot be determined with precision.

A Mr. Wilson of Elizabh. Town, in the State of New Jersey called here to know on wht. terms I would dispose of my tract of Land in Fayette & Washington Counties. These I gave him agreeably to what I had mentioned in my letter to Colo. Jno. Cannon.

At Fredericksburgh, I was informed by Mr. Chs. Yates, a Gentleman on whose veracity entire confidence may be placed, that he has tried the experiment of raising Irish Potatoes by laying them on unbroken, hard, or grassy ground & covering them with straw and found them to succeed admirably. The following he gave as an instance—viz.—an irregular piece of ground 28 of his Steps one way which he computed might be abt. 23 yards—18 wide at one end, and 8 or 10 at the other, reduced in the same proportion will not exceed 255 sqr. yards. These he says produced 36 bushls. of fine large well tasted Potatoes, and 12 bushl. of Seed Potatoes. In this proportion an Acre would yield 900 Bushels but as Mr. Yates said that he computed at the time upon 700 bushls. it is probable there may be some mistake as to measurement of the ground or Roots. The way he managed was this—In April he laid the Seed Potatoes (after cutting them in the usual manner) on the ground (no matter what sort of land he thinks) in rows 2 feet a sunder, and the cuttings 8 or 9 inches apart in the rows. The whole of this Space was then covered 6 inches thick with straw. When the Potatoe vines had risen 6 Inches through this bed of straw another layer of equal thickness—that is 6 inches—was spread between the rows and close up to the Stems—after which nothing more was done with them. The Land on which these Potatoes grew was perfectly cleansed of weeds &ca. when the Potatoes and Straw were taken of and ameliorated.

Mr. Yates also mentioned another matter worthy of attention, respecting Potatoes; which was discovered accidentally—viz.—that some in a Corn field which had remained over (being left when the rest were dug, or unattended to) being covered with Corn stalks in the usual manner when they are cut down and thrown into heaps grew (the tops) through the stalks and yielded abundantly of very fine Potatoes. Query whether this covering, laid on thicker will not do instead of Straw.

It seems to be agreed by the farmers about Fredericksburgh that 6 bushels of Clover in the pug, or chaff is equal to 16 lbs. of clean Seed and that either is sufficient for an Acre. Colo. Carter sows 2 Bushels of Orchard grass (when alone) to an Acre and One peck when unmixed with other Seed, of Timothy. When clover and Orchard grass are sown together he gives 10 lb. of the first and a bushel of the latter.

Sowed the Turnip patch, and last years Cowpens in front of the Mansion house with Oats 11 bushels—Orchard Grass 3 Bushels, and Clover 1 Bushel. The qty. of ground my Farmer thinks is near 4 Acres but I believe this is large guessing. Perhaps there may be about [      ].

MY TRACT OF LAND IN FAYETTE & WASHINGTON COUNTIES: GW advertised for sale his two tracts of land in Pennsylvania: a 2,800-acre tract in Washington County and a 1,650-acre tract, originally in Washington County and subsequently in Fayette County when that county was formed in 1784 (advertisement for sale of lands, 22 Sept. 1786, DLC:GW). In this postrevolutionary period a number of the new settlers in southwestern Pennsylvania were from New Jersey (George McCarmick to GW, 31 Oct. 1786, and Israel Shreve to GW, 7 April 1787, DLC:GW). Col. John Cannon was GW's agent in that area (GW to Cannon, 13 April 1787, DLC:GW; and see entry for 18 Sept. 1784, n.3). Charles Yates (1728–1809), the son of Rev. Francis Yates of Whitehaven, Eng., emigrated to Virginia in 1752 and settled in Fredericksburg, where he became a prosperous merchant (*Va. Mag.*, 7 [1899–1900], 91–92). He probably had a plantation in Spotsylvania County, for in 1783 he owned 37 slaves there, and he was interested in agricultural experimentation (GW to Charles Carter, 10 Jan. 1787, DLC:GW; *Va. Mag.*, 4 [1896–97], 297).

Thursday 3d.    Mercury at [      ] in the Morning—[      ] at Noon and [      ] at Night.

Clear all day, wind at No. Wt. and cold all the forenoon—but little wind and that Southerly afterwards.

Rid to the Fishing landing—and thence to the Ferry, French's Dogue run, and Muddy hole Plantations with my Nephew G. W. to explain to him the Nature, and the ordr. of the business at each as I would have it carried on during my absence at the Convention in Philadelphia.

At the Ferry the same work going on as yesterday.

Likewise at French the same.

The Same also at Dogue Run.

And at Muddy hole nothing differing from yesterday. At the latter the Corn ground will go near to be. broke up this day.

Friday 4th.  Mercury at [    ] in the Morning–[    ] at Noon and [    ] at Night.

Morning clear and cool, tho the Wind was Southerly; and in the afternoon fresh with appearances of rain.

Rid into the Neck to explain to G.W. the business to be done there, and mode of conducting it.

At this place the Post and rail fence around field No. 9 would be closed, and entirely compleated (except the ditch) by Noon. Harrowing, drilling, and listing in field No. 3 going on as usual. The first planted Corn in this field appears to have been much destroyed by the birds and the first planting of *all* not to have come up. Finished planting in field No. 9, the So. Wt. cut and began the middle cut with the Corn from Nomeny.

At Muddy hole finished breaking up the Corn ground, ordered the two plows from French's home; and the plows of the Plantation to cross plow the 9th. square allotted for experiments (to be previously dunged as the others had been) in order to receive the bunch homeny bean, the common homeny bean, and the common black eyed Pease.

At Dogue run, the Harrow, drill, and other plows were working as yesterday. Finished Hooing the Tobacco grd. which had been inclosed by French's for Corn. And sowed 9 gallons of Clover Seed on the Barley in the Island in the Great Meadow and ordered it to be rolled in.

At French's the Harrow at work as usual–the two Plows from Muddy hole would return home to their work after dinner And the Rest of the People were grubbing along the sides of the Meadow, and preparing them for grass.

A Person calling himself Hugh Patton dined here & returned to Alexandria afterwards.

HOMENY BEAN: *Phaseolus vulgaris,* kidney bean or common garden pole bean. The bush or "bunch" variety is *P. vulgaris humilis.* "The Hominy-Bean is a sort of kidney-bean, and very productive" (PARKINSON, 2:341). GW raised both red and white varieties in the climbing and bush forms. Later he tried the lima bean, *P. limensis,* sending a packet to William Pearce 27 April 1794, with instructions that they were to be planted the first of May (NBLiHi). He also tried *Vicia faba,* broad or Windsor bean, which both he and Jefferson called the horse bean. Jefferson wrote John Taylor, 29 Dec. 1794, "The President has tried it without success" (BETTS [2], 221). It failed for Jefferson, too, perhaps because it was not suited to the hot Virginia summers.

A Hugh Patton (d. 1790) was a merchant in Richmond after the Revolution (*Va. Mag.,* 13 [1905–6], 427).

Saturday 5th.    Mercury at [      ] in the Morning–[      ] at Noon and [      ] at Night.

A few drops of rain fell in the Night–the Morning cloudy and the Wind brisk from the Southward. A good shower abt. 10.

Rid to the Fishing landing, Ferry, French's and D. run Plantations.

At the first Plantation One Plow was listing in the Stoney field, another crossing in the flat, and the harrow preparing for the drill plow. The Women preparing, & hoeing the New grd. in front of the House;

At Frenchs two Plows were set to plowing alongside the Meadow, where the roots and Grubs had been taken out in order to prepare it for grass seeds but making bad work my farmer thought the grd. cd. not be made fit to receive them this Spring. One harrow was harrowing as usual And the rest of the People grubbing. The clover seemed to be coming up pretty thick in places among the flax. The flax & Barley seemed to grow pretty well.

At Dogue-run, one Plow was crossing in the last years Tobo. grd. for Corn. In the laps of the fence Inclosg. it 139 pumpkin hills were Planted. Drilling corn, & listing going on as usual there.

At Muddy hole, the Plows began to break up the ground which was in drill Corn last year for Turnips, Pease, Potatoes &ca. Finished Plantg. their parts of the New ground in front of the home house with Corn–in every other 4th. row of which and 10th. hill two Pumpkin seeds were planted through the whole ground.

Ordered this to be done on the other side by the Ferry People.

Mr. Bull–A Delegate in Congress from South Carolina on his return to that came here to dinner and stayed all Night.

John Bull (c.1740–1802) was returning home, his third (and last) one-year term having expired on 21 Feb. 1787 (SALLEY [1], 34–35; JCC, 30:410).

Sunday 6th.    Mercury at [      ] in the Morng.–[      ] at Noon and [      ] at Night.

Wind Southerly, lowering at times till about 12 Oclock when it began to rain and continued to do so slowly for an hour but not so as wet more than a thin Surface of the Earth.

Colo. Fitzgerald, Doctr. Stuart and Doctr. Craik came here to dinner and returned afterwards.

Monday 7th.    Mercury at [      ] in the Morng.–[      ] at Noon and [      ] at Night.

Clear, with the wind pretty fresh at No. Wt. all day but not cold.

At home preparing for my journey to Philadelphia.

In the Afternoon Cols. Simms and Darke came in, the first expecting to meet the Governr. here, the other on business of the Potomack Compy. Both returned in the Evening.

THE GOVERNR.: Edmund Randolph had been elected governor of Virginia in Nov. 1786.

Tuesday. 8th.    Mercury at [      ] in the Morning–[      ] at Noon and [      ] at Night.

The Weather being squally with Showers I defer'd setting off till the Morning. Mr. Chas. Lee came in to dinner but left it afterwards.

Following his entry for 8 May 1787 GW set off for Philadelphia to attend the Constitutional Convention scheduled to convene on 14 May. He soon realized, however, that his current Mount Vernon diary (which he had numbered volume eight [Regents' No. 33]) had, he wrote George Augustine Washington, "by mistake" been "left behind" (27 May 1787, CSmH). Before arriving in Philadelphia GW bought another blank leaf booklet, probably in Baltimore, and began another journal (Regents' No. 34) with an initial entry for Friday, 11 May 1787, the day he left Baltimore on his journey to Philadelphia. The first part of this Philadelphia journal covers the period of the Constitutional Convention and ends with GW's return to Mount Vernon on 22 Sept. He apparently intended at first to transfer his Philadelphia journal entries into the diary he had left at Mount Vernon but decided instead to make the 23 Sept. entry in his Philadelphia volume, and he continued to make his Mount Vernon entries in the Philadelphia volume until the last blank page was filled with his entry of 15 Nov. At this point GW returned to volume eight of his Mount Vernon diary (Regents' No. 33) where, following his entry for 8 May, he proceeded to copy (and expand) all of his entries from his Philadelphia journal through 22 Sept., the date he had returned to Mount Vernon. GW turned next to abstracting the farm reports that George Augustine Washington had sent to him during his absence in Philadelphia but quickly realized that such elaborate recopying of other records would be a waste of time and effort, as he explains in the diary. He then went on to transfer into volume eight of the Mount Vernon diaries the remainder of his daily entries from his Philadelphia journal (i.e., his Mount Vernon entries beginning with his entry of 23 Sept.). When this volume was full he was only through 27 Oct. 1787. He then began a new volume (nine [Regents' No. 35]), completing his transfer into that volume seriatim through the last entry in his Philadelphia journal, that of 15 Nov. 1787.

Now well into his ninth volume of postwar Mount Vernon diaries, GW resumed making his original entries with that for 16 Nov. 1787, in which he noted: "remained within doors all day." It may have been on this rainy day that he did his copying from his Philadelphia journal into the eighth and ninth volumes of his Mount Vernon diaries. This date seems particularly likely because when he copied his entry of 15 Nov. from the Philadelphia journal he added the information that Mr. O'Kelly and George Steptoe Washington had appeared at Mount Vernon on the fifteenth. The remainder of his 1787 diary appears in the ninth manuscript volume of the postwar Mount Vernon diaries. It should be noted here that when GW copied in his daily entries from his Philadelphia journal to volumes eight and nine of his Mount Vernon diaries he added temperature readings taken each day at Mount Vernon, presumably from his nephew's farm reports. After the Philadelphia volume was copied, it was probably stored away and seldom referred to, for it is in much better condition than the regular Mount Vernon diaries to which GW often turned to check previous weather and crop entries.

GW's second and more complete (revised) version of his entries from 9 May through 15 Nov. (found in Regents' Nos. 33 and 35) is used as the text in this edition of the diaries. Although the information contained in the two versions does not differ greatly, there is considerable variation in length, wording, and tone. The original version of the entries from 9 May through 15 Nov. (Regents' No. 34) is therefore printed in reduced type in this volume immediately following the diaries for 1787.

A concise acct. of my Journey to Philadelphia, and the manner of spending my time there, and places where, will now follow—after whih. I shall return to the detail of Plantation occurrances as they respect my Crops & intended experiments agreeably to the reports which have been made to me by my Nephew Geo: Auge. Washington in my absence.

Wednesday 9th.     Crossed from Mt. Vernon to Mr. Digges a little after Sun rise & pursuing the rout by the way of Baltimore—dined at Mr. Richd. Hendersons in Bladensbg. and lodged at Majr. Snowdens where feeling very severely a violent hd. ach & sick stomach I went to bed early.

Thomas Snowden (1751–1803) lived at Montpelier about 20 miles south of Baltimore in Prince George's County (BOWIE, 439; W.P.A. [2], 310; and see RICE, 2: pl. 127).

Thursday 10th.     Very great appearances of rain in the morning, & a little falling, induced me, tho' well recovered, to wait till abt. 8 Oclock before I set off. At one Oclock I arrived at Baltimore. Dined at the Fountain, & Supped & lodged at Doctr. McHenrys. Slow rain in the Evening.

The Fountain Inn, which GW had visited several times before, was now in its new location on Light Lane (*Md. Journal*, 3 Dec. 1782). The inn was probably copied after the old George Inn at Southwark, Eng., with balconies surrounding an open courtyard, and was considered one of the outstanding public houses in the United States. Daniel Grant, the builder and first proprietor, advertised the business for sale in 1795, and the description in the advertisement reveals something of the size and appearance of the house. "The House is 100 feet front, and 44 deep, and laid out in the following manner, viz. Excellent Cellars, floored and properly divided, under the whole House, six Parlours, or Rooms of different sizes, for company to meet in.

James McHenry, attributed to
James Sharples. (Independence
National Historical Park Collec-
tion)

Twenty-four Bed-Rooms, eight Garrets for servants, three kitchens with Garrets over them, a Laundry, Spring-House, and Larder, Ice-House, and Barber's Shop, four Brick Stables containing 84 Stalls. . . . The principal part
of the inside work of the House, is finished with Mahogany" (ANDREWS, 17,
44, 62–63, 67) .

James McHenry (1753–1816) immigrated in 1771 from Ireland to Philadelphia, where he studied medicine with Benjamin Rush. During the Revolutionary War he was an aide to GW and later to Lafayette. After the war
he settled in Baltimore and served several years as a Maryland delegate to the
Continental Congress, and was chosen one of the five Maryland delegates to
the Constitutional Convention. McHenry had a town house at the corner of
Baltimore and Fremont streets and a country estate, Fayetteville, near the
city.

Friday 11th.    Set off before breakfast. Rid 12 miles to Skirretts
for it. Baited there and proceeded without halting (weather
threatning) to the Ferry at Havre de gras where I dined but could
not cross the wind being turbulent & squally. Lodged here.

SKIRRETTS: Skerrett's tavern, at the head of the Bird River in Baltimore
County, went through many changes of owners and names. It was probably
the "Cheyns's" tavern GW recorded having breakfast at on 7 May 1775.

Saturday. 12th.    With difficulty (on acct. of the Wind) crossed
the Susquehanna. Breakfasted at the Ferry house, on the East side
—Dined at the head of Elk (Hollingsworths Tavern) and lodged

at Wilmingtons at O'Flins. At the head of Elk I was overtaken by Mr. Francis Corbin who took a seat in my Carriage.

Hollingsworth's tavern, at Head of Elk on Elk Creek, Cecil County, Md., is shown in COLLES, 172.

O'FLINS: Patrick O'Flynn (1748–1818), an immigrant from Ireland, was a Delaware militia captain in the Revolution. He settled in Wilmington, where he opened a tavern, Sign of the Ship. Located on Third and Market streets, it was a popular tavern for ceremonial dinners, including occasional meetings of the Delaware Society of the Cincinnati (O'BRIEN, 48–51).

Francis Corbin was apparently on a trip to Philadelphia. When, in late June, a vacancy occurred in the Virginia delegation, Corbin, who was a member of the Virginia legislature and already in Philadelphia, was recommended to fill that vacancy. No appointment, however, was made (George Mason to Beverley Randolph, 30 June 1787, MASON [2], 3:918).

Sunday. 13th.     About 8 Oclock Mr. Corbin and myself set out, and dined at Chester (Mrs. Withy's) where I was met by the Genls. Mifflin (now Speaker of the Pennsylvania Assembly) Knox and Varnum—The Colonels Humphreys and Minges and Majors Jackson and Nicholas—With whom I proceeded to Philada. At Grays Ferry the City light horse commanded by Colo. Miles met me, and escorted me in by the Artillery Officers who stood arranged & saluted me as I passed. Alighted through a crowd at Mrs. Houses—but being again warmly and kindly pressed by Mr. & Mrs. Rob. Morris to lodge with them I did so and had my baggage removed thither.

Waited on the President, Doctr. Franklin as soon as I got to Town. On my arrival, the Bells were chimed.

The inn of Mary Withy (Withey), located on the northeast corner of Market and Fifth streets in Chester, was well known for the quality of its food (CHASTELLUX, 1:315).

Thomas Mifflin (1744–1800), who began service in the Revolution as GW's first aide-de-camp and later resigned as quartermaster general under a cloud, was now a Pennsylvania delegate to the convention. From 1790 to 1799 he was governor of Pennsylvania.

James Mitchell Varnum (1748–1789), of Rhode Island, served as a brigadier general in the Continental Army and was with GW at Valley Forge. After the Revolution he became a founder of the Society of the Cincinnati, now holding a general meeting in Philadelphia, and was, in 1787, a member of the Continental Congress for Rhode Island.

MINGES: Col. Francis Mentges (d. 1805), born in France, was a dancing teacher in Philadelphia before the Revolution. He joined the Pennsylvania line in 1776 and was with GW at Valley Forge. In 1781, following the victory at Yorktown, he supervised military hospital services in Virginia and resigned from the army in 1783. He was an active member of the Cincinnati and at this time was inspector general of the Pennsylvania militia (*Pa. Mag.*, 45 [1921], 385).

Maj. William Jackson (1759–1828), born in England and raised in South Carolina, served in the Revolution in the southern theater. After returning from a mission to Europe in 1781 he was appointed assistant secretary at war and subsequently settled in Philadelphia, where he studied law and became an active member of the Society of the Cincinnati (*Pa. Mag.*, 2 [1878], 353–69). NICHOLAS: Maj. Francis Nichols (d. 1812), of Pottsgrove, Pa., participated in the seige of Quebec (1775) and retired from the Continental Army as a major in the 9th Pennsylvania Regiment. He was later appointed United States marshal for the eastern district of Pennsylvania (*Pa. Mag.*, 20 [1896], 504; Nichols to GW, 21 Aug. 1789, DLC:GW).

GRAYS FERRY: The Lower Ferry over the Schuylkill took its name from George Gray, who ran it in the 1740s. A floating bridge, built at the Middle Ferry by the British during their occupation of Philadelphia (1777–78) was, upon their evacuation in 1778, moved by the Americans downstream to Gray's ferry, where it remained until swept away by a flood in 1789. The bridge was crossed by GW in his march to Yorktown in 1781 and in his trip to be sworn in as president of the United States in April 1789 (SCHARF [1], 1:454, 3:2141, 2143; SNYDER, 152).

Col. Samuel Miles (1739–1805), of Montgomery County, Pa., who had served in the Braddock expedition, was commissioned colonel of the state's rifle regiment in 1776 and later served as auditor, quartermaster, and brigadier general of state forces. In 1790 he was elected mayor of Philadelphia. From 1786 to 1788 he was captain of the First City Troop of Light Horse, founded in 1774 as a gentlemen's arm of the local militia which participated in public ceremonies (*Pa. Mag.*, 46 [1922], 72–73).

Mrs. Mary House's boardinghouse, on the southwest corner of Fifth and Market streets, was just a few doors down Market Street from the Morris house. Within the week George Read, a delegate from Delaware, found that "Mrs. House's, where I am, is very crowded" (FARRAND, 3:25). Benjamin Franklin was at this time president of the Supreme Council of Pennsylvania. BELLS WERE CHIMED: The *Pennsylvania Packet*, 14 May 1787, reported the next day that "His Excellency General Washington, a member of the grand convention, arrived here. He was met at some distance and escorted into the city by the troop of horse, and saluted at his entrance by the artillery. The joy of the people on the coming of this great and good man was shewn by their acclamations and the ringing of bells."

Monday 14th. This being the day appointed for the Convention to meet, such Members as were in town assembled at the State Ho[use]; but only two States being represented—viz.—Virginia & Pensylvania—agreed to attend at the same place at 11 'Oclock to morrow.

Dined in a family way at Mr. Morris's.

Tuesday 15th. Repaired, at the hour appointed to the State Ho[use], but no more States being represented than were yesterday (tho' several more members had come in) we agreed to meet again to morrow. Govr. Randolph from Virginia came in to day.

A view of the State House, Philadelphia, from the *Columbian Magazine,* June 1787. (New-York Historical Society)

Dined with the Members, to the Genl. Meeting of the Society of the Cincinnati.

Edmund Randolph, in his capacity as governor of Virginia, was the head of the Virginia delegation. Randolph was active in the convention but disapproved of some of the provisions of the Constitution and refused to sign it. Later, however, he supported its ratification by the state of Virginia. CINCINNATI: GW was dining with about 20 delegates of various state societies of the Cincinnati, in Philadelphia for the second general meeting of the society. The general meeting reelected GW president.

Wednesday 16th. No more than two States being yet represented, agreed till a quorum of them should be formed to alter the hour of Meeting at the State house to One oclock.

Dined at the President Doctr. Franklins and drank Tea, and spent the evening at Mr. Jno. Penns.

Benjamin Franklin later commented on this dinner: "We have here at present what the French call *une assemblée des notables* a convention composed of some of the principal people from the several States of our confederation. They did me the honor of dining with me last Wednesday" (Franklin to Thomas Jordan, 18 May 1787, FARRAND, 3:21). Franklin's dining room seated

24 comfortably, which was about the number of delegates in the city by this date.

John Penn (1729–1795) of Lansdowne, a grandson of William Penn, was the last proprietary lieutenant governor of Pennsylvania. After 1776 he lived in political retirement, dividing his time between his country estate, Lansdowne, and his town house in Philadelphia.

Thursday 17th.     Mr. Rutledge from Charleston and Mr. Chs. Pinkney from Congress having arrived gave a representation to So: Carolina and Colo. Mason getting in this Evening placed all the Delegates from Virginia on the floor of Convention.

Dined at Mr. Powells and drk. Tea there.

John Rutledge, who had been a war governor of South Carolina, was later appointed a justice of the United States Supreme Court. Charles Pinckney (1757–1824), cousin of Charles Cotesworth Pinckney, was a member of Congress from South Carolina from 1784 until Feb. 1787 and a prime mover for the Constitutional Convention, where he played an active role. Four times elected governor of South Carolina, he subsequently left the Federalists to become a leader of the Republicans in South Carolina.

The Virginia General Assembly, through a joint ballot of both houses, elected a seven-man delegation (any three providing a minimum for a quorum), which could cast Virginia's vote in the convention by a majority vote within the delegation. The returns show GW first, followed by Patrick Henry, Edmund Randolph, John Blair, James Madison, George Mason, and George Wythe (FARRAND, 3:561). Of the seven originally chosen, GW vacillated for months before accepting (see FREEMAN, 6:75–84). Only Patrick Henry declined outright. To Henry's place Governor Randolph appointed Thomas Nelson, who declined. Randolph then turned to Richard Henry Lee. Lee declined, on account of poor health. Finally on 2 May Randolph appointed Dr. James McClurg (1746–1823), a member of the Virginia Council of State, who was at that time in Philadelphia (FARRAND, 3:21, 558, 561). Hence, GW's notation on 16 May in his Philadelphia journal that "Doctr. McClerg of Virginia came in" probably records McClurg's first day of attendance at the convention.

COLO. MASON: Three days after his arrival, George Mason wrote to his son, George Mason, Jr.: "the Virg[ini]a Deputies (who are all here) meet and confer together two or three Hours, every Day; in order to form a proper Correspondence of Sentiments" (MASON [2], 3:880).

Samuel Powel's house was on the west side of Third Street between Spruce and Walnut streets (GW ATLAS, pl. 44; BAKER [2], 75n).

Friday 18th.     The representation from New York appeared on the floor to day.

Dined at Greys ferry, and drank Tea at Mr. Morris's—after which accompanied Mrs. [Morris] and some other Ladies to hear a Mrs. O'Connell read (a charity affair). The lady being reduced in circumstances had had recourse to this expedient to obtain a little money. Her performe. was tolerable—at the College-Hall.

# May 1787

GREYS FERRY: The recently opened public gardens on the west bank of the Schuylkill at Gray's ferry were an innovation in public amusement gardens for Philadelphia. Patterned after the public gardens of London, the Gray's ferry gardens placed artificial grottoes and waterfalls among beds of flowers and exotic plants, set in several acres of the natural landscape along the Schuylkill River. Here concerts, illuminations, and fireworks were presented, especially on holidays. Refreshments and meals were served at the ferry inn, incorporated into the gardens (SCHARF [1], 2:942–44).

MRS. O'CONNELL: On this day the *Pennsylvania Packet* reported: "THE Lecture which was to have been read by a LADY in the University last evening was postponed until tonight, at the particular desire of several ladies and gentlemen of distinction. The Lecture to be read THIS EVENING is a continuance of the Dissertation on Eloquence, which commenced in the first course."

Saturday 19th.    No more States represented.

Dined at Mr. Ingersolls. Spent the evening at my lodgings–& retird. to my room soon.

Jared Ingersoll (1749–1822), originally of Connecticut, became a prominent attorney in Philadelphia. In 1785 his residence was near the northeast corner of Fourth and Market streets, but by 1791, when in his first term as attorney general of Pennsylvania, he had moved to a house on Chestnut Street across from the Pennsylvania State House. An early advocate of a revision of the Articles of Confederation, he became a Pennsylvania delegate to the convention (GW ATLAS, pl. 44; JACKSON [3], 110).

Sunday 20th.    Dined with Mr. & Mrs. Morris and other Company at their farm (called the Hills). Returned in the afternoon & drank Tea at Mr. Powells.

THE HILLS: While visiting Philadelphia in July 1787 Manasseh Cutler recorded how he rode "out of the city on the western side . . . in view of the Schuylkill, and up the river several miles, and took a view of a number of Country seats, one belonging to Mr. Robert Morris. . . . His country seat . . . is not yet completed but it will be superb. It is planned on a large scale, the gardens and walks are extensive and the villa situated on an eminence has a commanding prospect down the Schuylkill to the Delaware" (*Pa. Mag.*, 12 [1888], 105; and see SNYDER, 140, 188).

Monday 21st.    Delaware State was represented.

Dined, and drank Tea at Mr. Binghams in great Splender.

MR. BINGHAMS: William Bingham (1752–1804), scion of an old Pennsylvania family, was born in Philadelphia, graduated from the University of Pennsylvania (1768), and was a British consul in Martinique before the Revolution and an American commercial agent in the West Indies during the Revolution. In 1780 he returned to Philadelphia with a large fortune and married Anne Willing (1764–1801), a daughter of Thomas Willing and renowned as a great beauty and a brilliant hostess. After spending several years in Europe the Willings returned to Philadelphia to build an elaborate town house on the west side of Third Street above Spruce Street, where they entertained extensively during the 1790s.

**Tuesday 22d.** The Representation from No. Carolina was compleated which made a representation for five States.

Dined and drank Tea at Mr. Morris's.

**Wednesday 23d.** No more States being represented I rid to Genl. Mifflins to breakfast—after which in Company with him Mr. Madison, Mr. Rutledge and others I crossed the Schuylkill above the Falls. Visited Mr. Peters—Mr. Penns Seat, and Mr. Wm. Hamiltons.

Dined at Mr. Chews—with the Wedding guests (Colo. Howard of Baltimore having married his daughter Peggy). Drank Tea there in a very large Circle of Ladies.

Mifflin's country seat, overlooking the falls of the Schuylkill, was one of his three homes; the other two were a farm in Berks County and a town house in Philadelphia (ROSSMAN, 174; and see SNYDER, 157, 193).

Richard Peters (1744–1828), secretary of the Board of War (1776–81), was later appointed by GW a judge of the United States District Court for Pennsylvania. His country seat, Belmont, where he carried out large-scale agricultural experimentation, was on the west side of the Schuylkill below the falls (BAKER [2], 76n). MR. PENNS SEAT: Lansdowne, an Italianate house built c.1773 by lieutenant governor John Penn. Located on the west side of the Schuylkill about halfway between the falls and the Middle Ferry, Lansdowne was later incorporated into Fairmount Park (see SNYDER, 169, 173).

William Hamilton (1745–1813), a wealthy Philadelphia patron of the arts, was particularly devoted to landscape gardening. Hamilton employed trained gardeners and was responsible for the introduction of many new plants. When Meriwether Lewis sent plant specimens back from the Lewis and Clark expedition (1804–6), some were forwarded to Hamilton by Thomas Jefferson for experimentation. In Mar. 1792 Hamilton shipped a small collection of plants and cuttings to Mount Vernon, including several species which GW had not planted before. Today GW is visiting Hamilton at Bush Hill, located just north of the city. He had inherited the property from his uncle James Hamilton upon the latter's death in 1783 (see SNYDER, 156, 159).

Benjamin Chew's daughter Margaret (Peggy) Chew (1760–1824) married John Eager Howard (1752–1827) on 18 May 1787. Howard had served as an officer of Maryland troops under Nathanael Greene during most of the Revolution, participating in the Jersey campaigns with GW before being reassigned to the southern theater, where he distinguished himself. In 1788 Howard was elected governor of Maryland. This party was probably at the town house of Benjamin Chew, on Third Street between Walnut and Spruce streets. The house, built in the 1770s for William Byrd III of Westover, was later bought by Benjamin Chew, who was proscribed as a Tory during the Revolution. During the winter of 1781–82, GW made the Chew town house his headquarters (see EBERLEIN, 103–27; VIRKUS, 5:730).

Bush Hill, one of the estates of William Hamilton, on the Schuylkill River. From *New-York Magazine*, February 1793. (New-York Historical Society)

A view by William Strickland of the falls of the Schuylkill River from the portico of Thomas Mifflin's house. (New-York Historical Society)

Thursday 24th.   No more States represented.

Dined and drank Tea at Mr. John Ross's.

One of my Postilion boys (Paris) being sick, requested Doctr. Jones to attend him.

Dr. John Jones (1729–1791), who had studied medicine in Europe, helped organize the medical department of the Continental Army, published several important medical papers, and was an organizer and first vice-president of the College of Physicians of Philadelphia.

Friday 25th.   Another Delegate coming in from the State of New Jersey gave it a representation and encreased the number to Seven which forming a quoram of the 13 the Members present resolved to organize the body; when, by a unanimous vote I was called up to the Chair as President of the body. Majr. William Jackson was appointed Secretary and a Comee. was chosen consisting of 3 Members to prepare rules & regulations for conducting the business and after [ap]pointing door keepers the Convention adjourned till Monday, to give time to the Comee. to report the matters referred to them.

Returned many visits to day. Dined at Mr. Thos. Willings and sp[en]t the evening at my lodgings.

A unanimous vote for GW as president had been generally expected by the delegates. Benjamin Franklin, the only other possible candidate for the honor, had planned to nominate GW, but he was unwell and Robert Morris made the nomination, seconded by John Rutledge. James Madison's notes described the scene: "General [Washington] was accordingly unanimously elected by ballot, and conducted to the chair by Mr. R. Morris and Mr. Rutlidge; from which in a very emphatic manner he thanked the Convention for the honor they had conferred on him, reminded them of the novelty of the scene of business in which he was to act, lamented his want of [better qualifications], and claimed the indulgence of the House towards the involuntary errors which his inexperience might occasion" (FARRAND, 1:3–4).

William Jackson, who later served as one of GW's secretaries, was not the only candidate for secretary of the convention. John Beckley, clerk of the Virginia House of Delegates, accompanied Governor Randolph to Philadelphia "in *expectation of being appointed clerk*" of the convention (James Monroe to Thomas Jefferson, 27 July 1787, JEFFERSON [1], 11:631). William Temple Franklin, secretary to his grandfather Benjamin Franklin when he was in Paris, was nominated by the Pennsylvania delegation, but Jackson, who actively solicited GW and other delegates for support, was elected (FARRAND, 1:4, 3:18). In Nov. 1795 GW attended Jackson's wedding to Eliza Willing, daughter of Thomas Willing, GW's dinner host today (*Pa. Mag.*, 2 [1878], 366, 21 [1897], 27).

Thomas Willing's three-story town house was on Third Street just below Walnut Street.

Saturday 26th.    Returned all my visits this forenoon. Dined with a club at the City Tavern and spent the evening at my quarters writing letters.

MY VISITS: In 1781 Chastellux remarked that following breakfast, "we went to visit the ladies, according to the Philadelphia custom, where the morning is the most proper hour for paying calls" (CHASTELLUX, 1:135).

For the City Tavern, see entries for 4 Sept. 1774, 12 May 1775, and 26 July 1786.

Sunday 27th.    Went to the Romish Church—to high Mass. Dined, drank Tea, and spent the evening at my lodgings.

ROMISH CHURCH: Of the two Roman Catholic chapels in Philadelphia at this time GW probably attended the larger, St. Mary's, on Fourth below Spruce Street. The chapel had been extensively renovated in 1782 (SCHARF [1], 2:1372).

Monday 28th.    Met in Convention at 10 Oclock. Two States more—viz.—Massachusetts, and Connecticut were on the floor to day.

Established Rules—agreeably to the plan brot. in by the Comee. for the governmt. of the Convention & adjourned. No com[municatio]ns without doors.

Dined at home, and drank Tea, in a large circle at Mr. Francis's.

NO COM[MUNICATIO]NS WITHOUT DOORS: GW is referring to the secrecy rule which was proposed in the convention on this day. It was referred to the rules committee and adopted on the following day (FARRAND, 1:13, 15).

Tench Francis, Jr. (1730–1800), was the son of Tench Francis (d. 1758) and an uncle of Tench Tilghman, one of GW's aides during the Revolution. In 1787 he lived on Chestnut Street between Third and Fourth streets. He later became first cashier of the Bank of North America (*Pa. Mag.*, 11 [1887], 299, n.2, 49 [1925], 82).

Tuesday 29th.    Attended Convention and dined at home—after wch. accompanied Mrs. Morris to the benifit Concert of a Mr. Juhan.

BENIFIT CONCERT: Members of the local music community, made up of native Americans and post-Revolution musical migrants from England and the Continent, sometimes participated in benefit concerts in which the musician who benefited took the financial risks and received all the profits (SONNECK, 123). Today's concert, which featured pieces by the contemporary European composers Haydn, Sarti, and Martini (Schwartzendorf), also included "A New Overture" by Alexander Reinagle, the local musical impresario, a flute concerto by the local composer and organist William Brown, a "Concerto Violoncello" by Henry (Henri) Capron, whom GW later hired as a music teacher for Nelly Custis, and several pieces for violin and piano by "Mr. Juhan" (*Pa. Packet,* 29 May 1787; PHi: GW Household Accounts, 1793–97; see entry for 28 May 1795; and see COVEY, 517).

In the spring of 1783 James Juhan (Joan, Juan), who advertised himself as a teacher of harpsichord, violin, flute, "Tenor Fiddle," violincello, and guitar, and also as a maker of harpsichords and "the great North American fortepianos," arrived in Philadelphia, and on 6 Aug. presented "a grand Concert of MUSIC, Vocal and Instrumental" (*Pa. Gaz.,* 25 June, 6 Aug. 1783; SONNECK, 123–24, 265). He may have been related to Alexander Juhan, Jr., who advertised himself as *"Master of Music,* lately arrived in this city," who offered to teach "the Harpsichord and Violin" as well as singing, and who cosponsored a series of subscription concerts in 1786–87 in Philadelphia (*Pa. Packet,* 23 Dec. 1783; SONNECK, 80).

**Wednesday 30th.    Attended Convention.**

Dined with Mr. Vaughan. Drank Tea, and spent the evening at a Wednesday evenings party at Mr. & Mrs. Lawrence's.

Mr. Vaughan is probably Samuel Vaughan rather than one of his sons. The elder Vaughan was in Philadelphia until about Dec. 1787 when he sailed to visit his holdings in Jamaica. He returned to Philadelphia by 1789 but left again in 1790 to take up permanent residence in England (STETSON [3], 472–74).

John Lawrence (1724–1799), who in the colonial period had been a mayor of Philadelphia and a judge of the Pennsylvania Supreme Court, was proscribed a Tory during the Revolution. Mrs. Lawrence was Elizabeth Francis Lawrence (1733–1800), a sister of Tench Francis, Jr., whom GW visited twice this week, and an aunt of GW's wartime aide Lt. Col. Tench Tilghman. In 1790 Lawrence lived on Chestnut Street below Sixth Street (*Pa. Mag.,* 24 [1899], 403; HEADS OF FAMILIES, PA., 225).

[Thursday 31st.]    The State of Georgia came on the Floor of the Convention to day which made a representation of ten States.

Dined at Mr. Francis's and drank Tea with Mrs. Meredith.

THE STATE OF GEORGIA: In his Philadelphia diary GW specified William Houstoun (1757–1812), who was an active convention participant, and William Pierce (d. 1789), who participated little but left some notes of the convention, including character sketches of delegates (FARRAND, 1:xxi, 3:87–97).

MRS. MEREDITH: Margaret Cadwalader, daughter of Dr. Thomas Cadwalader (d. 1799) and a sister of Lambert and John Cadwalader, both of whom served under GW. She married Samuel Meredith (1741–1817) in 1772.

# [June 1787]

Friday 1st. June.    Attending in Convention and nothing being suffered to transpire no minutes of the proceedings has been, or will be inserted in this diary.

Dined with Mr. John Penn, and spent the evening at a superb entertainment at Bush-hill given by Mr. Hamilton—at which were more than an hundred guests.

Saturday 2d.    Majr. Jenifer coming in with sufficient powers for the purpose, gave a representation to Maryland; which brought all the States in Union into Convention except Rhode Island which had refused to send delegates thereto.

Dined at the City Tavern with the Club & spent the evening at my own quarters.

Although the state of Maryland appointed five delegates to the Constitutional Convention, their official instructions provided that the presence of a single delegate was enough to fully represent the state. James McHenry, the first of the five Maryland delegates to join the convention (28 May), was still the only Maryland delegate present when he was forced to leave on 1 June because of illness in his family. Hence the arrival on 2 June of Daniel of St. Thomas Jenifer, the second Maryland delegate to join the convention, again allowed the state to be fully represented (FARRAND, 1:xxi, 3:586).

Sunday. 3d.    Dined at Mr. Clymers and drank Tea there also.

George Clymer (1739–1813) was a Philadelphia merchant and financier and an early advocate of independence. As a member of the Continental Congress (1776–78, 1780–83) he was active on committees dealing with finance, prisoners of war, Indian relations, commissary reform, and penal law revision. Clymer was a Pennsylvania delegate to the Federal Convention and a representative in the First Congress. In 1785 he resided on Fourth Street between Walnut and Spruce streets (*Pa. Mag.*, 11 [1887], 300n).

Monday 4th.    Attended Convention. Representation as on Saturday.

Reviewed (at the importunity of Genl. Mifflin and the officers) the Light Infantry—Cavalry—and part of the Artillery, of the City.

Dined with Genl. Mifflin & drk. Tea with Miss Cadwallader.

MISS CADWALLADER: probably either Rebecca Cadwalader (1746–1821) or Elizabeth Cadwalader (1760–1799), daughters of Dr. Thomas Cadwalader of Philadelphia. Rebecca, who some time after 1791 became the second wife of Philemon Dickinson, and Elizabeth, who never married, were probably the "Misses" Cadwalader listed in 1790 as "Spinsters" living next door to Philemon Dickinson on Chestnut Street in Philadelphia (HEADS OF FAMILIES, PA., 225).

Tuesday 5th.    Dined at Mr. Morris's with a large Company, & Spent the Evening there. Attended in Convention the usual hours.

The Residence of Washington in High Street— 1795.
2d door below 6th Street south side of Market St.

Robert Morris's house in Philadelphia. (Historical Society of Pennsylvania)

**Wednesday 6th.** In Convention as usual. Dined at the Presidents (Doctr. Franklins) & drank Tea there—after which returnd. to my lodgings and wrote letters for France.

**Thursday 7th.** Attended Convention as usual. Dined with a Club of Convention Members at the Indian Queen. Drank Tea & spent the evening at my lodgings.

The Indian Queen, on Fourth Street between Market and Chestnut streets, was the lodging house for a number of delegates to the convention. It was described by a visitor that summer as being "kept in an elegant style" (*Pa. Mag.*, 12 [1888], 103).

**Friday 8th.** Attended the Convention. Dined, drank Tea, and spent the evening at my lodggs.

**Saturday 9th.** At Convention. Dined with the Club at the City Tavern. Drank Tea, & set till 10 oclock at Mr. Powells.

**Sunday 10th.** Breakfasted by agreement at Mr. Powell's, and in Company with him rid to see the Botanical garden of Mr. Bartram; which, tho' Stored with many curious plts. Shrubs & trees,

many of which are exotics was not laid off with much taste, nor
was it large.

From hence we rid to the Farm of one Jones, to see the effect of
the plaister of Paris which appeared obviously great—First, on a
piece of Wheat stubble, the ground bearing which, he says, had
never recd. any manure; and that the Wheat from whence it was
taken was so indifferent as to be scarcely worth cutting—The white
clover on this grd. (without any seed being sown & the plaister
spread without breaking up the soil) was full high enough to
mow, and stood very thick. The line between this and the herbage
around it, was most obviously drawn, for there nothing but the
naked stubble, some weeds & thin grass appeared with little or no
white clover. The same difference was equally obvious on a piece
of mowing grd. not far distant from it for where the Plaister had
been spread the White and red clover was luxuriant and but little
of either beyond it and these thin. The Soil of these appeared
loamy—slightly mixed with Ising-glass and originally had been
good; but according to Jones's account was much exhausted. He
informed us of the salutary effect of this plaister on a piece of
heavy stiff meadow (not liable however to be wet) where it tran-
scended either of the two pieces just mentioned in the improvement.

This manure he put on the 29th. of October in a wet or moist
spot, and whilst the Moon was in its increase, which Jones says
he was directed to attend to (but this must be whimsical) and at

William Bartram, by Charles
Willson Peale. (Independence
National Historical Park Collec-
tion)

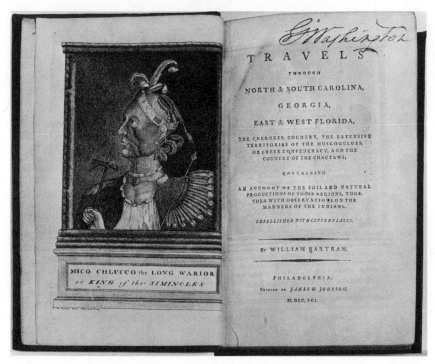

Title page of William Bartram's *Travels,* from Washington's library. (Boston Athenaeum)

the rate of about 5 bushls. to the Acre. When it is laid on grass land or Meadow he advises harrowing, previously, to the laying it thereon in order to raise the mould for incorporation.

From hence we visited Mr. Powells own farm after which I went (by appointment) to the Hills & dined with Mr. & Mrs. Morris. Returned to the City abt. dark.

William Bartram (1739–1823) operated a botanical garden with his brother John, Jr. (1743–1812), on the west bank of the Schuylkill three miles from Philadelphia. The establishment was still called John Bartram & Sons although it had passed into the hands of the sons upon the death of its founder, John Bartram (1699–1777). William's reputation as a traveler-naturalist was enhanced by the publication in 1791 of his *Travels through North and South Carolina.* GW was a subscriber to the book but declined a request that it be dedicated to him. On 2 Oct. 1789 GW sent word to Clement Biddle, his agent in Philadelphia, that he wanted the Bartrams' list of plants plus a note about the care of each kind (PHi: Washington-Biddle correspondence). In Mar. 1792 he obtained plants of 106 varieties, the surviving list bearing the heading "Catalogue of Trees, Shrubs & Plants, of Jno. Bartram" (DLC:GW). These plants were sent to George Augustine Washington,

GW's manager at Mount Vernon, and a second shipment was sent down in November to replace the plants that had not flourished. While it is assumed that GW purchased the plants, it is quite possible that they were a gift from Bartram. MR. POWELLS OWN FARM: Samuel Powel owned land across the Schuylkill River southwest of Philadelphia.

Monday 11th.    Attended in Convention. Dined, drank Tea, and spent the evening in my own room.

Tuesday 12th.    Dined and drank Tea at Mr. Morris's. Went afterwards to a concert at the City Tavern.

This benefit concert, with tickets at 7s. 6d., was for Alexander Reinagle (1756–1809), born into a musical family of Austrian descent who lived in England. He was accomplished both as a composer and a performer on several instruments. In 1786 he immigrated to America and soon became Philadelphia's leading musical impresario. This concert, scheduled to begin at "exactly" 7:45 P.M., opened with an overture by Bach, and included compositions by the then current European composers Sarti, André, Fiorillo, and Piccini as well as pieces by the local musicians Henry Capron and William Brown. The concert concluded with two works by Reinagle, a piano sonata and "a new Overture" (*Pa. Packet,* 12 June 1787; SONNECK, 80, 131–32).

Wednesday 13th.    In Convention. Dined at Mr. Clymers & drank Tea there. Spent the evening at Mr. Binghams.

Thursday 14th.    Dined at Major Moores (after being in Convention) and spent the evening at my own lodgings.

Although there were several Major Moores in Philadelphia at this time, GW is probably visiting Maj. Thomas Lloyd Moore (d. 1819), on Pine Street between Second and Third streets. At the end of the Revolutionary War, GW referred to Moore as among "the best Officers who were in the Army" (GW to Thomas Mifflin, 21 Dec. 1783, DNA: PCC, Item 152).

Friday 15th.    In Convention as usual. Dined at Mr. Powells & drank Tea there.

Saturday 16th.    In Convention. Dined with the Club at the City Tavern and drank Tea at Doctr. Shippins with Mrs. Livingstons party.

Anne Hume Shippen (1761–1841) was the daughter of Dr. William Shippen (1736–1808). She married (1781) Henry Beekman Livingston, son of Judge Robert R. Livingston (1718–1775), but at this time the Livingstons were separated.

Sunday. 17th.  Went to Church. Heard Bishop White preach, and see him ordain two Gentlemen Deacons—after wch. rid 8 Miles into the Country and dined with Mr. Jno. Ross in Chester County. Returned in the Afternoon.

William White (1748–1836), a native of Philadelphia, was the assistant minister and then, during the Revolution, the successor to Jacob Duché as minister for Christ and St. Peter's Anglican churches in Philadelphia. White had recently returned from England, where earlier this year he had been consecrated an Anglican bishop, thus becoming empowered to consecrate deacons for the newly formed Protestant Episcopal Church of the United States of America, which he was instrumental in organizing following the Revolution. White's sister Mary was the wife of GW's Philadelphia host Robert Morris.

DEACONS: One of the deacons was apparently a son of Dr. Gerardus Clarkson (*Pa. Mag.*, 12 [1888], 105).

John Ross's farm, Grange Farm, or The Grange, was located on the old Haverford Road near Frankford in Chester County. He bought the property, formerly called Clifton Hall, from his father-in-law, Capt. Charles Cruikshank, in 1783 and renamed it in honor of Lafayette's home in France (*Pa. Mag.*, 23 [1899], 77–85).

Monday 18th.  Attended the Convention. Dined at the Quarterly meeting of the Sons of St. Patrick—held at the City Tavn. Drank Tea at Doctr. Shippins with Mrs. Livingston.

SONS OF ST. PATRICK: Founded in 1771 in Philadelphia by Irish-American merchants and their friends, the Society of the Friendly Sons of St. Patrick strongly supported the American Revolution and several of its dinners were attended by GW, who was "adopted" by the society (DOUGHERTY, 1–21).

Tuesday 19th.  Dined (after leaving Convention) in a family way at Mr. Morris's and spent the Evening there in a very large Company.

Wednesday. 20th.  Attended Convention. Dined at Mr. Meridiths & drank Tea there.

MR. MERIDITHS: Samuel Meredith (1741–1817) had been a brigadier general under GW during the New Jersey campaigns (1777–78) and was now a Pennsylvania delegate to Congress. In 1789 GW appointed him first treasurer of the United States. His home was on Front Street between Arch and Race streets.

Thursday 21st.  Attended Convention. Dined at Mr. Pragers, and spent the evening in my Chamber.

Mr. Prager is probably Mark Prager, Sr., a member of the Jewish mercantile family that came to Philadelphia shortly after the Revolution. The firm, at first called Pragers, Liebaert & Co., was some time before 1791 changed to Pragers & Co. GW had written William Fitzhugh on 23 July 1784 introducing Mr. Prager, who had been strongly recommended to him as "a Gentleman who is very extensively engaged in Trade, & a partner in several very capital Houses in Europe. He is taking a review of the State of our Trade & Ports, & probably, if he finds them answerable to his wishes, will fix a House in this State" (DLC:GW). Prager evidently found Philadelphia more to his liking.

**Friday 22d.** Dined at Mr. Morris's & drank Tea with Mr. Frans. Hopkinson.

Francis Hopkinson, lawyer, musician, composer, and poet, and, as a delegate from New Jersey, signer of the Declaration of Independence, was at this time a judge in the admiralty court of Pennsylvania. During the Revolution he wrote and published a series of satiric essays and pamphlets supporting the American cause, and in 1787–88 wrote essays supporting the proposed new Constitution. In this year Hopkinson published a collection of his compositions, *Seven Songs,* which he dedicated to GW. GW was pleased, but took exception to the dedication, pleading that although he would "defend your performance, if necessary, to the last effort of my musical Abilities . . . what, alass! can I do to support it? I can neither sing one of the songs, nor raise a single note on any instrument to convince the unbelieving" (GW to Hopkinson, 5 Feb. 1789, DLC:GW).

**Saturday 23d.** In Convention. Dined at Doctr. Ruston's & drank Tea at Mr. Morris's.

Dr. Thomas Ruston, a native of Chester County, Pa., attended the College of New Jersey and received a medical degree from the University of Edinburgh in 1765. He practiced in England until after the Revolution. In 1785 Ruston returned to Philadelphia where he became an associate of Robert Morris in land speculations. He was jailed for debt in 1796 (RUSH, 1:92, n.1). Ruston had been introduced to GW by George William and Sally Fairfax in a letter of 2 July 1785 as "not only a good American by birth, but also in sentiments" (DLC:GW). Ruston had a town house built for him on Chestnut Street. In the 1790 census he appears on West Market Street between Eighth and Ninth streets (*Pa. Mag.,* 8 [1884], 111; HEADS OF FAMILIES, PA., 226; JACKSON [3], 232).

**Sunday 24th.** Dined at Mr. Morris's & spent the evening at Mr. Meridiths—at Tea.

**Monday 25th.** Attended Convention. Dined at Mr. Morris's— drank Tea there—& spent the evening in my chamber.

**Tuesday 26th.** Attended Convention. Partook of a family dinner with Govr. Randolph and made one of a party to drink Tea at Grays ferry.

Edmund Randolph first boarded at Mrs. House's, where George Read had been obliged to give up a larger room "for Governor Randolph, it being then expected he would have brought his lady with him, which he did not, but she is expected to follow some time hence" (Read to John Dickinson, 21 May 1787, FARRAND, 3:25). A week later Randolph "engaged a couple of rooms in a House at a small distance" from Mrs. House's. "As Mr. Randolph expects his lady his situation is too Confined in this House. He is to dine at our Table" (Read to Dickinson, 25 May 1787, FARRAND, 4:61). A week later Randolph wrote his cousin Lt. Gov. Beverley Randolph: "the prospect of a very long sojournment here has determined me to bring up my family" (FARRAND, 3:36).

**Wednesday 27th.** In Convention. Dined at Mr. Morris's. Drank Tea there also and spent the evening in my chamber.

**Thursday 28th.** Attended Convention. Dined at Mr. Morris's in a large Company— (the news of his Bills being protested, arriving last night a little mal-apropos). Drank Tea there, & spent the evening in my chamber.

Over a month earlier, Robert Morris's "£50,000 sterling of . . . bills of exchange" had been protested in London. The protest interrupted the financier's purchase of American tobacco and threatened to disrupt the American tobacco trade with France, for which Morris had an exclusive contract with the French Farmers General (James Maury to Thomas Jefferson, and William Short to Jefferson, 21 May 1787, JEFFERSON [1], 11:370–71, 373).

**Friday 29th.** In Convention. Dined at Mr. Morris and spent the evening there.

**Saturday 30th.** Attended Convention. Dined with a Club at Springsbury—consisting of several associated families of the City —the Gentlemen of which meet every Saturday accompanied by the females of the families every other Saturday. This was the ladies day.

In his original Philadelphia journal GW refers to the club at Springettsbury as the Cold Spring Club. SPRINGSBURY: One of the original manors set aside by William Penn for his family was named Springettsbury, taking its name from the family name of Penn's first wife, Gulielma Maria Springett. Much of the original manor, encompassing thousands of acres just north of the original city, was gradually sold off, but a portion retaining the manor name was kept in the family and developed in the mid-eighteenth century by William Penn's son Thomas Penn (1702–1775). The manor house, within an easy walk from Bush Hill, was the temporary country home of Robert Morris in 1779 and 1780. In the 1780s its overgrown gardens, random springs, and abandoned buildings offered a gothic setting for pastoral outings (see SNYDER, 200; BAKER [2], 81n).

# [July 1787]

July. 1st.    Dined and spent the evening at home.

Monday. 2d.    Attended Convention. Dined with some of the Members of Convention at the Indian Queen. Drank Tea at Mr. Binghams, and walked afterwards in the state house yard.

Set this Morning for Mr. Pine who wanted to correct his portrt. of me.

For Robert Edge Pine's visit to Mount Vernon to paint this portrait, see entry for 28 April 1785.

Tuesday. 3d.    Sat before the meeting of the Convention for Mr. Peale who wanted my picture to make a print or Metzotinto by.

Dined at Mr. Morris's and drank Tea at Mr. Powells—after which, in Company with him, I attended the Agricultural Society at Carpenters Hall.

Charles Willson Peale, now living in Philadelphia, wrote GW of the "great desire I have to make a good mezzotinto print" of him assuring GW he would "make the business as convenient to you as possible . . . by bringing my

Peale's mezzotint of Washington hung at Mount Vernon. (Mount Vernon Ladies' Association of the Union)

Pallette and Pensils to Mr. Morris's that you might sett at your leisure" (29 May 1787, May–June, 1787, PPAmP: Charles Willson Peale Papers; see also SELLERS, 1:257–58; EISEN, 2:378).

On this day a local diarist recorded: "Before breakfast went with my daughter Hannah to the meadow. . . . On returning we met his Excellency General Washington taking a ride on horseback, only his coachman Giles with him" (HILTZHEIMER, 128).

The Philadelphia Society for Promoting Agriculture, founded in Feb. 1785 to promote agriculture in the United States, consisted of active (resident) members living in or near Philadelphia and honorary (later corresponding) members. GW became one of the latter in 1785. Samuel Powel was president from 1785 to 1794. The regular monthly meetings, drawing between 10 and 20 members, were held in Carpenters' Hall, on Chestnut Street near Third Street. Built in 1770 by the Carpenters' Company of Philadelphia, the hall had been the meeting place of the First Continental Congress (1774), to which GW had been a delegate (see GAMBRILL, 410–39).

Wednesday 4th.     Visited Doctr. Shovats Anatomical figures and (the Convention having adjourned for the purpose) went to hear an Oration on the anniversary of Independance delivered by a Mr. Mitchell, a student of Law—After which I dined with the State Society of the Cincinnati at Epplees Tavern and drank Tea at Mr. Powells.

DOCTR. SHOVATS ANATOMICAL FIGURES: The surgeon and anatomist Abraham Chovet (1704–1790) was born in England, studied in France, practiced in England and the West Indies, and in 1774 opened his "Anatomical Museum" of wax human figures on Vidal's Alley off Second Street in Philadelphia. Chastellux, impressed with Chovet's work, was even more impressed with Chovet: "a real eccentric: his chief characteristic is contrary-mindedness; when the English were at Philadelphia he was a Whig, and since they left he has become a Tory" (CHASTELLUX, 1:146, 311). Chovet remained in Philadelphia, where he practiced medicine, taught anatomy, and helped found the College of Physicians (1787).

CINCINNATI: "Gen. Washington presents his Complts. to The honle. The Vice Presidt. of the Pensa. State Society of Cincinnati and will do himself the honor of dining with the society on the 4th of July agreeable to Invitation" (GW to Thomas McKean, 29 June [1787], PHi: McKean Papers). EPPLEES TAVERN: Henry Epple (d. 1809) kept The Sign of the Rainbow, a popular tavern on the north side of Sassafras (Race) Street, above Third. Epple, who ran the tavern until 1794, had served as an officer in the army during the Revolution.

Thursday 5th.     Attended Convention. Dined at Mr. Morris's and drank Tea there. Spent the evening also.

Friday 6th.     Sat for Mr. Peale in the Morning. Attended Convention. Dined at the City Tavern with some members of Convention and spent the evening at my lodgings.

Saturday 7th.    Attended Convention. Dined with the Club at Springsbury and drank Tea at Mr. Meridiths.

Sunday 8th.    About 12 Oclock rid to Doctr. Logans near German town where I dined. Returned in the evening and drank Tea at Mr. Morris's.

Dr. George Logan (1753–1821), a strict Quaker and an active pacifist, took his medical degree from the University of Edinburgh in 1779 and returned to Pennsylvania to settle at his family home, Stenton, near Germantown, Pa., where he pursued experimental agriculture, and where GW is visiting this day.

Monday 9th.    Sat in the Morning for Mr. Peale. Attended Convention. Dined at Mr. Morris's & accompanied Mrs. Morris to Doctr. Redmans 3 Miles in the Country where we drank Tea and returned.

On 8 July Charles Willson Peale wrote GW: "the Drapery and background of your Portrait is painted and if it is convenient to your Excellency to favor me with a sitting tomorrow morning, I will have my pallit sett with fresh ground Colours" (PPAmP: Charles Willson Peale Papers).

Although there were several Dr. Redmans in Philadelphia at this time GW is probably visiting Dr. John Redman (1722–1808), who was trained in Edinburgh and Leyden and practiced in Paris and London before returning home to Philadelphia. Here he specialized in obstetrics and trained many local physicians, including George Logan and Benjamin Rush. From 1786 to 1804 Redman served as first president of the College of Physicians of Philadelphia.

Tuesday. 10th.    Attended Convention. Dined at Mr. Morris's. Drank Tea at Mr. Binghams & went to the Play.

The play was performed at the Southwark Theater, located just south of the city boundary. Because of a state law (1779) prohibiting theatrical performances, the building was called an opera house by the American Company, which played there from 25 June to 4 Aug. To skirt this same law the plays presented were billed under false titles that could still be recognizable by the theater-going public. Hence, in this evening's "concert" James Townley's *High Life below the Stairs* was billed as an "entertainment" called "the Servants Hall in an Uproar," while the farce *Love in a Camp, or Patrick in Prussia* was advertised as a "Comic Opera" (SCHARF [1], 2:965–67; SEILHAMER, 2:217–21).

Wednesday 11th.    Attended Convention. Dined at Mr. Morris's and spent the evening there.

Thursday 12th.    In Convention. Dined at Mr. Morris's & drank Tea with Mrs. Livingston.

Friday 13th.    In Convention. Dined, drank Tea, & Spent the Evening at Mr. Morris's.

Saturday. 14th.    In Convention. Dined at Springsbury with the Club and went to the play in the Afternoon.

The play was Shakespeare's *The Tempest,* adapted by John Dryden (SEIL-HAMER, 2:219).

Sunday 15th.    Dined at Mr. Morris's & remaind. at home all day.

Monday 16th.    In Convention. Dined at Mr. Morris's and drank Tea with Mrs. Powell.

Tuesday 17th.    In Convention. Dined at Mrs. Houses, and made an excursion with a party for Tea to Grays Ferry.

On this day Jacob Hiltzheimer went "in the afternoon . . . to Mr. Gray's ferry, where we saw the great improvements made in the garden, summer houses, and walks in the woods. General Washington and a number of other gentlemen of the present Convention came down to spend the afternoon" (HILTZHEIMER, 128).

Wednesday 18th.    In Convention. Dined at Mr. Milligans and drank Tea at Mr. Meridiths.

In 1790 James Milligan (d. 1818) lived on south Second Street (HEADS OF FAMILIES, PA., 237). As auditor and then as comptroller general of the treasury under the Articles of Confederation he had audited many of GW's Revolutionary accounts.

Thursday 19th.    Dined (after coming out of Convention) at Mr. John Penn the youngers. Drank Tea & spent the evening at my lodgings.

John Penn (1760–1834), son of Thomas Penn, grandson of William Penn, and a first cousin of John Penn of Lansdowne, returned from England to Philadelphia in 1784 and built a home, The Solitude, on the west bank of the Schuylkill, later incorporated into Fairmount Park. Penn probably also had a house in town. He returned to England in 1788, where he promoted philanthropic causes, including the Outinian Society to promote matrimony, although Penn himself died a bachelor (see SNYDER, 131–32).

Friday 20th.    In Convention. Dined at home and drank Tea at Mr. Clymers.

Saturday 21st.    In Convention. Dined at Springsbury with the Club of Gentn. & Ladies. Went to the Play afterwards.

The play was the tragedy *Edward and Eleanora,* by the Scots poet James Thomson (SEILHAMER, 2:221).

Sunday 22d.    Left Town by 5 oclock A.M. Breakfasted at Genl. Mifflins. Rode up with him & others to the Spring Mills and returned to Genl. Mifflins by Dinner after which proceeded to the City.

SPRING MILLS: Spring Mill was an old grist mill on the east side of the Schuylkill River, about two miles below Conshohocken in Montgomery County, Pa. It was powered by the combined waters from several springs in a small area. The diary of Peter Legaux, a French immigrant who lived near Spring Mill, has the following entry for this date: "This day Gen. Washington, Gen. Mifflin and four others of the Convention did us the honor of paying us a visit in order to see our vineyard and bee houses. In this they found great delight, asked a number of questions, and testified their highest approbation with my manner of managing bees" (BAKER [2], 84n).

Monday 23d.    In Convention as usual. Dined at Mr. Morris's and drank Tea at Lansdown (the Seat of Mr. Penn).

Landsdown *the Seat of the late* W.ᵐ Bingham Esq.ʳ *Pennsylvania.*

*Drawn Engraved & Published by W.Birch Springland near Bristol Pennsylv.ᵃ*

Lansdowne, home of former governor John Penn on the Schuylkill River. From W. Birch's *Country Seats of the United States*, Springfield, Pa., 1808. (Beinecke Rare Book and Manuscript Library, Yale University)

On this day GW wrote Elizabeth Powel that he would "do himself the honor of calling upon her at, or before 5. oclock (in his Carriage) in hopes [of] the pleasure of conducting her to Lansdown this Evening" (ViMtV).

**Tuesday 24th.** In Convention. Dined at Mr. Morris's and drank Tea, by appointment & partr. Invitation at Doctr. Rush's.

Dr. Benjamin Rush (1745–1813), republican and reformer, and an earnest supporter of the American cause, developed the practice and teaching of medicine in Philadelphia, where he was a center of medical controversy. He campaigned for the ratification of the Federal Constitution and in the early years of the new nation worked for reforms in the fields of prisons, insane asylums, poverty, education, and public medical care and campaigned for the abolition of slavery.

**Wednesday 25th.** In Convention. Dined at Mr. Morris's, drank Tea, & spent the evening there.

**Thursday 26th.** In Convention. Dined at Mr. Morris's, drank Tea there, and stayed within all the Afternoon.

**Friday 27th.** In Convention, which adjourned this day, to meet again on Monday the 6th. of August that a Comee. which had been appointed (consisting of 5 Members) might have time to arrange, and draw into method & form the several matters which had been agreed to by the Convention as a Constitution for the United States.

Dined at Mr. Morris's, and drank Tea at Mr. Powells.

Here GW was relying too much upon his memory, for his Philadelphia diary (see entry for 8 May 1787) had no notation of the date of adjournment, which was actually 26 July (FARRAND, 2:118, 128).

**Saturday 28th.** Dined with the Club at Springsbury. Drank Tea there and spent the Evening at my lodgings.

**Sunday 29th.** Dined and spent the whole day at Mr. Morris's principally in writing letters.

**Monday. 30th.** In company with Mr. Govr. Morris, and in his Phaeton with my horses; went up to one Jane Moores in the vicinity of Valley-forge to get Trout.

Before setting off on this fishing expedition GW, in a note to Mrs. Elizabeth Powel dated "Monday Morning," wrote: "Genl. Washington presents his respectful compliments to Mrs. Powell, and would, with great pleasure, have made one of a party for the *School* for *Scandal* this evening; had not everything been arranged, & Mr. Govr. Morris and himself on the point of stepping into the Carriage for a fishing expedition at Jenny Moores; at Which place Mr. & Mrs. Robt. Morris are to be tomorrow, to partake of the successes, of Mr. Govr. Morris & himself this day. The Genl. can but regret that matters have turned out so unluckily, after waiting so long to receive a lesson in the School for Scandal" ([30 July 1787], ViMtV) . Mrs. Jane Moore's Montgomery County farm bordered on Trout Creek and was within the old Valley Forge encampment (FREEMAN, 6:102) .

Tuesday 31st.    Whilst Mr. Morris was fishing I rid over the old Cantonment of the American [army] of the Winter 1777, & 8. Visited all the Works, wch. were in Ruins; and the Incampments in woods where the ground had not been cultivated.

On my return back to Mrs. Moores, observing some Farmers at Work, and entering into Conversation with them, I received the following information with respect to the mode of cultivating Buck Wheat, and the application of the grain. Viz.—The usual time of sowing, is from the 10th. to the 20th. of July—on two plowings and as many harrowings at least—The grain to be harrowed in. That it is considered as an uncertain Crop being subject to injury by a hot sun whilst it is in blossom and quickly destroyed by frost, in Autumn—and that 25 bushls. is estimated as an average Crop to the Acre. That it is considered as an excellent food for horses, to puff and give them their *first* fat—Milch cattle, Sheep, and Hogs and also for fatting Beeves. To do which, 2 quarts of Buck Wheat Meal, & half a peck of Irish Potatoes at the commencemt. (to be reduced as the appetite of the beasts decrease or in other words as they encrease in flesh) mixed and givn. 3 times a day is fully competent. That Buck wheat meal made into a wash is most excellent to lay on fat upon hogs but it must be hardened by feeding them sometime afterwards with Corn. And that this meal & Potatoes mixed is very good for Colts that are weaning. About 3 pecks of Seed is the usuall allowance for an Acre.

On my return to Mrs. Moores I found Mr. Robt. Morris & his lady there.

# August. [1787]

Wednesday 1st.    About 11 oclock, after it had ceased raining, we all set out for the City and dined at Mr. Morris's.

Thursday 2d.    Dined, Drank Tea, & Spent the Evening at Mr. Morris's.

**Friday 3d.** In company with Mr. Robt. Morris and his Lady and Mr. Gouvr. Morris I went up to Trenton on another Fishing party. Lodged at Colo. Sam Ogdens at the Trenton Works. In the Evening fished, not very successfully.

Samuel Ogden (1746–1810), an iron founder who had supplied iron products to GW's army during the Revolution, had also served as a colonel in the New Jersey militia. In 1775 he married Euphemia Morris, a younger sister of Gouverneur Morris (MINTZ, 39, 47, 70; SWIGGETT, 15, 48).

**Saturday 4th.** In the morning, and between breakfast & dinner, fished again with more success (for perch) than yesterday.

Dined at Genl. Dickenson's on the East side of the River a little above Trenton & returned in the evening to Colo. Ogden's.

Philemon Dickinson (1739–1809), a brother of John Dickinson, was a brigadier general and major general in the New Jersey militia and participated in the 1777 New Jersey campaign. In that year John Adams "walked . . . [from Trenton] to General Dickinsons House," which he found to be "a Scaene of Desolation" from the war (ADAMS [1], 2:264). In 1784 Jacob Hiltzheimer found Dickinson "busy looking after the stone house he is having built at the end of his wooden building, about a mile out of Trenton" (HILTZHEIMER, 65). Dickinson was John Cadwalader's second in a duel (4 July 1778) with Thomas Conway over the latter's criticism of GW's abilities as a general.

**Sunday 5th.** Dined at Colo. Ogdens, early; after which in the company with which I came, I returned to Philadelphia at which we arrived abt. 9 Oclk.

**Monday 6th.** Met, according to adjournment in Convention, & received the rept. of the Committee. Dined at Mr. Morris's and drank Tea at Mr. Meridiths.

**Tuesday 7th.** In convention. Dined at Mr. Morris's and spent the evening there also.

**Wednesday 8th.** In Convention. Dined at the City Tavern and remained there till near ten oclock.

**Thursday 9th.** In Convention. Dined at Mr. Swanwicks and spent the Afternn. in my own room—reading letters and accts. from home.

John Swanwick, who became a partner of Thomas Willing and Robert Morris in 1783, later served in the United States House of Representatives (1795–98).

Friday 10th.    Dined (after coming out of Convention) at Mr. Binghams and drank Tea there. Spent the evening at my lodgings.

Saturday 11th.    In Convention. Dined at the Club at Springsbury and after Ten returnd. home.

Sunday 12th.    Dined at Bush hill with Mr. William Hamilton. Spent the evening at home writing letters.

Monday 13th.    In Convention. Dined at Mr. Morris's, and drank Tea with Mrs. Bache, at the Presidents.

Sarah Franklin Bache (1744–1808), daughter of Benjamin Franklin and wife of Richard Bache (1737–1811), served as her father's hostess after his return from France to America in 1785.

Tuesday 14th.    In Convention. Dined, drank Tea, and spent the evening at home.

Wednesday 15th.    The same—as yesterday.

Thursday 16th.    In Convention. Dined at Mr. Pollocks & spent the evening in my chamber.

In 1790 Oliver Pollock lived on Chestnut Street below Sixth Street (HEADS OF FAMILIES, PA., 225).

Friday 17th.    In Convention. Dined and drank Tea at Mr. Powells.

Saturday 18th.    In Convention. Dined at Chief Justice McKeans. Spent the afternoon & evening at my lodgings.

Thomas McKean (1734–1817) began his law career in Delaware and in 1777 became chief justice of Pennsylvania, serving until 1799 when he was elected governor of Pennsylvania. In 1790 he lived on the east side of Third Street (HEADS OF FAMILIES, PA., 238).

Sunday 19th.    In company with Mr. Powell rode up to the white Marsh. Traversed my old Incampment, and contemplated on the dangers which threatned the American Army at that place. Dined at German town. Visited Mr. Blair McClenegan. Drank Tea at Mr. Peters's and returned to Philadelphia in the evening.

WHITE MARSH: about 12 miles north and west of Philadelphia, the last camp of GW's army (Nov.–Dec. 1777) before he moved his men to Valley Forge for the winter. See FREEMAN, 5: chap. 21. GERMAN TOWN: the scene of a confused battle between the Continental Army and the British (3–4 Oct. 1777) a few miles north of Philadelphia on the east side of the Schuylkill River. Blair McClenachan, a Philadelphia merchant, had bought Cliveden, the Chew country home in Germantown, from Benjamin Chew in 1779, which is probably where GW is visiting this day. In the American attack on Germantown this house, stubbornly held by British troops, was the center of intense fighting and cannonading by GW's troops.

Monday 20th.    In Convention. Dined, drank Tea and spent the evening at Mr. Morris['s].

Tuesday 21st.    Did the like this day also.

"We have lately made a rule to meet at ten and sit 'til four, which is punctually complied with" (David Brearley to William Paterson, 21 Aug. 1787, FARRAND, 3:73).

Wednesday 22d.    In Convention. Dined at Mr. Morris's farm at the Hills. Visited at Mr. Powells in the Afternoon.

Thursday 23d.    In Convention. Dined, drank Tea & spent the evening at Mr. Morris's.

Friday 24th.    Did the same this day.

Saturday 25th.    In Convention. Dined with the Club at Springsbury & spent the afternoon at my lodgings.

Sunday 26th.    Rode into the Country for exercise 8 or 10 miles. Dined at the Hills and spent the evening in my chamber writing letters.

Monday 27th.    In Convention. Dined at Mr. Morris's and drank Tea at Mr. Powells.

Tuesday 28th.    In Convention. Dined, drank Tea, and spent the evening at Mr. Morris's.

Wednesday 29th.    Did the same as yesterday.

Thursday 30th.    Again the same.

Friday 31st.    In Convention. Dined at Mr. Morris's and with a Party went to Lansdale & drank Tea with Mr. & Mrs. Penn.

LANSDALE: Lansdowne. John Penn's wife, Ann Allen Penn, was the daughter of William Allen, the former chief justice of Pennsylvania.

## September. [1787]

Saturday 1st.    Dined at Mr. Morris after coming out of Convention and drank Tea there.

Sunday 2d.    Rode to Mr. Bartrams and other places in the Country, dined & drank Tea at Grays ferry and returned to the City in the evening.

Monday 3d.    In Convention. Visited a Machine at Doctr. Franklins (called a mangle) for pressing, in place of Ironing, clothes from the wash. Which Machine from the facility with which it dispatches business is well calculated for Table cloths & such Articles as have not pleats & irregular foldings and would be very useful in all large families. Dined, drank Tea, & spent the evening at Mr. Morris's.

Tuesday. 4th.    In Convention. Dined &ca. at Mr. Morris's.

Wednesday 5th.    In Convention. Dined at Mrs. Houses & drank Tea at Mr. Binghams.

Benjamin Franklin from Charles Willson Peale's mezzotint, executed in 1787 and hung at Mount Vernon during Washington's lifetime. (Mount Vernon Ladies' Association of the Union)

Thursday 6th.    In Convention. Dined at Doctr. Hutchinson's and spent the afternoon and evening at Mr. Morris's.

Dr. James Hutchinson (1752–1793) lived on south Second Street between Walnut and Spruce streets (*Pa. Mag.*, 11 [1887], 307). He was surgeon general of Pennsylvania (1778–84), taught at the University of Pennsylvania, and died while fighting the 1793 yellow fever epidemic in Philadelphia.

Friday 7th.    In Convention. Dined and spent the afternoon at home (except when riding a few Miles).

Saturday 8th.    In Convention. Dined at Springsbury with the Club and spent the evening at my lodgings.

Sunday 9th.    Dined at Mr. Morris's after making a visit to Mr. Gardoqui who as he says came from New York on a visit to me.

Today GW wrote George Augustine Washington that he thought the convention would adjourn within a week. "God grant I may not be disappointed in this expectation, as I am quite homesick" (John Rylands Library, Manchester, Eng.).

On 19 May 1787 Diego de Gardoqui (1735–1798), Spanish representative in the United States, wrote GW from New York requesting "the honor of a personal acquaintance with your Excellency" (DLC:GW). GW replied on 31 May: "I look with much pleasure to the moment which promises me the honor of a personal acquaintance with your Excellency" (DLC:GW). Gardoqui was in the third year of frustrating negotiations regarding American rights to navigate the lower Mississippi River, which then ran through Spanish territory. GW's cryptic entry here may reflect his concern at being dragged into the emotional and nationally divisive debate of "the *Spanish negociation*," lately described as being "in a very *ticklish situation*" (James Madison to Thomas Jefferson, 23 April 1787, MADISON, 9:400; see also GW to Gardoqui, 28 Nov. 1787, DLC:GW).

Monday. 10th.    In Convention. Dined at Mr. Morris's & drank Tea there.

Tuesday 11th.    In Convention. Dined at home in a large Company with Mr. Gardoqui. Drank Tea and spent the evening there.

Wednesday 12th.    In Convention. Dined at the Presidents and drank Tea at Mr. Pines.

Thursday 13th.    Attended Convention. Dined at the Vice Presidents Chas. Biddles. Drank Tea at Mr. Powells.

Charles Biddle (c.1745–1821) was the son of William Biddle, a native of New Jersey, and Mary Scull Biddle of Pennsylvania. When Biddle was chosen vice-president of the Supreme Executive Council of Pennsylvania in 1785 he was living on Front Street. He later moved to a house on Chestnut Street below Fifth Street.

**Friday 14th.** Attended Convention. Dined at the City Tavern, at an entertainmt. given on my acct. by the City light Horse. Spent the evening at Mr. Meridiths.

**Saturday 15th.** Concluded the business of Convention, all to signing the proceedings; to effect which the House sat till 6 Oclock; and adjourned till Monday that the Constitution which it was proposed to offer to the People might be engrossed and a number of printed copies struck off. Dined at Mr. Morris's & spent the evening there.

Mr. Gardoqui set off for his return to New York this forenoon.

**Sunday 16th.** Wrote many letters in the forenoon. Dined with Mr. & Mrs. Morris at the Hills & returned to town in the Eveng.

**Monday 17th.** Met in Convention when the Constitution received the Unanimous assent of 11 States and Colo. Hamilton's from New York (the only delegate from thence in Convention) and was subscribed to by every Member present except Govr. Randolph and Colo. Mason from Virginia & Mr. Gerry from Massachusetts. The business being thus closed, the Members adjourned to the City Tavern, dined together and took a cordial leave of each other—after which I returned to my lodgings—did some business with, and received the papers from the secretary of the Convention, and retired to meditate on the momentous wk. which had been executed, after not less than five, for a large part of the time Six, and sometimes 7 hours sitting every day, sundays & the ten days adjournment to give a Comee. opportunity & time to arrange the business for more than four Months.

Elbridge Gerry (1744–1814), one of the most active delegates in the convention and a frequent advocate of compromise, listed a series of objections to his signing the completed document (see FARRAND, 2:632–33, 635–36, 646–47, 649). Other delegates besides the three mentioned by GW opposed the Constitution, but they had already left the convention.

THE PAPERS: "Major Jackson, after burning all the loose scraps of paper which belong to the Convention, will this evening wait upon the General with the Journals and other papers which their vote directs to be delivered to His Excellency" (William Jackson to GW, 17 Sept. 1787, DLC:GW).

Tuesday 18th.    Finished what private business I had to do in the City this forenoon. Took my leave of those families in wch. I had been most intimate. Dined early at Mr. Morris's with whom & Mr. Gouvr. Morris I parted at Grays ferry and reached Chester in Company with Mr. Blair who I invited to a seat in my Carriage 'till we should reach Mount Vernon.

Wednesday 19th.    Prevented by rain (much of which fell in the Night) from setting off till about 8 Oclock, when it ceased, & promising to be fair we departed. Baited at Wilmington—dined at Christiana and lodged at the head of Elk—at the bridge near to which my horses (two of them) and Carriage had a very narrow escape. For the rain which had fallen the preceeding evening having swelled the Water considerably there was no fording it safely. I was reduced to the necessity therefore of remaining on the other side or of attempting to cross on an old, rotten & long disused bridge. Being anxious to get on I preferred the latter and in the attempt one of my horses fell 15 feet at least the other very near following which (had it happened) would have taken the Carriage with baggage along with him and destroyed the whole effectually. However, by prompt assistance of some people at a Mill just by and great exertion, the first horse was disengaged from his harness, the 2d. prevented from going quite through and drawn off and the Carriage rescued from hurt.

Thursday. 20th.    Sett off after an early breakfast. Crossed the Susquehanna and dined in Havre de gras at the House of one Rogers and lodged at Skirretts Tavern 12 Miles short of Baltimore.

HOUSE OF ONE ROGERS: John Rodgers's ferry house was at this time on the east bank of the Susquehanna River at Perryville. GW must have dined at a house Rodgers still owned on the west bank. He at one time owned a house on what is now W. Washington Street and an estate, Sion Hill, near the river, two and one half miles off the main highway (W.P.A. [2], 323).

Friday 21st.    Breakfasted in Baltimore—dined at the Widow Balls (formerly Spurriers) and lodged at Major Snowdens who was not at home.

SPURRIERS: site of the town of Waterloo in Howard County, Md., twice chosen during the Revolution as an encampment for Rochambeau's army (RICE, 1:160, 2: pl. 128).

Saturday 22d.    Breakfasted at Bladensburgh and passing through George Town dined in Alexandria and reached home (with Mr. Blair) about Sunset after an absence of four Months and 14 days.

The following
Is a diary of the Weather, occurrances on, and management of, my farms; together with the progress of the Crops thereon, during my absence; as taken & reported to me by my Nepw. G. A. Washington.

M.  N.  Night

Wednesday 9th. May.    Thermometer—50—65—58.  Morning Cloudy—afternoon from 2 to 4 Showery.

Began to plant Corn in the commn. way at the Ferry on Monday last. Nearly finished it to day. The drill corn nearly finished planting at this place. A few fish heads, guts &ca. ordered to be put into some of the Corn hills, to try the effect of them as a manure. Two plows preparing for the planting of Potatoes Pease &ca. at Frenchs.

At Frenchs the people were still in the swamp at work and two ploughs breaking up, and the harrow preparing ground designed for Turnips &ca.

At Dogue run. Finished planting the Corn in the small field by Frenchs & began to plant Pumpkins in the angles of the fence around the drilled Corn—4 plows preparing for Parsnips—1 sent to the Shop.

NOTE. After entering upon the above, it was found that too much time for my convenience, would be required either to insert the report as it had been made, or to make a proper digest of it; and therefore both are declined. The reports must accompany this volume and be refered to as part thereof, for the purpose of information as above whilst I continue my own diary from the day on which I returned home.

# [September 1787]

Sunday. 23d.    Thermometer at 60 in the morning—70 at Noon and 70 at N. Foggy Morning—calm & clear afterwards.

Mr. Blair remained. Colonels Fitzgerald, Simms, Ramsay &

Lyles; Mr. Hunter, Mr. Murray & Mr. Taylor and Doctr. Stuart, Mrs. Stuart, and the girls came to dinner: All, except Mr. Blair, Doctr. & Mrs. Stuart went away afterwards.

Monday. 24th.　Thermometer at 62 in the Morning—70 at Noon and 70 at Night.

Wind Westerly with some Clouds. After breakfast I rid to the Plantatns. at the Ferry—Frenchs—Dogue run & Muddy hole.

At the first, the hands were getting out Wheat & Rye; and the Plows were putting in Wheat in field No. 6.

At the next, 4 plows were putting in Rye in No. 6 and the rest of the hds. grubbing in the New Meadow.

At Dogue run the plows were covering Wheat in No. 6 and the other hands employed chiefly in grubbing the Swamp between the upper Meadows.

At Muddy hole the Plows were (3 of them) following for Wheat in No. 4—the other people gathering fodder.

In the Afternoon Doctr. Stuart, Mrs. Stuart & the Girls returned to Abingdon.

Tuesday 25th.　Thermometer at 62 in the Morning—68 at Noon and 64 at Night. Calm in the Morning—cloudy afterwards—wind, what there was of it—So. Wt.

Mr. Blair left this before Sun rise in my carriage which carried him to the junction of the Roads at Boggess' where he met the Stage.

After breakfast I rode into the Neck—hands chiefly employed in getting fodder.

Robert Boggess's house was on the Cameron-Colchester stage road, at the intersection of the road from Gum Springs.

Wednesday 26th.　Thermometer at 63 in the Morning—74 at Noon and 72 at Night. Foggy morning—calm, & clear for the most part of the day.

Rid to all the Plantations—the hands at each employed nearly as they were yesterday.

Thursday 27th.　Thermometer at 68 in the morning—76 at Noon and 74 at Night. Cloudy in the Morning—clear afterwards—wind at South all day.

Visited all the Plantations—same employment at each as yesterday.

Friday 28th.    Thermometer at 62 in the Morning—66 at Noon and 65 at Night. Clear all day with variable winds.

Rid to the Plantations at the Ferry, Frenchs, Dogue run, and Muddy hole—engaged in the same work at each.

Mrs. Jenifer came here to dinner.

Saturday 29th.    Thermometer at 54 in the Morning—62 at Noon and 62 at Night. Clear all day, with the Wind at No. Wt.

Rid into the Neck and set Six plows to breaking up the Orchard Inclosure (wch. was an Oat Stubble) for Wheat & grass Seeds, &ca.

After Breakfast Mr. Corbin Washington and his wife, and Miss Fanny Ballendine (who came here on Thursday afternoon) returned and after dinner Majr. G. A. Washington left this for Fredericksbg.

Sunday 30th.    Thermometer at 57 in the Morning—66 at Noon and 62 at Night. Clear all day with the wind at No. Wt. in the morning & Southerly afterwards.

# October [1787]

October 1st.    Thermometer at 56 in the Morning—64 at Noon and 62 at Night—Cloudy in the Morning but clear afterwds. with variable winds.

Mrs. Fanny Washington, and the Children, and Mrs. Jenifer went up to Abingdon.

Colo. Gilpin and Mr. Willm. Craik dined here. The latter stayed all Night.

Rid to all the Plantations. Work at each as usual except that the Plows at Dogue run were putting in rye in field No. 6. North part of it.

Daniel Overdonck & 5 Negro Ditche[r]s went to work at Muddy hole to ditch between fields—3 & 4.

Mr. Craik went away very early this morning.

Tuesday 2d.    Thermometer at 55 in the Morning—70 at Noon and 67 at Night. Cloudy in the Morning & clear afterwards—Wind No. Et. in the forenoon & Southerly afterwards.

Rid to all the Plantations. Sent 2 plows from Frenchs to Muddy hole—The other two preparing a piece of ground which had been twice plowed before on the side of the Meadow for Rye & grass

Seeds—on which 1½ B. of Rye was sown and therewith on the No. part of the grd. 1½ Bushls. of Sainfoin & 6 lbs. of Trafoil adjoining the Road. The lower part of the grd. had 2 quarts of Timothy Seed sown with the Rye.

**Wednesday 3d.**   Thermometer at 62 in the Morning 70 at Noon & 67 at Night. Foggy Morning but clear afterwards. Westerly Wind in the forenoon & No. Wt. afterwards.

Went up with Mrs. Washington to Abingdon. Dined at Mr. Herberts in Alexandria on our way.

MRS. WASHINGTON TO ABINGDON: appears in the manuscript as "Mrs. Abingdon to Washington."

**Thursday. 4th.**   Thermometer at 50 in the Morning 60 at Noon and 60 at Night. Clear all day, Wind Northerly in the forenoon & Southerly afterwards.

Dined at Abingdon and came home in the afternoon. Brot. Fanny Washington with us.

Found two more plows from Frenchs at work at Muddy hole.

**Friday 5th.**   Thermometer at 50 in the Morning—70 at Noon and 67 at Night. Clear all day with the Wind at South.

Rid to all the Plantations. Having finished sowing Rye at Dogue run, 22½ Bushels, sent one of the Plows to Muddy hole. The rest of the horses, & hands, were employed in treading out wheat—the Fodder there being also secured.

Finding it in vain to attempt following the whole of No. 4 for Wheat, I quitted breaking up any more till the whole should be crossed, and accordingly set all the plows to the latter work.

In the Afternoon Mr. Alexr. Donald came in.

On 12 Nov. 1787 Alexander Donald wrote to Thomas Jefferson of this visit: "I staid two days with General Washington at Mount Vernon about Six weeks ago. He is in perfect good health, and looks almost as well as he did Twenty years ago. I never saw him so keen for any thing in my life, as he is for the adoption of the new Form of Government. As the eyes of all America are turned towards this truly Great and Good Man, for the First President, I took the liberty of sounding him upon it. He appears to be greatly against going into Publick Life again, Pleads in Excuse for himself, His Love of Retirement, and his advanced Age, but Notwithstanding of these, I am fully of opinion he may be induced to appear once more on the Publick Stage of Life. I form my opinion from what passed between us in a very long and serious conversation as well as from what I could gather from Mrs. Washington on the same subject" (JEFFERSON [1], 12:345–48).

Saturday 6th.　　Thermometer at 56 in the Morning—72 at Noon & 70 at Night. Clear all day with the Wind at South.

Rid to the Plantations at the Ferry, Frenchs, Dogue run, and Muddy hole.

At the first, having got out all the Wheat & Rye, the fodder next claimed attention and was accordingly set about.

Colo. McCarty & his wife; Mrs. Craik and her daughters Mrs. Jenifer & Mariamne; and Mrs. Ann Jenifer came here to dinner & returned afterwards. Towards evening Mr. & Mrs. Powell of Philadelphia came in.

MRS. CRAIK: In the original Philadelphia journal GW had written "Mrs. Craik & Sally & two Mrs. Jenifers came." Sally was, of course, Mrs. Sarah Craik Jenifer. He made the correction when copying the entry into the final version.

Sunday 7th.　　Thermometer at 58 in the Morning—70 at Noon and 63 at Night. Clear in the forenoon & cloudy afterwards with variable Winds.

After breakfast Mr. Donald went away and whilst we were at dinnr. Mr. Bushrod Washington & his wife came in.

Monday. 8th.　　Thermometer at 56 in the Morning—56 at Noon & 56 at Night. Cloudy all day with the Wind at No. Et. & Et.

Julia Ann (Nancy) Blackburn Washington, wife of Washington's nephew Bushrod. (The Supreme Court of the United States)

Rid with Mr. Powell to my Plantations at Muddy hole, Dogue run Frenchs & the Ferry.

Work going as usual.

Tuesday 9th.　Thermometer at 56 in the Morning—59 at Noon & 57 at Night. Clouds, Mists & Sunshine alternately. Wind at So. Et. & So.

Rid with Mr. & Mrs. Powell to view the Ruins of Belvoir.

Called on my return at Frenchs where I had begun with grass Scythes (a cradle having been found not to answr.) to cut the Pease which had been sown broadcast. The first sowing of these appeared pretty ripe, & the vines pretty full. The others were quite green. Whether this is owing to their being too late sown—or to the drought which kept them back I am unable to determine—to the latter however it is ascribed. In cutting these vines, the Pods of many of them were left without means of getting them up without picking them by hand. Hence it is evident that the Surface of the grd. after the Pease are sown ought by rolling and otherwise to be laid quite smooth that it might be raked easily and effectually. Without this many of them will always be lost—left at least on the ground where they would be excellent for falling weathers which would undoubtedly glean them compleatly—but [in] this case there should be nothing in the same enclosure that they can injure or destroy. Raked the Pease into small heaps.

Finished ditching up to the lane by the Overseers house.

Doctr. Griffith came in and stayed all Night.

Wednesday 10th.　Thermometer at 52 in the Morning—63 at Noon & 60 at Night. Clear with variable Winds.

Mr. & Mrs. Powell, Mr. Bushrod Washington & wife, and Mr. Griffith going away after an early breakfast I rid to all the Plantations and found the same work at ea. going forward.

Thursday 11th.　Thermometer at 54 in the morning—64 at Noon and 62 at Night. Foggy Morning & clear afterwards—wd. at N. Wt. & Wt. all day.

Rid to all the Plantations. Began to sow Wheat and Sainfoin in the orchard in the Neck—the ground being first plowed—then crossed—on which the Wheat was sown and harrowed in with a heavy harrow the way it was last plowed—then followed the Sainfoin and harrowed in the same way, with the same harrow—so that, on the whole the Oat Stubble had two plowings and two harrowings.

Charles Cotesworth Pinckney, by John Trumbull. (Yale University Art Gallery)

Finding the Pease at Muddy hole riper than the latter sowed ones at Frhs. I ordered the Scythes there to morrow leaving the greenest for the last to see if they would fill & ripen more.

In the evening Genl. Pinkney and his Lady came in on their return to South Carolina from the Federal Convention.

Friday 12th.    Thermometer at 56 in the Morning—62 at Noon and 60 at Night. Weather clear and Winds variable—viz. N.E.: N.W. & S.W.

Genl. Pinkney and Lady going away after breakfast I rid to Muddy hole Dogue Run & Frenchs.

At the first finding great waste in Cutting the Pease (owing as has been observed to the cloddy & uneven surface of the grd.) I attempted to pull them by hand but found it so tedious as to oblige me to return to the Scythes notwithstanding the loss.

Sent the Plows belonging to Frenchs and Dogue run to their respective plantations.

Saturday 13th.    Thermometer at 52 in the Morning—62 at Noon and 56 at Night. Cloudy in the Morning and clear afterwds. with the Wind at No. Wt.

Rid to Dogue run, French's & the ferry Plantns.

At the two first took an Acct. of the Horses Cattle and Sheep wch. are as follow—viz.—

At Dogue run.

| | | Horses height | Age | | |
|---|---|---|---|---|---|
| Dabster | a grey | 14½ | 10 | ⎫ | |
| Columbus | bay | 14 Camp | | ⎬ Ploughers Horss. | |
| | bay | 14¼ Ferry | | ⎭ . . . . 3 | |
| | bro: bay | 14½ Camp | | ⎫ | |
| | 2d. bodd. Do. | 13¼ | | ⎪ | |
| | Milk & Cydr. | 14¼ | | ⎬ Working Horses | |
| | Bay | | | ⎪ | |
| | Dark bro: | | | ⎭ . . . . 5 | |
| A Bay Mare, stabled at Mansn. Ho[use] last year | | 14½ | 10 | ⎫ | |
| A Black—blaze face 2 hind feet white | | | | ⎪ | |
| A bay, off hind foot whe. | | | | ⎪ | |
| A bla. Snip & Star—2 hind feet white | | | | ⎪ | |
| From Milk & Cyder. | | | | ⎪ | |
| Bay—Stabled last year | | 13½ | 4 | ⎬ Mares unbroken—or not used | |
| Bay. like her, rather Smaller No white | | | | ⎪ | |
| Chesnut—likely | | | | ⎪ | |
| Bay—No white | | | 3 | ⎪ | |
| Bay. blaze—near fore and 2 hind feet wh[it]e | | | | ⎪ | |
| Sorrel—no white | | | 1 | ⎭ . . . . 11 | |
| Bay. stabled last year | | | 4 | | |
| Grey, breaking | | | | | |
| Sorrel—sml. Star—2 fore feet light—not wh[it]e | | | 1 | . . . . 3 | |
| Bay. horse colt sml. Star | | | spg. | | |
| Bay. Mare Do. no white | | | Do. | | |
| Yellow bay—blaze face | | | Do. | . . . . 3 | |

Not belongg. to the Plantn.

| old Partner | ⎫ | Charr[io]t Horses | |
|---|---|---|---|
| Old Valiant | ⎬ | | |
| Jersey—Mare | ⎫ | | |
| Augusta Do—bay | ⎭ | . . . . 4 | |

In all . . . . 29

## Cattle

| | | | |
|---|---|---|---|
| Oxen | | | 7 |
| Cows | in the pasture | 20 | |
| | at home house | 2 | |
| | Mill besides a calf | 1 | 23 |
| Heifers | 4 years old | 1 | |
| | 3 years old | 0 | |
| | 2 Do. Do. | 5 | |
| | 1 Do. Do. | 8 | |
| | Calves (cows) | 11 | 25 |
| Steers | 4 years old | 5 | |
| | 3 Do. Do. | 8 | |
| | 2 Do. Do. | 6 | |
| | 1 Do. Do. | 1 | |
| | Bull Calves | 6 | 26 |
| Bulls | 4 yrs. old | 1 | |
| | 1 Do. Do. | 1 | 2 |
| | | | 83 |

Calf at the Mill . . . . . . . . . . 1

In all . . . 84

1 Steer—&
1 Cow ⎫ on the M: Meadw. for Sla:

Sheep—of all sorts . . . . . . . . . . 99

## At French's
## Horses.

The same as had from Robinson, and particularly ⎫
enumerated and described the 1st. day of Jany. ⎬ 11
last, as registered in the Diary of that date ⎭

A Sorrel horse colt last Spring from the Sorrel Mare    1

in all . . . 12

## Cattle.

| | | | |
|---|---|---|---|
| Oxen | | | 4 |
| Cows | (Includg. the Farmers) | | 7 |
| Heifers | 1 year old | | 1 |
| | cow calves | | 3 |
| Steers | 1 year old | | 4 |
| | spring calves | | 1 |
| | In all | | 20 |

Sheep . . . . . in all . . . . 29

At French's sowed a narrow slipe of the grd. off which Pease had been taken next the Meadow Ditch with Wheat. The Wheat was sown on the ground without breaking and plowed in which it did in a very mellow & pulverized state, although the grd. in common never was drier or harder to work. In short, had the grd. been often plowed it could not have been in a better state of culture than it appeared (as did the whole field) to be in—which evinces, if Pease is not an exhauster, that land cannot be better prepared for an Autumnal sowing than by raising a crop of them previous thereto.

Finished cutting, and putting into small heaps the Pease at Muddy hole.

Sunday 14th.    Thermometer at 50 in the Morning—60 at Noon and 56 at Night—weather clear—Wind at No. W. in the Morning, & So. Wt. in the afternoon; A severe frost this Morning, which killed Pease Buckwheat, Pumpkins, Potatoe Vines &ca. turning them quite bla[ck].

Monday. 15th.    Thermometer at 52 in the Morning 56 at Noon and 52 at Night. Clear all day—Wind at So. Wt. in the Morning and at No. Wt. afterwards.

Ordered the Buckwheat to be immediately cut—beginning with that at Dogue run (abt. 12 Acres) which was accordingly done this forenoon (when the frost was likewise severe) before the moisture was off the Straw. Put the Buck Wheat, as cut (with scythe and cradle) into small heaps to dry. Note—Whether this grain has std. out too long, or not I am not sufficiently acquainted with the nature of it to decide. There appeared to be as much shattered on the grd. as fully to sow it again, & at the same time there was at least as much Green Seed as had shed & many Blossums also on the Straw.

Rid to Muddy hole and into the Neck. Took an Acct. of the Horses Cattle and sheep at each as follow.

### In the Neck.
### Horses.

| | | | age | | |
|---|---|---|---|---|---|
| Doctor | white | 15 hands | 12 | | |
| Prentis | dark bay | 15 | 16 | | |
| Randolph | grey | 14½ | 9 | | |
| Jack | Black | 15 | 11 | Plow Horses | |
| Grunt | Bright bay | 14½ | 12 | | |
| Pompey | Dark bay | 14½ | 9 | | |
| Dick | Dingy bay | 14½ | 5 | | |
| Ranger | Black | 14 | 5 | | |
| Diamond | White | 14 | 10 | | |
| Possum | Flea bittn. grey | 15½ | 9 | | |
| | | | | . . . | 10 |
| Betsy | Bay | 14½ | 10 | | |
| Fanny | Black | 15 | 11 | | |
| Betsy | Dun | 13½ | 15 | | |
| Kate | Brown | 14 | 11 | Work Mares | |
| Punch | Grey | 14½ | 10 | | |
| Jenny | Grey | 14 | 12 | | |
| Patience | Bright B. | 13 | 15 | | |
| Brandy | Black | 13½ | 9 | | |
| Nancy | Sorrel | 14½ | 9 | . . . | 9 |
| Davys | M: Bla. | 14½ | 13 | . . . | 1 |

| | |
|---|---|
| A Brown or black – 14½ – 4 years right hind foot White sml. Star | |
| A Black – 13 hds. – 5 yrs. Sml. Star | |
| A black. 13 hands – 3 yrs. old white all fours – blaze fa. | Unbroke Horss. |
| A black Colt: 1 year old blaze face right fore foot white & the left hind ft. do. | |
| A Bay gelding 1 yr. old no white handsome | |
| A Bay Stallion Colt – Ho. | |

. . . 6

| |
|---|
| A Black 14 hands. 4 yrs. old |
| A Brown 13½ Do. 3 yrs. two hind feet white – right eye wh[it]e |
| A Bla: 13 hands. 2 yrs. old. Star and right hind foot white |
| A White 14 hands 4 yrs. old. |

. . . 4

Horses  .  .  In all  .  .  .  30

Cattle

| | | | | |
|---|---|---|---|---|
| Oxen | | | | 8 |
| Cows | | 15 yrs. old | 1 | |
| | | 12.Do. | 2 | |
| | | 11.Do. | 1 | |
| | | 10.Do. | 1 | |
| | | 9.Do. | 4 | |
| | | 8.Do. | 3 | |
| | | 7.Do. | 2 | |
| | | 6.Do. | 11 | |
| | | 5.Do. | 4 | |
| | | unknown | 1 | |
| | | at the Mansn. Ho[use] | 10 | |
| | | | | 40 |
| Heifers | | 4 Years old | 7 | |
| | | 3 Do. | 3 | |
| | | 2 Do. | 9 | |
| | | 1 Do. | 15 | |
| | | Calves | 11 | |
| | | | | 45 |
| Steers | | 7 Years old | 4 | |
| | | 6 Do. | 2 | |
| | | 5 Do. | 3 | |
| | | 4 Do. | 2 | |
| | | 3 Do. | 1 | |
| | | 2 Do. | 5 | |
| | | 1 Do. | 4 | |
| | | Calves | 6 | |
| | | | | 27 |
| Bulls | | 4 Years old | 1 | |
| | | 3 Ditto | 1 | |
| | | 1 Ditto | 2 | |
| | | | | 4 |

On the Plantn. to be accounted for          124

Besides the above
1 Cow & Calf to the Farmer          2
2 Cows & 2 Calves to G. A. W.          4
                                          6

Fattg. at the Mill Meadow.  Steers    5
                            Cows    3
                                          8

Not on the Plantation          14

Sheep.

In great Pasture . . . . . . . . 92
    River Ditto . . . . . . . . . 83
    Field—No. 1 . . . . . . . . . 24

                                     . . 199

Stock at Muddy hole
Horses

Diamond H[orse]
Jockey Do.
Dobbin Do.
Phoenix M[are]           Plow beasts . . . .   6
Jenny Do.
Old Fly Do.

A Grey mare; old—with foal by the Jack 13½
    hands high
A bay Mare 13½ hands said to be 8 yrs. old—no
    white
A bay (brandy) 13½ hands with foal by the Jack.
    Slender—2 hd. feet white—narrow blaze &
    Snip—8 or 9 yrs. old.
a dark bay (Jenny) 13½—6 or 7 yrs. old & un-
    sightly a small streak & Snip—2 hind feet white
A Brown Mare (Simpson) 14 hands—5 years old.
A Bay 13½ hands—7 yrs. old slight & unsightly—
    a small star 2 hind feet and off fore foot white.
A Bay not 13 hands. 7 yrs. old with a very dim &
    sml. Star.
A Grey 2 yrs. old well grown & strong, but not
    sightly
A Grey 14 hands—9 yrs. old Slight
A dark brown or black (it was not noted whether
    horse or mare) 2 yrs. old—near fore & hind foot
    w. very small Star.
A Sorrel—1 year old no wh. sent from the house
A Sorrel 1 year old, blaze face 4 feet white
A Brown spring colt from Simpson—got in the
    Woods

Unbroke Mares & M. Colts

                                       . . 13

A Bay 2 yrs. old—a very dim and small Star—but one eye near fore, & off hind foot white—small but tolerably likely.

A black 2 yrs. old—small & unsightly—no white but the off hind foot.

A Sorrel year old Colt from Phoenix—got by Magnolio No white.

A [      ] year old from brandy blaze face—2 hind feet White—wall eye & not sightly.

A [      ] spring Colt—no white except a very dim Star small but sightly—got by Magnolio

Unbroke Horse Colts

. . 5

In all . . 24

### Cattle.

| | | | | |
|---|---|---|---|---|
| Oxen | | | | . . 6 |
| Cows | 6 yrs. old | 3 | | |
| | 4 Do. | 6 | | |
| | | | | . . 9 |
| Heifers | 2 Do. | 1 | | |
| | 1 Do. | 2 | | |
| | Calves | 3 | | . . 6 |
| Steers | 4 Years old | 1 | | |
| | 3 Ditto | 2 | | |
| | 2 Ditto | 1 | | |
| | Calves | 3 | | . . 7 |
| Bulls | 2 yrs. old | 1 | | |
| | 1 Do. | 3 | | . . 4 |
| At Mansn. House | Cow | | | . . 1 |
| | To be accounted for | | | . . 33 |

| | |
|---|---|
| Fatting—Steers | 4 |
| Cows | 1 |
| In the Mill Meadw | 5 |

### Sheep.

| | |
|---|---|
| Rams | 1 |
| Weathers | 3 |
| Ewes | 17 |
| In all— | 21 |

Finished Sowing the Orchard in the Neck with Wheat & Sainfoin seed. Of the first it took [      ] bushels and of the latter [      ]

bushels. Note—This grd. has been plowed & cross plowed—then Wheat sown & harrowed in—with the heavy harrow—Next sown with Sainfoin and harrowed in like manner (both the way the ground was plowed last) —after which 50 lbs. of Trefoil was sown over the whole and harrowed with the double harrows cross the former.

Tuesday 16th.    Thermometer at 46 in the Morning 50 at Noon and 46 at Night. Clear all day with the Wind at No. Wt. & fresh.

Rid to the Ferry, French's Dogue run & Muddy hole Plantations.

At the former took an Acct. of the Horses—Cattle & Sheep as follow.

### Horses.

Note—The Acct. of the Horses being mis-laid, cannot be entered here; but will come in when a fresh one can be taken—see Decr. 15th. 1787.

### Cattle

| | | | |
|---|---|---|---|
| Oxen | | | 5 |
| Bulls—4 yrs. old | | 1 | |
| 2 Do. | | 1 | |
| | | | 2 |
| Cows | 8 years old | 2 | |
| | 7 Ditto | 3 | |
| | 6 Ditto | 3 | |
| | 5 Ditto | 2 | |
| | | | 10 |
| Heifers | 4 years old | 3 | |
| | 3 Ditto | 2 | |
| | 2 Ditto | 2 | |
| | Calves | 7 | |
| | | | 14 |
| Steers | 5 years old | 1 | |
| | 4 Ditto | 3 | |
| | 3 Ditto | 8 | |
| | 2 Ditto | 5 | |
| | Calves | 2 | |
| | | | 19 |
| | On the Plantatn. to be accd. | | 50 |

Besides the above.

Cows with the Farmrs. . . . . . . 1
In the Meadw. fattg. . . . . . . 2

     . . . 3

Steers    Do.   Do. . . . . . . . . . . 1
Oxen . . . . . . . . . . . . . . . 2

Not in care of the Overr. . . . 6

Sheep.

Rams . . . . . . 1
Wethers—old . . . . 1
      young . . . 20
Ewes . . . . . . . 19 . . . 41

At Muddy hole put the Buck Wht. which was this day cut into very small heaps and dug the Country Potatoes which measured as follow from the half Acre of experimental ground (the half of which had received dung—viz. 50 Bushels) —viz.—The No. Wt. quarter of the Piece, which had been dunged, and was in hills, yielded 4 bushels of eatable, and 3½ which were fit only for seed. The So. Wt. quarter also in hills but not dunged yielded 2½ Eatable & 3½ Seed. The No. Et. quarter which had been dunged & was in 4 feet drills produced 2½ eatable and 2 of Seed and the So. Et. Quarter 2½ eatable and 2 of Seed. In the whole 11½ of eatable and 11 of Seed. The Potatoes in the dunged part of the ground were much the largest and yielded

|  | eatable |  | seed |
|---|---|---|---|
| from the Hills . . . . . . | 4 B. | & | 3½ |
| In 4 feet rows | 2½ |  | 2 |
|  | 6½ |  | 5½ |
| Undunged |  |  |  |
| In Hills . . . . . . | 2½ |  | 3½ |
| 4 feet Rows . . . . . . | 2½ |  | 2 |
|  | 5 |  | 5½ |
| difference | 1½ |  |  |
|  | 6½ |  | 5½ |

Note.

Upon remeasurg. of these after they came to the Mansion House they turned out (heaped measure) only 7½ Bushls. of eatable and 10½ of Seed.

Short in the eatable     4 bush.
Seed     ½    4½

Whether this was occasioned by the difference of measure or theft of the Carter is not certain.

At Dogue run Treading out And at French's plowing and filling up Gullies in the New Meadow.

At the Ferry pulling Pease.

Wednesday 17. Thermometer at 40 in the Morning—50 at Noon and 46 at Night. Clear all day with the Wind at No. Wt.

Rid to all the Plantations except the Ferry.

In the Neck cut the Buck Wheat. a good deal of which shattered but perhaps (it is a grain I am not accustomed to) not more than common & therefore I cannot undertake to decide whether it stood too long or not. Finished getting in the fodder at this place (which concluded this business at all the places—Sowed as yesterday and to day (Wind preventing it sooner) 50 lbs. of Trefoil on the Wheat and Sainfoin in the Orchard in the Neck and began to sow at the No. Wt. Corner of this enclosure under furrow the Winter Vetches crossing by so doing the first plowing after which a light harrow followed to level the ground.

The Pease in broad cast at French's were much injured by the frost. It was unfortunate that they had not been cut a day or two sooner.

### Note.

The ground in which Pease and Buck Wheat are sown ought always to be rolled when it is expected the Crops are to be cut. Without this they can never be got off clean. The Pease however that are left would be fine for Sheep and in that case the waste is of no great signification but in this case there must be nothing else in the inclosure that they can injure.

WINTER VETCHES: *Vicia villosa*, hairy or winter vetch. The spring or common vetch, also called tare, is *V. sativa*.

Thursday 18th. Thermometer 38 in the morning—52 at Noon and 48 at Night. Clear all day with the Wind at No. West.

Rid into the Neck, to Muddy hole & Frenchs Plantations.

At the first doubled the small heaps of Buck Wheat in the Morning whilst the dew was on. Finished plowing Sowing & harrowing in 6 Bushels of red clover Seed between the branch which runs from the gate to the Spring and the road which leads from the gate also the Quarters and thence into the Creek field.

At Muddy hole finished late in the afternoon the ditch round the Barn and Dug the Irish Potatoes in the half acre of experi-

mental ground (adjoining the ½ acre of Sweet or Country Potatoes) which being of the red and white in alternate rows through
the piece yielded as follow

|  | red | | white |
|---|---|---|---|
|  | Bushls. | | |
| In the ½ wch. had been dungd. . . . | 11 | & | 8¼ |
| ½ which had no dung . . . | 6 | | 3½ |
|  | 17 | | 11¾ |
|  | 11¾ | | |
| Total of both sorts | 28¾ | | |
|  | 5 | | |
| Difference betwn. the red & Wh[it]e is | 4¾ | | 4¾ |
| Of both together | 9¾ Bush. | | |

All the hands from the House, except the Carpenters, that were
employed in the Neck yesterday went to French's to day to assist
in securing as many of the Pease there as they could—great loss by
the frost—The ripe pease opening and sheddg. and the green ones
with the vines on which they grew had turned quite black loking
like a thing parboiled. Carried the Pease and the Vines which
appeared to be cured into one end of the Tobo. House in field
No. 1.

In the Evening Mr. Houston and lady & Miss Maria Livingston
her Sister came in and stayed all Night.

MR. HOUSTON: probably William Houstoun of Georgia. Houstoun, the son of
Sir Patrick Houstoun, Bart., and Lady Priscilla Dunbar Houstoun, went to
England to study law at the Inner Temple during the Revolution, returning
to America in time to obtain a commission and serve briefly in the army. He
served in the Continental Congress from 1784 to 1787 and in 1785 was one
of the commissioners to settle the boundary line between Georgia and South
Carolina. Houstoun was a delegate to the Constitutional Convention; although he took an active part in the convention, urgent personal business
called him away before the signing of the Constitution. Houstoun's "Lady"
was his future wife Mary Bayard (c.1766–1808), daughter of Nicholas Bayard
and Catherine Van Brugh Livingston Bayard of New York. They were to
marry the following year. Maria Livingston, her traveling companion, was
probably one of her numerous Livingston cousins.

Friday 19th.    Thermometer at 40 in the Morning—52 at Noon
and 50 at Night. In the Morning the weather was hazy—at Noon
Cloudy and in the evening raining.

Mr. Houston going away abt. 10 Oclock I rid to French's the
Ferry Dogue run & Muddy hole.

At the Ferry the hands were making a farm pen.

At French's about the Pease as yesterday. The Vines of some of them appeared to me to be not sufficiently cured.

At Dogue run getting out Wheat and removing brush from the Swamp to the gullies.

At Muddy hole began to ditch between fields No. 1. 2. 3. & 4 and to sow Wheat with a Barrel 6 feet long—perforated with holes strapped round with leather bands in order with intention to drop the wheat in clumps 6 Inches square but the leather not binding equally alike in all parts it discharged Seeds from the Sides and sowed it broad.

On my return home I found a Mr. Dunlap (a West Indian) Mr. Cary Mr. Donaldson, and Mr. Porter here who returned to Alexa. after dinner.

Joseph Cary (Carey) was a partner of Thomas and John Williams in the Alexandria firm of Williams, Cary & Williams (*Va. Journal,* 29 Mar. and 15 Nov. 1787; SPROUSE [2], 2:19).

Robert Donaldson, an Alexandria merchant, in 1785 was selling imported goods from the West Indies (*Va. Journal,* 30 June 1785). In the 1790s he was a partner in the firm of Hartshorne & Donaldson.

Saturday 20th.    Thermometer at 44 in the Morning—48 at Noon & 46 at Night. Wind at No. Et. with a continued rain since it began yesterday afternoon.

No out doors work done this day.

Sunday 21st.    Thermometer at 46 in the Morning—50 at Noon and 50 at Night. Wind at No. Et. till the afternoon then No.— Cloudy all day with some rain—at home alone.

Monday 22d.    Thermometer 46 in the Morning—58 at Noon and 56 at Night. Clear and exceedingly pleasant all day—with the Wind Northerly in the Morning and Southerly in the evening.

Went up to a meeting of the Potk. Company at George Town. Called at Muddy hole Plantation in my way. Did the business which called the Comy. together. Dined at Shuters Tavern, and returned as far as Abingdon at Night.

Whilst at Muddy hole, finding that the Barrel continued to scatter the Wheat, and not having time to try new expedients to alter it; the Season for sowing this grain being far advanced; I directed that it should proceed as it was.

Tuesday 23d.    Thermometer at 46 in the Morning—66 at Noon and 58 at Night—Weather calm & clear.

After a very early break fast at Abigdon I arrived at Muddy hole Plantation by 8 oclock and took the Bands off the Barrel that the grain might drop without interruption from the holes therein.

Went round by Dogue run, Frenchs and the Ferry Plantation.

At the first getting out Wheat.

At the 2d. (Frenchs) securing Pease and

At the Ferry Treading out Oats.

Wednesday 24th. Thermometer at 43 in the Morning—62 at Noon and 61 at Night. Morning Foggy but clear afterwards with the Wind at So. Wt. & South.

Rid to all the Plantations. In the Neck found that the Sowing of the orchard Inclosure with Wheat had been compleated on Monday last and that such parts thereof as have not been already enumerated, had been sown with Wheat alone. The Orchard part had received the workings already mentioned as also the part which was sown with the winter Vetches. The Part which had been sown with Wheat & clover, as already mentioned had been plowed & cross plowed—the Wheat then harrowed in, after which the clover seed was Sown over which a bush passed to scratch in the Seed and level the grd. That part which had Wheat alone had also been plowed—crossed plowed—& the Wheat harrowed in.

Ordered the Buck Wheat at every place to be got in and threshed out. yield—exclusive of abt. 1/4 at the So. Wt. Corner of the Sqr., which had perished by, it is apprehended the lowness of the situation, as follow 3¾ bushls. & ½ a peck whereof 2¼ grew on the dunged part of the half acre.

At Frenchs, the Pease would be all got in this Night (but with great loss) —and

at the Ferry the people were cleaning Oats which were tread out yesterday.

Mr. Richard Lee & his Sister came here in the evening.

These visitors were probably Richard Bland Lee and his eldest sister Mary Lee, children of Henry Lee of Leesylvania, who died earlier this year. Mary later (c.1792) became the third wife of Philip Richard Fendall of Alexandria (LEE [5], 296–98).

Thursday 25th. Thermometer at 56 in the Morning—66 at Noon and 66 at Night. Clear all day, with the Wind at So. Wt.

Rid to all the Plantations. In the Neck, began with 4 plows to flush plow field No. 6 (in 6 feet Ridges) for Indian Corn & Potatoes next yr. and began also to draw the Buck Wh. together, and to get up the Hogs at this place for killing.

At Muddy hole began also to get in, and thresh out the Buck Wheat. An half acre of the experimental grd. at this place which had been divided into 3 equal parts and planted with the Bunch homeny Beans—Of the commn. homony bean and with the small round Pease yielded as follow—viz.—of the first which had been gathered before I came home 3 pecks—of the 2d. (just now gathered) 1 peck only and of the other viz. Pease the 2d. & last gathering of which has been just made—3 pecks. Note each of these Thirds contained the 6th. of an acre. Of the experimental half acres there are 3 yet to obtain the crops from—viz.—Jerusalem Artichokes (of which, out of 1442 hills 417 are missing)—Carrots and Turnips. In the half acre of Irish Potatoes there were 27 Rows 4 feet a part & 60 in length. These were also missing in places, and more in the undunged than dunged part. Had the Rows been nearer, the Crop would have been greater. Ordered the Irish Potatoes at this place wch. had been planted under Straw &ca. for experiments to be taken up.

Yield as follow.

| | Bushls. |
|---|---|
| From 400 Sqr. yards laid on Green sward & covd. w. str. | 3¾ |
| From 56 sqr. yds. laid on a poor washed knowl—gulld. | 3 Pecks |
| From a sqr. made by Fence rails & raised lair above lair with Straw & Potatoes | ¾ of a Peck |
| From 160 sqr. yds. laid in grn. Sward & covd. with Corn Stalks | 1 Peck |

At Dogue Run the hands were getting in & threshing out Buck Wheat.

At Frenchs—The Hoe people and Cart were filling up gullies and two plows were at work.

At the Ferry two plows began to break up part of No. 2 for Indian Corn & Potatoes. The rest of the Negroes were measuring and carrying off Oats—Stacking blades and otherwise securing the fodder.

At the Mansion House setting Turnips raised from the Seed sent me by Mr. Young to propagate Seed from.

On my return home found Mrs. Stuart and her two youngest daughters here—and Mr. & Miss Lee whom I had left.

MR. YOUNG: GW had included turnip seeds in the list of items requested on 6 Aug. 1786 of Arthur Young, the English agriculturist (PPRF).

Friday. 26th.    Thermometer at 57 in the Morning—68 at Noon and 67 at Night. Clear all day & wind pretty fresh from the So. Wt.

Rid to all the Plantations after Mr. & Miss Lee went away.

In the Neck, the Buck Wheat was all drawn to a yard in the field for the purpose of threshing and it was accordingly done and removed to the Barn but not measured. 6 plows at Wk. there to day.

At Muddy hole finished Sowing with the Barrel, the ground on the left of the road leading from the gate on the Ferry road, to the Barn with 18½ Bushls. of Wheat—and thinking this quantity inadequate I had more holes perferated in the Barrl. to sow the other part on the right of the above road. Got all the Pease into the Barn yard which had been cut down with the Scythes—also the remains of the Buck Wheat.

At Dogue run gathered in to the Farm yard & began to thresh and clean it.

At Frenchs filling gullies & Plowing (2 plows) part of field No. 2 which had been left unbroke in the Spring & Summer.

At the Ferry treading out Oats began with 2 plows to break up the lay part of field No. 2.

Saturday 27th.    Thermometer at 56 in the Morning 67 at Noon and 64 at Night. The Morning was calm and mild but the Wind blew fresh afterwards from the Westward.

Went to the Woods back of Muddy hole with the hounds. Unkennelled 2 foxes and dragged others but caught none—the dogs running wildly and being under no command.

Passed through Muddy hole Plantation & returned home by way of Dogue run, French's and the Ferry.

At the first, Sowed in 6 Oblong Squares at the West end of field No 4 (on the Wheat just sown) abt. an acre in each, the following grass Seeds. viz.—on the most Westerly square (being a breadth across the field) and divided, as all the others are, by a partition furrow 8 lbs. of rib grass—Next to this 20 lbs. of red clover—in the 3d. 2 Bushls. of Orchard grass—In the 4th. 20 lbs. of Hopclover—In the 5th. four Bushls. of Ray grass and in the 6th. 2 bushls. of Sainfoin. After sowing these Seeds the ground was first rolled and then harrowed with a bush. The square containing Sainfoin had the Seed first harrowed in with the Wheat over and above what is mentioned to have been done with respect to the others.

At Dogue run finished threshing cleaning and measuring the Buck Wht. wch. amounted to 121 Bushls. from about 12 Acres.

At Frenchs cleared up the shattered Pease and threshed those wch. had been picked off the grd. wch. together amounted to 9 Bushls.

At the Ferry set 3 plows to work. Put the girl Eby to one of them.

The tryal that was made in the Neck of differt. qties. of Oats to the acre turned out as follow.

That wch. had 2 bushls. yielded . . . . 8½
       3  Do.   Do.   . . . . 7
       4  Do.   Do.   . . . . 5½

The above 3 acres were adjoining each other and as nearly alike as possible in quality of Soil, levelness and other circumstances. The grd. was prepared in all respects alike and sowed at the same time.

EBY: GW calls her Edy in the 18 Feb. 1786 entry of the *Diaries* and in his 1799 list of slaves. She was about 14 years old at this time (list of Negroes belonging to GW, c.June 1799, NjP:Armstrong Collection, photostat).

Sunday 28th. Thermometer at 52 in the Morning—58 at Noon and 54 at Night. Clear all day with the Wind at So. Wt. in the Morning and No. Et. in the Evening.

Went to Pohick Church—Mr. Lear & Washington Custis in the carriage with me.

Mr. Willm. Stuart came from Church with me & Mr. Geo. Mason Junr. came in soon after.

Monday 29th. Thermometer at 45 in the Morning—48 at Noon and 46 at Night. Raining slowly at day breaking—how much earlier it began is not known; continued to do so, mixed with flakes of Snow till one oclock, when it cleared away pleasantly; but little wind all day, & that at East.

Spread, whilst it was raining, 2 Bushels of the Plaster of Paris had from Philadelphia on the So. half of the lawn beyond the break or small fall therein—quantity about half an acre.

After dinner Mr. George Mason went away.

Tuesday 30th. Thermometer at 44 in the Morning—44 at Noon and 46 at Night. Cloudy in the Morning with the Wind at So. Wt. About 8 oclock it began a slow & misling rain which encreased till it came on to rain fast which it continued to do until 11 Oclock when it ceased. A variable afternoon, but upon the whole pleasant.

Rid to Muddy hole and Dogue run, in the Morning but being

driven in by the Rain I rode after it ceased to the Ferry & French's.

At Muddy hole cleaning up the Buck Wheat—57 bushls. of it only from 18 acres of ground.

At Dogue run 4 plows were at Work—the other hands agrubbg.

At French's 2 plows were at Work and the other hands weeding 2 yards for treading out grain.

At the Ferry the 3 plows were at work and the other people grubbing.

Wednesday 31st.    Thermometer at 42 in the Morning—44 at Noon and 41 at Night. Clear pleasant and warm in the forenoon. Towards Noon it grew cold the Wind being hard at No. Wt.

Rid to all the Plantations. In the Neck 6 plows were at Work and two more just added—one of which broke immediately. The other hands were digging Potatoes in the further cut opposite to Mr. Digges in No. 3.

At Muddy hole, finished sowing Wheat on the right of the road leading from the gate on the Ferry road to the Barn—in which 12½ bushls. of Seed was deposited and put in as that on the other side was. The hands getting the Remainder of the frost bitten Pease; and taking up those Turnips in the experimental grd. (which, not havg. the tops taken of being intended for seed) the yield could not be ascertained.

At Dogue run—The plows and People were employed as yesterday.

The Ditchers went to Frenchs this Morning.

Mrs. Stuart and her two youngest Children and Mr. William Stuart went from this Yesterday morning.

## November 1787

Thursday 1st.    Thermometer at 34 in the Morning—44 at Noon and 42 at Night. A frost this morning which crusted the grd. and formed Ice. Early it was calm & not unpleasant but the Wind blew fresh from the No. Wt. & grew cold afterwards.

Rid by the way of Muddy hole where the people were taking up Turnips to transplant for Seed to Alexandria to attend a meeting of the Directors of the Potomack Company. Also the exhibition of the Boys of the Academy in this place. Dined at Leighs Tavern & lodged at Colo. Fitzgeralds after returning abt. 11 Oclock at Night from the performance which was well executed.

## November 1787

THE EXHIBITION OF THE BOYS: part of "the public Examinations of the several Schools in the Alexandria Academy, antecedent to the autumnal Vacation. . . . In the Evening the Pupils of the Rev. Mr. M'Whir delivered public Orations before a large and respectable Audience, among whom were present General Washington, and the greater Part of the Principal Inhabitants, Ladies and Gentlemen, of the Town and the Neighbourhood: After which Prizes were distributed" (*Va. Journal*, 8 Nov. 1787). George Steptoe Washington, GW's nephew, won a prize in Latin and ancient geography. LEIGHS TAVERN: George H. Leigh operated the Bunch of Grapes Tavern on the corner of Fairfax and Cameron streets.

Friday 2d.    Thermometer at 32 in the Morning—46 at Noon and 44 at Night. Last Night being very cold the grd. this morning was hard frozen. The Weather however through the day was very pleasant.

After breakfast I returned home by way of Muddy hole, Dogue run, Frenchs and the Ferry.

At the first 3 plows were breaking up the remains of field No. 4. The other hands were taking up the Jerusalem Artichoke from the half Acre of experimental ground adjoining the half Acre in which the Irish Potatoes grew. Yield 58½ bushls. The quantity in the dunged, and undunged part was equal but the roots of the 1st. were largest.

At Dogue run all hands were engaged in treading out Wheat.

At Frenchs except the two Plows which were at work, they were employed in digging Irish Potatoes.

At the Ferry in treading out Oats.

Saturday 3rd.    Thermometer at 34 in the Morning—48 at Noon and 47 at Night. Clear weather & very pleasant with but little wind.

Rid to all the Plantations. Digging Potatoes at the River, Muddy hole, and Frenchs—at all of which the Plows were also at work. Treading Wheat at D. Run & Oats at the Ferry.

Sunday 4th.    Thermometer at 42 in the Morning—52 at Noon and 51 at Night. Clear & pleasant with but little Wind.

After the Candles were lighted Mr. & Mrs. Powell came in.

Monday 5th.    Thermometer at 48 in the Morning—58 at Noon and 56 at Night. But little Wind, clear & pleasant all day.

Mr. & Mrs. Powell remaining here I continued at home all day.

Tuesday 6th.    Thermometer at 48 in the Morning—60 at Noon and 56 at Night. Little or no Wind. Clear and pleasant all day.

Mr. & Mrs. Powell crossing the river to Mr. Digges a little after Sunrise I accompanied them that far & having my horse carried into the Neck I rid round that and all the other plantations.

From the cut of drilled Corn in the Neck (in wch. the Tobo. house stands) came 45 bushls. of Irish Potatoes from every 3d. interval between the Corn Rows. From the So. Cut on the river came 38 Bushels from the 4 rows and from the Farm yard cut 4th. rows came 98 Bushels in all 181 whereof 21 only were red. Eight Plows were at work here.

At Muddy hole 2 plows were at Work. The driver of the 3d. was after Hogs. The rest of the hands getting Potatoes from a 10 acre cut of Corn, adjoining the experimental ground from whence (every 4th. row) came 25 bushls. of white & 22¾ of red—alternate rows of each sort—In all 47¾.

At Dogue run all hands were engaged in cleaning wheat, stacking the Straw &ca.

At Frenchs two plows were at Work—all the other hands diggg. Potatoes.

At the Ferry 3 plows were at Work. The other hands were gettg. Corn from the New ground in front of the Mansn. House.

In his original Philadelphia journal GW included the notation that "Mr. Rid[ou]t dind & returned."

Wednesday 7th.   Thermometer at 46 in the Morning—57 at Noon and 60 at Night. A Very thick fog in the morning, & but little wind all day—the fog continuing till near 12 oclock.

Rid to Muddy hole, Dogue run, Frenchs and the Ferry.

At Muddy hole 2 plows only at work—the other hands getting Corn in the New ground in front of the Mansion house.

At Morris 4 plows were at Work. All the other hands were digging Potatoes on the right of the road leading from the gate to the Houses. Entered upon this business this morning.

At Frenchs 2 plows were at work. The rest of the hands were digging Potatoes which they finished—quantity 84½ Bushls. from 46 rows 170 yds. long each.

At the Ferry the same work as yesterday.

Majr. Geo. Auge. Washington and his wife returned this evening from Berkley.

Thursday 8th.   Thermometer at 44 in the Morning—56 at Noon and 54 at Night. Wind Southerly and morning soft. Between 9 and

10 oclock it began to rain moderately & continued to do so (very slowly) for about two hrs. and warm and damp afterwards.

Went up to Alexandria to meet the Directors of the Potomack Compy. Dined at Mr. Leighs Tavern and retd. in the afternoon.

The Ferry part of the New grd. Corn in front of the Mansion house being gathered and measured turned out as follow.

Of that wch. was sound       24

    Rotten              4½    28½

Stopped the Plows at Muddy hole to assist in digging the Potatoes there.

Friday 9th.     Thermometer at 48 in the Morning—60 at Noon and 59 at Night. Wind at So. Wt. Weather mild & clear.

Went this day to the back line of my land in order to run a strait line 30 feet within the marked trees for a ditch leaving that space without for a road. Was not able to compleat it.

Passed by the Ferry, Frenchs and Dogue run in going and Muddy hole in returning.

At the 3 first the plows as usual were at work. At the latter the drivers were assisting with the Potatoes.

At the Ferry the hands were husking & securing the Corn they had gathered.

At Frenchs they were grubbing and stopping gullies before the Plows.

At Dogue run they were digging Potatoes.

At Muddy hole doing the same.

Saturday 10th.     Thermometer at 44 in the Morning—54 at Noon and 52 at Night. The morning was mild & pleasant with the Wind at South. About 5 oclock it thundered & began to rain which it continued to do more or less till 10 oclock at Night.

Went again on the business I quitted yesterday without finishing it.

Passed by the Ferry, Frenchs and Dogue run, and returned by Muddy hole.

At the Ferry the Plows were at work as usual and the other hands were digging Potatoes.

At Frenchs they were employed as yesterday but were ordered to remove the trash out of the wet part of the Meadow (that had been grubbed) before it got wet.

At Dogue run only 2 plows were at work—the other hands digging Potatoes.

At Muddy hole all were digging Potatoes.

On my return home found the Widow Graham and her daughter here who stayed all Night.

The widow Graham was probably Mrs. Elizabeth (Cocke) Graham, whose husband John Graham of Graham Park near Dumfries died in 1787. They had two daughters: Margaret Graham, who married Dr. Richard Gustavus Brown in 1769, and Jean Graham (b. 1768).

Sunday 11th.    Thermometer at 48 in the Morning—58 at Noon and 56 at Night. Morning clear & pleasant with the Wind westerly but not hard nor cold.

After breakfast Mrs. Graham & her daughter went away and to dinner came my Nephew Geo. Steptoe Washington and young Mr. McCrae. In the Evening Colo. Richd. Henry Lee came in.

McCRAE: probably John McCrea (McCrae), a son of Robert McCrea of Alexandria and a schoolmate of George Steptoe Washington (*Va. Journal,* 8 Nov. 1787).

Monday 12th.    Thermometer at 46 in the morning—52 at Noon And 52 at Night. Wind Southerly, weather mild but lowering all day. Towards noon, and from thence till 4 oclock it had much the appearance of Snow after wch. the clouds thinned and the prospect of fair weather brightned.

Colo. Lee went away about 11 Oclock and the young men after dinner. I did not ride as usual.

Finished digging the Irish Potatoes at Dogue run in the cut they began on thursday last—quantity from every 4th. interval between the Corn rows 120 bushl—63 of wch. were red. Red & white were in the rows alternately.

Tuesday 13th.    Thermometer at 52 in the Morning—70 at Noon and 69 at Night. Very mild & soft morning with the wind Southerly.

Rid to all the Plantations. At the River Quarter 8 Plows were at work. The rest of the people were gathering Beans, and threshing out Pease.

At Muddy hole all hands digging Potatoes. Sent the small gang from the House there to assist, and ordered the Ferry People except the Ferry men & those drawing the Plows to go there tomorrow for the same purpe.

At Dogue Run, 4 plows were at Work. The other hands aided by the People from Frenchs were digging Potatoes on the left of the road leading from the gate to the Houses.

At Frenchs two plows were at Work.

At the Ferry 3 plows were at Work. The other hands having finished digging the Potatoes; qty. 41 Bushls. whereof 6½ were red and 34½ white were picking the remainder of the frost bitten pease.

Wednesday 14th.   Thermometer at 56 in the Morning–66 at Noon and 67 at Night. Clear and very mild in the morning. Cloudy afterwards with slight sprinklings of Rain. Wind at So. West.

Rid to the Ferry, Frenchs, Dogue run & Muddy hole.

At the Ferry 3 plows were at Work. All the other hands except the Ferry men had gone to Muddy hole.

At French's they had got done abt. ⅔ of the Stack of Barley and were treading of it. Finding the weather unsettled ordered that which was tread out and the other part in the Stack to be well covered. The Plow horses being employed in treading the Plows were stopped this day.

At Dogue run 4 plows were at work–the other hands about the Potatoes.

At Muddy hole all hands, except the 3 plow people (who were plowing) together with the House people & those from the Ferry were digging Potatoes in No. 1 by the quarter, having yesterday afternoon finished the Corn grd.–The quantity of wch. exclusive of those wch. grew on the 10 Acre cut amounted to 54½ bushels of red and 59½ of white and added thereto makes 84½ of White and 77¼ of red–in the whole 161¾ Bushels from every 4th. interval between the Corn Rows.

Recd. this evening, the last of the Potatoes from the Neck; amounting in the whole, to 181 Bushels; whereof 42 grew in the Easternmost cut of Corn in field No. 3–every 3d. row betwn. the Corn–39 in the Southernmost cut on the river every 4th. row and the remainder (100 Bushls.) in the Farm yard cut. From the whole of this there came only 21 bushls. of red from seed which had got intermixed (it is presumed at planting) with the White. From this place also came 56½ Bushls. of spring Barley which grew near the Barn in front of the Overseers House in grd. which had been in Turnips last year and might be about 4 acres. 31 Bushels of sound and good Pease were also brought home from thence; and 7½ more of those which had been bit by the frost in a great degree too some of them. These Pease came from the Field No. 3 between the 3d. Corn row in the first mentioned cut & the 4th. of the other two cuts–in like manner the Potatoes–the whole field containing 130 acres.

Thursday 15th.   Thermometer at 63 in the morning—62 at Noon and 62 at Night. Morning mild and very heavy—the Wind having blown very fresh from the So. West all night. About 10 oclk. (after some previous sprinklings) it began a constant rain which continued till near three oclock without intermission, and at times very powerfully. After this till Night it ceased, but recommenced sometime after dark and continued it is supposed thro' the Night.

Went to Alexandria to an Election of a Senator, for the district of Fairfax & Prince William. Was accompanied by Mr. William Stuart who with Mrs. Stuart & his Sister came here last evening. Gave my suffrage for Mr. Thos. West who with a Mr. Pope from the other County were Candidates and returned home to dinner through the midst of the rain from an apprehension that the weather was not likely to abate in the evening.

The last of the Potatoes were brought from the left hand cut at Dogue run making therefore 113½ Bushels whereof 57¾ were red and 56½ were white. These added to those on the other side of the road, make 120¾ of red, and 113½ of White; In all 234¼ Bushls. from the 4th. Intervals of the Corn rows. The No. of Acres in Corn may be abt. 57.

In the Evening Mr. Kelly the Dancing Master and my Nepw. G. Steptoe Washington came in.

Thomas West, eldest son of John West, Jr., and Catherine Colvill West, served in one session (1784–85) of the House of Delegates for Fairfax County. In the polling for this Virginia Senate seat West lost to John Pope, of Prince William County, who remained in the Senate until 1791, after which he served several terms in the House of Delegates for Prince William County (see SWEM and WILLIAMS). MR. KELLY: John B. O'Kelly of Alexandria (O'BRIEN, 52).

Friday 16th.   Thermometer at 57 in the morning—56 at Noon and 57 at Night. A continued rain all day—some times powerful, by which the grd. was made very wet. Wind in the forenoon Southerly—afternn. Easterly—and towards Night at No. West but not hard at any period of it.

Remained within doors all day.

Saturday 17th.   Thermometer at 44 in the morning—56 at Noon And 55 at Night. A very clear and pleasant Morning. Day fine, Wind tho' not much of it at No. West.

Rid to the Ferry, French's, Dogue run and Muddy hole.

At the first ground being too wet to Plow I sent them to Frenchs which was something drier being lay land.

At the other, cleaning the Barley, aided by some of the Dogue run people—but was not able to finish it.

At Dogue run four plows were at work. The other hands were filling gullies before the Plows.

At Muddy hole 3 plows were at Work. The other people & the small gang from the House were digging Potatoes tho' it was bad doing it on acct. of the wetness of the earth.

Mrs., Miss Stuart and the Miss[es] Custis together with Harriot W. went up to Abingdon, & Mr. Kelly & Geo. Steptoe Washington to Alexandria, after breakfast.

The dancing class was over on this day and GW paid O'Kelly for "one quarter's instruction" of Lawrence and George Steptoe Washington (LEDGER B, 256). The class, organized in August, also included their younger sister, Harriot Washington (1776–1822), and Eleanor Parke Custis (LEDGER B, 248).

Sunday 18th.    Thermometer at 41 in the Morning—56 at Noon and 51 at Night. Weather clear and pleasant. The Wind in the morning was at No. Et.—at Noon East and at Night Southerly.

Geo. Auge. Washington and his wife went up to Abingdon. To Dinner came Mr. Potts his wife and Brother and Mr. Wilson from Alexandria and soon after them Colo. Humphreys. The first company went away after dinner and in the evening Mr. Corbin Washington came in.

John Potts, Jr., was married in June 1786 to Eliza Ramsay (*Va. Journal,* 29 June 1786). She was the daughter of Mrs. Elizabeth Ramsay of Alexandria, the widow of Patrick Ramsay, a Scottish merchant, formerly of Blandford, Prince George County, Va.

Monday 19th.    Thermometer at 40 in the Morning—53 at Noon and 51 at Night. Morning clear and calm, with a red sky in the Eastern horizon and some fog on the River.

Rid before breakfast to the Plantations at Frenchs, Dogue run & Muddy hole. Had the Barley at the former fanned, cleaned and Measured—quantity 126½ bushls. from about 9 acres of ground.

At Dogue run, laid down the Barley to tread out.

At Muddy hole digging Potatoes. The hands from the Ferry, and sml. gang from the Mansn. house assisting. The Ploughs would abt. finish breaking up field No. 4 this evening. Mr. Robt. Morris, Mr. Gour. Morris & Doctr. Ruston came in before Dinner.

On 13 Nov. Samuel Powel wrote GW from Philadelphia to thank the Washingtons for their hospitality, adding: "Messrs. Robert & Gouverneur Morris left this City Yesterday & will probably be with you before the Arrival of this Letter. They will be able to give you a full and ample Detail of all

Matters relative to our grand Question, I mean the Acceptation of the federal Constitution" (DLC:GW). The Morrises were in Virginia for several months "to straighten out difficulties connected with Robert's contract for a monopoly on the sale of American tobacco to the French Farmers General" (MINTZ, 205).

Tuesday 20th.   Thermometer at 54 in the Morning—57 at Noon and 55 at Night. Morning pleasant, very lowering afterwards. Wind at So. Et., and moderate in the forenoon—but fresh afterwards—veering more Easterly.

Colo. Lyles, Mr. Hunter, Mr. Rumney, Mr. Lowry, Mr. Abernathy, Mr. Monshure, Mr. Nelson, and Doctr. Craik came to Dinner and returned in the evening. Mr. Corbin Washington went away after breakfast.

Wednesday 21st.   Thermometer at 51 in the Morning—51 at Noon And 46 at Night. A great deal of rain fell in the Night. Cloudy morning but clear afterwards. Wind at No. West all day but neither very hard, nor cold.

Messrs. Morris's, & Doctr. Ruston went away after Breakfast. With the first two I rid a few miles and then visited my plantations at Frenchs, Dogue run & Muddy hole on my return.

At the first, the Ferry Plows were aiding those of the Plantatn., their own grd. being too wet and the other hands were assisting the Muddy hole people in digging Potatoes. The rest of French's hands were filling up gullies before the Plows.

At Dogue run 4 plows were at work. The other hands were fillg. up gullies.

At Muddy hole the Plows (three) only finished breaking up No. 4 last night, instead of doing it the eveng. before, as I expected. And began this morning to plow No. 3. The other hands with those from the Ferry were about the Potatoes.

In the Neck, finished breaking up field No. 4.

Thursday 22d.   Thermometer at 50 in the Morning—51 at Noon And 45 at Night. Cloudy morning with the Wind fresh all day at No. West. About Noon it was clear. Lowered again in the Afternoon.

Rid into the Neck and to Muddy hole.

At the first, began to Plow (next the Mouth of Carneys gut) field No. 9 as the first preparation for a wheaten Crop, next fall— to receive in the Mean while Buck Wheat, & some other fallow Crops. 6 plows only at work.

At the Plantation at Muddy hole 2 plows only were at work in No. 3. The third had come down to the House to be repaired; all the other hands, together with those from the Ferry, were digging Potatoes. Examined the squares which I had sowed at this place with grass seeds; and found that the red clover, hop clover, Ray grass, and orchard grass were all up very thick. None of the rib grass could I perceive up and very little if any of the Sainfoin.

The Winter Vetches, red clov. and trafoil which had been sowed in the Neck were also up the two last very thick & well; but I could perceive none of the Burnet, and very little of the Sainfoin above ground.

Friday 23d.     Thermometer at 44 in the Morning—52 at Noon and 50 at Night. Wind at No. Wt., but neither cold nor very fresh. Cloudy in the forenoon but clear afterwards.

Rid to the Ferry, Frenchs, D. Run and Muddy hole.

At the first the plows belonging to the Plantation were at work at frenchs. The other hands were getting Corn in the flat below the hill in No. 1.

At Frenchs, the Plows were stopped, in order that the Horses might tred out Oats: all hands employed in this business.

At Dogue run, finished cleaning the Oats raised from the Seed sent me by Genl. Spotswood, from an Acre of grd.; 41½ Bushels. The remainder of the Barley, 6¾ bushls. was brot. from this place, which made the whole raised at it 74¼ bushls.—total at all the places 257¼ bushls. 3¼ bushls. of the black Spelt was brot. home from this place also. 4 Plows were at Work. The other hands (after cleang. Oats) were spreadg. Buck Wheat straw and threshing the common Spelts.

At Muddy hole, 3 plows were at work; the other hands, belonging to the Plantation, were digging Potatoes, which they finished doing about Noon. These have not been measured, but spread in the Barn that they might get dry and be sorted. Note—The digging of Potatoes has been too long postponed this fall. The proper season to do this work in is, as soon as the top dies & before it becomes so dry as to fall. At so late a Season the earth is wet, clings to the Potatoes; makes them very dirty, & difficult to dry; from whence many are spoiled without much troubles & attention. Note also. It is too late, where there are not Barns, on the floors of which grain can be threshed dry, & with safety, to have Wheat, Oats, or other Crops of this kind remaining in the Straw. Dirt yards, on which they are tred, get damp; & much grain is buried in the earth; to keep them from freezing is not only troublesome, but difficult; and the freqt. rains which fall at this Season, are not sufficiently counteracted by the Sun to prepare them for use before they are endangered by a repetition of more.

Saturday 24th.    Thermometer at 48 in the morning—48 at Noon And 45 at Night. Wind at No. Et. all day with heavy clouds, & great appearances of rain till the evening, when the Clds. broke and the prospect brightned a little.

Rid to the Ferry, Frenchs, Dogue run, & Muddy hole Plantns.—also to the Carpenters in the Woods.

At the Ferry, the Plows were as yesterday at work at Frenchs. The other hands were husking & lofting of Corn and gathering Beans.

At Frenchs all hands and Horses were treading out Oats.

At Dogue run 4 plows were at Work. The rest of the People were threshing & cleaning the common Spelts—qty. 35½ Bushls. which were left there for the use of the Plantation Horses.

At Muddy hole 3 plows were at Work. The other hands were gathering & husking of Corn, & sorting the Irish Potatoes.

Mrs. Lee (wife of Colo. Henry Lee) came here to dinner and in the afternoon he & Judge Harrison of Maryland arrived.

**Mr. Lear** went up to Alexa. today on my business.

Sunday 25th.    Thermometer at 44 in the Morning—50 at Noon and 45 at Night. Clear & pleasant all day—Notwithstanding the Wind (though not brisk) continued at No. East.

Colo. Simms, Mr. Porter, and young Mr. Bowen came here to dinner, and returned afterwards.

Monday 26th.    Thermometer at 46 in the Morning—49 at Noon And 47 at Night. Wind at No. Et. and great appearances of rain all day. About Noon it began to Mizzle after which the clds. broke & the weather looked less threatning.

Colo. Lee & his Lady, & Colo. Harrison going away after breakfast I rid to French's, Dogue run, and Muddy hole.

At the first, 2 plows were at work; the other hands were cleaning Oats.

At Dogue run, all hands were engaged in getting out Oats, for which purpose the Plows were stopped.

At Muddy hole, 3 plows were at work; the other hands were gathering Corn;

Three plows were at Work at the Ferry. Mrs. Jenifer came here.

Tuesday 27th.    Thermometer at 46 in the Morning—49 at Noon and 47 at Night. Wind at No. Et. all day and weather very heavy and threatning.

Rid to the Plantations in the Neck, Muddy hole, Dogue run, Frenchs and Ferry. At the first gathering, and measuring Corn. The whole produce of field No. 3 amounted to no more than [     ] Barrls. 6 plows were at work.

At Muddy hole, 3 plows were at work—the other hands gathering Corn & husking it.

At Dogue run, 4 plows were at Work. The other hands were cleaning the Oats which had been tread out yesterday.

At French's 2 plows were at Work. All the other hands were cleaning Oats.

At the Ferry 3 plows were at Work. All the rest of the hands were gathering & husking Corn.

Wednesday 28th.    Thermometer at 44 in the Morning—48 at Noon and 47 at Night. Wind variable, sometimes East, and sometimes West of North. Began to drop rain by or before Sun rise. About 10 Oclock it encreased so as to rain pretty fast; which it continued to do, more or less till abt. 4 oclock when it cleared & the Sun.

Rid to the Plantations at the Ferry, French's, Dogue run & Muddy hole.

The Plows were at Work at all of them till abt. 10 Oclock when they were stopped by rain—as all other outdoors work was.

Thursday 29th.    Thermometer at 38 in the Morning—44 at Noon and 49 at Night. Clear and calm in the fore part of the day, & in the afternoon. Cloudy from 12 Oclock till 3, with appearances of Snow & wind at No. West.

In Company with Colo. Humphreys Majr. Washington & Mr. Lear went a hunting, found a fox about 11 Oclock near the Pincushion. Run him hard for near 3 quarters of an hour & then lost him.

Mr. Lund Washington who joined us, came & dined with us and returned afterwards.

Passed through Muddy hole Plantation. 3 plows were at Work, the other hands were gathering & husking Corn.

Friday 30th.    Thermometer at 38 in the Morning—44 at Noon and 39 at Night. Cloudy in the Morning but clear afterwards. Early in the Morning the Wind was about So. West after which it got to No. Wt. but neither blew hard nor cold. In the evening it was calm & quite clear.

Rid to the Plantations at the Ferry, French's, Dogue run & Muddy hole.

At the first three plows were at work in field No. 3, Number 2 being two wet to plow. The rest of the hands were gathering and husking Corn.

At French's 2 plows were at Work. The other hands were filling gullies before the Plows. The last load of Oats from the stack which had been tread were brot. to the Mansion house from this place—qty. 287½ bushls. from this Stack.

At Dogue run, 4 plows were at Work. The other hands were making drains to let of the water (wch. was ponding in wet weather) from fields No. 4 & 6, now in grain. Brot. the last of the Oats from this place which grew in the ground (abt. 25 acs.) that was winter fallowed in No. 1, adjoining the Ferry road. Qty. 139½ Bushls. All these (last mentioned) Oats, were deposited in the Seed loft, over the Green Ho.

At Muddy hole 3 plows were at work. The other hands were gathering and husking corn.

Mrs. Jenifer went away about Noon.

## December 1787

Saturday first.  Mercury at 46 in the Morning—58 at Noon and 57 at Night. Calm and remarkably clear and pleasant all day. A large white frost in the Morning & grd. froze.

Went with Colo. Humphreys, Majr. W. & Mr. Lear a fox hunting. Found a fox abt. 9 Oclock & run him hard till near 10 and lost him.

Passed through Muddy hole Plantation, & returned through those of Dogue run, Frenchs, & the Ferry, after the Hunt.

At the first 3 plows were at Work. The other hands were gathering & husking Corn.

At Dogue run, all hands (Plows being stopped) were treading out Oats.

At Frenchs—the same.

At the Ferry 3 plows were at Wk. in No. 3. The other hands were gathering & measuring Corn.

Sunday 2d.  Thermometer at 48 in the Morning—60 at Noon and [    ] at Night. Clear, mild & pleasant in the Morning with but little Wind and that Southerly. About 11 Oclock it shifted to No. Wt. & blew pretty fresh but not cold.

At home all day. Mr. G. W. Lewis and Geo. Steptoe Washington who with Mr. Wm. Booth came here yesterday to dinner returned this afternoon to their respective homes.

MR. WM. BOOTH: probably William Aylett Booth, son of Col. William Booth of Westmoreland and Frederick counties. GW was one of the trustees appointed to dock the entail of some of Colonel Booth's land for the benefit of William Aylett Booth (William Aylett Booth to GW, 16 April 1787, DLC:GW; HENING, 8:640).

Monday 3d.    Thermometer at 46 in the Morning—62 at Noon and 60 at Night. Very little wind. Mild & pleasant all day. In the first of the Morning, what wind there was came from the No. Et. Afterwards it was Southerly.

Mr. Booth going away after Breakfast I rid to all the Plantations.

In the Neck 6 Plows were at Work. All the other hands were gathering & husking of Corn.

At Muddy hole 3 plows were at Work—the other hands gathering & husking of Corn.

At Dogue run 4 plows were at work. The rest of the force were cleaning the Oats which were tread out on Saturday last.

At Frenchs all hands were treading the remainder of the Stack of Oats which was began on Saturday.

At the Ferry 3 plows were at work in field No. 2. The other hands were gathering & husking Corn.

On my return home found a Mr. Jones of No. Carolina, and Doctr. Craik here. The former stayed all Night. The latter returned to Alexandria.

Tuesday 4th.    Thermometer at 47 in the Morning—47 at Noon And 46 at Night. Wind Southerly all day—varying sometimes to the East, & then to the [      ]. Morning very heavy with slight rain. Clear afterwards & very pleasant.

After Mr. Jones went away I rid to the Ferry, Frenchs, Dogue run & Muddy hole Plantations.

At the first 3 plows at Work in field No. 2. The other hands finished measurg. the Corn qty. as follow—24½ frm. New grd. 7 frm. drilled do. 17 frm. Stony hill & 20 fm. flat—In all 68½ sound besides 3 picked ⟨up in⟩ difft. fields—& soft Corn 22 Bar[rls.]

At Frenchs two plows began to work abt. 11 Oclock. The other hands were cleaning Oats.

At Dogue run 4 plows were at Work. The other hands were gathering & husking of Corn.

At Muddy hole 3 plows were at Work. The other hands had just finished husking & measuring Corn—qty. 30 Barrls. sound & 11 Hog Corn—7 rotten of wch. 9 Barrls. of the first & 1 of the other grew on the first 10 ac[res] next the experimental Squares. A large proportion of the Corn at all my Plantations is soft & rotten this year.

Turned every species of Stock of my Clover at Muddy hole and the five acre lott in the Neck.

Took up some Turnips for Table use to day at Muddy hole.

Wednesday 5th.    Thermometer at 47 in the Morning—47 at Noon and 46 at Night. The Wind getting to No. Wt. in the Night blew hard but lulled in the Morning, & by Nine Oclock, grew calm and very cloudy. About noon it dropped rain and had appearances of a wet afternoon tho' it turned out otherwise—a bright horizon about Sundown.

Went out, in Company with Colo. Humphreys, with the hounds after we had breakfasted. Took the drag of a Fox on the side of Hunting Creek near the Cedar gut. Carried it through Muddy hole Plantation into the Woods back of it and lost it near the Main road.

After which I went to Muddy hole, Dogue run, Frenchs, and the Ferry Plantations.

At the first (Muddy hole) 2 plows only were at Work; the third being at the Shop. The other hands after securing their Corn in the Barn began to dig the Carrots in the (quarter of an Acre of the) experimental ground.

At Dogue run, the Corn in the East cut of field No. 4 measured 27 barrls. and that which grew in the Small field by Frenchs measured 15 barrls. of sound Corn. The Plows were stopped, and all hands were employed in treading out the only remaining Stack of Oats. The last Stack turned out 129 bushls.; 37½ of wch. came to the Mansn. Ho. & 91½ remd. for the Plantn.

At French's 2 plows were at work, the other hands were employed in cleaning Oats.

At the Ferry, three plows were at Work. The other hands were cleaning the tailings of Wheat & threshing out Pease.

Thursday 6th.    Thermometer at 40 in the morning—[     ] at Noon and [     ] at Night. Cloudy & raw in the morning, wind being at No. Et. Abt. Noon it veered to the East, and then to the So. Et. Many changes in the appearance of the Weather, it sometimes threatning immediate Snow or rain, and then promised to be fair. Once or twice a few flakes of Snow fell.

Rid to all the Plantations. In the Neck, finished husking and measuring the Corn in the South part of field No. 9—quantity [    ] Barls. including what had been given to the Hogs. Plows were stopped in order to tread a stack of Oats whch. grew in the No. Et. part of field No. 2—The hands engaged in this work and housing the Corn.

At Muddy hole finished digging the carrots which grew on the half of the half-acre of experimental grd. (the other half thereof, had been sowed with Turnips, and taken up by mistake without Measuring, or weighing) . That part of the grd. which had received the usual quantity of 50 bushls. of dung (to the *half* acre) produced 12 Bushls. of Carrots; and the other part of the ground which had not been dunged yielded 12 Bushels. In the size of the Carrots there was but little difference. In both they were short, and *mostly* forked; many of them however were thick. Three plows were at Work. In one I put the mule which worked very well. The horse mule is intended also for this Plantation.

At Dogue run 5 plows were at work. Moll, with the old dray Mare, & another Mare bot. for me by Mr. Muse ware set to this business. The other hands were cleaning Oats & threshing Pease.

At Frenchs two Plows were at Work—the other hands cleaning Oats.

At the Ferry 3 plows were at work in field No. 2. The other hands after finishing cleaning the tailings, Pease, & Beans were employed in getting the Cedar Berries. The quantity of Sound Pease *only* amounted to 3½ Bushls. and the Beans to 1¼ Bushls. 54 Pumpkins were sent from this place to the Mansion Ho. for the Cows.

Taking up Turnips, at Dogue by the small gang from the Mann. House. Three men from Do. cutting broom straw for litter.

Friday 7th.    Thermometer at [    ] in the Morning—42 at Noon and 40 at Night. Raining good part of the Night moderately. Wind at No. Wt. in the Morning; and continued so pretty fresh through the day and cool. For the most part cloudy.

Visited all the Plantations. In the Neck 5 plows only were at work—not more through the week. Finished cleaning and measurg. the Stack of Oats wch. was tread out yesterday from the Eastermost cut of field No. 2 quantity 109 bushls. from about 8 acres of grd. After this all hands were employed (except those with the five plows) in gathering Corn.

At Muddy hole two plows only were at work—the 3d. at the Smiths shop. Measured the ¼ of an Acre of Carrots which were taken from the experimental ground—quantity 24 Bushls. half of wch. was from the undunged part, and of equal quality with those which grew on the dunged part (as noticed yesterday). Dug those which grew on the first 10 acres of Corn, adjoining to the experimental grd. (in every 4th. Corn Row). These were of the Orange sort, and very large, but a good deal missing—quantity 22 bushels. The 4th. rows which had been in Irish Potatoes & had yielded 47¾ bushls. as appears by the entry on the 6th. of last Month which makes the difference of 25¾ bushls. in favor of the Potatoes wch. were much less miss[in]g.

At Dogue run, 4 plows only were at work; the other hands, after cleaning the Oats & putting them away, quantity 96 bushls.; threshed, cleaned and sent to the Mansn. house the Pease—viz.— 14½ bushls. of sound & 6 ditto of frost bitten ones.

At Frenchs, 2 plows were at Work. The other hands cleaning of Oats.

At the Ferry, 3 plows at work. Other hands preparing and littering the Farm pen and doing other Jobs.

Saturday 8th.     Thermometer at 31 in the Morning—44 at Noon and 42 at Night. Clear Morning and a large white frost. The forenoon was calm but in the afternoon the wind coming briskly from the Southward it clouded & felt raw.

Went a hunting after breakfast; about Noon found a fox between Muddy hole & Pincushion, which the Dogs run for some time in woods thro which there was no following them so whether they caught, or lost it is uncertain.

I returned home by way of Dogue run & Frenchs.

At Dogue run 5 plows were at Work. 3 Men were felling timber for rails to inclose field No. 7. The rest of the hands were getting in and husking Corn.

At French's 2 plows were at Work. The other hands, after cleaning & sending to the Mansion House the remainder of the Oats which had been tread out from the 2d. Stack (quantity 287¾ bushels and which made the whole yield of field No. 5 wch. had been in Oats, amount to 33 Acres 575¼ bushels or 17½ bushls. to the Acre) were employed in preparing and covering the yard at the Tobacco house in order to tread out the Wheat & Oats there.

At Muddy hole the remainder of the Carrots in the other 10 Acres (sowed with Seed from the Mansion House) were dug & measured—yield 6 bushels only. These were very much missing, and of an inferior quality, to the orange—Much so in point of size.

Sunday 9th.     Thermometer at 32 in the Morning—38 at Noon And 36 at Night. The Wind having shifted to the No. Wt. in the

Night it cleared and grew cold. In the Morning the ground was hard froze & the Weather very clear as it continued to be all day— the wind tho' not hard remaining at No. Wt.

Colos. Fitzgerald & Gilpin, Captn. Conway & Mr. Herbert, Mr. Hartshorne & Doctr. Craik Junr. came here to Dinner & returned afterwards.

Monday 10th.    Thermometer at 31 in the Morning—36 at Noon and 34 at Night. Morning & day clear. Wind varying from West to No. Wt. and very cold all day. Ground hard froze—plows stopped till it softened—Ice 3/4 of an Inch thick in places.

Rid to all the Plantations. In the Neck, gathering and husking Corn with all the hands till the plows could work.

At Muddy hole began to put up the Fence between fields No. 3 & 4.

At Dogue run gathering and husking Corn—5 plows at Work.

At Frenchs all hands treading Wheat—plows stopped for this purpose.

At the Ferry 3 plows were at Work. The other hands were getting up taking an Acct. of the Stock & Tools previous to Hezekh. Fairfaxs leaving the place—afterwards grubbing in the slash between this Plantan. & Frenchs.

This day agreed to give the two Brothers of Cornelius Mc-Dermot Roe 20 guineas as Ditchers or labourers till the 1st. of Novr. next the Younger of the two to Work at Brick laying when Cornelius is so employed.

Cornelius McDermott Roe's two brothers were Edward and Timothy (LEDGER B, 236; O'BRIEN, 186–87).

Tuesday 11th.    Thermometer at 27 in the Morning—37 at Noon And 35 at Night. Wind at West varying some times to the No. ward & sometimes to the Southward. Cold & raw with appearances of Snow towards evening.

Rid to Muddy hole, D. Run Frenchs and the Ferry Plantns.

Too hard frozen the ground to Plow any where.

At Muddy hole Fencing.

At Dogue run cutting Rail stuff with the Men—women husking Corn.

At Frenchs Treading out the remainder of the Wheat.

At the Ferry—grubbing in the slash as mentioned yesterday.

In the Evening Mrs. Bushrod Washington (brought by my Chariot from Colchester) and Mr. Fendal, came here.

Wednesday 12th.    Thermometer at 28 in the Morning—32 at Noon And 30 at Night. Clear and cold but not unpleasant. Wind at No. Wt. all day. Grd. very hard froze. Creeks covered with Ice.

No plowing any where to day.

Mr. Fendall going away after breakfast Mrs. Washington, Mrs. Bushrod Washington, Colo. Humphreys & myself dined at Mr. Lund Washingtons.

I rid by the Ferry, Frenchs, and Dogue run Plantations as I went.

At the Ferry, grubbing in the swamp as yesterday.

At French's cleaning up the Wheat that had been tread out.

At Dogue run, after finishing husking Corn, the Women were employed in cleaning up the swamp in the Meadow above the Houses.

Killed the following Hogs to day viz.—

| | | | |
|---|---|---|---|
| from the Neck. | 22 | weight | 3119 |
| Ferry | 23 | Do. | 3000 |
| Dogue run | 21 | Do. | 2498 |
| Muddy hole | 17 | Do. | 1594 |
| Total | 83 | | 10211 |
| Also at the Mill | 7 | Do. | 1166 |
| Together | 90 | | 11377 |
| Out of these the Miller recd. | | | 599 |
| Bishop 100 & R. B. Walker 100 | | | 200 |
| remain | | | 799 |

The last Potatoes having been brought home from Muddy hole, from the grd. by the Quarters, the qty. in that piece amounted to 275¾ Bls. and makes the whole from that Plantation 468 Bushls. From all the Plantations 997¾ Bushls. whereof 409 Bushels of large white 153½ bushls. of large red—246 bushls. of Small White and 60 bushls. of small red were put into the Cellars. The deficiency have been made use of and got injured and were given to the Cows.

Thursday 13th.    Thermometer at 31 in the Morning—35 at Noon And 30 at Night.

Clouds & Sunshine alternately, sometimes great appearances of Snow. Wind West—varying Sometimes to the No. & sometimes to the So. of it.

Rid to all the Plantations except the Neck.

Ground too hard froze to plow at any of them.

At the Ferry, all hands grubbing the Swamp except 1 man getting stakes for fence.

At Frenchs—all hands cleaning Wheat. Cornelius & his two brothers began to deepen the parting ditch betwn. this Plantation & the ferry.

At Dogue Run—the women were digging Carrots—grd. very improper for it, being hard froze, & wheat hurt by it. Men cutting rail timber except those who were at the Mansn. House abt. the Hogs.

At Muddy hole, the Men being employed at the Mansn. house abt. the Hogs the women were cutting Corn stalks.

Friday 14th.    Thermometer at 27 in the Morning—41 at Noon and 38 at Night. Clear and Cold all day the Wind continuing steadily at No. Wt.

Rid to all the Plantations. The grd. continuing hard frozen all day an entire stop was put to plowing.

At the River Plantation, all hands were employed in gathering, husking and housing Corn.

At Muddy hole, the people were employed in putting up fencing.

At Dogue run the Men were cutting & Mauling rails—the Women grubbing in field No. 5. Ordered them to Frenchs tomorrow to clean out the meadow, before the wetness of it shall put a stop to it.

|  | Barrls. |
|---|---:|
| The Corn in the left hand cut measured of sound | 22 |
| The right hand ditto | 27 |
| The New grd. by Frenchs | 15 |
| Total | 64 |

The Carrots brot. from thence measured [      ] Bushels—one row remains undug.

At Frenchs, finished cleaning the Wheat and sent it to the Mill qty. 47½ Bushls. besides tailings which were brot. to the Mansn. House [      ] bushels.

At the Ferry, all the Women were grubbing.

In the evening Messrs. Rumney Monshur & Porter came down.

Saturday 15th.    Thermometer at 30 in the Morning—42 at Noon And 39 at Night. Wind at No. West all day, and abt. Noon pretty fresh. Ground hard froze all day.

No plowing.

A little after Sun rise, in company with the Gentlemen who

came yesterday—Colo. Humphreys, Majr. Washington & Mr. Lear, went a hunting; but did not get a fox on foot nor is it certain we ever touched on the trail of one. The Gentlemn. and Lund Washington (who joined us) came home to dinner, & returned home afterwards.

The Acct. of the horses at the Ferry Plantation, which had been mislayed (after taking it the 16th. of Octr.) is as on the other side.

|  | yrs. old |  |
|---|---|---|
| A bla. horse. Prince 15 hds. high a striek of wh. down the face | 20 | Horses |
| A bla. horse—Dick—14 hands Star in the forehead | unkn. |  |
| A Small bay Mare Kitty 13 hands Star in her forehead | 13 | Working Mares |
| A bla. Mare Nancy—14 hands. Small star left fore foot white. | 7 |  |
| A Grey Mare Peggy—14 hands | 14 |  |
| A Sorrel Do.—Bonny—14½ Do.—Star in her forehead | 14 |  |
| A Grey Do.—Fly—13½—black legs | 9 |  |
| A Black horse 13 hands—3 yrs. old next spring—small Starr—dam Nancy. Sire Robinsons horse |  | Unbroken Horses and Mares |
| A bla. ditto—3 yrs. old in the Spring blaze face, white noze, and two hind feet white |  |  |
| A bay horse 13½ hands 4 years old next Spring—dam dead Sire Leonidas |  |  |
| A Bay Mare 12½ hands. 3 y. old next Spring—black legs dam Kitty—Sire the dray |  |  |

Sunday 16th.    Thermometer at 32 in the Morning—37 at Noon and 37 at Night. Wind at No. Et. in the morning—then calm—then So. Et. Cloudy all day with great appearances of Snow.

Monday 17th.    Thermometer at 34 in the Morning—40 at Noon and 38 at Night. But little wind all day, & that at No. Et. Weather much more moderate than it has been. In the morng. and alternately through the day, great appearances of Snow. At times a little fell, but not enough to whiten the ground. In the afternoon the Sun appeared.

Rid to the Ferry, French's, & Muddy hole Plantations.

No Plowing any where. A hand from each Plantation sent to the

Mansn. Ho. to cut wood for Christmas—the Carts from the Ferry, Frenchs & Dogue run accompanying them in order to draw it in, & to carry out dung.

At the Ferry the Women were grubbing the Slash.

At Frenchs they were getting out Oats.

At Dogue Run, except the Men who were at home, getting Rail timber, the rest were at Frenchs cleaning the Meadow as they had been on Saturday agreeably to the order given on Friday.

At Muddy hole the Women were fencing between fields No. 5 & 6.

On Saturday last brot. home the 2 Maltese Jennys, and 2 Mules one from the bla. dray Mare at D. run—the other from a Grey Mare at the Ferry—Also the 2 Stallion Colts from the Neck—to Winter. The Bullocks which had been in the Mill Meadow and intended for Stall feeding—6 in number—were brot. home to their racks this day also.

Tuesday 18th.   Thermometer at 31 in the Morning—42 at Noon And 38 at Night. Wind Northerly and variable.

Rid to the Ferry, Frenchs and Muddy hole.

At the first grubbing the Swamp or slash.

At French's, Treading out Oats.

The hands from Dogue run cleaning up the Meadow at this place as yesterday.

At Muddy hole fencing. Finished gathering, husking and Housing the Corn at the River plantation—qty. as follow.

|  |  | Sound barrls. | Soft or Rottn. Barrels |
|---|---|---|---|
| From field No. 3 | drilled | 92½ | 8 |
| Wood cut 9 |  | 17 | 2 |
| Old gate do. | do. | 86½ | 17 |
| Next Wms. | do. | 8 | 6 |
| New gate cut | do. | 93½ | 49 |
| East cut | do. | 44 | 48 |
|  |  | 341½ | 130 |
| Of the above sound Corn 290 was Housed, the rest eaten by Hogs &ca. |  |  |  |
| Crop at Muddy hole |  | 30 | 18 |
| Ferry |  | 71½ | 22 |
| Dogue run |  | 64 | unknown |
| Total |  | 507 | 170 |

Wednesday 19th.    Thermometer at 34 in the Morning—44 at Noon And 40 at Night. Wind variable from No. Et. to So. East. Snowing by spirts & sometimes fast (but never so as to whiten the ground) from Sun rise till 11 Oclock.

Rid to all the Plantations. At the Neck—Men getting Posts for Fencing, & some, with the Women, covering & getting Farm pen in order. Brought the (Waggon here to assist in getting in wood) .

At Muddy hole—The people were fencing.

At Dogue run, except those who were mauling & cuttg. Rails they were cleaning the Meadow at Frenchs as yesterday.

At Frenchs, on acct. of the weather, no Oats were tread out to day but those which had been tread out were cleaning up.

At the Ferry cleaning up the Swamp which had been grubbed.

Thursday 20th.    Thermometer at 34 in the Morning—43 at Noon and 36 at Night. Perfectly clear all day. Morning calm. Wind fresh & cold from the No. Wt. afterwards till towards sundown when it became calm & pleasant.

Rid to the Ferry, Frenchs and Muddy hole Plantations.

At the first the People having cleaned up the slash or swamp they were directed to level the ditch in No. 2 (which formerly divided this Plantation from French's) and to grub on the sides of it. Ordered 4 of the fatting hogs from hence to the Mansn. Ho. to be slaughtered—1 Sow which appeared to be with pig to be turned out for a breeder & 3 to be left for the Farmer.

At French's all the hands that were at home were employed in Treading out Oats. At this place also—in the Meadow the D. Run people were at work and would finish the Meadow—that is taking out the Trees which had fallen and other trash.

At Muddy hole—Fencing as yesterday—the partition between fields No. 4 & 5 would be compleated to day. That between fields 3 & 4 was so yesterday.

Ordered the remainder of the Hogs, except 3 for Overseer to be brot. to the Mansion Ho. this evening to be slaughtered.

The Ditchers went to cut & ditch between fields No. 1 & 4 to day at Frenchs but having a fence which was on the line to remove, previous thereto they would scarcely enter thereon to day.

Friday 21st.    Thermometer at 33 in the Morning—38 at Noon And 35 at Night. Morning clear and tolerably pleasant. Wind Westerly, but getting to No. Wt. it blew fresh & turned cold but continued clear & not unpleast.

The frost since it set in being a continued one, has stopped all plowing. The ground quite dry and roads dusty.

Rid to Muddy hole, Dogue run French's & the Ferry Plantatns.

At Muddy hole began to fence between No. 1 & 2. Brought two Sorrel Colts from thence rising two. Magnolio's.

At Dogue run the people having finished the Meadow at Frenchs yesterday were (the Women, the Men getting rails) employed in cleaning their own Meadow. Counted all the Stock at this place and brot. to the Mansn. House to be wintered 8 Mares with fold – 2 Sorrl. Colts rising two – a young bay mare rising three – a young bay horse for Washington Custis and the Chariot horse Partner.

At French's all the hands that were at home, were cleaning Oats and that this business might be dispatched I sent 4 hands from the Ferry to work a 2d. Fan.

At the Ferry the women were levelling the Ditch in No. 2 ordered to be done yesterday.

Killed the following Hogs to day.

| | | | |
|---|---|---|---|
| From the Neck | 18 | weight | 1650 |
| Ferry | 4 | Do. | 335 |
| | | | 1985 |

Disposed of them as follow

| | |
|---|---|
| Thos. Bishop & T. Green | 800 |
| Richd. B. Walker | 152 |
| Overseer Morris | 300 |
| Ditto at Frenchs | 300 |
| Ditto Muddy hole | 228 |
| Carpenter Isaac | 202 |
| | 1982 |

Overseer Da[v]y retained 3 of his Hogs agreeably to order, as did the Farmer at the Ferry. The first weighed 311 lbs.: of the weight of the latter – if killed, no acct. has yet been rendered. The 2 reserved by him when the first hogs came from the Ferry weighed 243 lbs.

The General Acct. stands thus.

| | | hogs | |
|---|---|---|---|
| Early killg. from the Mill Novr. 12th. | | 7 | 1342 |
| 2d. Killing – 12th. Inst. – viz. includg. 2 to the Farmer | | 92 | 11620 |
| 3d. Killing, exclusive of 3 left for him & includg. 3 left for Davy | | 25 | 2286 |
| Total | | 124 | 15248 |
| Disposed of to the Ovrs. & others pr. the foregoing Accts. remaing. for Fam[il]y | | | 12712 |

Saturday 22d.    Thermometer at 27 in the Morning—27 at Noon And 26 at Night. Wind at No. Et. & the weather varient till abt. Noon when it turned very cold & cloudy. Towards Night it began to Snow & continued to do so whilst I sat up but in the Night it turned to rain. The Snow was not more than 2 Inches deep and is the first time the ground has been whitened with it this Fall or Winter.

After our usual breakfasting, Colo. Humphreys, Majr. Washington & myself with Mr. Lear went out with the hounds. Dragged up the Creek to the Gum Spring and then the Woods between Muddy hole, Dogue run & Colo. Masons Quarters, without touching on the trail of a fox.

I visited the Plantations (in going out & coming home) except the Neck.

At Muddy hole the people were Making the fence they were upon yesterday.

At Dogue run cleaning the swamp as yesterday.

At French's cleaning Oats &

At the Ferry grubbing a small part of the Swamp that runs into Frenchs Plantation.

In the Afternoon Mrs. Stuart and her 4 Children and Mr. George Calvert came here.

Sunday 23d.    Thermometer at 33 in the Morning—36 at Noon And 34 at Night. Mizling at times and Cloudy all day. Wind at No. Wt. but not very cold.

At home all day.

Monday 24th.    Thermometer at 35 in the Morning—38 at Noon And 36 at Night. Wind at No. West all day—the fore part of which was clear, the latter part cloudy—moderate.

Rid to all the Plantations.

At the River Plantation, the Men were preparing Posts & Rails —the Women cleaning out the Stables & heaping dung about the Barn.

At Muddy hole the Men were getting trunnels for fencing and the Women were threshing Pease.

At Dogue run the Men were making Pens &ca. for feeding the outlying horses. The Women were cleaning up the swamp they have lately been at work in.

At Frenchs the Men were cutting & carting Wood—the Women cleaning & securing Oats.

At the Ferry—the Men were cutting wood & getting stakes for

fencing. The Women, except the four which were at work at Frenchs were grubbing in the Swamp as before.

Mr. Snow came here.

Tuesday the 25th.    Thermometer at 34 in the Morning—46 at Noon And 42 at Night. Wind at No. West but not much of it.

Wednesday 26th.    Thermometer at 35 in the Morning—43 at Noon And 40 at Night. Morning calm, & pleasant for the Season, about Noon the Wind rose at No. West but it did not grow cold.

Mr. Snow returned to Alexandria. Colo. Humphreys, the Gentlemen of the Family & myself went out with the hounds but found nothing tho much ground was gone over. G. & L. W. came.

G. & L. W.: George Steptoe Washington and Lawrence Augustine Washington.

Thursday 27th.    Thermometer at 35 in the Morning—44 at Noon And 40 at Night. Calm and very mild, with but little wind & that at South.

Mr. Lund Washington & his wife and Miss Nancy Stuart came here to Dinner. The latter remained.

Friday 28th.    Thermometer at 35 in the Morning—44 at Noon and 40 at Night. Cloudy during the fore part of last with appearances of Snow or Rain but the Wind springing up fresh at No. Wt. it cleared. Very pleasant all day—morning calm & not hard. Abt. Noon the wind rose at No. Wt. but neither hard nor cold. In the afternoon it got to the Southward.

Mr. Willm. Craik & his two Sisters, & Mr. Kelly the dancing Master came down to dinner and stayed all Night.

Went out with the hounds to day. Took the drag of a fox with in my Muddy hole Inclosures, and found him in Stiths field (lately Herberts). Run him hard about half an hour—came to a cold drag & then lost him.

Mr. Willm. Craik and his Sisters Mariamne & Nancy and Mr. OKelly the Dancing Master came to Dinner and stayed all Night.

STITHS FIELD (LATELY HERBERTS): Buckner Stith (d. 1800), son of Capt. Buckner Stith of Brunswick County and his wife, Ann Walker Stith, had earlier in the year purchased from William Herbert two adjoining tracts of land containing a total of 301½ acres on Little Hunting Creek. The land adjoined that of Thomson Mason on the road from Gum Springs to Cameron Run (deeds of Stith to Herbert, Fairfax County Deeds, Book Q-1, 492–95, 497–500, Vi Microfilm; SPROUSE [2], 2:32).

Saturday 29th. Thermometer at 38 in the Morning—52 at Noon and 48 at Night. Remarkably fine, clear & moderate. Very little Wind & that Southerly.

Rid (the hollidays being ended) to the Plantations at the Ferry, Frenchs Dogue run, and Muddy hole.

At the Ferry the Men were getting Stakes for fencing, and the Women levelling the ditch in field No. 2.

At Frenchs all hands were cleaning Oats.

At Dogue run 5 Men were cutting & mauling rails & the rest cleaning up the swamp between the Meadows.

At Muddy hole—the People were about fencing except 1 Man getting stakes for Do. & 3 after Noon plowing.

Doctr. Craik and Mr. Roger West came to Dinner; and in the evening, with Mr. Wm. Craik & the two girls, returned; but the Postillion boy, Paris, getting his Jawbone broken by the kick of a horse; the Doctr. was pursued & brought back after he had got as far as Dorrels hill.

DORRELS HILL: Darrell's Hill, a mile south of Alexandria, was formerly the home of Sampson Darrell.

Sunday 30th. Thermometer at 34 in the Morning—35 at Noon And 32 at Night. Wind at So. Et. and Snowing fast all or the greater part of the day—but being wet it did not accumulate fast.

Doctr. Craik and Mr. OKelly went away after breakfast and abt. 11 Oclock Mr. Paradise & his Lady lately from England but now of Williamsburgh came in on a visit.

The Englishman John Paradise (1743–1795), who was pro-American during the Revolution, married Lucy Ludwell (1751–1814), daughter of Philip Ludwell (1716–1767), of London, Eng., and of Green Spring, James City County, Va. The Paradises arrived in Virginia from England in Sept. 1787, and after a stay at Green Spring were visiting friends and family, including many of the Lees, to whom Mrs. Paradise was related by marriage (see SHEPPERSON).

Monday 31st. Thermometer at 28 in the Morning—34 at Noon And 30 at Night. Clear and not unpleasant—being but little Wind from the No. West.

Mrs. Stuart and Miss Nancy Stuart went to Mr. Lund Washingtons.

I remained at home all day. Mr. Chs. Lee came here to dinner and stayed all night.

The following diary is GW's Philadelphia journal (Regents' No. 34), a rough diary (from 11 May through 15 Nov. 1787) from which GW drew information for his more complete diary entries for those dates which appear earlier in this volume (see entry for 8 May 1787).

## [May 1787]

**Friday 11th.** Set out before breakfast and rid 12 Miles to Skirrets Tavern, where we baited, and proceeded to the Ferry at Havre de grass to dinner. The wind being high, & the weather Squally I did not cross the river—frequent Showers thro' the day with Mists and sun shine alternately.

**Saturday 12th.** Crossed the river early in the morning and breakfasted at the ferry house on the east side. Dined at the head of Elk and lodged at Wilmington. At the head of Elk Mr. Corbin joined me, and took a seat in my carriage to Wilmington.

**Sunday 13th.** About Nine o'clock Mr. Corbin and I set out, and dined at Chester, where I was met by Genls. Mifflin, Knox & Varnum—Colonls. Humphreys and Minges and Majors Jackson and Nicholas. After dinner we proceeded for the City. At the Ferry (Grays) I was met by the Troop of City light horse by whom (and a large concourse, I was escorted to Mrs. Houses—after passing the Artillery officers (who saluted) at the entrance of the City. On my arrival a peal was rung and Mr. Robt. Morris & his Lady again pressing me to lodge with them I had my baggage moved and took up my Quarters at their House—after paying my respects to the President of the State Doctr. Franklin.

**Monday 14th.** This being the day appointed for the meeting of the Convention such members of it as were in town assembled at the State House where it was found that two States only were represented—viz. Virginia and Pensylvania. Agreed to meet again tomorrow at 11 Oclock. Dined (in a family way) at Mr. Morris's & dr[an]k Tea there.

**Tuesday—15th.** Repaired to the State Ho. at the hour appointed. No more States represented, tho' there were members (but not sufficient to form a quoram) from two or three others—viz. No. Carolina, & Delaware as also Jersey. Govr. Randolph of Virginia came in to day. Dined with the Society of the Cincinnati.

**Wednesday 16th.** Only two States represented. Agreed to meet at one oclock. Doctr. McClerg of Virginia came in. Dined at Doctr. Franklins. Drank Tea & spent the Evening with Mr. Jno. Penn.

**Thursday. 17th.** Mr. Pinkney of So. Carolina coming in from New York and Mr. Rutledge being here before formed a representation from that State. Colo. Mason getting in this Evening from Virginia compleated the whole number of this State in the delegation.
Dined at Mr. Powells and drank Tea there.

Friday 18th. The State of New York was represented. Dined at a club at Greys ferry over the Schuylkill & drank Tea at Mr. Morris's—after wch. went with Mrs. Morris & some other Ladies to here a lady read at the College Hall.

Saturday. 19th. No more States represented. Agreed to meet at one Oclock on Monday. Dined at Mr. Ingersolls and spent the evening at home—going to bed soon.

Sunday 20th. Went into the Country with Mr. & Mrs. Morris and dined at their place at the Hill. Returned in the afternoon and drank Tea at Mr. Powells.

Monday 21 Delaware State was represented. Dined and drank Tea at Mr. Binghams—great splender shewn.

Tuesday. 22d. North Carolina represented. Dined and drank Tea at Mr. Morris's.

Wednesday 23d. No more States represented. Rid to Genl. Mifflins to breakfast—after wch. in Company with him Mr. Madison, Mr. Rutlidge & others, crossed the Schuylkill above the Falls. Called at Mr. Peters's Mr. Penns and Mr. Hamiltons and repaired at the hour of one to the State House. Dined at Mr. Chews with the wedding guests & drank Tea there in a large Circle of Ladies.

Thursday 24th. No more States represented. Dined and drank Tea at Mr. Ross's. One of my Postilion boys (Paris) being ill sent for Doctr. Jones to him.

Friday 25th. Another delegate coming in from the State of New Jersey made a quoram; and Seven States being now represented, the body was Organized and I was called to the Chair by a unanim. vote. Major Jackson was appointed Secretary—and a Com[mitt]ee consisting of Mr. Wythe, Mr. Hamilton, and Mr. Chs. Pinkney chosen to prepare rules & regulations by which the Convention was to be governed. To give time for this it adjourned till Monday 10 Oclock. Returned many visits in the forenoon and dined at Mr. Thos. Willings. Spent the Evening at my quarters.

Saturday 26. Returned all my visits this forenoon (where I cd. get an Acct. of the Lodggs. of those to whom I was indebted for them). Dined at a club at the City Tavern and spent the Evening at my Quarters writing lett[ers].

Sunday 27th. Went to the Romish Church, to high Mass. Dined, drank Tea, and spent the evening at my lodgings.

Monday 28th.    Met in Convention at 10 Oclock. Two States more—viz., Massachusetts and Connecticut being represented, made nine on the floor. Proceeded to the establishment of rules for the government of the Convention and adjourned about 2 Oclock.

Dined at home and drank Tea in a large Circle at Mr. Francis's.

Tuesday 29th.    Dined at home and went to Mr. Juhans benefit Concert at the City Tavern. The same Number of States met in Convention as yesterday.

Wednesday 30th.    Convention as yesterday.

Dined with Mr. Vaughan. Drank Tea and spent the Evening at Mr. & Mrs. Lawrences.

Thursday. 31st.    Convention representation encreased by the coming in of the State of Georgia occasioned by the arrival of Majr. Pierce & Mr. Houste[n].

Dined at Mr. Francis's and drank Tea with Mrs. Meridith.

# [June 1787]

Friday June 1st.    Convention as yesterday. Dined with Mr. John Penn and Spent the evening at Bush-hill at a very elegant entertainment given to a numerous company by Mr. Hamilton the owner of it.

Saturday. 2d.    Majr. Jenifer coming in with powers from the State of Maryland authorizing one member to represent it, added another State (now eleven) to the Convention.

Dined at Club, at the City Tavern, and Spent the evening at my q[uarte]rs.

Sunday—3d.    Dined at Mr. Clymers and drank Tea there.

Monday—4th.    Convention as on Saturday. Dined with Genl. Mifflin. Reviewed the light Infantry—Cavalry—and part of the Artillery of the City and dined. Drank Tea with Miss Cadwalader.

Tuesday. 5th.    Dined at Mr. Morris's with a large Company and spent the evening there.

Wednesday 6th.    Dined at the Presidents with a large Company & drank Tea there after wch. came home & wrote Letters for France.

Thursday—7th.    Dined at a Club at the Indian Queen. Drank Tea & spent the evening at home.

Friday—8th.    Dined—drank Tea and spent the Evening at home.

Saturday 9th.    Dined at the Club at the City Tavern. Drank Tea and sat till 10 oclock at Mr. Powells.

Sunday 10th.    Breakfasted by agreemt. at Mr. Powells; and in company with him, rode to see the Botanical Garden of Mr. Bartram—which though stored with many curious Trees, Shrups, & flowers was neither large nor laid off in much taste.

From hence we rode to the Farm of one Jones to see the effect of the Plaister of Paris. This appeared obvious—first on a piece of Wh. stubble, which he says has never recd. any Manure, and the Wheat so indifferent as to be scarcely worth cutting; The White clover on this (without any Seed be putting in the grd., & the Plaister laid on the Stubble without breaking) was full high to Mow and very thick. The line was fairly, & most obviously drawn between the grass where the powder was spread and that where it ended, for in the latter the grass was not only thin, and very indifferent, but scarcly any of the White clover. The same difference was equally apparent on a piece of mowing ground. The grass there, principally White clover, with a mixture of Red far overstepped, and was much thicker than that which surrounded it. The Soil of these pieces appeared to be a loam—very slightly mixed with Isenglass originally good, but according to Mr. Jones's acct. a good deal exhausted. He informed us of the effect of the Plaister on a piece of heavy, stiff meadow (not subject however to be wet) and that it was still more obvious here.

This manure according to his acct. was laid on the 29th. of October in damp or wet weather, & at the rate of about 5 bu. to the Acre—Moon in the Increase (2d. quarter) wch. he says (though there certainly can be nothing in it) the farmers tell him ought to be attended to. When it is laid on grass land, or Meadow, the ground ought first to be well furrowed, so as to raise the mould.

From hence visited Mr. Powells farm, after which I went to Mr. Morri[s's] country seat to dinner by appointment and returned to the City about dusk.

Monday. 11th.    Dined—Drank Tea and spent the Evening (in my own room) at Mr. Morris['s.]

Tuesday 12th.    Dined at Mr. Morris's & drank Tea there. Went afterwards to the Concert at the City Tavern.

Wednesday 13.    Dined at Mr. Clymers & drank Tea there. Spent the evening at Mr. Bing[h]ams.

Thursday—14th.    Dined at Majr. Moores and spent the evening at my own lodgings.

Friday—15th.    Dined at Mr. Powells & drank Tea there.

Saturday—16th.    Dined at the Club at the City Tavern and spt. the evening at my own lodgings.

Sunday 17th.    Went to Church. Heard Bishop White Preach & see him Ordain two Gentlemen into the Order of Deacons.

After which rid 8 Miles into the Country dined with Mr. Jno. Ross and returned to Town agn. about dusk.

Monday—18th.    Dined at the Quarterly meeting of the Sons of St. Patrick at the City Tavern and drank Tea at Doctr. Shippens with the party of Mrs. Livingston.

Tuesday. 19th.    Dined in a family way at Mr. Morris's and spent the evening there in a large party.

Wednesday—20th.    Dined at Mr. Meridiths and drank Tea there.

Thursday 21st.    Dined at Mr. Pragers and spent the evening in my own room.

Friday—22d.    Dined in a family way at Mr. Morris's and drank Tea at Mr. Francis Hopkinsons.

Saturday 23d.    Dined at Doctr. Rustons and drank Tea at Mr. Morris's.

Sunday—24th.    Dined at Mr. Morris's and spent the Evening at Mr. Meridiths in drinking Tea only.

Monday. 25th.    Dined at Mr. Morris's. Drank Tea there and spent the Evening in my own Room.

Tuesday—26th.    Took a family dinner with Govr. Randolph and made one of a party to drink Tea at Grays ferry.

Wednesday. 27th.    Dined at Mr. Morris's drk. Tea there, & spent the Evening in my own room.

Thursday—28th.    Dined at Mr. Morris's in a large Compy. Drank Tea there & spent the Evening in my own room.

29th. Friday.    Dined at Mr. Morris's and spent the Evening at home.

Saturday 30th.    Dined at a Club of Genn. & Ladies at the Cool Spring—Springsbury and spt. the Evening at home.

# July [1787]

Sunday 1st.    Dined and spent the Evening at home.

Monday. 2d.    Dined with some of the Members of Convention at the Indian Queen. Drank Tea at Mr. Binghams & walked afterwards in the State Ho. yard. Sat for Mr. Pine.

# July 1787

Tuesday [3d].  Sat for Mr. Peal This Morn. Dined at Mr. Morris. Drank Tea at Mr. Powells and went with him to the Agricultural Society at Carpenters hall.

Wednesday 4th.  Visited Dr. Chuvats Anatomy. Heard at the Calvanist church, an Oration on the Anniversary of Independence. Dined afterwards with this State Society of Cincinnati and drank Tea at Mr. Powells.

Thursday 5th.  Dined at Mr. Morris's. Drank Tea and spent the Evening there.

Friday—6th.  Sat for Mr. Peale to draw my Picture in the Morning. Dined at the City Tavern with some gentn. of the Convention and spent the evening at home.

Saturday 7th.  Dined at the Cold Spring, with the Club. Returned in the evening, and drank Tea at Mr. Meridiths.

Sunday—8th.  About 12 Oclock rode to Doctr. Logans near Germn. Town where I dined. Returned in the Evening and dk. Tea at Mr. Morris's.

Monday—9th.  Sat in the Morning for Mr. Peale. Dined at Mr. Morris's and drk. Tea at Dr. Redmans.

Tuesday 10th.  Dined at Mr. Morris's—Drank Tea at Mr. Binghams and went to the Play.

Wednesday 11th.  Dined at Mr. Morris's and spent the evening at home.

Thursday 12th.  Dined at Mr. Morris's and Drank Tea with Mrs. Livingston.

Friday 13th.  Dined at Mr. Morris's, Drank Tea, there, & spent the Evening.

Saturday 14th.  Dined at the Cold Spring Club and went to the Play in the Afternoon.

Sunday—15th.  Dined at Mr. Morris's & Remained there all the afternoon.

Monday 16th.  Dined at Mr. Morris's, & drank Tea at Mr. Powells.

Tuesday—17th.  Dined at Mrs. Houses, & made an excursion with a party to Grays Ferry to Tea.

Wednesday 18th.  Dined at Mr. Milligan's and drank Tea at Mrs. Meridiths.

Thursday. 19th. Dined at Mr. John Penns (the Younger) drank Tea, and spent the evening at home.

Friday—20th. Dined at home, and drank Tea at Mr. Clymers.

Saturday 21st. Dined at the Cold Spring Club, and went to the Play in the afternoon.

Sunday 22d. Left town by 5 Oclock, breakfasted at General Mifflins—rode up to the Spring Mills and returnd. to Genl. Mifflins to Dinner, after which came to the City.

Monday 23d. Dined at Mr. Morris's, and drank Tea at Lansdown—the Country Seat of Mr. Jno. Penn. Returned in the evening.

Tuesday—24th. Dined at Mr. Morris's and drank Tea at Doctr. Rush's.

Wednesday—25th. Dined at Mr. Morris's. Drank Tea & spent the evening at home.

Thursday. 26th. Dined at Mr. Morris's. Drank Tea there & stayed within all the afternoon.

Friday—27th. Dined at Mr. Morris's & drank Tea at Mr. Powells.

Saturday—28th. Dined at the Cold Spring Club and after drink Tea there—returned to Mr. Morris's & spent the eveng. there.

Sunday 29th. Dined and spent the whole day at Mr. Morris's.

Monday 30th. In company with Mr. Governr. Morris went into the Neighbourhood of the Valley Forge to a Widow Moores a fishing at whose house we lodged.

Tuesday—31st. Before breakfast I rid to the Valley forge and over the whole Cantonment & works of the American Army in the Winter of 1777–8 and on my return to the Widow Moores found Mr. & Mrs. Rob: Morris. Spent the day there fishing &ca. & lodged at the same place.

## [August 1787]

Wednesday Augt. 1st. Returned abt. 11 Oclock with the above Company to Philadelphia.

    In this Town I understood—that the usual time of Sowing Buck Wheat was from the 10th. to the 20th. of July—that the grd. ought to be Twice plowed and *at least* as often harrowed & the grain harrowd. in—That it is considered as an uncertain Crop—liable to injury (whilst in the blossom) by a hot Sun—and very apt to in[ju]ry by frost in Autumn—That it is excellent food for Horses (to puff them up) Milch Cattle, Sheep, Hogs, also for fattin[g] beeves; and to feed Colts when they are weaned.

That 2 quarts of Buck Wheat meal, & ½ a peck of Potatoes (at first, the quantity to be reduced as the fatting creature falls off in stomach, or in other words encreases in fat) given 3 times a day is fully sufficient. That the Buck Wheat ground into Meal & given in wash—is most excellent to lay on fat for Hogs (to be hardened with Corn) & that this meal and Potatoes (given raw, but washed, and cut small, is excellent for the weaning of Colts. And that the quantity to the acre is (on an average) 25, Bush. About 3 pecks of Seed is sufft. for an Acre of ground.

Thursday 2d.  Dined at Mr. Morris's—drank Tea—and spent the evening there.

Friday—3d.  Went up to Trenton on a Fishing party with Mr. & Mrs. Robt. Morris, & Mr. Govr. Morris. Dined and lodged at Colo. Saml. Ogdens. In the evening fished.

Saturday—4th.  In the Morning, and betwn. breakfast and dinner fished. Dined at General Dickensons, and returned in the evening to Colo. Ogdens.

Sunday—5th.  Dined at Colo. Ogdens and about 4 oclock set out for Philadelpa. Halted an hour at Bristol and reached the City before 9 Oclock.

Monday—6th.  Again met in Convention agreeably to adjournmt. & recd. the report of the Com[mitt]ee. Dined at Mr. Morris's and drank Tea at Mr. Meridiths.

Tuesday—7th.  Dined at Mr. Morris's and drank Tea no where. Spent the evening at home.

Wednesday 8th.  Dined at the City Tavern and remained there till near 10 Oclock.

Thursday 9th.  Dined at Mr. Swanwicks and spent the evening in my own room—reading letters & accts. from home.

Friday—10th.  Dined and drank Tea at Mr. Binghams. Spent the evening at home.

Saturday 11th.  Dined at the Cold Spring Club and after Tea returned & spent the evening at home.

Sunday 12th.  Dined at Bush-hill with Mr. William Hamilton. Spent the evening at home—writg.

Monday. 13th.   Dined at home and drank Tea with Mrs. Bache at the Presidents.

Tuesday 14th.   Dined & drank Tea at home.

Wednesday 15th.   Did the same.

Thursday 16th.   Dined at Mr. Pollocks & spent the evening in my own room.

Friday—17th.   Dined and drank Tea at Mr. Powells.

Saturday 18th.   Dined at Chief Justice McKeans & spent the evening at home.

Sunday 19.   In company with Mr. Powell rode up to the White Marsh. Dined at German Town—drank Tea at Mr. Peters's & returned home in the eveng.

Monday 20th.   Dined and drank Tea at home.

Tuesday 21st.   Did the same.

Wednesday 22d.   Dined at the Hills—Mr. Morris's and visited at Mr. Powells in the Evening.

Thursday 23d.   Dined at home and drank Tea there.

Friday 24th.   Dined at home.

Saturday 25th.   Dined at the Club and spent the evening at home.

Sunday 26.   Rode into the Country 8 or 10 Miles. Dined with Mr. Morris at the Hills & spent the Evening writing letters.

Monday 27th.   Dined at Mr. Morris's and drank Tea at Mr. Powells.

Tuesday—28th.   Dined at home and drank Tea there.

Wednesday 29th.   Did the same.

Thursday 30th.   Did the same.

Friday—31st.   Dined at home and in Company with others went into the Country and drank Tea with Mr. Penn.

## [September 1787]

Saturday. Sepr. 1st.    Dined at home and drank Tea there.

Sunday—2d.    Rode to Mr. Bartrams & other places in the Country and dined & drank Tea at Mr. Grays.

Monday 3d.    Dined and drank Tea at home.

Tuesday 4th.    Dined and did the same after visiting a machine at Doctr. Franklins for smoothing Clothes, instead of Ironing of them after washing which appears to answer exceeding well for every species of them that has not pl[e]ates & folds.

Wednesday 5th.    Dined at Mrs. Houses, and drank Tea at Mr. Binghams.

Thursday 6th. Dined at Doctr. Hutchinsons and spent the afternoon & evening at home.

Friday—7th.    Dined and spent the afternn. at home (except whilst riding a few miles).

Saturday. 8th.    Dined at the cold spring club and spent the afternoon at home.

Sunday—9th.    Dined at home after paying a visit to Mr. Gardoqui (Minister from Spain) who had come from New York on a visit to me.

Monday 10th.    Dined at home and drank Tea there.

Tuesday 11th.    Dined at home in a large Company & drank Tea & spent the evening there.

Wednesday 12th.    Dined at the presidents & drank Tea at Mr. Pines.

Thursday. 13th.    Dined at the Vice Presidents Chs. Biddles, & drank Tea at Mr. Powells.

Friday 14th.    Dined at the City Tavern at an entertainment given on my Acct. by the City Troop of light horse. Spend the Evening at Mr. Meridithes.

Saturday 15.    Finished the business of the Convention all to signing the proceedings to do which the House set till 6 Oclock. Spent the evening at my lodgings.

Sunday 16th.    Wrote many letters in the forenoon. Dined with Mr. & Mrs. Morris at the Hills & returned to Town in the Evening.

Monday 17th.    Met in Convention & Signed the proceedings—all except Govr. Randolph, Colo. Mason & Mr. Gerry. Dined all together at the City Tavern & returned to my lodgings.

Tuesday. 18th.    Finished what private business I had to do this forenoon. Dined abt. 1 Oclock at Mr. Morris's and set off afterwards—in Company with Mr. Blair, who took a Seat in my Chariot with me—on my return home. Reached Chester, where we lodged.

Wednesday 19th.    Prevented by Rain much of wch. fell in the Night f[ro]m setting off early. Baited at Wilmington—dined at Christiana bridge and lodged at the head of Elk—at the bridge near whch. I narrowly escaped an ugly accidt. to my Chariot & horses. One fell through & another with the Chariot was on the point of following but by exertions was saved.

Thursday 20th.    Sett off after an early breakfast. Crossed the Susquehannah & dined in Havre de grass at the Ho. of Colo. Rogers & lodged at Skirretts Tavern.

Friday 21st.    Breakfasted in Baltime.—dined at the Widow Balls formerly Spurriers and lodged at Majr. Snowdens.

Saturday 22d.    Breakfasted at Bladensburgh—passed thro George Town— dined at Alexandria and reached home by Sun set after being absent 4 Months & 14 days.

———————

Sunday—23d.    Mr. Blair remained here Cols. Fitzgerald, Simms, Ramsay & Lyles, Mr. Hunter, Mr. Murray Mr. Taylor Doctr. & Mrs. Stuart & the Girls dined here, all of whom except Mr. Blair Doctr. & Mrs. Stuart, went away afterwards.

Monday 24th.    After breakfast I rid to the Plantn. at the Ferry—Frenchs Dogue run, & Muddy hole. At the first the hands were getting out wheat & rye, and the plows putting in wheat in No. 6. At the next the Plows 4 were putting in Rye in No. [    ] and the other hands grubbing in the New Meadow. At Dogue run the Plows were covering wheat in No. [    ] and the other hands employed chiefly in grubbing the Swamp between the Meadows. At Muddy hole the plows were fallowing in No. [    ] for wheat— the rest gathering fodder.

   In the afternoon Doctr. Mrs. Stuart & the girls returned to Abingdon.

Tuesday 25th.    Mr. Blair set out before Sun rise, in my Chariot, to meet the stage at Boggess's.

After breakfast I rid into the neck—hands chiefly employed in getting fodder.

Wednesday 26th.    Rid to all the Plantations where the hands were generally employed as yesterday & gettg. Fodder.

Thursday 27th.    Did the same & the same work was going on.
   In the evening Mr. Corbin Washington, his wife and Miss Fanny Ballendine came in.

Friday 28th.    Rid to the Plantns. at the Ferry—French's, Dogue run & Muddy hole—work as usual.
   Mrs. Jenifer came here to dinner.

Saturday 29th.    Rid into the Neck and set 6 plows to breaking up the orchard Inclosure for Wheat and grass Seeds.
   After breakfast Corbin Washington, his wife and Miss Ballendine left this & in the afternoon Majr. G. A. W. set off for Fredericksburgh.

Sunday 30th.    Mrs. Fanny Washington, Mrs. Jenifer, and Nelly Custis & Hariot Washington went up to Abingdon.
   Colo. Gilpin & Mr. Wm. Craik came to dinner. The latter stayed all Night.

## [October 1787]

Oct.—Monday—1st.    Rid to all the Plantations—work as usual—except that the Plows at Dogue run were putting in Rye in the same field No. [      ]. Mr. Craik went away Ditchers went to Muddy hole—&

Tuesday. 2d.    Rid to all the Plantations. Sent 2 Plows from Frenchs to Muddy hole—the other 2 preparg. ground within the Meadow for Rye & grass Seeds—on which 1½ bushels of Rye was sown and therewith 1½ bushls. of sainfoin and 6 lbs. of Trefoil on the part next the road, & on the lower part adjoining the branch 2 quarts of Timothy Seed.

Wednesday 3d.    Went up with Mrs. Washington to Abingdon. Dined at Mr. Herberts in Alexa. on our way up.

Thursday 4th.    Dined at Abingdon and came home afterwards. Brot. Fanny Washington with us.
   Found 2 more plows from Frenchs at Muddy hole.

Friday 5th.    Rid to all the Plantns. Havg. finished sowing rye 22½ Bls. at Dogue run, sent one plow to Muddy hole. The rest of the horses & hands were employed in treading out Wheat—the Fodder being also secured. W[en]t to cross[in]g at M. H. being late finishg. ditch to ferry road.

In the Afternoon Mr. Alexr. Donald came in.

Saturday. 6th.    Rid to the Plantations at the Ferry, French's, Dogue run & Muddy hole. At the first having got out all the Wheat and Rye the Fodder next employed the hands. Colo. McC. & Wife & Mrs. Craik & Sally & two Mrs. Jenifers came here & retd.

In the Afternoon Mr. & Mrs. Powell of Phila. came in.

Sunday. 7th.    After Breakfast Mr. Donald went away and to dinner Mr. Bushrod Washington and his wife came.

Monday—8th.    Rid with Mr. Powell to my Plantations at Muddy hole, Dogue run, Frenchs, and the Ferry. Work as usual.

Tuesday 9th.    Rid with him and Mrs. Powell to see the Ruins of Belvoir. Called at Frenchs as we returned where I had begun with grass Scythes (a Cradle having been found not to answer) to cut the Pease wch. had been sown in broadcast—part being ripe and many green—owing either to their being too late sown or kept back by the drought wch. had been so severe. In cutting these Pease the Pods [or] heads of many were left without means of getting them up without picking them up by hand. Hence, the grd. shd. always be rolled to give it a smooth Surface that the rakes may gather better. Note this loss would not be very material if there had been no other crops in the same field to prevent the turng. in of Sheep. Doctr. Griffth came. Raked the Pease into small Cocks. Finishd. ditch to lane.

Wednesday 10th.    Mr. & Mrs. Powell & Mr. B. W. & wife went away after an early breakfast; I rid to all the Plantations after Doctr. Griffith who came here last Night went away. Same kind of Work going on.

Thursday—11th.    Rid to all Plantations. Began to sow Wheat and Sainfoin in the Orchard in the Neck. Finding the Pease at Muddy hole riper than those remaining to be cut at Frenchs ordered the Scythsmn. to go there tomorrow and leave the greener ones to the last.

In the Evening Genl. Pinkney & his Lady came in.

Friday. 12th.    Genl. Pickney going away after breakfast I rid to Muddy hole Dogue run & Frenchs—also to the Ferry.

Attempted (to avoid the loss by cutting) to pull up the Pease by the roots but found it too tedious & returned to the Scythes again. Sent Dogue run & Frenchs Plows home.

Saturday 13th.    Rid to Morris, Frenchs & the Ferry. At the two first took an Acct. of the horses Cattle & Sheep. Finished cutting & putting into sml.

Cocks the Pease at Muddy hole. Sowd. W[heat] on P[ease] w[ithou]t plowg.—but plowed them in—abt. [     ].

Sunday 14th.    At home all day. Wind having got to the No. Wt. abt. Noon Yesterday it turned very cold and this Morning the frost was so severe as to bite the Buck Wheat, Pease, Potatoe Vines Pompions &ca. & turn them quite black.

Monday—15th.    Ordered the Buck Wheat to be immediately cut—beginning with that at Dogue run abt. 15 Acres—which was fin[ishe]d this Morning (the frost being likewise severe) before the Moisture was off the Straw. Had it this also put into small Cocks to dry. Apprehend the Cutting of this grain has been delayed too in expectation of more of its ripening; a good deal of the Seed shed.

Rid to Muddy hole and into the Neck. Took an Acct. of the Stock at both places. Finished Sowing the Orchard with Wheat & Sainfoin—of the first [     ] bushls. and of the latter [     ] bushls. Note this grd. has been plowed & cross plowed—then Wheat sown & harrowed with the heavy harrow—then sowed with Sainfoin & harrowed in like manner—both the way it was last plowed. Ordered 50 lbs. of Trafoil to be sown over the Whole & harrowed with the dble. harrows cross the formr.

Tuesday—16th.    Rid to the Ferry, Frenchs, Dogue, & Muddy hole Planns. At the former took an account of the Stock. At the latter cut & put the buck Wheat into small shocks & dug the Country Potatoes—waste as at Morris's. At Dogue run treading out Wheat and at Frenchs Plowing & filling gullies in the New Meadow. At the Ferry pulling Pease.

Wednesday 17th.    Rid to all the Plantations except the Ferry. Cut the Buck Wheat in the Neck. A good deal of it shattered but whether it ought to have been cut sooner I cannot (for want of more knowledge of it) determe. Finished getting in the Fodder in the Neck the last at all the Places. Sowed yesterday & today (wind preventing it sooner) the trefoil 50 lbs. on the Wheat & Sainfoin in the Orch[ard] in the Neck and began to sow under furrow the Winter Vetches at the No. end of the same inclosure crossing therewith the first plowing and intending to run the light dble. harrows over the grd. after Sowing.

The Pease in broadcast at French's were much injured by the frost. It was unfortunate that they had not been cut a day or two sooner. Note the ground in which Pease & Buck Wheat are sowed ought always to be rolled if it is expected the Crop is to be taken off clean. The Pease however that are left would be fine for Sheep—especially fatting wethers. The Sweet Potatoes made at Muddy hole from the half Acre of experimental ground are as follow—viz.—the No. Wt. quarter wch. was in hills, & dunged as formerly mentioned, produced 4 bushels eatable, & 3½ fit only for Seed; the So. Wt. qr. also in Hills but not dunged, produced 2½ eatable & 3½ for seed—The No. Et. qr. in 4 foot rows and dunged, produced 2½ bushls. eatable, and 2 Seed—and the So. Et. qr. 2½ eatable & 2 Seed—In all 11½ of bush⟨ls.⟩ eatable and 11 bushls. of seed. The Potatoes in the dunged part of the ground were much the largest and turned out from

|  | eate. |  | seed |
|---|---|---|---|
| The hills . . . . . . . . . . . | 4 | . . | & 3½ |
| In 4 feet rows . . . . . . . . | 2½ | . . . | 2 |
| Undunged | 6½ |  | 5½ |
| In Hills . . . . . . . . . . | 2½ |  | 3½ |
| In 4 feet Rows . . . . . . . . | 2½ |  | 2 |
|  | 5 |  | 5½ |
| differe. . . . . . . | 1½ |  |  |
|  | 6½ |  | 5½ |

Upon remeasuring of the foregoing Potatoes. after they came home they turned out (heaped measure) only 7½ Bushls. eatg. Potatoes & 10½ of Seed —short in

The eatable . . . . . . . . . . . . . . . . . 4 bush.
Seed . . . . . . . . . . . . . . . . . . . ½ Bl.

Whether this was occasioned by the diffe. of measure or Stolen by the driver of the Cart remains to be discovered.

Thursday 18th.    Rid into the Neck, to Muddy hole, and French's. At the first dbled. the small heaps of buck Wheat in the Morning whilst the dew was on. Finished sowing & plowing the 6 Bls. of Winter vetches and harrowing in half a bushel of red clover seed between the branch by the Orchard, and the Road leading to and from the Negro quarters.

At Muddy hole finished late in the Afternoon the ditch round the Barn and dug the Irish Potatoes in the experimental ground (adjoining the ½ Acre of Sweet Pot[atoe]s) which being half of the red and half of the white in alternate rows through the pie[ce] (half acre) turned out as follow—

|  | red B[ushels] | Wht. B[ushels] |
|---|---|---|
| In the ½ wch. had been dunged— | 11 | 8¼ |
| ½ wch. had no dung— | 6 | 3½ |
| Total ½ acre | 17 | 11¾ |
| diffe. betwn. red & whe. | 5 | 4¼ |

In the afternoon of yesterday the hands from the Ho., except the Carpenters, went after they returned from the Neck, to French's; to get up, and secure as much of the Pease there as they could & with the hands belonging to the Plantation were employed in the same manner today—great loss by the frost —the ripe pease opening and shedding and the green ones—together with the vines turned quite black and as if parboild. Carried the Pease and Vines which appeared to be cured, into one end of the Tobo. House in field No. [   ].

In the evening Mr. Houston & Lady, and Miss Maria Livingston her Sister, came in and stayed all Night.

Friday. 19th.    Mr. Houston &ca. going away about 10 Oclock I rid to the Ferry, Frenchs, Dogue run & Muddy hole. At the first the People were making a farm Pen—at the next getting in Pease as yesterday—some of which (Vines) appeared to me to be not sufficiently cured.

At Dogue run, getting out Wheat & removing brush frm. the Swamp to gullies.

At Muddy hole began this morning to ditch between the fields No. 1, 2, 3, & 4. and to sow Wheat with a Barrel 6 feet long perforated with holes strapped Round with leather bands in order to drop the Wheat in sqrs. of 6 Inches—but the leather not being equally stretched and binding in all parts equally, and the sides opening a little—it discharged Seeds from the Sides as well as from the holes wch. in some measure defeated my intention.

On my return home found Mr. Dunlap (a West Indian) Mr. Cary, Mr. Donaldson, and Mr. Porter here who went away after dinner.

In the afternoon it began to rain slow & moderately with the wind (tho' not much of it) from the No. Et.

Saturday 20th.    The rain which began in the afternoon of yesterday, continued fm. appearances in the same slow manner through the Night and until the night of this day in which it rained much faster—Wind continuing at No. Et. all the while.

No out doors work done this day on acct. of the Rain.

Sunday. 21st.    Cloudy all day, but little or no rain. At home alone.

Monday. 22d.    Went up to a meeting of the Potomack Company at George Town. Called at Muddy hole Plantation to see how a barrel, which I had designed to drop 5 or 6 grains of Wheat in clusters at 6 Inches equidistant from each other performed. Found instead of doing this that it scattered the grains and having no time to alter, I directed it to proceed in that manner till I returned.

After finishing the business I got back to Abingdon.

Tuesday—23d.    Left this place before Sunrise. Coming to Muddy hole by 8 oclock and finding the alterations which were intended to be made in the barrel were not easy to be effected without some materials of which I was not possessed and the season not admitting of delay I took the bands from the barrel in order that it might sow more regular & thicker in broadcast.

Went round by Dogue run, French's, & the Ferry Plantations; At the first getting out Wheat—at the second securing Pease & at the last Treading out oats.

Wednesday 24th.    Rid to all the Plantations. In the Neck, found that the Sowing of the Orchard Inclose. had been compleated on Monday last—That what may *properly* be called the Orchard part of it had been sown with Wheat—Sainfoin—and Trafoil as has been mentioned—That the slipe between the Water course from the Road to the Spring & the Road *to* and *from* the Quarters had been sown with Wheat & red Clover as has been noted—That the No. Wt. part of the Inclosure had been sown (to a stake) with the Winter vetch *alone* and *all* the other part with Wheat *alone*. The Orchd. Part had been plowed & cross plowed—Then the Wht. harrowed in—next the Sainfoin harrowed in; both the same way the ground had been last plowed—and lastly, after the Trafoil was sown—the whole cross harrowed with a light harrow. The part that had the clover sown, was plowed & cross plowed as above, the Wheat then harrowed in & cross harrowed to bury the clover Seed. The ground in wch. Vetches were sown was cross plowed, which plowing, put them in—after which, it was harrowed to Smooth it. The remainder of the Inclosure which only had Wheat, was plowed—cross plowed and the Wheat harrowed in. Ordered the Buck Wheat at every place to be got in, and threshed out, as soon as possible.

Had that in the half Acre of experimental ground at Muddy hole, cut. About 1/4 at the So. Wt. corner was entirely missing (occasioned, I believe, by the low situation of the ground)

At Frenchs they would about get in all the Pease (tho' with great loss) tonight and at the ferry the people were cleaning the Oats which had been tread out yesterday. Mr. R. Lee & Sistr. came here in the evening yesterday.

Thursday 25th.    Rid to all the Plantations. In the Neck Began with 4 plows to break up flush field No. 4 (in 6 feet ridges) for Indn. Corn & Potatoes next yr. and began also to get to a yard wed for the purpose the Buck Wheat—also to get up the Hogs for Porke.

At Muddy hole began also to get in, and thresh out the Buck Wheat. That which grew on the experimental half acre yielded only 3¾ Bushls. & ½ a peck—Whereof 2¼ Bushl. grew on the dunged part the residue on the un-dunged part whereof one half (that is a quarter of the whole) was missing. The half acre of experimental grd. at this place which had been divided into 3 equal divisions yielded as follow—of the bunch homony beans (gathered before I came home) 3 pecks—of the Common homony bean, just gathered only 1 peck—and of the small round bla. eyed pease (the 2d. gathering of which lately accomplished) 3 pecks. Each of these 3ds. contained the 6th. of an Acre. Note, of the experimental ½ acres, there remains to be got—Jeru-salem Artichokes (of which 417 hills out of 1442 are missing) —Carrots, & Turnips—the last of which are much missing & very thin. In the half Acre of Irish Potatoes there were 27 Rows 4 feet apart & 60 yards long. These were also missing in places & more in the undunged, than dunged part.

Ordered the Irish Potatoes at this place, wch. had been planted under Straw & Corn Stalks, to be taken up. The first were in two spots the largest (intended to be 20 yards square) wch. had been laid on green sward. The smallest, 14 by 4 yards, had been laid on a poor washed yellow clay. The other (under the Corn Stalks) had been laid on green sward 20 by 8 yards.

At Dogue run the hands were getting in, & threshing out Buck Wheat.

At Frenchs the Hoe people & Cart were filling up Gullies whilst two Plows were at Work.

At the Ferry, two plows began to break up No. 2 for Barley & Oats. The rest of the Negroes were measuring & carrying off Oats—Stacking blades & otherwise securing the fodder.

At home house Setting Turnips (raised from the seed sent by Mr. Young) to propogate Seed.

On my return home fd. Mrs. Stuart & her two youngest Children here and Mr. & Miss Lee whom I had left.

Friday—26th.   Clear, Wind pretty fresh from the Southward.

Rid to all the Plantations. In the Neck finished gathering to a yard in the field all the Buck Wheat which was threshed & cleaned & got to the Barn but not measured—6 Plows at work there to day.

At Muddy hole finished sowing (with the Barrel) the grd. on the left of the road going from the ferry road up to the Barn with 18½ Bushl. of Wht. and thinking this quantity inadequate ordered the Barrel home to be perforated with more holes. Got all the Beans into the Barn yard at this place which were cut down with Scythes—also the remains of the Buck Wheat.

At Dogue Run gathered all the Buck Wheat to the Wheat yard & began to thresh & clean it.

At French's, filling gullies, & plowing (2 plows) part of field No. 2 left unharrowed in the Spring.

At the Ferry treading out Oats. Began with two ploughs to break up field No. 2, the lay part of it.

Saturday 27th.   Went to the Woods back of Muddy hole with the hounds. Unkennelled two foxes & dragged others but caught none. The dogs run wildly & ⟨were⟩ under no command.

Passed through Muddy hole Plantation and ordered grass Seeds to be sown in the following places, manner, & quantities—viz.—taking a breadth from field No. 4 across to No. 3 of eql. width with the farm yd. & containing abt. 5 acres, I had it divided into 5 oblong squares (seperated by a parting furrow) —In the westermost of which was sown 8 lbs. of rib-grass—in the next 20 lbs. of red clover—in the 3d. 2 Bushels of Orchard grass—in the 4th. 20 lbs. of Hop clover—In the 5th. 4 bushels of Ray grass and in the 6th. 2 bushels of Sainfoin. After sowing these seeds the ground was first rolled & then harrowed with a bush. The sqr. containing Sainfoin had the Seed harrowed in at the same time the Wheat was over and above the bush harrowing & rolling that the others received.

Took up the Potatoes that had been planted under straw for experiments; as mentioned on thursday. Yield as follow.

|  |  | Bushls. |
|---|---|---|
| The 20 yds. sqr. | Green swd. | 3¾ |
| 4 by 14 yds. | washed knoll | ¾ |
| Corn stalks—20 by 8 |  | ¼ |
| and from a rail pen |  | Do ¾ |

Returned by way of D. Run, French's & Ferry. At the first finished threshing cleaning & measuring the buck Wheat & had it brot. to the Mansion house—qty. 121 bushls. from abt. 12 Acres.

At frenchs cleaned up the shattered Pease & threshed those that had been picked of the grd. qty. 9 bushls. & 1 peck.

At the Ferry set 3 plows to work. Put the girl Eby to learning.

The Trial that was made in the Neck of different qties. of Seed Oats to the Acre turned out as follow—

|  |  | Bls. |
|---|---|---|
| 2 bushls. | yield | 8½ |
| 3 bushls. | Do. | 7 |
| 4 Do. | Do. | 5½ |

The above 3 Acres were adjoining and as nearly alike as possible in quality of Soil & Situation. They were all sown [the same] day & managed in all respects alike—the grd. on wch. they grew being quite level.

Sunday—28th.   Went to Pohick Church—Mr. Lear & Washington Custis in the Church with me. Mr. Willm. Stuart came home with me and George Mason came in sooner after. Both stayed all Night.

Monday 29th.   Raining slowly at day break, how long before I know not. Continued to do so (mixed with flakes of Snow) till One Oclock, when it cleared away pleasantly. But little Wind all day; that at East.

Spread 2 bushels of the Plaster of Paris (whilst the Snow and rain was falling) on the So. half of the lawn, beyond the break or small fall therein, qty. about half an acre.

After dinner Mr. Geo: Mason went away.

Tuesday. 30th.   Cloudy in the morning with the Wind fresh from the So. Abt. 8 Oclock it began a slow and misling rain which encreased till it came on to rain fast till ab. 11 Oclock when it ceased.

The afternoon a little variable but upon the whole pleasant.

Rid to Muddy hole and Dogue Run. In the Morning driven in by the Rain and after it ceased rode to The Ferry and Frenchs's—Cleaning up the Buck Wheat at the first place—only 57 Bls. of it from 18 Acres of grd. At the 2d. (D[ogue] R[un]) 4 plows were at work, & the other people grubbing & filling gullies before them.

At The Ferry the 3 plows were at work, & the other people grubbing.

At Frenchs 2 plows were at work and the other hands weeding 2 yards for treadg. out grain.

Wednesday. 31st.   Clear pleasand & warm in the forenoon. Towards Noon it grew cold. Wind hard at No. West.

Rid to all the Plantns. In the Neck 6 plows were at work & 2 more were put at it this morning one of wch. broke immediately. The other hands were getting Irish Potatoes in the further cut (Tob. Ho.) in Timber landg. f[iel]d.

At Muddy hole—finished Sowing Wheat 12½ bushls. in the cut right of the road leading to the Barn with the Barrel—The other hands getting the remainder of the frost-bitten Pease and taking up those turnips in the experimental grd. (which not having the tops taken of, as they were for seed, the yield cannot be ascertained).

At Dogue run the Plows and People were employed as yesterday.

At French's the same Ditchers went to this pl[ac]e this Morng.

## November [1787]

Thursday 1st.    A frost this Morning which crusted the ground and formed Ice. The Morning early was calm and not unpleasant but the Wind blew fresh and cold afterwards at No. Wt.

Rid, by the way of Muddy hole (where the People were taking up Turnips to transplant for seed) to Alexandria to attend a meeting of the Directors of the Potomack Company and the Exhibition of the Boys at the Alexa. Academy. Dind. at Leighs Tavern and Lodged at Colo. Fitzgeralds after returning abt. 11 at Night from the performance which was very well executed.

Friday 2d.    The past Night being very cold, the ground this Morng. was hard froze. The weather however through the day was mild and pleasant.

After breakfast I returnd. home by way of Muddy hole Dogue run Frenchs & the Ferry.

At the first—three plows were breaking up in field No. 4. The other hands were taking up the Jerusalem Artichokes—qty. 58½ bushls.—in dunged & undunged eql.—the 1st. largest.

At Dogue run all hds. were engaged in treading out Wheat.

At Frenchs except the two plows wch. were at work, they were employed in digging Irish Potatoes and at the Ferry in treading out Oats.

Saturday 3d.    Day clear and very pleast. with but little Wind.

Rid to all the Plantations. Digging Potatoes at the River—Muddy hole, and Frenchs Plantations—at wch. the Plows were also at work—Treading Wheat at Morris and Oats at the Ferry.

Sunday [4th.]    Clear and pleasant with but little wind. After candles were lighted Mr. and Mrs. Powell came in.

Monday—5th.    Clear and pleasant with very little wind at any time of the day. Mr. and Mrs. Powell remaining here I continued at home all day.

Tuesday—6th.    Clear and pleasant all day with but little Wind.

Mr. & Mrs. Powell crossed the river a little after Sun rise to Mr. Digges in order to pursue their journey to Philadelphia. I accompanied them over, and havg. my horse carried into the Neck, I rid round that and all the other Plantations in my way home.

From the cut of drilled Corn in the Neck next Mr. Digges's, there came from every 3d. row 45 Bls. of Irish Potatoes. In the next on the river shore

38 Bls. from every 4th. and in the 3d. by the gate & farm pens 77 [ ( ] 7 of wch. red [ ) ] bush.—from every 4 Row—in all 154. 8 Plows at work here.

At Muddy hole, 2 plows breaking up—the driver of the 3d. Will after outlying Hogs—People gathering Potatoes from the 10 acre Stakes 25 bushls. of White and 223 of Red came from the grd.—In all 47¾. These grew in every fourth interval between the Corn. Had ev[er]y inter[va]l been plantd. the qty. pro[bably] wd. have b[een] 190.

At Dogue run, all hands were engaged in cleaning wheat, stacking the straw &ca.

At Frenchs, 2 plows w[er]e at work and all the other hands were digging Potas.

At The Ferry 3 plows were at work—the rest of the hands getting Corn from the New grd. in Front of the House. Mr. Rid[ou]t dind & returned.

Wednesday 7th.    Very little Wind all day—a very thick fog which contd. till near 12 oclock.

Rid to Muddy hole D[ogue] R[un] Frenchs and the Ferry—at the first 2 plows only at work—the other hands getting Corn in the N. Grd.

At Morris's 4 plows at Wk. all the other hds. digg[in]g Potatoes right of the Road—began to day.

At Frenchs 2 plows at Wk. rest of the People digging Potatoes—finished —the whole qty. 84½ B. from 46 rows 170 yds. long each.

At the Ferry—the same work as yesterday.

Majr. G. W——n & wife retd. this evening.

Thursday—8th.    Wind Southerly and Morning soft. Between 9 and 10 Oclock it began to rain moderately & contd. to do so (very slowly) for about two hours—continuing warm and damp afterwards.

Went up to Alexandria to meet the Directors of the Potomack Company. Dined at Mr. Leighs Tavern and returned in the aftern.

The Ferry part of the New grd. Corn (in front of the Mansn. House) being all gathered & measured, was found to yield

|  | Barls. |
|---|---|
| of that wch. was sound | 24 |
| Rotten | 4½ |
| In all | 28½ |

3 Barls. had been given to the Hogs at this place from the other fields.

Stopped the Plows at Muddy hole to assist in digging the Potatoes there.

Friday. 9th.    Wind at So. West and weather clear and mild.

Went this day to the back line of my Tract in order to run a strait course between Colo. Mason & my self 30 feet within my bounds in order to digg a ditch, and make a road without it. Was not able to compleat it. Went by the Ferry, Frenchs and Dogue Run Plantations and returned home by Muddy hole.

At the 3 first the Plows as usual were at Work. At the latter the drivers were aiding with the Potatoes.

At the Ferry the hands were securing the Corn they had gathered.
At Frenchs they were grubbing, & stopping gullies before the Plows.
At Dogue run they were digging Potatoes.
At Muddy hole the same.

Saturday—10th.  Morning Mild & pleasant with the Wind at So. Abt. 5 ock. it thundered began to rain & contd. to do so more or less till 10 oclk. at night.

Went again on the business I was upon yesterday, but could not finish it.

Passed by the Ferry, Frenchs and Dogue run Plantations, and returned home by Muddy hole.

At the first, the Plows were at work as usual, and the other hands were digging Potatoes.

At French's they were employed as yesterday but were ordered to remove the trash out of the wet part of the Meadow (that had been grubbed) before it got wet.

At Dogue run only 2 plows were at work—the other hands digging Potatoes.

At Muddy hole all were digging Potatoes.

On my return home found the Widow Graham & her daughter here who stayed all Night.

Sunday. 11th.  Morning, clear and pleast. with the Wind Westerly but not fresh nor cold.

After Breakfast Mrs. Graham & daughter went away. To dinner Geo. Steptoe Washington and a Son of Mr. McCrae's came and in the evening Colo. R. Hy. Lee.

Monday. 12th.  Wind Southerly—Weather mild but lowering all day. Towards Noon & from thence till 4 Oclock it looked much like Snow—after which the Clouds thinned and it seemed inclind. to be fair.

Colo. Lee went away after breakfast & the 2 young men after dinner.

I did not ride as usual to day.

Finished digging the Irish Potatoes at Dogue run in the cut of Corn which is on the right hand of the road which leads from the Gate to the Houses— quantity 120 bushls. whereof 63 were red—the number and length of these Rows & the white being equal.

Tuesday 13th.  Very mild & soft morning—wind at South.

Rid to all the Plantns. At the Neck 8 plows were at work the rest of the People gathering beans & threshing out Pease.

At Muddy hole all hands digging Potatoes. Sent the small gang from the Mansion House there; and ordered the Ferry People to assist them to morrow.

At Morris's, 4 plows at wk.; the other hands (aided by the People from Frenchs) were digg[in]g Potatoes on the left of the Road leading from the gate to the Houses.

At Frenchs—two Plows at Work.

At the Ferry 3 plows were at Work. The other hands had finished digging the Potatoes and were getting the remainder of the Frost bitten Pease that they might go to Muddy hole in the Morning.

Wednesday. 14th.    Clear and very mild morning—Clouds afterwards and a sml. Sprinkle—Wind abt. So. W.

Rid to the Ferry, French's D. Run & Muddy hole.

At the first 3 plows at work, all the other hands execpt the Ferry men, were sent to Muddy hole.

At Frenchs treading out Barley—Plows stopped for this purpose.

At D. Run 4 plows at Wk. The other hands digging Potatoes.

At Muddy hole all hands digging Potatoes—the Small gang from the H[ous]e and the Ferry People assisting. The quantity of Potatoes taken from the remg. part of the Corn ground at this place amounted to 54½ Bls. of red, and 59¼ white—which added to those that came off the 10 acres in the same corn field make 84½ Whe. & 77¼ red—In all 161½ Bushels from the Corn ground—every 4th. row.

Received 14¾ bushls. of Irish Potatoes from the Neck to day—wch. added to those that were brot. over on Saturday make 21¼ bushls. of red and 160 bushls. of white—In all 181¼ Bushels. Recd. from the same place 56½ Bushls. of Barley which grew on about 5 Acres near the Barn wch. had been in Turnips last year—also 31 Bushls. of Pease sound and good; and 7½ of Ditto which had been bit with the frost in different degrees—some very bad.

Thursday 15th.    Morning mild and very heavy with the wind fresh from So. Wt. Which produced sprinkling rain till abt. 10 Oclock and constant rain afterwards till about 2 Oclock when it moderated, but continued very cloudy with slight drippings all the afternoon.

Went to Alexandria to an election of Senator for this district—Mr. Thos. West of Fairfax & Mr. Pope of Prince William being the Candidates. I gave my vote for the first & immediately as the weather promised to be getting worse.

The last of the Potatoes from Dogue run came home to day; viz. 113½ Bushels, where⟨of⟩ 57¾ were red, and 56½ White. ⟨Th⟩ese came out of the cut on ⟨the⟩ left of the road leading from ⟨the⟩ gate to the houses and with ⟨th⟩ose of the other cut, make ⟨12⟩0¾ of red and 113½ of white—In all 234¼ Bushels from every 4 row between the Corn rows.

# At Mount Vernon

## 1788, January–February 1789

### January 1788

[Tuesday 1st.]    Thermometer at 25 in the Morning–30 at Noon and 27 at Night. Clear and moderate in the forenoon there being but little Wind and that Southerly. Towards night it clouded–after which the wind getting to No. Wt. it cleared and turned cold.

Mr. Lee returned to Alexandria after breakfast–as Mrs. Stuart did from Mr. Lund Washington's.

I remained at home this day also.

Wednesday 2d.    Thermometer at 21 in the morning–30 at Noon and 25 at Night. Clear Morning but variable afterwards–not much wind, but that Southerly & cold–at least raw.

Colo. Humphreys & Myself accompanied Mr. Paradise and his lady to Alexandria. Dined with Mr. Charles Lee and returned in the Evening–leavg. Mr. & Mrs. Paradise there.

On the ride home GW contracted "a very severe cold" and for the next week or more was plagued almost continually by a bad cough and "slow fevers" (GW to John Fitzgerald, 9 Jan. 1788, DLC:GW).

Thursday 3d.    Thermometer at 25 in the Morning–30 at Noon And 26 at Night. Clear all day and Cool. Wind for the most part at So. Et.

Visited the Plantations at the Ferry, Frenchs, Dogue run, and Muddy hole.

At the first the Women were taking up and thinning the Trees in the swamp which they had before grubbed. The Men were getting stakes & trunnels for fencing & making racks to feed the Creatures in. Began yesterday & would about finish today sowing the New Meadow at this (which was too thin of timothy) with a quart of timothy Seed to the Acre.

At Frenchs they were putting up Racks to feed the Cattle in. One man was getting stakes for fencing.

At Dogue run–The Women began to hoe the Swamp they had

grubbed in order to prepare it for Sowing in the Spring with grain and grass Seeds. The Men were cutting the Tops of the Trees which had been fallen for rails into Coal Wood.

At Muddy hole, the Women after having threshed out the Pease, went about the fencing—two Men getting Stakes &ca. for it. All the Pease from the broadcast sowing at this place, amounted to no more than ⟨7 bushels of good⟩ & 5 pecks of defective ones which was far short of expectation bad as the year proved.

Friday 4th.    Thermometer at 35 in the Morning—30 at Noon And 25 at Night. The morning was neither cold nor unpromising but the Wind coming out from the No. Wt. about 10 Oclock it blew fresh & keen.

Rid to all the Plantans. In the Neck the Men were getting Posts & rails for fencing; & the Women were threshing Oats.

At Muddy hole, the Men were getting rails and the women makg. fences.

At Dogue run, the Men were cutting Coal wood and the Women Hoeing Swamp as yesterday.

At Frenchs the Men were cuttg. & mauling fence Stakes and the women levelling old ditches and grubbing. From this Plantation 120 Bushls. of clean Oats had been sent to Muddy hole, 108 brot. to the Mansn. House and 100 left for the Plow horses on the Plantation. These with some which had been carried to Muddy hole in the straw, and what the Plow horses have all the Fall & Winter been fed on, constitute the amount of what grew in field No. 1 whereof 15 acres were in Wheat leaving abt. 40 in Oats.

At the Ferry—the Men were getting Stakes, making Racks &ca. & the Women thinning trees in the Swamp.

Doctr. Craik dined here & returned afterwards to Alexandria.

A Vessel with 130 Barls. of Corn, sent by Colo. Mercer arrived here but from mismanagement of the Overseer on board no notice thereof was given till Sundown. Consequently no endeavor used to land it tho' the Weather indicated a severe frost.

"The almost total loss" of GW's 1787 corn crop "by the drought" obliged him "to purchase upwards of eight hundred Barrels of Corn" for use at Mount Vernon until the next harvest (GW to Charles Lee, 4 April 1788, DLC:GW). John Francis Mercer's 130 barrels cost GW £102 18s. 4d., a sum which was credited against a large debt owed GW by the estate of Mercer's father, John Mercer of Marlborough (LEDGER B, 221; GW to John F. Mercer, 11 Jan. 1788, DLC:GW).

Saturday 5th.    Thermometer at 17 in the Morning—21 at Noon And 19 at Night. Day clear, wind (though not hard) at No. Wt.

and very cold. The river a good deal covered with Ice wch. prevented any attempts to land Corn till after Noon when 16 Barls.
only were got on Shore & deposited in the Corn loft.

Majr. G. Washington & his Wife set off abt. 11 Oclock for
Eltham—to take the Marriage of Mr. Burwell Bassett with Miss
McCarty of Pope's Creek in their way down but their horses (being unused to a Phaeton &) running restive they were obliged to
return after having proceeded abt. 5 Miles on their journey.

I remained at home all day. About Eight oclock in the evening
we were alarmed, and the house a good deal endangered, by the
soot of one of the Chimneys taking fire & burning furiously, dis-
charging great flakes of fire on the roof—but happily, by having
aid at hand and proper exertion no damage ensued.

Burwell Bassett, Jr., of Eltham married Elizabeth McCarty, daughter of
Daniel McCarty (d. 1795) of Popes Creek, in Westmoreland County, on 10
Jan. 1788 (wmq, 1st ser., 15 [1906–7], 187).

Sunday 6th.    Thermometer at 14 in the Morning—21 at Noon
And 19 at Night. Notwithstanding the Wind blew fresh all night,
the River was quite closed this Morning and the Ice on the flats
hard, and sufficiently thick to bear a Man.

The Major & his wife, recommenced their journey to day, aided
by a pair of my horses to take them over the worst of the roads.

George Augustine Washington was to return to Mount Vernon from this
trip some time in February, but Fanny, who was now about six months
pregnant, planned to remain at Eltham until she had her child. "Her ill
luck with her first child," Martha Washington wrote Elizabeth Willing
Powel 18 Jan. 1788, "is the only reason of her wishing to change the place
of her laying inn this time, If her child lives, it will be sometime in may
before she can come up, and the distance is two farr for me to goe down
to see her." Fanny was, Mrs. Washington confessed, "as a child to me, and
I am very lone some when she is absent" (ViMtV). For Fanny's first child,
see entries for 10 and 25 April 1787.

Monday 7th.    Thermometer at 17 in the Morning—24 at Noon
and 22 at Night. But little Wind all day—weather much moderated; but variable with respect to Sunshine & clouds—the appearances of Snow, at times being great. What wind there was, came
from the So. Wt. but no thawing.

Visited the Plantations at Dogue run & French's. At the first the
Women (though the grd. was too hard frozen to Hoe) were grubbing & otherwise preparing the Swamp for Meadow. The Men
were cutting as usual.

At Frenchs (except Abram who was cutting stakes) the rest were threshing out Pease.

Set the Women belonging to the Ferry, and to Muddy hole, to grubbing the woods in front of the House, adjoining the last years Corn.

Began to day to fill my Ice house, and for expediting the business, brought 3 Carts from the Plantations & some hands.

The ground being too hard to Ditch, the Dutchman came home & broke flax and the Negro men were employed in cutting rail stuff and Brick Wood.

THE DUTCHMAN: Daniel Overdonck.

Tuesday 8th.    Thermometer at 26 in the Morning—32 at Noon and 32 at Night. Wind at East in the Night, and this fore noon— afterwards at West. About 2 Inches of Snow fell in the Night. About day break it turned to hail, and then to rain, which continued till after 12 oclock when the Sun came out.

I remained at home all day. My Carriage brot. Betsy & Patsy Custis down—their mother having gone to Maryland occasioned by the death of her father—the Honble. Benedict Calvert Esqr.

Benedict Calvert died at his Prince George's County home, Mount Airy, on 9 Jan. 1788 (NICKLIN [2], 314; BOWIE, 101).

Wednesday 9th.    Thermometer at 27 in the Morning—34 at Noon And 32 at Night. Clear and cold, frost hard again, the wind having got to No. West.

Colo. Carrington came here to Dinner. I continued at home all day.

Yesterday & this day, employed as Monday in collecting for, and ramming Ice, in my Ice house.

Thursday 10th.    Thermometer at 26 in the Morning—32 at Noon and 32 at Night. Clear and tolerably pleasant—the Wind being at So. Wt. all day.

Colo. Carrington left this after breakfast (on my horses) for Colchester; to meet the Stage.

Giles, who with a pair of my horses assisted G. A. Washington on his journey, returned about Noon.

Getting Ice as yesterday, House not yet half full.

The slave Giles served GW as a driver and stabler for more than 20 years (see entry for 18 Feb. 1786).

Friday 11th.   Thermometer at 16 in the Morning–20 at Noon and 19 at Night. The Wind having shifted in the night to the No. West and blowing pretty fresh it turned very cold but continued clear all day.

Visited the Plantations at Muddy hole, Dogue run, Frenchs & the Ferry.

The hands at Muddy hole, except 2 men who were cutting & mauling rails were grubbing at the Mansion house & some about the Ice.

The hands at Dogue run were grubbing (that is the women) in the Mill swamp and had been so since Tuesday–Men cutting Wood & Mauling rails.

At French's the Women that were well (except one at the Ice house) were ⟨thres⟩hing pease–one man cutting and mauling stakes for fences.

At the Ferry the Women were grubbing at the Mansion Ho. The Men getting Stakes &ca.

Collecting, filling & pounding Ice for the Ice house as had been the employment of the Week.

Saturday 12th.   Thermometer at 19 in the morning–24 at Noon and 24 at Night. Wind at So. Et. and weather variable. About Noon, & before, there were great appearances of Snow–some falling. Afterwards it brightned and the afternoon became clear, mild & pleasant.

Upon which, Colo. Humphreys & myself set off for the meeting of the Directors of the Potomack Co., to be held at the Falls of Shanandoah–but meeting a letter from Colo. Fitzgerald enclosing one from Governer Johnson requesting that the meeting might be postponed till Tuesday we turned back & I returned home by the way of Dogue run.

Getting Ice as usual, which makes the 6th. day (except some interruption from the Weather on Tuesday) that as many people & Carts have been engaged in this work as could be advantageously employed altho' Six feet of Space was yet left.

The purpose of this meeting was to inspect the progress made in clearing the upper falls of the Potomac. GW expected to be gone from home for ten or more days of "cold houses and Bad Beds" (GW to John Fitzgerald, 9 Jan. 1788, GW to Lafayette, 10 Jan. 1788, and GW to John Francis Mercer, 11 Jan. 1788, DLC:GW).

Sunday 13th.   Thermometer at 24 in the Morning–28 at Noon and 24 at Night. Weather more temperate with respect to cold but about 11 oclock it began to Snow and continued to do so more or less till 9 Oclock at Night adding about 2 or 3 Inches to what had fallen before. Wind was at So. East all day but at Night shifted to No. Wt.

The Weather prevented my settg. out for the meeting at Shanandoah.

Colo. Hooe, a Mr. Wickoff and a Captn. Thomas came here to dinner and returned in the evening.

MR. WICKOFF: Isaac Wikoff (d. 1814) or Peter Wikoff, both merchants of Philadelphia (RUSH, 2:676, n.10; PA. ARCH., 2d ser., 8:274–75, 3d ser., 10:664–65, 14:166, 171, 298).

Monday 14th.    Thermometer at 10 in the Morning–20 at Noon, and 16 at Night. Wind, though not hard, continued at No. Wt. all day & was exceedingly keen.

The cold–apprehension of the Horses balling with the Snow that had fallen–and insufficiency of time to reach the place of meeting agreeably to appointment induced me to relinquish the journey altogether.

I remained at home all day–employed as last week getting & pounding Ice for the Ice house.

Tuesday 15th.    Mercury in the ball this Morning the cold being very intense–25 at Noon And 24 at Night. Wind in the early part of the morning was at East, and afterwards at So. Et. which occasioned a considerable abatement of the cold, but very little thaw.

Rid to the Plantations at Dogue run, French's, & the Ferry. At the first, the Men were cutting and mauling of rails; & the women grubbing in the Mill swamp.

At Frenchs, the Women were still threshing Pease, and two Men cutting trunnels for Fences.

At the Ferry, the Men were gettg. stakes & trunnels; and the Women grubbing at the Mansn. House.

As were also the People belonging to Muddy hole.

Employed at the Mansion House as yesterday in getting Ice into the Ice [House] but did not compleat it, it wanting near three feet to fill it.

Wednesday 16th.    Thermometer at 32 in the Morning–37 at Noon and 36 at Night. Wind at So. Et. & pretty fresh all day with constant rain–notwithstanding which little or no impression was made on the frozen ground by either for it still continued hard. Snow in the open grd. almost entirely carrd. away.

Thursday 17th.    Thermometer at 34 in the Morning—39 at Noon And 38 at Night. The Wind shifting in the night to the No. Wt. blew fresh, and froze hard. Towards Noon it moderated, and the afternn. became very pleasant & thawing.

Visited all the Plantations. In the Neck the [men] were getting Posts and Rails for Fencing. Women, in part were cleaning Oats and in part cutting down Corn Stalks in No. 9.

At Muddy hole 2 Men were getting Rails—one Carting of them and the Women that were well, were grubbing at the Mansn. House.

At Dogue run, the Men were getting Rails, and the Women, as the Mill swamp had a good deal of Water in it, with the Overseer came to the home house to grub.

At French's except two Men who were getting stakes and trunnels for Fencing the rest were cleaning the Pease which had been threshed.

At the Ferry, the women were at the New ground at home—the Men getting stakes &ca. for Fencing.

Friday 18th.    Thermometer at 25 in the Morning—35 at Noon And 35 at Night. In the Morning the Wind was at East, afterwards Southerly, clear, moderate & thawing but not more than an Inch in the ground.

Rid to the Mill, French's & Ferry Plantation.

Work at all the places as yesterday.

Saturday 19th.    Thermometer at 32 in the Morning—36 at Noon and 34 at Night. Raining at times, & mizling all day, with the Wind at So. Et.

I remained at home all day. From Muddy hole there was brought 21 Bushls. of Pease whereof 9 only were sound & good. The others were hurt by the frost & rotten.

A Mr. Copley (a considerable Manufacturer of Cloth) from Leeds in Yorkshire came here in the evening introduced by letter from Doctr. McHenry of Baltimore.

Burrow Copley of Hunslet Parish, borough of Leeds, Eng., was among the first cloth makers in the Leeds area to use water-powered machinery to card and slub wool (CRUMP, 32:11–12).

Sunday 20th.    Thermometer at 36 in the Morning—42 at Noon and 36 at Night. A thick vapour or fog in the Morning early but

Primitive painting of Mount Vernon (1797) showing fencing on the Mansion House plantation. (Mount Vernon Ladies' Association of the Union)

the wind coming out, a little after Sun rise very fresh from the No. Wt. it soon dispelled & the day became clear.

Mr. Ingraham, and Mr. Porter came here to dinner and returned to Alexandria in the evening.

Mr. Bushrod Washington and his wife came here in the afternoon.

Monday 21st. Thermometer at 28 in the Morning—38 at Noon And 36 at Night. In the Morning the wind was at No. West. Afterwards it shifted to the So. Ward & became calm & lowered a little in the evening.

Rid to the Ferry, French's, Dogue run, & Muddy hole Plantations.

The Women of the first were at wk. in the new grd. The Men were set to getting Rails.

At Frenchs—two Men were cutting Trunnels for Fences and the Women were carrying Rails from the Swamp side to the division fence between the two Plantations.

At Dogue run, The Men were cutting & Mauling of Rails—the Women at the New ground at the home House.

At Muddy hole 2 Men were cuttg. & mauling—1 Carting and the Women at the New ground.

From the Neck eight Women were also at this place grubbing.

Tuesday 22d.    Thermometer at 30 in the Morning—36 at Noon and 32 at Night. But little wind all day—& that Easterly & Southerly: towards Noon it clouded & about 3 Oclock began to Snow but not more than would barely cover the earth.

The Ice on the river began to break this morning and move with the tide, for the first time since the river closed.

Visited the Plantations in the Neck, Muddy hole, & Dogue run.

At the former the Men were getting Posts & rails—some of the women cutting down Corn Stalks & gathering them into heaps— 8 others of them at the Mansn. House.

At Dogue run the hands were all of them were employed as yesterday.

So likewise were those of Muddy hole.

On my return home found Mrs. & Miss Stuart, and Mr. Lund Washington here. And just after we had dined Doctr. Ruston came in—all of whom except Mr. L. Washington stayed all Night.

Wednesday 23d.    Thermometer at 30 in the morning—42 at Noon And 36 at Night. Early in the Morning the wind was at So.

Wt. tho there was but little of it. Soon after it inclined to the West, & No. West and grew colder and towards Night it got more round to the Northward & Eastwd.

Doctr. Ruston going away about 10 Oclock I rid to the Plantations at the Ferry, Frenchs and Dogue run.

At all of them, as also at Muddy hole and in the Neck, the hands were employed as usual, except at French's where the People were carrying Rails improperly.

From this place 13½ Bushels of Pease were brought which with those brought from thence in the fall were all, except the frost bitten ones that were raised at this place in broadcast.

Those which suffered by frost were considerable, and as has been observed formerly great waste was experienced in gathering them from the uneveness of the ground.

Thursday 24th. Thermometer at 23 in the Morning—23 at Noon and 22 at Night. Wind at No. Et. all day with threatning appearances of Snow all the forenoon. About 12 Oclock it sett in to do [so] and continued without intermission till some time in the Night when the Wind shifting to the No. West and blowing violently it ceased but the Snow drifted much.

Mrs. & Miss Stuart, and Betcy & Patcy Custis went away after breakfast.

I continued at home all day.

Ten-year-old Patsy was "a little unwell" during her stay at Mount Vernon, but apparently improved (GW to David Stuart, 18 Jan. 1788, ViU).

Friday 25th. Thermometer at 22 in the Morning—24 at Noon and 23 at Night. The Wind high, & disagreeably cold all day from the No. West—tho' by the Thermometer was not so high as it has been some other days. The Snow drifted a good deal. River closed again.

At home all day.

Saturday 26th. Thermometer at 26 in the Morning—26 at Noon And 26 at Night. But little Wind—morning cloudy with appearances of Snow but about Noon it cleared. The wind got to the Southward and grew pleasant.

Rid to the Ferry & French's. The hands at the first employed as before.

At French's part of them were in the New ground at the Mansion House where they began to Work on Thursday and the others were repairg. fences wch. had been blown down.

Sunday 27th.    Thermometer at 14 in the Morning—[     ] at Noon and [     ] at Night. Morning cold, but pleasant afterwards wind tho' not fresh being at So. Wt. Thawed a little.

At home all day.

Monday 28th.    Thermometer at 30 in the Morning—38 at Noon and 38 at Night. Wind Southerly, but not fresh. Fore part of the day clear & pleasant—latter part mild & lowering.

Tuesday 29th.    Thermometer at 35 in the Morning—47 at Noon and 47 at Night. Wind at So. Wt. and moderate all day. A good deal of rain fell in the course of the Night which with the dissolution of the Snow, occasioned much water in the Brooks and places from whence [it] had no discharge. The Thaw also to day was great⟨er than it has been since the 10th.⟩ of Decr. and yet the top of the ground only was softened not more than an Inch deep.

Rid to the Ferry, Frenchs, and Dogue run Plantations. Found Colo. Gilpin on my ret[urn]

Employed as usual at each. 3 Men began to cut rail timber yesterday afternoon at Dogue run for the fence which is to divide fields No. 2 & 3.

Wednesday 30th.    Thermometer at 30 in the Morning—32 at Noon and 30 at Night. The wind having got to No. Wt. in the Night it froze hard again. It continued at this point all day and was very raw and cold, with great appearances often of Snow till towards evening when it became clear.

Rid into the Neck—To Majr. Washingtons Plantation—to Muddy hole and the Carpenters. The fence between the Majr. and me was nearly compleated to the River above the Fish House at Johnsons.

Hands at all the places at Wk. as usual.

Thursday 31st.    Thermometer at 20 in the Morning—30 at Noon and 30 at Night. Morning clear and calm. What little air stirred was from the Southward—at which point it continued all day but freshened & was cool with but little thawing.

Visited the Plantation at Dogue run. Men there cutting and Mauling as usual. The Women were putting up cross Fences in the Meadow by the Overseers House.

Hands at all the other places employed as Usual.

# February [1788]

Friday 1st.    Thermometer at 25 in the Morning—38 at Noon and 38 at Night. Morning clear & pleasant with the Wind (but not much of it) Southerly, at wch. point it continued all day, & grew Milder. The top of the ground for about an Inch thawed—but not deeper.

Visited the Plantations at Muddy hole, Dogue run, Frenchs and the Ferry.

Work at all as usual. The Women belonging to Dogue run having returned to the New ground at the Mansion house.

Employed the five Negro Ditche[r]s who had been cutting wood for burning Bricks in getting the same out of the Swamp where it grew.

Saturday 2d.    Thermometer at 32 in the Morning—42 at Noon and 42 at Night. Wind Southerly, & day moderate.

Visited my Ferry, Frenchs & Dogue run Plantations.

At all, the same work as usual, except that the Dogue run Women were employed in pulling up a cross fence in the Meadow by the Overseers house—being the 2d. cross fence in this Meadw.

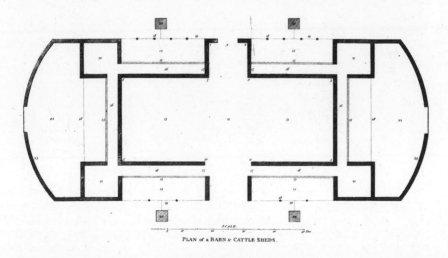

PLAN of a BARN & CATTLE SHEDS.

Arthur Young's plan, used by Washington for his new barn, appeared in *Annals of Agriculture,* 1791. (University of Virginia Library)

Set the home house gang to cording the Wood which had been cut for Bricks.

Began with a pair of Sawyers, this day, to cut the flooring planks for a Barn, proposed to be built between the Ferry & French's Plantations of 2 Inch Oak.

Doctr. Craik came down to visit Mathew Baldridge but returned before dinner.

My Nephew Geo. Steptoe Washington came here this Evening to proceed to Lancaster to visit his Brother Ferdinando Washington who lay dangerously ill of a Consumption.

The barn was to be a two-story brick structure built according to a plan obtained from Arthur Young the previous year, but with some changes by GW to adapt it to his particular needs. Jacques (Jean) Pierre Brissot de Warville, a French visitor who saw GW's new barn in an advanced stage of construction later this year, described it as "a huge one . . . about one hundred feet long and of an even greater width, which was to store all his grain, potatoes, turnips, etc. [from Ferry and French's plantations]. Around it he had also built stables for all his cattle, horses, and donkeys [on those two plantations]. . . . The barn is so well planned that a man can fill the racks with hay or potatoes easily and without any danger." Because most of the building materials came from Mount Vernon, the cost of the whole undertaking, GW told Brissot, "amounted to no more than £300." The barn and barnyard, Brissot noted, "were innovations in Virginia, where they have no barns and do not store fodder for cattle" (BRISSOT, 343; SCHOEPF, 2:48). GW wrote Young 4 Dec. 1788 that he believed his barn to be "the largest and most convenient one in this Country" (DLC:GW).

Sunday 3d.    Thermometer at 42 in the morning—46 at Noon and 45 at Night. Mild, Wind tho' not much of it Southerly & thawing. Towards evening it lowered and at Night began to rain.

Colo. Fitzgerald, Messrs. Porter, Ingraham, Murray & Bowen, Doctr. Stuart & Craik Junr. and a Mr. O'Conner came to Dinnr. & returned except Doctr. Stuart.

John O'Connor, who styled himself "a barrester at law of the kingdom of Ireland," arrived in America in 1787 and was now traveling through Virginia, peddling subscriptions for a proposed multivolume geographical and topographical history of the Americas, "Collected and compiled" by himself (*Md. Gaz.*, 6 Dec. 1787). That work, he told subscribers in Alexandria, was now "nearly finished, and . . . the first volume was absolutely in Press at Philadelphia." However, one subscriber who had occasion to visit Philadelphia in April inquired at the printing office about the progress of O'Connor's history and was greatly surprised to learn that the printers had not "received one shilling" from the author, nor had they "ever seen the manuscript" (*Md. Journal*, 22 April 1788). Although O'Connor continued for the next year and a half to assure everyone of his determination to publish his work as advertised, it never appeared (*Md. Journal*, 13 May 1788; O'Connor to GW,

5 Oct. 1789, DNA: PCC, Item 78; O'BRIEN, 44–45). GW did not subscribe to O'Connor's history.

**Monday 4.** Thermometer at 32 in the Morning—42 at Noon And 38 at Night. Clear with the Wind at South in the Morning—West afterwards, & violent. The Ice very much broken by it.

Visited the Plantation at Dogue run. Women still about the cross fence.

Attempted to plow, but found it impracticable the ground not being thawed more than two or 3 Inches.

All other work as usual. Doctr. Stuart went away after Dinner.

**Tuesday 5th.** Mercury in the Ball of the Thermometer in the Morning, from whence it never rose the whole day, being intensely cold. In the preceeding Night the wind having got to No. Wt. blew at times, exceeding hard. It continued to blow hard all day, and was very piercing from Morng. to evening.

The River, which had opened very much yesterday and promised a free Navigation was entirely closed again to day, in all the malignancy of the frost.

I remained within all day. Mr. Lear went up to Mr. Porters Wedding—in Alexandria.

At Alexandria on this date, according to reports heard by the British traveler John Enys when he reached the town a few days later, "farenhights Thermomether was so low as ten Degrees, others say so low as seven or Eight within doors." When Enys visited Mount Vernon on 13 Feb., David Humphreys told him that the mercury in GW's Fahrenheit thermometer "which is . . . placed in an exposed Situation was in the Ball for some hours" on 5 Feb. (ENYS, 349, n.21).

"The Navigation of this river," GW today wrote Henry Knox, "has been stopped for near five weeks. At this moment we are locked fast by Ice, and the air of this day is amongst the keenest I ever recollect to have felt" (MHi).

Thomas Porter married Sarah (Sally) Ramsay, daughter of William and Ann McCarty Ramsay of Alexandria.

**Wednesday 6th.** Mercury in the Ball all day and the weather exceeding cold but not so piercing as yesterday. In the Morning the Wind was at East. Afterwards it was abt. So. Wt.

Rid out, but finding the cold disagreeable, I returned. Hands of all the places (except the Men) working in the New ground at the Mann. House.

**Thursday 7th.** Mercury in the Ball in the Morning. By noon it rose to 24 and by Night was at 26. The Wind tho' not much of it, was at So. Wt. all day. The appearance of the Weather varient—

sometimes threatning Snow—at other times promising to be fair.

At home all day. Mr. Lear returned about 2 oclock from Alexa.

Friday 8th.    Thermometer at 24 in the Morning—29 at Noon and 28 at Night. Wind tho not much of it, was at No. Et. in the Morning, and continued there all day with fine snow & sometimes Mists.

Visited the Plantations at Frenchs and the Ferry; at Work at both as usual.

The Neck & Muddy hole people, with the Women belonging to the above two, were at Work in the New Grd. in front of the House.

The Dogue run [people] were not there but at work in the Great Meadow at the Mill. Sowed yesterday and to day, on the fallowed Wheat at the Ferry (about 25 Acres) at the rate of a quart of clean Timothy Seed & 5 lbs. of red Clover Seed to the Acre on the Snow wch. was about 2 or 3 Inches deep & very level.

Saturday 9th.    Thermometer at 30 in the Morning—39 at Noon And 38 at Night. Clear Wind at No. Wt. all day but neither fresh nor cold. Thawing.

Visited all the Plantations except the Neck.

At All, working as usual—that is the Men getting Materials for fencing and the Women, except those of Dogue run, grubbing at the Mansion house. The Dogue run Women grubbing in the G. Meadow.

Sunday 10th.    Thermometer at 24 in the Morning—42 at Noon And 40 at Night. Wind at So. Wt. all day—moderate and pleasant. The Snow in the open ground had almost disappeared.

At home all day. Majr. G. A. Washington returned from New Kent about 1 oclock and just before Dinner Doctr. Stuart, Mrs. Stuart, Miss Stuart & Betcy & Patcy Custis came in.

Monday 11th.    Thermometer at 42 in the Morning—50 at Noon And 48 at Night. Wind at So. Wt. & fresh till toward Sun down when it veered more to West & then got to No. Wt. in the Night, but not very hard. Snow quite gone.

Visited the Plantations at Muddy hole & Dogue-run.

The Women from every place were in the New Ground at home. Those at Dogue run were in the G. Meadow at home but there was too much Water to Work to advantage.

Tuesday 12th.    Thermometer at 40 in the Morning—54 at Noon and 53 at Night. Clear, pleasant & thawing. Wind at So. Wt. & pretty fresh; Ice breakg. for the 3d. time.

Doctr. Stuart (alone) returned to Abingdon after Breakfast.

I visited the Plantations of Muddy hole, French's & the Ferry.

The People at all of them, and in the Neck at the usual work. The Women from Dogue run had, on account of the wetness of the Swamp come to the New ground at the Mansn. House It appearing that the ground would be sufficiently thawed I ordered the whole of them to take their Tools home & try to put up their Fences, and do other work at their respective Plantations.

Ordered the Plows also to be tryed to morrow.

Wednesday 13th.    Thermometer at 45 in the Morning—54 at Noon and 50 at Night. Clear and pleasant with the Wind at So. Wt. all day.

The Marqs. de Chappedelaine (introduced by letters from Genl. Knox, Mr. Bingham &ca.) Captn. Enys (a British Officer) Colo. Fitzgerald, Mr. Hunter, Mr. Nelson & Mr. Ingraham came here to Dinner—all of whom returned after it except the last.

I remained at home all day. The Plows at Muddy hole were usefully employed.

At Dogue run it seems the grds. were in bad order.

At the Ferry & Frenchs they cd. not work for the Frost and In the Neck they were not set to work till late.

Silhouette of Lt. John Enys. (Owned by present members of the Enys family; photograph courtesy of Adirondack Museum)

This party of visitors intended to come to Mount Vernon on 11 Feb. to congratulate GW on the occasion of his fifty-sixth birthday, but bad weather that morning and an Alexandria town election the next day forced postponement of their visit to this day (ENYS, 244–45).

The marquis de Chappedelaine, "a Captain in the first Regt of french Dragoons" who was touring the United States, had previously visited New York, Philadelphia, and Baltimore (ENYS, 238–40). "The Marquis . . . ," wrote Henry Knox in his letter of introduction to GW, "thinks that he should have come to America to little purpose were he to depart without having seen your Excellency" (Knox to GW, 2 Nov. 1787, DLC:GW). Although Chappedelaine may not have actually been a marquis, he was apparently a member of the noble Breton family of Chappedelaine, for in late 1790 or early 1791 he and several Breton nobles fleeing from the French Revolution landed on the island of Sapelo off the coast of Georgia, where they established an émigré colony for a time (ENYS, 341–42, n.81; Chappedelaine to GW, 9 Jan. 1791, DLC:GW; LOVELL, 97). Chappedelaine may have been Jean René Chappedelaine (b. 1766), an officer in the Regiment de Barrois, who was said to have emigrated in 1792, or Jean Baptiste Marc de Chappedelaine, comte de Boslan (1741–1819), an officer in the Regiment de Soubise, who was said to have emigrated in 1791. Both men later returned to France (DICT. BIOG. FRANÇAISE, 8:434).

John Enys (1757–1818) was commissioned an officer in the 29th Regiment of Foot in 1775 and served with that unit on garrison duty in Canada 1776–82 and 1784–87. Before returning to England, he made a tour of scenic and historical places in the United States, passing through Albany, N.Y., New York City, Princeton, N.J., Philadelphia, Baltimore, and Alexandria on his way to Norfolk where he took a ship for home. Letters of introduction to John Fitzgerald and William Hunter, Jr., enabled Enys to include Mount Vernon in his itinerary. "We had no sooner alighted," Enys wrote of his visit, "than the Immortal General came to receive us at the door and conducted us into his Parlour." After some conversation about the new federal Constitution and a tour of the grounds, dinner was served. "It was a very good one," Enys reported, "but the part of the entertainment I liked best was the affable easy manners of the whole family. . . . The Ladies left the room soon after Dinner but the Gentlemen continued for some time longer. There were no public toasts of any kind given, the General himself introducing a round of Ladies as soon as the Cloath was removed, by saying he had always a very great esteem for the Ladies, and therefore drank them in preference to any thing else." The visitors did not leave until "it was near dark" (ENYS, xviii–xxxv, 244–52).

Thursday 14th.    Thermometer at 46 in the Morning–54 at Noon And 50 at Night. The wind was at No. West all day & about Noon blew hard, but moderated towards evening–not very cold.

Visited all the Plantations.

In the Neck 7 Plows were at Work in the field by the Barn– frost some interruption to the Plows. The Women grubbing along the Branch below the Spring. Men at work as usual.

At Muddy hole 3 plows going on very well. Women grubbing before them.

At Dogue run 4 plows were at work in field No. 3, but it was so wet that I ordered them to Muddy hole after they had fed the Horses. Women in N[ew] Gr[oun]d Ho[me] H[ouse].

At neither French's nor the Ferry could the Plows Work. The Women at each were levelling the old ditches.

Began yesterday to Ditch again at French's and with Cornelius & his two Brothers to dig the foundation for the Barn between the Ferry & French's Plantations.

On my return from riding, I found the Marqs. de Chappedelaine and Doctor Lee here—both of whom stayed all Night.

Friday 15.    Thermometer at 36 in the Morning—34 at Noon and 32 at Night. Cloudy with the Wind at No. Et. all day during which it snowed twice fast but not enough fell to cover the ground. At Night it began to rain, and continued to do so quite through it.

Let out a Fox (which had been taken alive some days ago) and after chasing it an hour lost it.

The Marquis de Chappedelaine & Mr. Ingraham returned to Alexandria after Dinner.

Saturday 16th.    Thermometer at 34 in the Morning—36 at Noon and 34 at Night. The Wind remained at No. Et. till near night when it came out fresh from No. Wt. and cleared till when it rained and sleeted so as to surcharge the Trees and every thing else with Ice.

At home all day.

Sunday 17th.    Thermometer at 34 in the Morning—36 at Noon and 30 at Night. Early in the Morning the Wind was at So. Wt. but it soon shifted to No. Et. and overcast. About Noon it began to Snow & continued to do so till Sun down when it ceased soon after wch. the Wind got to No. Wt. blew fresh and grew cold. The Snow was about two Inches deep.

At home all day with the Family. Mrs. Stuart, Miss Stuart & Betcy and Patcy Custis going away after breakfast.

Monday 18th.    Thermometer at 22 in the Morning—32 at Noon, & 29 at Night. Morning clear with the Wind at No. Wt. but towards evening shifted to the So. Wt. keeping clear; Navigation again stopped.

Visited the Plantations at Muddy hole and Frenchs.

The Ploughs were stopped every where.

The Women of Dogue run, Frenchs and the Ferry were all at Work in the New ground at the Mansn. House.

At Muddy hole they were spreading dung.

George Steptoe Washington who went down to see his Brother Ferdinand who died before he got to Lancaster returned about 12 oclock. And Mr. Harry Peake dined here.

Finished landing the last of the Corn sent here by Colo. Jno. Fras. Mercer.

Henry Peake (b. 1762) was a son of Humphrey and Mary Stonestreet Peake (MCDONALD, 449).

Tuesday 19th. Thermometer at 25 in the Morning—40 at Noon And 38 at Night. Morning clear with the wind, tho' not much of it at West & Cool tho' it thawed a good deal in the middle of the day.

Visited the Plantations in the Neck and at Muddy hole. At the first the Men were getting & preparing for fencing. The Women, some were grubbing and others throwing down old fences in order to erect them a New.

At Muddy hole, The Women had just finished spreading dung on part of No. 1.

At the other places the Men were cutting & mauling and the Women grubbing at the Mansion House.

Wednesday 20th. Thermometer at 30 in the Morning—40 at Noon and 38 at Night. The Wind was at No. Wt. and the frost severe. River close this Morning but opened with the tide & by the wind.

Rid to the Plantations in the Neck and at Muddy hole.

In the Neck the Women were putting up (as far as rails were in place) the fence between fields No. 7 & 8.

At Muddy hole they were sprouting the stumps & taking up grubs in the Winter fallow of No. 4.

The People at the other places and at the Mansion house were working as usual.

SPROUTING: removing sprouts from.

Thursday 21st. Thermometer at 30 in the Morning—32 at Noon and 28 at Night. Wind at No. Wt. with Clouds and appearances of Snow.

Rid to Muddy hole, Dogue run Frenchs and Ferry.

At the first working as yesterday.

*February 1788*

At Dogue run the same; except that the cutters and maulers had shifted to the East Side of the Plantation in order to get rails to repair the meadow fence.

Friday 22d.   Thermometer at 24 in the Morning—28 at Noon and 26 at Night. Wind at No. Et. and North; and fresh & cold. About 10 Oclock last Night it began to Snow & continued to do so all Night and till afternoon this day—but as it drifted much the depth cd. not be ascertained.

Colo. Wm. Heth, who came here to dinner yesterday was sent by me to Alexandria to pursue his journey to New York in the Stage.

I remained at home all day.

William Heth (1750–1807), a wealthy Henrico County landowner and distinguished veteran of the Continental line, was going to New York as commissioner for the state of Virginia to settle with Congress the state's accounts "for the expences incurred in the acquisition and Defence of the Western Territory"—the lands north of the Ohio that Virginia had ceded to the Confederation in 1781 (VA. COUNCIL JLS., 3:514; 4:209, 226, 244). After spending the night of 20 Feb. with George Mason, Heth had set out for Mount Vernon after breakfast on 21 Feb. "I was fortunate enough," he recorded in his diary, "to find the General without any other company than Colo. Humphreys who has been here some months. Dined & spent an agreeable day—find that the General is very anxious to see the proposed federal constitution adopted by all the States. He recd. letters this evening from Boston & New York informing him that the Convention of Massachusetts then sitting would unquestionably accept of it" (DLC). Definite word of Massachusetts's ratification arrived on the evening of 22 Feb. (George Augustine Washington to Frances Bassett Washington, 22 Feb. 1788, ViMtV; Heth's obituary is in *Va. Gaz.* [Richmond], 1 April 1807; see also LEE [7], 275–76).

The northern stage at this time left Alexandria from George H. Leigh's Bunch of Grapes Tavern on the corner of Fairfax and Cameron streets (*Va. Journal,* 11 Oct. 1787).

The accumulation of snow on this day, according to George Augustine Washington, amounted to "5 or 6 Inches" (George Augustine Washington to Frances Bassett Washington, 22 Feb. 1788, ViMtV).

Saturday 23d.   Thermometer at 27 in the Morning—36 at Noon and 35 at Night. Wind at No. Wt. Fresh & cold all day but clear.

I remained at home all day.

Sunday 24.   Thermometer at 30 in the Morning—42 at Noon and 40 at Night. Clear Morning with the Wind still at No. W. where it continued all day but went down with the Sun.

In the Evening the Revd. Mr. Fairfax came in.

[ 279 ]

Monday 25th.    Thermometer at 32 in the Morning—48 at Noon and 46 at Night. Calm and clear Morning. Wind Southerly afterwards which occasioned a considerable thaw.

Mr. Fairfax going away directly after breakfast I rid to the Plantations in the Neck—at Muddy hole and Dogue run.

At the first (that is the Neck) the Women were grubbing & fencing along the Creek.

At Muddy hole doing the same. The Women from Dogue run, Frenchs & Ferry were at work in the New grd. at the Mansn. house.

Tuesday 26.    Thermometer at 38 in the Morning—46 at Noon And 42 at Night. Clear Morning & calm, but the Wd. soon rose & blew fresh from the No. Wt. till evening when it ceased. It thawed pretty considerably to day but not sufft. to admit the Plows.

Rid to Muddy hole, Dogue run, French's & the Ferry Plantations.

At all, the People belonging to them were at work.

Set in the Inclosure below the Garden, Seven bushels of Carrots to raise Seed from—6 of which, on the upper side, were of the Lemon kind. The other Bushel were of the Orange sort; and are between the 2d. & 3d. Stakes, reckoning from the upper one.

Wednesday 27th.    Thermometer at 30 in the Morning—32 at Noon and 28 at Night. The wind came hard from the No. Wt. about day break and blew violently all day. The ground was hard frozen and the day very cold—but little thawing.

Rid to all the Plantations. No plowing at any. Grubbg. at most.

Thursday 28th.    Thermometer at 20 in the Morning—30 at Noon and 32 at Night. Clear and very cold. The River frozen to the Channel. Wind at No. Wt. all day.

Mr. Porter & his wife, and Mr. Ingraham and a Mr. Koch a dutch Gentleman came here to dinner. The two first stayed all night. The latter returned to Alexandria.

I remained at home all day.

Nathaniel Ingraham, who was to sail to Amsterdam within a few weeks, agreed to try to procure a Dutch gardener for GW. He returned by way of Philadelphia in late November but apparently brought no gardener (GW to Ingraham, 22 Mar. 1788, DLC:GW; GW to Clement Biddle, 27 Nov. 1788, PHi: Washington-Biddle Correspondence; *Pa. Packet*, 11 Oct. and 13 Nov. 1788; see also entry for 15 Nov. 1788).

Friday 29th.    Thermometer at 22 in the Morning—38 at Noon and 36 at Night. Clear with the Wind at No. Wt. but moderate and towards night not unpleast.

Rid to the Plantations at the Ferry, Frenchs, D. Run & Muddy hole.

Cutting down Corn stalks at the first, grubbing at the other, and fencing at the two latter.

# March [1788]

Saturday the first.   Thermometer at 24 in the Morning—24 at Noon and 24 at Night. The Wind, which had considerably encreased in the Night, blew cold from the No. Wt. and clouded up. About 11 Oclk. it began to Snow, and continued to do so fast till about 2 Oclock covering the grd. about an Inch & half when it ceased and the Sun came out.

Rid to the Plantations at Muddy hole, D. Run and Frenchs.

Fencing at the first, cutting corn stalks at the 2d., & grubbg. at the other.

Having sent my Waiter Will to Alexandria to the Post Office he fell at Mr. Porters door and broke the Pan of his other Knee & was not able to return.

The Letters were sent down by Mr. Ingraham by his assistant.

For William Lee's first knee injury, see entry for 22 April 1785.

Sunday 2d.   Thermometer at 18 in the Morning—28 at Noon And 28 at Night. Wind high from the No. Wt. and cold all day. Weather clear.

At home all day.

Monday 3d.   Thermometer at 26 in the Morning—32 at Noon And 32 at Night. Wind at No. Wt. (but not hard) till evening when it veered round to the Eastward with encreasing & thickning clouds.

Visited the Plantations at Muddy hole, Dogue run, Frenchs, and the Ferry—The weather being too hard to grub.

At Muddy hole and Dogue run, the Women were fencing.

At Frenchs they were carrying trash to, & filling up Gullies and

At the Ferry they were cutting down & picking up Corn Stalks.

Tuesday 4th.   Thermometer at 28 in the Morning—32 at Noon And 32 at Night. About 9 Oclock last Night it began to Snow and continued to do so through the Night and till 8 oclock this morning by which time it appears to have been at least 6 Inches deep on a level. In the early part of the Morning the Wind was at No.: after which getting to the No. West it cleared and was cold.

**Wednesday 5th.**    Thermometer at 28 in the Morning—42 at Noon and 38 at Night. Clear and the wind fresh all day from the Wt. But little thaw.

Rid to the Plantations at Muddy hole, Dogue run, & French's.

At the two first the women were fencing—at the latter removing rails for the same purpose.

The Ferry Women were at work in the New grd. at the Mann. House.

**Thursday 6th.**    Thermometer at 32 in the Morning—43 at Noon and 38 at Night. Early in the Morning the Wind made some feeble efforts to blow from the So. Wt. but shifting to No. Wt. Before 8 Oclock it was fresh, but not very cold, all day.

Rid to the Plantations in the Neck Muddy hole, Dogue run and Frenchs.

At the first some of the Women were grubbing, & some fencing —the Men getting rails.

At Muddy hole the Women were grubbing, as they also were at French's.

At Dogue run they were making fences.

Men at all the places getting Rails &ca.

On my return home found Doctr. Stuart & Mr. Jno. Calvert here.

Colo. Humphreys & Majr. G. Washington went up to Alexandria, and returned in the evening.

John Calvert was a younger brother of Dr. Stuart's wife, Eleanor (BOWIE, 102–3).

**Friday 7th.**    Thermometer at 36 in the morning—44 at Noon and 43 at Night. Clear morning with the breeze from the So. West. which soon shifted to No. Wt. and blew fresh & cold all day—but little thawing & that at top only.

Doctr. Stuart and Mr. Calvert going away after breakfast I rid to the Plantations at Muddy Hole, Dogue run, Frenchs & the Ferry.

Work going on at each as pr. the Weekly report.

**Saturday 8th.**    Thermometer at 38 in the Morning—42 at Noon And 36 at Night. Morning pleasant, with the Wind at So. Wt. &

appearances of mildness but shifting. Before 8 Oclock it blew fresh clouded & turned cold, and remained so all day.

Rid to the Plantations in the Neck at Muddy hole and Dogue run.

Work at each pr. Report Book. Majr. G. A. Washington set of this afternoon for Colo. Bassetts—where his wife was.

Sunday 9th.    Thermometer at 34 in the Morning—46 at Noon and 44 at Night. Morning cloudy with the Wind disagreeably cold from the No. Wt. the greatest part of the day. Towards evening it seemed to moderate & grow milder.

Mr. Wm. Hunter, a Mr. Phillis and a Captn. Parnel came here to dinner. The two latter went away after it.

Monday 10th.    Thermometer at 39 in the Morning—[    ] at Noon And 46 at Night. Morning calm and pleasant, but the Wind rising at No. Wt. & blowing hard it became disagreeable.

Mr. Hunter went away after breakfast.

I rid to all the Plantations. Began the Meadow fence in the Neck with some of the Women, while others were grubbing.

At Muddy hole finished grubbing in field No. 4.

At Dogue run grubbing below the Meadow by the Quarters.

At Frenchs grubbing along the swamp sides and

At the Ferry filling gullies with trash.

Tuesday 11th.    Thermometer at 36 in the Morning—52 at Noon And 52 at Night. The Wind still at No. Wt. & fresh and Cold in the forenoon. In the afternoon it lulled & was more moderate.

Rid to Muddy hole, Dogue run, Frenchs & the Ferry.

At the first Began to plow—Women making fence on ditch round the Barn, and in lane. The frost below the surface (2 or 3 Inches) stopped in places the plow but I ordered them to proceed.

Directed the Plows at Dogue run to begin to morrow.

At Frenchs two plows were at work and the Women began to fence between fields No. 1 & 4.

At the Ferry I directed the Plows to work to morrow. Women still filling gullies and the Men preparing to fence on the long ditch.

Mr. Lund Washington and his wife dined here.

Wednesday 12th.    Thermometer at 42 in the Morning—55 at Noon and 55 at Night. The morning calm & very pleasant which continued through the day.

Rid to the Plantations in the Neck, Muddy hole, Dogue run, Frenchs & the Ferry.

At the River Plantation, the Plows were unable to work on acct. of the frost. The Women were fencing between fields No. 1 & 2 except those who were grubbing; having finished the fence by the Meadow.

At Muddy hole the Plows were going on very well and the other People were repairing the outer fence (along the Ferry road) of field No. 4.

At Dogue run 5 plows began to Work in field No. 3 and in the part intended for Barley. The ground in pretty good order. Women grubbing by the Quarters.

At Frenchs Plowing & Fencing going on as yesterday.

At the Ferry, the Plows began to Work in field No. 3. The other people were employed in fencing. The grd. at this place was not in good order on acct. of the frost for Plowing.

Thursday 13th.    Thermometer at 45 in the Morning—62 at Noon and 62 at Night. Very pleasant, warm, & growing—the Wind tho not very fresh, at South.

Rid to the Plantations at Muddy hole, Dogue run, Frenchs & the Ferry.

Work as usual at all (except at Dogue run, where the Women havg. finished grubbing by the Quarters were employed in grubbing a piece of fencing Round field No. 7).

Began this day to Sow the imported Beans and Pease at Frenchs which when finished the place kinds & manner of putting it will be noticed.

Transplanted the last of my Carrots for Seed to day.

Friday 14th.    Thermometer at 52 in the Morning—60 at Noon And 60 at Night. The Wind pretty fresh from the Southward and weather exceedingly hazy with heavy clouds but no rain.

Went with Mrs. Washington to Alexandria. Visited Captn. Conway Doctr. Craik, Colo. Saml. Hanson, Mr. Murray, & Mr. Porter with the last of whom we dined. Returned in the Eve.

Samuel Hanson of Samuel had served as a lieutenant colonel of the Charles County, Md., militia during the Revolution (SCHARF [4], 2:194). He was at this time boarding GW's two nephews, George Steptoe and Lawrence Augustine Washington, while they attended the Alexandria Academy (LEDGER B, 151; GW to George Steptoe Washington, 23 Mar. 1789, DLC:GW).

Saturday 15th.    Thermometer at 46 in the Morning—58 at Noon And 56 at Night. The Wind, tho' there was but little of it, was at No. Wt. Mild and warm.

Visited all the Plantations. At all of them, the full compliment of Plows were at work and going on very well.

In the Neck, the Women were spreading Dung on the ground intended for Oats and Barley—being the West part of No. 2. At this place ⟨also⟩ I causd to be sown a bed of Reynold's Turnip rooted Cabbages for the purpose of raising plants to put in my Corn Rows.

At Muddy hole the Plows finished breaking up the remains of Fd. No. 3 yesterday afternoon and finding that part of No. 4 intended for Oats too wet to cross they went into field No. 1 to plow for Barley this Morning. The Women fencing r[oa]d the same.

At Dogue run, The Women began to Hooe the ground they had grubbed at the lower end of the Meadow; gave Scotts Cabbage Seed to be sown at this Place on Monday on a bed to be barned [burned].

At French's the Women were Fencing. The Farmer finished yesterday sowing the Pease and Beans on the No. side of the Middle Meadow in the following Manner—viz.—in the upper land, adjoining the fence, the Pease (1 bushel) were sown. The Next land to this a bushel of Berkshire Beans from Mr. Peacy was sown. In the 3d. 4th. 5th. & half the sixth lands the Beans from Mr. Young 3¼ (said by my farmer to be the same of the last) were sown and in the other half of the 6th. land and the 7th. were a bushel of the Gloucester Beans from Mr. Peacy.

At the Ferry the Women were still about the fence of field No. 6.

TURNIP ROOTED CABBAGES: *Brassica napobrassica,* rutabaga. The first leaves resemble cabbage leaves.

William Peacey (d. 1815), a noted gentleman farmer of Northleach, Gloucestershire, Eng., employed GW's farmer, James Bloxham, for 15 years before Bloxham came to America (George W. Fairfax to GW, 23 Jan. 1786, DLC:GW). Several casks of seeds of various kinds had arrived from Peacey during the previous year aboard the same ship that brought Bloxham's wife and children to join him. GW paid Peacey £10 1s. 1d. for the seeds and was generally pleased with their condition even though some had been damaged from being stored in the hold of the ship (GW to Peacey, 16 Nov. 1786, PHi, and 7 Jan. 1788, ViMtV; GW to Wakelin Welch & Son, [8 Jan. 1788], DLC:GW; see also ABBOTT, 180–81).

Sunday 16th.   Thermometer at 43 in the Morning—55 at Noon and 50 at Night. Morning clear with the wind at No. Wt. & rather cooler than it was yesterday. Afterwards it freshned and blew pretty strong all day.

Monday 17th.   Thermometer at 37 in the Morning—[    ] at Noon and [    ] at Night. Clear all day and pleasant. Wind a little variable–in the Morning Easterly–in the evening Southerly.

Went up (accompanied by Colo. Humphreys) to the Election of Delegates to the Convention of this State (for the purpose of considering the New form of Governmt. which has been recommended to the United States) ; When Doctr. Stuart and Colo. Simms were chosen without opposition. Dined at Colo. Fitzgeralds, and returned in the Evening.

The Virginia Ratifying Convention was to meet in Richmond on 2 June. Election of delegates took place in each county on its appointed court day in March. "Our elections," GW wrote John Jay 3 Mar. 1788, "form an interesting epocha in our Annals. After the choice is made, the probable decision on the proposed Constitution (from the characters of memebers) can with more ease be conjectured; for myself I have never entertained much doubt of its adoption" (DLC:GW). The results, which were not fully known for several weeks, indicated a thin margin in favor of the friends of the Constitution (FREEMAN, 6:133–34). Both Dr. David Stuart and Charles Simms supported the new form of government (*Md. Journal*, 28 Mar. 1788).

Tuesday 18th.    Thermometer at 39 in the Morning–46 at Noon and 40 at Night. Wind at East & So. Et. Cloudy all day with small sprinkles in the forenoon. Towards Night it became stormy, the Wind blowing very fresh from the So. Et. and raining hard which it continued to do most part of the Night.

Visited all the Plantations. In the Neck, found that the Plows had finished breaking up the Barn Inclosure last Night and all, except one (which went to laying of fd. No. 6 for planting Corn &ca.) were plowing for Oats in the No. Wt. corner of No. 2. The Women were clearing the hedge Row in the same field & preparing for fencing. The Men were fixing posts & Rails for fencing No. 6 &ca. and making the lane betwn. them and fields No. 1 & 2.

The Ditchers–to wit–Dl. Overdonck, Boatswain, Robin, Charles & Bath began yesterday to ditch for same.

At Muddy hole, finding the ground (intended for Oats in No. 4) had got tolerably dry the plows were shifted from No. 1 thither yesterday after breakfast and this day the grd. wch. they had plowed in No. 1 by the quarters was sowed with Barley & harrowed in. The Women were partly fencing, & partly picking up Corn Stalks. Harrowed with Oxen which made an awkwd. hand.

At Dogue Run–The Plows finished yesterday afternoon the ground intended for Barley in field No. 3 & began to plow that part of the same field wch. was designed for Oats. The women were partly hoeing (as on Saturday) & partly grubbing before the Plows. The Cabbage Seed was sown at this place on Monday.

At Frenchs, the Plows (now three) having finished breaking the ground in the lower meadow had gone this Morning to breaking up in No. 3 but were ordered to plow to morrow the So. part of No. 2 for Oats. The Women were fencing on the dividing line.

Yesterday 6 bushels of English Oats (sent me by Mr. Young) was sowed on abt. 2 Acres of grd. on the No. side of the Middle meadow—the ground once plowed, and the Seed harrowed—in good tilth.

At the Ferry, the Ploughs went yesterday to plough (cross) the grd. in No. 6 wch. was intended for Oats and it worked well, except being rather too wet. The Women were fencing.

At the Mansion house, began the circular Post & rail fencing in front of the lawn yesterday Morning.

Mr. Madison on his way from New York to Orange came in before dinner and stayed all Night.

The slave ditchers working with Daniel Overdonck were from different plantations: Boatswain from Home House, Robin from Dogue Run or River plantation, Charles from Muddy Hole, and Bath from River plantation (see entry for 18 Feb. 1786).

James Madison, Jr., who had been fulfilling his duties as a congressman in New York since the end of the Constitutional Convention, was going home to be present on 24 Mar. when Orange County was to elect its two delegates to the state ratifying convention. Madison was chosen as one of Orange's delegates and subsequently was one of the leaders in the fight for the Constitution in the convention (MADISON, 10:542, n.4).

Wednesday 19th. Thermometer at 50 in the Morning—58 at Noon and 56 at Night. Wind fresh from the So. Wt. Towards evening it veered more to the Westward and in the Night got to No. Wt. The whole day the air (considering the Wind) was rather cool.

Remained at home all day.

Thursday 20th. Thermometer at 40 in the Morning—42 at Noon and 40 at Night. The Wind came from the No. Wt. and blew pretty fresh and cool all day with clouds; & once (about 8 Oclk.) with threatning appearances of Snow.

Mr. Madison (in my Carriage) went after breakfast to Colchester to ⟨fall⟩ in with ⟨the Stage⟩.

I visited all the Plantations. In the Neck began yesterday to Sow Oats—the other work going on as usual.

At Muddy hole the Rain that fell on Tuesday Night made the grd. intended for Oats too wet to plow. They therefore returned to that wch. was designed for Barley in No. 1 & plowed there. The

Women having finished fencing were grubbing in the sunken part of No. 3.

At Dogue run the Plows five were plowing for Oats & the Women hoeing.

At Frenchs the Plows were at work in No. 2 for Oats & the Women fencing. 1¾ Bushls. of Summer Wht. (sent by Mr. Young) was sowed at this place yesterday below the Beans and Pease in the Middle Meadow. At the same time better than half a Bushel of orchard grass-seeds & 18 lbs. of Clover were Sown in the same Meadow on the English Oats by the old bridge and the ground cross harrowed. The Wheat was harrowed in.

At the Ferry the Plows were crossing in No. 6 for Oats. The other hands were fencing.

Friday 21st.    Thermometer at 37 in the Morning—50 at Noon And 50 at Night. Clear Morning and Mild, but a hard crust on the Surface by the frost. Clear all day.

Rid to all the Plantations. In the Neck, Oat sowing, and other Work going on as usual.

At Muddy hole, continued sowing and harrowing in Barley, after the ground got thawed & a little dried at Top.

At Dogue run, working as yesterday.

At French's the same and the ground which had been sowed with English Oats and Grass-seeds was rolled.

At The Ferry, the work was the same as yesterday.

On my return home, found a Mr. Rogers of New York here who dined and proceeded to Alexandria afterwds.

John Rodgers (1727–1811), a renowned Presbyterian clergyman, served the Presbyterians of New York City as pastor from 1765 to 1810, except during the Revolution when he chose to live outside the British-occupied city. Although he attended no college or university, the University of Edinburgh conferred the degree of doctor of divinity on him in 1768 at the instigation of the evangelist George Whitefield, who greatly influenced Rodgers's life from an early age. Rodgers was also for many years a trustee of the College of New Jersey and during the spring of this year served as a member of the committee that revised the standards of the Presbyterian Church in America. At the end of the War of Independence, he had written GW proposing that each discharged Continental soldier be given a copy of an American translation of the Bible, a scheme that GW warmly approved in general terms, but politely forestalled on the practical grounds that nearly two-thirds of the army had gone home by the time Rodgers's letter arrived (Rodgers to GW, 30 May 1783, and GW to Rodgers, 11 June 1783, DLC:GW).

Saturday 22d.    Thermometer at 42 in the Morning—48 at Noon and 46 at Night. Southerly Wind all day, clear & pleasant.

Visited all the Plantations. In the Neck sowing Oats & Grass Seeds—viz. 5 pints of red clover, & 2 pints of timothy to the acre—which being cross plowed in was afterwards rolled.

At Muddy hole Sowed the same quantity of red Clover & timothy to the acre as above, on the Barley wch. had been sown & some of it having been in the ground 2 or 3 days and a rain fallen thereon I did not incline to disturb the grain with an Iron lined [tined] harrow, and therefore rubbed a bush harrow over it to smooth the surface, and to bury the grass seed.

At Muddy [Dogue] Run, began to Sow Oats this morning all of which was harrowed in & cross harrowed.

At Frenchs, & The Ferry the Work was the same as yesterday and the hands of the former compleated the fencing of field No. 3 except the part wch. divides it from the Middle Meadow.

On my return home, found Colo. Jno. Mercer here, who remained all Night.


Sunday 23d.    Thermometer at 46 in the Morning—46 at Noon And 46 at Night. Clear Morning, & a fresh Wind from the So. Et. About Nine O'clock a very black cloud arose in the So. Wt.: and about 10 it began to rain, which it continued to do moderately till past Noon when it ceased but continued cloudy. The Wind shifting to So. Wt. & then West and turning Cooler.

To dinner came Doctr. Stuart, Mrs. Stuart & Miss Stuart and the 4 children and after it Colo. Mercer went away.


Monday 24th.    Thermometer at 36 in the Morning—44 at Noon and 40 at Night. Clear day, with the wind very hard (and turning cold) from the No. Wt. The ground a little crusted this Morning with the frost.

Mr. Jno. Dawson came here a little before dinner, & proceeded after it to Alexandria.


Tuesday 25th.    Thermometer at 36 in the morng.—46 at Noon and 44 at Night. Morning clear, ground hard frozen, Wind from So. Wt. in the Morning early. Afterwards it veered to West, blew fresh & cold. In the evening it got to So. Wt. again and became moderate.

Visited all the Plantations. The ground at all was too hard frozen and when thawed too wet to sow and harrow till afternoon.

Mr. Benja. Dulany came here dined and returned afterwards.

Benjamin Tasker Dulany today brought £120 annual rent that he owed GW for 376 acres of land on Hunting Creek (LEDGER B, 132; see entry for 3 Feb. 1785).

Wednesday 26th.   Thermometer at 37 in the Morning—44 at Noon and 44 at Night. Morning clear, & Wind at So. Wt. but afterwards it shifted to No. W. and blew very hard—turng. cold.

Doctr. Stuart went away after breakfast.

I visited all the Plantations. Sowing, harrowing, & rolling retarded at each on Acct. of the frost in the Morning, & stickiness of the earth afterwards, till towards Noon.

Finished sowing so much of the West cut of No. 2 in the Neck as recd. the Oats raised from the Seed of Genl. Spotswood; and Clover & timothy thereon; & harrowed & cross harrowed them in, but could not roll them on acct. of the damps on the Surface. Began to Sow Oats in the Eastermost cut of this field which was finished plowing this Morning and to plow in the middle cut for Barley.

At Muddy hole, finished Sowing & harrowing in Barley up to the road in No. 1, from the quarters and by mistake the plows went to work in the Same field on the lower side of the Quarter— but were ordered to go to field No. 4 to morrow & cross plow for Oats.

Sowing Oats, and other work doing as yesterday at D. Run.

At French's the Plows at wk. as yesterday and the Women filling gullies in the lower Meadow.

At the Ferry the Plows having yesterday finished cross plowing for Oats began this day to Sow. The Women cleaning the swamp in No. 2 & thinning the Trees there.

Thursday 27th.   Thermometer at 36 in the Morning—47 at Noon and 46 at Night. Clear with the Wind at No. Wt. but not hard. Ground frozen hard. Towards Noon it became calm and in the evening a breeze from the Southward.

Went to Alexandria (consequent of a Summons, to give evide. in a Suit betwn. the Admrs. of Mr. Custis and Mr. Robt. Alexander) dined at Colo. Hooes & returned in the evening. Mrs. Washington, Mrs. Stuart, & Colo. Humphreys also dind. at Colo. Hooes.

Passed thro' Muddy hole Plantation where grass-seeds were harrowing in on the Barley, & the ground cross harrowing.

The Plows had begun this Morning to cross for Oats as ordered Yesterday. The Women of this place, except those who were engaged with the Plows & Harrows came yesterday to, and were engaged to day in, the Ground in front of the Mansion House—preparing it for Corn.

Dr. David Stuart had succeeded Bartholomew Dandridge as administrator of John Parke Custis's estate after Dandridge's death in the spring of 1785. The suit between the estate and Robert Alexander concerned the Abingdon property which Custis had bought from Alexander in 1778 at a price that GW considered embarrassingly exorbitant (see entry for 12 Mar. 1785). In dispute now was the mode of payment: whether or not the price and the compound interest on it could be paid before the end of the 24 years given for payment, thereby saving the estate a great amount of interest, and whether or not the payment had to be made in specie or could be rendered in any currency, including inflated Revolutionary money. The documents passed between Custis and Alexander were vague or contradictory on these points, and apparently no reliable witnesses to the transaction could be found. It was, as GW exclaimed, "a very strange Affair" (GW to Stuart, 21 Sept. 1789 and 23 Mar. 1790, Stuart to GW, 2 April 1790, DLC:GW; GW to Stuart, 11 April 1790, ViMtV). GW, who had washed his hands of John Parke Custis's business matters many years earlier, was involved in the suit only as acting guardian of George Washington Parke Custis, principal heir to the estate. The suit was later settled out of court with Alexander agreeing to take the property back in return for a fair rent paid for the period during which Custis and his administrators had held it (HENING, 13:99–100; STETSON [1], 25–31).

Friday 28th.    Thermometer at 40 in the Morning—51 at Noon And 50 at Night. Wind at So. Wt. all day and in the evening very high—day clear.

Visited all the Plantations. In the Neck, Plowing, Sowing (Oats & Grass seeds) fencing & picking up Corn Stalks. Conceiving that putting in Grass Seeds before harrowing across with the dble. harrows, buried them too deep, I ordered the Grain should be first harrowed in & cross harrowed and then the Seeds sown & run over with a bush harrow & afterwards rolled.

At Muddy hole did the same where the efficacy of the measure & consequence of harrowing in with an Iron tined harrow the Grass seeds may be seen—the So. E. Corner of the ground as far & rather beyond the old farm pen being put in, in this manner. As was those in the Neck in which Spotswoods Oats were sown on the No. side of the West cut.

At Dogue run, the Plows, yesterday finished plowing for Oats and went to breaking up the ground between fields No. 5 & 6.

The Women having also hoed up the ground below the Meadow, were employed in doing the like in a slash in field No. 5. Sowing & harrowing Oats as usual.

At French's began yesterday to harrow & Sow Oats—the other hands filling gullies in the lower meadow.

At the Ferry, Sowing & harrowing in Oats. The plows went on thursday to finish breaking up field No. 2 for Corn & were employed there to day—and the women were hoeing the slash in the same field.

Mr. & Mrs. L. Washington dined here, & returned afterwards.

Saturday 29th.    Thermometer at 43 in the Morning—47 at Noon And 46 at Night. Cloudy morning with the Wind at No. Wt. & cool. Clear afterwds. with the wind in the same place and rather more pleasant.

Visited all the Plantatns. In the Neck the Plows (this morning) finished plowing the West cut of No. 2 for Barley, & went into the Middle cut of the same field. Sowed the East cut of the same field with 46 Bushls. of Oats which were all harrowed & cross harrowed except the last sowed to do wch. there was not time—nor to sow the Whole with grass-seeds.

At Muddy hole, finished sowing & harrowing in with a bush, grass Seeds on the Barley that had been sowed at Muddy hole.

At all the other Plantations the Work was the same as yesterday.

A Mr. Cay, Undertaker of the Plaistering of the Capitol, came here (with a letter from the Govern.) to look at my New room. He dined & went away afterwards and in the evening Mr. Fendal came.

Joseph Kay (died c.1793) of Henrico County was responsible for the plastering at the new state capitol at Richmond (vsp, 5:248, 6:179–80). Gov. Edmund Randolph's letter has not been found.

Sunday 30th.    Thermometer at 39 in the morning—51 at Noon and 50 at Night. Morning calm clear & pleasant as it continued to be all day, with smoke.

Colonels Hanson & Ramsay, Mr. Powel & Messrs. Jenks & Winsor dined here in addition to those who were here before & returned afterwards.

Mrs. Jenifer also dined here & returned after it.

Olney Winsor (Winzor) was a partner in Jenckes, Winsor & Co., of Alexandria (see entry for 26 Nov. 1786). In 1790 he was listed as a trustee of Alexandria (hening, 13:175).

Monday 31st.    Thermometer at 42 in the Morning—54 at Noon And 51 at Night. Clear with the Wind at South, but cloudy afterwards and towards Night slow rain.

Doctr. Stuart, Mrs. Stuart and the Girls, together with Nelly

Custis set out for Abingdon. And a Son of Revd. Mr. Griffiths came here on business of his fathers & stayed to dinner.

Visited all the Plantations. In the Neck, began to sow Barley in the So. Wt. part of the west cut of No. 2 but had not finished sowing grass-seeds in the East cut.

At Muddy hole, began to sow Barley & grass-seeds which had been sown in No. 1.

At Dogue run, finished Sowing & harrowing Oats in No. 3—qty. of Oats [    ] bushls. Began Saturday afternoon to plow for Engh. Barley in the Turnip ground at this place.

At French's, having finished plowing the ground (but not sowing it) intended for Oats, two plows Wh[i]le the other team was harrowing in the Oats went to breakg. the ground in the same field No. 2 for Barley. The Women, in part, were filling gullies in No. 3 and the other part, and the Cart, gettg. dung to the gullies which had been levelled in the lower meadow.

At the Ferry, harrowing in Oats with one harrow. The Plows would, this afternoon, abt. finish breaking field No. 2 for Corn. Women hoeing in the Swamp as before.

In my Botanical Garden—Next the necessary house, was sown 3 rows of Grass-seeds sent me from Kentucke by Colo. Marshall name unknown and the next 3 rows to these were sown with what this Gentleman calls wild rye but it more resembles Oats. All the other rows of this were of the painted lady Pease. Put in cuttings of the Weeping Willow, behind the Post & rail fence along the road leading to the Gate in the hollow at the distance of a foot from each other. This work was unavoidably delayed too late as the buds were not only much swelled but the leaves of most of them beginning to unfold.

Rev. David Griffith had at least two sons: David Griffith, Jr., and Richard Griffith (deed of Bryan Fairfax to David Griffith, Jr., 16 May 1793, Fairfax County Deeds, Book W-1, 355–57; SPROUSE [2], 2:84). The son who came to Mount Vernon today brought a letter from his father asking GW to pay his annual subscription for the minister's support which had been due since 1 Aug. 1787 (31 Mar. 1788, DLC:GW). The son, however, apparently left without any money (LEDGER B, 265).

Thomas Marshall in Oct. 1788 sent GW seeds and nuts of several plants native to the region around his Fayette County, Ky., home: "some of the different specias of wild rhye, a few of the Coffee [tree] nuts, Buckeye, the seeds of the Papaw-apple, a few acrons [acorns] of an excellent specias of the white oak," and "some of the natural grass seed of that country." The grass seed, Marshall wrote GW, "is of a very luxuriant growth and as far as I have tried it appears to be excellent for hay, but as I have only cultivated a small spot, sow'd last fall in my garden, I can as yet judge of it with no great certainty: it does not require a wet soil, but the ground it is sow'd in ought to be rich & made fine. Feby. will be a good time, & sow it about as thick as Tob[acc]o seed" (27 Oct. 1787, DLC:GW).

PAINTED LADY PEASE: *Lathyrus odoratus*, sweet pea.


# April [1788]

Tuesday 1st.    Thermometer at 52 in the Morning—65 at Noon And 64 at Night. Morning heavy with the Wind at South. Clear afterwards & very warm.

Went with Mrs. Washington and Colo. Humphreys to visit Mr. & Mrs. Rogr. West. Dined there & returned in the afternoon.

Previous to this I visited all my Plantations.

At the Ferry, the Plows began to work in field No. 3—the Harrow putting in Oats & grass Seeds and the women hoeing the swamp.

At Frenchs the Work was going on as yesterday. Grass Seeds at the rate of 3 pints of Timothy and 6 of red clover—sowing to the Acre.

At Dogue run, the Harrows, after crossing the Sown Oats, were layed aside, & 2 plows went to crossing the grd. destined for Barley. The Women were hoeing the Swamp in the Middle meadow by the Overseers house.

At Muddy hole, Plowing, sowing, Harrowing & rolling were going on. The women not engaged in these were at Work at the Mansn. Ho[use] New ground.

In the Neck, the ground intended for Barley in the West cut of No. 2 that was stiff, & did not work fine at first was cross plowed, & harrowed till it was brought into fine order. Finished harrowing in Oats & grass-seeds in the East cut of this field but not rolling some part of the roller havg. given way.

Made a draught with the Sein this evening at the Ferry Landing, and caught 15 Shad and a few hundreds of Herrings at one hawl.

Mariamne Craik, daughter of Dr. James Craik, Sr., had recently become Roger West's second wife (see entries for 28 Dec. 1787 and 21 July 1788). His first wife was Nancy Macrae West, daughter of Allan Macrae of Dumfries. The Wests lived near the mouth of Hunting Creek at the house they called West Grove, the same house that had belonged to Roger's father, Col. John West (see entry for 8 Jan. 1760).

Wednesday Second.    Thermometer at 50 in the Morning—56 at Noon And 54 at Night. In the forenoon the Wind was at No. Wt. and cold. In the Evening it was Southerly & warm.

The ground had got dry, and somewhat (in places) baked. Moderate & warm rain wanting.

Rid to the Plantations at the Ferry, Frenchs, Dogue run and Muddy hole.

At the two first, and last, the Work was going on precisely as yesterday.

At Dogue run, began to sow grass Seeds on the Oats, at the rate of 3 pints of Timothy & 6 pints of red clover to the acre.

Sowed in drills, in the Section of my Botanical garden between the Salt House & the other, and amg. the Pride of China Plants [    ] rows of the Grass-Seed sent me by Colo. Marshall of Kentucke, being the same with the 3 rows sowed in the West pt. of the other Section, on Monday last.

Transplanted from a box in the Garden, 13 plants of the horse chesnut into the shrubberies by the Garden Walls.

Thursday 3d.    Thermometer at 46 in the Morning—44 at Noon And 43 at Night. Heavy morning with the Wind at So. East—at which it continued all day—at sometimes fresher than others. Abt. 8 oclock it began a slow, light rain, which with mists continued till Night and moistened, tho' it did not wet the ground much.

Continued at home all day.

Friday 4th.    Thermometer at 46 in the Morning—60 at Noon And 60 at Night. Calm, clear, and very pleasant all day.

Rid to all the Plantations. In the Neck, Plowing, sowing Barley & Grass Seeds, and other work as on Wednesday.

At Muddy hole, stopped the roller in order that two harrows might be covering Oats. At this place the first sown Barley was coming up & appeared to be thick.

At Dogue run the usual work was going on.

At the French's began to sow Barley in the No. part of No. 2. At this place perceived the English Oats, & the Pease were coming up the ⟨1⟩st. tolerably thick.

At the Ferry, the harrow having finished (yesterday) covering the Oats & grass Seeds—all three of the Plows were breaking up in No. 3.

Caught 500 and odd Shad to day. In my Botanical Garden on thursday morning, before the rain, I sowed in the Section next the spinning house, one row of Rhubarb seed, sent me by Mr. Jay— the Seeds 3 Inches a part. These were placed along the Walk— parallel to the Ho.

John Jay, by Joseph Wright.
(New-York Historical Society)

RHUBARB: *Rheum rhaponticum.* John Jay wrote from New York 3 Feb. 1788 that he had obtained some rhubarb seed from an Englishman who vouched for its high quality, and he was sending "a little Parcel of it" to Mount Vernon so that GW might try it in the soil and climate of Virginia (DLC:GW).

Saturday 5th.     Thermometer at 51 in the Morning—64 at Noon And 63 at Night. Clear and warm all day, but little wind and that at Easterly.

Visited all the Plantations. In the Neck, the same work as yesterday was going forward.

At Muddy hole the same also.

At Dogue run the same. The two plows at this place finished breaking up the turnip ground in No. 1 about dinner time yesterday & went afterwards to crossing in No. 2 for Barley.

At Frenchs the same work going forward and

At the Ferry also.

Sunday 6th.     Thermometer at 46 in the Morning—60 at Noon and 60 at Night. What wind there was, was from the Southwd., but not much. Clear and very pleast.

Sent my two Jackasses to the Election at Marlborough in Maryld. that they might be seen.

The Maryland General Assembly set 7 April as the day for electing all delegates to the state convention that was to meet in Annapolis two weeks later to consider ratification of the federal Constitution (STEINER, 30–31). Many planters, therefore, would be at the Prince George's County courthouse in Upper Marlboro on Monday to choose the county's four delegates. It would, GW knew, be a good opportunity to display his two jackasses, Royal Gift and Knight of Malta, whose stud services had been advertised in the Annapolis and Baltimore newspapers for the past few weeks (*Md. Gaz.,* 13 and 20 Mar. and 3 April 1788; *Md. Journal,* 11, 18, 21, and 25 Mar. 1788). The jackasses were taken to Upper Marlboro by Peter, a lame dower slave who normally worked on the Home House plantation as a knitter (LEDGER B, 265; see entry for 18 Feb. 1786).

Monday 7th.    Thermometer at 50 in the Morning—50 at Noon And 50 at Night.

The Wind was at So. Et. & East all day; abt. 7 Oclock it sprinkled rain and abt. 1 Oclock, began a slow & thin Rain, which continued with intervals the remainder of the day and in the Night a good deal fell.

Visited all the Plantations. In the Neck, the Posting, Railing & ditching was compleated this Morning up to the Gate; and the other part, to the Gut, set about. The Plows would, about Noon, finish breaking up the Middle cut of No. 2 and a particular part of wch. being very cloddy & stiff, I ordered it to be crossed and the whole of What was not already sown with Barley to be gone over once, or oftener with the harrows before it was sowed, that it might be the better prepared for the reception of this grain and Grass-Seeds. The Women would about have done picking up & heaping the Corn Stalks in No. 3 to day (having finished those in No. 7) and would repair the fence round No. 6 and Orchard Inclosure.

At Muddy hole, the Plows wd. finish to day, crossing the ground for Oats—and would go into No. 1 to break up the remainder of that allotted for Barley. Ordered the Women from the New Ground to Hoe along the fence where the ground had been grubbed in the Oat field for the better reception of this grain.

At Dogue-run, the Women wd. about compleat hoeing the Swamp in the middle Meadow. Removed the Plow that was laying off for Corn to assist in crossing for Barley in No. 2. Finished Sowing grass-seeds this morning & harrowing them in the Oats in the same field qty. 2 bushls. of Clover and 1 of Timothy.

At Frenchs, two plows and a harrow were putting in Barley & grass-seed as usual, and the women filling gullies in field No. 3.

At the Ferry 1 plow began to lay off Corn rows in No. 2 and one other being stopped on acct. of the failure of one of the plow beasts I sent a Mare from the Mn. Ho. (wch. had been brought from the Neck) there to assist. The Women were hoeing an old hedge row in No. 2.

In the Vineyard Inclosure below the Stables I sowed in a bed in the No. Et. Cornr. the Seed of the Runkel Recbar or Root of Scarcity and adjoining this in two other beds—ranging therewith —the Seeds of Sulla were sown; the Middle bed was the freshest Seeds. Next below these, in drills, is the Seeds sown which was sent by Mr. Peacy to my Farmer. Below these again will be Sown the Seeds of the Fancy grass, given to me by the Revd. Mr. Massey but night coming on prevented its being done this evening. In the lawn West of the House & West part of it, I sowed 3½ bushels of Blue grass Seeds from the fall therein to the walks. The No. half was mixed with 3 bushels of the Plaister of Paris & the South half with[ou]t having had Plaister spread thereon in the last Autumn on a slight snow.

ROOT OF SCARCITY: *Beta vulgaris,* mangel-wurzel. A large coarse beet grown chiefly as a food for cattle, this plant was attracting much attention among English agriculturalists at this time. The seeds that GW planted today were apparently ones that had arrived from Richard Peters of Philadelphia within the past few days, but GW may have also had seeds from some roots that a neighboring lady sent Mrs. Washington in the fall of 1785 (Peters to GW, 12 Mar. and 27 April 1788, DLC:GW; GW to Elizabeth French Dulany, c.23 Nov. 1785, MdHi, photostat). Later this month Benjamin Rush of Philadelphia sent GW a small quantity of mangel-wurzel seeds that he had recently received from England together with a pamphlet describing "the method of cultivating . . . & useful qualities of this extraordinary vegetable" (Rush to GW, 26 April 1788, DLC:GW; see entry for 29 Oct. 1788).

SULLA: *Hedysarum coronarium,* often called sulla clover. GW was given these seeds during the Constitutional Convention by the French essayist, Hector St. John de Crèvecoeur. "This plant . . . ," GW later reported to Crèvecoeur through James Madison, "came to nothing. . . . The seed vegitated partially, and not being able to find the name in any botanical list of plants in my possession or to ascertain the properties of it; and it appearing at the sametime not to be grateful for the *first* attentions which were bestowed on it, not much care was taken of it afterwards" (GW to Madison, 17 Nov. 1788, DLC:GW).

Tuesday 8th.    Thermometer at 46 in the Morning—50 at Noon and 50 at Night. Wind Easterly all day. Besides the Rain which fell in the Night it was Showery all day. In the course therefore of the 24 hours much rain had fallen.

About 10 Oclock, in company with Colo. Humphreys, Mrs. Washington Harriott Washington and Washington Custis I set of for Abingdon—where we dined and stayed all Night.

Wednesday 9th.    Thermometer at 52 in the Morning—64 at Noon And [      ] at Night. Clear and temperate with the Wind variable, but chiefly from the So. W.

Dined at Abingdon and returned home in the evening—all, except Harriot Washington.

Thursday 10th.    Thermometer at 50 in the Morning—62 at Noon and 62 at Night. Clear with the wind what little there was in the Morning at No. Et. In the afternoon at So. Wt., and much fresher & warmer.

Visited all the Plantations. In the Neck, the Plows having crossed the ground (which left it in as rough a state as before) that was intended for Flax, began this morning (Six of them) to list No. 6 for Corn. Previous to this the laying off furrow was deepned, and two thrown into it. Every other one of these was left for the vegitable tribe to fill hereafter. The Women were repairing the fencing from the lane to the Barn and the Harrows were putting in Barley & grass Seeds in the middle cut of field No. 2.

At Muddy hole, the Plows as was expected finished crossing for Oats in field No. 4 and went into No. 1 to plow for Barley. The Women having hoed up the ground along the fence in this field were spreading what dung remained in heaps on the South half of the half Acre sqrs. of experimental ground last yr. intended for Barley this.

At Dogue-run, Began, as soon as the grd. was in order after the rain, to harrow in Barley & grass seeds after the Plows—4 of wch. were at Wk. & 2 harrows; one of them (single) drawn by Oxen. The Women were prevented from finishing hoeing the Meadow on acct. of the Rain and went yesterday to putting up the Logs wch. were in place betwn. fields No. 2 & 3 and to day were pickg. up Corn Stalks in No. 4.

At Frenchs—The Plows and Harrows were putting in Barley and grass-Seeds. The Women having filled the gullies in fd. No. 3 were heaping dung for the Cart, & spreading it when carted in the places wch. had been filled up in the lower Meadow.

At the Ferry the Women were levelling the old ditch betwn. this Plantn. & French's having hoed up the hedge row in No. 2— One plow laying off for Corn and 2 breakg. up No. 3.

At the Mansn. House, sowed as was intended, in the Vineyard inclosure, below the Seed sent by Mr. Peacy, in drills, the Fancy grass and below the Fancy grass, what Burnett I had left in drills also. And adjoing. these below, were sowed, or rather planted, the everlasting (or Lady Pease) sent me by the Honble. James Mercer.

Friday 11th. Thermometer at 54 in the Morning—[ ] at Noon And [ ] at Night. Clear & very pleasant all day with but little wind, and that Northerly in the morning and Southerly afterwards till eveng. when it was fresh fm. So. Et.

Rid to Muddy hole, Dogue run, Fr[enc]hs and the Ferry plantations and to the Fishing landing.

At Muddy hole, finished sowing Oats qty. [ ] bushls. but would not more than get them harrowed in by Night & crossed. The Women were spreading dung as yesterday and the Plows at Work as yesterday, for Barley.

At D. Run, The Ploughs and harrows were employed in gettg. in Barley & grass-seeds in No. 2. The women at this place began to cross hoe the grd. they had broke up in the lower end of the Ho. Meadw. in order to prepare it for Flax and grass. Send a hand from this place to the fishing landing.

At French's the women were levelling the old ditch in No. 3 some of them, whilst others were employed in heaping dung. Plows and Harrows putting in Barley & grass Seeds.

At the Ferry, the Plows were at work as yesterday. The Women repairing fence around No. 7.

Caught a good many fish to day, both shads & herring.

Saturday 12th. Thermometer at 54 in the Morning—54 at Noon And 54 at Night. Wind at So. Et. in the Morning, and pretty fresh. Weather lowering. A red Sky in the East horizon at sun rising, & a bur round the Moon last Night. Before 8 Oclock it began to sprinkle a little, which it continued to do by intervals till about 10 oclk. when it set into a constant, but not a hard rain till past 12 & ceased. Afternoon clear.

Visited the Neck, Muddy hole, and Dogue run Plantations; and was prevented going to the others by the Rain.

In the Neck, the Sowing, Seeding with grass, harrowing &ca. of 100 Bushels of Barley was compleated but the cross harrowing of the So. Et. part was not accomplished till after the Rain & being in part done (for dispatch) with the large or drag harrow it is not improbable but that the grass-seeds may be buried too deep. This Barley was sown on a single plowing, which was insufficient, but where the ground was stiff & clody I ordered it to be harrowed till it was tolerably well reduced before the Barley should be sown and being harrowed & cross harrowed afterwards upon the whole might be said to be in good order. The Post & Rail fence to the gut was compleated this afternoon. Women repairing fences, & ploughs listing for Corn.

At Muddy hole, recommenced Sowing of Barley in No. 1; North of the Quarter & following the Plows. The women returned to the New ground to Work.

At Dogue-run, Plowing for Sowing & harrowing in Barley and grass Seeds. Women cross Hoeing as yestery.

BUR: circle.

Sunday 13th.    Thermometer at 54 in the Morning—70 at Noon and 68 at Night. Very little wind and that Southerly. Clear and warm.

Went to Church at Alexandria accompanied by Colo. Humphreys Mr. Lear, & Washington Custis. Brought Hariot Washington home with us who had been left at Abingdon & came to Church with Mrs. Stuart.

Monday 14th.    Thermometer at 58 in the Morning—64 at Noon And 60 at Night. Grey, or rather a heavy morning with a red Sun & the Wind tho' not much of it at So. Et. Bur round the Moon last Night—also a dim circle. About 10 Oclock there came on a heavy mist which soon end in a moderate rain for 2 hours or more when it ceased and towards evening became clear. Visited the Plantations at Muddy hole, Dogue run Frenchs and the Ferry— also the Fishing landing.

At Muddy hole, Plowing & harrowing in Barley in No. 1. Women making Hills in No. 3 for Sweet Potatoes.

At Dogue Run, cross plowing for and harrowing in Barley and grass Seeds. The Women were cross hoeing in the Meadow, but were sent with their hoes & Baskets to break the grass tussucks in the Barley ground in the low parts thereof, which neither the Plows nor harrows could accomplish and to pile the grass.

At Frenchs, Plowing for, & sowing, harrowing in Barley & grass Seeds—Women grubbing & filling gullies in No. 3.

At the Ferry, besides the Plow wch. was laying off in No. 3 for Corn, the other two came this afternoon to listing after it. The Women were repairing fences & heaping Dung.

Caught about 50,000 herrings at a draught this afternoon.

Put in slips of the Weeping Willow along the Walks to the gate —the leaves of these were more than an inch long.

The Reverd. Mr. Fairfax came here to dinner and stayed all Night.

Tuesday 15th.    Thermometer at 60 in the Morning—71 at noon and 64 at Night. Warm with the Wind Southerly. Clouds and Sun shine alternately thro' the day.

Rid to all the Plantations (Mr. Fairfax going away after breakfast).

At all of them, the same work was going on as yesterday.

At Dogue run, the Plows finished crossing for Barley in fd. No. 2 and two of them began to cross for flax in the same field, and a third to break up a piece of ground for Do. wch. is to be taken into the Meadow next the Overseers house.

In the Neck harrowing in Oats & grass-seeds—the Women beating Tussicks & carrying off grass from part of the Barley ground.

The remains of my everlasting Pease were put in the grd. in the Neck to day—in the Orchard Inclosure.

Buck Wheat in all the ground that produced a crop of it last year is coming up from the shattered seed and in places thick.

Wednesday 16.    Thermometer at 58 in the Morning—70 at Noon and 68 at Night. Clear and pleasant all day. Very little wind, & that Northerly in the Morning. More of it, and that Southerly in the Afternn.

Visited the Plantations at Muddy hole, D. Run, Frenchs & the Ferry—and the Fishing landing.

At Muddy hole the Plows would finish about 10 Oclock plowing for Barley in No. 1 and the grd. would receive the Barley—qty. 48 Bushels. In this grd. was also sown [      ] pints of Red Clover and [      ] pints of Timothy Seeds. The Women having finished hilling as much grd. as would do for the Sweet Potatoes, I ordered them to remove the Farm Pen, & to heap the dung.

At D. Run finished sowing Barley in No. 2 qty. 55 Bls. With the Barley was sown [      ] pints of red Clover and [      ] pints of Timothy Seeds. The Plows harrows, & Women employed as yesterday at this place.

At Frenchs, the same work as yesterday. Examined the ground at this place which had been sown with English seeds, and found matt[er]s to stand, as follow—viz.—The Oats had come up well, & were sufficiently thick. The Pease had been either sown too thin, or being damaged, had come up badly; not being sufficiently thick; the Berkshire Beans adjoining to them (from Mr. Peacy) were up, but too thin also. Next to these (said also to be) Berkshire Beans from Mr. Young none were up, and it is supposed never would come up. The Gloucester Beans below were up, but too thin. The Summer Wheat next to these again, were almost entirely missing—not more than a plant here and there to be seen. The american cabbage seed was up tolerably thick which had been sown in beds.

At the Ferry the Plows were listing and the Women heaping dung.

Thursday 17th.   Thermometer at 57 in the Morning—57 at Noon and 58 at Night. But little wind in the Morning and that at So. Et. with clouds & a red sky at the Eastern horison. About 11 it began to Rain & continued to do so all the remaining part of the day, and very constantly with the wind fresher from the No. Et.

Visited all the Plantations & the Fishing Landing.

In the Neck, the Plows began yesterday morning to cross so much of the ground in the orchard Inclosure, as lay East of the New Post & Rail Fence for Oats; & part of them were sown & harrowed in before the Rain. Attempted with the harrow, to reduce the ground wch. had been crossed in the Barn inclosure for Flax, but finding it impracticable, I ordered the Hoes to follow the harrows, & beat the grassy clods to pieces in order to prepare it for Flax. Finished sowing Oats in field No. 2 qty. besides the 42 Bushls. from Spotswoods seed 77 Bushls. On this & the 100 Bushls. of Barley in the same field were sown [      ] pints or lbs. of Red clover Seed and [      ] pints or lbs. of Timothy Seed. Began to day to Roll the Barley, but was obliged to desist on Acct. of the Rain. Finished crossing abt. 11 Oclock, the grd. before mentioned East of the New fence & the Plows returned to listing again in No. 6.

At Muddy hole, the Plows began yesterday a little before dinnr. to Plow the 5 Acrs. of experimental grd. in No. 2 for Barley. Would have half finished it by the same time to day, but for the Rain. By mistake he was (that is the Overseer) crossing the sown Barley before the grass seeds were Sown. Would not be able to compleat this before the Rain. On this crossing he was sowing Seeds with intention to Bush harrow them in. All the grd. sown before the Rain will not *now* need this. Women removing Farm Pen & heaping dung in No. 3.

At Dogue run. The Plows finished breaking up the slipe, to be included within the Meadow, about breakfast time & had gone to crossing the Turnip grd. in No. 1 for Barley. Sowed, harrowed, & crossed with grass-Seeds as on Oats and Barley 3 Bushels of Flax Seed in the No. Et. Corner of No. 2 (at D. Run). Chopped about the Stumps in order to put the Seed in the better.

At French's, the Plows finished about Noon breaking up No. 2 for Oats & Barley. Began to Roll the Oats in this field, which were three inches high among which Clover & Timothy had been just sown. This work was stopped by the Rain. The Women were filling gullies in No. 3.

At the Ferry, the Roller wch. was going over the Oats (also up 2 or 3 Inches) was stopped by the Rain. The Plows at this place was listing & the Women were filling gullies in No. 3.

Charles Hagan came to Brick making to day—set him to makg. a cover for the Bricks before he began to Mould. Gunner and Sam were sent to Work with him.

Charles Hagan signed a contract with GW on 5 Jan. 1788, agreeing to begin work at Mount Vernon "as early in the spring as the state of the ground will admit" (DLC:GW). His pay was set at a rate of £4 10s. a month, allowing 26 working days or nights to the month. In addition, he was to be given provisions and a half a pint of rum a day. Hagan apparently was a diligent laborer, for between this date and 12 Nov. 1788, when he stopped working for GW, he accumulated a total of 7 months and 14 days in working time, earning £33 18s. (LEDGER B, 271).

The slaves Gunner and Sam were laborers on the Home House plantation (see entry for 18 Feb. 1786).

Friday 18th.    Thermometer at 59 in the Morning—70 at Noon and 70 at Night. A thick Fog & showers in the Morning. Cloudy all the day with a brisk wind from the Southward.

Rode to the Fishing landing—the Plantations at the Ferry, Frenchs, Dogue run, and Muddy hole—also to My Mill where the heavy rain of last Night had blown up my lower tumbling dam, or waste, and broke the race in other places which was the more unfortunate as all my People were busily employed in other Work.

The Ditchers, however, and two Carpenters, were sent to repair the damage.

At the Ferry, the abundance of rain which fell in the course of yesterday & last Night rendered plowing in the Corn grd. impracticable. The plows therefore were shifted to the hill in No. 7.

At Frenchs, from the same cause they were removed to No. 3, to break up for Corn—having finished plowing No. 2 (all but the So. Et. corner) & unable to cross in the lower meadow. Women filling gullies in No. 3 but ordered to grub & sprout the clover ground in the upper meadow at this place.

At D. Run the Plows were stopped entirely. The Women & plow people were beating the Clods & removing the grass from the Barley ground.

At Muddy hole, the Women were heaping dung; and cross harrowing of Barley being stopped, the three plows were employed in the 5 Acres of experimental ground in No. 2, to break it up, & to prepare it for Barley &ca.

The Rain having washed up many of the Willow cuttings wch. had been set by the Post & Rail fence near the road I had them (late as it is in the Season) replaced tho' there is little hope of their living.

Saturday 19th.    Thermometer at 67 in the Morning—75 at Noon and 72 at Night. Wind at So. Wt. all day and in the afternoon very high. After dark there were Showers of Rain with distant thunder.

Rode to all the Plantations—to the Mill, Brick yard, and fishing landing.

In the Neck the Plows were stopped yesterday. And to day the grd. being too wet to list, I ordered them into field No. 9 till the water had subsided. Harrows and Rollers unable to work. Women heaping dung, rotten straw, and other trash about the Barn and Farm yard.

At Muddy hole, the Plows about Noon finished plowing the 5 Acres of (exp[erimenta]l grd.) in No. 2 which was sown with 10 bushls. of Barley & harrowed in length ways. The first Acre (or 2 half Acre Squares) was also sown with 6 lbs. of White Clover (imported) but remained unharrowed (cross wise) till 4 bushels of Sainfoin wch. was in soak should be sown there on likewise. Women heaping dung, old Straw &ca. about the Barn.

At Morris's (Dogue run) the Plows this morning began to work in the grd. which had been hoed in the meadow (all others being too wet) to prepare it for Flax & Orchard grass. The women began to chop that which was plowed on the other side of the Meadow. Cabbage Seed at this place had come up tolerably well, and the plants stood tolerably thick.

At French's, finding the field No. 3 in which the plows were at work too wet—I ordered them into No. 5 to break it for B. Wheat as a fallow and Manure for Wheat. The Women having Sprouted, & cleaned the Clover in the upper meadow were again filling gullies in the field No. 3 & Meadow adjoining.

At the Ferry, the Plows were still on the Hill in No. 7—Corn grd. being too wet to list. The Women were filling gullies in No. 3. At this place, the effect of the fish manure wch. was put into the Corn hills in May last was visible with the Wheat, almost as far

as the latter could be seen. The lower meadow appears very indifferent—scarce any grass but in the low & wet part of it, and no
great appearance of Timothy there.

Sunday 20th.    Thermometer at 48 in the Morning 50 at Noon
And 45 at Night. Wind hard & cold from the No. Wt. all day.

Mr. Herbert, Mr. Hunter, Mr. Fendall and Doctr. Stuart came
here to Dinner and returned afterwards. Mrs. Stuart and her three
daughters came to Dinner and stayed all Night.

Monday 21st.    Thermometer at 40 in the Morning—[    ] at
Noon And [    ] at Night. Wind at No. Wt. all day—in the evening it lulled.

Went to Alexandria to the Election of a Senator for the district
and delegates for the County in the General Assembly—when Mr.
Pope was chosen for the first and Mr. Roger West, and Doctr.
Stuart for the latter. Dined at Doctr. Crks. and came home in the
evening. Fd. Mrs. Stuart & her two eldest daughters gone—and
Mr. Tracy here.

In my way up, I passed thro' the Plantations of Muddy hole and
Dogue run.

At Muddy hole, sowed the Sainfoin on the grd. allotted for it;
which with the White Clover was harrowed in. This had been in
soak (being very hard & dry) since friday morning. Also sowed,
in the next two squares, or Acre, 8 lbs. of Trafoil—in the 3d. Acre
or two squares 10 lbs. of Row grass—In the 4th. Acre or dble.
Square Two bushels of Orchd. grass Seeds and in the last two
Squares or Acre 16 lbs. of red Clover were sown. But the harrow
was not able to cross the whole before night. Roller running over
Barley 3 or 4 Inches high & 2 or 3 leaves on it. This being pressed
down, and appearing to be bruised, I apprehended, notwithstanding it was done by my Farmers advice that it wd. be injured, and
therefore had a place left unrolled in the Middle of the sqr. that
was rolling to try the difference. One Plow went from here to
French's this Morning and another about Noon after it laid off
some grd. for Irish Potatoes &ca. The women were heaping dung
abt. Barn & Farm yard.

At Dogue run, the plows having finished crossing the hoed grd.
had returned to crossing the Turnip ground they had left on Acct.
of the rain for English Barley. The first was sown with Flax Seed
and the harrows covering of it but for want of a previous harrowing before sowing the Seed was put in very badly and in danger
of being buried. Ordered 5 bushls. of Orchard grass to be sown on

this grd.; to be crossed harrowed, and the work to be made good with the hoes afterwards as there were a good many Stumps in it. Women hoeing the ground opposite to this.

Thomas Tracy, who had previously served Arthur Middleton of South Carolina, was employed by David Stuart to teach the oldest two Custis girls, Elizabeth and Martha, "Music & other branches of Education," including arithmetic and penmanship (HOYT [1], 97–99).

Tuesday 22.    Thermometer at 48 in the Morning—55 at Noon And 55 at Night. Wind Southerly in the Morning & cold. About sun rise it began to rain and continued to do so with small intervals till about 2 Oclock When it ceased with appearances of clearing but towards sunset it began to rain again.

At home all day.

Wednesday 23d.    Thermometer at 45 in the Morning—55 at Noon And 55 at Night. Wind at No. Wt. in the Morning which veered round to the Eastward and was at So. Et. in the Afternoon, & became warm.

Visited all the Plantations. In the Neck, the Plows on Monday were listing, but the Rain yesterday drove them into field No. 9 again, to day, except the one which was laying off Corn rows. The Harrow on Monday was employed in the ground intended for Flax, and the Hoes following of it, to prepare it for sowing. The Roller was engaged towds. the Afternoon, to Roll the Barley but was Stopped yesterday. The Women Monday and as much of yesterday as they could work out, were engaged in chopping after the harrow in the flax ground. To day they were chopping in the Flax which the Overseer was sowing. Grd. in tolerable good order —except having a good many grassy clods which were not quite broken with the Hoes. The last of the Oats were sown, harrowed & cross harrowed within what is now the Orchard Inclosure. This grd. was plowed before Christmas, lately cross plowed—the Seed Sown, harrowed in & cross harrowed.

At Muddy hole, the two plows that went to French's continue there. The Harrow (crosswise) all the Sqrs. of experimental grd. except that which recd. the Row-grass which was too wet to cross; and went to harrowing by the ground which had been laid off for Potatoes and Jerusalem Artichokes in No. 3. The Women planted about ½ a bushel of Sweet Potatoes in the same field (all the Seed I had in 500 hills) and went to work in the New ground in front of the Mans[io]n Ho[use]. The Overseer sowing grass-seeds on clover in fd. No. 1.

At Dogue run the Orchard grass seeds were sown and harrowed in on the Flax as directed on Monday and afterwards chopped. The ground looks *now* to be in good order—5 bushels of Flax & 5 bushels of Orchard-grass were sown qty. of ground, by estimation abt. 3 Acres. The ground on the other side, except a small piece at the lower end, had also been chopped over but would require to be harrowed (when drier) before it is sown. The Plows having crossed this Morning, the Turnip grd. for Barley were laying off & listing in No. 5. The Women were removing the Meadw. fence so as to include the grounds wch. have been lately worked on the sides of it.

Sent the fatting Steers, and an old work oxen to No. 1, at D. Run, to Pasture.

At French's, the remains of the Barley, abt. 7 Bushels, making in all at this place—43 bush. was sown harrowed in, & was cross harrowing. 4 plows (two from Muddy hole) were breakg. up field No. 5 to sow with B. Wheat &ca. The Women were cuttg. the Sprouts, taking up grubs &ca. in this field.

At the Ferry, the Women were filling gullies in No. 3 and the plows breaking up No. 7.

At the fishing landing there was plenty of custom & no fish. Last week there was plenty of fish & no custom.

The Wild Oats, & other grass Seeds from Colo. Marshall in the Botanical garden was up, & coming up thick—as was the fancy grass in the Vineyard Inclosure.

WILD OATS: *Avena fatua,* wild oat, is today considered by farmers a common and undesirable weed.

Thursday 24th.    Thermometer at 45 in the Morning—61 at Noon And 56 at Night. Wind at So. Et. all day, with appearances of Rain in the Afternoon but none fell.

Rid to all the plantations.

In the Neck, finished listing No. 6 for Corn. The ploughs again went into field No. 9 to break it up. Finished sowing flax—8 bushels on abt. 6 Acres by the Barn. After which the Women went to heaping dung at the farm pen & removing rails out of the Way.

At Muddy hole, finished sowing grass seeds on Barley in No. 1, but could not harrow it, as the grain was up. Rolling this till the Iron staple gave way. The Plows at Frenchs. Harrow preparing that part of field No. 3 for Buck Wheat wch. lies East of the branch. Women hoeing in the New ground at the Mansn. Ho.

At Dogue run, the Plows having overtaken the layer off (for

Corn) in field No. 5; went to French's after dinner, 4 of them. The Women finished the lower part of the Meadow fence at this place. Perceived the Clover & timothy which had been sown amongst the Barley & Oats here to be coming up.

At French's, the Farmer finished Sowing Barley, Oats & grass Seeds in field No. 2, except the rough ground on the East side of it, and harrowed & cross harrowed them all in. The Women were taking up grubs, and cleaning No. 5 in which the Plows fm. Muddy hole & Dogue run, as well as those belonging to the Plantatin. were.

At the Ferry, the Plows were in No. 7 breaking up for Buck Wheat. The women were filling gullies—but ordered them to make fence around the Brick yard and to put up that betwn. No. 2 & 3.

Not many fish caught today. Two little Carts employed in carrying out the heads & guts of the Fish upon the Corn grd. at the Ferry.

Perceived at the Mansion Ho[use] that the Burnett which had been sown in the Vineyard inclosure was coming up thick and that the Fancy grass was also coming up—but could discover nothing of this kd. in the everlasting Pease or Seeds from Mr. Peacy. Here & there a seed of the Sulla was to be seen up, but none of the Scarcity plant—or nothing that I thought was it, was discoverable.

Friday 25th.    Thermometer at 56 in the Morning 70 at Noon and 66 at Night. Early in the morning the Wind was at No. Et. and cloudy—it afterwards shifted to the So. Et. but there was very little of it all day—Cloudy & Sun shine alternately—warm & growing. In the afternoon Rain.

R:d to all the Plantations.

At the Ferry the same work was going forward as yesterday. But few fish caught this Morning.

Began yesterday to mould Bricks.

At Frenchs, the Plows this Morng. began to cross the grd. that had been broke up in the lower meadow. The drag harrow followed the Plows, and the Women (after they had spread the Dung there) followed the harrow, in order to knock the clods to pieces & remove the grass, to fit it for Oats—Clover, & orchard grass.

At Dogue run 1 Plow was laying off, & the Roller going over the oats; which were 3 or 4 Inches high. The Women were chopping, & preparing the lower end of the Meadow (West side) for Flax seed, & grass Seeds. The first sown Flax seed at this place was appearing above grd. as was the Clover & Timothy seeds.

At Muddy hole, planted all the Jerusalem Artichokes, that were preserved (not more than 3 pecks in field No. 3 by the gate. By these Irish Potatoes (red kind) in 4 feet rows & 10 Inches apart in the rows were also planting; and adjoining to these again, began, on the ground that was harrowed yesterday, to sow Buck Wheat at the rate (if directions was attended to) of ½ a bushel to the Acre. The Potatoes were planted, or dropped in the Rows which had been laid off for them, & a furrow turned on them. The ground which had been sown with Barley & Row grass, and which on acct. of the Rain which fell before the latter could be covered & went unharrowed, was forced to be bushed in to day, the Barley being sprouted.

In the Neck, the Plows were breaking up No. 9 and the Women heaping dung at the Farm yard & removg. Rails.

A Mr. Rinaldo Johnston dined here yesterday & went away after it.

Rinaldo Johnson (c.1755–1811) of Aquasco, Prince George's County, Md., was a well-to-do planter who married George Mason's eldest daughter, Ann Eilbeck Mason, in 1789 (COPELAND, 241).

Saturday 26th.    Thermometer at 60 in the Morning–58 at Noon and 54 at Night. Morning very heavy, with the Wind at No. Wt. –then No. Et. and East and afterwards So. Et. Clouds & heavy appearances of rain continued all day.

Rode to all the Plantations–the Fishing landing & brick Makers.

But few fish caught to day. At the Ferry, the Plows continued breaking up No. 7. The Women puttg. up fence between No. 2 & 3, & round the Brick yard.

At French's, the Plows (same as yesterday) were breaking up No. 3 for Corn, and this was full wet. The ground they crossed yesterday, & began to harrow, in order to prepare it for Oats and grass-seeds was in much worse condition by the Rain of yesterday than it was before the Plows crossed it. The Women were (as yesterday) endeavouring to cleanse it of the grass & rubbish.

At Dogue-run, the Plows were employed as yesterday and the Women, after chopping the ground for Flax in the Meadow were employed in taking up the Persimon grubs in No. 7.

At Muddy hole, the Plows were at Frenchs, as yesterday. The harrow was employed in putting in Buck Wheat in No. 3. So. of the road in the East cut; in which was sown 4 bushels–too much by one half. This was harrowed in one way, and part (South) but not the whole, crossed. Finished Planting the Irish Potatoes East part of the above cut 11¼ bushls.—covered as yesterday.

In the Neck, the same work, precisely, going on as yesterday.

Sunday 27th.    Thermometer at 50 in the Morning—48 at Noon and 47 at Night. Much rain fell in the course of last Night. Very heavy all day with Mists at times. Wind at East and No. Et.

Monday 28th.    Thermometer at 47 in the Morning—56 at Noon and 60 at Night. Rain again last Night. Morning very cloudy & dull. Wind at So. Et. where it continued till night and then changed to No. Et.—thundered, lightned, & rained a good deal. About 2 O'clock the Sun came out & the weather till towards Sun down looked as if it would be fair.

Visited all the Plantations—the fishing landing, Brick yard, and Mill. The continual rains had so absorbed the ground that scarcely any work could be done to advantage.

At the Ferry, I had assembled the Carts from French's, D. Run, & Muddy hole with which & the one belonging to the Plantn. the offal of the Fish were carried to field No. 7 where they were spread & plowed in (plows still being in that field). The Women were employed in gathering them into heaps at the landing & spreading them in the field—as also filling the gullies there.

At French's, the Plows (those from D. Run & M. Hole being still there) wd. by dinner have finished breaking up fd. No. 3 for Corn and were ordered to go next into the middle meadow adjoining to plow a piece of ground for flax. Nothing but necessity, arising from the lateness of the Season, can justify the plowing of land so wet as it now is.

At Do. Run, one plow (as usual) laying off—the Women taking up the grubs in No. 7—and the Men repairing the fencing of No. 1.

At Muddy hole, the Women were levelling the Hills which had been made for Sweet Potatoes (before the defection of the Seed was discovered) in order to sow when the grd. should be dry enough with Flax seed. Sowed the No. side of the little cut, by the gate with Buck Wheat, [    ] bushls. & harrowed & cross harrowed it in.

In the Neck, as at D. Run, the planting of Corn had been suspended on acct. of the rains, and extreme wetness of the Earth. The Plows (the work was bad) were still breaking up in No. 9 and the Women heaping dung. Began the brick work of the Dairy at this place to day. And ordered the holes for the Reception of

Corn to be made to morrow, altho the Corn shd. not be planted that the work might be forwarded thereby.

Few fish were caught in the forenoon of this day.

Charles Hagan, the Brickmaker, not at Work to day.

No work could be done in the breach of the Mill race to day, on Acct. of the wetness of the Earth.

Tuesday 29th.    Thermometer at 56 in the Morning—62 at Noon And 62 at Night. Raining a little in the Morning and very cloudy, without wind, which afterwards came out at No. Wt. tho' not fresh but which dispersed the clouds.

Visited all the Plantations.

At the Ferry, the Carts, as yesterday were taking out the heads, guts &ca.—the Plows in the same field plowing for Buck Wheat & the Women filling up gullies therein.

At French's, the Plows finished the grd. intended for Flax; and went about an hour by sun to breaking up part of No. 5 for Buck Wheat. The women grubbing, & removing the impediments therein.

At D. Run, 1 Plow was laying off for Corn (the rest at Frenchs). The Women were making a fence around that part of No. 1 which lays East of the swamp intended for English Barley &ca.

At Muddy hole, 1 harrow preparing No. 1 for Buck Wheat— (the Plows 2 at Frhs.) —the Women hoeing in the New ground.

At the River Plantation, the Plows finished breaking up that part of No. 9 that lay on the division line, between it and No. 8. The Women havg. finished heaping the dung at the farm pen, began, in the afternoon to make holes in No. 6 for planting Corn.

No fish caught to day, of any Consequence.

Charles Hagan was at work in the Brick yard.

No Work on the Breach in the Mill race on acct. of the wetness of the earth.

The Ditche[r]s, after finishing the Ditch on the ferry road (about breakfast time) went to Work in a ditch dividing No. 1 from No. 6.

A Mr. Tayler dined here.

Wednesday 30th.    Thermometer at 56 in the Morning—66 at Noon and 62 at Night. Clear all day. Wind at No. Et. in the Morning and South in the evening—and though not warm, yet pleasant.

Visited all the Plantations.

At the Ferry the Plows still in No. 7. The Women, though the ground was extremely wet, had begun to make holes in No. 2 for planting Corn. Drawing, with the Plantation Carts, & Waggon, the Scantling from the landing to the New barn.

At Frenchs, the Ploughs at Work as yesterday, except two, in laying off for Corn in No. 2. The women were repairing fences around field No. 5.

At Dogue run, one plow laying off for Corn. The Overseer & Women makg. holes to plant it. Ordered all the Stock of every kind to be removed from the Mill Meadow this Afternoon.

At the River Plantation, the plows, after breaking up, & listing the farm Pen, in No. 6, went (except one) to plow that part of No. 9 which has been lately added, West of the Post & Rail fence; Nat was ordered to run 3 feet furrows in the Barn yard enclosure for the purpose of hilling more regularly for Pease, Beans &ca.— The Women & the rest of the people making Corn holes—ground being too wet to plant.

All the Flax which has hitherto been sown was up, and seemingly well.

Few or no fish caught to day, at the time I was at the landing.

Brick making going on. The Ditchers Carpenters &ca. went to work on the breach in the Mill race to day.

Majr. George Washington returned from below (Colo. Bassetts) to day.

Although most of the materials for the new barn were obtained at Mount Vernon, GW bought ready-cut lumber for the roofing from the Alexandria firm of Peterson & Taylor so that his carpenters would be available for haying rather than using their time cutting scantling and plank (BRISSOT, 343; GW to Peterson & Taylor, 5 and 7 Jan. 1788, DLC:GW; see entry for 28 May 1788). The 21,922 board feet of pine scantling being transported today consisted of sleepers, joists, plates, rafters, window beams, studs, and rails all cut to order (GW to Peterson & Taylor, 5 Jan. 1788, DLC:GW). GW wanted this scantling delivered no later than 1 Mar. so that the carpenters would have adequate time to frame it before they were sent to the fields, but ice in the Potomac prevented Peterson & Taylor from getting timber from the Eastern Shore in time to meet his deadline (Peterson & Taylor to GW, 13 Feb. 1788, DLC:GW). GW was further disappointed to discover that 21 pieces of the scantling that he had ordered were missing and that 15 pieces not ordered were included (GW to Peterson & Taylor, 10 May 1788, and Peterson & Taylor to GW, 2 June 1788, DLC:GW). The ship that brought GW this scantling from Peterson & Taylor also brought him 1,300 board feet of one-inch thick pine plank and 2,300 feet of one-and-a-quarter-inch pine plank from the firm. The balance of GW's order, 10,000 board feet of the one-inch plank, arrived in another ship on 5 June (Peterson & Taylor to GW, 18 April 1788, DLC:GW; see entry for 5 June 1788). In all GW paid Peterson & Taylor £108 5s. 9d. for lumber for his barn (LEDGER B, 266).

The slave Nat had been a laborer on River plantation apparently since 1762 (GW tithable lists 1762–73, DLC: Toner Collection; see entry for 18 Feb. 1786).

## [May 1788]

Thursday 1st. of May.    Thermometer at 56 in the morning—76 at Noon And 76 at Night. Clear & warm, with the Wind Southerly.

Visited all the Plantations—the Fishing Landing, Brick yard & Mill.

At the Ferry, the Plows were removed from No. 7 to No. 2, & were plowing for Corn (laying off & listing). The Women were planting of it, but thinking the grd. too wet I made them desist, & return to making holes for this grain till it should get a little dryer.

At French's, two plows were laying off rows for Corn in No. 3. The rest seven in Number were breaking up No. 5 for Buck Wheat.

At Dogue run, one plow continued laying off, the Women having made holes for Corn as far as the ground was listed went to making pumkin hills in the Angles of the fence ard. field No. 5.

At Muddy hole, putting in Buck Wheat with one harrow. The Womn. were at Work in the New ground.

In the Neck, the work the same in all respects as yesterday.

Friday 2nd.    Thermometer at 69 in the Morning—80 at Noon And 70 at Night. Lowering Morning with a Shower but not heavy or much of it betwn. 3 & 4 Oclock.

Rid to all the Plantations except that in the Neck and finding the appearances of rain great—ordered the holes which had been made for Corn at the Ferry, Dogue run & the River Plantations to be immediately planted, & for this purpose, that the Muddy hole hands should assist at Dogue Run—and the hands at Frenchs to go to the Ferry. Accordingly

At Dogue run, the hands at work there would have planted all the holes by 12 Oclock. At Dogue run. The grd. in the Meadow West side of it was sown with flax seed 2 bushels and 6 qrts. of red Clover seed & 6 qrts. of Timothy seed. The Farmer also began to sow the Engh. Barley on that part of No. 1 at this place which lays East of the Swamp. The grd. in which the above flax was sown was previously harrowed, and twice harrowed afterwards— once for the grain, and again for the Seeds.

At the Ferry theres would be done about dinner time when others would be made & planted by the two gangs of hands above mentiond. The plows laying off and listing.

At Frenchs, two plows listing as yesterday, and about Noon the others would have finished that part of No. 5 which lyes East of the which runs through the field & the two belonging to the Plantation and one from Muddy hole would begin to list in No. 3. Those belonging to Dogue run wd. return home.

At Muddy hole 1 harrow crossing the Buck Wheat which had been sown.

The Vessel from York River arrivd this day with Corn had from Doctr. Stuart from the Plantns. of the decd. Mr. Custis— 290 Barls.

In the afternoon Mr. Fendal and Mr. Willm. Craik came and stayed all Night.

The vessel from York River belonged to Edward Pye Chamberlayne (1758– 1806) of King William County. GW paid Chamberlayne's skipper Gibb Jackson £20 for bringing this load of corn and £20 for another shipment which arrived on 30 May (LEDGER B, 265, 269; Chamberlayne to George Augustine Washington, 22 April 1788, ICHi). In all GW obtained 600 barrels of corn from John Parke Custis's estate at a cost of £450, a sum that was more than covered by the £525 "Rent or Annuity" that he received from the estate this year (LEDGER B, 272).

Saturday 3d.    Thermometer at 64 in the Morning—74 at Noon and 68 at Night. Wind at So. Wt. About 3 oclock there was a pretty smart shower of Rain.

Mr. Fendall and Mr. Craik went away directly after breakfast & I visited all the Plantations.

In the Neck, all hands except the Plowers & Carters were planting Corn—one plow laying off in the Barn Inclosure for Sundries —one harrow for Buck Wheat—3 plows listing for Car[ro]ts and Cabbages—2 Teams in the Waggon Carting rails to the fence betwn. fields No. 8 & 9.

At Muddy hole, two of the Plows still at Frenchs, harrow putting in (or crossing Buck Wheat). Women making Pumpkin hills in the borders of No. 3.

At Dogue run, one harrow was covering the Barley which was sown agreeable to the order of yesterday viz.—8 bushls. of that sent by Mr. Young—about a peck from Genl. Spotswood and about a pottle of the Naked Barley (Colo. Lees sort). The first was on the South Side adjoining the Road—the other two in the *next* land, North of it, the Naked Barley in the East part of it—up to two Stakes. On this Barley were sown 32 lbs. of Hop clover seed (from Engd.).

At Frenchs, Two plows were laying off & 2 listing—the Cart employed in getting up the Scantling &ca. to the Barn. Overseer Women & boys assisting in Planting Corn at the Ferry.

At the Ferry, the Plows were laying off & listing for Corn and the other hands planting of it.

Few or no fish being caught to day I ordered them to discontinue drawing the Sein after Monday unless they were more successful on that day.

NAKED BARLEY: a variety in which the grain is loose in the chaff. Henry Lee sent GW a few bushels of "Naked Italian Barley" in 1785 and described it as a short, stout plant with a drooping head which should be harvested by pulling rather than by cutting (16 April 1785, DLC:GW).

Sunday 4th.    Thermometer at 60 in the Morning–72 at Noon And 70 at Night. A good deal of rain fell last night with thunder & lightning. Wind high all day from the So. West. Weather clear.

Monday 5th.    Thermometer at 62 in the Morning–75 at Noon And 73 at Night. Wind at So. Wt. in the Morning but at No. Wt. afterwards & fresh, but not cold. Flying clouds, but upon the whole clear.

Visited all the Plantations.

In the Neck–except the plow that was laying off, the rest were cross plowing the rough parts of No. 9 for Buck Wheat 5 in number–2 teams in the Waggon, drawing Rails to inclose it. A harrow also preparing for Buck Wheat in this field.

At Muddy hole, 1 harrow preparing for & putting in Buck Wheat–Overseer planting of Pumpkin Seed and the rest of the hands (except the two plow people at Frenchs) working in the New ground.

At Dogue Run–The harrow finished crossing the Seeds that were sown in No. 1 on Saturday. 1 plow laying off in No. 5 for Corn and 3 listing after it. Finished planting Pumpkins around the above field in the laps of the fence &ca. and then went to making holes for Planting Corn.

At Frenchs–Two plows laying off, & two listing. The Overseer and the rest of the hands (except the Carter) planting Water Mellen Seeds. Cart drawing Logs & other trash from the Meadw. to the gullies in No. 5.

At the Ferry–The Plows were at Work as yesterday. The other hands were planting Corn.

No fish being caught to day I ordered the Hogsheads, and everything else to be secured, and the People to repair to their respective places, and businesses.

WATER MELLEN SEEDS: *Citrullus vulgaris,* watermelon. The quantity being sown here indicates the use of the melon as a field crop. GW's instructions of Dec. 1799 for the operation of Union Farm specify that field no. 3 in the clover lot was to be planted to pumpkins, cymlings (summer squash), turnips, and melons, all apparently intended for livestock feed.

Fish sales brought GW £60 18s. 4d. in cash this spring. In addition, he delivered 68,000 herrings worth £17 to the firm of Peterson & Taylor in partial payment for their lumber (LEDGER B, 265, 266, 269).

Tuesday 6th.    Thermometer at 65 in the Morning—75 at Noon And 75 at Night. Weather clear and wind at So. Wt. all day. At home all day.

Wednesday 7th.    Thermometer at 56 in the Morning—69 at Noon and 69 at Night. Clear and very pleasant all day. The Wind in the Morning was at No. Et. and in the afternoon at So. Et.

Visited all the Plantations—Mill, & Brick Yard.

In the Neck, five plows and 2 Harrows were preparing for, and putting in Buck Wheat—one laying off as before, for Pease &ca. in the Barn Inclosure. Yesterday sowed 13 rows (betwn. the Corn in No. 6) with Carrots. These rows were first listed as for Corn (the middle furrow being deepned) then a light triangular harrow was run twice, & oftener where the ground was cloddy or rough, to level & make it fine. The Seed, (a pint being mixed in half a bushel of Ashes) was next sown, so thick as that one could be seen within an inch and half of another, and covered with a bush harrow. The rest of the People were planting Corn. Finished the brick work of the Dairy here yesterday.

At Muddy hole—One harrow preparing for, & putting in Buck Wheat. One Woman planting Mellons by the Overseers House. And the rest of the People at work in the New ground at the Mansion house—preparing for Corn.

At Dogue run. One harrow putting in the Indian Pease & Clover in that part of No. 1 East of the swamp, & adjoining the Barley. Of the Pease 4 bushels were sown, & the Farmer thinks two thin, especially the North part; for he thinks there are 5 Acres in pease. Of the clover 55 lbs. were sown. Four plows were listing for, and the other people planting of, Corn.

At Frenchs. Two ploughs were laying off, and three were listing. The Drag harrow, was harrowing the grd. in the lower Meadow to prepare it for Oats & grass Seeds. The other People were plantg. Corn.

At the Ferry, the plows were listing, & the other people planting of Corn.

At the Mill, the hands had so nearly compleated the repairs of the race that I ordered the Carpenters to quit it, to Night, and the Mill people to finish it.

Thursday 8th.    Thermometer at 60 in the Morning—75 at Noon And 72 at Night. Clear in the Morning, with the Wind at So. Wt. Cloudy afternoon and rain about 8 Oclock.

Visited the Plantations at the Ferry, Frenchs, Dogue run, and Muddy hole—also the Brick yard and Mill race.

At the Ferry, the Ploughs wd. have finished to day—laying off and listing for Corn in field No. 2 and the People would about finish planting Corn, when they were ordered to join the hands at French[s] for that purpose. A plow & harrow would begin to prepare some of the intermediate rows for Carrots.

At Frenchs. The plows having finished laying off were (4 of them) listing. 2 harrows were *attempting* to prepare the ground in the lower Meadow for Oats and grass Seeds but from wetness, cloddiness, &ca. it was badly executed. Having on Acct. of the arrival of a Barrel of Barley frm. Minorca, I directed that part of the ground in the upper Meadow wch. had been sown in Summer Wheat & Beans (neither of which had come up) to be plowed up, to receive this grain.

At Dogue run. Only finished this Morning, to harrow for the last time, the grd. in No. 1 which had recd. the 4 bushels of Pease & 55 lbs. of clover Seed. Also finished Listg. No. 5 for Corn, & began with one plow and harrow to list, Sow, and harrow in Carrots, between the Corn Rows. After the Plows had left No. 5 they went, in the evening, to plow in the Middle Meadow which had been hoed. The other hands were planting Corn.

At Muddy hole, One harrow was preparing for, and putting in Buck Wheat. All the other hands were at Work in the New grd. at Mansn. House.

Mr. & Mrs. Porter & Mr. Monshur came here to dinner & stayed all Night and in the evening Colo. Harry Lee & Doctr. Craik came in and did the same.

Friday 9th.    Thermometer at 56 in the Morning—69 at Noon And 60 at Night. Much rain fell in the Night & this morning— cloudy most part of the day with a Shower in the afternoon. Wind variable from No. Et. to No. Wt.

I remained at home all day, Colo. Lee went away before breakfast & Doctr. Craik soon after it.

To dinner Mrs. Craik and Mr. & Mrs. Roger West came, & after it, with Mr. & Mrs. Porter and Mr. Monshur returned to their respective home's.

Doctr. Craik, who had been to Portobacco, got back in the eveng.

Saturday 10th.    Thermometer at 49 in the Morning—54 at Noon and 50 at Night. Fresh, & cold No. easterly Wind in the Morning with thick Drizzling weather which continued through the day with Showers.

Visited all the Plantations.

At the Ferry all the corn, except a small piece at the No. Et. Corner of the field was planted on thursday and this the excessive rains and consequent wetness of the Earth rendered impracticable —after wch. all the ground which from the same causes could be hilled was planted with Pumpkins. The Rains prevented any preparation of the grd. at this place for Carrots. The plows therefore went (yesterday) to breaking ground in field No. 7 as the only spot they could do tolerably good work in. The Women I sent to day to the New grd. at the Mansn. Ho. to assist the Muddy hole People.

At French's, No plowing cd. be done, and but little of any thing else. About 10 Oclock I ordered 4 plows from this place to join those at the Ferry in No. 7. Some of the Women were making Pumpkin hills (tho' the grd. was too wet for it). On Thursday afternoon about half the ground in the lower Meadow at this place was sown with Oats, but there not being time to sow grass seeds thereon the wet has prevented it since and now there can be no cross harrowing as the grain will be up before Tuesday.

At Dogue run, the Plows were all stopped and all hands were making, or finishing the Pole fence round the Barley & Pease in Field No. 1.

At Muddy hole—No harrowing, all the People that were well were in the New grd. at the Mansn. House.

In the Neck. The Plows, tho' the ground was very wet, was crossing for Buck Wheat. The other hands after having made the fence betwn. fields 8 & 9 as rails were in place 6 or 7 to a pannel began to make Pompkin hills but the grd. being wet did not plant the Seed. No Buck Wheat sown here since Thursday on Account of the Wet.

Doctr. Craik went away after breakfast and Mr. Hartshorn came in before Dinner to get notices (to the Subscribers to the Potomack Co. that motions would be made for judgments upon their

Arrearages at the next Genl. Court) signed. He returned after dinner.

The Potomac Company, according to the acts of incorporation passed by the Virginia and Maryland assemblies in 1784, was to recover unpaid subscriptions by selling the shares of delinquent subscribers at public auction after "giving at least one month's notice of the sale in the Virginia and Maryland Gazettes" (HENING, 11:514). However, that procedure proved inadequate for collecting the considerable balances owed the company, and in Dec. 1787 the assemblies of both states passed bills permitting a majority of the directors to recover sums from delinquent subscribers in the states' general courts after giving ten days' notice to those subscribers (HENING, 12:508–9). Unfortunately, the new procedure produced little immediate improvement in the company's troubled financial situation (BACON-FOSTER, 81–83).

Sunday 11th.   Thermometer at [      ] in the Morning–[     ] at Noon and [      ] at Night. Wind Westerly, and No. Wt. and rather cool.

At home all day.

Counted the number of the following Articles which are contained in a pint–viz.–Of

The small & round pease commonly called Gentlemans Pease } 3144

Those brot. from York Rivr. by Majr. G. Washington } 2268

Those brot. by Do. from Mrs. Dangerfields   1375
Those given by Hezh. Fairfax   1330
Large, & early black eye Pease   1186
Bunch homony Beans   1473

Accordingly–a bushel of the above, allowing 5 to a hill, will plant the number of hills wch. follow. Viz.

1st. kind . . . . . . . 40243
2. Ditto . . . . . . 29030
3. Ditto . . . . . . 17200
4. Ditto . . . . . . 17024
5. Ditto . . . . . . 15180
6. Ditto . . . . . . 18854

Monday 12th.   Thermometer at [     ] in the Morning–[     ] at Noon and [     ] at Night. Wind variable, with clouds, and appearances of rain. In the Morning early it was at So. Wt.–then West–No. Wt. &ca.

Went, in Company with Colo. Humphreys to Mr. Rozers. Dined & returned in the Afternoon.

Tuesday 13th. Thermometer at 57 in the Morning—66 at Noon and 62 at Night. Wind at No. Wt. all day—in the forenoon fresh —in the Afternoon moderate, and towards night calm. Clouds the greater part of the day.

Visited all the Plantations and the Brick yard.

At the Ferry, 6 plows were at Work in No. 7. Viz.—3 belonging to the Plantation—2 from Frenchs and 1 from Muddy hole. Two Men were Planting the remainder of the Corn ground; and the Women were in the New grd. at the Mansn. House.

At French's. The drag was harrowing the ground intended for flax with oxen. One Plow (from Muddy hole was replowing the ground which had received the Spring Wheat, and English Beans, that did not come up, in order to sow it with Barley from Minorca. The double harrow was putting in the remainder of the Oats in the lower meadow wch. could not (on acct. of the wet) be done on Saturday last. (The other hands were planting Corn) —[    ] bushls. Oats sown.

At Morris's—that is Dogue run—all hands were on the New grd. at the Mansn. House; Plow people as well as others. The English Barley sown at this place in fd. No. 1 was up, but rather thin. The naked barley was also up, & pretty thick—but of that sent me by Generl. Spotswood very little appeared. The Pease were Sprouting, & some coming up wch. were sown in this field, adjoining the Barley.

At Muddy hole—one harrow was preparing for, and putting in Buck Wheat. The other hands were in the New ground at the Mansn. House.

In the Neck. Finished planting Pumpkins around the Corn fd. No. 6 and the Women began to hill in the Barn Inclosure for Pease. 5 plows turning into 3 feet ridges the ground (which had been laid of this distance) before them, to expedite the work. Two harrows preparing for, & putting in Buck Wheat. Waggon Carting rails for the fence between fields No. 8 and 9. The first planted Corn at this place was comeing up, but looked yellow. The first sowed Oats and Barley here, in No. 2, looks very well— appearing to be very little injured by the Wet—the first not at all.

Wednesday 14th. Thermometer at 56 in the Morning—67 at Noon and 66 at Night. Little or no Wind with a hazy appearance in the Morning. Southerly Wind afterwards and great appearances of Rain.

Visited all the Plantations.

At the Ferry, the Plows of the Plantation were still in No. 7.

Those of French's and Muddy hole returned to the former. The two Ferry men were planting Pumpkins after finishg. Plantg. Corn —the Cart drawing Rails to the fence between fields No. 3 & 4. The other hands were at the New grd. as yesterday.

At Frenchs. Four plows were listing—One harrow levelling the plowing intended for the Minorca Barley before sowing and harrowing it in afterwards—3½ Bushls. This appears to be a large rough grain—called by some of the People about me Bear and esteemed a Winter grain. My Farmer sowed red Clover & Orchard grass Seeds on the Oats in the lower Meadow at this place but these were not harrowed—intended to be rolled. Planting Corn here.

At Dogue run. Five plows began to break up field No. 7 for B. Wheat as a preparative for Wheat. The other hands were at the New ground. Only 5 rows had yet been sown at this place with Carrots & 2 and a piece had been planted with the [    ] Cabbage wch. appeared to be growing very well. The Self sown Buck Wheat here (wch. stands pretty thick on the grd.) is blossoming, tho' much of it is not more than 4 Inchs. high, and scarcely any more than 8 Inches. The New River grass (which appears to be a course kind of grass) is beginning to seed—as well that which was sown broad as that that is in drills.

At Muddy hole. One harrow preparing for & putting in Buck Wht. The others (such as are well) are at Work in the New grd. as yesterday. The B. Wheat at this place & in the Neck that was up looked red and sickly as tho' it had been hurt with frost.

In the Neck. Precisely the same work was going on to day as yesterday. In the ground which had been ridged here for Pease &ca. 5 Men (besides the Overseer, who only worked occasionally) 11 Women, and one boy made 72 rows of Hills, which rows would average about 300 hills each—in the whole betwn. 21 and 22 thousand hills in the day.

Thursday 15th.    Thermometer at 58 in the Morning—60 at Noon and 58 at Night. Wind, tho' not much of it at So. Et. in the Morning with a sprinkling of Rain. In the Afternoon it veered to the East, and then to No. Et. No Sun all day—mists & sometimes fine rain.

Visited all the Plantations and the Brick yard—where a small kiln of Brk. were forming to Burn.

At the Ferry—the plows having finished breaking up No. 7 for Buck Wheat had returned to the Corn field No. 2 and were listing a few rows to Sow with Carrots, and plant with Cabbages between the Corn. The two ferry men were still planting Pumpkins. The Women were in the New grd. at the Mansn. House.

At Frenchs—The Plows were yet listing but would finish to day —After which, one would list betwn. the Corn rows for Carrots and Cabbages and the others would go into No. 5 to break the grd. up for Pease. The other hands were planting Corn. Cross harrowing the Barley that was sown yesterday, and putting the remainder of the grd. in Flax.

At Dogue run—Five Women were planting the remainder of the Corn grd. wch. on Acct. of the Wet had been left undone. 4 plows were breaking up No. 7. And one of the dble. Harrows was harrowing between the Corn rows, to prepare it the better for plowing. The other hands were in the New grd. at the Mansn. House.

At Muddy hole—One harrow was preparing for, and putting in B. Wheat. The other hands were at the N. Grd. At this place the Irish Potatoes & Jerusalem Artichokes were coming up—As was the Flax (which had been sown before the last rains tho' not noted at the time). One bushel.

In the Neck. Forty rows of the Hills in the Barn Inclosure (South side next the fence were planted with the bunch homony beans 5 in a hill. These 40 rows would make about 12,000 hills. Directed the Cabbage plants to be set out betwn. the Corn rows— in No. equal to those of the Carrots. Hilling—plowing—Harrowing for (with two Harrows) & putting in B. Wheat as usual.

At the Mansion House—in the Vineyard Inclosure, I planted 3 rows of the Seeds of the Scarcity root; the rows one yard a part, & the seeds 18 Inches asunder. In the first two rows, a single seed (being picked ones) *only* was planted; in the third row, two seeds (being more indifferent) were planted; next to these, below, the plants of this root in 11 Rows were transplanted, according to directions; and next to them, in an equal No. of rows that is 14 (the same distance a part) was sown the Red Hoorn Carrots— (had from Mr. Prager). Both these squares had Stable dung (from the long shed) at the rate of 11½ bushels to every square rod, or 16½ feet, put on them. The like will be done on the same qty. of grd. adjoining for Irish Potatoes, that a comparative view may be taken of the yield & value of these vegitables. The hills for Corn in the New Grd. (the part cleared this year would be compleated to day. Hills begun in the old ground tomorrow and planting be begun thro the whole.

Friday 16th.    Thermometer at 60 in the Morning—65 at Noon
and 67 at Night. A thick Mist, with the Wind, tho' very little of it,
at No. East; where it continued till Noon when it shifted to So.
Wt. Misting more or less all day—no Sunshine.

Visited the Ferry, Frenchs, and Dogue run Plantations.

At the Ferry. The Plows were breaking up No. 3. Three women
were planting Cabbages from Frenchs—finished 3 rows. Before I
got there they had planted them at two feet asunder in the rows
but I altered it to 3 feet. Sowed nine rows of Carrots here to day
4 pints of seed. The other Women were employed in the New
ground at M. Ho.

At Frenchs. Sowing and harrowing in Flax Seed, south side of
the Meadow adjoining the Corn fd. One team listing & harrowing
for Carrots—3 Plows breaking up No. 5. The other people planting Corn. This was done up to a green Oak about the Middle of
the field with the Corn from the Neck (Lees Corn). They then
began on the East side of the field and planted with the sort
brought from Mr. Custis's Estate on Pamunky. The Ditchers after
breakfast to day began to Work on the line between No. 1 & 2.

At Dogue run—Finished Planting Corn—& Sowing Carrot Seed.
Of the latter 15 rows were Sown which must have been greatly too
thin. Planted 1½ rows of Cabbages which makes 4 in all planted
at this place—No more plants large enough to transplant. About
Noon 4 plows began to cross the unoccupied Corner of No. 6 in
order to sow it with Oats.

At Muddy hole—One harrow preparing for & putting in Buck
Wheat. The rest that were well—were planting Corn in the New
ground.

A Mr. Van Praddle, and a Mr. Duplaine and Colo. Gilpin dined
here & returned in the Afternoon.


Saturday 17th.    Thermometer at 64 in the Morning—76 at Noon
and 77 at Night. Lowering morning with the Wind at So. Wt.
Clear afterwards with the Wind at So. Et. till about 5 Oclk. when
their fell a heavy Shower of rain.

Visited all the Plantations and the Brick yard.

At the Ferry—the Plows were at work as yesterday and the
women in the New ground. As (besides the three whole rows of
Cabbages which were planted yesterday) three rows were begun
but not finished with the Cabbage plants taken from F[renc]hs—
I directed these rows, & three others making 9 in all (equal to the
Number in Carrots) to be planted from the Farmers beds—the
Seed from which they came being sent by Mr. Peacy.

Mary White Morris, wife of Robert Morris, by Charles Willson Peale. (Independence National Historical Park Collection)

At Frenchs—Five and half bushels of Flax Seed were sown on the grd. which had been prepared for it in the middle meadow (adjoining the Corn ground). And at the East end of it, to a stake, about half a bush. of a Seed sent to me by the Stage (but when or by whom, it having lain by for sometime is not recollected) was sown; mixed with red clover. This seed was either Orchard or Rye Grass from the appearance of it, but seemed rather large for the former. The other part of the Ground was sown with Clover & Timothy mixed. This ground by frequent harrowings appeared to be got in very good order. After these Seeds were harrowed in, the Harrow was ordered into No. 5 to prepare the grd. that had been plowed there, South side, for Buck Wheat. The ploughs were at Work as usual and the other hands were plantg. Corn. Sowed 3½ pints Carrt. seeds in 8 Rows.

At Dogue Run—Finished Plantg. Corn about 10 oclock, and not yesterday as was expected after which the hands that did it, went to chopping the hoed grd. in the middle meadw. The plows were crossing as yesterday and the other hands at the New grd. at the Mansn. House.

At Muddy hole—the Harrow preparing for and putting in Buck Wheat. The other hands planting Corn &ca. at the New ground.

In the Neck—Six plows and two Harrows were preparing for and putting in Buck Wheat—1 plow laying off for Pea hills—The rest of the hands making these. Yesterday, at this place, next the

(40) rows of Bunch homony beans was planted one row of a small parcel of Pease brought by Majr. G. Washington from Mrs. Dangerfields as a valuable kind. Next to these were *two* rows more of a sort given to me by Hezekiah Fairfax, said also to be a fine kind and next to these two rows, the Planting of the large, white black eye Pease (early sort) commenced.

Mrs. Morris, Miss Morris and her two Sons (lately arrived from Europe) came here about 11 Oclk. and to Dinner came Mr. Hunter, a Mr. Braithwait, and Mr. McPherson who returned to Alexandria afterwards.

Robert Morris, who was still on business in Richmond (see entry for 19 Nov. 1787), had sent his servants and horses to Philadelphia a few weeks earlier to bring his wife, Mary White Morris, to Mount Vernon for a long-planned visit (Robert Morris to GW, 29 April 1788, DLC:GW). Miss Morris is probably the Morrises' older daughter, Esther (Hetty) Morris (1774–1816), who married James Markham Marshall (1764–1848) of Virginia in 1795, but could be their other daughter, Maria Morris (1779–1852), who married Henry Nixon of Philadelphia in 1802. The two sons, Robert Morris (b. 1769) and Thomas Morris (1771–1849), had been studying in Geneva, Switzerland, 1781–86, and at the University of Leipzig, Germany, 1786–88. Both later became lawyers (MORRIS [2], 1:277, n.18; BOOGHER, 28, n.2, 33, n.3, 37, n.1, 38, n.1; HART, 168–69).

Mr. McPherson is probably Daniel McPherson or Isaac McPherson, both merchants of Alexandria.

Sunday 18th.    Thermometer at 68 in the morning—80 at Noon and 70 at Night. Clear and calm in the forenoon. About two, clouds arose, and with thunder & lightning, produced frequent Showers of Rain in the afternoon.

At home all day.

About one 'Oclock, Colo. Andrew Lewis of Bottetourt came in —dined, & returned to Alexandria in the afternoon.

Monday 19th.    Thermometer at 69 in the Morning—78 at Noon and 77 at Night. Very little Wind all day—what blew was from the So. Wt. Clear till towards evening when it clouded but did not rain here.

Rid to the Ferry & French's Plantations, & to the Brick yard.

At the Ferry—Two plows were at Work breaking up No. 3— The harrow was preparing No. 7 for the reception of Buck Wheat —Two ferry men were planting Cabbages (of Mr. Peacys kind, as already mentioned) and the other hands were at Wk. in the Newground.

At Frenchs—Four Plows were breaking up No. 5. Two harrows crossing in do. for sowing Buck Wheat—one of them having got there, about Noon, from Muddy hole; where all the Buck Wheat intended for that place, was put in, and covered. The other hands were planting Corn.

Tuesday 20th.    Thermometer at 67 in the morning—82 at Noon and 80 at Night. Wind at East in the Morning, and very heavy. Clear afterwards with the Wind at So. Wt.

Rid in Company with Mrs. Morris, Mrs. Washington, the two Mr. Morris's & Colo. Humphreys to my Mill, and returned home thro' Frenchs & the Ferry Plantations, & by the Brick yard.

Began to Sow Buck Wheat today at the Ferry. Business in other respects at the above places going on as yesterday.

Finished planting Corn in the New ground at the Mansn. House on the No. side of the Road.

Doctr. Craik came here to Breakfast—proceeded on to Portobacco and returned in the afternoon. Mrs. Craik, Mrs. Porter, and Mr. Munsher came here to dinner & returned in the Afternoon.

Wednesday 21st.    Thermometer at 72 in the Morning—78 at Noon And 70 at Night. Clouds with the Wind pretty fresh from So. W. in the Morning. Easterly afterwards with the Rain in the Afternoon.

Visited all the Plantations, and the Brick yard.

Invitation to Mr. and Mrs. Thomas Porter for dinner on Tuesday, 20 May 1788. (Mount Vernon Ladies' Association of the Union)

In the Neck. The Plows & harrows were preparing for, and putting in Buck Wheat & the other hands were planting the Early black eye pease.

At Muddy hole—all the hands except those with the Plows and harrows (at French's) were in the New ground at the Mansion house.

At Dogue run—The Plows having crossed the grd. in No. 6, had returned to No. 7. The harrow was putting in Oats & Barley in the former. The other hands, after transplanting a row & half of Carrots between the Corn rows in No. 5, returned to the New grd. at the Mansn. Ho.

At French's—Four plows were breaking up the West cut of No. 5 and two harrows were preparing for, & putting in Buck Wheat in the East cut. The other hands were planting Corn in No. 3.

At the Ferry. One harrow was preparing for, and putting in Buck Wheat—two plows were planting Corn—beginning on the South side. The other hands (yesterday afternoon and this Morning) were transplanting Carrots. A quarter part of one row [      ] end, next the sown Carrots, had a little part of the Tap root taken of. The next 1/4 to this, had the top Cut off. The other two quarters were planted as they were taken out of the Bed—after doing this they went to the New ground.

In my Botanical garden, I transplanted two roots of the Scarcity plant— but they were so dry & appeared to be so perished, as to leave little hope of their ever vegetating. Also (in the same place) from a Box which came by the Philadelphia Packet I set out a number of cuttings of what I took to be the Lombardy Poplar. These had been so long in moss as to have white sprouts issuing from many of the buds at least two or three Inches long.

The Philadelphia packet boat, the sloop *Charming Polly* captained by John Ellwood (Elwood), Jr., sailed regularly between Alexandria and Philadelphia carrying freight and passengers. GW used Ellwood's freight service for many years, and Ellwood often did GW the favor of dropping off his goods at the Mount Vernon dock, saving a trip into Alexandria. The *Charming Polly* apparently stopped at Mount Vernon today on her way upriver; she arrived at Alexandria the next day (*Pa. Packet*, 13 Mar. and 30 May 1788; GW to Charles Petit, 2 Oct. 1787, and GW to Clement Biddle, 20 July 1788, DLC: GW).

LOMBARDY POPLAR: *Populus nigra italica*. Reportedly introduced by William Hamilton in 1784, it soon became a very common ornamental tree (HEDRICK, 146). GW may have planted some of these trees as early as 1765. An entry for 1 Jan. 1765 notes the purchase from Bryan Allison of eight poplar trees for more than £2 sterling (LEDGER A, 68). Since the native poplar was abundant, such a price could only have been paid for an exotic such as the Lombardy poplar. GW used Lombardy poplars first along his walks and later had them planted in hedges on various parts of his farms to act as "live fences" (GW to Anthony Whitting, 18 Nov. 1792, DLC:GW).

**Thursday 22d.** Thermometer at 65 in the Morning—66 at Noon And 62 at Night. A great deal of rain fell in the Course of last Night. Drizling all the Morning and cloudy the remainder of the day, with showers around us, but little rain fell here. Wind at No. West, & towards evening fresh & cool.

Mrs. Morris having (by the Stage of yesterday) received a request from Mr. Morris to proceed to richmond, set off for that place abt. 9 Oclock this Morning, with her two Sons & daughter. Colo. Humphreys & myself accompanied her to Colchester, & returned to dinner. Found Mr. Rozer here, & soon afterwards came in a Mr. Andrews from Peterburgh. The first went after dinner the Other stayed all night.

Began to lay the foundation of my Barn, for the Ferry and French's Plantations, of Brick.

Robert Morris, who found that he could not yet get away from his business in Richmond to return north, was anxious to be reunited with his family "after so (unexpectedly) long absence." He met them at Bowling Green in Caroline County on 25 May and accompanied them the rest of the way to Richmond (Morris to GW, 18 and 26 May 1788, DLC:GW).

Although GW built his new barn of brick, he did not do it on the recommendation of Arthur Young. "I have seen," Young wrote in 1791, "very expensive barns in Ireland, which the owners have boasted would confine a mouse;—so much the worse: there cannot be too much air all around: the sides, for this reason, should be neither of brick nor stone. . . . The best barns (for corn) are of boards; and the more air those boards admit, the better will the straw be for the cattle; and the brighter the sample of corn in a ticklish season" (ANNALS, 16: 150–51).

**Friday 23d.** Thermometer at 55 in the Morning—65 at Noon And 72 at Night. Clear, with but little wind in the Morning, from No. Wt. Cool.

Visited the Plantations at the Ferry, French's, and Neck and the Brick yard.

At French's—Three Ploughs, & two harrows were at work—the first preparing for Pease—the latter for, and putting in Buck Wheat. The other hands planting Corn.

At the Ferry—One harrow preparing for & putting in Buck Wheat—two plows weeding Corn and the other hands at work in the New ground at the Mansn. House.

At Dogue Run, all hands (Plow People as well as others) were planting Corn in the New ground at the Home Ho.—the Plows being stopped by the Rain.

At Muddy hole – except the Plow People, the others were planting Corn at the Mansn. House the doing of which was compleated this Afternoon and all hands went to Hoeing up the Balks between – beginning on the No. side, next the Road.

In the Neck – The Plows began to weed every other Corn Row – turning the furrow from the Corn. Two harrows were at Work, preparg. for, & putting in, Buck Wheat. The other hands were employed in planting the Black-eye Pease.

HOEING UP THE BALKS: using the hoe to smooth the unwanted ridges or balks produced during plowing.

Saturday 24th.    Thermometer at 65 in the Morning – 77 at Noon And 76 at Night. Morning clear, with but little wind, & that at West. About One Oclock a cloud, with a pretty heavy shower of rain came up, & Wind at No. Wt. and cool.

Rid to all the Plantations. At the Ferry & Frenchs – same work as yesterday – finished. Planting Corn.

At Dogue run – Four plows began to Weed Corn, and at the same time to prepare the ground for Potatoes. The plowing, this first time – as is the case in the Neck, and at the Ferry, turned the Furrow *from* the Corn. The other hands were at the New grd.

Muddy hole people employed as yesterday.

In the Neck. One plow (in the Corn) was Stopped, and two single harrows put to work in its place to harrow the grd. which they had gone over, to render it more fit for the reception of Potatoes. The other hands were planting Pease which they would go near to finish to Night.

Mrs. Geo. Washington & Child and Doctr. Lyon came here before breakfast this Morning, from Maryland.

Anna Maria Washington (1788–1814), daughter of George Augustine and Frances Bassett Washington, was born 3 April, apparently at Eltham.

Dr. James Lyons of Studley, Hanover County, was a friend of the Dandridge and Bassett families. He graduated from the College of William and Mary in 1776 and subsequently studied medicine at the University of Pennsylvania and the University of Edinburgh, graduating from the latter university in 1785 (DANDRIDGE [2], 154; BLANTON, 75, 82, 87).

Sunday 25th.    Thermometer at 67 in the Morning – 70 at Noon and 71 at Night. Clear Morning with the Wind at West. Afterwards at So. Wt. with clouds.

Doctr. Stuart, Mrs. Stuart, and her three oldest daughters and Miss Nancy Stuart came here to dinner and Stayed all Night. Mr. Waltr. Stone came to dinner and went away after it.

Monday 26th.    Thermometer at 67 in the Morning—70 at Noon and 71 at Night. Heavy showers of rain fell before day and lighter one's afterwards with the Wind at [      ].

Visited the Plantations at the Ferry, Frenchs and Dogue run.

At the Ferry—the ground being wet, the Women worked in the New ground at the Mansion House. Two plows weeding Corn, and preparing for the reception of Potatoes.

At Frenchs the Plows and Harrows were at Work as before. The other People were planting, and replanting Pumpkins. The Cart as it had been for many days was assisting the Ferry Cart in getting rails to enclose No. 3 at that Plantation.

At Dogue run—Began to Plant Potatoes on the West side of the Corn field. The Plows and harrows were preparing for it. Sowed with Oats the last of the ground between the Corn and Wheat in No. 6.

Added Thos. Davis, Reuben, and Billy to the Brick layers to day, by which means five were thus employed. The necessary attendance was given them.

Also set Gunner to making Bricks, along with Charles Hagan, with attendance also.

Tuesday 27th.    Thermometer at 68 in the Morning—69 at Noon And [      ] at Night. Clear day, with the Wind at North in the Morning, and very fresh from. So. W. all the remaining part of the day.

Rid to all the Plantations.

In the Neck. Two harrows were preparing for, and putting in Buck Wheat. Seven plows and one harrow—Weeding Corn & preparing for the reception of Potats. between the Rows—the other hands replanting of Corn. Finished planting of Pease here yesterday—the last [      ] rows of which, No. side were of the small round Gentleman Pease. The others (except the 3 rows formerly noted—one of Fairfax's Sort, & two of Mrs. Dangerfields) were of the large and early blackeye. Planted pumpkins between the Pease & Corn.

At Muddy hole, The Plows and Harrow were as usual at Frenchs—all the other hands, with three Women from French's, were hoeing balks in the New ground. The Irish Potatoes at this place were all up, and few or none missing; but do not look very flourishing. The Artichokes (Jerusalem) on the contrary were very much missing.

At Dogue run—The Plows and Harrows were at Work in the Corn preparing for the reception of Potatoes; but the latter being employed yesterday to put in the Oats, the Women this forenoon were engaged in Hoeing up the Swamp in the Middle Meadow, till they (that is the harrows) could make way for them again.

At Frenchs–The Plows, Harrows and Cart, at work as on yesterday, the overseer, one woman and a boy were replanting Water Mellons &ca. Three women as before mentioned were in the N. Ground.

Set the Ditchers yesterday to levelling the dirt which remained by the sunk fence in front of the Mansion House.

Doctr. Stuart and family went away after breakfast.

Wednesday 28th.    Thermometer at 60 in the Morning—70 at Noon and 68 at Night. In the Morning the Wind was at North, but it soon shifted to So. Wt. and blew very fresh, with clouds, and sprinklings of Rain. In the afternoon it shifted to No. Wt.

Rid to the Ferry, Frenchs & Dogue run Plantations, and to the Brick yard.

At the Ferry–Finshed this Morning replanting of Corn and began on the South Side of the field to plt. Potatoes between the Corn Rows. The Plows and harrows were at the same work, and for the same purposes as yesterday–a light harrow drawn by the two mules from Muddy hole was set to work (in addition) to day, to harrow after the Plows for Potatoes.

At Frenchs–Finished Sowing the Buck Wheat but not harrowing it in. Nor will the ground (at least part of it) be well prepared having got too hard for the harrows to penetrate deep enough to stir up a sufficient depth of Earth. This circumstance & many others, which from time to time have occurred has convinced me that on putting in all Sprg. Crops (as the Season produces heavy & frequent rains, & the ground apt to bake) it would be best to plow harrow and sow in such squares as are proportioned to the size of the farms, & strength of the teams than to break the whole up first; unless *repeated* plowings is intended and can be given. The Plows finished breaking up the West pt. of field No. 5 at this place and were ordered into the Corn field to weed, and prepare that for Potatoes. Replanting Corn here (3 hands at the New grd.) and rolling the Oats & grass in the lower Meadow.

At Dogue run–The Plows and Harrows were (as yesterday) weeding Corn, & preparing for the Planting of Potatoes–The other hands planting them, and when the Plows were overtaken replanted Corn.

Began, yesterday, with the Carpenters and Cowpers to cut grass & make Hay and with Thomas Green & Mahony to frame the lower floor of the Barn which is about. This day, after manuring in the same proportion which had been done for the Plants of Scarcity and for Carrots—I planted, adjoining the latter, 14 rows (the same as had been done of the other two) of Irish Potatoes, red sort, and whole—3 feet a part, & the sets 9 Inches asunder. And below these again in rows 3 feet a part I sowed 5 of lucern.

Thomas Mahony, a house carpenter and joiner who had worked at Mount Vernon from 1 Aug. 1786 to 1 Aug. 1787, was again employed by GW on 15 April 1788 and continued to work for him until the spring of 1792. Mahony received £24 a year plus board and other amenities for his services (articles of agreement between GW and Mahony, 1 Aug. 1786, 15 April 1788, and 7 May 1789, DLC:GW; LEDGER B, 236, 271, 331).

Thursday 29th.    Thermometer at 56 in the Morning—56 at Noon And 66 at Night. Clear All day, and cool in the forenoon. Wind being fresh from the No. Wt.

Visited all the Plantations.

In the Neck—All the Plows and Harrows were at Work in the Corn—Weeding the same and preparing the intervals between the Rows for the reception of Potatoes in drills. Began yesterday afternoon to plant the latter, having finished replanting Corn, and Pumpkins. Examined the Oats here, growing from Spotswood's Seed, which are very fine. The Wheat in No. 7 is thin, in places None, having been injured both by the Frosts of Winter and the rains of this Spring. The Barley is but indifferent being in places low, thin, and yellow at bottom.

At Muddy hole—Except the Plow people at French's—all hands were at Work in the New ground.

At Dogue run—The Plows and Harrows were weeding Corn and preparing for the reception of Potatoes. The other hands, when the plows were overtaken by the latter work, were replanting of Corn.

At French's—The Plows were weeding Corn. The Harrows after breakfast, began to cross the plowing for Pease, in order to prepare the grd. for the reception of them. The Roller had finished rolling the Oats in the lower Meadow and returned to the Carting of Rails at French's. The other hands were replanting of Corn.

At the Ferry. The Plows and a single harrow, drawn by the Mules were weeding Corn and preparing for Potatoes. The double harrows were putting in Buck Wheat wch. would be compleated tomorrow. The other hands were planting Potatoes.

In the Afternoon, a Mr. Walke and a Mr. Woodville came in and stayed all Night.

Anthony Walke III of Fairfield, Princess Anne County, and John Woodville (1763–1834), of Spotsylvania County, were returning to their homes from Philadelphia where they had been recently ordained priests of the Protestant Episcopal Church. Walke was inducted 3 July 1788 as rector of Lynnhaven Parish, Princess Anne County, a position that he held until 1800 (KELLAM, 176–78). Woodville, who had come to Virginia from England during the previous year and had lived with a Spotsylvania County family as a tutor, was appointed head of the Fredericksburg Academy in 1791. He became rector of St. George's Parish, Spotsylvania County, in 1792 and a year or two later moved to the rectorship of St. Mark's Parish, Culpeper County, where he remained until his death (SLAUGHTER [2], 59–61, 192–93).

Friday 30th.    Thermometer at 56 in the Morning—66 at Noon and 64 at Night. Morng. clear, wind at So. Wt. all the forenoon & briskly from the So. Et. in the Afternoon with clouds and appearances of Rain. A good deal of which fell in the night.

Visited the Plantations at the Ferry—French's & Dogue Run.

At the first, finished sowing Buck Wheat. In every other respect the work was the same as yesterday.

At French's—It was precisely the same as it was yesterday at this place. And the same likewise at Dogue run.

Began to cut such parts of the Clover in No. 1 at Frenchs, as Stood sufficiently thick, having cut the blew grass on the sides of the lower meadow at this place.

Having worked up the Bricks of the first Kiln—the Brick layers went to get & lay in a stock of Sand—but the second load of Corn from York River arriving the Boat would be occupied in landing of it to morrow.

Mr. Ludwell Lee & his Lady came here this afternoon and stayed the N.

Saturday 31st.    Thermometer at 60 in the Morning—[    ] at Noon And [    ] at Night. A good deal of Rain fell in the Night. The Morning very cloudy with the Wind at So. Et. and towards 10 Oclock pretty smart Showers. The ground being wet, I transplanted the remains of my plants of the Scarcity Root (to make good the dificiency of the last transplanting) except some of the smallest of them which were intended not to be removed, but by remaining to prove the efficacy of both modes.

After an early dinner, in company with Colo. Humphreys, I set out for a meeting of the Directors of the Potomack Company to be held at the Falls of Shenandoah on Monday next. Reached Mr. Fairfax's about an hour by Sun, who with his lady were at Alexandria; but a cloud which threatend rain induced us notwithstanding to remain there all night.

# [June 1788]

Sunday. June 1st.    About Sun rise, we set out for the Great Falls, where having met Mr. Smith (the assistent Manager who resides at the works at the Seneca falls) we examined the Canal, banks and other operations at this place and were pleased to find them in such forwardness and so well executed. The upper part of the Canal, however, still requires to be widened—Stones &ca. removed out of it and the lower side banked. From hence we proceeded by a Small cut, & wall About a mile higher up the River to the Seneca falls, where much digging & blowing had been performed for the purpose of conducting the Navigation through one of the Swashes on the Virginia side and a good deal of Substantial Wall erected but the whole being in a rude & unfinished state no judgment could be formed of the time necessary to execute it; but Mr. Smith supposes 20 hands will be able to accomplish it this Summer as a like number wd. do that at the Great falls above the Lock Seats. At this place we breakfasted, and in Company with Mr. Smith continued our journey. Dined at Leesburgh & lodged at Mr. Jno. Houghs.

Monday 2d.    About 5 Oclock, after an early breakfast, we set off, pilotted by Mr. Hough thro' by roads, over the short hills—by the House & Mill of one Belt for the Mo. of Shenandoah where we arrived partly by a good, & partly by a rugged road, at half after eight Oclock—distance about 12 Miles. Soon after came Govr. Johnson, and about 10 Oclock Govr. Lee & Colo. Gilpin arrived. We then, together, crossed the River, walked up to the head of the Canal on the Maryland side & viewed all the Works. Found that the Canal At the head was accomplished, & appeared to be well walled on both sides; and a tow path on the Maryland side for some distance below—but that much of the work remained yet to do How[eve]r the supposition is, that it may be so far compleated as to open the navigation in the course of the Summer for the passage of Boats tho much more labour will be necessary to perfect it. After dinner the board set—proceeded to the examination of Sundry accts. and other business which came before them; but that for which it principally met at *this place*—viz. —an investigation of complaints exhibited against Mr. Richardson Stuart, was postponed on acct. of his non-attendance occasioned as was said by a Law suit on the Genl. Court at Annapolis at which he was obliged to be prest. The board however conceiving that a

Manager without an Assistant was suffict. to superintend the works and thinking Mr. Smith the most competent of the two, resolved to discontinue Mr. Stuart at the expiration of the year for which he was engaged – viz. – the 15th. of July and to vest the chief direction in him.

The four directors informed Richardson Stewart of their decision by a letter written this same day. "The present funds or prospects will not warrant our continuing two managers . . . ," they explained. "It is with reluctance we found ourselves under the necessity to make an arrangement which at this point of time may possibly be thought by your enemies to be occasioned by the charges against you, but it has proceeded solely from our duty and inclination to promote the Company's interest without being influenced in any degree by facts alleged and not examined into. The preference given to Mr. Smith is on different principles and we expect cannot surprise you or hurt your feelings" (BACON-FOSTER, 82) .

To James Smith the directors recommended that "the most vigorous efforts" be made to open the navigation at all three falls by summer and that, with that view in mind, the work force "be increased as the occasion may require and opportunity will serve" (BACON-FOSTER, 83) .

Tuesday 3d.    Having accomplished all the business that came before the board by 10 Oclock, the members seperated and I (Colo. Humphreys having returned the day before) went to my Brothers about eight miles off – dined there and continued on in the Afternoon to Colonel Warner Washington's where I spent the evening.

Wednesday 4th.    About 7 Oclock I left this place, Fairfield, bated at a Small Tavern (Bacon fort) 15 miles distant – dined at the Tavern of one Lacey 14 Miles further and lodged at Newgate 16 Miles lower down.

Joseph Lacey apparently began renting and operating Charles West's tavern in Loudoun County some time before West's death in 1786 and subsequently purchased the place (HARRISON [1], 495–96) .

Thursday 5th.    After an early breakfast I continued my Journey by the upper and lower churches of this Parish & passing through my Plantations at Dogue run, Frenchs, and the Ferry and the New Barn I reached home about Noon in about 28 Miles riding where I found Colo. Humphreys who had just got in before me from Abingdon.

The Weather and Thermometer by the Accounts rendered – stood as follow.

Saturday afternoon a heavy rain, mixed with hail and a violent wind (which blew down much of my fencing at French's) .

Sunday—Clear Morning and evening, cloudy mid-day. Wind No. in the Morning—No. W. at Noon & So. W. at Night.

Munday—Cloudy Morning, clear afterwards. Wind at No. Et. in the Morning, & South afterwards.

Tuesday—Cloudy with the wind at So. Et.

Wednesday—Much rain fell last Night, and this day, till 12 or 1 Oclock; Cloudy afterwards. wind at No. Et. in the Morning—So. Et. afterwards.

Thursday—Cloudy or foggy morning clear afterwards with very little or no wind.

|           |        |    | Mercury. |    |       |    |
|-----------|--------|----|------|----|-------|----|
| Sunday    | Morng. | 61 | Noon | 68 | Night | –  |
| Monday    |        | 62 |      | 72 |       | 69 |
| Tuesday   |        | 64 |      | 68 |       | 68 |
| Wednesday |        | 67 |      | 69 |       | 72 |
| Thursday  |        | 70 |      | 79 |       | 78 |

On Saturday, the Ditchers finished weeding the honey locusts in the vineyard. Planted in the No. Garden, between the Green house & quarter 10 grains of early Corn; given to me (from So. Carolina) by Genl. Spotswood. And finished replanting Corn at Dogue Run.

On Monday—Finished plantg. every other Corn Row with Potatoes at Dogue run & began the intermediate ones (next the Carrots. Planting Potatoes at the Ferry, after repairing the Fencing which had blown down at this place & French's. Listing & harrowing for Potatoes at all the Plantns. Finished cutting grass (that was fit for it) at French's about 12 Oclock to day—but the Rains had much injured the first hay. Sent Materials for the Dairy in the Neck to day—Churns &ca.

On Tuesday—Muddy hole People, as had been the case at the Ferry, Dogue run &ca., had cut Rye out of their Wheat & were hoeing baulks in the New grd. At the Ferry the Potatoe planters having overtaken the Plows & Harrows, went to weeding Corn, with their hoes, as was the case at Frenchs—that is weeding Corn with Hoes. Made the Pole fence at D. Run round the English Barley in field No. 1. Chopped in (the Potatoe Planters having overtaken the Hoes & harrows) Oats & Timothy seed in the ground that had been prepared in the Swamp, in the middle meadow at this place. At the River every other Row of Patoes had been planted, & up to the farm pen of the intermediate ones when the Plows being overtaken the Planters were employed in weeding Water Mellons & taking Wheat from the Rye.

Seperated the Rams from the Ewes. Finished landing Corn from Chamberlains Vessel—viz. —425 at the Mill & 1004 at the Mansn. House.

On Wednesday—Transplanted part of a Row of Carrots to compleat an unfinished one at the ferry. Recd. 10,000 ft. of Inch pine plank from Messrs. Peterson & Tayler. Discharged Mr. Chamberlns. Vessel.

The upper church of Truro Parish was Payne's Church; the lower one was Pohick Church (see main entry for 9 Sept. 1768).

Friday 6th.    Thermometer at 72 in the Morning—82 at Noon And 80 at Night. Clear, Calm and warm all day.

Visited all the Plantations.

In the Neck the Plows & harrows were Weeding Corn, & preparing for the Reception of Potatoes between. The other hands were planting them till they overtook the harrows; then employed in taking Rye from Wheat. Shearing Sheep &ca.

At Muddy hole, except the Plow people, the other hands were engaged in the New ground at the Mansn. House, assisted by the Dogue-run hands.

At Dogue run—the Plows & harrows were weeding Corn, & preparing for the Reception of Potatoes. The other hds. were (as above) at the New grd. except 2 Shearing of Sheep.

At French's, the ground being too wet to plant & cover Potatoes I ordered the People (except those with the Plows & harrows) to weed Corn, & cut Rye from the Wheat. Harrowing in Pease in the West part of field No. 5. This was done after the ground had been plowed & twice harrowed—3 harrowings afterwards but notwithstanding the ground by the frequent and hard rains which had fallen af[ter] it was plowed, was settled & too closely bound together. The Hay at this place was opened, & stirred but had received great injury.

At the Ferry—The plows and harrows were weeding Corn, & preparing for Potatoes. The hoes, the grd. being too wet to plant them, were weeding Corn.

Saturday 7th.    Thermometer at 74 in the Morning—82 at Noon and 82 at Night. Clear morning—but clouds arising about Noon, produced one or two showers (of no long continuance) about one Oclock, with thunder & lightning—but little Wind.

Visited the Ferry, & Frenchs Plantations. At the first, the Plows & harrows were at Work as usual and the other hands planting

Potatoes, but as the ground was very heavy (especially in places) I directed them to desist and go to weeding Corn.

At Frenchs the People were planting Potatoes—but improperly on Account of the wetness of the ground. Plows in the Corn & one harrow following them—two harrowing in Pease.

Finished yesterday afternoon hoeing up the balks in the *New* part of the New grd. and went to replanting the Corn there, which would be compleated to day.

Ditchers after having made up the fence along the ferry road were about a similar one at Frenchs between fields No. 1 & 2.

Stirring, and endeavouring to secure what hay was down but it is scarcely worth the trouble, from the injury it has sustained.

Sunday 8th.    Thermometer at 72 in the Morning—70 at Noon and 69 at Night. A very heavy Shower of rain for an hour fell after dark last night with continual lightning and loud thunder. Wind at No. Et. all day with very clouds but no rain.

Monday 9th.    Thermometer at 62 in the morning—76 at Noon and 75 at Night. Thick foggy morning, with the Wind at So. Et. Clear towards noon with the Wind at So. Wt.

Captn. Barney, in the Miniature Ship Federalist—as a present from the Merchants of Baltimore to me arrived here to Breakfast with her and stayed all day & Night.

Remained at home all day.

The *Federalist,* a fifteen-foot-long boat rigged as a ship, was a showpiece designed to represent Baltimore's maritime trades and to symbolize the proposed federal union. "Highly ornamented" and mounted on a horse-drawn carriage frame, the little ship had been pulled through the main streets of Baltimore on 1 May as part of a great procession of merchants, artisans, and professionals celebrating Maryland's ratification of the new Constitution five days earlier. Miniature ships, named the *Federalist* or the *Union,* were features of many Federalist victory parades before and after Maryland's ratification. However, in Baltimore a group of Federalist merchants took the further step of launching their vessel after the celebration and dispatching it to Mount Vernon under the command of Joshua Barney (1759–1818), a naval hero of the Revolution and a staunch Federalist, for presentation to GW "as an Offering . . . expressive of their Veneration of his Services and Federalism" (*Md. Journal,* 6 May 1788 and 3 June 1788; GW to William Smith et al., 8 June 1788, anonymous donor).

Tuesday 10th.    Thermometer at 70 in the Morning. 80 at Noon and 79 at Night. Wind at So. Wt. A hard shower of Rain about 5 Oclock in the Afternoon which continued half an hour or more.

Between 9 and 10 Oclock set out for Fredericksburgh, accompanied by Mrs. Washington, on a visit to my Mother. Made a visit to Mr. & Mrs. Thompson in Colchester & reached Colo. Blackburns to dinner, where we lodged. He was from home. The next Morning, about Sun rise we continued our journey. Breakfasted at Stafford Court House and intended to have dined at Mr. Fitzhughs of Chatham but he & Lady being from home we proceeded to Fredericksburgh—alighted at my Mothers and sent the Carriage & horses to my Sister Lewis's—where we dined and lodged—As we also did the next day, the first in company with Mr. Fitzhugh, Colo. Carter & Colo. Willis and their Ladies, and Genl. Weeden. The day following (Friday) we dined in a large Company at Mansfield (Mr. Man Page's). On Saturday we visited Genl. Spotswoods dined there & returned in the Evening to My Sisters. On Sunday we went to Church. The Congregation being alarmed (without cause) and supposg. the Gallery at the No. End was about to fall, were thrown into the utmost confusion; and in the precipitate retreat to the doors many got hurt. Dined in a large Company at Colo. Willis's—Where, taking leave of my friends, we re-crossed the River, and Spent the Evening at Chatham. The next Morning before five Oclock we left it—travelled to Dumfries to breakfast—and reached home to a late dinner and found that Captn. Barney had left it about half an hour before for Alexandria to proceed in the Stage of Tomorrow for Baltimore.

Upon examination of the Accts. of the Work & Weather at home, during my absence, found them to be as follow.

Charles Carter of Ludlow, encumbered by heavy debts, had a few months earlier been obliged to sign over Ludlow farm and his other property in Stafford County to three trustees for public sale in order to satisfy his many anxious creditors (*Va. Herald*, 27 Mar. 1788). He and his wife, Elizabeth Chiswell Carter (d. 1804), were probably now living in Fredericksburg, where the following year Mrs. Carter advertised that she would take in "a few young gentlemen" as boarders at the rate of £25 a year (*Va. Herald*, 20 Aug. 1789; SHACKELFORD, 394, 402).

Lewis Willis (1734–1813), of Willis Hill near Fredericksburg, was the son of GW's aunt Mildred Washington (1696–c.1745) and her second husband, Col. Henry Willis (c.1691–1740). Lewis Willis served as a lieutenant colonel in the 10th Virginia Regiment during the War of Independence and was for many years a vestryman of St. George's Parish, Spotsylvania County. His first wife was Mary Champe of King George County, and after her death he married his present wife, Ann Carter Champe, widow of his brother-in-law John Champe, Jr. (d. 1775).

At St. George's Church, Mrs. Washington "perceived the Tomb of her Father the late John Dandridge Esqr. to be much out of sorts." GW subsequently wrote Charles Carter asking him "to have it done up again." GW bore the expense of the work, £1 10s. (28 June 1788, DLC:GW; LEDGER B, 270).

Wednesday 11th. Thermometer at 69 in the Morning—75 at Noon and 75 at Night. Clear with the Wind at No. Wt. in the Morning and So. Wt. in the afternoon.

That the Plows from French's and Muddy hole—as also the hands of those places, had been at work in the Mansion House New ground since Sunday and the Plows (except one to throw a furrow to the Corn) from Dogue run had come there yesterday.

That at the Ferry, and Dogue run, (the ground being too wet to *plant* Potatoes) the Plows at both places on Monday, and at the first yesterday and to day, were plowing Corn & throwing a furrow on each side to the plants (whilst the Hoes were weeding the same) —also prepg. for Pots.

That in the Neck, the ground not being quite so wet, the hands *continued* planting Potatoes on Monday & yesterday—plowing & harrowing as usual for them.

That four Mowers went on Tuesday (yesterday) to cut the Clover in the Neck; Tom Davis one of them.

That Cornelius, his Brother, and the two boys, returned to bricklaying again yesterday.

And that the following Gentlemen dined here—to wit—Colo. Fitzgerald & Messrs. Digges & Carroll, and Doctr. Hall & Brother from Maryland; and Messrs. Rumney, Hodgsden, Munsher, Cary & Williams from Alexandria.

That the Muddy hole hands this day (Wednesday) had wed the Pumpkins & Sweet Potatoes.

The Dogue run hands weeding Corn with the Hoes after the furrows had been thrown to it.

At Frenchs, the hands were grubbing Bushes in the ground which was receiving Pease; & the farmer showing and covering them near Manleys Houses with two pair of Harrows.

At the Ferry, the Plows were throwing furrows to the Corn & preparing as usual for Potatoes between it. Hoes weeding the Corn.

Finished cutting the Clover in the Neck about 12 Oclock to day.

Among the several Dr. Halls living in Maryland at this time was the prominent Harford County physician and educator Dr. Jacob Hall (1747–1812), but the Dr. Hall who visited Mount Vernon on 11 June was probably Dr. Elisha Hall (1754–1814) of Fredericksburg. He had one or more brothers living in Maryland, and he treated GW's mother for what was apparently breast cancer during her final days in the summer of 1789 (PLEASANTS, 217–26; JOHNSTON [6], 297–99, 381–82; BLANTON, 359–66).

William Hodgson (1765–1820) came to Alexandria from White Haven, Eng., about 1785 and established himself as a merchant, an occupation in which he engaged for many years.

Thursday 12th.    Thermometer 70 in the Morning. 78 at Noon. and 77 at Night. Wind at So. & So. W. A hard rain in the evening with some Hail.

At the Mansion Ho. New ground 6 Plows were at Work—viz. — 4 from D. Run 1 from Frenchs, & 1 from M. Hole which would by Noon have finished breaking up the balks on the So. Side of the Road.

At Muddy hole, the hands belonging there, were hoeing up balks in the above New ground where the Plows could not conveniently run.

At the Ferry 3 plows were weeding Corn & preparing for Potatoes—the Hoes weeding Corn also.

At French's, the Hoes were weeding Corn—two Plows doing the same. and two harrows preparing for, and putting in Pease in Field No. 5 broadcast.

At D. Run, all hands were weeding Corn—1 plow throwing furrows to it.

Cutting Clover at French's.

Friday 13th.    Thermometer at 71 in the Morning—69 at Noon and 70 at Night. Wind at No. Et. & rain till 8 Oclock moderately then hard till 4 Oclock.

Five plows, when the Weather would permit, were working in the Mansn. House New grd.—as were the hands from Muddy hole.

At the Ferry, the hands had been attempting to weed corn (wet as the grd. was).

At Frenchs weeding Water Mellens.

Saturday 14th.    Thermometer 66 in the Morning—69 at Noon and 68 at Night. Wind at No. E. and Showery all day.

Hoeing and plowing balks in the New grd. at Mansn. Ho. with the People from Muddy hole & 2 plows from the Ferry, 3 from Frenchs, and 1 from Muddy hole.

At Muddy hole threw a furrow to the Irish Potatoes (back of the one that first covered them).

At the River Plantation, all hands were planting Potatoes & weeding Corn. The Plows were throwing a furrow (on each side) to the Corn, covering Potatoes, &ca. The Pumpkins were also weeded and the Planting of Potatoes compleated at this place; qty. 269¾ Bushels. Plows prevented working here yesterday—but this day after putting in & compleating their work for the Potatoes plowed between the Pumpkins & then went into field No. 8 to prepare what remained of the unsowed part for Buck Wheat &ca.

At Dogue Run the hands were yesterday & to day weeding Corn —3 plows previously throwing a furrow on each side to it—little or no plowing here yesterday owing to the rain.

At French's weeding Pumpkins and setting Corn.

At the Ferry they were employed in doing the latter.

Finished cutting the Clover at French's.

Colo. Harrison and Mr. Corbn. Washington came here to Dinner, and stayed all Night.

Sunday 15th.    Thermometer at 62 in the Morning—68 at Noon And 68 at Night. Wind at No. Et. in the Morning—then So. Et.

Colo. Harrison & Mr. C. Washington went away after Breakfast. Cap. Barney (who went to Alexa. on Wednesday last) returned here this Morning—dined at Mr. Lund Washington's with Colo. Humphreys—came back afterwards.

Monday 16th.    Thermometer at 62 in the Morning, 70 at Noon and 70 at Night. Wind at So. Et. Morning & evening clear but cloudy between.

Finished plowing the New grd. at the Mansn. House about Noon to day. The ferry Plows went home—the others to Plowing at French's for Pease. The hands from Muddy hole were weeding the New ground Corn with their Hoes.

At the Ferry, Frenchs, D. Run and River Plantations the People were Weeding of Corn with Hoes. The Plows throwing furrows to it and at the River breaking up for B. Wheat.

Returned home this evening as has been mentioned already.

Tuesday 17th.    Thermometer at 67 in the Morng.—78 at Noon and 77 at Night. Morning and evening clear, midday cloudy.

Visited all the Plantations except that in the Neck. Examined the grain at each, and find the fields as follow.

At Muddy hole, the Wheat in No. 2, as might be expected from the exhausted state of the Land, was *generally* thin, and in some places scarcely worth reaping. The Rye (in the same field) though indifferent in places is full as good as could reasonably be expected from the Land, except the defect in the head. The Wheat in No. 4, where the ground had any strength, exceeded (considering the late sowing of it) my expectations. Other parts was good for nothg. and upon the whole very indifferent. The Oats in this field may be deemed above mediocrity—being, (though not high or stout) very regular & even. The Wht. in No. 1 (self sown, being the shattered grains which were plowed in when the Buck Wheat was sown) was very thin in places and not sufficiently thick in any. The Barley in this field (except being very much mixed with Oats) may be deemed tolerable. That part of the grd. wch. had been sprinkled with dung bore the best grain and next to it, that which had been in Potatoes. The whole was too thin. The Clover, *generally*, which had been sown with this Barley looked full as well as could be expected.

At Dogue run, The Wheat & Rye in field No. 4 (except the defect in the head) may be considered as very good for Corn grd. Wheat. The fallowed Wheat in field No. 6 is very stout on the East side of the field but too thin even there. Another part of the field was, in a manner, Intirely lost by the Winters frosts, aided in the lowest places by the continual Rains which have fallen this Spring and Summer. Upon the whole, though it was (partly) put in late, and in bad order. It exhibits an evidence of its superiority over Corn ground. The Rye in the No. part of the field with the exception beforementioned may (tho thin in places) be deemed good. The Barley at this place, contrary to my expectations, is much inferior, except in spots, to that at Muddy hole; & will turn out very indifferently: whether from the nature of the Soil, which was not able to bear the wet so well, the Land being *more* worn, which I do not conceive to be the case, or to some other cause I am not able to decide. The Oats in the same field (No. 2) are tolerably good, rather preferable to those at Muddy hole. The Clover is fully equal to my expectations which was sown among them. The Flax at this place may be called very good—but the rankest & best of it was twisted and laid down by the repeated Rains, and Wind.

At French's, the Wheat, generally, is thin—Scarcely any good and much of it very indifferent. The Rye is partly good, and partly very indifferent. The Barley at this place is some good, and some very indifferent. It is, however, much better than that at Dogue run & perhaps upon the whole preferable to that at Muddy hole. The Oats here, with scarcely any exception, may be esteemed fine and the Clover which was sown among them, and the Barley very promising in general. The English Pease & Beans which had been sown here were entirely destroyed with weeds. The Minorca Barley (but this was late sown) appeared as if it would come to little—nor did the English Barley & other small parcels which were sown at D. Run promise much. None of the Buck Wht. at this place looked well. The last sown was, *almost* entirely destroyed and in every, even the best parts of the field there were spots, and in some places large ones, where the B. Wht. after coming up, seemed to have been drowned, and drowning even where the Water did not lay & where the Soil was good.

At the Ferry, there was *no* good Wheat. That which was sown in the fallowed ground (late) was miserable—only parts of the grd. havg. any. The Corn ground Wheat was thin, except in the Hills which had been manured with fish guts &ca. and there it appeared, tho' rank, to be fired and entangled. The Rye (which was early sown, and looked remarkably well, & stood very thick in the fall) is exceedingly bad, being thin, week, & much broken down by the winds and rain. The Oats stand regular, & equal through the whole, and may be deemed middling.

Remarks—No rust appeared in any of the Wheat, though from the continual rains & cloudy weather it was much expected. This grain, however, and the Rye more so, is a good deal injured by the speck; that is, from the farina's being beat off before the grain was fully impregnated by which whole heads, parts of heads and grains here & there have not filled which must diminish the quantity considerably. Having suffered nothing to feed upon my grain this year, the Crop *would* have been much the better for it, but the frosts of Winter (when the Snows were blown off) destroying some parts of the fields entirely & thinning it in others and the constant rains since the middle of March drowning that which was in the low parts—though it brought forward others which otherwise would have come to nothing has rendered the prospect of a crop very indifferent. The grain which is not injured appears to be full, & seems as if it would be large—but it (the Wheat) is exceedingly intermixed with cheat and must be very much injured thereby.

Weeding Corn at all the Plantations with the Hoes, and throwing furrows to it with the Plows—also plowing the intervals between for Potatoes and at French's plowing & harrowing for Pease.

Wednesday 18th.  Thermometer at 70 in the Morning—75 at Noon And 72 at Night. Clear in the Morning; at Noon & Night Cloudy with rains about 10 Oclock for an hour. Wind at South.

Rid into the Neck and to all the Plantations.

Examined the grain in the Neck which appears as follow—viz.— The Wheat in field No. 7 which I expected would have been very fine scarcely merits the epithet—Middling the whole being too thin being injured by the frosts of Winter & the wet of this Spring. Of the red wheat which was sown in this field scarce any is to be seen and of the white (both imported from England) the ground was but thinly Covered. The Corn ground Wheat in No. 3 was too thin every where—in places scarcely any. In the Orchard the Wheat in places was good—in other places indifferent—upon the whole scarcely to be denominated middling. No rust appeared among it, but the speck was as much here as in other fields—but I think not quite so much cheat. The Rye at this place may, upon the whole, be deemed Middling though a good deal injured by the Speck. In some places it stands thick & well—in others thin and much fallen down. The Barley, *generally,* was but indifferent; some parts of the field being *low, thin,* & having scarcely any head. Other parts again (particularly on the So. & West sides of the field) were pretty good. The Oats, in the aggregate may be called good and those growing from General Spotswoods Seed are very fine. The Clover in both Barley & Oats (where the grd. is tolerable) is very good. The flax is also good, but the best of it is a good deal entangled by the Winds, and beat down with the Rain. Finished plowing the Corn here to day and all the plows went to cross plowing of field No. 8 for B. Wheat but were directed to plow the So. part of it for Pease to be sown in Broad cast. Set one plow with a single horse to plow between the Pease which were planted in hills and which were getting foul.

At Muddy hole the plows were throwing the So. part of field No. 3 into three feet Ridges—to be hilled for Pease. The Hoes were in the New ground at the Mansn. House.

At Dogue run, Two plows were plowing for Pease. The other 3 and the Hoes were weeding Corn.

At Frenchs, three plows and a Harrow were preparing for, and putting in Pease in Field No. 5. The other Plow was throwing a furrow to the Corn before the Hoes which were weeding it.

At the Ferry the Plows & Hoes both were in the Corn.

Thursday 19th.    Thermometer at 70 in the Morning—73 at Noon And 70 at Night. Wind in the Morning and evening No. Et. —at Noon So. Raining in the Morning and evening with Showers between.

Rid to the Ferry, French's, Dogue run & Muddy hole Plantations.

At the three first, Work the same as yesterday. At the last, I had a piece of ground, containing 500 hills four feet a part, spaded up the depth of the Spade—half a bushel of well rotted farm yard dung put upon each 4 feet Square, and chopped in; after which the above number of Hills were made, & planted with Tobacco

Plants (of the common kind) given to me by Mr. Abednego Adams.

Began to cut grass in the large Meadow at the Mill to day.

Friday 20th.    Thermometer at 64 in the Morning—72 at Noon And 62 at Night. Wind in the Morning & evening No. W. and at Noon So. Wt. Forenoon clear, Afternoon Cloudy with a heavy shower in the evening.

Visited the Plantations at Muddy hole, Dogue run, Frenchs & the Ferry.

At the first the Plows were in the ground intended for Pease, and the Hoes setting Corn in the New ground at the Mansn. House.

At the other three the work the same as yesterday and before, except that about Noon, the Plows at Frenchs finished plowing for Pease and went into the Corn at that place.

In the Morning, while we were at Breakfast, Mr. Jno. Mason, Son to Colo. Mason came in to ask my commands for France. After breakfast he returned.

John Mason (1766–1849) had recently become a partner with the brothers James and Joseph Fenwick of Maryland in a trading company based in Bordeaux. He sailed for Bordeaux 22 June and returned two years later (COPELAND, 245–61).

Saturday 21st.    Thermometer at 62 in the Morning—72 at Noon And 71 at Night. Weather clear, Wind at No. Wt. in the forepart of the day & at North the latter part.

Visited all the Plantations.

In the Neck, the Plows were employed in preparing for Pease, & the Harrows putting them—one plow weeding the Potatoes in hills—all the Hoes in the Corn.

At Muddy hole—both Plows & Hoes were weeding Irish Potatoes.

At Dogue run three plows and the Hoes were in the Corn.

At Frenchs—The Plows and Hoes were in the Corn as usual, and the Harrow finished covering the last Pease—quantity sown 33 bushels. The ground being a little cloddy, that wch. was sown next the slash (running thro the field) was rolled.

At the Ferry both Plows, Hoes & harrow were in the Corn.

Sunday 22d.    Thermometer at 67 in the Morning—78 at Noon And 76 at Night. Clear all day with the Wind at So. Wt.

Mr. Fendall, and Mr. Willm. Craik came to dinner and went

away afterwards – the latter to Alexandria and the former to Westmoreland.

Monday 23d.    Thermometer at 72 in the Morning – 88 at Noon And 78 at Night. Clear forenoon and very warm, the Wind being Southerly; About 3 Oclk. a cloud arose to the Westward which about 4 Oclock produced much rain and wind and entangled the flax that was rank very much.

Visited all the Plantations.

In the Neck, all the Hoes were weeding & setting Carrots where they were missing. Set two plows with single horses into the Corn with orders to throw the furrows towards the Corn – A small triangular harrow to level them and to tare the clods & grass asunder. One plow weeding the Pease in Hills and the others, & harrows preparing for, and putting in Pease broad-cast.

At Muddy hole, the Plows and Hoes finished, about 9 Oclock, weeding the Irish Potatoes. The first went to Frhs. and the others came to the New ground at the Mansn. Ho. & finished setting Corn – after which they came into the vineyard Inclosure to Weed Potatoes Carrots &ca. but the rain drove them in and the wetness of the ground prevented further working there.

At Dogue run, The Hoes, and the Plows were weeding Corn. The other 2 Plows being at Frenchs were ordered home this Evening.

At French's – the 3 plows from Muddy – the two from Dogue run & the three belonging to the place were plowing the Corn – one, following the rest – turning the Mould to the Plant. Stopped one of the Plows & set in lieu of it two harrows to preparing the Newly plowed ground for Potatoes. The Hoe people were pulling weeding from some foul pease about Manleys Houses.

At the Ferry – Both Hoes & Plows were weeding Corn and a harrow preparing the Intervals betwn. for Potatoes.

Tuesday 24th.    Thermometer at 67 in the Morning – 78 at Noon And 67 at Night. Wind at No. Wt. in the Morning and weather clear but about One Oclock a cloud came up and produced rain but neither hard or much of it – afterwhich it turned cool – the Wind being at N. W.

Rid to all the Plantations.

In the Neck – the ground being too wet to plow in the Corn ground, those & the harrow which were there, were obliged to quit and return to the Pease ground – the rest working as usual. About 10 Oclock the Hoe people finished weeding & transplanting Carrots, and all (except Ben who was left to Sow Pease, as the ground could be prepared—Lydia for the purpose of Milking, & Will because he was unable to walk and all 3 to weed the Pease in hills) came to the New ground at the Mansn. House.

At Muddy hole, the Hoes were in the New grd. and the Plows at French's.

At Dogue run all the Plows (the two being returned from Frenchs) were plowing the Corn and the Hoes weeding it.

At Frenchs the same work as yesterday—but a plow was ordered to open furrows for Potatoes & the People to go about Planting of them tomorrow.

At the Ferry—One Plow opening furrows for Potatoes—the others weeding Corn. The Hoe people planting Potatoes after an Interval, occasioned by the continual rains and very wet ground of 16 days.

Began, yesterday, to set another Brick Kiln.

Ben, who was about 59 years old, and Lydia, who was about 39, were both dower slaves (list of Negroes belonging to GW, c.June 1799, NjP: Armstrong Collection).

Wednesday 25th.    Thermometer at 56 in the Morning—62 at Noon And 60 at Night. Morning clear & cool with the wind fresh from No. Wt. at which point it continued all day.

Rid to the Ferry, French's and Dogue run Plantations.

At the Ferry—The Plows, Hoes and harrows were preparing for, and putting in Irish Potatoes. Began, and finished cutting the Rye at this place not so much because it was ripe, as because it was of little worth, and because the grain would get nothing by remaining and the Straw would grow worse. To what cause, unless to its being Sown too early, or too thick, to ascribe the meanness of this Rye, I know not; in the Autumn it looked the most promising of any I had.

At French's—Began to Plant Potatoes. The Plows and harrows were preparing for it as yesterday.

At Dogue Run, The Plows and Hoes were in the Corn. Set two Harrows to preparing for the reception of Potatoes between the Carrots Cabbages &ca.

Set fire to another Brick kiln to day—qty. said to be 35,000.

Mrs. Stuart who went to Maryland on Sunday, returned this Morning accompanied by her brothr. George Calvert. Mr. Tracey came here this evening.

George Calvert (1768–1838) was apparently the second oldest of Benedict Calvert's surviving sons (BOWIE, 102–3).

Thursday 26th. Thermometer at 60 in the Morning—68 at Noon And 68 at Night. Clear all day with the Wind Southerly.

Rid to the Ferry, Frenchs, Dogue Run and Muddy hole Plantation.

At the Ferry—the Hoe People were (as yesterday) planting Potatoes. One harrow preparing for them—a Plow opening for, and covering of them and the other two Plows throwing a furrow to the Corn on each side one.

At French's, The Plows having got through the Corn ground about 10 'Oclock those belonging to Muddy hole returned home. The Work at this place being backward, I put the 6 hands which had been cradling, and all that could be spared from the Hay, to planting Potatoes and Weeding Corn—also to setting it in the Missing parts.

At Dogue run. The Hoes having finished weeding Corn, as was the case also with the Plows, the first were employed in planting Potatoes, two harrows preparing before them. Two plows (when one of them was not opening furrows for, & covering the Potatoes) were engaged in plowing between every other Corn-row (those first planted with Potatoes) and in the following manner—viz.— *to* the Corn, on *each* side, three furrows were thrown, wch. brought the Plows as near to the Potatoes which grew between as could be done with propriety. This plowing was immediately followed by the light triangular harrow which went *four* times between the Corn—i.e. twice between it and the Potatoes—once as near the latter as the tines could run without injuring them & next, as near the Corn as it could go without breaking it down, or touching it. This operation drew loose earth to both kinds of plants. Pulverised the ground—levelled the furrows and gave the whole a very good & garden like appearance. At this place, for an experiment, I caused *five* of the short rows of Potatoes at the No. Wt. corner of the field to be harrowed. This was done by running *one* of the double harrows *twice* upon the Potatoes (which had been just plowed). The *ground* by this means was put in fine order but some of the Potatoes were drawn up by the Roots—many appeared to be loosened and covered with the dirt. Time must shew how far they have been destroyed, or injured by this operation. The rows, especially the fifth; seemed to be as well taken as those adjoining.

At Muddy hole—One plow (which came from Frenchs last Night was employed in checquering at the distance of 3 feet the three feet ridges which had been plowed for Pease and the others were to open these furrows, to see if the time & trouble of hilling could not be saved by it and the Pease equally well planted. The Hoes (as those also from the Neck) were in the New-ground, after they had wed the things in the Vineyard inclosure.

Friday 27th. Thermometer at 62 in the Morning—67 at Noon and 66 at Night. A brisk So. Wt. Wind all day. Morning tolerably clear but the Clouds soon began to gather, & by Noon it was very thick & now & then dropping rain but none fell though it continued very Cloudy.

Mr. Griffith, who came in yesterday afternoon, staying to dinner prevented my riding to day. Colo. Wren (Commr. for receiving the list of Taxable property) came in before dinner & went away with Mr. Griffith.

James Wren (c.1728–1815) of Long View, Fairfax County, was appointed tax commissioner in "Truro district" by the Fairfax County court 22 Jan. 1788 and took the oath of office 19 May 1788 (Fairfax County Order Book for 1783–88, 488, 505, Vi Microfilm). Born in King George County, he moved to Fairfax County by 1756. He was a vestryman of Fairfax Parish by 1766 and became a justice of the Fairfax County court in 1783 (STEADMAN [2], 471–78).

Saturday 28th. Thermometer at 64 in the Morning—[ ] at Noon and 66 at Night. Wind at So. Wt. and Morning very cloudy, but no rain had fallen in the Night; it afterwards cleared and became pleasant.

The Inhabitants of Alexandria having received the News of the ratification of the proposed Constitution by this State, and that of New Hampshire and having determined on public rejoicings, part of which to be in a dinner, to which this family was envited Colo. Humphreys my Nephew G. A. Washington & myself went up to it and returned in the afternoon.

On my way up I visited all my Plantations and

At the Ferry, found that the Planting of Potatoes had been compleated last night—quantity 128 bushls. That the Hoe people were gathering up, & shocking the Rye which had been cut down on Wednesday. And that three plows were throwing, as at Dogue run and in the Neck, 6 furrows to the Corn, 3 on each side; followed by the light harrow and one of the dble. harrows (drawn by the Mules) was going to work where the Potatoes had been Planted in the No. part of the field for the purpose of levelling the covering over them and tearing up the grass where the ground was harder.

At French's—Precisely the same work was going forward as on Thursday with some additional hands from the Meadows yesterday and to day.

At Dogue-run—the Hoe people had finished planting (last evening) Irish Potatoes and were weeding, and thinning the Carrots in Rows between the Corn.— qty. of Potats. 124½ Bls.

At Muddy hole—the Plows were at Work for Pease and the Hoes were in the Mansion house New ground.

In the Neck—The Hoe People except two Men, two boys, and a Woman who were weeding Pease (in hills) were in the Mansion Ho. New ground. The Plows that were not in the Corn ground, and the Harrows, having just finished preparing for, and putting in Pease & Beans in broadcast had returned to, and were preparg. for Buck Wht. All the ground in field No. 8, South of the road leading to the Creek landing was Sown with Pease; to do which it took 21 bushels: Whereof 13¾ bushels were of the large redish crowder kind which was on the East part next to the gate—as far as a line of stakes—the remainder 7¼ bushls. in the West part, were of the common Sort of Pease. On the other, or No. side of the Road, & next the Creek, were 2¾ bushls. of homony beans sown in broadcast.

The New Hampshire Convention ratified the Constitution 21 June by a vote of 57 to 46, and Virginia's Convention did the same four days later with a vote of 89 to 79. As the ninth and tenth states to ratify, they made it legally possible to implement the new Constitution.

Alexandria received news of Virginia's ratification during the previous evening and of New Hampshire's action a short time later. "Foederal to a man," the Alexandrians promptly illuminated their town "in an elegant manner" and communicated "the agreeable intelligence . . . to . . . neighbours, up and down the river, by a well timed discharge of cannons." The dinner held this day was at John Wise's tavern. GW "was met some miles out of town by a party of Gentlemen on horseback, and escorted to the tavern, having been saluted on his way by the light infantry company in a respectful manner. His arrival was announced by a discharge of ten cannon," and after dinner ten toasts were drunk, each punctuated by a cannon shot (GW to Charles Cotesworth Pinckney, 28 June 1788, DLC:GW; GW to Benjamin Lincoln, 29 June 1788, MH; *Pa. Packet,* 11 July 1788).

Sunday 29th.    Thermometer at 62 in the Morning—68 at Noon And 68 at Night—Wind at No. Wt. with flying clouds & cool all day. Towards evening the appearances of rain encreased but none fell.

Monday 30th.    Thermometer at 60 in the Morning—72 at Noon And 72 at Night. Morning clear & cool, the Wind being at No. W. but shifting afterwards to the So. Wt. it grew warm.

Rid to the Ferry, French's and Dogue run Plantations; and to the Brick yard.

At the Ferry—three plows & two harrows were at work as mentioned yesterday & the other people were gathering up & Shocking the Rye which had been cut down.

At French's. The Muddy hole plows came there about 8 Oclock; and the *Hoe* People from D. Run (except the two old women) about 11; in order that my Corn might be hoed and my Potatoes get Planted. And abt. 5 Oclock in the Afternoon 12 hands from the Neck were also added to them. The whole employed in Weeding & setting Corn, & planting Potatoes. Two harrows and one plow were preparing for, and covering the latter—While 4 plows threw a single furrow on each side of the Corn to facilitate the Hoe work.

At Dogue Run—the Hoes, until I ordered them to French's were weeding and thinning Carrots; but seeing no prospect of their accomplishing it today, and the work above mentioned being more essential the change of course was made. Three plows were Plowing Corn as usual. The little harrow following. Moll being Sick the 2d. harrow (newly-fitted up) was stopd.

At Muddy hole—the Plows having checquered the ground intended for Pease went, as before mentioned, to French's. The Hoe people having, abt. 5 Oclock, finished the Mansion House New ground, recd. the Pease sent me by Colo. Spaight & those brought from York river by my Nephew, and went to planting them in the following manner—viz.—the small white Peas picked from the others, which were red, and which hardly exceeded a pint were to be planted in the South Corner of the ground. Then leaving an interval of a Row, the Red Pease of do. were to be planted, & then after another interval of a Row, those from York River were to follow.

Moll, a laborer, may be the cook Molly, age 45, who was at Dogue Run in 1799 (see entry for 18 Feb. 1786; list of Negroes belonging to GW, c.June 1799, NjP: Armstrong Collection).

The peas from Richard Dobbs Spaight came to Mount Vernon "by way of Baltimore." GW sent his thanks to Spaight on 25 May, promising to "cultivate the Pease with care—this year in hills, to accumulate Seed—Next year in broadcast, for a crop" (Nc-Ar).

# [July 1788]

July first.    Thermometer at 68 in the morning—74 at Night and 78 at Night. Wind at So. West in the forenoon but calm afterwards.

Rid to the Ferry, French's, Dogue run & Muddy hole Plantations.

At the first, the Plows and harrows were at work, as usual. The other people having gathered up, and put the Rye in shocks, went this morning to assist in Weeding Corn & Planting Potatoes at French's.

At French's. The hands which were there yesterday, with the addition of those from the Ferry, were employed in Weeding Corn & planting Potatoes. The first was accomplished with the Hoes about 4 Oclock. Eight Cradlers were employed here, who cut down the Rye in No. 6 by 10 Oclock—next the ripest of the Wheat on the Creek side and then went about the Rye by the road in the Meadow.

At Dogue-run, 4 plows and a harrow following, were in the Corn as usual, and

At Muddy hole—the Hoe people, (except three sick) were planting Pease. The Plows at French's as before.

Began to lay the frame for the lower floor of the New Barn—1st. the part for the threshing floor.

Miss Nancy Stuart came here this evening from Mr. L. Washingtons.

Wednesday 2d.    Thermometer at 68 in the Morning—78 at Noon and 76 at Night. A little rain fell in the Night. Morning clear with the wind at No. Wt. but calm afterwards.

Rid to the Ferry, Frenchs, and Dogue run Plantations.

At the Ferry—The Plows were going as usual and the Assembled force, after the business was accomplished at French's, repaired hither and wed out the Carrots and Cabbages.

At Frenchs—the hands which had been brought from the several quarters, finished Planting the Potatoes 136 bushels, all of the red Sort and wed out the Carrots. The Plows also got over the Corn grd. and two from Muddy hole, and one belonging to the plantation with a small harrow began it again on the West side—the harrow to follow the Plows as at the other places.

At Dogue Run four Plows and a harrow were at work as usual and about 10 Oclock got over the first Planted Potatoe Rows East of the Carrots and went back to plow the intermediate ones subsequently planted. Began with 8 Cradles to cut Rye here to day.

At Muddy hole. Finished planting the ground with Pease which had been prepared for them—which took all those sent me by Colonl. Spaight of No. Carolina—and abt. 3 pecks of those brought from York River. Intervals between them as has been mentioned.

Mr. Bushrod Washington, and Mr. Richd. Blackburn came here to dinner; & Mrs, Stuart &ca. went away.

Richard Scott Blackburn was Bushrod Washington's brother-in-law.

Thursday 3d.    Thermometer at 68 in the morning—82 at Noon. And 72 at Night. Clear and quite calm in the morning. In the Afternoon the wind sprung up & blew tolerably fresh from the So. Et. About 4 Oclock a cloud arose to the Westward & approached in the Winds eye & began to rain very moderately, and continued to do so in the same manner for ¾ of an hour, without Wind.

Rid to all the Plantations.

At the Ferry—two Cradlers began to cut Wheat in No. 1 on Stoney hill but it being rather green, in places, it was thought best to let it lay a day before binding. The People therefore went into and wed the Corn which was in the low part of the field—2 Plows and harrows at Work as usual there.

At French's—three plows, and two harrows were at Work—one of the double harrows going before the Plows (over the Newly planted Potatoes) and the small (triangular one following after them). Will (the Overseer) and 4 of his own Women—Delia being taken from Spinng.—Davy from the Mill and Sinah and Lilly from the House were employed in taking up the Wheat and Rye that was cut down on Tuesday last.

At Dogue Run. Two plows and a Harrow were at work in the Corn. All the other hands, with Mima from the House, were engaged in securing the Rye that was cut yesterday. The Dutchman & Simms were cutting the cape Wheat, and other Wheat in the little field by French's—Seven Cradlers were at work cutting Rye in field No. 6 by Colo. Masons—viz.—Isaac, Cooper Tom, Ben, Adam, Jack, Paschal & Abram—which they began pretty early this Morning after finishing that in fd. No. 4.

At Muddy hole—5 Cradlers—viz.—Mink Will, Cowper Jack, Tom Nokes Charles and Gabriel (newly put to it) were cutting Rye. All the other hands with Virgin from the House, were securing it.

In the Neck—Two plows and a harrow were yet preparing part of field No. 8 for Buck Wheat; that part of this field which had been sown with Pease had come up very well. Two plows and the little harrow were in the Corn field—And 1 plow was in the hilled

Pease. The other two were stopped that the drivers might assist in the harvest field. Began with Seven Cradlers—viz.—James, Tom Davis, Boatswain, Sambo, Smith George, Essex & Ned to cut Rye. All the other hands were securing it after them.

The names of the slaves mentioned here illustrate GW's efforts to make full use of his labor force in the fields at harvest time. All four of the slaves at the mill—miller Ben and coopers Davy, Tom, and Jack—were sent to the fields as were the four Home House carpenters: Isaac, James, Sambo, and Tom Nokes. Other Home House slaves who were given harvest duties were the carter Simms, bricklayer Tom Davis, blacksmith George, laborer Boatswain, and four young girls: Sinah, age 16; her sister Mima, age 12; and Lilly and Virgin, both age 13. Adam and Jack were laborers normally assigned to Dogue Run; Mink Will, Charles, and Gabriel were Muddy Hole laborers; and Essex and Ned were River plantation laborers. Will, the overseer at French's plantation, was apparently one of the slaves rented from Penelope Manley French, as were Delia, Paschal, and Abram (see entry for 18 Feb. 1786; deed of Penelope Manley French to GW, 18 Oct. 1786, Fairfax County Deeds, Book Q-1, 392–96, Vi Microfilm).

Friday 4th.    Thermometer at 70 in the Morning—74 at Noon— And 74 at Night. A very heavy Morning with the Wind at South where it continued all day with sparse dripping rain at Intervals till One or two Oclock when the clouds broke; but another arising at dusk it rained hard for about 20 Minutes.

Visited all the Plantations in the Morning, and all except that in the Neck in the afternoon.

At the Ferry—The same Plows as yesterday, were at Work. The other hands were following the Cradlers; binding & putting the Wheat in small shocks.

At French's—The Rye which had been cut down being too wet to bind—the People were Hoeing, till the Afternoon, Corn; Three plows and two harrows were at work as yesterday.

At Dogue Run—The same cause preventing the binding of Rye, the Hoe People went to thinning and weeding of Carrots. Two Plows and a harrow at Work. The Cradlers having cut down the Rye in field No. 6, went, after breakfast to cutting the ripest & thickest set Barley in No. 2—where they were ordered to remain till dinner time and then repair to Muddy hole and cut the forwardest of the Barley there till Night and then to proceed into the Neck to do the like at that place tomorrow.

At Muddy hole. Being interrupted by the dripping Rains, the binders fell a good way behind the cradlers, but when the State of the grain would permit they returnd to this Work. The Cradlers (4, Jack having cut himself) would nearly finish the Rye this Evening.

In the Neck—The Cradlers continued to cut, but the grain being too damp to bind, the People for the greater part of the time were weeding the Pease in hills. Two Plows & a harrow were in the Corn—One in the hilled Pease—and two Plows & a harrow were preparing for & putting in Buck Wheat.

In the Afternoon, Mr. Madison and Doctr. Stuart, with a Son of Mr. Willm. Lee, arrived from Richmond.

James Madison was returning to New York from the Virginia Ratifying Convention in Richmond to resume his congressional duties. Bothered somewhat by ill health recently, he had been urged by GW in a letter dated 23 June 1788 "to take a little respite from business" and to tarry at Mount Vernon for that purpose. "Moderate exercise, and books occasionally, with the mind unbent, will be your best restoratives," GW advised (NjP).

William Ludwell Lee (1775–1803) was the only living son of William and Hannah Philippa Ludwell Lee.

Saturday 5th.  Thermometer at 70 in the Morning—79 at Noon and 74 at Night. Morning pure, and day clear till evening when there were great appearances of Rain but little or none fell here—The body of the cloud passing to the Southward of us.

Doctr. Stuart, after breakfast left this and Colo. Humphreys, who went with Mrs. Stuart to Abingdon on Wednesday returned home.

I remained at home all day with Mr. Madison.

Sunday 6th.  Thermometer at 70 in the Morning—78 at Noon—And 79 at Night—heavy morning with Clouds all day—In the afternoon a slight Shower & about dusk a pretty heavy one for 15 or 20 Minutes.

Colo. Fitzgerald and Doctr. Craik came here to Dinner and after Dinner, Colo. Gilpin and Mr. Hartshorn on business of the Potomack Company called—all of whom went away in the Afternn.

Monday 7th.  Thermometer at 71 in the Morning—82 at Noon And 82 at Night. Morning clear with the wind pretty fresh from South, which continued all day. About Sundown a cloud from the Westward produced a hard rain for 12 or 15 minutes with strong wind. Some thunder and lightning.

After dinner—Mr. Madison, and the Son of Mr. Lee went (in my Carriage) to Alexandria in order to proceed on to New York in the Stage tomorrow.

I remained at home all day.

Tuesday 8th.    Thermometer at 76 in the morning—82 at Noon and 82 at night. Morning clear with the Wind pretty fresh from the Southward which continued all day.

Visited all the Plantations.

At the Ferry—Only one plow at Work (the driver of the other being sick). About Noon sent two more Cradlers to this place—one from Dogue run & the other from Muddy hole to assist in cutting down Wheat that the Oats here which were getting very ripe might be set about.

At French's—The grain that had been cut down, being too wet, from the Rain of yesterday evening, to gather up but that which was standing being drier, and to be bound with safety the Cradlers and their followers were set about the standing Wheat untill that which was down should dry. The ground being wet I stopped the Plows to assist with the grain. The Barley at this place was cut down yesterday.

At Dogue run—the same cause produced the same effect with respect to the management of the standing, & lying down grain; but three Cradlers *only* were at work here (the two belonging to French's having gone home, the Cradle of another being broke, and a fourth having been sent to the Ferry). As soon as the Rye, which was on the ground, was dry enough to take up & bind (which happened by 10 Oclock, it was set about; and the Cradlers went to cutting the remainder of the Barley. Stopped the two plows which were at Work here (the driver of the third being unable to follow it) on acct. of the wetness of the grd. and to assist in the harvest.

At Muddy hole. Till the cut grain was dry enough to take up, the force here was employed in cutting down & securing Wheat. About 10 Oclock the Cradlers as well as others—went to raking & binding Barley.

In the Neck—the Morning was spent in cutting down and securing Wheat—after which in taking up Rye & Barley. But my forward Oats (from Spotswoods seed) in field No. 2, being lodged, and in a ruinous way, I set the Cradlers into these about One 'clock to cut them down. Finished covering the last of the Buck Wheat here this Morning—Four Plows and a harrow at work here.

Wednesday 9th.    Thermometer at 76 in the Morning—75 at Noon and 73 at Night. Wind fresh from the Southward. Soon after day light it began to Rain, accompanied by thunder and the former Continued till about Seven Oclock. About Noon, clouds again arose and at intervals produced Rain thro the whole afternoon but not violent.

Visited all the Plantations. Harvest very much interrupted at them by the frequent Showers.

Stopped two Plows at French's, & sent the drivers of them into the harvest field at this place.

In this & the other fields much time is lost in shifting from one sort of work to another in order to get the grain down and secured.

A Captn. Gregory (a french Gentlemn. who served in the American Navy last War & now in the Service of Rob. Morris Esqr.) came here by Water from Dumfries. Dined, Supped and returned.

Stephen Gregory served as a lieutenant in the Continental navy and was now commanding merchant vessels for Robert Morris. He had come to Dumfries from Richmond on business and had brought with him a letter of introduction to GW from Morris (Morris to GW, 3 July 1788, DLC:GW; HOWARD, 100–102, 108, 209).

Thursday 10th. Thermometer at 72 in the Morning—81 at Noon and 76 at Night. Morning clear, with the Wind fresh from the So. Wt. In the Afternoon, about 4 O'clock a very heavy & severe rain fell for about ten or 15 minutes which set every thing on float.

Visited all the Plantations. The work at each very much impeded by the Rains—the Grain in places broken down by them, and the Wheat being very ripe, and the Oats getting so very fast, makes an unfavourable prospect in the Harvest fields.

Work as usual at all.

Friday 11th. Thermometer at 72 in the Morning—85 at Noon And 82 at Night. Clear Calm in the Morning, with the Wind at So. Wt. afterwards & clear all day.

Visited the Ferry, Frenchs, Dogue run & Muddy hole Plantations and after going to the last returned back by the former on my way home.

The Wet occasioned by the Rain of yesterday afternoon, and the very heavy dew of this morning rendered it impracticable to do any thing to good effect with the grain and the Plowing being very heavy I directed the Plows to be stopped and the drivers to go to the harvest field.

At the Ferry—Finished cuttg, but not binding & shocking all the

Oats and the Cradlers went into the best of the Wheat about One Oclock.

At French's—Having got up all the Wheat that was down, the Rakers went into the Barley that had been cut down since Monday and the Cradlers to cutting down the English Oats.

At Dogue Run—The Cradlers and Rakers (the Barley in the Morning not being fit to Rake up) went into the field No. 4 and by Dinner time would have cut all that part next the House down and got it secured. After which the workers would return to the Barley again.

At Muddy hole—The Cradlers & Rakers in the Morning were employed in the Wheat—after which all hands returned to getting up the Barley.

Began to set another Brick kiln to day.

Saturday 12th.    Thermometer at 78 in the Morning—86 at Noon And 85 at Night. Morning calm & clear—So. Westerly Wind thereafter.

Visited the Plantations at the Ferry, Frenchs, Dogue run and Muddy hole.

At the first—Four Cradlers were cutting Wheat in No. 6 and binding it—but after cutting that which stood tolerably well would go to French's.

At French's—all hands (Plow drivers included) were getting up the Barley.

At Dogue Run. The Cradlers about 10 Oclock would have finished cutting down the Barley & would go into the ripest Oats. All the other hands (except two at the Plows) were securing the Barley.

At Muddy hole. About Eleven Oclock, both Barley & Rye would be in Shock that had been cut down when the five Acres of Barley in the experimental ground would be next cut down.

To a late Breakfast Mr. & Mrs. Robt. Morris, their two Sons & Daughter and Mr. Gouvr. Morris came.

Sunday 13th.    Thermometer at 78 in the Morng.—84 at Noon and 79 at Night. Calm & clear in the Morning, but about two O'clock a cloud arose in the No. Wt. quarter which produced very heavy rain for 15 or 20 Minutes with violent wind, which laid down a great deal of my standing grain—grass—and flax; Blew down much of my fencing; the caps of all the shocks of grain and in many places (where they had been lately made) the Shocks themselves. About dark another gust came which discharged more rain but with less Wind than the former and both together made the ground exceedingly wet.

Doctr. & Mrs. Stuart and the three girls, and Mr. George Lee of Maryland came here to Breakfast and Mr. Lowry with a Mr. Tate and a Mr. Hamilton (the first from England and the other from the West Indies) and Mr. Williams came here to Dinner—after whh. all of them went away except Doctr. Stuart and family.

Monday 14th.     Thermometer at 74 in the morning 79 at Noon and 76 at Night. Calm Morning, with very little wind all day, & that variable.

Rid before Breakfast to the Plantations at the Ferry, Frenchs Dogue run and Muddy hole—at all they were putting up the Fences which were blown down yesterday—after which,

At the Ferry the hands went to cutting & securing Wheat (which, tho' standing, was very damp).

At Frenchs the hands were united with those from the Ferry in the above work. Plows were stopped on acct. of the heaviness of the ground.

At Dogue-run—after putting up the Fencing, the hands with the Cradlers (which had been cutting Oats till then) went into field No. 6 to cut the ripest and strongest Wheat. No plowing here to day.

At Muddy hole—after rectifying the Fencing all hands went to cutting and securing Wheat in field No. 2.

Tuesday 15th.     Thermometer at 74 in the Morning—80 at Noon and 78 at Night. Cloudy Morning with droppings of Rain but more clear afterwards with variable winds.

Early in the Morning Mrs. Stuart and family left this and about 11 Oclock Mrs. Washington & myself accompanied Mr. Mrs. Morris &ca. as far as Alexandria on their return to Philadelphia. We all dined (in a large Company) at Mr. Willm. Hunters; after which Mr. Morris & his family proceeded and Mrs. Washington, Colo. Humphreys & myself retd.

Wednesday 16th.     Thermometer at 74 in the Morning—80 at Noon and 78 at Night. The Morning was cloudy, a good deal of Rain having fallen about day break. Wind at East & varying between that and South. Cloudy all day.

Visited all the Plantations—Plows stopped at all by the wet, & heaviness of the ground except in the Neck. Harvest impeded by the former—but I directed the grain at all to be cut down (tho' it could not be bound up in the Morning) as it had got quite ripe and the Wheat in many places broke down.

Thursday 17th.    Thermometer at 74 in the morning—83 at Noon And 83 at Night. Close morning with the Wind at South, but not much of it at any time of the day.

Rid to the Plantations at the Ferry, Frenchs, Dogue run & Muddy hole.

At the first, finished getting up & shocking all the Oats—after which the hands (except the Ferry men, and the drivers of a Plow & harrow which were in the Corn) went to French's.

At French's—The Cradlers having Cut all the grain at that place were gone (Six of them) to cutting Oats at Dogue run. The other people were re-shocking Wheat & binding and Shocking Oats. No plows at Work here to day.

At Dogue run—Four Cradlers, as usual, were cutting Wheat in field No. 6 and the hands of the place securing it after them. Six Cradlers from French's were cutting Oats in No. 2.

At Muddy hole—four Cradlers were cutting Wheat in field No. 4 having finished what was in No. 1 by breakfast this morning. Rakg. & binding at this place is up with the cutters.

Agreed with [    ] to sink a well at my Barn for the doing, and walling of which, wch. is to be 3 feet in the clear I am to give him 4/6 pr. foot; & and if any uncommon impediments should interpose (such as rocks, gravel that cannot well be penetrated, or quicksands that cannot be kept up) I am to make a further reasonable allowance. He is to do all the labouring and walling work, and is to obtain 6, or 5½ ft. water and when water is come to, and the Kirb [curb] about to be sunk he is to attend in Person to the execution.

In the Afternoon Mr. John Bassett—his wife, Miss Brown his Wife's sister and Patcy Dandridge came.

John Sullivan received £3 9d. on 1 Aug. for "diging & walling" the well at GW's new barn (LEDGER B, 270).

Elizabeth Carter Browne Bassett had two sisters: Judith Carter Browne (1773–1830), who later married GW's nephew Robert Lewis (1769–1829), and Mary Burnet Browne, who married Herbert Claiborne of King William County. PATCY DANDRIDGE: probably Martha Washington Dandridge, daughter of Mrs. Washington's brother Bartholomew Dandridge. She was a cousin of John Bassett (CARY [2], 36).

Friday 18th.    Thermometer at 74 in the Morning—86 at Noon And 77 at Night. Morning clear with the Wind Southerly, and fresh all day. About 2 oclock a cloud from the Westwd. produced for 10 or 15 minutes a good deal of rain and wind from No. Wt. which cooled the Air very much.

Visited all the Plantations.

At the Ferry—one plow and harrow were at work, and the other people in the Morning weeding Potatoes. Afterwards till the Rain, assisting at French's to bind & shock Oats. The whole then, went into their respective Corn fields.

At Frenchs—One plow and harrow were at Work. The other people with the assistance, and in the manner above were securing of Oats.

At Dogue run—The Cradlers would, about 11 Oclock, have finished cutting down the Wheat in fd. No. 6, & would proceed to cut down what was left standing in No. 4. The other Cradlers, by Night, would have finished cutting down the Oats, & were to unite. The hands of the Plantation were binding & shocking Wheat (a good way in the rear of the Cradlers) in No. 6. Except 2 plows at work.

At Muddy hole—all hands were in No. 4 Cutting & securing Wheat and had their work all up; that is, the binding & shocking even with the cutters.

In the Neck—It was the same and about the half of field No. 7 was secured. Five plows and a harrow was in the Corn field at work.

Saturday 19th.     Thermometer at at 66 in the Morning—75 at Noon And 74 at Night. Clear and tolerably pleasant all day. Wind at No. Wt. in the Morning but not much of it then, or at any other time of the day.

Visited all the Plantations.

In the Neck—5 Plows and a Harrow were at Work in the Corn field. All the other hands were in the Wheat in No. 7.

At Muddy hole the two setts of Cradlers which had finished cutting down the grain last Night at Dogue run had come to this place and having finished Cutting the Wheat before breakfast were in the Oats which they would have cut down about or a little after dinner and wd. join the rakers in getting up the Wheat.

At Dogue run—All hands, except the Cradlers and two people at the Plow were getting up the Wht. that had been cut down. And after breakfast, Frenchs & the Ferry People came here to get up the Oats.

At French's—A Plow and Harrow were at Work—the other hands (as above) after getting their Oats in to Shock had gone to Dogue run.

At the Ferry. The hands from this place had also gone to the same place. Two plows and a harrow were at Work here.

Sunday 20th.    Thermometer at 69 in the Morning—75 at Noon and 72 at Night. Clear and calm in the forepart of the day—some clouds and an Easterly wind afterwards.

Mr. & Mrs. Herbert, Mr. & Miss Muir, Doctr. Brown & his wife and Mrs. Conway came here to dinner and returned in the Afternoon.

Miss Muir was probably John Muir's only sister, Elizabeth (KING [4], 51).

Monday 21st.    Thermometer at 68 in the Morning—74 at Noon And 70 at Night. Cloudy with the Wind at East in the Morning at which it continued varying Northerly all day.

Visited all the Plantations.

At the Ferry—two Plows and a harrow were at Work in the Corn. The other hands were all at Dogue run in the Harvest field.

At French's—Three plows and a harrow were in the Corn. All the other people were at Dogue run.

At Dogue Run. Two plows and a harrow were in the Corn—the other hands, with those mentioned above from the Ferry & Frenchs, were all in the Harvest field. About Noon, all the Wheat was got into Shocks and by Night the Oats were also secured in like manner.

At Muddy hole—The Rakers were employed in getting up the Oats—all the Cradlers went into the Neck.

In the Neck—Five plows and a harrow were in the Corn—the 1st. of which would finish Plowing the alternate rows about 4 Oclock, and would next go into the Pumpkins. The Cradlers from Muddy hole would, about dinner time, finish cutting the Wheat in the Orchard Inclosure. The others wd. not be able to compleat the cuttg. of Field No. 7.

Two men, sent by [      ] began about 10 Oclock to sink a Well at my New Barn.

Mr. & Mrs. Porter and a Mr. Ingraham, and Young Doctr. Craik and his Sisters Mrs. West & Nancy Craik came here to Dinner & returned afterwards.

The two well diggers were apparently sent by John Sullivan.

This Mr. Ingraham may be Duncan Ingraham, Jr., of Philadelphia, who was in the Dutch trade. He was probably related to Thomas Porter's partner, Nathaniel Ingraham, who was on a voyage to Amsterdam at this time (*Pa. Packet,* 7 Nov. 1788; Fairfax County Order Book for 1789-91, 144, Vi Microfilm; see also entry for 28 Feb. 1788).

Tuesday 22d.   Thermometer at 62 in the Morng.—76 at Noon, and 72 at Night. Morning clear with the Wind at No. East—continued clear all day.

Visited all the Plantations.

At the Ferry. Two plows and a harrow were at work in the Corn grd. as *were* and *had* been the two Ferrymen. The other people were in the Harvest at Muddy hole.

At French's—Three plows and a Harrow were in the Corn—the rest of the hands were at Muddy hole.

At Dogue run—Two plows and a harrow were in the Corn field and the two old Women were weeding Pumpkins. The other people were at Muddy hole.

At Muddy hole—All hands were binding and securing Oats which was accomplished about dinner after which all hands (except the Women who had young Children) went into the Neck.

In the Neck—the Oats were cut down about Noon, & the last of the Wheat about five Oclock, when the Cradlers assisted in binding and securing the grain. One harrow in the Corn and the five Plows finished Weeding the Pumpkins after dinner.

Got Water which seemed to be good, and in tolerable plenty in about ten feet digging at my New Barn.

Mr. and Mrs. Fendall came here in the afternoon.

Wednesday 23d.   Thermometer at 70 in the Morning—74 at Noon and 74 at Night. Morning heavy with the Wind at No. East Where it continued fresh all day with mists in the forenoon and a smart shower about 2 'Oclock.

Visited all the Plantatns.

At the Ferry—Two plows and a harrow were at Work. The Plows began on the So. part of the field and were employed in throwing a furrow to both the Corn & Potatoes. The two ferry men were employed in weeding and hilling the former. The harrow in levelling the former plowings, and taring up the grass. The other hands were in the Neck closing the harvest at that place.

At French's—The Plows having got through the Corn, the two belonging to Muddy hole were sent home. The other was employed in throwing a furrow to the first Pla[n]ted Potatoes. The Harrow was engaged as usual. The other People were in the Neck, except a woman with a young Child who was weeding Pumpkins.

At Dogue run—Two plows and a Harrow were in the Corn. The two old Women, & two young ones with Children, were weeding Pumpkins. The rest were in the Neck.

At Muddy hole—The two women with young children, and the

two Plow Women who had just returned from Frenchs were employed in Weeding Pumpkins. the other hands were in the Neck.

In the Neck—Five Plows and a harrow were in the Corn. The first, beginning on the West side, were going through every other row—throwing one furrow to both Corn and Potatoes &ca. The other hands were binding & shocking the last of the Wheat; which finishing about the hour of One, they, with those from the other plantations went, after the rain ceased to pulling flax.

The Men who were *digging* the well compleated *their* work this afternoon and returned to Alexandria—having, as they say, obtained 6½ feet of what *appears* to be good & constant water.

Thursday 24th.    Thermometer at 70 in the Morning—71 at Noon and 74 at Night—A very high No. Et. Wind all Night, which, this morning, being accompanied with Rain, became a hurricane—driving the Miniature Ship Federalist from her Moorings, and sinking her—blowing down some trees in the groves & about the houses—loosning the roots, & forcing many others to yield and dismantling most, in a greater or lesser degree of their Bows, & doing other and great mischief to the grain, grass &ca. & not a little to my Mill race. In a word it was violent and severe—more so than has happened for many years. About Noon the Wind suddenly shifted from No. Et. to So. Wt. and blew the remaining part of the day as violently from that quarter. The tide about this time rose near or quite 4 feet higher than it was ever known to do driving Boats &ca. into fields were no tide had ever been heard of before—And must it is to be apprehended have done infinite damage on their Wharves at Alexandria—Norfolk—Baltimore &ca.

At home all day.

The sudden shift in wind direction indicated the passing of the eye of the storm. GW's apprehension about the damage done elsewhere was well founded. This hurricane ravaged Bermuda on 19 July, and after sinking many vessels on the North Carolina coast, it struck Norfolk about 5:00 P.M. on 23 July. There, according to a newspaper account, the storm "continued for 9 hours—wind at start from NE—at 0030 [hours] it suddenly shifted to S and blew a perfect hurricane—tearing up large trees by the roots, removing houses, throwing down chimneys, fences, etc., and laying the greatest part of the corn level. . . . Only two ships in Hampton Roads survived the gale" (*Phila. Independent Gaz.,* 8 Aug. 1788, quoted in LUDLUM [2], 30–31). At Alexandria the storm was reported to have "brought in the highest tide that was ever known in this river, and the damage done to Tobacco, Sugar, Salt, &c. in the Warehouses in this town, is computed at five thousand pounds. Several inhabitants on the wharves were obliged to retire to their chambers, and some were taken out of their houses in boats. . . . The damage in the country to the wheat, growing tobacco, Indian-corn, &c. is beyond description; and many planters and farmers, who flattered themselves with much greater crops than have been known for many years past, had their hopes blasted by the violence of the storm" (*Md. Journal,* 5 Aug. 1788). The center of the hurricane skirted Annapolis, causing little or no damage despite an unprecedented high tide (*Md. Gaz.,* 31 July 1788). However, at Baltimore this evening "The Wind . . . blew with unabated Fury, (accompanied with heavy Rain) for upwards of Twelve Hours, which occasioned a most dreadful Inundation of the Sea, that deluged all the Wharves, Stores, and low Grounds near the Bason and at Fell's Point, producing a Scene of Devastation and Horror not to be described. . . . Immense Quantities of Sugar, Rice, Salt, Dry Goods, and other valuable Merchandise, were entirely ruined" (*Md. Journal,* 25 July 1788). North of Baltimore the storm apparently diminished rapidly, possibly exhausting itself in the Appalachian Mountains to the northwest (LUDLUM [2], 30–31).

**Friday 25th.** Thermometer at 72 in the Morng.–84 at Noon and 80 at Night. Fore part of the day clear–with a very warm sun –the remaining heavy and frequent showers–Wind at S.W.

Rid to all the Plantatns. Found the ground too wet either to plow among Corn, or set it up–It having been beat flat to the ground and a great deal of it broke short of.

At the Ferry–one cradler was cutting the thin wheat that remained. The other hands unable to do any thing in their Corn ground were sent to Frenchs.

At Frenchs–One Cradler was cutting the Oats which had been left. The other hands went abt. Wheat which was overflowed with the tide and then with the Ferry hands went to Dogue Run.

At Dogue-run all hands, with those of Muddy hole *all* day and The ferry & Frenchs part of the day were pulling flax except some of the men who were sent to repair the breaches in the Mill race.

At Muddy hole–the three plows were plowing in Buck Wheat & those from Dogue run were ordered to join them tomorrow as they could not work in their own Corn ground.

In the Neck–all the River Fence being carried away, All hands (plow people as well as the rest) were collecting rails to repair it, to keep the Stock out of the fields of grain except One or two who were righting some Shocks of grain and Setting up Flax which had been pulled and blown all abt.

**Saturday 26th.** Thermometer at 72 in the Morning–[      ] at Noon and [      ] at Night. More or less cloudy all day, with the Wind Southerly.

Remained at home.

**Sunday 27.** Thermometer at 70 in the Morning–75 at Noon and 76 at Night–More or less cloudy with a heavy Shower of Rain about 3 oclock. Wind Southerly.

Whilst we were at Dinner Judge Harrison of Maryland came in and stayed all Night.

Monday 28.    Thermometer at 74 in the Morng.—80 at Noon and 79 at Night. Morning very heavy with the Wind Southerly—About 7 Oclock it began to rain and continued to do so for half an hour, fast; after which through the day there were light showers and close funky weather.

Rid to the Plantations at the Ferry, Frenchs, Dogue Run & Muddy hole.

At the first—three plows were plowing in Buck Wheat—the other hands were repairing the fence which had been washed away by the tide.

At French's—all hands were at Dogue Run pulling flax. Ordered two of the Plows belonging to this place (the 3d. being disabled) to repair tomorrow the Ferry to plow in Buck Wheat.

At Dogue run—Four plows were at Work at Muddy hole and some hands on the Mill race. All the rest with those from Frenchs were pulling flax—the ground at every place being too wet to plow or Hoe in the Corn fields. The flax at this place as well as in the Neck, has been greatly injured by the continual rains which has beat a great deal of it to the ground which has rotted and by the immense growth of Weeds from which it was impracticable to seperate it unless each plant, in a manner was individually pulled.

At Muddy hole—The three plows belonging to the Plantation and the four from Dogue run, were plowing in Buck Wheat. The other hds. were weeding a yard for the reception of grain and imprudently opening the shocks till they were ordered to do them up again.

The continual rains—the heat and closeness of the Weather conspiring was sprouting all the outside sheaves of the Shocks of every kind of grain that had been examined except Rye—and without the speedy interposition of dry weather—sun—and Wind must soon ruin it.

Tuesday 29th.    Thermometer at 74 in the morning—81 at Noon and 79 at Night. Little or no wind—Morning though somewhat clear about sun rise soon became very thick foggy and heavy—after which the Wind came out—first at No. Wt. and then shifted to the No. Et. at which it continued.

Visited all the Plantations.

At the Ferry—Five plows were turning in Buck Wheat two of

Francis Adrian Van der Kemp. (Unitarian Church of Barneveld, New York)

them from Frenchs. The other hands were weeding their Wheat yard.

At French's—Except the two Plows which were at the Ferry, all were pulling flax at Dogue run.

At Dogue run—Four Plows were at work at Muddy hole. All the rest were pulling flax.

At Muddy hole—Seven plows were turning in Buck Wheat. The other People were weeding a yard for treading Wheat.

In the Neck—Eight Plows were turning in Buck Wheat. The rest of the hands, except some who were preparing the yard for the reception of grain and getting Corn Stalks to bottom the Stacks with Were weeding Pease.

Sowed Turnips yesterday in a square below the Stables—Norfolk Globe.

And began yesterday to cut Hay in the Neck. Finished this evening, except such parts of the Meadows as were under Water.

A Mr. Vender Kemp—a Dutch Gentn. who had suffered by the troubles in Holland and who was introduced to me by the Marquis de la Fayette came here to Dinner.

Francis Adrian Van der Kemp (1752–1829), Dutch soldier, scholar, and Mennonite minister, had been imprisoned in his homeland during a part of the previous year for revolutionary activities connected with the Patriot party, a group of Dutch liberals who wished to implement the republican ideals of the American Revolution in their country. Upon being freed in December, Van der Kemp found himself much reduced in fortune and faced with further political repression in the Netherlands. For some time he had thought of going to America to become a farmer, and in Mar. 1788 he sailed with his wife and children for New York. To ease his way Dutch friends obtained for him several letters of introduction to prominent Americans, including a letter from Lafayette to GW (6 Mar. 1788, PEL). Soon after his arrival in New York on 4 May, Van der Kemp dispatched the letters to their intended recipients (Van der Kemp to GW, 15 May 1788, DLC:GW). GW's reply of 28 May contained a cordial invitation to visit Mount Vernon when convenient, an invitation that Van der Kemp could not decline, having a great desire "to know that man, to whom america so much was indebted for her liberty" (Van der Kemp to GW, 16 July 1788, DLC:GW; GW to Van der Kemp, 28 May 1788, PHi: Autograph Letters of the Presidents).

Van der Kemp found Mount Vernon, as did many visitors, to be a place "where simplicity, order, unadorned grandeur, and dignity, had taken up their abode," although he detected in his host "somewhat of a repulsive coldness . . . under a courteous demeanour" (VAN DER KEMP, 115–16; JACKSON [2], 64–67, 142–43). Van der Kemp became an American citizen in 1789 and lived the remainder of his life in upstate New York farming and pursuing his scholarly interests.

Wednesday 30th. Thermometer at 74 in the Morng.—78 at Noon and 76 at Night. A heavy morning with sprinklings of Rain; one of which, about 10 oclock, was a pretty heavy shower about Dogue run. Afternoon less cloudy with the wind brisk from the No. Et. & East. A red light (supposed to be the Aurora Borealis) in the North.

Rid to the Ferry, French's and Muddy hole Plantations. At the Ferry—five Plows were at wk. The other hands were setting up Corn.

At Frenchs—Binding and shocking the Oats which were on the ground and the little Wheat in No. 2—The hands from D. Run assistg.

At Muddy hole. Seven plows were at Work; which where the Buck Wheat was Rank and stood thick on the ground turned it in very indifferently—nor no contrivance I could make seemed to have any good effect. The other hands after pulling the flax, weeded some of the foulest of the Pease in order to come into the New grd. Corn tomorrow.

The Man (Sullivan) who was to Wall up my Well, came to day to do it. Mr. Vender Kemp returned.

Thursday 31st. Thermometer at 68 in the Morning—74 at Noon and 72 at Night. Wind still at No. Et. but not hard at any time of the day—tolerably clear.

Rid to all the Plantations.

At the Ferry—five Plows were at Work as yesterday. The other hands were hilling or hoeing Corn, though the ground was very heavy and wet.

At French's—The People with those from Dogue Run were pulling flax and cutting a few latter Oats.

At Muddy hole—Seven Plows (including those from D. Run) were at work. The other hands (except 5 in the Corn grd. at the Mansn. Ho. were employed in gettg. in & stacking Barley.

In the Neck—9 Plows were turning in B. Wheat. The other hands were weeding Pease, & getting in & stackg. Oats.

Mrs. Dulany & her daughter, and Doctr. Craik & Mr. B. Grymes dined here all of whom went away afterwards.

Elizabeth French Dulany and her husband, Benjamin Tasker Dulany, had six daughters and six sons. The daughters were Elizabeth French, Julia, Rebecca, Ann Bladen, Louisa, and Henrietta Maria Dulany.

# August 1788

1st.    Thermometer at 68 in the Morning—75 at Noon—and 74 at Night—Not much wind, and that at So. Et.—Morng. clouded but tolerably clear afterwards.

Rid to the Plantations at the Ferry, Frenchs, Dogue Run and Muddy hole.

At the Ferry—the same plows as yesterday were at work in the B. Wheat. The other hands, except the Carter, who was drawing rails to the Wheat yard, were Hoeing Corn.

At French's after getting up the Oats &ca. the People began to clean their Wheat yard.

At Dogue run—The same work was going forward together with the getting in Wheat from field No. 4. Four plows were at Muddy Ho.

At Muddy hole—The Cart, with proper assistance, was drawing in Wheat. The other hands were examining the Shocks of Oats &ca.

A Mr. Obannon—D. Surveyer in the Western Country—came here with some executed Land warrants—dined & proceeded on to Richmond afterwards.

John O'Bannon (d. 1813), a deputy surveyor of the Virginia Military Reserve lands northwest of the Ohio River, had surveyed for GW three tracts near present-day Cincinnati, Ohio, during the previous winter and spring. Totaling 3,051 acres, these tracts were surveyed on two military warrants purchased by GW: one for 3,000 acres issued to John Rootes for service in the

French and Indian War and the other for 100 acres issued to Thomas Cope for service in the War of Independence. O'Bannon apparently deposited GW's warrants and surveys in the Virginia Land Office in Richmond, and on 1 Dec. 1790 GW received a patent for the three tracts from the state. However, an act of Congress passed 10 Aug. 1790 stipulated that surveys for Virginia military lands northwest of the Ohio must be recorded with the secretary of state and federal patents issued (1 STAT. 182–84). This was not done for GW's three tracts during his lifetime, and although GW's heirs later attempted to make good his titles, they were unable to do so (Virginia Land Grants, Book 23, 420–23, and Virginia Surveys, Book 23, 846–48, Vi Microfilm; RANDALL, 303–18.

O'Bannon, a resident and militia officer of Fauquier County during the American Revolution, moved about 1784 to Kentucky, where he eventually became a prominent citizen of Woodford County (EVANS [2], 319–27). George Augustine Washington today paid O'Bannon £4 3s. for the surveys (LEDGER B, 270).

Saturday 2d.    Thermometer at 68 in the Morning 77 at Noon and 73 at Night. Wind Southerly all day and tolerably clear.

Visited all the Plantations. At the Ferry—Six plows were turning in B. Wheat—three of them from Frenchs. Tried the Patent Plow sent me by Major Snowden, whh. run easy and did good work. Gathered up the thin wheat wch. had been cut down some days ago.

At Frenchs—The hands were still preparing the Wheat yard, and the Cart drawing Rails to enclose it.

At Dogue run—five plows were at work at Muddy hole. The other hands and the Cart were getting in and stacking Wheat from field No. 4.

At Muddy hole—Eight plows were turning in B. Wheat. The other hands were getting in and stacking Wheat from field No. 2 and drying Barley shocks in the same field.

In the Neck—Eight Plows were turning in B. Wheat—One harrow preparing for Turnips between Corn Rows (left for the purpose, 13 in number, and which were sown with the Green Turps.) in No. 6. The rest of the hands, and two Carts, were getting in and stacking both wheat & Bar[le]y.

Mr. John Bassett & Wife and child, and Miss Brown, went away very early this Morning.

GW ordered the plow from Thomas Snowden 9 May 1787 when he stopped at Snowden's place in Maryland on his way to Philadelphia (GW to George Augustine Washington, 27 May 1787, CSmH). He was so pleased with this type of plow that he decided to employ it generally at Mount Vernon. On 3 Oct. 1788 he wrote Snowden requesting another plow exactly like the first one, as perfectly made as possible in both iron and wood, to serve as a model for others to be made in Mount Vernon's workshop. He also asked for "two dozen iron shears . . . of the proper sort and size to be manufactured with as little labour as may be into Ploughs" (DLC:GW).

The Bassett's first child, Virginia Bassett, was born 2 Sept. 1787.

Sunday 3d.    Thermometer at 70 in the Morng.—81 at Noon and 79 at Night. Wind South; and raining moderately from about five Oclock till nearly 7 when it ceased, and cleared—the Wd. remaining in the same place and continuing warm.

At home all day.

Monday 4th.    Thermometer at 70 in the Morning—81 at Noon and 79 at Night. Very little Wind and warm—towards the afternoon Sultry.

Went up to alexandria to a meeting of the Potomack Company; the business of which was finished about Sun down—but matters which came more properly before the Directors obliged me to stay in Town all Night.

Dined at Wise's and lodged at Colo. Fitzgeralds.

GW today delivered the annual report of the company's directors to the general members. "The unusual height of the Waters this Spring & Summer," he told them, "have greatly retarded our Operations on the River but should the Weather become more favorable we have reason to believe that a partial though not a perfect Navigation may be effected this fall & winter from Fort Cumberland to the Great Falls—at which place the Canal is nearly completed. Our principal force has been applied to the Shenandoah & Seneca Falls, which considering the number of hands & the unfavorable Season are in as great forwardness as we could expect" (BACON-FOSTER, 83–84).

Tuesday 5th.    Thermometer at 72 in the Morning—82 at Noon and 79 at Night. Warm with but little wind.

The business before the Board of Directors detaining till near two Oclock (I dined at Colo. Fitzgeralds) and returned home in the Afternn.

Called by the Plantation at Muddy hole. Found the Cart and some hands getting in the grain to the Barn and yard and others chopping down weeds in the Corn at the Mansion house.

At Mount Vernon this evening GW found his nephew Lawrence Augustine Washington, who had run away from Samuel Hanson's home apparently with the aid of his brother George Steptoe Washington. Lawrence complained of ill treatment by Hanson and "offered to shew . . . some bruises he had received." GW severely reprimanded the boy for running away, threatened to punish him with his own hands, and sent him back to Hanson the next day after obtaining a promise "that there should be no cause of complaint against him for the future" (GW to Samuel Hanson of Samuel, 6 Aug. 1788, GW to George Steptoe Washington, 6 Aug. 1788, and Hanson to GW, 7 Aug. 1788, DLC:GW).

Wednesday 6th. Thermometer at 70 in the Morning—76 at Noon—and 74 at Night. Very warm with the Wind Southerly & great appearances of Showers all the forenoon, but no rain fell here.

Rid to the Plantations at the Ferry, French's, Dogue run & Muddy hole.

At the first—The Rows between the Corn, which had been planted with Cabbages and had perished, had been plowed and harrowed and were sowing with the Green (Norfolk) Turnip. One Plow was at Work before the Hoes in the Corn ground, & the other two, with the three belonging to Frenchs, had gone to that Place about 10 Oclock to plow in the Buck Wheat, weeds, &ca. in field No. 5 for Wheat—where 4 plows frm. Dogue run—& 3 from Muddy hole had gone for the same purpose yesterday. The Hoes except Cupid were hilling & Weeding Corn.

At Frenchs—all hands—with the Ferry Cart, & the Waggon from the mansn. Ho. were getting in the Wheat & Rye from field No. 6.

At Dogue Run, One plow was preparing the Intervals which was designed for Turnips between the Corn for sowing—Six hands were weeding & hilling Corn—and the others with the Cart were getting in and stacking the Wheat & Rye of No. 4.

At Muddy hole—Six hands were chopping down the Weeds in the Corn at M. Ho. The others were getting in and Stacking the Barley.

Cupid, a dower slave, was one of Ferry plantation's laborers (see entry for 18 Feb. 1786).

Thursday 7th. Thermometer at 74 in the Morning—79 at Noon and 76 at Night. Clear with the Wind at No. West and tolerably pleasant.

Visited all the Plantations. In the Neck—Nine hands were weeding & hilling Corn, one plow going before them to throw a furrow on each side. The rest with the Waggon & two Carts were getting (Spotswood's) Oats—The Barley and wht. in the Orchard having been brot. in and stacked. Six plows were turning in Buck Wheat.

At all the other Plantations the Work was precisely the same as yesterday.

Friday 8th. Thermometer at 66 in the Morning 69 at Noon and 70 at Night—Morning clear & rather cool—with appearances of dry weather—Wind North. About one Oclock however it overcast

A pit for breeding mules, illustrated in Thomas Hale's *Compleat Body of Husbandry,* London, 1758. (Mount Vernon Ladies' Association of the Union)

and betwn. 3 & 4 began a *very* slow rain wch. increased in the Night and a good deal fell.

Visited the Plantations at the Ferry, French's D. Run & Muddy Ho.

At French's — they would have finished, about two 'Oclock, getting in and stacking all the grain in No. 6; and would proceed to fencg. the yard, & securing the Inclosure — after which if there was time for it they would begin to get in and stack the Barley & Oats in No. 2. Plows in No. 5.

At the Ferry — One Plow, and the Hoe people were weeding and Hilling of Corn.

At Dogue Run — the Cart and necessary attendance for that, and Stacking, were employed about the Rye (Six besides the Overseer). The rest Seven, with two plows were in the Corn.

At Muddy hole. Having finished getting in, and stacking the Barley all hands about 1 Oclock came to the Corn grd. at the Mansn. Ho. but the Cart was ordered tomorrow to assist in getting in the Rye at D. Run.

Brought the Jenny with the Jack Colt from Muddy hole, and turned them, with the other Maltese Jenny — the two yearling Mule Colts and the 4 Sorrel Colts, into the Clover Paddock. The other Mares and Colts which were in No. 1 at Muddy hole were carried to No. 1 at Dogue Run for the benefit of the pasture.

Mr. Geo. Digges & a Dr. Kelty came to Dinr. & retd.

William Kilty (1757–1821) of Prince George's County, Md., was born in London, attended school in France as a youth, and before the War of Independence moved with his parents to Annapolis, where he studied medicine under a local physician. He became a surgeon's mate in the Maryland Continental line in 1778 and two years later was promoted to surgeon. Captured at the Battle of Camden 16 Aug. 1780, he was later paroled and then returned to Annapolis, where he began studying law. He served as chief judge of the District of Columbia 1801–6 and as chancellor of the state of Maryland 1806–21 (KOOPMAN, 103–4).

Saturday 9th.   Thermometer at 62 in the Morning–72 at Noon and 70 at Night. Raining about day break–very heavy afterwards with the Wind at No. East till towards noon, when it cleared.

Visited all the Plantations. At the Ferry. One Plow and the Hoes were in the Corn.

At French's–The Plows would have finished turning in the Buck Wheat & Weeds in the East part of No. 5. The other hands were repairing the fences around fields 1 and 6.

At Dogue run–the rain which fell in the Night prevented the removal of grain till Noon, when the Cart &ca. continued getting in Rye. The other hands, were in the Corn as yesterday.

At Muddy hole all hands were threshing Rye.

In the Neck–The Carts were stopped by the wet. The Plows 8 of them were turning in B. Wht. and the other People were weeding Pease which were most abominably foul.

Mrs. Jenifer who came here yesterday to dinner returned home this afternoon.

Colo. Humphreys went to Abingdon and George Town.

Sunday 10th.   Thermometer at 60 in the Morning–67 at Noon and 67 at Night. The Wind was a little to the Eastward of No.– and as much to the Westward of it at Noon. The Morning lowered, but the weather brightned afterwards and looked more settled.

Monday 11th.   Thermometer at 60 in the morning–76 at Noon and 66 at Night. Clear all day with the wind at North.

Visited all the Plantatns. At the Ferry–3 plows were at wk. in the Corn, and all the Hoes (except Cupid, who was stacking Barley at French's) were weeding and Hilling of Corn.

At French's–The Waggon and two Carts began to draw in Barley for Stacking–the hands engaged in loading, unloading, and Stacking it. 3 plows were at work in the Corn–turning two furrows to that, and to the Potatoes. Ordered the Flax that was set together (but not properly shocked) to be opened, thoroughly dried and put into a Stack.

At Dogue run—five plows were at Work, throwing (as at Frenchs) two furrows to the Corn and two to the Potatoes. The other hands (except those about the Stock) were hilling Corn—which by this time was so grassy as in a manner to be lost, and the wk. not practicable to do, as it shd. be with either plows or Hoes. Overlooked the Stock at this place. Drew two Steers, & 3 old Cows out of the Cattle to be sent to a fresh Pasture at Frenchs for feeding. Withdrew the Lambs 49 in number from the other sheep for the purpose of weening them and placed them in the upper meadow. Also sorted the Sheep and set apart 3 old ewes and 25 old weathers for my own killing and for Market—The rest—viz. [     ] ewes and [     ] weathers for breeding & for Store sheep. Ordered the Horse Chevalier and a poor Mare to be turned into No. 1 to get fat for selling.

At Muddy hole. The hand were all at the Mn. Ho. Corn ground. Seperated 3 lambs & 5 Weathers from the rest of the Sheep, leaving [     ] yearling sheep for breeding. Drew a work Steer from the Cattle, to be sent to the feeding Pasture at Frenchs —also two young Mares to be broke in the Room of Jocky & Diamond (two old wk. Horses) which are to be sent to the Pasture at Frenchs to be fatted. Directed the Mare called Simpsons to the Ferry, to be broke in lieu of the bay Mare wch. came last year from the Neck and wch. is allotted for a breeder (not to work) –& a brown Mare to the Past[ur]e a[t] F[renc]hs.

In the Neck—Eight Plows were turning in Buck Wheat—one going over the Corn turning two furrows to it. The other hands, except those attending the Carts & stacking were brushing over the Pease which in a very rough and imperfect manner would be accomplished to day. Overlooked the Stock here, and seperated 13 (besides 2 Work Steers which will follow as soon as they can be spared) to go to the feeding Pasture at French's viz.—5 Steers & 9 cows. Seperated the Lambs 45 in number from the Ewes, & put them in Field No. 2. Drew 12 old weathers and 38 old ewes for killing and Marked and put them in Field No. 7. The residue— viz. 29 weathers & 79 ewes were turned in the Common Pasture. Ordered a Mare called Davy's and her Colt to Frenchs to recruit.

In the Evening Colo. Humphreys returned—accompanied by Mr. Geo. Calvert.

Tuesday 12th.    Thermometer at 59 in the Morning—[     ] at Noon and 68 at Night. Wind Northerly all day but not much of it.
    The whole family, accompanied by Colo. Humphreys and Mr.

Calvert crossed the River—dined with Mr. Geo. Digges—& returned in the Evening.

Wednesday 13th. Thermometer at 64 in the Morning—70 at Noon and 70 at Night. Wind still Northerly and Morning clear. In the afternoon it shifted to the Southward and became warmer.

Visited the Ferry, French's, Dogue run & Muddy hole Plantations.

At the first—Three Plows and all the hands were at Work in the Corn ground except Cupid—who was stacking at Frenchs. Examined the Stock at this place; and sent an old Steer and Cow to the fatting Pasture at Frenchs. Of the Sheep there was but one old weather which was brought to the Ho[use]; and there being but one of what might be called old ewes that was in danger of not standing the Winter, it was left to take its chance with the rest— wch. are as follow—

   1 old ewe

  14 Young & middle aged—Do.

  22 Young Weathers—&

  23 Lambs—Ewes & Weathers

In all 60 Sheep. Cattle, besides the two which were sent to Frenchs are as follow

  2 Bulls

  6 Work Oxen

 26 grown Cattle

  9 Yearlings

  8 Calves

  4 Ditto from Mn. House

  2 Cows at Ditto.

In all 57. The Horses were agreeable to the former acct. & reports—viz.—8 Workers—besides the one lately sent there from Muddy hole for that purpose & the two Mules—A bay Mare (young) with a small sorrel horse Colt.

At Frenchs—The Waggon and two Carts and all hands, except three people with the Plows, in the Corn field, were getting in and Stacking the Oats. Examined the stock here and put two old Cows, and five old weathers into the fatting field for killing or Market. Remainder of the Sheep were 32 Ewes and 16 Lambs. The horses were found agreeable to the list taken the first of Jany. 1787 and the reports since—as also the Cattle.

At Dogue Run—all the Ploughs and Hoes were in the Corn.

At Muddy hole—The Plows were crossing the Pease. All the

other hands were chopping down Wds. in the Corn at the Mansn. House.

Thursday 14th.     Thermometer at 62 in the Morning—73 at Noon and 79 at Night. Wind Southerly all day with appearances of rain after noon.

Went into the Neck, and to Muddy hole.

At the first—8 Plows were turning in Buck Wheat & one in the Corn. Two Carts and Ten hands were getting in and stacking Oats. All the rest were Weeding and hilling of Corn.

At Muddy hole—The three plows were employed as yesterday and all the other hands were threshing wheat for Seed.

Friday 15th.     Thermometer at 67 in the morning—72 at Noon and 70 at Night. Wind though very little of it, at East in the morning about Sun rise, with a small sprinkling of Rain; Abt. Noon a pretty serious shower fell with frequent sprinklings afterwards.

Visited the Plantations at the Ferry, Frenchs and Dogue run.

At the first—the Plows and Hoes were employed as they were yesterday and the day before, that is the Plows were breaking up the grd. between the Corn and Potatoes—and the Hoes were weeding and drawing dirt to the latter—havg. hilld the Corn.

At Frenchs the wet morning prevented working among the grain. All hands therefore went to weeding a yard for the purpose of treading out the Barley & Oats in field No. 2.

At Dogue run the 5 plows would have finished throwing a furrow to the Corn & Potatoes by Noon and would begin on the West side of the field to plow up the balks between these two furrows. At Night the Hoes compleated the hilling of the Corn.

At Muddy hole—The Hoe people were all in the Corn at the Mansion House. The plows finished crossing the Pease, and breaking up the ground which had been in flax in No. 3.

Saturday 16th.     Thermometer at 67 in the Morning 69 at Noon And 67 at Night. Wind at East, & No. Et. all day—Showery in the Night & this morning but moderate & without wind—also towards Sundown.

Rid to the Plantations at the Ferry, Frenchs, Dogue run and Muddy hole.

At the Ferry—the same work, precisely, was going on as yesterday.

At Frenchs—No Carting or Stacking of grain. 3 plows were in

the Corn—the other hands weeding a yard to tread out the English Oats No. of the Branch.

At Dogue run—3 Plows were at work—one was stopped on acct. of sickness—and another to Harrow. The other hands were weeding and drawing dirt to the Potatoes.

At Muddy hole All hands were threshing Wheat.

Sunday 17th.    Thermometer at 66 in the Morning—72 at Noon and 70 at Night. Wind at No. Et. with clouds and appearances of Rain but none fell—except what fell in the Night.

Monday 18th.    Thermometer at 66 in the Morning—69 at Noon and 68 at Night. Wd. still at No. Et. and raining more or less, moderately, all day.

Remained at home.

Tuesday 19th.    Thermometer at 70 in the Morning—75 at Noon and 73 at Night. Wind at No. Et. in the forenoon with mists and light showers—In the afternn. it was at So. a little West and clear —though the Sun set in a bank.

Rid to the Plantations at the Ferry, French's, Dogue run, and Muddy hole.

At the first—three plows were in the Corn and all the other hands were drawing dirt to the Potatoes.

At Frenchs—The Ploughs were stopped, till I set them to work abt. 11 Oclock. All hands till that time and the rest afterwards were hoeing the Corn.

At Dogue run, Four plows (one plowman being still sick) and all the rest of the hands, except one Woman sick, were among the Corn—The latter Weeding, and drawing dirt to the Potatoes. Ordered all except the Plow people & Carter, the latter with his Cart to Muddy hole, to go to Frenchs tomorrow to Hoe Corn.

At Muddy hole—three ploughs were crossing the East cut by the gate of Field No. 3 for Wheat. This ground did not work well. The Buck Wheat had not been buried long enough to have got sufficiently rotted; consequently the Ploughs choaked. The Waggon from the House, and the Cart were taking out dung to spread on the poor knowls in the field. Some hands were spreading it— and the others weeding, & drawing dirt to the Irish Potatoes and Jerusalem Artichokes adjoining.

Wednesday 20th.    Thermometer at 66 in the Morning—76 at Noon and 76 at Night. Clear and warm all day, with little or no Wind.

Went up to Alexandria with Mrs. Washington. Dined at Mr. Fendalls and returned in the evening.

Thursday 21st.    Thermometer at 69 in the Morning—79 at Noon and 79 at Night—Very little wind from the Southward—clear and warm all day.

Visited all the Plantations. At the Ferry—began with 3 plows & a harrow, to sow and cover Wheat in field No. 7—The ploughs crossing the lately plowed in Buck Wheat and the harrow covering the grain at twice—that is—going as the plows do the first time— next, crossing it. Every other land was also sowed with Buck Wheat—for the experiment of its falling with the frost, and by laying on the Wht. during the winter keeping it warm and from being hove out of the grd. The Hoe people were weeding and drawing dirt to the Potatoes.

At French's—The ploughs finished throwing on each side of the Corn a furrow—and begun on the West side of the field to break up the balks between. The other hands were employed—some in getting in and stacking the grain and the rest with those from Dogue-run and Muddy hole in hilling and weeding of Corn.

At Dogue run—three plows and a harrow were breaking up, and levelling the balks between the Corn & Potatoes. The Overseer and five hands were getting in & stacking the Rye that grew in field No. 4. The rest of the hands that were well—were at work at Frenchs.

At Muddy hole. Two plows & a harrow were putting in Wheat in the East cut of field No. 3. The Overseer & five hands were getting in and stacking the Wheat that grew (voluntarily) in No. 1. The rest of the hands—except Nancy, who was sick were at Work at French's.

In the Neck—Six plows were turning in B. Wheat. Two and a harrow were breaking up and levelling the balks between the Corn & Potatoes. Two Carts with the necessary attendance were getting in and stacking the Remainder of Spotswoods Oats, which would be finished this day (9 Stacks) and proceed to bringing in Wheat from No. 7. The rest of the hands (one pressing Cyder) were weeding Pease.

The slave Nancy, now about 17 years old, was the wife of Abram, one of the slaves that GW had hired from Penelope French. Her oldest child Oliver was born about 1788 (list of Negroes belonging to GW, c.June 1799, NjP: Armstrong Collection).

Friday 22d.    Thermometer at 78 in the Morning 82 at Noon and 80 at Night. Quite clear, calm and warm all day.

Rid to the Ferry, Frenchs, Dogue run, & Muddy hole plantations.

At the first, and two last the Work was precisely the same as yesterday.

At Frenchs—the getting in, stacking and securing the last of the grain would be compleated abt. Noon. About which time or a little after the Hoes would nearly have got over the Corn and would begin to weed & draw dirt to the Potatoes.

Mr. Richard B. Lee and his brother Theodk. Lee came here to dinner and stayed all Night.

Saturday 23d.    Thermometer at 74 in the Morning—83 at Noon and 82 at Night. The Morning was very clear, calm, and Warm; but a pretty fresh Southwester blew afterwards and towards Evening the Weather looked hazy & lowering.

Visited all the Plantations. In the Neck—Eight Plows and a harrow were at work in the Corn. The Waggon and two Carts were drawg. in Wheat from field No. 7 and the rest of the hands were about finishing weeding the Pease & *pulling* the large weeds from among the Pompions—after which would gather up the apples under the Trees.

At Muddy hole, the Plows and harrow were plowing for and putting in Wheat. The other hands were getting in & Stacking Oats and working at French's as yesterday.

At Dogue run—The Plows and harrow were in the Corn. The other hands were at Frenchs except such as were employed in getting in and stacking the Barley.

At Frenchs—The Plows as yesterday were breaking up the balks. All the rest were weeding and drawing dirt to the Potatoes.

At the Ferry—The Plows and harrow were crossing for, & putting in Wheat. One land of which, designated by a stake drove into it, was trench plowed; or dble. plowed in the same furrow to break the ground 8 or 10 Inches deep to try the effect. This *ought* to have been done in the *fall*.

A Mr. George Thompson, from the Academy in Alexandria, with a letter to me from his father Doctr. Thompson respecting his Son in law Doctr. Spence; and Geo. Step. Washington came here to dinner & stayed all Night.

Dr. William Spence was the stepson of Dr. Thomas Thomson of Westmoreland County. As a boy Spence was sent to Great Britain for his education, which was culminated in 1780 by his taking a medical degree at Glasgow University. In Sept. 1781 he sailed for New York with a wife and child aboard the *Buckskin Hero,* but the vessel disappeared without a trace after having last been seen by another vessel two or three days' sail out of New York harbor. It was assumed that the *Buckskin Hero* had sunk with all aboard until a report in the spring of 1788 from a man claiming to be a former Algerian prisoner gave some hope that the vessel had been captured by Algerian pirates and the crew and passengers carried into slavery. That report prompted Dr. Thomson's letter, dated 12 Aug. 1788, to GW (DLC:GW). Although Thomson did not know GW personally, he was confident that GW would assist the family by asking French officials to make inquiries about the fate of Dr. and Mrs. Spence and their child. Strongly doubting the truth of the report, GW wrote for further information to Thomas Barclay of Philadelphia, who had been involved with American affairs in North Africa. Barclay confirmed GW's suspicions. The *Buckskin Hero* was not among the vessels captured by the Algerians, a fact that was further substantiated later by Thomas Jefferson through James Madison (GW to Thomson, 24 Aug. and 18 Sept. 1788, GW to Barclay, 31 Aug. and 18 Sept. 1788, DLC:GW; Madison to Jefferson, 8 Oct. 1788, Jefferson to Madison, 12 Jan. 1789, JEFFERSON [1], 14:3–4, 436–38).

George Thomson, a son of Dr. Thomson by his first wife, was apparently a schoolmate of George Steptoe Washington at the Alexandria Academy.

Sunday 24th.    Thermometer at 75 in the morning—84 at Noon and 82 at Night. Morning clear with but little Wind and that at No. Wt.—very warm.

Mr. & Mrs. Roger West & Miss Craik and Mr. Chas. Lee & his Sister and Miss Ballendine came here to dinner, all of whom stayed all night except Mr. & Mrs. West.

Monday 25th.    Thermometer at 74 in the Morning—84 at Noon and 84 at Night. Wind at So. Wt. all day and clear.

Rid to the Ferry, Frenchs, D. Run and Muddy hole Plantations. At The Ferry—Three plows and the dble. Harrows were putting in Wheat and two Carts & the other hands getting in and stacking of Oats.

At French's—All hands, including those from D. Run & Muddy hole were weeding & earthing the Potatoes. 3 Plows were at work, but not able to keep before the Hoes.

At Dogue Run—Four Plows and a harrow were in the Corn. The Cart and some hands were getting in & Stacking Barley. The Rest were at Frenchs.

At Muddy hole. Two Plows and a harrow were preparing for and putting in Wheat—Six hands getting in Oats and stacking them and the rest were at Frenchs.

At the Mansion House, began with 8 Scythes to cut the Lawn on the West front of the House which they only accomplished by Night.

Mr. Lee & the young Ladies—and my Nephews, Geo. & Lawe. Washington returned to alexandria after Breakfast.

Tuesday 26th.    Thermometer at 79 in the Morning—82 at Noon and 76 at Night. But little wind in the Morning & that at So. Wt. Afterwards—about Noon, a black cloud arose to the Northward which seemed highly charged with Wind or rain, a small part of the latter, only, came to our share.

Rid to all the Plantations. In the Neck—8 Plows and a harrow were in the Corn and all the hands except those who were with the Carts & Waggon getting in Wheat and stacking of it were weeding & Earthing Potatoes which work they began yesterday.

At Muddy hole—the same work going on as yesterday.

At Dogue run—The Plows havg. finished the Balks in the Corn field went after Dinner yesterday to French's and were there to day, where the same hands from Muddy hole and this place were at Work.

At Frenchs, the same work with the addition of 4 Plows from D. Run were going on.

At the Ferry—The Oats were got in just before the Rain And the Wheat on Stoney hill was next set about. The Ploughs, harrows, and other hands were employed as usual.

At the Mansion House—the Lawn East of the House was nearly cut down to day.

Wednesday 27th.    Thermometer at 70 in the Morning—80 at Noon and 80 at Night. Clear Morning with the Wind at No. West —but calm, and warm afterwards.

Visited the Plantations at the Ferry, Frenchs, Dogue run and Muddy hole.

At the first the same work precisely, as yesterday.

At Frenchs the same till the Plows finished breaking up the balks in the Corn—when trying, & finding the Buck Wheat which had been plowed in at this place not sufficiently rotted to cross they went to the Ferry to prepare for and put in Wheat at that Plantation.

At Dogue run—the same work going forward as yesterday.

And at Muddy hole the same. Mrs. Stuart, Miss Nancy Stuart, a Brother of the Doctors and their children came to Dinner, as did Commodore Brooke. In the evening Doctr. Stuart came.

The brother of David Stuart who came today was Richard Stuart (1770–1835) of King George County (see entry for 29 Aug. 1788).

Thursday 28th.    Thermometer at 70 in the Morning—80 at Noon and 78 at Night. Morning clear and calm.

Visited the Plantations at the Ferry, Frenchs, Dogue run and Muddy hole—accompanied by Doctr. Stuart.

At the first—Ten plows and a Harrow were at Work—preparing for and putting in Wheat. The other hands with the Waggon and two Carts were getting in and stacking the grain from the fields.

At French's—The Plows having finished the Corn went as has been observed to the Ferry yesterday And the Hoes having wed the Potatoes & earthed them all went this morning to D. Run.

At Dogue-Run, The Hoes from French's & Muddy hole—Six from each—having joined those of the Place were at Work in weeding & earthing the Potatoes. The Plows were at the Ferry and a Cart and Six hands were getting in & Stacking the Oats.

At Muddy hole—Two Plows & a harrow were preparing for Wheat & the Cart & Six hands were getting in, and Stacking what was in the fields. The other hands were at Dogue run.

Friday 29th.    Thermometer at 80 in the Morning—83 at Noon; and 81 at Night. Wind at So. W. clear & very warm.

Visited all the Plantations. In the Neck—The Waggon & 1 Cart were getting in Wheat—the other was at Mill. The other hands except those at Plow and employed in getting in and Stacking the Wheat—were threshing out Oats, & pressing Cyder.

At Muddy hole—The Plows wch. had just finished preparing for, & putting in Wheat at the Ferry (with the Ferry Plows) set into work after dinner. All the other hands were employed as yesterday.

At Dogue run—The same hands were at the same work as yesterday.

At Frenchs—The Hoe & Plow people were, as before mentioned, at the other places.

At the Ferry—The Plows went after dinner to Muddy hole—the rest were employed in getting with the carts & Waggon the Grain.

Doctr. Stuart & his Brother Richard left this before Breakfast for their Fathers.

David and Richard Stuart's father, Rev. William Stuart (1723–1798), rector of St. Paul's Parish, King George County, lived at Cedar Grove in the Chotank area. The estate had been a wedding gift to William and his wife, Sarah Foote Stuart, from her father. Richard Stuart later inherited Cedar Grove and lived there until his death (EUBANK, 17–18; ST. PAUL'S, xxii–xxiii, 134–36).

Saturday 30th.    Thermometer at 79 in the Morning 84 at Noon and 79 at Night. Calm, & clear till towards 3 Oclock when there was a pretty hasty shower for a few minutes.

Rid to the Plantations at Muddy hole—Dogue run—Frenchs and the Ferry.

The work at all, was precisely the same as yesterday.

Finished to day, getting in and stacking all the grain at the Ferry.

Cleaned up a stack of Oats wch. had been threshed out in the Neck which yielded 81 Bushls. The stack was small, but of the shortest Oats. The Wheat from the English seed was also threshed & cleaned—of the red there was but 3 pecks. Of the other (White or Harrison Wheat) 13¼—vast loss in both—the goodness of the sort, of both, much questioned.

The quantity of ground sowed at the Ferry in Wheat may be abt. 30 acres—on which [    ] Bushels was bestowed—viz. 18 bushls. from Muddy hole 18 bushls. from Captn. Speak and 3 bushls. of the White or Harrison Wheat from England. NB. This last was sown on the North part of the field next the Woods and Stoney field.

Francis Speake of Charles County, Md., was a privateer captain during the War of Independence and afterwards served as tobacco inspector at Chicamuxen warehouse for many years. GW had reprimanded Speake earlier this year for ferrying passengers across the Potomac River without authorization, thus depriving GW's public ferry of revenue it otherwise would have received. "I find the Ferry," GW declared, "inconvenient, and unprofitable enough without this, to wish the discontinuance of it" (GW to Speake, 30 Mar. 1788, DLC:GW).

Sunday 31st.    Thermometer at 76 in the Morning—76 at Noon and 72 at Night. A Little Rain, with some thunder & lightning fell in the Night. Morning & most part of the day cloudy with appearances of Rain but none fell—the Wind at No. Et., & sometimes Easterly all day.

Mr. Murray and his wife, Colo. Fitzgerald; a Mr. Hancock and Son, the former a Merchant of London, a Mr. Aitkinson (all three introduced by Colo. Fitzgerald), and Captn. Gregory came here to dinner and returned to Alexandria afterwards. Mr. Tracy who came here last night remained.

# September 1788

Monday 1st. Septemr.    Thermometer at 69 in the Morning—74 at Noon and 74 at Night. Morning cloudy with the wind still at No. East. Misting at intervals through the day—but no rain fell.

Rid to the Plantations at the Ferry, Frenchs, Dogue run and Muddy hole.

At the First—Weeding Turnips—The Plows at Muddy hole.

At Frenchs—all hands except the Plow People, were at Dogue run.

At Dogue run—the Same Work as on Saturday was going on. The Oats would be all in and Stacked to day And the Potatoes nearly wed out.

At Muddy hole—The Plows of the Ferry, French's, & Dogue run were at work, preparing for the Sowing of Wheat. Began about Noon to sow the red wheat raised from English seed, in drills. Of this there was 3 pecks, very indifferent; which occupied 3 lands, 6 feet & better broad, next the pease, South side the field. Next to these—in like manner, sowed the White, or Harrison Wheat [     ] bushels up to the next Stake (the first stake being drove between the red & this). Finding that the barrel disposed of too much seed—after 7 rows were sowed with the Harrison wheat I altered it—wch. alteration continued to the end of the drills thinner.

Doctr. Stuart returned here last Night from his Fathers and Mr. Tracy who came here on Saturday went away this Morning.

Tuesday 2d.    Thermometer at 68 in the Morning—76 at Noon and 72 at Night. Wind at No. W. fresh—clear—and cool.

Rid to the Plantations at Muddy hole—Dogue run—Frenchs and the Ferry.

At the first—the Plows would, about 12 Oclock, have crossed the Buck Wheat & would then go into the Pease. The Barrel Plow was sowing Wheat & 2 Harrows covering after it—going twice (once each) in the same row the same way. The other work the same as yesterday.

At Dogue Run—The Plows were at Muddy hole. The Potatoes wd. be wed out by Noon—and the hands from French's and Muddy hole wd. return home.

At French's—The Plows were at Muddy hole and the other People at Morris's.

At the Ferry. The Plows were at Muddy hole—the other hands preparing ground to re-sow Turnips between Corn Rows—where the first sowing were chiefly cut off by the fly.

Captn. Gregory dined here and went away afterwards.

Wednesday 3d.    Thermometer at 64 in the morning—76 at Noon and 75 at Night. Clear morning with the Wind fresh from No. Wt. after which it became calm.

Visited all the Plantations. In the Neck—6 Plows were crossing the B. Wheat field for sowing Wheat; one harrow in the Corn.

The Waggon & Ox Carts were getting in Wheat. The other hands (not with the Carts and at the Stacks) were Weeding and Earthing the Potatoes.

At Muddy hole—The Pease having had a furrow thrown to them, all the Plows, except those belonging to the Plantation, went yeste[r]night to French's. The other hands were getting in Wheat, and threshing out Rye.

At Dogue run—The Oats and Barley being all in, & the other People having got through the Potatoes—all hands were employed in fencing Around the above stacks—repairing the Meadow & other fences of field No. 2 and preparing it for the reception of small stock—Into wch. 3 old Ewes and 4 Calves from the Mansion House were put. The Plows were at Work at French's.

At Frenchs—The Plows belonging to the Ferry—Dogue run and the Plantation, were crossing the East part of Field No. 5 (where Buck Wheat had been plowed in) in order to sow Wheat therein. The hands of the place were getting the Seed from the Flax in order to rot it. The cross plowing of the above ground was done miserably bad—owing to the B. Wheat & Weeds not being rotted and by choaking the Plows every 3 or 4 steps preventing them from penetrating the earth.

At the Ferry—The Plows were employed as above—the Ferry men cleaning the shattered Wheat & other grain in the Yard and the other hands were brushing over some of the foulest of their Corn.

From the Mansion house. Three old Ewes, and 4 Calves were sent to field No. 2 at Dogue run.

Thursday 4th.　　Thermometer at 64 in the Morng. 76 at Noon and 76 at Night. Calm morning with a very heavy fog—Wind afterwards at So. Wt.

Rid to the Plantations at Muddy hole—Dogue run—French's and the Ferry.

At the first. The Harrison Wheat, 10 Bushels having been sown in drills and covered in—Three harrows were putting in Wheat adjoining thereto, the Seed of which was brot. from the Neck.

At the other 3 plantations the work was precisely the same as yesterday.

Mrs. Craik, and Miss Craik, came here to dinner.

Friday 5th.　　Thermometer at 71 in the Morning—83 at Noon and 82 at Night. But little wind and that from the So. Wt.

Rid to the Plantations at Muddy hole, Dogue run, French's and the Ferry.

At Muddy hole—Only one harrow remained to cover the Wheat. The other two went to French's—getting in Wheat and Stacking it. The other hands were spreading the trash that was raked together by the Harrows to prevent, by laying in heaps the destruction of the Wheat.

At Dogue run—Getting in and stacking the Wheat from field No. 6. The other hands were repairing the fencing between the Corn field and Meadow by the Ho., inclosing the Hay Stacks—and Wheat yard. Turned 3 old Ewes and 25 Weathers into field No. 2 at this place, for feeding—and brought 28 head of Cattle from French (which had been put into the clover of field No. 1) into the large Meadow at the Mill also 2 Calves. The blind Cow was left at Frenchs. One being killed and another having died makes the number (31) that was sent to the above pasture.

At French's—The Plows from Dogue run, Ferry, & Muddy hole were preparing for sowing Wheat. Three harrows, one pair being added from the ferry were covering the Seed which the Farmer began to sow to day. The Harrow was run over, after the Plows, & before Sowing, to level the ground and rake the grass & Weeds into heaps; but the ground was miserably rough notwithstanding they were to pass twice after sowing. The People at this place were getting the Seed from the flax in order to spread it.

At the Ferry—The Hoe people were brushing over the most grassy Potatoes in the Corn ground—Three Plows at Frenchs.

Mrs. Craik and her daughter went away after dinner to Colo. McCarty's.

Saturday 6th.     Thermometer at 76 in the Morng.—76 at Noon and 72 at Night. Wind at No. Et. with appearances of rain towards evening.

Visited all the Plantations. In the Neck—One harrow was covering the Wheat that had been sown (viz. 12½ Bushels). All the other hands were getting in Wheat, and treading out a bed. Waggn. & 2 Carts employd.

At Muddy hole—One harrow was employed in covering the Wheat, the sowing of which was now finished at this place (except a little of the Cape Wheat wch. is to be sown where the Irish Potatoes and Jerusalem Artichokes are now growing) and which is as follow in field No. 3 viz.—In the small cut East of the Branch 10 Bls. Next the Pease three pecks of red imported Wheat in drills —3 rows. This grain was much shrivelled & bad. Next to these, in drills also, was 10 Bushels of White imported Wheat (called Harrison) large, but not full & plump—then 14 Bushls. of the common Wheat—Seed from the Neck. On the North side of the road leading from the Gate to the Barn 21 bushls. of common wheat also from the Neck was sown—making together—drilled and broad 55 Bushels. The other hands were stripping the Seed from the Flax—getting in and Stacking Wheat.

At Dogue Run—The Waggon from the Mansn. House aided the Cart in getting in Wheat. The Plows were at Frenchs and the other hands were stacking and making fences round the Wheat Yard.

At French's—All the Plows were at Work as yesterday; and would finish crossing all the B. Wht. grd. this afternoon. The part South of the road from the Bars was sown—harrowed and compleated—but in a rough manner. Part on the other, or North side of this road was also sown, and the harrows covering it. The Pease ground at the No. end of this field which had been plowed in were cross plowed—part harrowed (across the last plowing) and a bushel of the plain white Wheat, sent me by Beale Bordley, Esqr., sown thereon in drills—[    ] rows. The hands of this Plantation were beating the seed from the flax in order to spd. it.

At the Ferry. The Plows were at Frenchs as yesterday and the other hands brushing over the Potatoes in the Corn.

John Beale Bordley's wheat seed arrived at Mount Vernon between 1 and 17 Aug. together with some barley and madder. "No Wheat that has ever yet fallen under my observation," GW wrote Bordley, "exceeds the *White* which some years ago I cultivated extensively; but which, from inattention during my absence from home of almost nine years has got so mixed or degenerated as scarcely to retain any of its original characteristic properties. But if the march of the Hessian Fly, Southerly, cannot be arrested; . . . this *White Wheat* must yield the palm to the *yellow bearded,* which alone, it seems, is able to resist the depredations of that destructive insect. This makes your present of it to me more valuable. It shall be cultivated with care" (17 Aug. 1788, MHi: Waterston Papers) .

Sunday 7th.    Thermometer at 70 in the Morning—67 at Noon and 64 at Night. The Clouds of yesterday evening produced Rain about 9 Oclock last Night, which they continued to do, more or less, through the whole of it and part of the forenoon of this day— Wind remaining at No. Et. and continuing cloudy all day.

Colo. Gilpin dined here, and went away in the afternoon for Colchester.

Monday 8th.    Thermometer at 65 in the Morning—72 at Noon and 70 at Night. Thunder & Rain a little before day—heavy

Morning with the Wind (tho' not much of it) a little to the East of North in the forenoon and So. Wt. afterwards, & clear.

Brought 12 Ploughs, with all the hands that could be spared from the Wheat yard in the Neck—viz.—all from Muddy hole—all from D. Run except the 2 old Women & two that were sick—and all from Frenchs and the Ferry that were not sick; making in the whole [    ] in order, while the ground was in its present moist State, to get the Corn ground in front of the Mansion house, expeditiously sown with Wheat; began by the White gates, on the South Side of the Road.

The Waggon, and Carts from D. Run, Ferry and Frenchs, were Carting Brick Wood.

Spread all the Flax, wt. the Hay makers, the Seed of which had been taken off at French's.

At French's, Harrowing in Wht. on the No. Cut, where the Harrows were on Saturday; the ground since the Rain harrowing better than it did before—also sowing, with the Barrel Plow, One bushel of the White bearded Wheat sent me by Beale Boardly Esqr. adjoining to the plain Wht. sowed on Saturday—and adjoining this again (likewise in drills) 9 Gallons of the Cape Wheat from that Gentleman also. Note—the Plain White which was sown on Saturday (in drills) was either not covered, or covered so thinly as to have *much* of it left quite bare by the late rains. This, in a degree, was the case of that sown broad in the same field— South side of the Et. cut.

Tuesday 9th.    Thermometer at 68 in the Morning—74 at Noon and 66 at Night. A good deal of distant Thunder and lightng. in the Night, but no rain. Wind this Morning at No. Wt. & pleasant —the same through the day.

Work going on as yesterday in the Corn ground at the Mansion house. About One Oclock the Wheat on the South side of the road was sown and Hoed & plowed in—and the other side begun. Began also to sow the South side with Timothy Seed on the Wheat. Ordered a gallon of clean seed to be allowed to the Acre.

Finished sowing Wheat in the cut at Frenchs where the harrows were at work yesterday. In both sides of this cut (East of the Branch) 32 Bushels of Wheat were Sown. That on the So. side of the road from the Bars, by the Cabbins, to the Gate, was harrowed once before sowing and twice afterwards—but that on the No. side of the said road, was not, at least the No. East end of it, harrowed till after sowing. Finished sowing, in drills, the Wheat by the Gate and Manleys Ho.; & not having enough of the Cape Wheat from

[ 391 ]

Mr. Bordley to do this I sent half a bushel of my own to compleat it—which with three pecks more was all the sound & clean seed that was raised of this sort of Wheat last year and added to other circumstances which have been heretofore remarked of it, proves that it is of too precarious a kind to be depended on for a crop—for in the first place it will not stand hard frost—and in the next place it does not fill kindly and is subject to rust.

The Waggon & Carts that were drawing Brick Wood yesterday, were at it again to day. About 12 Oclock to day the Brick layers compleated the 12th. course of Bricks, of the 14 Inch Wall from the second floor in the New Barn.

Wednesday 10th.    Thermometer at 60 in the morning—68 at Noon and 66 at Night. Morning clear with the wind at No. Wt. wch. afterwards shifted (though there was but little of it) to the East veering Northerly—clear & pleasant all day.

Visited the Plantations in the Neck, Muddy hole and Frenchs Plantations.

At the first—the Waggon and two Carts were drawing in Wheat and People as usual employed and stacking of it—Five plows and one harrow preparing for, and putting in Wheat—one triangular harrow running betwn. the Corn Rows—3 Women picking up Apples & threshing rye. The others at the Corn ground at the Mansion House.

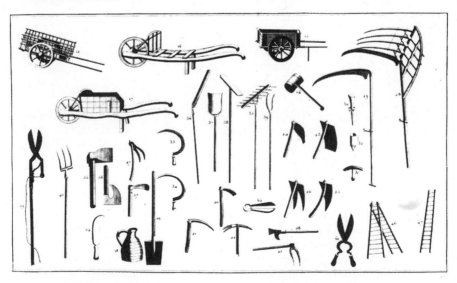

Farm implements shown in *La Nouvelle Maison Rustique,* Paris, 1798. (Mount Vernon Ladies' Association of the Union)

At Muddy hole. *All* hands were in the Corn field at the Mansion House. The Wheat sowed in drills at this place seems to be coming up very thin. Whether more is to arise, or the ground was not sufficiently seeded cannot as yet be decided on. The latter is to be feared—nor is it perfectly in drills being too much scattered. Note —to do this work well furrows should be opened for the seed to fall in.

At Dogue run—except the two old Women, the rest of the hands were at the Mansn. House.

At Frenchs—Two Women and a boy were spreading the trash which had been raked into heaps in the newly sown Wheat ground and hoeing around the Stumps—all the rest were at the Mansion House.

At the Ferry—all were at the Mansion House. The Carts of the last 3 places were engaged at the Brick yard.

At the Mansion House—finished sowing the Wheat in the Corn ground 35½ bushls. from the Neck on both sides the road up to the last cleared ground. On the South Side of the road 13 gallons of clean timothy seed (mixed with Sand) was sown. More ought to have been sown—24 at least as I directed a gallon to be allowed to the Acre. On the other, or No. Side of the road Orchard grass was sown—viz.—[      ] Bushels. As the whole was not chopped in this afternoon—the hands from Muddy hole and the Ferry were ordered to compleat it to morrow.

Thursday 11th.    Thermometer at 58 in the Morng.—72 at Noon and 70 at Night. Clear Morning with a breeze from the No. East which cond. through the day.

Mrs. Plater and her two daughters, and Mr. George Digges and his Sister came here to dinner and stayed all night.

Mr. Lear returned home to day.

George Plater, of St. Mary's County, Md., married Elizabeth Rousby (d. 1789) of Calvert County, Md., in 1764. Their daughters were Rebecca Plater (b. 1765) and Anne Plater (b. 1772).

The sister of George Digges who came today was probably his unmarried sister Ann, who apparently lived at Warburton until her death about 1804. George Digges's other two living sisters were married: Elizabeth to Daniel Carroll (d. 1790) and Jane to John Fitzgerald (BOWIE, 258).

Tobias Lear had set out from Mount Vernon sometime in May to visit his family and friends in Portsmouth, N.H. Although he planned to remain in New England six to eight weeks, several matters relating to settlement of his father's estate obliged him to stay longer (Lear to Benjamin Lincoln, 2 May and 6 June 1788, MHi: Lincoln Papers; Lear to GW, 2, 22 June and 31 July 1788, DLC:GW).

Friday 12th.    Thermometer at 62 in the morn. 72 at Night and 72 at Night. Cloudy with the Wind to the Eastward of North in the Morning with clouds & Sunshine alternately thro the day. Wind continuing in the same qr.

Visited all the Plantations. In the Neck. The Ploughs and harrows from the different Plantations were at Work, preparing for, and putting in Wheat—one harrow in the Corn and the Waggon & Carts drawing in Wheat. The other hands were cleaning Wheat (which had been tread out yesterday) and picking up apples.

At Muddy hole—The Cart was drawing in Rye—others spreading Flax the seed of which had been taken of and measured 2 Bushels.

At Dogue run—Two Carts (one from French's) and the Mans[io]n Ho[use] Waggon were drawing in Wheat and those who were not employed in loading & Stacking were getting the Seed of the Flax.

At French's the People were Hoeing round the stumps in the field No. 5 Newly sown with Wheat and taking up the grubs.

At the Ferry the People were about there fencing—the Ploughs as those of the other Places being in the Neck.

Saturday 13th.    Thermometer at 66 in the Morning—76 at Noon and 76 at Night. A very thick fog this morning, which continued until 10 'Oclock.

George Plater of Maryland. 1825 copy by Charles Willson Peale after John Wollaston. (Government House, Annapolis, Maryland Commission on Artistic Property)

Rid with Mrs. Plater and Mrs. Washington to the Mill and New Barn.

Colo. Plater, Mr. Hall & a Mr. Mathews came here (from Mr. Digges's) just after we had dined—stayed all N.

Sunday 14th.   Thermometer at 70 in the Morning—74 at Noon and 71 at Night. Cloudy morning with the Wind at No. East—clear afterwards but the Wind still remaining at the same point.

Colo. Plater, his Lady & daughters; Mr. Digges & his Sister; and Mr. Hall and Mr. Mathews went away after breakfast.

Monday 15th.   Thermometer at 66 in the Morning—78 at Noon and 74 at Night. Clouds, with the Wind still Easterly in the morning; About noon it shifted to the Southward and there were great appearances of rain but none fell. At Night it got to No. West.

Visited all the Plantations. In the Neck—21 plows and Harrows were employed in preparing for, and putting in Wheat—The Harrow that was in the Corn having finished that Work. The Carts and Waggen were drawing Grain from field No. 3. Some of the People were stacking and others spreading the trash raked together by the Harrows.

At Muddy hole—Getting in and stacking the Rye and threshing it out.

At Dogue run—The Cart from Frenchs, and the Waggon from the Mansn. House were assisting in getting in the grain—some of the people assisting in this and in Stacking. The rest with the People from the Ferry, were getting the Seed from the Flax.

At French's—The People had just finished about 12 Oclock getting the Seed from the flax and spreading it, after which they were ordered to Dogue Run.

At the Ferry—The Plows were in the Neck, and the other People were, as above, at Dogue run.

Tuesday 16th.   Thermometer at 73 in the Morning—77 at Noon and 76 at Night. Wind Southerly and warm, with appearances of rain till Night when the wind got round to the No. W.

Rid to Muddy hole, Dogue run, French's & the Ferry.

At the first—Having got in the grain, the Cart, after carrying a load of Rye to the Mill went into the Neck to assist with the grain there. Some of the other hands were employed in cleaning the Rye wch. they had threshed and others came to the Corn at the Mansn. Ho. to cut the tops. Note—this Corn, since the working it received to put in the Wheat and grass Seeds, has fired most astonishingly except the part which was worked since harvest. This seems rather to be benifitted—tho' after that working it fired a good deal but recovered its colour again. Now it is too to do this by that wch. has lately fired.

At Dogue run—The same hands, with the addition of those from Frenchs were employed as yesterday and in spreading the flax from which the Seed had been taken. Finished getting in all the grain this Evening.

At French's & the Ferry—the Plows & People were abroad as already mentioned.

Wednesday 17th.    Thermometer at 64 in the Morning—72 at Noon and 70 at Night. Morning clear and Wind at No. Wt.—pleasant all day.

Rid to all the Plantations. In the Neck—Finished sowing Wheat in No. 8 last Night; and the Plow horses were engaged to day in treading out a bed of Rye, and another of Oats. Some Plows, were engaged in the ground where the bunch homony beans grew. 1061½ bushels of Wheat were sown in the above field. The Carts from Muddy hole and French's were assisting here to get in the grain and except those who were employed in loading the Carts and stacking the People were attending the treading out of the above grain.

At Muddy hole—The hands except those who were with the Plows were about the Fodder in the Mansion House Corn field.

At Dogue run—the same hands as yesterday, were employed about the Flax. Some still remained at the Stacks, the grain not being all secured.

At French's and the Ferry the hands were absent as before mentioned, with the flax at D. R.

Thursday 18th.    Thermometer at 66 in the Morning—76 at Noon and 76 at Night. Wind at No. Wt. in the morning and Southerly afterwards—perfectly clear.

Rid to the Ferry, Frenchs & Dogue run Plantations.

At the first—began with the Plows belonging to it and those of Frenchs to break up field No. 3 for Corn next year, but the ground had got so hard as to oblige them to go twice in the same furrow. The hands of this place (except the Ferry men) still at D. Run about the Flax.

At Frenchs—the Plows were employed as above—the hands at Dogue run.

At Dogue Run—Four of the Plows belonging to the place and

the 3 from Muddy hole began to break up No. 7 for Corn, next year. All the other people together with those from French's and the Ferry were getting the Seed from, & spreading of the Flax.

The People from Muddy hole except one who was cutting and attending the Tobacco, were about the Fodder at the Mansion House.

Friday 19th.    Thermometer at 64 in the Morning—76 at Noon and 70 at Night. Morning clear with the Wind at South—towards evening it got to So. Wt. & began to lower.

Visited all the Plantations. In the Neck—The Carts &ca. would have finished (by Night) getting in all the grain. The other people after cleaning up the Oats & Rye which had been tread out—viz.—43½ of the first, & 72 of the latter were employed in pulling the blades of the Corn from which the tops had been taken yesterday—No Plows at Work here to day—nor since the Wheat was Sown.

At Muddy hole—All hands, except those with the Plows and Cart were employed with the Fodder at the Mansion House.

At Dogue run. Seven plows were at Work. The other hands, with those from the Ferry and French's were about the Flax which would be stripped of the Seed & spread to day.

At Frenchs—the Plows and other People were employed as yesterday.

At the Ferry—Five Plows were at Work one from Frenchs wanting repairs.

Saturday 20th.    Thermometer at 69 in the Morning—70 at Noon And 70 at Night. Morning heavy with the Wind at No. East. Cloudy all day, with grt. appearances of rain towards night.

Rid to the Plantations at the Ferry, Frenchs and Dogue run.

At the first—The Plow horses of this place and Frenchs were treading out a bed of Rye—The other hands attending.

At Frenchs—The people were cleaning the flax Seed which had been beat out some days ago 4¾ bushl., & Hoeing the waste ground adjoing. the fences of field No. 5 in which to put Wheat.

At Dogue Run—The Plow horses were engaged in treading out Rye—the People in attending the work, and cleaning flax Seed—which was sent to the Mansn. House—qty. 22½ bushels.

Colonel Harrison, and Colo. Hoe came here to dinner and stayed all Night.

Sunday 21st.    Thermometer at 60 in the morning—62 at Noon and 60 at Night. Morning clear with the Wind a little to the East of North—after wch. it shifted more Easterly but still continued tolerably clear.

Mr. John Nisbet, & a Mr. Cunningham from the West Indies came here to dinner and stayed all Night.

Colo. Hooe returned to Alexandria after dinner.

Monday 22d. Thermometer at 56 in the Morning—62 at Noon and 63 at Night. Morning cloudy with the Wind about North a little Et.

Rid to the Plantations at the Ferry, Dogue run and French's.

At the first the People began to get fodder—aided by the hands from the latter. Six plows were at work, breaking up field No. 3 twice in a Furrow. The Carts (Frenchs joined) were drawing Rails to enclose the Wheat and Hay stacks.

At French's—Hands employed as above at the Ferry.

At Dogue run—Eight Plows were at Work breaking up field No. 7—twice in a furrow. The other hands were employed in getting fodder.

At Muddy hole—The whole force was about getting in, and securing the fodder at the M. Ho.

Mr. Nisbet, Mr. Cunningham, & Colo. Harrison went away after breakfast. Majr. Powell—Sub. Sheriff came here on business before dinner & dined.

GW today paid Joseph Powell, Jr., £14 5s. 7½d. for the current parish levy on his 153 tithables plus clerk's fees (LEDGER B, 268, 275). Powell was sworn a Fairfax County subsheriff 17 Jan. 1785 and apparently served to the end of 1788 or early 1789 (Fairfax County Order Book for 1783–88, 105, and Fairfax County Order Book for 1788–91, 243, Vi Microfilm).

Tuesday 23d. Thermometer at 58 in the Morning 72 at Noon and 72 at Night. But little Wind and that Westerly in the Morning—towards evening what there was of it was Southerly.

Visited all the Plantations. In the Neck—Seven Plows began yesterday to break up Field No. 9. The rest of the hands were about the fodder.

At Muddy hole—All hands, and the Cart, were engaged with the fodder.

At Dogue run—The Cart was drawing Rails for a fodder Stack. All the other hands were engaged in pulling Blades. Seven plows were at Work breaking up No. 7.

At Frenchs—The Plows and Cart, and all the hands were at the Ferry.

At the Ferry—Six plows were at Work in field No. 3. The Carts were drawing Rails to enclose the Wheat and the other hands were about the fodder.

Wednesday 24th.    Thermometer at 60 in the Morning—72 at Noon and 72 at Night. A heavy fog in the Morning which cleared away between 8 and 9 Oclk. but little wind in the forenoon—in the afternoon a breeze from the So. Et. and lowering.

Rid to the Ferry, French's and Dogue run Plantations.

At all of which the same work as yesterday—precisely—so likewise at Muddy hole.

Thursday 25th.    Thermometer at 60 in the Morning—72 at Noon and 72 at Night. A fog in the morning, but clear afterwards, & warm all day.

Dined at Mr. Benja. Dulany's but passed through the Plantations at the Ferry, Frenchs & Dogue run.

At all of which the same work was going on—both with the Plows and other people—as yesterday.

Friday 26th.    Thermometer at 63 in the morning—78 at Noon and 73 at Night. Clear morning with little or no Wind—So. Et. afterwards with appearances of Rain in the evening which went off by the winds shifting to the No. Wt.

Rid to all the Plantations. In the Neck—Six plows only were at Work. All the other hands were engaged about the Fodder.

At Muddy hole—The three Plows belonging here were at Dogue run and the other hands at the Mansion house about the Fodder whh. would be compleated this Night.

At Dogue run—French's and the Ferry the same work as usual both with the Plows and Hoe People was going on.

Mr. & Mrs. Crawford (of Maryland) who came here on Wednesday evening went away this Morning after breakfast.

Saturday 27th.    Thermometer at 60 in the morning—68 at Noon and 72 at Night. Clear Morning with the Wind at No. Wt. Calm afterwards, or very little wind from So. Et.

Rid to the Ferry, Frenchs and Dogue run Plantations.

The same work at all three, as in the days preceeding—with the Muddy hole hands in aid at the latter.

Turned the Mares & Colts from the Pasture at the home house into that at the Ferry to day.

Received a Bull calf from Mr. Digges's to day.

Mr. Chas. Lee came here in the afternoon & stayed all Night.

Sunday 28th.    Thermometer at 60 in the Morning—71 at Noon and 73 at Night. Clear morning with the Wind (though not much of it) at South where it continued all day, and towards night lowered a little.

Monday 29th.    Thermometer at 66 in the Morning—75 at Noon and 73 at Night—Wind at South and Morning hazy, or lowering. Cloudy afterwards—and at Night a slow and moderate rain.

Visited all the Plantations. In the Neck—All the tops were cut and blades pulled from the Corn on Saturday last, but not got in being too green. All hands, except 5 people at the Plows, getting them in to day.

At Muddy hole—All hands were at Dogue run.

At Dogue Run—Six plows only were at Work. All the other hands with those from Muddy hole, were getting fodder—except the Carter who was drawing Rails to make the division between fields No. 5 & 6.

At French's—All hands were at the Ferry—and

At the Ferry—Six plows were at work—and the other hands were about the Fodder.

Began to cut with Scythes the Indian Pease at Frenchs in field No. 5.

Put the Rams to the Ewes at all the Planns.

Tuesday the 30th.    Thermometer at 70 in the Morng. 65 at Noon and 63 at Night. Cloudy Morning with the wind fresh from the Northward. Raining more or less all last Night.

Rid to the Plantations at the Ferry, French's & Dogue run.

At the first—The Six plows were at Work and all the hands of both Plantations about the fodder which would be all down but not dry enough to secure to day.

At Frenchs—The Plows and other force, were at the Ferry as above.

At Dogue run—Seven plows were at Work. The other hands with those from Muddy hole were about the fodder which would be all down to day—but not got in.

A Mr. Cary (who came here to enquire into his right to Lands under the claim of one Williams his father in law) dined here and returned to Alexandria afterwards.

John Cary (Carey) married Elizabeth Williams, daughter of John Williams, in Lancaster County 23 Aug. 1785. John Williams had served under GW as a lieutenant in the Virginia Regiment Sept. 1755 to June 1757 but had apparently died without receiving his share of veterans' lands. Cary did not succeed in making good his father-in-law's claim until 12 Dec. 1792 when the Virginia Assembly passed an act authorizing warrants to be issued to Cary and to Williams's unmarried daughter Martha for 1,000 acres each (HENING, 13:610).

## October 1788

Wednesday 1st. day.    Thermometer at 56 in the Morning—56 at Noon and 56 at Night. Cloudy morning with the Wind at No. East. Lowering afterwards till about 2 Oclock when it began to Rain & continued to do so pretty steadily till bedtime—probably all night.

Visited all the Plantations. In the Neck—The Fodder not being dry enough to take in, the People were employed in pulling up the Blackeye pease by the Roots. Seven plows were at work in No. 9.

At Muddy hole—all the hands with the Cart were at Dogue run.

At Dogue run—Seven plows were at Work. All the other hands (that were well) with those from Muddy hole were turning flax.

At Frenchs—the hands of the Plantation, with those from the Ferry, were turning flax & getting Poles & forks for a fodder House.

At the Ferry—Six plows were at Work. The other hands, except one or two who were about their fodder house were as above, at French's.

Thursday 2d.    Thermometer at 53 in the Morning—62 at Noon and 62 at Night. Morning very thick & cloudy with the Wind at No. Et.—Clear afterwards and tolerably pleasant.

Rid to the Plantations at Muddy hole, Dogue Run, Frenchs and the Ferry.

At the first—All the hands were still at Dogue run—also the Plows.

At Dogue run—in the forenoon the hands (with those of Muddy hole) were employed about a cross fence betwn. fields No. 5 & 6—Afterwards in opening & spreading the fodder. Six Plows only were at work here.

At Frenchs—The Plows & people were, in the forenoon, working at the Ferry. In the Afternoon the latter were engaged about their fodder House except 3 who went to Dogue run.

At the Ferry—Six Plows were at Work. The other hands (with those from Frenchs) were in the forenoon making & compleating the Fence between fields No. 3 & 4. In the afternoon they were opening and turning their fodder.

Yesterday before the Rain fell, & partly while it was falling I sowed 19 Rows of the Yellow bearded Wheat between the Rows of the Mangel Wurzel & those of the Carrots—placing the grains about one inch apart.

Friday 3d.    Thermometer at 56 in the morning 64 at Noon and 64 at Night. Clear & pleasant Morning with the Wind still at No. Et. Cloudy in the afternoon with appearances of Rain.

Went with Mrs. Washington to Abingdon, to visit Mrs. Stuart who was sick.

Saturday 4th.    Thermometer at 60 in the Morning—64 at Night and 63 at Night. Raining till about 9 or 10 Oclock with the Wind Easterly. Cloudy all the rest of the day. Towards dusk the wind shifted to the No. Wt. and it grew cool.

At Abingdon still.

Sunday 5th. Thermometer at 50 in the Morning—58 at Noon and 56 at Night—Cool, the Wind being at No. Wt. in the morning—North & a little Easterly afterwards with appears. of Rain.

Returned home after breakfast and reached it about 11 ock.

Monday 6th.    Thermometer at 50 in the Morning—52 at Noon and 52 at Night. Morning very heavy with the Wind a little to the Eastward of North. About Noon it began to sprinkle rain and in the Afternoon (towards Night) it set in to close raining with but little wind and continued so through the night.

Rid to the Plantations at the Ferry, French's, Dogue run and Muddy hole.

At the Ferry—Six plows were at work which was done much better since the rain. Some of the hands were stacking blades and the rest were at work at French's.

At French's—all hands were pulling blades from the Corn from which the tops were taken on Saturday last.

At Dogue Run—Seven plows were at Work. All the other hands were getting in and securing fodder.

At Muddy hole. The Plows were at Dogue Run. The other hands were repairing a fence through the Swamp which incloses field No. 4 untill it began to Rain—after which they began to thresh.

Tuesday 7th.    Thermometer at 50 in the Morning—54 at Noon and 50 at Night—Wind at No. Et. with unceasing tho remitting rain till Noon and very cloudy the remaing. part of the day.

Did not stir from home.

Wednesday 8th.    Thermometer at 55 in the Morning—65 at Noon and 63 at Night. A very thick fog till nine Oclock—after which the Sun came out and it was very pleasant till about Noon when there was Sun shine and clouds alternately afterwards—Wind at So. Wt. in the morning which veered more to the northward afterwards.

Rid to the Plantations at Muddy hole, Dogue run, Frenchs & the Ferry.

At Muddy hole, after pulling up the Early (or Carolina) Pease, the hands about Noon, went to Dogue run to assist about their fodder.

At Dogue run—The people were opening & spreading the fodder. 7 Plows were at work and the Cart as that of Muddy hole, Frenchs and the Ferry also were, were carting brick wood at the New Barn.

At French's—After opening the Tops, the People were employed in taking up the Flax which had been spread and was supposed to be rotten enough.

Sent Mr. Lear to Alexandria to day on business.

Thursday 9th.    Thermometer at 58 in the Morning—63 at Noon and 63 at Night. Clear calm, warm and remarkably pleasant all day. Towards night a light breeze came up from the Eastward.

Visited all the Plantations. In the Neck—the People having pulled up all the Pease that were planted in Hills had begun to dig the Irish Potatoes between the Corn rows in order to Sow Rye. The Carts and Waggon were getting in the Pease and one man was cutting down with a scythe those Pease which had been sown in Broadcast. Six plows were plowing the grd. where the Pease grew in Hills for wheat & 1 pr. of dble. harrows covering it, but finding the ground to work very loose & mellow I directed what remained unplowed of the ground to be sowed *before* plowing that the Wheat might be plowed in—the harrows to follow after; first as the plows run, & then to cross; that the ground might be made level and fit for the reception of Seeds.

From Muddy hole, all the hands had gone to Dogue run.

At Dogue run—Two Carts, and all the other hands were employed in getting in the Fodder which they finished doing in the evening.

With the Ditchers, House People &ca. the Flax at this place was taken up tied in bundles, and heaped to be Housed.

At French's—all hands, together with those from the Ferry were employed in and about the fodder, and sending to the Mansion House the rotted Flax.

At the Ferry—the People were aiding as above at French's.

Cut the young bay Stallion Colts which (at first) were designed for stud Horses—the one rising 3 & the other 2 Years old. Also cut 3 sorrel & a black colt from frenchs. One of the first must have been 3 years old last spring—another of them 2 years old and the third one year old. The black was two years old last Spring.

The Revd. Mr. Keith, and Doctr. Craik dined here and went away afterwards.


Friday 10th.    Thermometer at 57 in the Morning—57 at Noon and 57 at Night. Wind at No. Et. all day and very cloudy. After dark it rained pretty briskly for some time.

Rid to the Plantations at the Ferry, Frenchs & Dogue run.

It was this day, and not yesterday, that the above Horses were cut.

At the Ferry the hands were assisting about the Fodder. At French's—all hands were engaged about the Fodder.

At Dogue run—after having got all the Flax which had been taken up the overnight into the Tobacco Ho. the People assisted by those of Muddy hole set about taking up the Irish Potatoes in order to prepare the ground for Wheat. 7 Plows at Work.

Saturday 11th.    Thermometer at 62 in the Morning—68 at Noon and 68 at Night. Clear with the Wind at No. Wt. all day, and not unpleasant.

Rid to all the Plantation's. In the Neck—Seven Plows and a harrow were at Work in the Pease grd. by the Barn which by Night would be sowed with Wheat. On the South side of this field [    ] bushls. of the Wh. English Seed Wheat was sown. Next to this (a small space being left) was a Wheat sent me by Mr. Jno. Barns—about 3½ bushels and the residue of the grd. was sown with Wheat raised on the Plantation 19½ bushels. The other hands were turning Pease and digging Irish Potatoes. Of the latter, from 23 rows comprehended between the first & last Carrot Rows were taken 135 Bls. & put into the Corn Ho.

From Muddy hole—all hands were gone to Dogue R.

At Dogue run—The whole force were employed (except the Plows) in getting up & carrying in Potats. Seven Plows were at work.

At French's—The hands of the Plantation, with those of the Ferry, were employed about the fodder; finished at this Place with the House gang & Ditchers, cuttg. down the Pease which had been sown in Broadcast in field No. 6 but, though some of them had been cut down more than a week none were dry enough to stack, or put away.

At the Ferry—Six plows (as usual) were at work in field No. 3 which was nearly broke up.

Cut at the Mann. Ho. to day—the 2 Working Stallions from Frenchs; 1 Year old Mule Colt; 3 Mule Colts of this Spring; and 1 horse Colt belonging to the Black Mare at Frenchs and likewise a spring (sorrel colt with a blaze face) at Dogue run, & one in the Neck.

Mr. Hunter and a Captn. Oudebards (a French Gentleman from the West Inds.) dined here to day and returned to Alexandria in the Evening.

Sunday the 12th.    Thermometer at 55 in the Morning—70 at Noon and 66 at Night. Wind at West in the Morning—abt. No. Wt. at Noon and So. Wt. at Night. Clear warm and pleasant all day.

A Mr. Whiting of Berkeley, on his way from Gloucester (with a letter from Mr. Francis Willis Junr.) called here—& dined, after which he proceeded to Alexandria. This Gentleman was requested to inform Mr. Willis, in answer to his letter to me—dated 24th. of Septr. last—that if the sum for which he sold the Negroes (of which Mrs. Washington the Widow of my deceased Brother Saml. Washington died possessed, & by Will gave to her Son, by him, to whom I am heir) with Interest thereon from the time of her death and my interest therein commenced that I shall neither *reclaim* the Negros—nor give him any trouble for the illegality of the Act of disposing of them.

Francis Willis, Jr. (1744–1791), of Whitehall, Gloucester County, was the executor of the will of his sister-in-law, Susannah Perrin Holding (Holden) Washington, fifth wife of Samuel Washington. In her will Susannah bequeathed five slaves supposedly given to her by her brother to her only son, John Perrin Washington (1781–1784). When the son died a short time after his mother's death, Willis sold the slaves for £240 not realizing that they were to pass to GW. Willis's letter of 24 Sept. 1788 was the second one that he sent to GW apologizing for his error and asking for instructions on settling the matter (DLC:GW). GW requested the £240, not for his own use, but for the use of Samuel Washington's daughter Harriot who had been left only a pittance by her father. However, it was later discovered that Susannah Washington had no legal title to the five slaves, her brother having failed to make a proper conveyance. Her estate actually included only one slave left to her by her mother. For that slave GW agreed to take £100 from Willis, a sum which was to be applied to the "immediate support" of Harriot (Willis to GW, 4 Aug. 1793, DLC:GW; GW to Willis, 25 Oct. 1793, ViMtV).

Monday 13th.    Thermometer at 56 in the Morning—65 at Noon and 64 at Night. Clear and very pleasant all day with the wind Southerly.

Rid to all the Plantations and to Majr. Geo. Washingtons to give him, at his request, my opinion respecting the spot on which to place his Houses.

In the Neck—The Plows began to put in Rye in the Corn ground—the Pease in Broad cast not being removed from the ground, so as to admit the Sowing of Wheat—Turning the Pease which had been pulled up by the Roots in order to cure & Stack them—Pulling Pumpkins and threshing Oats.

Muddy hole hands at Dogue run—the Cart belonging to that place drawing Pease together at French to Stack.

At Dogue Run—Seven Plows were at Work and would, by dinner time, finish (with what was plowed in the Spring) breaking up field No. 7 for Corn next year. The Cart was drawing Rails to fence the Hay Stacks in the middle & upper Meadow. All the other hands, with those from Muddy hole were digging Irish Potatoes. From the short Rows between the first Carrot row on the West side of the Field & the Woods 126½ bushls. of Potatoes were dug. At French's. Two Carts, and all the hands of that & the Ferry Plantation were employed about the Fodder—the Ferry men excepted. The House gang were employed at this place in curing, getting up, & Stacking the Pease which had been cut here.

The Ditchers went into the Neck to cutting the broadcast Pease there.

At the Ferry 5 Plows only were at Work.

THE SPOT ON WHICH TO PLACE HIS HOUSES: George Augustine Washington began to build a house on the Clifton's Neck property a few years later to house his growing family, but after his death in 1793 Fanny discontinued the construction (GW to Anthony Whitting, 9 Dec. 1792 and 3 Mar. 1793, DLC: GW).

Tuesday 14th.    Thermometer at 60 in the Morning—64 at Noon and 64 at Night. Wind Southerly with great appearances of Rain all the forenoon but clear afterwards.

Rid to the Ferry, Frenchs, and Dogue run Plantations.

At the Ferry, only 5 plows were at Work. The driver of the other got hurt. The other hands were at French's.

At French's, two Carts and all the hands were about the Fodder. Stirring the Pease at this place with the small gang about the Mann. House. 3 Men began to ditch below Manleys houses up to the Ferry road.

At Dogue run—Two Plows and a harrow began to put in Wheat among the Corn (from whence the Potatoes were taken) on the west side of field No. 5. The other 4 Plows began on the South side of No. 3 to break it up for Spring grain next year. All the other hands with those from Muddy hole were digging Potatoes.

A Mr. Brown clerk to Mr. Hartshorn came here on business of the Potomk. Company.

Wednesday 15th.   Thermometer at 60 in the morning—65 at Noon and 63 at Night. Morning clear and calm.

Visited all the Plantations. In the Neck—the Mowers having cut down all the Pease (in broad Cast) in field No. 8 were employed in cuttg. down the grass and Weeds where the flax grew in order that it might be spread and rot. The Hoe People were digging Potatoes, chopping in Rye and wd. go to getting the Pease from field No. 8 in order that Wheat might be sowed therein. Seven plows and two harrows were employed in putting in Rye.

The Muddy hole people were employed with their Plows at D.R. as usual.

At Dogue run—Four Plows were breaking up field No. 3 and three others were plowing in Wheat, but finding more plows necessary for the latter purpose two from the former were added. All the others were digging Potatoes—of which, between the Eastern-most and Westernmost Carrot rows came 198½ Bushels from 34 Rows.

At Frenchs—about 1 Oclock—the last of the blades were pulled and some of the Pease ground in field No. 6 got in order for plowing in Wheat.

At the Ferry—5 plows were at work and would by Night compleat breaking up field No. 3. The other hands were at Work at Frenchs.

Colo. Carrington and Mr. Robt. Purviance of Baltimore, and Mrs. Jenifer and Miss Wagener came here to dinner and stayed all Night.

Robert Purviance (d. 1806) and his brother Samuel Purviance, Jr., were prominent merchants and civic leaders in Baltimore for many years. Born in

Ireland, they settled in Baltimore during the 1760s and soon established a prosperous distillery and shipping business. They were active in local Presbyterian affairs and in revolutionary politics. In 1788 Samuel was captured by Indians while on an expedition to the Ohio Country and was never seen again. About this time Robert's fortunes were declining. On 19 May 1789 he wrote GW soliciting a minor post in the Baltimore naval office (DLC:GW). GW appointed him to the position and in 1794 he became collector of the port, an office he retained until his death (SCHARF [2], 54, 299; *Md. Hist. Mag.*, 42 [1947], 27n, 61 [1966], 350, 63 [1968], 16, 71 [1976], 296–99).

MISS WAGENER: probably one of the daughters of Peter Wagener (1742–1798): Sinah, Mary Elizabeth, Ann, or Sarah (Sally). Mary Elizabeth later married her cousin William Grayson (1766–1806) of Prince William County (GRAYSON, 263; KING [4], 62).

Thursday 16th.    Thermometer at 55 in the Morning—70 at Noon and 68 at Night. Clear morning & day with the Wind pretty fresh from So. Wt.

After breakfast Mrs. Jenifer Miss Wagener and Mr. Purviance went away. Colo. Carrington and myself rid to the Ferry, French's and D. R. Plantations and to the New Barn.

At the Ferry the hands were assisting at Frenchs in getting in the Fodder. The 3 plows belonging to the Plantation were breaking up the head lands in field No. 3.

At Frenchs—Two Plows began to cover Wheat in the Pease ground in field No. 6. All the other hands were about the fodder.

At Dogue run—Five Plows and Harrows were covering Wheat in the Corn ground—and two breaking up in field No. 3. All the other hands of this & Muddy hole Plantation were employed in this work also, & digging Potatoes. Turned the Mare & Colts yesterday into the upper Meadows which were opened to field No. 6.

Friday 17th.    Thermometer at 57 in the Morning—72 at Noon and 71 at Night. Clear and calm in the Morning. Pleasant all day.

Colo. Carrington going away after breakfast—I vis[i]ted all the Plantns.

In the Neck—All the Plows were stopped to tread out Wheat and all the hands were employed about the same.

From Muddy hole all the hands were at Dogue run.

At Dogue run—some hands from the Ferry had joined those of Muddy hole & this place in digging Potatoes, and putting in Wheat. Ordered the two Ploughs which were breaking up in field No. 3 for Spring grain to join those in the Corn field, in order to expedite the Sowing of Wheat.

At French's—5 plows and harrows were putting in Wheat on the Pease ground. The other hands were getting in and securing the

Fodder. The Ditch would be nearly finished this Evening—the Pease turning with the House gang.

At the Ferry—Five hands were stacking blades and doing other odd jobbs.

Saturday 18th.    Thermometer at 60 in the Morning—70 at Noon and 70 at Night. Cloudy morning with great appearances of Rain all the forenoon and a little sprinkle of it—but clear warm and pleasant in the Afternoon.

Went up to Alexandria agreeably to a summons to give evide. in the Suit between the Estate of Mr. Custis & Robt. Alexander, but the latter not appearing nothing was done & I returned home to dinner.

Sunday 19th.    Thermometer at 60 in the Morning—60 at Noon —and 58 at Night. Wind at No. Et. in the Morning & cloudy which it continued to be all day & at Night began to rain.

Mr. OKelly the Dancing Master Mr. O'Kelly the Lawyer, Mrs. O'Conner of Alexandria—Mrs. Peake & her Son Harry & her Nephew Eaglan Dined here, all of whom except Mrs. O'Conner went away after it.

Eliza Harriet O'Connor, wife of the John O'Connor who had visited GW 3 Feb. 1788, opened an academy for young ladies in Alexandria earlier this year and tried unsuccessfully to induce GW to serve as one of the school's official visitors (Eliza H. O'Connor to GW, 17 June 1788, and GW to Eliza H. O'Connor, 20 June 1788, DLC:GW). She was now preparing to leave Alexandria to join her husband, who, she said, had obtained a public office and superintendency of an academy in Edenton, N.C. Wishing to reopen her own school in Edenton, Mrs. O'Connor asked GW to give her a letter of introduction to North Carolina's governor, Samuel Johnston, a request that GW refused on grounds that he did not know Governor Johnston and had never corresponded with him (Eliza H. O'Connor to GW, 7 Oct. 1788, and GW to Eliza H. O'Connor, 17 Oct. 1788, DLC:GW). However, GW did permit her to come to Mount Vernon for "advice upon some matters of very material consequence" concerning her decision to leave town, a decision of which her students' parents did not approve (Eliza H. O'Connor to GW, 18 Sept. 1788, DLC:GW). Mrs. O'Connor did soon leave Alexandria, but if she went to Edenton, she probably did not stay there long; her husband by the fall of 1789 was at Georgetown, Md., still professing his intention to publish his history of the Americas (John O'Connor to GW, 5 Oct. 1789, DNA: PCC, Item 78; O'BRIEN, 45).

EAGLAN: apparently one of the several sons of Mrs. Peake's sister Sarah Stonestreet Edelen of Prince George's County, Md. (BRUMBAUGH, 59; see main entry for 9 May 1770).

Monday 20th.    Thermometer at 49 in the Morning—54 at Noon and 54 at Night. Much Rain (with the wind high from No. Et.)

fell in the Night and continued to do so until past Noon when it moderated and towards Night entirely ceased but continued very cloudy.

At home all day.

Tuesday 21st. Thermometer at 54 in the Morning—54 at Noon and 54 at Night. Flying clouds all day, with the Wind very hard from the No. Wt.

Went up to Alexandria to move the Court to appoint Commissioners to settle the Accts. of the Administration of Colo. Thos. Colvills Estate to whose Will I was an Executor. Colo. Fitzgerald, Mr. William Herbert & Mr. Robt. McCrae being nominated for this purpose—any two to act—I dined at Mr. Fendalls & came home in the afternoon.

Wednesday 22d. Thermometer at 49 in the Morning 60 at Noon and 60 at Night. Clear all day with the Wind (especially in the Night) fresh from So. Wt. Sent Mrs. O'Conner to Alexa.

Rid to the Plantations at the Ferry, French's & Dogue run.

At the latter, the hands from the two first except the Ferry men & Carts, together with their plows as were the Plows of Muddy were all at work digging Potatoes & plowing & Hoeing in Wheat among the Corn.

At Muddy hole—the Hoe People were pulling up their Pease wch. had been planted in Hills. They were in a manner green but the apprehension of a frost induced this Measure. Those Pease which were sent me by Colo. Spaight and planted at this place at the same were quite ripe and had been pulled great part of them many days ago—qty. of these latter about 9 bushels from about [    ] Acres of grd. These are a very forward kind, and must be reserved for Seed.

Thursday 23d. Thermometer at 56 in the Morning 70 at Noon and 72 at Night. Clear, Warm & exceedingly pleasant all day, with [wind] (tho' but little of it) at So. West.

Rid to all the Plantations. In the Neck—the Plows had, about Noon, just finished sowing the last of the Wheat in field No. 9 qty., South of the Road leading to the Creek landing, [    ] bushels; which with a small Corner on the No. Side of the Road that had been in Homony Beans make [    ] bushels in all in this field. This compleats the last sowing of Wheat at this Plantation. The Hoe People were digging Potatoes; & for want of having them out of the way of the Plows to be putting in Rye, these were obliged to return to field No. 8 to breaking up till the Hoe People should get sufficiently ahead with the Potatoe digging between the Corn Rows.

At Dogue Run—the hands and Plows of all the other Plantations were at Work.

The Ditchers & Mansn. House Gang, with the Waggon & two Carts were getting in and stacking the Pease at French's.

Friday 24th.    Thermometer at 60 in the Morng.—75 at Noon and 75 at Night. Clear and warm with but little Wind & that Southerly.

Rid to the Ferry, Frenchs and Dogue run Plantations.

From the Ferry, the Plows were gone to French's to put in Wheat—and the other hands except the Ferry men were at Dogue run digging Potatoes.

At Frenchs 5 plows were at Work putting in Wheat in No. 6. The other hands were at D. Run digging Potatoes.

At D. Run Seven plows and Harrows were covering Wheat among the Corn in field No. 6. All the other hands were following with the Hoes & digging Potatoes before them. Muddy hole people aiding.

Saturday 25th.    Thermometer at 63 in the Morning—73 at Noon and 73 at Night. Clear calm & warm all day.

Rid to the Ferry, French's and Dogue run Plantation to make a fresh distribution of the Mares Colts and other Horses that do not work but not being able to finish it the relation of it is postponed.

At these three plantations & Muddy hole—the same work precisely was going on as yesterday.

But at Frenchs, all the Wheat except the garden at, and a small spot just by, Manleys Houses was sown with Wheat—plowed & harrowed in *once* but some part had not received the cross harrowing.

Sunday 26th.    Thermometer at 63 in the Morning 75 at Noon and 74 at Night. Clear, calm, warm & very pleasant.

Went to Pohick Church and returned home to dinner. Found Dr. Stuart at Mt. Vernon—who dined there & returned home afterwards.

Monday 27th.    Thermometer at 63 in the Morning 76 at Noon and 75 at Night—Clear, calm and very warm.

[ 411 ]

Rid to all the Plantations. In the Neck 8 plows were covering Rye among the Corn. All the other hands were digging Pots. before them, or Hoeing in Rye in the Step, after them.

The hands from Muddy hole were at D. Run.

At Dogue Run, 7 Plows and Harrows were putting in Wheat as yesterday. All the other hands, consisting of those from the Ferry, Frenchs & Muddy hole, were putting in Wht. in the Step between the Corn behind the Plows—and digging Potatoes before them.

At Frenchs 5 plows and a harrow were putting in Rye, in the Middle part of field No. 6, between the newly, & first sown Wheat, at this Place.

Getting up the Hogs for killing at the Ferry, quantity 25—feeding them with Potatoes.

Made the following distribution of the Mares, Colts and Horses that do not work—viz.—

At Dogue Run in the Upper Meadows. 22 Mares, besides Doctr. La Moyeurs. For breedg. work or Sale.

In the Ferry Meadows, & fields adjoining, under the same Inclosure.

| | | | yrs. |
|---|---|---|---|
| Jennies | | 2 | |
| Washingtons horse | 1 | age | 5 |
| Peters          Ditto | 1 | 2 | 5 |
| Stallion Colts from Mn. Ho. | | 2 | 3 & 2 |
| The sett—viz.—4 sorrels each 2 yrs. old; 2 Horses & two Mares little or no Wh. | | 4      each | 2 |
| A Sorrel horse colt—oldest of French's—W. | | 1 | 4 |
| A Sorrel mare frm. Frhs. | | 1 | 3 |
| A Sorrel horse—blaze face light feet & legs from French's | | 1 | 2 |
| A Sorrel Mare Blaze face White feet—frm. M. Hole | | 1 | 2 |
| A Sorrl. horse colt blaze face White feet. Frhs. | | 1 | 1 |
| A Sorrl. colt small blaze face 2 hd. feet White—Ferry | | 1 | spring |
| A Bay Mare—blaze face Dogue run | | 1 | 2 |
| A Bay do. no white D.R. | | 1 | 2 |
| A small bay horse Colt with a very small & dim Star—D.R. | | 1 | 1 |

| | | |
|---|---|---|
| A small bay Do. from D. Run. no white | } 1 | 1 |
| A likely bla. horse from Ferry | 1 | 2 |
| A bla. horse Colt with a small snip – Frhs. | } 1 | 2 |
| A bla. or brown Mare Colt Star & near hd. foot Wh. | } 1 | 1 |
| A Black or brown Mare Colt from Davys Mare a star & 2 hind ft. Wh. | } 1 | Spring |
| A Bla. horse Colt – no white – from French | } 1 | Spring |
| Doctr. La Moyeurs – a sorr. | 1 | 1 |
| A Black or dark bro. with a blaze face fm. Neck | } 1 | 2 |
| In all | 27 | |

Tuesday 28th.    Thermometer at 63 in the Morning – 57 at Noon and 55 at Night. Wind pretty fresh from the No. Et. with encreasing clouds as the Sun rose. About 11 Oclock it began to rain, and continued to do so with intermission till after 2 oclock – from thence till night it remained cloudy & misty.

Rid to the Ferry, Frenchs and Dogue run Plantations.

At the first the Plows & Harrows were putting in Rye at Frenchs in field No. 6. The other hands, except the Ferry men, were at Dogue Run.

At Frenchs putting in Rye as above. The other hands were at D. Run.

At D. Run – Seven Plows and harrows were putting in Wheat and all the hands above mentioned with those of the Plantation and Muddy Ho. were digging Potatoes & covering Wheat in the Step between the Corn.

Wednesday 29th.    Thermometer at 42 in the Morning – 53 at Noon and 50 at Night. Clear morning with a frost. Wind at No. West all day & cold.

Rid to all the Plantations. In the Neck – the hands were digging Potatoes but not being able to keep way before the plows, the latter went to breaking up field No. 8. Ordered the Pumpkins at this and all the other plantations to be taken up & secured as a severe frost might be expected.

The hands from the several places were at work as yesterday.

Took up the Mangel Wurzel, or Roots of Scarcity in the Inclosure below the Stable. Had those raised from the seeds sent me from Doctr. Rush (coming immediately from Doctr. Letsum) 48 in number—put by themselves; being of the grey or marble coloured sort. And those which approached nearly to this colour from the seed had from Mr. Peters was also put by themselves—both kinds to raise seed from for another year making together 2½ bushl. Those with red leaves, and leaves approaching nearly to this colour were laid aside for eating or giving to the Stock. The largest of these white leaved roots only weighed (after the leaves were taken of) 3 lbs. 6 oz. and altogether [    ] lbs. filling 6 bushels.

Colo. Symm on business respecting the Affairs of Colo. Geo. Mercer and his Mortgagees came here—dined, & returned afterwards.

John Coakley Lettsom (1744–1815) of London, a somewhat eccentric Quaker physician, corresponded with Benjamin Rush on a wide variety of subjects including, besides mangel-wurzel and medicine, the abolition of the slave trade, prison reform, and balloons. Born in the West Indies and educated at Edinburgh and Leyden, Lettsom enjoyed a large and lucrative medical practice in London, but expended much of his income on his elaborate suburban residence and various philanthropies. He was also the author of numerous medical, biographical, and philanthrophic works (RUSH, 1:313, n.1). Marble-colored mangel-wurzel was considered to be the best variety (GW to Francis Adrian Van der Kemp, 27 Sept. 1788, DLC:GW).

On this date GW received, undoubtedly from Charles Simms, £7 18s. 5d., the balance due upon a bond from the estate of James Kirk of Alexandria. At the same time, he paid Simms for bringing suit for the bond and for entering an action against his neighbor Robert Alexander for a long-standing debt (LEDGER B, 275).

The deceased George Mercer's affairs were no longer of much concern to GW. At the beginning of the War of Independence, GW had announced that he would cease acting as one of Mercer's trustees, and in Nov. 1782 the general court ordered all bonds and other papers in GW's hands relating to the 1774 sale of Mercer's lands to be turned over to James Mercer. Nevertheless, an unsuccessful attempt was made about this time to involve GW in some of the continuing legal problems of George Mercer's estate ("The Answer of George Washington to the Bill of Complaint exhibited against him by William Owens," 15 Feb. 1789, ViU).

Thursday the 30th.    Thermometer at 39 in the Morning—45 at Noon and 42 at Night. Clear Morning and severe white frost. Wind at No. Wt. & cold all day.

Rid to Muddy hole, Dogue Run, Frenchs & Ferry Plantations.

At Muddy hole—the Hoe people began to dig their Irish Potatoes in field No. 3. The Plows of this place wd. finish sowing Wheat at Dogue run to day, & return & put in their own Rye.

At Dogue Run—All the Potatoes wd. be dug to day; total qty., besides scattering ones yet to pick up after the plows, 1061½ bushels. Finished sowing wheat also in field No. 5 among Corn—qty. 64 Bushels.

At French's all the Rye wd. be sown this Evening—qty. [     ] bushels. This must be too thick, as the grd. in which it was put could not exceed [     ] acres. The grd. for this was first plowed, then the Seed sown & harrowed in—afterwards cross harrowed.

At the Ferry (as from Frenchs) the Hoe people were all at D. Run: would return home to Night—as would the Ferry Plows from Frenchs.

Sowed the remainder of the yellow bearded Wheat adjoining the last in the enclosure below the Stable in the ground where the Irish Potatoes grew—6 Rows.

Friday 31st.    Thermometer at 34 in the morning—45 at Noon and 44 at Night. Clear with the Wind at No. Et. in the morning and veering round got to So. Et. by Night with appearance of rain.

Finished pruning the Weeping Willows, & other Trees in the Serpentine walks front of the House and was on the point of Riding when Mr. William Fitzhugh Junr. (of Maryland) came in, about 10 Oclock—after whom, Colo. Henry Lee arrived. Both stay'd dinner and the latter all night.

Remained at home all day.

Henry Lee was returning to his home in Westmoreland County from New York where he had been attending Congress (Lee to GW, 13 Sept. 1788, DLC:GW; GW to Lee, 22 Sept. 1788, Vi).

## November 1788

Saturday the First.    Thermometer at 44 in the Morning—54 at Noon and 54 at Night. The Wind in the Morning was from the So. Wt. & pretty fresh. About 9 Oclock it clouded up and began to rain for 10 or 15 minutes pretty smartly after which two or three other scuds of rain for a few minutes passed over. Afternoon clear.

Colo. Lee went away after breakfast and I rid to all the Plantations.

In the Neck—all the Plows were putting in Rye, and all the Hoes employed in taking up Potatoes & hoeing in Rye between the Corn.

At Muddy hole—The Plows began to put in Rye in field No. 3

where the Pease grew in hills. The Hoe People continued digging the Irish Potatoes which they began on thursday last.

At Dogue run—The Plows were breaking up field No. 3 and the other hands were employed in taking up the scattering Potatoes & fallen Corn.

At Frenchs—both plows and Hoes were employed in breaking up the bouting Roes along the fence that they may be sowed wth. the grain the field has received.

At the Ferry—The plows were breaking up No. 5. The other people, some were cleaning up the Rye that was tread out yesterday, and some digging Potatoes.

Doctr. Craik was sent for, and came down this afternoon to visit Waggoner Jack, who had been sick two or three days.

The slave Jack, wagoner at the Home House plantation, apparently died in the fall of 1795 (GW to William Pearce, 25 Oct. 1795, NBLiHi).

Sunday 2d.   Thermometer at 50 in the Morning—[    ] at noon and 70 at Night. Wind at No. Et., with clouds, and appearances of rain till about Noon; when it cleared and became pleasant.

One of Madame de Bréhan's miniatures of Washington, made into a ring. (Yale University Art Gallery, The Lelia A. and John Hill Gordon Collection)

Nelly Custis, a miniature painted by Madame de Bréhan on ivory. (Yale University Art Gallery, The Mabel Brady Garvan Collection)

Mr. George Mason came here to dinner and returned in the Evening. After dinner word was brot. from Alexandria that the Minister of France was arrived there and intended down here to dinner. Accordingly, a little before Sun setting, he (the Count de Moustiers) his Sister the Marchioness de Brehan—the Marquis her Son—and Mr. du Ponts came in.

Eléanor François Elie, comte de Moustier (1751–1817), successor to the chevalier de La Luzerne as French minister to the United States, had arrived at New York in January. Although an officer in the French army from the age of 17, he spent most of his life in diplomatic service. He was appointed minister to the German state of Trier in 1778, was sent to London in 1783 to soothe relations between Britain and France's ally Spain, became minister to Prussia in 1790, and later served Royalist exiles of the French Revolution in negotiations with both the British and Prussians (BIOG. UNIVERSELLE, 29: 482–84). In the midst of this distinguished career, his mission to the United States was a failure almost from the start. "A very well informed man" sincerely desirous of promoting American-French commercial relations, he lacked the tact and insight needed to deal with American republicans (David Humphreys to Thomas Jefferson, 29 Nov. 1788, JEFFERSON [1], 14:300–304). "The Count de Moustier," wrote John Jay to Jefferson 25 Nov. 1788, "it seems . . . expected more particular and flattering Marks of minute Respect than our People in general entertain Ideas of, or are either accustomed or inclined to pay to anybody" (JEFFERSON [1], 14:290–91).

The marquise de Bréhan, an artist and much esteemed friend of Thomas Jefferson, proved to be a further detriment to Moustier's reputation in America. "Appearances (whether well or ill founded is not important)," Jay told Jefferson, "have created and diffused an opinion that an improper Connection subsists between him [Moustier] and the Marchioness. You can easily conceive the Influence of such an opinion on the Minds and Feelings of such a People as ours" (Jay to Jefferson, 25 Nov. 1788, James Madison to Jefferson, 8 Dec. 1788, JEFFERSON [1], 14:290–91, 339–42).

For her part Madame de Bréhan was already "furiously displeased with America" (Jefferson to Maria Cosway, 14 Jan. 1789, JEFFERSON [1], 14: 445–46). She came to America hoping to find a climate beneficial to her delicate health and a pastoral utopia where the simple virtues of rural life extolled by French intellectuals of the time really existed. The harshness of the American winters and the realities of American life both in towns and in the country soon gave the lie to those romantic preconceptions, leaving her with a feeling of betrayal (JEFFERSON [1], 14:300–304).

Madame de Bréhan's son, Armand Louis Fidèle de Bréhan (1770–1828), who later became the marquis de Bréhan, had been brought to America with the hope of giving him an education that would be "more masculine and less exposed to seduction" than in France (Jefferson to Abigail Adams, 30 Aug. 1787, JEFFERSON [1], 12:65–66). He was later commissioned a captain in the Royal Lorraine cavalry and accompanied Moustier to Berlin when the comte was appointed minister to Prussia. Although Bréhan joined the Royalist émigrés during the early years of the French Revolution, he returned to France in 1803 and became a baron of the empire under Napoleon. When Napoleon fell from power, he apparently accommodated himself to the new Bourbon regime with little difficulty (DICT. BIOG. FRANÇAISE, 7:196–97; *Md. Journal*, 11 Nov. 1788).

Victor Marie du Pont (1767–1827), eldest son of the French economist and diplomat Pierre Samuel du Pont de Nemours (1739–1817), had recently become an attaché to the French legation. When Lafayette became commander of the French national guard in 1789, Du Pont returned home to serve the marquis as an aide-de-camp. He subsequently held several diplomatic posts in the United States and in 1800 joined his father and other members of the family in establishing permanent residence in the new nation. His American business ventures, unlike those of his younger brother Eleuthère Irénée du Pont (1771–1834), were generally unsuccessful.

MR. GEORGE MASON: probably George Mason, Jr., of Lexington (see entries for 17 Dec. 1773 and 29 Nov. 1785).

Monday 3d.     Thermometer at 50 in the Morning—70 at Noon And 70 at Night. A thick fog untill 8 or 9 Oclock—Clear, calm & exceedingly pleasant afterwards.

Remained at home all day. Colo. Fitzgerald & Doctr. Craik came down to dinner—& with the copy of an address (which the Citizens of Alexandria meant to present to the Minister) waited on him to know when he would receive it.

Mr. Lear went to Alexandria to invite some of the Gentlemen and Ladies of the Town to dine with the Count & Marchioness here to morrow.

Alexandria's address, welcoming Moustier to Virginia and expressing hope for continued close political connections and growing trade between France and the United States, was warmly received by him on 6 Nov. (*Md. Journal*, 25 Nov. 1788).

Tuesday the fourth.     Thermometer at 58 in the Morning—75 at Noon and 72 at Night. Morning clear, calm and very pleasant—as the weather continued to be thro' the day.

Mr. Herbert & his Lady, Mr. Potts & his Lady, Mr. Ludwell Lee & his Lady, and Miss Nancy Craik came here to dinner and returned afterwards.

In MS "Tuesday" reads "Thuesday."

Wednesday 5th.     Thermometer at 63 in the Morning—75 at Noon and 73 at Night. Very clear, calm, warm & pleast. all day.

The Minister & Madame de Brehan expressing a desire to Walk to the New Barn—we accordingly did so and from thence through Frenchs Plantation to my Mill and from thence home compleating a tour of at least Seven Miles.

Previous to this, in the Morning before breakfast I rid to the Ferry, Frenchs, D. Run and Muddy hole Plantations.

At the Ferry some of the People were cleaning up the Rye

which had been tread out the day before. Others were digging Potatoes. The Plows were at work in No. 5.

At French's—the People were preparing the yard to tread out Oats which had remained in shocks at the yard.

At Dogue Run—some hands were cleaning up Rye and preparing to lay down a bed of Wht. and others digging a Cellar to Store Irish Potatoes in—The Plows yesterday & this day being stopped to tread out grain.

At Dogue run—The People were raising Mud for Manure. The Rye would be all in and covered to day.

Thursday 6th.    Thermometer at 63 in the Morning—73 at Noon and 72 at Night. Clear, calm, warm and exceeding pleasant.

About Nine Oclock the Minister of France, the Marchioness de Brehan & their Suit, left this on their return for New York. I accompanied them as far as Alexandria & returned home to dinner. The Minister proceeded to George Town after having received an address from the Citizens of the Corporation.

In the Afternoon Mr. Ferdinand Fairfax came in and stayed all Night.

Moustier and Madame de Bréhan originally planned to make a more extensive tour of Virginia including stops at Richmond, the Natural Bridge, and Monticello, home of their friend Thomas Jefferson. They cut short their visit to the state because, in their opinion, "the season was too far advanced" and they already "had so much suffer'd from the cold" on their travels. Nevertheless, they were greatly pleased with GW and Mount Vernon. "Every thing there," they wrote Jefferson, "is enchanting" (29 Dec. 1788, JEFFERSON [1], 14:399–400).

Ferdinando Fairfax, a godson of GW, had inherited most of the estate of his uncle George William Fairfax during the past year (GW to Warner Washington, 9 Nov. 1787, NHi: George and Martha Washington Papers).

Friday 7th.    Thermometer at 62 in the Morning 62 at Noon and 60 at Night. Brisk Wind from the So. Wt. with great appearances of much rain till towards evening when it cleared—Sprinklings now & then through the day.

Went with Mr. Fairfax to my New Barn and to the Plantations at the Ferry, French's, Dogue run and Muddy hole.

At the Ferry—five plows were breaking up Field No. 5. The other force was cleaning Wheat which had been tread out and digging Potatoes.

At French's—Two of the Plows were at the Ferry—the other was stopped. Some of these people were digging Potatoes at the Ferry and others cleaning up Oats.

At Dogue run—The Plows were at work in Field No. 3: that is five; one of them from Muddy hole. The People were cleaning Wheat.

At Muddy hole—The hands were getting up Mud & some endeavouring to get up Hogs.

Saturday 8th.    Thermometer at 52 in the Morning—62 at Noon and 62 at Night. Clear all day, with the Wind high from the No. Wt.

Went up to Alexandria, agreeably to a summons, to give testimony in the Suit depending between the Estate of Mr. Custis and Mr. Robt. Alexander. Returned by the New Barn which had got about half the Rafters up.

Found Mrs. Stuart, Miss Stuart, and all Mrs. Stuarts Children here when I came home.

Sunday 9th.    Thermometer at 44 in the Morning—52 at Noon and 52 at Night. Clear & pleasant without much Wind—that Easterly.

At home all day. One of the Bucks in the Paddock having much wounded the Young woman Dolshy, Doctr. Craik was sent for who came and stayed all Night.

Dolshy, a dower slave, was listed in 1799 as a spinner. She was then the wife of the slave carpenter Joe (list of Negroes belonging to GW, c.June 1799, NjP: Armstrong Collection).

Monday 10th.    Thermometer at 42 in the Morning—52 at Noon and 50 at Night. Wind Easterly all day & fresh with clouds and great appearances of Rain.

Doctr. Craik went away in the Morning. Rid to all the Plantations.

In the Neck—the Plows and all hands were putting in Rye and taking up Potatoes—except a few who were threshing out Oats.

At Muddy hole—Two Plows were gone to Dogue Run. The Plowman of the other, and the Overseer were endeavouring to get up some outlaying hogs. The other People were getting up Mud.

At Dogue run. The Plows were at work in No. 3. The other hands were cleaning up the Tailings of Wheat & preparing the Cellar for Potatoes.

At French's—The Overseer & one or two other hands were employed in putting in Wheat in the bouting rows, in field No. 6; especially in that part where the Wht. was sown in drills. The other hand & his plows were at the Ferry.

At the Ferry—five plows were at Work in No. 5. Part of the hands were cleaning Wheat which had been tread out and part were getting up Potatoes.

The New Barn would *nearly* if not *quite* have the Rafters up to day.


Tuesday 11th. Thermometer at 50 in the Morning—52 at Noon and 52 at Night. In the Night past the Wind shifted more to the Southward and blew most *violently*. About day it began to rain (which it had done by intervals durg. the Night) and continued to do so till about sun rise when it cleared but still continued to blow very hard at So. West the whole day.

All my People, except those in the Neck were on the public roads repairing of them to day: attended, in some measure, this business myself.

Mr. Lund Washington—Overseer of the Roads—dined here to day.

Lund Washington was appointed by the Fairfax County court on 20 Oct. 1785 to oversee two public roads that ran across the Mount Vernon plantation: from Gum Spring to the mill on Dogue Run and from Gum Spring to Posey's ferry (Fairfax County Order Book for 1783–88, 180, Vi Microfilm). His visit today was apparently an official one made to request GW to repair one or both roads with his slaves.


Wednesday 12th. Thermometer at 44 in the Morning—52 at Noon and 51 at Night. Wind at So. Wt. all day & pleasant—Clear in the morning, but a little lowering towards 3 oclock—clear afterwards.

The force of yesterday was employed in the roads to day.

Mrs. and Miss Stuart went away after breakfast. I rid to the repairers of the Road and to my New Barn—the Rafters of which were all raised about Noon.

Mr. Lund Washington dined here again to day.

GW bought about 100,000 eighteen-inch-long juniper shingles for the barn from Thomas Newton, Jr., of Norfolk at a cost of about £40, but unfortunately the last and largest load of shingles did not reach Mount Vernon until the middle of December (GW to Newton, 1 Aug., 10 Oct., and 17 Dec. 1788, DLC:GW). "The Season," GW wrote the comte de Moustier 15 Dec. 1788, "will be so far advanced before I shall have compleatly finished covering my Barn, that I can be able to do nothing more to it this year" (Arch. des Aff. Etr., Mémoires et Documents, Etats-Unis, vols. 5–6). George Augustine Washington oversaw the completion of the building the following spring (GW to George Augustine Washington, 31 Mar. 1789, DLC:GW).

Thursday 13th.    Thermometer at 42 in the Morning–[     ] at Noon and [     ] at Night. Clear calm, and very pleasant all day.

Began a Survey of the Road leading from my Ferry to Cameren and thence along the Back road by Mr. Lund Washingtons & Mr. Triplett to my Mill, & from thence *direct* to the Ferry–But meeting Doctr. Craik coming to introduce a Mr. Wilming and another German from Bremin, I turned back with them–after having got as far as Cameren. Dr. Craik retd.

GW wished to replace the public roads running through the Mount Vernon plantation with a single new road. Virginia law forbade the use of gates on public roads; to fence or ditch both sides of a road to keep livestock in or out was expensive. The new road would run from Posey's ferry past the new barn on Ferry plantation to the mill, thence generally with the millrace to the tumbling dam at the head of the race, and then east across Mount Vernon's northern boundary to join the "riverside old road" between Gum Spring and Cameron. The "Back road" on which Lund Washington and William Triplett lived was the main road from Alexandria to Colchester (GW to George Augustine Washington, 31 Mar. 1789, and GW to William Pearce, 28 Sept. 1794, DLC:GW; Fairfax County Order Book for 1788–91, 32, Vi Microfilm; map of roads and fences to be maintained for use of the ferry, [Oct. 1790], Vi; map of roads from Cameron to Posey's ferry and Robert Boggess's, n.d., ViMtV). MR. WILMING: Henrich Wilmans of Bremen, Germany.

Friday 14th.    Thermometer at 44 in the Morning–[     ] at Noon and 56 at Night. Wind Southerly in the forenoon, and thro' the day till evening, when it shifted to No. Wt. All the forenoon was very cloudy with great appearances of rain–some of which in a sprinkle or two, fell about 11 Oclock–afternoon clear.

Mr. Wilming–the German Gentleman above mentioned having offered to engage a Gardener for me and to send him in a ship from Bremen; I requested that it might not exceed the following conditions for him and his Wife (if he brings one) –viz.–Ten pounds sterling for the 1st. year–Eleven for the 2d.–Twelve for the 3d. and so on, a pound encrease, till the sum should amt. to £15. beyond which not to go. That he would be found a comfortable House, or room in one, with bedding, victuals & drink; but no clothes; *these* for *self* and *wife* to be provided at his own expence–That he is to be a compleat Kitchen Gardener with a competent knowledge of Flowers and a Green House. And that he is to come under Articles and firmly bound. His, or their passages to be on as low terms as it can be obtained–The Wife if one comes is to be a Spinner, dairy Woman–or something of that usefulness.

After Mr. Wilming went away as soon as breakfast was over I rid to all the Plantations.

In the Neck—The sowing of ten Bushels of Winter Barley, East side of field No. 6 between the Corn was just finished (for an experiment) —being delayed till this time for want of the Barley, from Mr. Wayles. The People were employed in digging Potatoes which they wd. finish doing to day. The Plows were, some breaking up No. 8 and others plowing in Rye the sowing of which would be compleated to morrow.

At Muddy hole—the hands were getting up Mud. Plows at D. Run.

At Dogue run—they were cleaning a bed of Wheat which had been tread out yesterday; & compleating the Potatoe Cellar.

At Frenchs—The People were repairing the Fences around field No. 5. The Plows were at the Ferry.

At the Ferry 6 plows were at Work—the People digging Potatoes.

Mr. Lear finished to day what was left undone yesterday of the Survey of the Roads.

Doctr. Logan and Lady of Philaa. and a Monsr. [    ] of Lyons in France came here to dinner and went away afterwards.

Henrich Wilmans sent a gardener named John Christian Ehlers to GW in the summer of 1789. Ehlers, who was later joined by his wife, began work at the rate of 12 guineas a year and received subsequent raises. GW dismissed him in the fall of 1797 (GW to Wilmans, 12 Oct. 1789, Wilmans to GW, 28 Feb. 1790, and GW to James Anderson, 7 April 1797, DLC:GW; LEDGER B, 313, 353; LEDGER C, 9).

Andrew Wales (c.1737–1799) operated a brewery in Alexandria for many years. Little barley of any kind was grown or sold in the Alexandria area, and Wales as a brewer was the only local person who maintained a supply of it (GW to Thomas Peters, 4 Dec. 1786, NN: Emmet Collection; GW to William Pearce, 23 Mar. 1794, DLC:GW).

Dr. George Logan married Deborah Norris (1761–1839) of Philadelphia 6 Sept. 1781. Granddaughter of a chief justice of Pennsylvania, she obtained an exceptionally good education for a woman of her times largely as a result of a self-directed program of study at home. Her many social connections in the Philadelphia area and her precise and well-informed mind make her *Memoir of Dr. George Logan of Stenton* (Philadelphia, 1899), written after her husband's death in 1821, and her extensive annotation of family manuscripts, also undertaken in her later years, valuable sources for historians.

Saturday 15th.    Thermometer at 43 in the Morning—52 at Noon and 50 at Night. Clear morning with the Wind at No. Wt. Pleasant all day & clear with less Wind.

Went with my Compass and finished the line of stakes from Dogue run (at the Tumbling dam) to Hunting Ck.; for a road on the border of my land adjoining to Colo. Masons. Also connected

Jacques (Jean) Pierre Brissot de Warville. From J. P. Brissot de Warville and Etienne Clavière, *The Commerce of America with Europe,* New York, 1795. (Rare Book Department, Alderman Library, University of Virginia)

this with the road leading from the Gum Spring to Alexandria and from the former run the courses and measured the distances to my Mill and from the Mill to the Mansion House.

On my return home in the Evening I found Mr. Warville and a Mr. de Saint Tries here—brought down by Mr. Porter who returned again.

Jacques (Jean) Pierre Brissot de Warville (1754–1793), French journalist and reformer, came to the United States in July of this year as an agent for three European financiers who were interested in investing in the American public debt and in public lands. However, Brissot also had reasons of his own for coming. A warm friend of the United States and an admirer of Jean Jacques Rousseau, he was thinking of settling in America, possibly in the Shenandoah Valley and was planning to write a history of the new country (BRISSOT, xi–xxi). It was this last project that brought him to Mount Vernon. Brissot, Lafayette wrote to GW 25 May 1788, "is . . . very desirous to Have a peep at Your papers, which Appears to me a deserved Condescension as He is Very fond of America, writes pretty well, and will set Matters in a proper light" (PEL). How much Brissot used GW's papers during his brief stay, if at all, is not known, but he was well received by GW and was given, he said, "a great deal of information both on the recent war and on present conditions in America" (BRISSOT, 345). From Mount Vernon, Brissot went to New York and sailed for France, where he soon became deeply involved in the French Revolution. He was a prominent member of the Paris Commune and a leader of the Girondist party, but during the Terror he fell from power and was guillotined.

The chevalier de St. Trys (St. Tries, St. Trise, St. Fris), "a Captain in a french Rgt of dragoons," had a letter of introduction to GW from Lafayette (4 May 1788, PEL). He had probably come to America on the ship that brought Brissot, but did not return to France with him (Thomas Jefferson to Charles Thomson, 1 May 1788, James Madison to Jefferson, 12 Dec. 1788, JEFFERSON [1], 13:122–23, 14:352–53; St. Trys to Benjamin Franklin, 25 July 1788, HAYS, 4:377).

Sunday 16th.    Thermometer at 42 in the Morning—52 at Noon and 50 at Night—Lowering all day with the Wind fresh from the So. Wt.—towards Night the Wind shifted to the Eastward, and in the course of it rained.

Monsrs. Warville and Saint Tres returned to Alexandria in my Chariot.

Monday the 17th.    Thermometer at 42 in the Morning—50 at Noon and 50 at Night. Warm and lowering.

It was this day and not yesterday that Mr. Warville and Mr. Staint trees went to Alexandria. An Officer in the Navy of the United Netherlands came here to dinner and stayed all Night—introduced by Mr. Jas. McHenry of Baltimore—his name Richard Daily.

I remained at home all day.

Tuesday 18th.    Thermometer at 44 in the Morning—48 at Noon and 48 at Night. Warm and pleasant.

Rid to the Plantations at the Ferry, Frenchs & Dogue run.

At the Ferry—Six plows were at Work. All the other force of this place & Frenchs were digging Potatoes.

At Dogue run—Seven plows were at Work. The other hands were cleaning up Wheat which had been tread out and grubbing and Sprouting in the field where the Plows were.

The Muddy hole began to gather Corn in the New grd. at the home house yesterday.

Mr. Roger West dined here to day.

Wednesday 19th.    Thermometer at 48 in the Morning—58 at Noon and 56 at Night. Lowering all day; but little wind and that from the Southward.

Rid to all the Plantations. In the Neck the Plows were at Work breaking up field No. 8. The other hands were stripping the Seed off the flax in order to Spread.

At Muddy hole—gathering & carrying home as on the preceeding days.

At Dogue run Sprouting the meadow—the weather being too heavy to tread Wheat.

At French's & the Ferry the same Work going on as yesterday.

Thursday 20th.    Thermometer at 46 in the Morning 56 at Noon and 56 at Night. A very heavy fog—and lowering Weather all day —with a light air from the No. East.

Went to Alexandria with Mrs. Washington. Dined with Colo. Henry Lee & Lady at Mr. Fendalls and returned home in the Evening. Found Doctr. La Moyeur here.

Matilda Lee and her mother, Elizabeth Steptoe Lee Fendall, were both very ill. Neither ever fully recovered her health, Mrs. Fendall dying the next spring, and Matilda in the fall of 1790. The Lees stayed in Alexandria until the middle of March (GW to Henry Lee, 30 Nov. 1788, and Lee to GW, 2 and 23 Dec. 1788 and 14 Mar. 1789, DLC:GW).

Friday 21st.    Thermometer at 52 in the Morning 56 at Noon and 56 at Night. Thick morning and dull through the day—without wind.

Visited the Plantations at the Ferry—Frenchs and D. Run.

At the two first—the Plows were at Work as usual. The other hands were digging Potatoes.

At Dogue run 7 plows were at Work—the other hands riddling Potatoes and putting them away in the Cellar which has been prepared for them.

Muddy hole People about Corn. Doctr. Lee came here to dinner and stayed all Night.

RIDDLING POTATOES: removing soil from potatoes with a coarse sieve.

Saturday 22d.    Thermometer at 50 in the Morning 66 at Noon and 66 at Night. A very thick fog in the Morning—but clear, calm & remarkably pleasant afterwards.

Docter Lee going away after breakfast I rid to all the Plantations.

In the Neck—Seven plows began to break up that part of field No. 8 wch. is directly opposite to Mr. [Abednego] Adams's on the point. The other hands having finished spreading the flax were employed in threshing out Pease.

At Muddy hole—finished gathering the Corn in the New ground & Carting it to the Plantation. The Grey Mare slunk her fold.

At Dogue run—Seven Plows as usual were at Work. The other hands were Riddling Potatoes.

At the Ferry & French's (which are now united under one management) Six plows were at Work as usual and the other People began to get Corn from the Ferry field No. part & to husk it.

Began at all the Plantations to feed my fatting hogs with Corn, not finding that they throve much on Potatoes altho' they eat them very greedily. This might be owing to their not having sufficient age, for they are all young and growing.

Ferry and French's plantations were put under the management of James Bloxham (GW to George Augustine Washington, 26 Aug. 1787, WRITINGS, 29:263–66; GW's instructions for James Bloxham, 1 Jan. 1789, DLC:GW). GW called this area "the United Plantations" or simply "Ferry & French's" until 1793 when he named it "Union Farm, or Plantation" (GW to Anthony Whitting, 27 Jan. 1793, DLC:GW).

Sunday 23d.    Thermometer at 47 in the morning—54 at Noon and 56 at Night. A good deal of rain fell in the course of last Night and this day.

Monday 24th.    Thermometer at 63 in the Morning—68 at Noon and 68 at Night. A brisk So. Wester with Clouds, Mists & Sun shine, alternately in the forenoon. Clear afterwards till Night, when the wind came out hard from the No. West but shifted to the No. Et. and rained a little in the Night. Visited the United Plantations, D. Run & Muddy hole.

At the first the People were husking Corn and the Plows at work in No. 7 at Frenchs breaking up for B. Wheat & Wheat next year.

At D. Run Seven plows were still at work in No. 3—the other hands riddling & stowing away Potatoes.

At Muddy hole—the Plows were at D. Run. The other hands were getting up Mud and threshing out Rye.

Messrs. Thos. and Ferdinand Fairfax came here to dinner and stayed all Night.

GW today wrote letters of introduction for Ferdinando Fairfax to Samuel Powel and Dr. Thomas Ruston, both of Philadelphia. Ferdinando was preparing to go to that city "for the laudable purpose of compleating his Studies" (GW to Powel, ViMtV; GW to Ruston, WRITINGS, 30:132).

Tuesday 25th.    Thermometer at 42 in the Morning—36 at Noon and 36 at Night. Wind at No. East with rain in the morning heavy all day and sometimes dripping Rain.

At home all day, intending if the weather would have permitted to have gone up to the Great & Seneca falls by appointment made with Colos. Fitzgerald & Gilpin.

After dinner the two Mr. Fairfaxs went away.

Wednesday 26th.    Thermometer at 40 in the Morning—46 at Noon and 46 at Night. Raining more or less all day—with the Wind at No. East.

Thursday 27th.   Thermometer at 44 in the Morning—49 at Noon and 48 at Night. Clear and tolerably pleasant, with the Wind at So. Wt.

Rid to the Plantations (United) & to D. Run & Muddy hole.

At the first—Six plows were at Wk. and all the other hands were Grubbing in fields No. 7 at Frenchs, where the plowing was going on.

At Dogue Run—The Plows (Seven) were still at Work in field No. 3 and the other People removing Potatoes.

At Muddy hole (the Plows being at D. Run) the People were threshing Rye.

Colo. Blackburn and Mr. Gustavus Scott of Maryland came here to dinner & stayed all Night—as did a Mr. Packet.

Gustavus Scott (1753–1800), of Cambridge, Md., was the youngest son of Rev. James Scott of Prince William County. A lawyer, he was educated at King's College, Aberdeen, Scotland, and at the Inns of Court, London. He represented Somerset County in the Maryland conventions of 1775 and 1776 and was a delegate from Dorchester County in the assembly 1780–81 and 1783–85. During the latter session he played an active role in the creation of the Potomac Company. He was elected to the Continental Congress in 1784 but was prevented from attending by bad health. GW appointed him a commissioner for the city of Washington in 1794 (GW to Tobias Lear, 28 Aug. 1794, DLC: GW).

Mr. Packet, who lived at Bushfield with Bushrod Washington apparently as an employee, today brought a letter from Bushrod to GW, dated 20 Nov. 1788, in which Bushrod announced his intention of moving to Alexandria. The demands of his plantation and of his legal career, Bushrod had found, were incompatible. "The life as well as the capacity of man," he wrote, "is insufficient to attain even a competant degree of perfection in more than one Study, and as my inclination is attached to that of Law, I wish not to be diverted from it." Packet was on his way "up to Alexandria to enquire about the Rent of Houses in that place" (ViMtV). This Mr. Packet may be the John Packett whom GW employed in some capacity from Aug. 1789 to Sept. 1791 (LEDGER B, 313).

Friday 28th.   Thermometer at 44 in the Morning—45 at Noon and 45 at Night. Wind at No. Et. all day, with heavy clouds and at times thick mists—in the evening it Rained.

Colo. Blackburn & Mr. Scott not going away until towards Noon together with the suspiciousness of the day prevented me from riding.

Saturday 29th.   Thermometer at 45 in the morning—54 at Noon and 50 at Night. Morning cloudy with the Wind at So. Wt. which veering round to the No. Wt. blew very hard & cleared.

Mr. Richd. Harrison, late Consul in Spain, Colo. Ramsay and

Mr. Snow came here to dinner and returned to Alexandria afterwards.

Rid to the two Plantations (united) to Dogue run, and to Muddy hole.

At the first, the Plows (6) were as usual at Work and all the others were digging Potatoes in the Ferry part.

At Dogue run—Seven plows were at Work. The other hands were digging, topping & stringing Carrots.

At Muddy hole. The Ploughs as usual, were at Dogue run. The other hand were (as yesterday) threshing Oats.

Sunday 30th.    Thermometer at 34 in the Morning—46 at Noon and 46 at Night. The Wind was fresh from the No. West in the Morning and the grd., for the first time, this fall, pretty hard frozen. Towards noon the wind lulled; and at Night came out from the So. Wt. and lowered a good deal blowing fresh. It was this day & not yesterday that Mr. Harrison &ca. were here.


# December 1788

Monday 1st.    Thermometer at 44 in the Morning—55 at Noon and 54 at Night. Wind at So. Wt., & very fresh all day, with clouds but no great appearance of Rain. Towards Night it shifted to No. Wt. & continued to blow hard—turning cold.

Visited all the Plantations on this side the Creek.

At the United ones—The Plows as usual were at Work. The other hands were in part digging the remainder of the Potatoes in the Ferry field No. 2 and would go when they were done, wch. would be about Noon, into French's No. 4 adjoining about the same work. The other part were cleaning Wheat at the Ferry wch. had been tread out before the late wet weather & part of it sprouted.

At Dogue run—The Plow horses, and part of the hands were getting out Wheat. The other part finished taking up the Carrots wch. after topping, stringing and washing turned 86 bushels. These grew on 17 Rows between the Corn—two of which were transplanted & yielded badly—being (generally) small short, & forked—running more into top than root. 34 Rows of Potatoes, also between the Corn & intermixed with the above Carrots, yielded as noted 15th. Oct. 198½ bush. The other mixtures among the Corn were Cabbages, which came to nothing and Turnips (in drills) which at this time, are not much better; five Rows of each; making together, of the vegitable tribe, 61 Rows, all of which were intermixed between 60 Rows of Indian Corn which are to be gathered, & measured seperately, to see the yield of each.

At Muddy hole the people were getting up Mud for manure.

Tuesday 2d.     Thermometer at 37 in the morning—47 at Noon and 46 at Night. Clear, with the Wind at No. Wt. but not strong.

Visited all the Plantations. In the Neck, the People were gathering Beans, corn, and drawing them in. Only 5 plows were at Work —the Waggon being employed in drawing in Corn. That part of the Corn which was intermixed with Carrots, would be gathered (tho' not measured) to day. It amounted to 49 rows—between which 23 rows of Irish Potatoes, yielding 135 bushls. (as observed the 10th. of Octr.) hath already been dug, & 13 rows of Carrots, 12 of Turnips, and one of the Turnip rooted Cabbage now remain.

The Hands from Muddy hole were some at Dogue run with their Plows and about the Carrots and some at Frenchs about the Potatoes.

At the two Plantations United, The Plows were at Work as usual. The other hands were employed, some in cleaning up the Wheat as yesterday and the rest about the Potatoes—where also the Ditchers, & such others of the weak gang from the House were also sent.

At Dogue run, the Plow Horses were getting out Wheat—the other hands in topping & sprouting the Carrots and preparing them for putting away.

Wednesday 3d.     Thermometer at 32 in the Morning—33 at Noon and 29 at Night. Clear with the Wind fresh from No. Wt. & cold—ground as yesterday froze hard.

Rid to the two Plantations united and to the New Barn.

The Plows at these places were at work as usual. After sending of the wheat to the Mill—the whole force with some hands from Muddy hole the ditchers &ca. from the House were employed in getting up & securing the Potatoes in field No. 4 at Frenchs in the Barn.

Thursday 4th.     Thermometer at 25 this Morning—42 at Noon and 40 at Night. Wind still at No. Wt. and fresh—but after the Morning the cold was not so severe as yesterday.

At home all day.

Friday 5th. Thermometer at 36 in the Morning—46 at Noon and 42 at Night—Wind Southerly and weather moderate—a few flakes of snow fell in the early part of the Morning—but not enough to whiten the grd. This is the first that has fallen *here* this fall. Clear & pleasant all day—but the Wind getting to No. Wt. again at Night it turned cold.

Visited all the Plantations. In the Neck the Plows were stopped by the frost which had frozen the ground quite hard. The greater part of the hands had been working on the public roads the two preceeding days. To day they were removing Potatoes into the Barn from the Corn House.

All the hands from Muddy hole were at Dogue run, & digging Potatoes at Frenchs. No plowing.

At Dogue Run—Plows were stopped. Part of the hands were gathering, drawing & husking corn and part cleaning up Wheat which had been tread out.

At the Ferry & Frenchs Plantations The Plows were at work and most of the other hands were from about 10 or 11 Oclock digging Potatoes. In the Morning, and all day yesterday the ground was too hard frozen to dig them up. Some of the People were cleaning up (at the Ferry) the last tread wheat.

Saturday 6th. Thermometer at 33 in the morning—46 at Noon and 44 at Night. Clear morning and day—first part of wch. was calm—the latter part the Wind was pretty fresh from the Southward.

Rid to the Ferry & Frenchs Plantn. Lofting Corn at the first—and digging Potatoes at the latter which were much injured and some entirely destroyed by the frost.

Mr. Dulany dined here yesterday.

Sunday 7th. Thermometer at 44 in the Morning—57 at Noon and 57 at Night. Clear, warm & pleasant all day.

Monday 8th. Thermometer at 50 in the Morning—[    ] at Noon and [    ] at Night. Clear warm & pleasant with the Wind at South.

Went up to Alexandria on business of the Estate of Colo. Thos. Colvill to whom I am an Executor. Returned in the Evening accompanied by Colo. Henry Lee.

Tuesday 9th. Thermometer at 60 in the Morning—60 at Noon and 60 at Night. Wind still Southerly and fresh—a good deal of rain fell in the course of last Night and the early part of this Morning.

Rid to the Plantations at the Ferry, Frenchs & Dogue run.

At the two first the Plows were at work in field No. 7 at French's and all the other hands with the assistance as mentioned last week were employed to day as they were yesterday in getting up Potatoes.

At Dogue run. The Plows finished about Noon, breaking up field No. 3 and the other hands compleated the Husking and measuring the Corn which grew in 60 rows between the Carrots—qty. 46 barrls. of sound Corn and 4 of what is called cow Corn—hence

| | |
|---|---|
| 60 Rows of Corn produced | 230 Bls. |
| 34 ditto of Irish Potatoes intermixed with these | 198½ |
| 17 ditto of Carrots—ditto | 86 |

Mr. Ludwell Lee & Mr. Elliot Lee came here to dinner and in the afternoon with Colo. Henry Lee returned to Alexandria.

Concluded my exchange after dinner to day with Colo. Hy. Lee of Magnolio for 5000 acres of Kentucke Land agreeably to the memo. which he gave to me—which in case it should have been disposed of by Doctr. Skinner (now deceased) is to be supplied by other Lands of equal value. This bargain was made in the presence of Colo. Humphreys, the two Mr. Lees above mentioned Mr. Lear, & my Nephew Geo. Auge. Washington.

GW was willing to part with Magnolia because the stallion was expensive to keep and had brought in little or no money for stud service during the past two and a half years despite frequent advertisement of that service (GW to Henry Lee, 30 Nov. 1788, DLC:GW; LEDGER B, 227). Dr. Alexander Skinner, of Richmond, who served as surgeon of Lee's Legion 1780–83, patented tracts of 2,000 and 3,000 acres on or near the Rough River in Jefferson (now Ohio) County, Ky. Lee obtained a deed for these two tracts by 17 Jan. 1789, and in February or March he conveyed his title to GW (BLANTON, 337; Henry Lee to GW, 2 Dec. 1788, 17 Jan., 6 and 14 Feb., and 14 Mar. 1789, GW to Henry Lee, 12 Dec. 1788, 20 Jan. and 14 Feb. 1789, DLC:GW).

Wednesday 10th.  Thermometer at 41 in the Morning—44 at Noon and 43 at Night. Clear, with the Wind fresh at No. Wt. all day.

Remained at home all day. William Gardener—my New Overseer for the Neck, arrived (by Water) with his family to day.

William Garner, of Charles County, Md., today signed a contract with GW, agreeing to serve as overseer of River plantation "with the utmost Industry, Sobriety and Honesty" in return for £36 a year (articles of agreement between Garner and GW, 10 Dec. 1788, DLC:GW). He was employed until 1792 when he was dismissed for the neglectful way in which he conducted that year's harvest (LEDGER B, 314; GW to Anthony Whitting, 13 Jan. and 26 May 1793, DLC:GW).

Thursday 11th.    Thermometer at 37 in the Morning—44 at Noon and 44 at Night—Clear & tolerably pleasant—the Wind being Southerly.

Rid to the Plantations at the Ferry & Frenchs—Dogue run & Muddy hole.

At the first, the 6 Plows having finished breaking up No. 7 at Frenchs began yesterday about dinner to plow in No. 4 at the Ferry. All the other hands assisted as before were digging Potatoes in No. 4 at Frenchs.

At Dogue run—the 4 plows at this place, and the 3 belonging to Muddy hole, began in the afternoon of Tuesday to plow in No. 5 at the latter plantation having finished breaking up No. 3 at the first. Some of the hands at this place were cleaning Wheat & the others about the Corn.

At Muddy hole—The Plows began in No. 5 as has been mentioned. Some hands were getting in a Stack of Oats and the rest were at French's.

Friday 12th.    Thermometer at 35 in the Morning—46 at Noon and 46 at Night—Clear in the forenoon with appearances of Snow, in the afternoon but these vanished before Night. Wind Southerly all day.

Visited all the Plantations. In the Neck 7 Plows were in No. 8 breaking it up. The other hands were pulling and getting in Corn; and topping Carrots.

At Muddy hole—3 plows were at work in No. 5. The other hands were in part threshing Oats and part at Frenchs about the Potatoes.

At Dogue run—the Plow horses were treading Wheat and the hands attending—getting in & husking Corn.

At the Ferry & Frenchs—6 Plows were at work in No. 5 at the Ferry. The other hands were all employed abt. the Potatoes.

Saturday 13th.    Thermometer at 38 in the Morning—52 at Noon and [    ] at Night. Clear, calm & pleasant.

Visited the Ferry & French's, & Dogue run & Muddy hole Plantations.

At the two first the Horses were getting out the remainder of the wheat—a small damaged stack and the Plow people attending. All the other hands were about the Potatoes which were dug & housed to day—quantity in the whole (at Frenchs) 1088 bushels—but many of them having suffered by frost—and all being put up wet, owing to the sloppiness of the ground occasioned thereby—the whole must be taken out, assorted & dried in order to preserve them. It is indispensable that this work should be, next year, & every succeeding one, be compleated before the ground begins to freeze—in short as soon as the tops of the Potatoes begin to fade & while there is Sun to dry them properly.

At Dogue run—treading Wheat again & the other hands employed as yesterday.

At Muddy hole—the Plows and other People were at Work as yesterday.

Sunday 14th.    Thermometer at 40 in the morning—[    ] at Noon and 50 at Night—Clear, warm & pleasant all day with the Wind at So. Et.

Monday 15th.    Thermometer at 46 in the Morning—60 at Noon and 50 at Night. A little lowering in the morning, but clear afterwards—Wind till about 10 'oclock was Southerly after wch. it came out at No. Wt. but neither hard nor cold.

Rid to the Plantations at the Ferry & Frenchs and to D. Run and Muddy hole.

At the first two, Six plows were at Work. The other hands were, some of them, digging Carrots in the Ferry field No. 2 and the remainder were taking the Potatoes out of the Barn with a view to dry them but it appeared to be a vain attempt as there were so many watery ones among them—occasioned by the frost—as to render it scarcely possible to save any without seperating them one by one which would be endless. However, to try the effect I had them spread thin in the sun, and stirred to see if they would dry—ordering them to remain out, in heaps if the appearance of wet, or frost shd. not be great and, after again spreading them tomorrow—to remove them into the Barn Cellar tho' they will be exposed there & to lay them thin there.

At Dogue run—some of the hands were cleaning up Wheat and others about the Corn. The 4 Plows of this place were at Muddy hole.

At Muddy hole—Seven plows were at Work—some hands were threshing out Oats and the rest were at D. Run.

Received the remainder of the Carrots which were made in the Neck—quantity 93 bushels.

Tuesday 16th.    Thermometer at 39 in the Morning—49 at Noon and 48 at Night; Went to Alexandria to day to lay before the Court a plan of the roads as they pass through my Mount Vernn. tract of Land to & from the Ferry with the hardships occasioned thereby and to ask relief agreeably to the alterations which were proposed and submitted by the said plan which was readily assented to.

Dined at Colo. Fitzgeralds and returned home in the afternoon.

The Fairfax County court today granted GW permission to alter and open public roads on his lands (Fairfax County Order Book for 1788–91, 77, Vi Microfilm; GW to William Pearce, 28 Sept. 1794, DLC:GW).

Wednesday 17th.    Thermometer at 31 in the Morning—32 at Noon and 28 at Night. Wind fresh from No. Wt. all the latter part of the Night with a little Snow and great appearances of its continuing in the Morning early—but about 9 oclock (before the grd. got covered) it ceased and before Eleven O'clock was quite clear but cold the Wind continuing fresh from the same point.

Rid to the Plantations at the Ferry and Frenchs and to Dogue run & Muddy hole.

At the two first—6 Plows were going. The other hands were, some about the Potatoes & others about the Carrots in Frenchs Corn field No. 4 those out of the Ferry field being topped & sent to the M. House quantity 21 bushels from 12 rows.

At Dogue Run—The Plows 4, were at Muddy hole. All the other hands with some from Muddy hole were about the corn.

At Muddy hole 7 Plows were at work. The other hands at home were threshing & cleaning Oats.

Thursday 18th.    Thermometer at 25 in the Morning—26 at Noon and 24 at Night. Not much wind which towards Night was Easterly with Snow after dark.

Rid to the Ferry & Frenchs only. Got up the Carrots at the latter & had them brought to the Mansion House—qty. 33 bushels from eight rows. The Plows were stopped. The other hands were about the Corn getting it out of the Ferry field.

Friday 19th.    Thermometer at 25 in the morning—30 at Noon and 32 at Night—but little wind—ground covered about an Inch deep with Snow.

Rid to the Plantations at the Ferry and Frenchs and to Dogue run & Muddy hole.

At all, the Plows were unable to move.

At the Ferry & Frenchs, all hands were employed about the Corn of the Ferry field.

At Dogue run—The People were also about the Corn, getting in & husking it and about cleaning Wheat which they had threshed out yesterday.

At Muddy hole—Except the hands which were aiding at Dogue run, the rest were employed in threshing & cleaning Oats.

Mr. Madison came here to dinner.

James Madison was going to Orange County to stand for election to the United States House of Representatives from his home district. In the voting, which occurred 2 Feb. 1789, he won by a large majority (Madison to GW, 2 Dec. 1788, and GW to Madison, 16 Feb. 1789, DLC:GW).

Saturday 20th.    Thermometer at 22 in the Morning—24 at Noon and 20 at Night. Wind having sprung up in the Night blew hard & cold all day from the No. Wt.

Remained at home with Mr. Madison. Sent my Carriage to Dumfries for Mrs. Washington of Bushfield & others—but expect it will find difficulty to cross Occoqn.

Sunday 21st.    Thermometer at 17 in the Morning 20 at Noon and 16 at Night. Wind hard & cold all day from the No. Wt.

Mr. William Craik, and Mr. [    ] Washington—Son of Mr. Lawrence Washington of Chotanck dined here and returned afterwards to Alexandria.

Lawrence Washington of Chotank had three sons: George Washington (b. 1758), who died young; Lawrence Washington, Jr. (d. 1809); and Needham Langhorne Washington (d. 1833), who inherited his father's home (WAYLAND [1], 333, 339; EUBANK, 20).

Monday 22d.    Thermometer at 13 in the Morning—16 at Noon and 20 at Night. The Wind though there was but little all day was Southwardly. In the Night it blew pretty fresh from the So. Wt. This morning the river was closed except holes in places. Yesterday a good deal of Ice was formed as there also was the day before.

At home all day.

The Corn which grew between the rows of Carrots at the Ferry, being in number 38 amounted to 28 barrls. or 140 bushls. Of the above 12 Carrot Rows three were Transplanted, and did not yield more than a peck each, which is an additional proof that this mode of Culture will not succeed.

The Carriage Returned from Dumfries without Mrs. Washington & the others for whom it went—but was obliged to head Occoquan on account of the Ice which had impeded the passage. Doctr. Stuart called here dined and contd. to Abing.

Tuesday 23d.    Thermometer at 20 in the Morning—20 at Noon and 20 at Night. Wind at No. Wt. again, snowing & cold.
At home all day.

Wednesday 24th.    Thermometer at 14 in the Morning—20 at Noon and 18 at Night. Clear & cold. Wind at No. Wt.—ground about 4 Inches covered with Snow.
At home all day.

Thursday 25th.    Thermometer at 14 in the Morning 24 at Noon and 18 at Night. Lowering in the Morning but clear afterwards and not very cold there being but little wind.
Sent Mr. Madison after breakfast as far as Colchester in my Carriage.

Friday 26th.    Thermometer at 19 in the Morning—30 at Noon and 27 at Night. Wind at No. West but not fresh—clear.
At home all day.

Saturday 27th.    Thermometer at 21 in the Morning—28 at Noon and 29 at Night—Wind at No. Et. and heavy all the fore part of the day; with a sleet at Night.
At home all day.

Sunday 28th.    Thermometer at 37 in the Morning—42 at Noon and 44 at Night—Wind still at No. Et. with fine rain, & Sleet in the Morning but thawing afterwards—by Night little or no Snow appeared.

Monday 29th.    Thermometer at 38 in the Morning—44 at Noon and 44 at Night. Cloudy in the Morning, & till near 11 O'clock—after which clear, moderate & pleasant, with the wind at So. Wt.
Rid to the Plantations at the Ferry and Frenchs and to Dogue run & Muddy hole.
At the two first all hands had began to gather, get in, & husk the Corn wch. grew at French's. Taking those rows which grew between the 8 rows of Carts. which in number were 28, these Rows yielded 80 bushels of sound & 10 bushls. of Rotten Corn—as the 8 rows of Carrots did 33 bushels of these Roots.

*January 1789*

At Dogue run—The Men were making a farm Pen, and the Women breaking & swingling flax and getting up the shattered Corn.

At Muddy hole—The Men were about a farm pen and the Women threshing Oats.

SWINGLING: swingeing; beating.

Tuesday 30th.    Thermometer at 46 in the morning—52 at Noon and 51 at Night. Wind at So. Wt. all day and weather variable— sometimes threatning rain at other times promising fair weather. About dusk it began to drizzle and by Nine Oclock rained fast. Snow all gone.

Rid into the Neck and to Muddy hole Plantations.

At the first the Men were about a farm Pen and the Women threshing.

At Muddy hole the Men were still about the Farm Pen & the Women threshing.

Wednesday 31st.    Thermometer at 50 in the Morning—[    ] at Noon and [    ] at Night. Cloudy in the Morning, with the Wind at No. Wt. Clear afterwards but not very cold.

Rid to the Ferry & Frenchs and to Dogue run and Muddy hole Plann.

At the two first all hands were about the Corn and dreadfully wet & disagreeable this work and proves however improper and injurious it is to have this business on hand so late in the year.

At Dogue run the Men (except those with the Plows) were about the Farm Pen and the Women abt. the flax.

At Muddy hole—Seven Plows were at work, 4 from D. Run and 3 from the Plann. The other hands were repairing fences on the Ferry road around field No. 5.

# January 1789

Thursday 1st.    Thermometer at 38 in the Morning—47 at Noon and 47 at Night. Clear Morning and wind tho' not much of it at No. Wt.—clear all day & pleasant.

Went out after breakfast to lay of or rather to measure an old field which is intended to be added to Muddy hole Plantation— after which marked out a line for the New road across from the Tumbling Dam to little Hunting Creek to begin [th]e Post and rail fence on.

In the Evening Mr. Bushrod Washington & his wife and Miss Polly Blackburn came in.

The new road from Posey's ferry to the Gum Spring–Cameron road was apparently never finished. On 29 Nov. 1790 the Virginia General Assembly passed an act discontinuing the ferry for lack of sufficient patronage. With the ferry closed, there was little or no reason for the public to use the old roads, and GW soon had gates erected on them, an action that the Fairfax County court later questioned but apparently never explicitly forbade (HEN-ING, 13:152; GW to William Pearce, 28 Sept. 1794, DLC:GW; map of roads and fences to be maintained for use of ferry, [Oct. 1790], Vi).

Bushrod and Nancy Blackburn Washington apparently were now living in rented quarters at Alexandria. Their furniture had been sent up from Bush-field on 12 Dec., and on 19 Jan., Bushrod took his oath as an attorney before the Fairfax County court. GW offered Bushrod the use of his town house in Alexandria rent free, but Bushrod declined, the house being out of repair and having no facilities for a lawyer's office (GW to Bushrod Washington, 25 Nov. 1788, DLC:GW; GW to Bushrod Washington, 16 Jan. 1789, Bushrod Washington to GW, 12 Dec. 1788 and 18 Jan. 1789, ViMtV; Fairfax County Order Book for 1788–91, 82, Vi Microfilm).

**Friday 2d.** Thermometer at 36 in the Morning—34 at Noon and 34 at Night. Wind at No. Et.—Drizzling & raining more or less all day.

**Saturday 3d.** Thermometer at 35 in the Morning 40 at Noon and 40 at Night. Wind still at No. Et. with the same kd. of weather as yesterday.

**Sunday 4th.** Thermometer at 40 in the morning—44 at Noon and 40 at Night. In the Morning the Wind was at So. West but soon shifting to No. Wt. it cleared and was tolerably & not cold overhead but exceedingly sloppy & deep under foot.

The Revd. Mr. Fairfax came here in the evening and stayed all Night.

**Monday 5th.** Thermometer at 32 in the Morning—44 at Noon and 40 at Night. Clear and cool with the wind at No. Wt.

Mr. Fairfax, and Mr. Bushrod Washington & wife, and Miss Blackburn went away after breakfast.

**Tuesday 6th.** Thermometer at 31 in the Morning—44 at Noon and 40 at Night. In the Morning the Wind was Southerly—but it soon shifted to No. west.

Rid to the Ferry & Frenchs Plantations—and to Dogue run and Muddy hole.

Wednesday 7th.    Thermometer at 32 in the Morning—39 at Noon and 39 at Night. Calm all day, but raw & chilly.

Went up to the Election of an Elector (for this district) of President & Vice President when the Candidates polled for being Doctr. Stuart and Colo. Blackburn the first recd. 216 votes from the Freeholders of this County and the second 16 Votes. Dined with a large company on venisen at Pages Tavn. and came home in the evening.

The Virginia General Assembly passed an act 17 Nov. 1788 authorizing election of the state's 12 presidential electors by districts. Fairfax County was in the district which also included Prince William, Loudoun, and Fauquier counties. Voting in all districts occurred on this day at the courthouses with all voters qualified to vote for General Assembly members eligible to participate (HENING, 12:648–53). David Stuart won his district by a margin of 347 votes (*Md. Journal*, 20 Jan. 1789). Virginia's electors met in Richmond on 4 Feb. and voted unanimously for GW for president as did electors of all the other ratifying states, who met that day also. GW was formally notified of his election on 14 April (FREEMAN, 6:157–66).

William Page (d. 1790) ran a tavern in Alexandria apparently for only a few years. The local Freemasons met there in 1788 (BROCKETT, 34).

Thursday 8th.    Thermometer at 31 in the Morning—40 at Noon and 40 at Night—But little Wind all day & that Southerly and a little lowering. In the Night it shifted to No. Wt. & blew fresh & cold.

Mess. Lund & Lawe. Washington—Mr. Willm. Thompson & Mr. William Peake dined here. I was at home all day.

Friday 9th.    Thermometer at 28 in the Morning—31 at Noon and 27 at Night. Wind fresh from No. Wt. all day and cold—in the evening calm.

Finished gathering Corn this day *only* at French's—quantity [      ] Barrels of yellow which is an indifferent sort—much shrivelled & rotten. [      ] Barrls. of White Corn of the kind had in 1787 from Colo. Richard Henry Lee and [      ] Barrls. of rotten or faulty. I remained at home all day.

Saturday 10th.    Thermometer at 28 in the Morning—29 at Noon and 28 at Night. Wind Southerly, but cold notwithstanding. At home all [day.]

Sunday 11th.    Thermometer at 25 in the Morning—27 at Noon and 27 at Night—Abt. Nine Oclock last Night it began to Snow, and continued to do so, more or less all Night & till about 10 oclock to day when it ceased but did not clear. The ground was covered about 4 Inches deep.

Monday 12th. Thermometer at 16 in the Morning—25 at Noon and 25 at Night—Clear and cold—with the Wind at No. Wt.— towards Night it lowered again.

This day sowed Clover & Timothy Seed (6 pints of the first & 2 of the latter on an acre) at bothe the Ferry & Muddy hole Plantations— On the Wheat—beginning at the South end of the field at the Ferry and by the Gate at Muddy hole.

Tuesday 13th. Thermometer at 25 in the Morning—28 at Noon And 29 at Night. Wind at So. Wt. with a mixture of Snow, hail, and sometimes drops of Rain till about Noon when the Clouds broke and the weather promised to be fair.

Wednesday 14th. Thermometer at 29 in the Morning—32 at Noon and 30 at Night. Variable wind, with a little Snow in the Morning but clear about Noon.

The Sleet, or hail that fell yesterday making a hard crust on the Snow to day, I discontinued sowing grass-Seeds as they could not bury themselves, & were liable to be blown of the surface of the Snow and drifted.

Thursday 15th. Thermometer at 26 in the Morning—30 at Noon and 27 at Night—Clear (with the Wind at No. Wt.) till after Noon when the Weather lowered with appearances of Snow.

Rid to the Plantations at the Ferry and Frenchs and to Dogue run & Muddy hole.

Friday 16th. Thermometer at 21 in the Morning—26 at Noon and 26 at Night. Clear all day; with the Wind at No. Wt. in the forenoon, & So. Wt. in the Afternoon.

Brought from Dogue run Plantation 15 Mares which were supposed to be with fold; and one that was thought not to be so to the Mann. Ho. Left 3 there to be added to the Plow horses—sent one to Muddy hole—and one to the Ferry for the same purpose And also brot. from the Ferry [    ] Young Horses & Mares to the Mansion House to be fed.

Began to put Ice into the Ice Ho. this day.

Doctr. Craik dined here & returned to Alexandria afterwards.

Saturday 17th. Thermometer at 30 in the Morning—36 at Noon and 32 at Night. Wind Southerly in the Morning & forenoon with great appearances of Snow—Afternoon clear with the Wind at No. West.

Rid to the Plantations in the Neck and at Muddy hole.

Sunday 18th.    Thermometer at 28 in the Morning—34 at Noon and 34 at Night. But little Wind all day and pleasant for the Season.

Monday 19th.    Thermometer at 32 in the Morning—37 at Noon and 40 at Night. Heavy lowering Morning and little Wind—drops of rain afterwards with the Wind at South and thawing.

    Rid to the Plantations at the Ferry & Frenchs and to Dogue run and Muddy hole.

    At Muddy hole, finding the top of the Snow to be sufficiently softened—I directed the Overseer to renew the sowing of grass Seeds on the Wheat.

Tuesday 20th.    Thermometer at 46 in the Morng.—50 at Noon and 50 at Night. Thick morning & raining more or less all the remaining part of the day with the Wind at So. Wt.—which together dissolved all the Snow.

    At home all day.

Wednesday 21st.    Thermometer at 42 in the Morning—42 at Noon and 42 at Night. Very heavy Morning, tho' last night was very clear—more favourable afterwards but not perfectly clear. At home all day.

    Mr. Lund Washington dined here.

Thursday 22d.    Thermometer at 32 in the Morning—36 at Noon and 32 at Night. Snowing, hailing & raining more or less all day— with the Wind at No. Et.

Friday 23d.    Thermometer at 32 in the Morning—38 at Noon and 37 at Night. Clear & calm in the Morning & continued to be so & very pleasant all day.

    Rid to the Ferry & French's Plantations and to Dogue Run & Muddy hole.

    At the first began to ditch across the New Meadow to inclose or rather seperate fields No. 1 & 2.

    At Dogue run the People were fencing in field No. 7.

    Doctr. Stuart came here to Dinner & stayed all Night.

Saturday 24th.    Thermometer at 36 in the morning—40 at Noon and 40 at Night—Morning heavy & lowering with the Wind at So. —Moderate all day with Sun shine at times.

    Went into the Neck—measured some fields there and laid off 8 Acres for Tobacco.

Sunday 25th.    Thermometer at 38 in the Morning 40 at Noon and 40 at Night. Lowering more or less all day with rain after dark.

Colonels Fitzgerald Lee & Gilpin dined here, and returned to Alexandria in the evening.

Monday 26th.    Thermometer at 45 in the Morning—50 at Noon and 44 at Night. A good deal of rain fell in the course of the Night —Varable Winds & Weather through the day, with rain again at Night.

Tuesday 27th.    Thermometer at 42 in the Morning—42 at Noon and 44 at Night. Much rain fell in the course of last Night—heavy forenoon, with the Wind at No. Et.—At Night a good deal of Rain.

At home all day.

Wednesday 28th.    Thermometer at 35 in the Morning—34 at Noon and 32 at Night. Wind at No. Et. Raw & cold. About Noon it began to Snow & continued to do so fast for about half an hour, but it soon disappeared—and in the Night rained hard again.

Rid to the Plantations at the Ferry Frenchs & to those at Dogue run and Muddy hole.

Renewed the Plowing in the two first—in field No. 4 at the Ferry—& finished breaking up field No. 5 at Muddy hole & began abt. Noon to plow No. 4 for Buck Wheat at the same place.

Major Washington set out for Berkley to see his father who had informed him of the low state of health in which he was.

Thursday 29th.    Thermometer at 35 in the Morning—35 at Noon and 44 at Night. So. Wt. & very lowering all day—towards Night it began to brighten a little and the sun set clear.

At home all day.

Friday 30th.    Thermometer at 36 in the Morning—35 at Noon and 34 at Night. Heavy morning with the Wind at No.—which afterwards getting to No. Et. brought on a fine Snow which continued.

Visited the Plantations at the Ferry & Frenchs and Dogue run & Muddy hole.

At the first two added another Plow to their number.

*February 1789*

Saturday 31st.    Thermometer at 29 in the Morning—26 at Noon and 27 at Night. The Snow which began yesterday afternoon continued without through the whole of last Night and till about Sun rising this Morning by which it was near a foot deep. Wind blowing hard all day from No. Wt. it became very cold.

# February 1789

Sunday 1st.    Thermometer at 14 in the Morning—22 at Noon And 20 at Night. Clear morning with the Wind at No. Wt. where it continued fresh & very cold, all day.

Mr. & Mrs. Herbert—Mr. & Mrs. Young and Mr. George Calvert came here to Dinner and stayed all Night.

Hugh Young, a Baltimore merchant, assisted GW several weeks later by forwarding some Irish gooseberry cuttings that arrived for him in Baltimore (Young to GW, 16 Feb. 1789, and GW to Young, 3 Mar. 1789, DLC:GW).

Monday 2d.    The Mercury was in the Ball of the Thermometer in the Morning—at 26 at Noon and 20 at Night.

Mr. Herbert and Mr. Young and their Ladies went away after breakfast.

I went up to the Election of a Representative to Congress for this district. [V]oted for Richd. Bland Lee Esqr. Dined at Colo. Hooes & returned home in the afternoon.

On my way home met Mr. George Calvert on his way to Abingdon with the Hounds I had lent him—viz.—

| | |
|---|---|
| Vulcan—&<br>Venus | } From France |
| Ragman &<br>two other dogs | } From England |
| Dutchess &<br>Doxey | } From Philadelpha. |
| Tryal<br>Jupiter &<br>Countess | } Descended from the French Hounds |

All ten of Virginia's allotted representatives were elected today. The district in which Fairfax County was located also included King George, Stafford, Prince William, Loudoun, and Fauquier counties. Everyone qualified to vote for members of the General Assembly was entitled to vote in this election (HENING, 12:653–56). Richard Bland Lee, a Federalist, won and was subsequently reelected twice.

# The Presidency and the New England Tour

## April, October–December 1789

### [April 1789]

[16 April 1789]   About ten o'clock I bade adieu to Mount Vernon, to private life, and to domestic felicity; and with a mind oppressed with more anxious and painful sensations than I have words to express, set out for New York in company with Mr. Thompson, and colonel Humphries, with the best dispositions to render service to my country in obedience to its call, but with less hope of answering its expectations.

Although GW evidently kept a diary for at least part of the spring and summer of 1789, the diaries for this period have disappeared. Only two entries for these months are presently available, both in printed form. The entry for 16 April 1789 is taken from MARSHALL [3], 5:154; it also appears in SPARKS, 10:461. The entry for 23 April is from IRVING, 4:505–6.

On 4 Feb. presidential electors of those states which had ratified the Con-

Charles Thomson, longtime secretary of the Continental Congress, delivered to Washington official word of his election to the presidency. (Mr. Armistead Peter III)

Hannah Harrison Thomson, wife of Charles Thomson. (Mr. Armistead Peter III)

stitution were scheduled to meet in specified cities to vote for the president and vice-president. The announcement of the results of the election was to be made by the new federal Congress, which was to convene in New York on 4 Mar. On the appointed day Congress failed to achieve a quorum and it was not until 6 April that the electoral votes were counted (DE PAUW, 1:6–11). Throughout the month, however, reports reaching GW from various sources made it clear that his election was virtually a certainty, and he reluctantly began preparations to leave Mount Vernon, feeling, as he informed Henry Knox, not unlike "a culprit who is going to the place of his execution, so

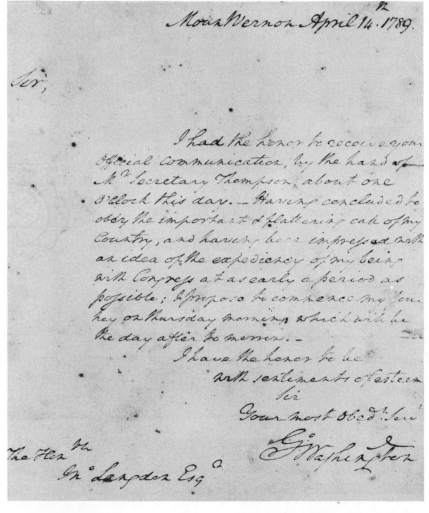

Washington's letter to John Langdon, president pro tempore of the Senate, accepting the presidency. (Lilly Library, Indiana University, Bloomington, Ind.)

unwilling am I, in the evening of a life nearly consumed in public cares, to quit a peaceful abode for an Ocean of difficulties" (1 April 1789, DLC:GW). On 14 April Charles Thomson, secretary of Congress, arrived at Mount Vernon, bringing GW the awaited confirmation of his election. Thomson had "left New York on Tuesday, the 7th of the present month; and though much impeded by tempestuous weather, bad roads, and the many large rivers I had to cross, yet, by unremitted diligence I reached Mount Vernon, the seat of his excellency General Washington, on Tuesday, the 14th, about 12 o'clock. I found his excellency at home; and after communicating to him the object of my mission and the substance of my instructions, I took an opportunity, on the day of my arrival, to address him as follows:

" 'Sir, the President of the Senate, chosen for the special occasion, having opened and counted the votes of the electors in the presence of the Senate and the House of Representatives, I was honored with the commands of the Senate to wait upon your excellency with the information of your being elected to the office of President of the United States of America. . . .

"To this his excellency was pleased to make the following reply:

" 'Sir, I have been long accustomed to entertain so great a respect for the opinion of my fellow-citizens, that the knowledge of their unanimous suffrages having been given in my favor, scarcely leaves me the alternative for an option. Whatever may have been my private feelings and sentiments, I believe I cannot give a greater evidence of my sensibility for the honor they have done me, than by accepting the appointment. . . .

"Upon considering how long time some of the gentlemen of both Houses of Congress have been at New York, how anxiously desirous they must be to proceed to business, and how deeply the public mind appears to be impressed with the necessity of doing it immediately, I cannot find myself at liberty to delay my journey. I shall therefore be in readiness to set out the day after to-morrow, and shall be happy in the pleasure of your company' " (ASP, MISC., 1:5–6).

For the ceremonies attending GW's journey north and his reception in New York City, see FREEMAN, 6:167–84; BAKER [2], 121–29; BOWEN, 19–36.

[23 April 1789]   The display of boats which attended and joined us on this occasion, some with vocal and some with instrumental music on board; the decorations of the ships, the roar of cannon, and the loud acclamations of the people which rent the skies, as I passed along the wharves, filled my mind with sensations as painful (considering the reverse of this scene, which may be the case after all my labors to do good) as they are pleasing.

Today's diary entry is a fragmentary account of GW's reception in New York City. The New York *Daily Advertiser*, 24 April 1789, was more explicit. "Yesterday arrived the illustrious George Washington, President of the United States, amidst the joyful acclamations of every party and every description of citizens. . . . The President was received at Elizabeth-Town, by a deputation of three Senators, five Representatives of the Congress of the United States, and three officers of the State and Corporation; with whom he embarked in the barge, built . . . and rowed by thirteen pilots of this harbour, dressed in white uniform; Thomas Randall, Esq. acting as cockswain.

"No language can point the beautiful display made on his excellency's approach to the city. The shores were crouded with a vast concourse of citizens, waiting with exulting anxiety his arrival. His Catholic Majesty's sloop of war the *Galviston,* (Mr. Dohrman's) ship North-Carolina, and the other vessels in port, were dressed and decorated in the most superb manner. His excellency's barge was accompanied by the barge of the Hon. Gen. Knox, and a great number of vessels and boats from Jersey and New-York, in his train. As he passed the Galviston, he received a salute of thirteen guns, and was welcomed by an equal number from the battery. . . .

"On his excellencys arrival at the stairs, prepared and ornamented, at Murray's wharf, for his landing; he was received and congratulated by his excellency, the Governor of this State, and the officers of the State and Corporation, and [a] . . . procession was formed . . . followed by an amazing concorse of citizens.

"The procession advanced through Queen street to the house fitted up for the reception of his Excellency, where it terminated, after which, he was conducted without form to the house of Governor Clinton, with whom his Excellency dined. In the evening the houses of the citizens were brilliantly illuminated."

# October 1789

Thursday 1st.    Exercised in my Carriage in the forenoon.

The following company dined here to day. viz.—

Mr. Read of the Senate, Colo. Bland and Mr. Madison of the House of Representatives—Mr. Osgood and his Lady Colo. Duer his Lady and Miss Brown Colo. Lewis Morris & Lady—Lady Christiana Griffin and her Daughter and Judge Duane & Mrs. Greene.

Mr. Thomas Nelson joined my Family this day.

Dispatched Many of the Comns. for the Judiciary Judges, Marshalls and Attorneys this day with the Acts.

George Read (1733–1798) was United States senator from Delaware. A signer of the Declaration of Independence, Read was a member of the Continental Congress 1774–77 and a delegate from Delaware to the Constitutional Convention where he represented the interests of the small states. He served in the Senate from 1789 to 1793 when he became chief justice of Delaware.

Theodorick Bland had been elected to the House of Representatives from Virginia in 1789.

James Madison had been elected to the House of Representatives from Virginia in 1789 with GW's quiet support. During the early months of his administration GW had frequently called upon Madison for advice on matters pertaining to appointments and protocol and requested his aid in drawing up such official papers as his first inaugural and other addresses and statements to Congress. In these months Madison assumed the role of an unofficial cabinet member and administration whip in the House (see BRANT, 3: 276–89).

Samuel Osgood (1748–1813) had been a member of the Continental Congress 1781–84 and of the Board of Treasury 1785–89. Although he opposed ratification of the Constitution, GW appointed him postmaster general 26 Sept. 1789, a post he retained until the federal government moved to Philadelphia in 1790. In 1786 he married Maria Bowne Franklin, widow of Walter Franklin of New York. Upon GW's arrival in New York he occupied a house facing Franklin Square built by Walter Franklin and now owned by Osgood. The house, "square, five windows wide, and three stories high," had previously been occupied by the president of the Continental Congress (DECATUR, 117). Congress had ordered Osgood 15 April 1789 to "put the same, and the furniture therein, in proper condition for the residence and use of the President of the United States, to provide for his temporary accommodation" (ANNALS OF CONGRESS, 1:149–50).

William Duer (1747–1799) was born in Devonshire, Eng., educated at Eton, and served in India as aide-de-camp to Lord Clive. He emigrated to America in 1768 and settled in New York where he became active in business and politics. Duer was a member of the Continental Congress in 1777 and 1778 and in Mar. 1786 was appointed to the Board of Treasury. His appointment as assistant secretary of the treasury in 1789 was one of GW's more controversial appointments since Duer's speculative ventures had already excited the suspicions of the Antifederalists. In 1779 Duer married Catherine Alexander, usually called Lady Kitty, daughter of William Alexander, Lord Stirling.

Anne Brown (Browne), who was born in 1754, was a daughter of William and Mary French Browne of Salem, Mass. (Some members of the family dropped the "e" from the family name.) Her parents died while she was still a child and she was sent to New York to live with relatives. In Dec. 1773 she and her older brother William Burnet Browne visited Mount Vernon (see entry for 11 Dec. 1773). In the note to this entry, the Brownes have been incorrectly identified as Dr. William Brown and his sister Frances. William Burnet Browne married Judith Walker Carter and the family lived at Elsing Green, King William County, Va. In the early 1790s the Brownes' daughter Judith Carter Browne married GW's nephew Robert Lewis. Anne Brown (Browne) was a cousin of Lady Kitty Duer.

Lewis Morris (1726–1798), a half brother of Gouverneur Morris, was born at the family estate, Morrisania, in Westchester County, N.Y., and educated at Yale. A signer of the Declaration of Independence, he served in the Continental Congress 1775–77 and in the New York legislature 1777–81, and as a member of the New York Ratifying Convention he had vigorously supported the Constitution. In 1749 he married Mary Walton, daughter of Jacob and Maria Beekman Walton. At his father's death in 1762 Morris had received the half of the estate of Morrisania lying west of Mill Brook, and in 1789 he was still engaged in restoring his property which had been extensively damaged by the British during the Revolution.

Lady Christiana Griffin (1751–1807) was the wife of Cyrus Griffin (1748–1810), a prominent Virginia jurist and the last president of the Continental Congress. In 1770 Griffin had married Lady Christiana Stuart, daughter of John Stuart, sixth earl of Traquair, in Edinburgh. In Aug. 1789 Griffin had been appointed a member of the commission to negotiate with the southern Indians (see entry for 16 Nov. 1789) and was now absent from New York. In Feb. 1790 GW appointed him federal judge of the district of Virginia.

James Duane (1733–1797), of New York City, was a member of the Con-

A 1790 print of Federal Hall in New York City during Washington's inauguration. (New-York Historical Society)

tinental Congress from 1774 to 1783 where he was particularly active in financial and Indian affairs. He was mayor of New York City from 1784 to 1789 and a member of the New York Ratifying Convention where he strongly supported the Constitution. In 1759 Duane had married Mary Livingston, daughter of Robert Livingston, third lord of Livingston Manor. GW appointed him first federal judge for the district of New York in Sept. 1789.

Catherine Littlefield Greene (1755–1814), a native of Shoreham, R.I., had married Nathanael Greene in 1774. During the Revolution the Greenes became close friends of the Washingtons. Greene died in 1786, leaving a plantation in Georgia and a legacy of debt to his wife and five children. At this time Mrs. Greene was spending part of her time in Newport, R.I., and part in New York City.

Thomas Nelson, Jr., was the son of Gov. Thomas Nelson of Virginia. Governor Nelson had died in Jan. 1789 leaving his wife and children impoverished and with extensive debts. David Stuart wrote GW, 14 July 1789, suggesting that some government position might be found for young Thomas. Since the governor had been an "old friend and acquaintance," GW decided to appoint the young man as one of his secretaries, although "I must confess there are few persons of whom I have *no* personal knowledge or good information that I would take into my family, where many qualifications are necessary to fit them for the duty of it—to wit, a good address, abilities above mediocrity—secresy and prudence—attention and industry—good temper—and a capacity and disposition to write correctly and well, and to do it obligingly" (GW to Stuart, 26 July 1789; GW to Nelson, 27 July 1789; Nelson to GW, 13 Aug. 1789, DLC:GW). Nelson resigned from GW's family in Nov. 1790 (Nelson to GW, 24 Nov. 1790, DLC:GW).

ACTS: These officers had been appointed under the provisions of "An Act to Establish the Judicial Courts of the United States" (1 STAT. 73–74 [24 Sept. 1789]).

**Friday 2d.** Dispatching Commissions &ca. as yesterday for the Judiciary.

The Visitors to Mrs. Washington this evening were not numerous.

Martha Washington held her levees, lasting about three hours, on Friday evenings at 8:00, and GW usually attended. "She gives Tea, Coffee, Cake, Lemonade & Ice Creams," Abigail Adams noted. "The form of Reception is this, the servants announce & Col. Humphries or Mr. Lear, receives every Lady at the door, & Hands her up to Mrs. Washington to whom she makes a most Respectfull courtsey and then is seated without noticeing any of the rest of the company. The Pressident then comes up and speaks to the Lady, which he does with a grace dignity & ease, that leaves Royal George far behind him. The company are entertaind with Ice creems & Lemonade, and retire at their pleasure performing the same ceremony when they quit the Room." Frequently the receptions were "as much crowded as a Birth Night at St. James, and with company as Brilliantly drest, diamonds & great Hoops excepted" (Abigail Adams to Mary Cranch, 9 Aug. 1789, 5 Jan. and 27 July 1790, MITCHELL, 18, 35, 55).

**Saturday 3d.** Sat for Mr. Rammage near two hours to day, who was drawing a miniature Picture of me for Mrs. Washington.

Walked in the Afternoon, and sat about two Oclock for Madam de Brehan to complete a Miniature profile of me which she had begun from Memory and which she had made exceedingly like the Original.

John Rammage (1763–1802), a skilled miniature painter and silversmith, had been a lieutenant in the Royal Irish Volunteers in Boston in 1775 and subsequently served in the British army in Halifax and New York, where he settled after the Revolution. Rammage, an Irishman, was "a handsome man of the middle size," a contemporary noted, who "dressed fashionably . . . a scarlet coat with mother-of-pearl buttons—a white silk waistcoat embroidered with colored flowers—black satin breeches and paste knee buckles . . . a gold-headed cane and gold snuff box, completed his costome" (DUNLAP, 1:267–68). Rammage's debts eventually forced him to flee to Canada where he remained until his death. The miniature Rammage was working on today was probably the Betty Washington–Stabler miniature, painted on ivory (see EISEN, 2:487).

The marquise de Bréhan and the comte de Moustier, who had visited GW at Mount Vernon in 1788 (see entry for 2 Nov. 1788) now lived in the Macomb House on Broadway, soon to be occupied by GW. Both Moustier and his sister were widely unpopular in the United States. "We have a French minister now with us," John Armstrong complained, "and if France had wished to destroy the little remembrance that is left of her and her exertions in our behalf, she would have sent just such a minister: distant, haughty, penurius, and entirely governed by the caprices of a little singular, whimsical, hysterical old woman, whose delight is in playing with a negro child, and caressing a monkey" (GRISWOLD, 93; see also John Jay to Jefferson, 25 Nov. 1788, JEFFERSON [1], 14:291). The marquise was a skilled miniaturist and had worked on a portrait of GW on her visit to Mount Vernon in 1788. She may have begun the work from one of Houdon's busts in Paris, and continued it at her visit to Mount Vernon and at this sitting. "Her painting was in cameo-relief in blue, white, and black, and looks like carved reliefs, though painted profiles. She made a number of copies" (EISEN, 2:454–55, 591–92).

**Sunday 4th.**   Went to St. Pauls Chappel in the forenoon. Spent the remainder of the day in writing private letters for tomorrows Post.

St. Paul's Chapel, opened in 1766, was one of two Protestant Episcopal chapels which had been established when Trinity Church needed additional parish facilities (SMITH [4], 136). GW attended St. Paul's regularly in 1789 and early 1790, probably because the rebuilding of Trinity, which had been destroyed by fire in 1776, was not yet completed. When the new building, erected on its original site at Broadway and Wall Street, was consecrated in Mar. 1790, it contained a pew for the president, and GW frequently attended Trinity for the remainder of his stay in New York.

**Monday 5th.**   Dispatched the Commissions to all the Judges of the Supreme and District Courts; & to the Marshalls and Attorneys and accompanied them with all the Acts respecting the Judiciary Department.

Exercised on horse back between the Hours of 9 and 11 in the forenoon and between 5 and 6 in the Afternn. on foot.

Had conversation with Colo. Hamilton on the propriety of my

St. Paul's Chapel, New York City. (New-York Historical Society)

makg. a tour through the Eastern states during the recess of Congress to acquire knowledge of the face of the Country the growth and Agriculture there of and the temper and disposition of the Inhabitants towards the new government who thought it a very desirable plan and advised it accordingly.

GW had appointed Alexander Hamilton secretary of the treasury on 11 Sept. 1789.

Tuesday 6th.    Exercised in a Carriage with Mrs. Washington in the forenoon.

Conversed with Genl. Knox (Secretary at War) on the above tour who also recommended it accordingly.

Signed Letters of Instructions to the Governor of the Western Territory respecting the situation of matters in that Quarter. And authorized him, in case the hostile disposition of the Indians was such as to make it Necessary to call out the Militia, & time would not allow him to give me previous notice of it, to apply to the States of Virginia & Pennsylvania for a Number not exceeding 1500; one thousand of which to be taken from the former and 500 from the latter.

Henry Knox had been appointed secretary of war by GW 11 Sept. 1789.

LETTERS OF INSTRUCTIONS: Section 5 of "An Act to recognize and adapt to the Constitution of the United States the establishment of the troops raised under the Resolves of the United States in Congress assembled, and for other purposes therein mentioned" (1 STAT. 95–96 [29 Sept. 1789]) authorized the president to call state militia into service if needed to protect the frontier from Indian raids. A copy of GW's letter to Arthur St. Clair, governor of the Northwest Territory, is in DNA: RG 233, Records of Reports from Executive Depts.—War Dept.

Wednesday 7th.    Exercised on horseback; & called on the Vice President. In the afternoon walked an hour.

Mr. Jay communicated the purpt. of the Instructions received by Sir John Temple British Consul from the Duke of Leeds Secretary for Foreign affairs—viz.

Trade. How many *foreign* Vessels—of what Nations—whether from Europe or their Colonies.

What Tonnage—whether any and what difference between *British* and others—what on American.

What *Port charges* on foreign Vessels—whether any and what difference &ca.

What *duties* on foreign Goods—whether any and what difference as to the *Countries* producing, and *Vessels* bringing them—Number of Vessels *built* where &ca.

Staple Commodities. Whether they encrease or diminish—which —in what degree—and why.

Manufactures—What—Where—Whether and how encouraged.

Emigrations—From *Europe* in what numbers—from where—whether and how encouraged &ca.

From *United States*—to British and Spanish Territories &ca.

Population—whether generally, or partially encreasing or diminishing and from what causes.

Justice—Whether there be any, and what obstructions, and where, to the recovery of British Debts according to Treaty.

Upon consulting Mr. Jay on the propriety of my intended tour into the Eastern States, he highly approved of it—but observed, a similar visit wd. be expected by those of the Southern.

With the same Gentlemen I had conversation on the propriety of takg. informal means of ascertaining the views of the British Court with respect to our Western Posts in their possession and to a Commercial treaty. He thought steps of this sort advisable, and mentioned as a fit person for this purpose, a Doctr. Bancroft as a man in whom entire confidence might be placed.

Colo. Hamilton on the same subject highly approved of the Measure but thought Mr. Gouvr. Morris well qualified.

Vice-President John Adams and his family were now living in a mansion on Richmond Hill, near Lispenard's Meadows at the corner of Varick and Van Dam streets (BOWEN, 18). "The House is situated upon a high Hill which commands a most extensive prospect. . . . You turn a little from the Road and enter a Gate. A winding Road with trees in clumps leads you to the House. . . . You enter under a piazza into a Hall & turning to the right Hand ascend a stair case which lands you in an other of equal dimensions of which I make a drawing Room. It has a Glass door which opens into a gallery the whole Front of the house which is exceeding pleasant. . . . The House is not in good repair, wants much done to it" (Abigail Adams to Mary Cranch, 12 July 1789, MITCHELL, 17–18).

John Jay, secretary of foreign affairs under the Confederation, had been named chief justice of the Supreme Court by GW on 24 Sept. 1789. GW had appointed Thomas Jefferson secretary of state 25 Sept. 1789, but Jefferson was on his way to America from his post as United States minister to France before he could be notified and did not learn of his appointment until his arrival in Norfolk, Va., 23 Nov. 1789. Jay continued in charge of the State Department until Jefferson arrived in New York 21 Mar. 1790 (MALONE [2], 2:243, 254–55).

Dr. Edward Bancroft (1744–1821), a native of Westfield, Mass., studied medicine in England and was living in London in 1776 when he became an unofficial agent for the American commissioners in Paris and remained a confidant of Benjamin Franklin and Silas Deane until the end of the war. At the same time, he was pursuing a highly successful career as a spy for the British ministry. Although considered ill-mannered and indiscreet by such contemporaries as John Adams (ADAMS [1], 4:71–74), only Arthur Lee seriously considered his activities treasonable. In 1789 Bancroft was living in London.

Hamilton's suggestion was undoubtedly a welcome one to GW. In addition to his own frequent and pleasant contacts with Morris after the Revolution, Morris's abilities had been prominently displayed at the Constitutional Convention where he had led the fight for a strong and independent presidency. He was already in Europe, having arrived in Paris in early 1789 to attend to the problems arising out of business associate Robert Morris's tobacco contract with the Farmers General and to engage in a highly speculative attempt to purchase the American debt to France. Since the mission to Britain was unofficial, the appointment would not have to run the gamut of the Senate where there was considerable suspicion of Morris's political principles and personal morality. GW wrote Morris two letters 13 Oct. 1789 requesting that he undertake the unofficial mission to London to discuss with the British ministry the possibility of a commercial treaty between Great Britain and the United States and attempt to reach an understanding on the major grievances between the two countries: the failure of American citizens to pay debts owed to British creditors and the retention by the British government of seven frontier posts in American territory (WRITINGS, 30:439–42). On the same day the president sent Morris a personal request that he procure for him "mirrors for a table, with neat & fashionable but not expensive ornaments for them;

such as will do credit to your taste" and "handsome & useful Coolers for wine *at* & *after* dinner" (DLC:GW).

Thursday 8th.    Mr. Gardoqui took leave, proposing to embark to morrow for Spain.

The following Company dined with Me to day. viz.

The Vice-President his Lady & Son and her Niece with their Son in Law Colo. Smith & his Lady. Governor Clinton & his two eldest daughters—Mr. Dalton and his Lady their Son in law Mr. Dubois and his lady and their other three daughters.

In the Evening the Count de Moustier & Madam de Brehan came in and sat an hour.

Mr. Madison took his leave to day. He saw no impropriety in my proposed trip to the Eastward; but with respect to the private agent to ascertain the disposition of the British Court with respect to the Western Posts & Commercial treaty he thought if the necessity did not press it would be better to wait the arrival of Mr. Jefferson who might be able to give the information wanted on this head—and with me thought, that if Mr. Gouvr. Morris was employed in this business it would be a commitment for his appointment as Minister if one should be sent to that Court or wanted at Versailles in place of Mr. Jefferson—and Moreover if either of these was his Wish whether his representations might not be made with an eye to it. He thought with Colo. Hamilton, and as Mr. Jay also does, that Mr. Morris is a man of superior talents—but with the latter that his imagination sometimes runs a head of his judgment—that his Manners before he is known—and where known are oftentimes disgusting—and from that, and immoral & loose expressions had created opinions of himself that were not favourable to him and which he did not merit.

Don Diego de Gardoqui, Spanish representative in the United States, lived in the Kennedy House at No. 1 Broadway where he entertained lavishly. Accompanied by his son and one of his secretaries, Gardoqui sailed for Bilboa on 10 Oct. on board the snow *San Nicholas* (*Gaz. of the U.S.*, 14 Oct. 1789).

Abigail Adams (1744–1818), born in Weymouth, Mass., married John Adams in 1764. From 1784 to 1787 she was in Europe with her husband during his diplomatic service at The Hague and in Paris and London. The Adams family had moved in the summer of 1789 from their home in Braintree to Richmond Hill in New York City (see entry for 7 Oct. 1789). Abigail quickly became Mrs. Washington's staunch social ally in the new capital. "We live upon terms of much Friendship & visit each other often," Abigail noted. "Mrs. Washington is a most friendly, good Lady, always pleasent and easy" (MITCHELL, 30). The Adams's son is either Charles Adams (1770–1800), who had accompanied the family to New York and was studying law with Alexander Hamilton, or John Quincy Adams (1767–1848), also living at Richmond Hill. HER NIECE: Louisa Smith, the daughter of Abigail Adams's brother William Smith, lived with the Adamses.

William Stephens Smith (1755–1816) had served as one of GW's aides-de-camp 1781–83 and had married the Adamses' daughter Abigail Amelia in London in 1786 while he was John Adams's secretary of legation. After touring Europe he returned to America in 1788 where he soon became heavily involved in land speculation. GW appointed him marshal for the district of New York in 1789.

George Clinton (1739–1812) had been governor of New York since 1777. A vigorous Antifederalist, he led the fight against ratification of the Constitution in the New York Convention. In 1789 he was the victor in a bitterly contested campaign against the Federalist candidate Robert Yates for the governorship. Clinton's two eldest daughters were Catharine Clinton (b. 1770) and Cornelia Clinton (b. 1774).

Tristram Dalton (1738–1817), merchant and farmer of Newburyport, Mass., graduated from Harvard in 1755, served in the Massachusetts legislature 1782–88, and was elected to the United States Senate in 1789. His wife was Ruth Hooper Dalton, daughter of Robert "King" Hooper, a wealthy Marblehead, Mass., merchant. MR. DUBOIS: The Daltons' daughter, Ruth Hooper Dalton, had married Lewis Deblois, a Boston merchant, 21 July 1789 (NEWBURYPORT VITAL RECORDS, 2:125).

Friday 9th.    Exercised on horse-back between the hours of 9 and 11. Visited in my rout the Gardens of Mr. Perry and Mr. Williamson.

Received from the French Minister, in Person, official notice of his having recd. leave to return to his Court and intended embarkation—and the orders of his Court to make the following communication—viz.—That his Majesty was pleased at the Alteration which had taken place in our Government and congratulated this Country on the choice they had made of a Presidt.

He added that *he* should take care to make a favourable representation of the present State of things here to his Master who he doubted not would be much pleased therewith. Hitherto he observed that the Government of this Country had been of so fluctuating a nature no dependence could be placed on its proceedings; whh. caused foreign Nations to be cautious of entering into Treaties &ca. with the United States—But under the present Government there is a head to look up to—and power being put into the hands of its Officers stability will be derived from its doings.

The Visiters this evening to Mrs. Washington were respectable both of Gentlemen and Ladies.

"Perry's garden was on the west side of the Bloomingdale road, west of the present Union Square. [David] Williamson's was a flower and nursery garden, and a place of public resort, on the east side of Greenwich Street, extending about three squares up from Harrison Street" (BAKER [2], 149).

The comte de Moustier had written to John Jay on 6 Oct. 1789 requesting an appointment to take leave of the president since he had received permission to return to France to improve his health and attend to private business (DNA: RG 59, Domestic Letters). Moustier sailed for France around 12 Oct. (SMITH [4], 243).

Saturday 10th.   Pursuant to an engagement formed on Thursday last—I set off about 9 Oclock in my Barge to Visit Mr. Prince's fruit Gardens & shrubberies at Flushing on Long Island. The Vice President—Governor of the State, Mr. Izard, Colo. Smith and Majr. Jackson accompanied me.

These Gardens except in the number of young fruit Trees did not answer my expectations—The shrubs were trifling and the flowers not numerous.

The Inhabitants of this place shewed us what respect they could, by making the best use of one Cannon to salute.

On our return, we stopped at the Seats of General, and Mr. Gouvernr. Morris and viewed a Barn of which I have heard the latter speak much belonging to his farm—but it was not of a Construction to strike my fancy—nor did the conveniencies of it at all answer the cost.

From hence we proceeded to Harlaem where we were met by

Ralph Izard by John Trumbull. (Yale University Art Gallery)

Mrs. Washington, Mrs. Adams and Mrs. Smith—Dined at the Tavern kept by a Captn. Mariner and came home in the evening.

William Prince's Linnean Botanic Garden at Flushing, Long Island, had been established by his father, also William Prince, in 1737. Although Prince's extensive nurseries for plants and trees had been severely decimated by British depredations during the Revolution, the gardens and orchards had largely recovered by 1789, and GW often ordered fruit for his table from Prince (DECATUR, 62, 93).

Ralph Izard (1742–1804) was born near Charleston, S.C., and owned extensive lands in the state. When the Revolution began Izard was traveling in Europe and in 1777 Congress appointed him commissioner to Tuscany. He was never received at that court and the time until his recall in 1779 was spent in Paris squabbling with Benjamin Franklin over his accounts and his diplomatic prerogatives. He returned to America in 1780, served in the Continental Congress 1782–83, and was United States senator from South Carolina 1789–95. A staunch Federalist, his connection with GW dated from 1780 when he had visited the commander-in-chief at headquarters (see GW to Samuel Huntington, 6 Sept. 1780, DNA: PCC, Item 152).

SEATS OF GENERAL, AND MR. GOUVERNR. MORRIS: Lewis Morris was now living on the portion of Morrisania, the family estate, lying west of Mill Brook, which he had received under the terms of his father's will. On the elder Lewis Morris's death in 1762, the eastern half of the estate and the manor house went to Morris's second son, Staats Long Morris, although Morris's second wife, Sarah Gouverneur Morris, and her children were permitted to occupy the house during her lifetime. Staats Long Morris had remained loyal to the crown during the Revolution and was living in England when, in 1787, his half brother Gouverneur Morris purchased from him his portion of the estate including the manor house, Morrisania (MINTZ, 13–16, 173–75).

Abigail Adams described this outing in a letter 11 Oct. 1789 to her sister Mary Cranch: "We yesterday had a very pleasant party together. The whole family of us dinned with the President on Thursday, and he then proposed an excursion to long Island by water to visit Princes Gardens, but as Mrs. Washington does not Love the water we agreed that the Gentlemen should go by water and the Ladies should meet them at a half way House and dine together, and yesterday we had a most Beautifull day for the purpose. The President, [the] V.P., Col. S[mith], Major Jackson, Mr. Izard &c. went on Board the Barge at 8 oclock. At Eleven the Ladies, namely Mrs. Washington, Mrs. Adams, Mrs. Smith, Miss Custos [Custis] set out in Mrs. Washingtons coach & six & met the Gentlemen at Harlem where we all dinned together & returnd in the same manner" (MITCHELL, 29–30).

William Mariner had been active in whaleboat warfare in the waters around New York during the early part of the Revolution. His tavern, sometimes called the Ferry House, was at present-day 126th Street and First Avenue. He may also have kept a tavern for a time on Ward's Island (DECATUR, 69; BAKER [2], 149).

Sunday 11th.    At home all day—writing private Letters.

Monday 12th.    Received the Compliments of the Count de Pentheve, commanding his most Christian Majestys Squadron in the harbour of Boston—these were sent by the Marquis de Traversy in the Active Frigate; who with all his Officers, were presented by the French Minister about One clock.

A squadron of the French navy consisting of two ships of 74 guns and four frigates, under the command of Henri Jean Baptiste, vicomte de Pontèves-Giens (1738–1799), had arrived in Boston harbor on 3 Sept. Jean Baptiste Prévost de Sansac, marquis de Traversay, and the *Active* had been dispatched to New York by Pontèves "to present the respects of the Officers of the squadron to the Chief Magistrate of the United States." During the Yorktown campaign the marquis had served with de Grasse's fleet on the Chesapeake. The *Active* anchored in New York harbor on Sunday 11 Oct. (*Gaz. of the U.S.*, 14 Oct. 1789; *Pa. Packet*, 3 Nov. 1789; CONTENSON, 245, 273).

Tuesday 13th.   At two Oclock received the Address from the People called Quakers.

A good many Gentlemen attended the Levee to day.

THE ADDRESS: presumably a statement of support for GW by "the Religious Society called Quakers, from their Yearly Meeting for Pennsylvania, New-Jersey, and the western Parts of Virginia and Maryland" (NHpR: Collection of Naval and Marine Manuscripts). The meeting was held 28 Sept.–3 Oct. 1789. A copy of GW's undated reply is in NHpR: Collection of Naval and Marine Manuscripts.

Wednesday 14th.   Wrote several Letters to France and about 7 Oclock in the afternoon made an Informal visit (with Mrs. Washington) to the Count de Mostier and Madame de Brehan to take leave of them. Into the hands of the former I committed these letters—viz.—to the Count de Estaing—Count de Rochambeau—the Marqs. de la Fayette and the Marqs. de la Rouirie.

Having resolved to write to Mr. Gouvr. Morris, to request, as a private Agent that he wd. sound the intention of the British Ministry with respect to their fulfilment of the Treaty and dispositions towards a Commercial Treaty with us the letters were prepared and lodged in the hands of Mr. Jay to forward.

LETTERS TO FRANCE: These letters, to the comte de Rochambeau, to the marquis de Rouerie, and to the comte d'Estaing, are all dated 13 Oct. in GW's letter books (DLC:GW). The letter to Lafayette is dated 14 Oct. (DLC:GW). For the letters to Gouverneur Morris, see entry for 7 Oct. 1789.

Thursday 15th.   Commenced my Journey about 9 oclock for Boston and a tour through the Eastern States. The Chief Justice, Mr. Jay and the Secretaries of the Treasury and War Departments accompanied me some distance out of the City. About 10 Oclock it began to Rain, and continued to do so till 11, when we arrived at

Alexander Hamilton in a portrait by James Sharples. (Metropolitan Museum of Art)

the house of one Hoyatt, who keeps a Tavern at Kings-bridge [1] where we, that is Major Jackson, Mr. Lear and myself, with Six Servants which composed my Retinue, dined. After dinner through frequent light Showers we proceedd. to the Tavern of a Mrs. Haviland at Rye; [2] who keeps a very neat and decent Inn.

The Road for the greater part, indeed the whole way, was very rough and Stoney, but the Land strong, well covered with grass and a luxurient Crop of Indian Corn intermixed with Pompions [pumpkins] (Which were yet ungathered) in the fields. We met four droves of Beef Cattle for the New York Market (about 30 in a drove) some of which were very fine—also a flock of Sheep for the same place. We scarcely passed a farm house that did not abd. in Geese. Their Cattle seemed to be of a good quality and their hogs large but rather long legged. No dwelling Ho. is seen without a Stone or Brick Chimney and rarely any without a shingled roof—*generally* the Sides are of Shingles also. The distance of this days travel was 31 Miles in which we passed through (after leaving the Bridge) East Chester New Rochel & Marmeroneck; but as these places (though they have houses of worship in them) are not regularly laid out, they are scarcely to be distinguished from the intermediate farms which are very close together and seperated, as one Inclosure from another also is, by fences of Stone which are indeed easily made, as the Country is immensely Stony. Upon enquiry we find their Crops of Wheat & Rye have been abundant

—though of the first they had sown rather sparingly on Acct. of the destruction which had of late years been made of that grain by what is called the Hessian fly.

¹ Caleb Hyatt had purchased this inn from George Dyckman.
² Mrs. Haviland was Tamar Haviland, who kept an inn called the Square House at Rye in Westchester County. She was the widow of Dr. Ebenezer Haviland, who had served as surgeon to several New York regiments during the Revolution.

Friday 16th.  About 7 Oclock we left the Widow Havilands, and after passing Horse Neck [Greenwich] Six Miles distant from Rye, the Road through which is hilly and immensely stoney and trying to Wheels & Carriages,¹ we breakfasted at Stamford which is 6 miles further (at one Webbs)² a tolerable good house, but not equal in appearance or reality, to Mrs. Havilds. In this Town are an Episcopal Church and a Meeting house. At Norwalk which is ten miles further we made a halt to feed our Horses. To the lower end of this town Sea Vessels come and at the other end are Mills, Stores, and an Episcopal and Presbiterian Church. From hence to Fairfield where we dined and lodged, is 12 Miles; and part of it very rough Road, but not equal to that thro' horse Neck. The superb Landscape, however, which is to be seen from the meeting house of the latter is a rich regalia. We found all the Farmers busily employed in gathering, grinding, and expressing the Juice of their Apples; the Crop of which they say is rather above Mediocrity. The Average Crop of Wheat they add, is about 15 bushels to the Acre from their fallow land—often 20 & from that to 25. The Destructive evidences of British cruelty are yet visible both in Norwalk & Fairfield; as there are the Chimneys of many burnt houses standing in them yet.³ The principal export from Norwalk & Fairfield is Horses and Cattle—Salted Beef & Porke, Lumber & Indian Corn, to the West Indies—and in a small degree Wheat & Flour.

¹ In 1788 Jacques (Jean) Pierre Brissot de Warville had traveled through the same area of western Greenwich on his way to New York. "The agreeable part of our journey ended at Fairfield," Brissot noted. "For thirty-three miles from this town to Rye we had to fight our way over rocks and precipices. I did not know which to admire more, the driver's daring or his skill. I cannot conceive how he succeeded twenty times in preventing the carriage from being shattered, or how his horses could check the coach when going down the veritable stairways of rocks. The word 'stairways' is no exaggeration. One of these, known as Horseneck, is nothing but a steep slope of boulders; if the

Ezra Stiles, painted in 1771 by Samuel King. (Yale University Art Gallery. Bequest of Dr. Charles C. Foote, great-grandson of Ezra Stiles)

horses slipped, the coach would tumble 200 or 300 feet down into the valley below" (BRISSOT, 121).

² Webb's tavern was at the corner of Main and Bank streets in Stamford, Conn. According to local tradition Mrs. Washington stayed at the tavern on her way to join GW at Cambridge in 1775 (CROFUT, 1:150).

³ In their attack on Norwalk 11 July 1779, the British burned over 100 houses and virtually destroyed the town. Brissot noted in 1788 that the "scars left by their infernal rage can still be seen. Most of the houses have been rebuilt, but those who knew the town before the war say that it was much finer then and that it was noted for its prosperous, even opulent, appearance" (BRISSOT, 121).

Saturday 17th.    A little after Sun-rise we left Fairfield, & passing through Et. Fairfield breakfasted at Stratford, wch. is ten Miles from Fairfield, and is a pretty village on or near Stratford Rivr. The Road between these two places is not on the whole bad (for this Country) —in some places very gd. especially through Et. Fairfield wch. is in a plain, and free from Stone. There are two decent looking Churches in this place—though small—viz.—an Episcopal and Presbeterian, or Congregationalist (as they call themselves). At Stratford there is the same. At this place I was received with an effort of Military parade; and was attended to the Ferry which is near a mile from the Center of the Town, by sevl. Gentlemen on horse back. Doctr. Johnson of the Senate visited me here, being with Mrs. Johnson in this Town (where he formerly resided).¹ The Ferry is near half a Mile; and sometimes much incommoded by Winds and cross tides. The Navigation for Vessels of about 75

Tonns extends up to Darby, ten Miles higher, where it is said there is a pretty brisk trade. At Stratford they are establishing a Manufactury of Duck, and have lately turned out about 400 bolts.[2] From the Ferry it is abt. 3 Miles to Milford, which is situated in more uneven and Stoney grd. than the 3 last Villages through wch. we passed. In this place there is but one Church, or in other words but one steeple—but there are Grist & saw Mills and a handsome Cascade over the Tumbling dam; but one of the prettiest things of this kind is at Stamford occasioned also by damming the water for their Mills; it is near 100 yds. in width, and the water now being of a proper height, and the Rays of the Sun striking upon it as we passed, had a pretty effect upon the foaming Water as it fell. From Millford we took the lower road through West haven, part of which was good and part rough, and arrived at New haven before two Oclock; We had time to Walk through several parts of the City before Dinner. By taking the lower Road, we missed a Committee of the assembly, who had been appointed to wait upon, and escort me into town—to prepare an Address and to conduct me when I should leave the City as far as they should judge proper.[3] The address was presented at 7 Oclock and at Nine I received another address from the Congregational Clergy of the place.[4] Between the rect. of the two Addresses I received the Compliment of a Visit from the Govr. Mr. Huntington [5]—the Lieutt. Govr. Mr. Wolcot [6] and the Mayor Mr. Roger Shurman.[7] The City of Newhaven occupies a good deal of ground, but is thinly, though regularly laid out, & built. The number of Souls in it are said to be about 4000. There is an Episcopal Church and 3 Congregational Meeting Houses and a College in which there are at this time about 120 Students under auspices of Doctr. Styles.[8] The Harbour of this place is not good for large Vessels—abt. 16 belongs to it. The Linnen Manufacture does not appear to be of so much importance as I had been led to believe—In a word I could hear but little of it.[9] The Exports from this City are much the same as from Fairfield &ca. and flax seed (chiefly to New York) . The Road from Kings bridge to this place runs as near the Sound as the Bays and Inlets will allow, but from hence to Hartford it leaves the Sound and runs more to the Northward.

[1] William Samuel Johnson (1727–1819) was a prominent Connecticut lawyer, who had served in the colony's legislature in the 1760s and from 1767 to 1771 was colonial agent for Connecticut in London. After the Revolution he served in the Continental Congress 1784–87. One of the ablest proponents of the Constitution in the Constitutional Convention, he was

elected United States senator from Connecticut in 1789. At this time he was also president of Columbia College. In 1749 he had married Ann Beach (d. 1796) of Stratford.

[2] The manufactory at Stratford for the production of duck, a closely woven durable fabric often made of cotton, was still largely a cottage industry (CLARK [4], 1:530; HAMILTON [2], 9:321).

[3] The committee of the Connecticut legislature waited for GW at Woodruff's tavern, about five miles from New Haven (John Chester to GW, 17 Oct. 1789, DLC:GW).

[4] The assembly's address and GW's reply, dated 17 Oct., are in DLC:GW. The address "of six Congregational Ministers" was presented by Ezra Stiles (STILES, 3:369). The address, 17 Oct., is in DLC:GW. GW's reply is in CtY: U.S. President's Collection. Both the addresses and GW's replies are printed in *Pa. Packet,* 29 Oct. 1789.

[5] Samuel Huntington (1731–1796) was a native of Windham, Mass. He was admitted to the Connecticut bar in 1758 and served the colony in various judicial capacities and in the legislature in the 1760s and 1770s. Huntington was a member of the Continental Congress 1775–84, serving as president 1779–81, and upon his resignation because of ill health GW had written him a warm letter of appreciation (25 July 1781, DLC:GW). In 1786 he was elected governor of Connecticut, a post he held for 11 years. A firm supporter of the Constitution, he had campaigned vigorously in his state for its adoption.

[6] Oliver Wolcott, Sr. (1726–1797), a native of Windsor, Conn., and a Yale graduate, had been active in Connecticut politics before and during the Revolution and had led Connecticut militia in the campaign against Burgoyne. He was elected to the Continental Congress in 1775 and, except for one term in 1779, served until 1783, although his attendance was interrupted periodically by his military service. He was elected lieutenant governor of Connecticut in 1787 and succeeded Samuel Huntington as governor in 1796. Although GW apparently had relatively little contact with the elder Wolcott, his son Oliver Wolcott, Jr. (1760–1833), was now serving as auditor of the treasury and in 1795 succeeded Hamilton as GW's second secretary of the treasury.

[7] Roger Sherman (1721–1793), a native of Newton, Mass., moved to Connecticut in 1743. He was admitted to the Connecticut bar in 1754 but by the 1760s had become a leading merchant in New Haven and Wallingford. Sherman was a conservative during the Revolution but supported the Patriot cause and served in the Continental Congress 1774–81, 1783–84. Although he at first favored strengthening the Confederation, he supported the Constitution at the Constitutional Convention. At this time Sherman represented Connecticut in the federal House of Representatives.

[8] Ezra Stiles (1727–1795) was born in New Haven, Conn., and educated at Yale. After some years as a tutor at Yale while he studied both law and theology, he was admitted to the bar in 1753 and in 1755 was ordained as a minister in the Congregational Church. A staunch Patriot during the Revolution, he became president of Yale in 1778 and held the post until his death.

[9] The linen factory at New Haven was under the management of Josiah Burr, and a large portion of the coarse linen produced there was shipped to the southern states and the West Indies. It was probably the same establishment visited in the mid-1790s by the duc de La Rochefoucauld, who described

Roger Sherman, by Ralph Earl.
(Yale University Art Gallery,
Gift of Roger Sherman White)

it as "a cotton-work at the distance of two miles from the town. The spinning
engine is put in motion by water; but the dereliction of this manufacture may
be foretold, as its success is opposed by all the obstacles common in similar
cases. Besides the expence upon the buildings has been far too considerable"
(HAMILTON [2], 9:319, 321; LA ROCHEFOUCAULD, 2:322).

Sunday 18th.   Went in the forenoon to the Episcopal Church and
in the afternoon to one of the Congregational Meeting Houses—
attended to the first by the Speaker of the Assembly Mr. Edwards,[1]
& a Mr. Ingersoll,[2] and to the latter by the Governor, the Lieutt.
Governor, the Mayor & Speaker. These Gentlemen all dined with
me (by Invitation) as did Genl. Huntington,[3] at the House of Mr.
Brown, where I lodged & who keeps a good Tavern.[4] Drank Tea
at the Mayors (Mr. Sherman's). Upon further enquiry I find that
there has been abt. [      ] yards of course Linnen manufactured at
this place since it was established and that a Glass work is on foot
here for the manufacture of Bottles. At 7 Oclock in the evening
many Officers of this State, belonging to the late Continental
Army, called to pay their respects to me. By some of them it was
said that the people of this State could, with more ease pay an additional 100,000£ tax this year than what was laid last year.

[1] Pierpoint Edwards (1750–1826), a New Haven lawyer and Yale graduate,
served in the Connecticut legislature 1777, 1784–85, 1787–90, and was speaker
in 1789. He was a strong supporter of the Constitution.
　[2] Mr. Ingersoll is probably Jonathan Ingersoll, a member of the Connecti-

cut legislature and a successful New Haven lawyer. In 1816 he was elected deputy governor of the state.

³ Jedediah Huntington (1743–1818) was a graduate of Harvard who had served with considerable distinction during the Revolution as a brigadier general in command of various Connecticut regiments. GW had appointed him collector of the customs at New London, Conn., in Aug. 1789.

⁴ Jacob Brown had opened his tavern in 1786 and in 1787 moved to the Hubbard House which stood at the intersection of George, Church, and Meadow streets in New Haven (CROFUT, 2:638).

Monday 19th.    Left New haven at 6 oclock, and arrived at Wallingford (13 Miles) by half after 8 oclock, where we breakfasted and took a walk through the Town. In coming to it we passed thro East haven about mid way; after riding along the river of that name 6 Miles on which are extensive Marshes Now loaded with hay stacks—the ride is very pleasant, but the Road is Sandy which it continues to be within a Mile of the Tavern (Carringtons which is but an ordinary house) ¹ at Wallingford. This and about five Miles of the Road beyond—that is West of New haven—is all the Sand we have met with on the journey. These Sandy Lands afford but ordinary Crops of Corn—nor has the Crops of this grain East of Stratford River appeared so heavy as on the West side of it. The Lands (Stone being less) are in part enclosed with Posts & Rails. At this place (Wallingford) we see the white Mulberry growing, raised from the Seed to feed the Silk worm. We also saw samples of lustring (exceeding good) which had been manufactured from the Cocoon raised in this Town, and silk thread very fine. This, except the weaving, is the work of private families without interference with other business, and is likely to turn out a benificial amusement. In the Township of Mansfield they are further advanced in this business. Walling ford has a Church & two meeting houses in it, which stands upon high and pleasant grd. About 10 Oclock we left this place and at the distance of 8 Miles passed through Durham. At one we arrived at Middletown on Connecticut River being met two or three Miles from it by the respectable Citizens of the place, and escorted in by them. While dinner was getting ready I took a walk round the Town, from the heights of which the prospect is beautiful. Belonging to this place I was informed (by a Genl. Sage) ² that there was about 20 Sea Vessels and to Weathersfield higher up 22 and to Hartford the like number. Other places on the River have their proportion, the whole amounting to about 10,000 Tonns. The Country hereabouts is beautiful and the Lands good. An average Crop of wheat from an Acre of fallowed Land is estimated at 15 bushels; sometimes they get as high as 25 and 30 bushls. to the Acre from their best lands—Indian Corn from 20 to 40 bushls. pr. Acre. Their exports are the same as from other places; together with Pot ash. Having dined, we set out with the same Escort (who conducted us into town) about 3 Oclock for Hartford, and passing through a Parish of Middletown & Weathersfield, we arrived at Harfd. about Sun down. At Weathersfield we were met by a party of the Hartford light horse, and a Number of Gentlemen from the same place with Colo. Wadsworth [3] at their head, and escorted to Bulls Tavern where we lodged.

[1] This tavern was kept by Jeremiah Carrington and was later called the Washington Hotel (CROFUT, 2:654).

[2] Comfort Sage (1731–1799) was a native of Middletown Upper House in the area of present-day Cromwell, Conn. He had served in the Connecticut militia during the Revolution. Under the Confederation, Sage had held the post of naval officer for the port of Middletown, Conn., and in the summer of 1789 had written GW asking that he be retained in the revenue service (31 July, 8 Aug. 1789, DLC:GW). On 18 Aug. 1789 GW replied, expressing his regret that the post for Middletown had already been filled (DLC:GW). According to local tradition, Sage was confined to his bed at the time of GW's visit (CROFUT, 2:469). Since Sage's pretensions were supported by such prominent citizens of Connecticut as Gov. Samuel Huntington (Huntington to GW, 19 Dec. 1789, DLC:GW), it is likely that GW's call was intended to soften his refusal. In Feb. 1790 the incumbent of the Middletown post resigned and Sage received the appointment (EXECUTIVE JOURNAL, 1:38, 40).

[3] Jeremiah Wadsworth was at this time a congressman from Connecticut. In the late 1780s he had turned increasingly from his more speculative business enterprises to the development of manufacturing and banking in Connecticut. He was interested in a distillery and a glassworks and was an investor in Josiah Burr's linen manufactory at New Haven. Wadsworth's major concern in 1789 was the Hartford Woolen Manufactory, founded in 1788, of which he was the largest shareholder. In 1789 he was living in the Wadsworth mansion at the corner of Asylum and Trumbull streets in Hartford (CROFUT, 1:238).

Tuesday 20th.    After breakfast, accompanied by Colo. Wadsworth, Mr. Ellsworth [1] and Colo. Jesse Root,[2] I viewed the Woolen Manufactury at this place which seems to be going on with Spirit. There Broadcloths are not of the first quality, as yet, but they are good; as are their Coatings, Cassimers, Serges and everlastings. Of the first that is broad-cloth I ordered a suit to be sent to me at New York and of the latter a whole piece to make breeches for my servants. All the parts of this business are performed at the Manufactury except the Spinning—this is done by the Country people who are paid by the cut.[3] Hartford is more compactly built than Middletown and contains more Souls; the computed Number of which amount to about dble. The number of Houses in Middletown are said to be 250 or 60. These reckoning eight persons to a house would make two thousand at least. The depth of Water which Vessels can bring to the last place, is about ten feet; and is as much as there is over Seabrook bar. From Middletown to Hartford there is not more than 6 feet Water. At Middletown there is one Episcopal & two Congregational Churches. In Hartford there is none of the first and 2 of the latter. Dined and drank Tea at Colo. Wadsworth and about 7 Oclock received from, & answered the Address of the Town of Hartford.[4]

[1] Oliver Ellsworth (1745–1807) was at this time Federalist senator from Connecticut. A native of Windsor, he had attended Princeton, studied law, and was admitted to the bar in 1771. A delegate to the Continental Congress 1777–84, he served on a number of committees which had brought him into contact with GW. Ellsworth was a member of the Connecticut delegation at the Constitutional Convention and played a prominent role in the convention's activities, particularly in negotiating the so-called Connecticut compromise. His home, Elmwood, was at South Windsor, Conn., where his wife, Abigail Wolcott Ellsworth (1756–1818), was a noted hostess.

[2] Jesse Root (1736–1822), a Hartford lawyer, was a delegate to the Continental Congress 1778–83. In 1776, when Root was in command of a company of Connecticut militia, GW had sent him to inform Connecticut officials of Howe's landing on Staten Island (GW to Root, 7 Aug. 1776, and GW to Jonathan Trumbull, 7 Aug. 1776, DLC:GW).

[3] The Hartford Woolen Manufactory began with a capital of £1,200 which by 1791 had been expanded to £2,800 and, although not incorporated, had received encouragement from the state of Connecticut in the form of tax exemptions and bounties. GW's examination of the new textile manufactory increased his interest in the possibility of introducing such a system of manufacturing in his own state or at least offering inducements to Virginia farmers to increase the number of sheep. He wrote Gov. Beverley Randolph of Virginia: "By a little Legislative encouragement, the Farmers of Connecticut have, in two years past, added one hundred thousand to their former stock. In my late tour thro' the Eastern States, I found that the Manufacturers of Woolens (for the Manufacture of Woolens is carried on there to very considerable extent and advantage) preferred the Wool raised in Virginia for its fineness, to that raised in more Northern parts of the Continent. If a greater quantity of Wool could be produced and if the hands (which are often in a manner idle) could be employ'd in the manufacturing it; a spirit of industry might be promoted, a great diminution might be made in the annual expences of individual families, and the Public would eventually be exceedingly benefitted" (GW to Randolph, 22 Nov. 1789, DLC:GW). In the spring of 1789 GW had received from the directors of the Hartford Manufactory "A Pattern of fine Cloth of our Fabrick which the Company flatter themselves Your Excellency will Receive as A Token of their support & Esteem" (Daniel Hinsdale to GW, 23 Mar. 1789, and GW to Hinsdale, 8 April 1789, DLC:GW).

[4] The address of the mayor, aldermen, and common council of Hartford and GW's reply are in DLC:GW.

Wednesday 21st.    By promise I was to have Breakfasted at Mr. Ellsworths at Windsor on my way to Springfield, but the Morning proving very wet and the rain not ceasing till past 10 Oclock I did not set out till half after that hour; I called however on Mr. Ellsworth and stay'd there near an hour. Reached Springfield by 4 Oclock, and while dinner was getting, examined the Continental Stores at this place which I found in very good order at the buildings (on the hill above the Town) which belong to the United States.[1] The Barracks (also public property) are going fast to destruction and in a little time will be no more without repairs. The Elaboratory, wch. seems to be a good building is in tolerable good repair and the Powder Magazine which is of Brick seems to be in excellent order and the Powder in it very dry. A Colo. Worthington,[2] Colo. Williams (Adjutant General of the State of Massachusetts),[3] Genl. Shepherd,[4] Mr. Lyman[5] and many other Gentlemen sat an hour or two with me in the evening at Parson's Tavern where I lodged and which is a good House.[6] About 6 Miles before I came to Springfield I left the State of Connecticut and entered that of Massachusetts. The Distance from Hartford to Springfield is 28 Miles — both on Connecticut River. At the latter the River is crossed in Scows, set over with Poles and is about 80 rod wide. Between the two places is a fall and ten miles above Springfield is another fall and others above that again — notwithstanding which much use is made of the Navigation for transportation in flats of about five tonns burthen. Seven miles on this side Hartford is Windsor a tolerable pleasant but not a large Village. Between Windsor and Suffield you pass through a level, barren & uncultivated plain for several Miles. Suffield stands high & pleasant — the Lds. good. From hence you descend again into another plain where the Lands being good are much better cultivated. The whole Road from Hartford to Springfield is level & good, except being too Sandy in places & the Fields enclosed with Posts & Rails generally their not being much Stone. The Crops of Corn, except on the Interval Lands on the River are more indifferent (tho' not bad) in the Eastern than we found them in the Western part of the State of Connecticut. There is a great equality in the People of this State — Few or no oppulent Men and no poor — great similatude in their buildings — the general fashion of which is a Chimney (always of Stone or Brick) and door in the middle, with a stair case fronting the latter, running up by the side of the latter [former] — two flush Stories with a very good shew of Sash & glass Windows. The size generally is from 30 to 50 feet in length and from 20 to 30 in width exclusive of a back shed which seems to be added as the family encreases. The farms by the contiguity of the Houses are small not averaging more than 100 Acres. These are worked chiefly by Oxen (which have no other feed than Hay) with a horse & sometimes two before them both in Plow & Cart. In their light Lands and in their sleighs they work Horses, but find them much more expensive than Oxen. Springfield is on the East side of Connecticut River; before you come to which a large branch of it called Agawam is crossed by a Bridge. It stands under the Hill on the interval Land and has only one Meeting house — 28 Miles from Hartfd.

[1] Springfield had been, because of its central location, a convenient depot for arms and ammunition during the Revolution and by 1779 Congress had established a permanent installation there. Both cannon and small arms were manufactured at the site after the war.

[2] John Worthington was a Springfield lawyer and a 1740 graduate of Yale University.

[3] GW is presumably referring to William Dennison (DIARIES, 4:29).

[4] William Shepherd (1737–1817), a farmer from Westfield, had seen military service during the French and Indian War. During the Revolution his position as lieutenant colonel and colonel of the 4th Massachusetts Regiment had brought him into frequent contact with GW. In 1786 he was appointed major general in the Massachusetts militia and defended the Springfield arsenal against the attack of the insurgents during Shays's Rebellion.

[5] William Lyman (1755–1811), a Yale graduate, was a member of the Massachusetts legislature in 1789. He had acted as major and aide-de-camp to General Shepherd during Shays's Rebellion. In 1793 he was elected as a Democratic-Republican to the United States Senate.

[6] Parsons's tavern was on Elm Street. It may have been operated by Zenas Parsons (HEADS OF FAMILIES, MASS., 125).

**Thursday 22d.** Set out at 7 Oclock; and for the first 8 Miles rid over an almost uninhabited Pine plain; much mixed with Sand. Then a little before the road descends to Chicabi River it is hilly, Rocky & Steep, & continues so for several Miles; the Country being Stony and Barren; with a mixture of Pine and Oak till we came to Palmer, at the House of one Scott [1] where we breakfasted, and where the Land though far from good, began to mend, to this is called 15 Miles. Among these Pines are Ponds of fresh Water. From Palmer to Brookfield, to one Hitchcocks; [2] is 15 Miles; part of which is pretty good, and part (crossing the Hills) very bad; but when over, the ground begins to get tolerably good and the Country better cultivated tho' the Crops of Corn do not look well and have been injured it is said by an early frost in September. A beautiful fresh water pond & large, is in the Plain of Brookland [Brookfield]. The fashion of the Houses are more deversified than in Connecticut, though many are built in their stile. The Inclosures have but indifferent fences—wood or Stone according as the Country abounds with the latter—of which it is full after passing the pine levels. At Brookland [Brookfield] we fed the Horses and dispatched an Express which was sent to me by Govr. Hancock—giving notice of the measures he was about to pursue for my reception on the Road, and in Boston—With a request to lodge at his House.[3] Continued on to Spencer 10 Miles further through pretty good roads, and lodged at the House of one Jenks who keeps a pretty good Tavern.[4]

[1] Presumably this was William Scott, who was a resident of Palmer, Hampshire County, Mass., with nine members in his household (HEADS OF FAMILIES, MASS., 120).

[2] Probably either Moses or David Hitchcock, both listed in HEADS OF FAMILIES, MASS., 214, as residents of Brookfield with a suitable number of retainers.

[3] John Hancock to GW, 21 Oct. 1789 (DLC:GW). On 22 Oct. GW replied, agreeing somewhat reluctantly to the plans for his reception. "But could my wish prevail I should desire to visit your Metropolis without any parade, or extraordinary ceremony. From a wish to avoid giving trouble to private families, I determined, on leaving New York, to decline the honor of any invitation to quarters which I might receive while on my journey and with a view to observe this rule, I had requested a Gentleman to engage lodgings for me during my stay at Boston" (DLC:GW).

[4] This is probably either Isaac or Lawrence Jenks, both listed in HEADS OF FAMILIES, MASS., 236, as householders in Spencer.

**Friday 23d.**   Commenced our course with the Sun, and passing through Leicester met some Gentlemen of the Town of Worcester on the line between it and the former to escort us. Arrived about 10 Oclock at the House of [    ] where we breakfasted—distant from Spencer 12 Miles. Here we were received by a handsome Company of Militia Artillery in Uniform who saluted with 13 Guns on our Entry & departure. At this place also we met a Committee from the Town of Boston, and an Aid of Majr. Genl. Brooke of the Middlesex Militia who had proceeded to this place in order to make some arrangements of Military & other Parade on my way to, and in the Town of, Boston; and to fix with me on the hours at which I should pass through Cambridge, and enter Boston.[1] Finding this ceremony was not to be avoided though I had made every effort to do it, I named the hour of ten to pass the Militia of the above County at Cambridge and the hour of 12 for my entrance into Boston desiring Major Hall, however, to inform Genl. Brookes that as I conceived there was an impropriety in my *reviewing* the Militia, or seeing them perform Manoeuvres otherwise than as a private Man I could do no more than pass along the line; which, if he thought proper might be under arms to receive me at that time. These matters being settled the Committee and the Aid (Colo. Hall) set forward on their return and after breakfast I followed; The same Gentlemen who had escorted me into, conducting me out of Town.[2] On the Line between Worcester and Middlesex I was met by a Troop of light Horse belonging to the latter, who Escorted me to Marlborough (16 Miles) where we dined, and thence to Weston (14 More where we lodged). At Marlborough we met Mr. Jonathan Jackson the Marshall of this State who proposed to attend me whilst I remained in it. A good part of the Road from Spencer to Worcester is Hilly, & except a little nearest the latter, very Stoney. From Worcester to Marlborough the road is uneven but not bad and from Marlborh. to Weston it is leveller with more Sand. Between Worcester & Marlborough the Town of Shrewsbury is passed and between Marlborough and Weston you go through Sudbury. The Country about Worcester, and onwards towards Boston is better improved & the lands of better quality than we travelled through yesterday. The Crops it is said have been good—Indian Corn, Rye Buck Wheat & grass—with Beef Cattle & Porke are the produce of their Farms.

[1] John Brooks (1752–1825) was a physician in Reading, Mass., at the beginning of the Revolution. He was appointed a major in the Continental Army in 1776 and rose to the rank of lieutenant colonel by the end of the war. In 1786 Gov. James Bowdoin appointed him major general in the Middlesex militia where he served during Shays's Rebellion.

On 21 Oct. Brooks had sent his aide, Maj. Joseph Hall, with a letter to GW explaining plans for his reception in Boston. As a testimony of the city's respect, Brooks proposed that "a body of about 800 men, will be under arms at Cambridge on the day of your entering into Boston. The troops will occupy the ground on which the continental army was formed for your reception in the year 1775" (DLC:GW).

[2] The committee at Worcester consisted of Joseph Barrell, Samuel Breck, and William Eustis, "a sub-committee of the committee of the town" (*Mass. Centinel*, 24 Oct. 1789). The party breakfasted at the United States Arms, a Worcester tavern. For a detailed account of GW's stay in Worcester, see *Conn. Courant*, 2 Nov. 1789.

**Saturday 24th.** Dressed by Seven Oclock, and set out at eight. At ten we arrived in Cambridge According to appointment; but most of the Militia having a distance to come were not in line till after eleven; they made however an excellent appearance with Genl. Brook at their Head. At this place the Lieutt. Govr. Mr. Saml. Adams, with the Executive Council met me and preceeded my entrance into town—which was in every degree flattering &

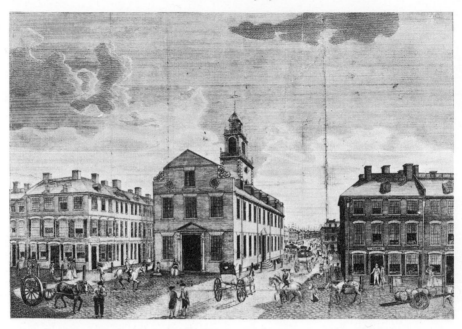

A view of the State House in Boston, from *Massachusetts Magazine,* July 1793. (I. N. Phelps Stokes Collection. Prints Division, New York Public Library, Astor, Lenox and Tilden Foundations)

honorable.[1] To pass over the Minutiae of the arrangement for this purpose it may suffice to say that at the entrance I was welcomed by the Select men in a body, Then following the Lieutt. Govr. & Council in the order we came from Cambridge (preceeded by the Town Corps very handsomely dressed) we passed through the Citizens classed in their different professions, and under their own banners, till we came to the State House; from which, across the Street, an Arch was thrown; in the front of which was this Inscription—"To the Man who unites all hearts" and on the other—"To Columbia's favourite Son" and on one side thereof next the State House, in a pannel decorated with a trophy, composed of the arms of the United States—of the Commonwealth of Massachusetts—and our French Allies, crowned with a wreath of Laurel was this Inscription—"Boston relieved March 17th. 1776." This arch was handsomely ornamented, and over the Center of it a Canopy was erected 20 feet high with the American Eagle perched on the top. After passing through the Arch, and entering the State House at the So. End & [as]cending to the upper floor & returning to a Balcony at the No. end—three cheers was given by a vast concourse of people who by this time had assembled at the Arch. Then followed an ode composed in honor of the President; and well sung by a band of select Singers [2] —after this three Cheers—followed by the different Professions, and Mechanics in the order they were drawn up with their Colours through a lane of the People which had thronged abt. the Arch under which they passed. The Streets, the Doors, Windows & Tops of the Houses were crouded with well dressed Ladies and Gentlemen. The procession being over I was conducted to my lodgings at a Widow Ingersolls [3] (which is a very decent & good house) by the Lieutt. Govr. and Council—accompanied by the Vice-President where they took leave of me. Having engaged yesterday to take an informal dinner with the Govr. to day (but under a full persuasion that he would have waited upon me so soon as I should have arrived) I excused myself upon his not doing it, and informing me thro his Secretary that he was too much indisposed to do it, being resolved to receive the visit.[4] Dined at my Lodgings, where the Vice-President favoured me with his Company.

[1] The revolutionary statesman Samuel Adams (1722–1803) served as lieutenant governor of Massachusetts 1789–93 and succeeded John Hancock as governor 1794–97.

The *Massachusetts Magazine,* Oct. 1789, noted that "At one o'clock, the President's approach was announced by federal discharges from . . . artillery at Roxbury—from the *Dorchester* artillery posted on the celebrated heights of that town—from . . . artillery at the entrance of the town—and from Castle William; by a royal salute from the Ships of his most Christian Majesty's squadron, and by the ringing of all the bells." The *Pennsylvania Packet,* 18 Nov. 1789, observed that the "President's dress, on his arrival . . . was the American uniform, with two rich apaulets. His other dress is black velvet."

[2] The "Ode to Columbia's Favorite Son: Great Washington, the Hero's Come . . ." is printed in *Pennsylvania Packet,* 4 Nov. 1789. It was sung by the Independent Musical Society. To some observers GW appeared uncomfortable: "A gentleman who was present at his arrival in Boston observed that when he came out of the State House to hear the Ode that was sung on the occasion, every muscle of his face appeared agitated, and he was frequently observed to pass . . . his handkerchief across his eyes" (*Hist. Collections of the Essex Institute,* 67 [1931], 299–300).

[3] Tobias Lear had written on 15 Oct. to Christopher Gore, a Boston attorney and member of the Massachusetts legislature, to engage lodgings in Boston for the presidential party. Gore replied, 22 Oct., that he had arranged lodgings at "Mrs. [Joseph] Ingersoll's house; at the corner of Court & Tremont Streets. . . . In the house are three parlours in the lower floor—three bed chambers on the second—and sufficient on the third to accomodate servants. In the neighborhood is a very good livery stable" (DECATUR, 80).

[4] After GW had refused Hancock's offer of lodging while the president was in Boston (see entry for 22 Oct. 1789), the governor had replied, 23 Oct., extending an invitation to GW and "the Gentlemen of your suit" to dine with him *"en famille,* at any hour that the circumstances of the day will admit" (DLC:GW). On the same day GW replied from Weston accepting the invitation (DNA: RG 59, Misc. Letters). The president had, however, assumed that the governor would make the first call. When it became apparent that Hancock's illness, real or feigned, would not be an acceptable excuse to the president, he sent GW a note stating that "the Governor will do himself the honor of paying his respects in half an hour. This would have been done much sooner had his health in any degree permitted. He now hazards every thing as it respects his health for the desirable purpose" (23 Oct. 1789, DLC:GW). Hancock's illness was reported to be gout. For public furor over the incident, see *Boston Gaz.,* 26 Oct., 2 Nov. 1789, and *Mass. Centinel,* 28 Oct. 1789.

**Sunday 25th.** Attended Divine Service at the Episcopal Church whereof Doctor Parker is the Incumbent in the forenoon, and the Congregational Church of Mr. Thatcher in the Afternoon.[1] Dined at my Lodgings with the Vice President. Mr. Bowdoin accompanied me to both Churches.[2] Between the two I received a visit from the Govr., who assured me that Indisposition alone had prevented his doing it yesterday, and that he was still indisposed; but as it had been suggested that he expected to *receive* the visit from the President, which he knew was improper, he was resolved at all hazds. to pay his Compliments to day. The Lt. Govr. & two of the Council to wit Heath & Russel [3] were sent here last Night to express the Govrs. Concern that he had not been in a condition to call upon me so soon as I came to Town. I informed them in explicit terms that I should not see the Govr. unless it was at my own lodgings.

[1] Rev. Samuel Parker (1744–1804), of Portsmouth, N.H., graduated from Harvard in 1764, was made rector of Trinity Episcopal Church in 1779, and in 1804 became second bishop of Massachusetts (SIBLEY, 16:76–84). Rev. Peter Thacher (1752–1802), a native of Milton, Mass., was a 1769 Harvard graduate. Ordained before the Revolution, he served in several military capacities in 1775 and wrote an account of the Battle of Bunker Hill. In 1785 he became minister of the Brattle Street Congregational Church, one of New England's most distinguished pulpits, and remained there until his death (SIBLEY, 17:237–47).

[2] James Bowdoin (1726–1790) was the revolutionary leader and former governor (1785–87) of Massachusetts. There was some comment in the press that GW had favored Bowdoin's company above that of Governor Hancock (*Mass. Centinel,* 14 Nov. 1789). Bowdoin's home was on Beacon Street near the corner of Bowdoin Street.

[3] William Heath and Thomas Russell.

Gov. John Hancock, a miniature by a British artist, Jeremiah Meyer. (Yale University Art Gallery, The Mabel Brady Garven Collection)

Monday 26th.    The day being Rainy & Stormy—myself much disordered by a Cold and inflamation in the left eye,[1] I was prevented from visiting Lexington (where the first blood in the dispute with G. Britn.) was drawn. Recd. the Complimts. of many visits to day. Mr. Da⟨l⟩ton and Genl. Cobb [2] dined with me and in the Evening I drank Tea with Govr. Hancock & called upon Mr. Bowdoin on my return to my lodgings.

[1] GW was apparently one of the early victims of an epidemic of colds and influenza that followed his visit to Boston. Because it afflicted many of the spectators who stood in the bitterly cold wind during the festivities, the ailment was thereafter referred to as the "Washington influenza." In fact, it was part of a widespread epidemic of respiratory ailments which had already swept through the central and southern states and was now spreading into New England (*Pa. Packet*, 18 Nov. 1789; *Am. Mercury*, 9 Nov. 1789).

[2] David Cobb (1748–1830), a graduate of Harvard, was practicing medicine at Taunton, Mass., at the beginning of the Revolution. In 1777 he became lieutenant colonel of Jackson's Regiment and was promoted to colonel of the 5th Massachusetts Regiment in Jan. 1783. Cobb was one of GW's aides-de-camp 1781–83 and was brevetted brigadier general in Sept. 1783. After the war he held a number of judicial posts in Massachusetts, was appointed major general in the state militia in 1786, and in 1789 was speaker of the Massachusetts House of Representatives. At this time he was living in Taunton with his wife, Eleanor Bradish Cobb, and nine children (SIBLEY, 16:351).

Tuesday 27th.    At 10 Oclock in the Morning received the Visits of the Clergy of the Town—at 11 went to an Oratorio [1] and between that and 3 Oclock recd. the Addresses of the Governor and Council—of the Town of Boston; of the President &ca. of Harvard College; and of the Cincinnati of the State; [2] after wch., at 3 Oclock, I dined at a large & elegant dinner at Fanuiel Hall, given

James Bowdoin, from *Massachusetts Magazine,* January 1791. (Boston Athenaeum)

by the Govr. and Council, and spent the evening at my lodgings.[3] When the Committee from the Town presented their Address it was accompanied with a request (in behalf they said of the Ladies) that I would set to have my Picture taken for the Hall, that others might be copied from it for the use of their respective families. As all the next day was assigned to various purposes and I was engaged to leave town on Thursday early, I informed them of the impracticability of my doing this, but that I would have it drawn when I returned to New York, if there was a good Painter there—or by Mr. Trumbull when he should arrive; and would send it to them.[4]

[1] The oratorio was held at King's Chapel (Stone Chapel) to raise money for an addition to the chapel (*Mass. Centinel,* 24 Oct. 1789). According to the *Pennsylvania Packet,* 5 Nov. 1789, "on account of the indisposition of several of the first performers, the music was postponed until Wednesday next. Several pieces were however given, which merited and received applause."

[2] These addresses and GW's replies, 27 Oct., are in DLC:GW.

[3] According to the *Pennsylvania Packet,* 5 Nov. 1789, Hancock "owing to severe indisposition," did not attend the dinner at Faneuil Hall.

[4] In spite of GW's refusal, Christian Gülager (1762–1827), a Danish artist living in Boston, apparently made some preliminary sketches in Boston which GW later approved. On 3 Nov., while in Portsmouth, N.H., he gave the artist a sitting for the Portsmouth Bust Portrait which Gülager probably completed

Faneuil Hall in Boston, from *Massachusetts Magazine,* March 1789. (Library of Congress)

from memory and which was eventually presented to the Massachusetts Historical Society (EISEN, 2:427–28). The painter John Trumbull (1756–1843) was in Europe at this time but planned to return to the United States at the end of 1789.

Wednesday 28th.    Went after an early breakfast to visit the duck Manufacture which appeared to be carrying on with spirit, and is in a prosperous way. They have manufactured 32 pieces of Duck of 39 or 40 yds. each in a week; and expect in a short time to encrease it to [      ]. They have 28 looms at work & 14 Girls spinning with Both hands (the flax being fastened to their waste). Children (girls) turn the wheels for them, and with this assistance each spinner can turn out 14 lbs. of thread pr. day when they stick to it, but as they are pd. by the piece, or work they do, there is no other restraint upon them but to come at 8 Oclock in the Morning and return at 6 in the evening. They are the daughters of decayed families, and are girls of Character—none others are admitted. The number of hands now employed in the different parts of the work is [      ] but the Managers expect to encrease them to [      ]. This is a work of public utility & private advantage.[1] From hence I went to the Card Manufactury where I was informed about 900 hands of one kind and for one purpose or another. All kinds of Cards are made; & there are Machines for executing every part of the work in a new and expeditious manr. especially in cutting & bending the teeth wch. is done at one stroke. They have made 63,000 pr. of Cards in a year and can under sell the Imported Cards—nay Cards of this Manufactury have been smuggled into England.[2] At 11 Oclock I embarked on board the Barge of the Illustrious Captn. Pentheve Gion, & visited his Ship & the Superb, another 74 Gun Ship in the Harbour of Boston, about 4 Miles below the Town.[3] Going & coming I was saluted by the two frigates which lye near the Wharves and by the 74s after I had been on board of them; as also by the 40 Gun ship which lay in the same range with them. I was also saluted going & coming by the fort on Castle Isld.[4] After my return I dined in a large Company at Mr. Bowdoins and went to the Assembly in the evening where (it is said) there were upwards of 100 Ladies. There appearance was elegant and many of them very handsome; the Room is small but neat, & well ornamented.[5]

[1] Boston Sailcloth Manufactory had been established in 1788 by a group of Boston merchants and businessmen under the leadership of Samuel Breck and Thomas Alkers, in hope of profiting from a bounty offered by the Massachusetts legislature in Mar. 1788 on the production of duck and sailcloth. The factory was erected in the area of what was then Nassau Street and Frog Lane (Boylston Street), and production was underway by early 1789. By 1792 "there were four hundred employees, and the weekly product was not less than fifty pieces of duck" (BAGNALL, 116). One observer noted that GW "made him self merry on this Occasion, telling the overseer he believed he collected the prettiest girls in Boston" (WEBB [2], 3:142–44).

[2] Presumably this was the cotton and wool card factory of Giles Richard and Co., on Hanover Square, supposedly the largest such establishment in Massachusetts. In 1791 Nathaniel Gorham, supervisor of the revenue for Massachusetts, reported that the company's improvements in machinery for carding had developed to such an extent that "models of two of their principal machines, were lately purchased by an English Gentleman for nearly one hundred pounds sterling. . . . At present the works are in such perfection, that Eight men can turn out Fifty dozen [cards] per day" (Gorham to Hamilton, 13 Oct. 1791, HAMILTON [2], 9:375).

[3] See entry for 12 Oct. 1789. The French captain and his officers, accompanied by the French consul, Philippe André Joseph de Létombe, had already paid a visit on 24 Oct. to GW at his lodgings (*Pa. Packet*, 4 Nov. 1789). For a further description of GW's visit to the French squadron, see *Pa. Packet*, 19 Nov. 1789.

[4] The fort on Castle Island was Castle William or Fort Adams, later Fort Independence.

[5] According to Joseph Barrell, a member of the Boston committee that had met GW at Worcester, "the Hall was elegantly decorated, behind his majesty was hung my handsomest Tapestry & before him as a Carpet the other. He was seated on a Crimson Settee with the Vice President, our Governor and Governor Bowdoin, the Ladies were very handsomely dressed, and

Joseph Pope's orrery. (Harvard University Collection of Historical Scientific Instruments)

every one strove here as every where else, who should pay the most respect. We had a very pretty Desert for Supper with 3 fine Cakes (one for each set) at 150£" (Barrell to Samuel B. Webb, 1 Nov. 1789, WEBB [2], 3:142–44).

Thursday 29th.    Left Boston about 8 Oclock. Passed over the Bridge at Charles Town and went to see that at Malden, but proceeded to the college at Cambridge, attended by the Vice President, Mr. Bowdoin, and a great number of Gentlemen: at this place I was shewn by Mr. Willard the President [1] the Philosophical Aparatus and amongst others Popes Orary (a curious piece of Mechanism for shewing the revolutions of the Sun, Earth and

The new bridge at Charlestown, Mass., opened for public use 17 June 1786. From *New-York Magazine,* September 1795. (New-York Historical Society)

A view of Harvard College, from *Columbian Magazine,* November 1788. (New-York Historical Society)

many other of the Planets) [2] – The library (containing 13,000 volumes) and a Museum. The Bridges of Charles town and Malden are useful & noble – doing great credit to the enterprizing spirit of the People of this State. From Boston, besides the number of Citizens which accompanied me to Cambridge, & many of them from thence to Lynn – the Boston Corps of Horse escorted me to the line between Middlesex and Essex County where a party of Horse with Genl. Titcomb [3] met me, and conducted me through Marblehead (which is 4 Miles out of the way, but I wanted to see it) to Salem. The Chief employmt. of the People of Marblehead (Males) is fishing – about 110 Vessels and 800 Men and boys are engaged in this business. Their chief export is fish. About 5000 Souls are said to be in this place which has the appearance of antiquity. The Houses are old – the streets dirty – and the common people not very clean. Before we entered the Town we were met, & attended by a Comee. till we were handed over to the Select Men who conducted us saluted by artily. in to the Town – to the House of a Mrs. Lee where there was a cold Collation prepared [4] – after partaking of which we visited the Harbour – their fish brakes for curing fish – &ca. and then proceeded (first receiving an Address from the Inhabitants) to Salem. At the Bridge, 2 Miles from this Town, we were also met by a Committee – who conducted us by a Brigade of the Militia, & one or two handsome Corps in Uniform,[5] through several of the Streets to the Town or Court House – where an Ode in honor of the President was sung – an address presented to him amidst the acclamations of the People – after which he was conducted to his Lodgings – recd. the compliments of many differt. Classes of People [6] – and in the evening between 7 and 8 Oclock went to an assembly, where there was at least an hundred handsome and well dressed Ladies.[7] Abt. Nine I returned to my Lodgings. The Road from Boston to this place is here and there Stoney tho' level; it is very pleasant: from most parts you are in sight of the Sea. Meads – arable Land and Rocky hills are much intermixed – the latter chiefly on the left. The Country seems to be in a manner entirely stripped of wood. The grazing is good – the Houses stand thick. After leaving Cambridge at the distance of 4 Miles we passed through Mistick – then Malden – next Lynn (where it is said 175,000 pairs of Shoes (womens chiefly) have been made in a year by abt. 400 workmen). This is only a row of houses & not very thick on each side of the Road. After passing Lynn you enter Marblehead wch. is 4 Miles from Salem. This latter is a neat Town and said to contain 8 or 9000 Inhabitants. Its exports are chiefly Fish Lumber & Provisions. They have in the East India Trade at this time 13 Sale of Vessels.

¹ Joseph Willard (1738–1804), a member of a prominent New England family and an ardent Federalist, was president of Harvard from 1781 to 1804. Through his extensive writings and correspondence he became well known as a scientist and mathematician and led the college out of the financial and academic disorganization caused by the Revolution. GW was received at Harvard in the "Philosophy-room of the University" (*Pa. Packet*, 13 Nov. 1789).

² The orrery at Harvard was the work of Joseph Pope, Boston watchmaker, who had worked on it from 1776 to 1787. "It was an elaborate structure based on the design of the grand orreries produced by the great English makers of the period, measuring 6½ feet in diameter and 6½ feet in height. It was covered with a glass dome with the signs of the zodiac painted on the glass side panels, and was supported on a hexagonal frame of mahogany in the Chippendale style. Twelve figures adorned its corners; these were said to have been carved in wood by Simeon Skillin and cast in bronze by Paul Revere." The instrument had been purchased for Harvard through a lottery sponsored by the Massachusetts legislature in Mar. 1789 (BEDINI, 384–85).

³ Jonathan Titcomb of Newburyport, Mass., had been in command of a Massachusetts regiment in 1775 and charged with securing supplies for the army during GW's tour of duty at Cambridge. By the end of the war he was a major general in the state forces. In June 1789 he solicited the post of naval officer for Newburyport, and GW appointed him in August (Titcomb to GW, 19 June 1789, DLC:GW; EXECUTIVE JOURNAL, 1:9, 12). Two members of the Titcomb family of Newburyport—Michael and Zebulon—had been members of the Commander-in-Chief's Guard during the Revolution (GODFREY, 259–60).

⁴ Mrs. Lee was Martha Swett Lee (d. 1791), daughter of Joseph and Hannah Swett of Marblehead and wife of Col. Jeremiah Lee, a prominent Marblehead shipowner. The Lee house, on Washington Street, was an elegant mansion constructed in 1768, and Mrs. Lee was a noted hostess. According to local tradition, silhouettes of eagles were placed in the windows of the house during GW's visit so they would show against the lighted candles (LORD, 234–36).

⁵ These military units included the Salem town regiment, "joined by a Regiment from Lynn, with the Horse from Ipswich, the Independant Company, & the Artillery. The Ipswich Horse were in blue with hats, the Independants in red, & the Artillery in black uniforms. The Militia were partly in Rifle frocks" (BENTLEY, 1:130).

⁶ To one observer GW's progress to the courthouse seemed less than triumphant: "His appearance as he passed thro' Court Street in Salem was far from gay, or making anyone else so. He looked oppressed by the attention that was paid him, and as he cast his eye around, I thought it seemed to sink at the notice he attracted. When he had got to the Court House, and had patiently listened to the ditty they sung at him, and heard the shouts of the multitude, he bowed very low, and as if he could bear no more turned hastily around and went into the house" (*Hist. Collections of the Essex Institute*, 67 [1931], 299–300).

While in Salem, GW lodged at the imposing Ward House on Court (now

View of the courthouse at Salem, Mass., from *Massachusetts Magazine*, 1790.
(Library of Congress)

Washington) Street, constructed between 1781 and 1785 by Samuel McIntire,
and presently owned by Joshua Ward. For GW's stay in Salem, see BENTLEY,
130–31; *Gaz. of the U.S.*, 14 Nov. 1789; RANTOUL, 68:1–19).

⁷ The inhabitants of Salem had sent GW an invitation to attend the entertainment, 23 Oct. 1789 (DLC:GW).

Friday 30th.    A Little after 8 Oclock I set out for Newbury-Port
and in less than 2 Miles crossed the Bridge between Salem and
Beverly, which makes a handsome appearance, and is upon the
same plan of those over Charles & Mistick Rivers; excepting that
it has not foot ways as that of the former has. The length of this
bridge is 1530 feet and was built for about £4500 lawful money—
a price inconceivably low in my estimation, as there is 18 feet
water in the deepest parts of the River over which it is erected.
This Bridge is longer than that at Charles town, but shorter by
[    ] feet than the other over Mistick. All of them have draw
bridges by which Vessels pass. After passing Beverley 2 Miles we
come to the Cotton Manufactury which seems to be carrying on
with Spirit by the Mr. Cabbots (principally).¹ In this Manufactury
they have the New Invented Carding and Spinning Machines—
one of the first supplies the work; and four of the latter; one of
which spins 84 threads at a time by one person. The Cotton is

prepared for these Machines by being first (lightly) drawn to a thrd. on the common wheel. There is also another Machine for doubling and twisting the threads for particular cloths. This also does many at a time. For winding the Cotton from the spindles, & preparing it for the Warp, there is a Reel which expedites the work greatly. A number of Looms (15 or 16) were at work with Spring shuttles which do more than dble. work. In short the whole seemed perfect, and the Cotton stuffs wch. they turn out excellent of their kind. Warp & filling both are *now* of Cotton. From this place with escorts of Horse I passed on to Ipswich about 10 Miles —at the entrance of which I was met and welcomed by the Select Men and received by a Regemt. of Militia. At this place I was met by Mr. Dalton and some other Gentlemen from Newbury-port— partook of a Cold Collation, & proceeded on to the last-mentioned place where I was received with much respect & parade, about 4 Oclock. In the evening there were Rockets & some other fire-works and every other demonstration to welcome me to the Town. This place is pleasantly situated on Merimack River, and appears to have carried on (here & about) the Ship-building business to a grt. extent. The number of Souls is estimated at 5,000.[2]

[1] The Beverly Cotton Manufactory was established in 1787–88 with John Cabot and Joshua Fisher as managers and George and Andrew Cabot as leading stockholders. In its early years the factory received considerable encouragement from the Massachusetts legislature—a grant of land in 1789 and a state lottery in 1791. It was incorporated 3 Feb. 1789 (BAGNALL, 93–94).

[2] For GW's reception in Newburyport, see *Essex Jl. and New Hampshire Packet,* 4 Nov. 1789; *Gaz. of the U.S.,* 14 Nov. 1789; *Pa. Packet,* 19 Nov. 1789). According to local tradition, GW left his carriage just outside of town and, mounting his horse, proceeded to South (Bromfield) and High streets where, accompanied by considerable fanfare, an ode dedicated to the president was sung. The party then proceeded to Tracy House, originally owned by Nathaniel Tracy but now occupied by Joseph Prince, where GW was to lodge (CURRIER, 408–10).

Saturday 31st.    Left Newbury-port a little after 8 Oclock (first breakfasting with Mr. Dalton)[1] and to avoid a wider ferry—more inconvenient boats—and a piece of heavy Sand, we crossed the River at Salisbury two Miles above; and near that further about— and in three Miles came to the Line wch. divides the State of Massachusetts from that of New Hampshire.[2] Here I took leave of Mr. Dalton and many other private Gentlemen who accompanied me—also of Genl. Titcomb who had met me on the line between Middlesex & Essex Counties—Corps of light Horse and Many officers of Militia—And was recd. by the President of the State of

New Hampshire—the Vice-President; some of the Council—
Messrs. Langdon & Wingate of the Senate—Colo. Parker Marshall
of the State, & many other respectable characters;[3] besides several
Troops of well cloathed Horse in handsome Uniforms, and many
Officers of the Militia also in handsome (white & red) uniforms
of the Manufacture of the State. With this Cavalcade we proceeded and arrived before 3 Oclock at Portsmouth, where we were
received with every token of respect and appearance of Cordiallity
under a discharge of Artillery. The Streets—doors and windows
were Crouded here, as at all the other Places—and, alighting at the
Town House, odes were Sung & played in honor of the President.
The same happened yesterday at my entrance into New-bury-
port—Being stopped at my entrance to hear it. From the Town
House I went to Colonel Brewsters Ta[ver]n[4] the place provided
for my residence and asked the President, Vice-President, the two
Senators, the Marshall and Majr. Gilman[5] to dine with me, which
they did—after which I drank Tea at Mr. Langdons.[6]

[1] Tristram Dalton's farm, where he engaged in extensive experimental
gardening, was five miles from Newburyport on the Merrimack River. A
contemporary traveler noted that it "is one of the most beautiful spots
imaginable and the view, one of the grandest I have ever seen, embraces a
panorama stretching over more than seven leagues. His farm is well kept;
I saw thirty cows, a good number of very fat pigs, some sheep, a well-stocked
larder, and a big vegetable garden" (BRISSOT, 368).

[2] On his way from Newburyport to Portsmouth, GW "passed through the
towns of Amesbury and Salisbury where several companies of Militia were
paraded which saluted as he passed. The Marine Society of this town prepared and decorated a handsome Barge, for the purpose of carrying the
President across Merrimack River, which was previously sent . . . opposite
to Amesbury Ferry, where it waited his arrival. The Barge men were all
dressed in white" (*Essex Jl. and New Hampshire Packet,* 4 Nov. 1789).

[3] John Sullivan (1740–1795) had been president of New Hampshire in
1786 and 1787 and was reelected in 1789. Appointed major of the New
Hampshire militia in 1772 and brigadier general in the Continental Army
in 1775, he brought his brigade to join GW's army outside Boston in 1775,
where he served throughout the siege of the city. He was promoted to major
general in Aug. 1776. His stormy military career during the Revolution included controversies with Congress and with the French command during the
Rhode Island campaign in 1778 and command of the expedition against the
Iroquois in western Pennsylvania and New York in 1779. Sullivan had served
intermittently in the Continental Congress during the Revolution, and in
Sept. 1789 GW appointed him federal judge for the district of New Hampshire (EXECUTIVE JOURNAL, 1:29–30).

John Pickering (c.1738–1805), one of New Hampshire's leading jurists,
was now vice-president of the state. In 1790 he was appointed chief justice
of the New Hampshire superior court and in 1795 GW named him to succeed

Sullivan as federal judge for the district of New Hampshire (EXECUTIVE JOURNAL, 1:172).

John Langdon (1741–1819) and Paine Wingate (1739–1838) were New Hampshire's two United States senators. Langdon, a former Portsmouth merchant, had seen military service at Saratoga during the Revolution and was a member of the Continental Congress 1775–76, 1783. At this time he was president *pro tempore* of the Senate. Wingate lived at Stratham, N.H., had served in the Continental Congress 1787–88, and was a United States senator until 1795.

In Sept. 1789 GW had appointed John Parker United States marshal for the district of New Hampshire (EXECUTIVE JOURNAL, 1:29–30).

⁴ The tavern was kept by William Brewster.

⁵ Nicholas Gilman (1755–1814), of Exeter, N.H., was appointed as regimental adjutant to the 3d New Hampshire Regiment in 1776 and served with New Hampshire Continental regiments to the end of the Revolution. From 1786 to 1788 he was a member of the Continental Congress. At this time he was a United States congressman.

⁶ John Langdon's mansion, built in 1784, was on Pleasant Street in Portsmouth.

## [November 1789]

November 1st. Attended by the President of the State (Genl. Sullivan) Mr. Langdon, & the Marshall; I went in the fore Noon to the Episcopal Church under the incumbency of a Mr. Ogden and in the Afternoon to one of the Presbeterian or Congregational Churches in which a Mr. Buckminster Preached.¹ Dined at home with the Marshall and spent the afternoon in my own room writing letters.²

¹ Rev. John Cosens Ogden was pastor of St. John's Episcopal Church from 1786 to 1793. Ogden had written GW, 30 Oct., extending an invitation to tea and mentioning, as an added inducement, that his mother-in-law was the widow of Brig. Gen. David Wooster and his sister the widow of Col. Francis Barber (DNA:PCC). GW attended services in Queen's Chapel of the church (*Pa. Packet*, 25 Nov. 1789). Rev. Joseph Buckminster became pastor of the North Congregational Church in Portsmouth in 1779 and held the post for 33 years (GURNEY, 140).

² Several newspaper accounts, including the *Pennsylvania Packet*, 19 Nov. 1789, state that on Sunday, 1 Nov., Tobias Lear was married in Portsmouth "to an amiable young lady of that town" and that GW attended the wedding. This is clearly in error since Lear did not marry Mary Long of Portsmouth until 18 April 1790. However, Lear family tradition holds that GW attended the engagement party on this day (DECATUR, 128).

Monday 2d. Having made previous preparations for it—About 8 Oclock attended by the President, Mr. Langden & some other Gentlemen, I went in a boat to view the harbour of Portsmouth;

John Langdon, by John Trumbull.
(Yale University Art Gallery)

which is well secured against all Winds; and from its narrow entrance from the Sea, and passage up to the Town, may be perfectly guarded against any approach by water. The anchorage is also good & the Shipping may lay close to the Docks &ca. when at the Town. In my way to the Mouth of the Harbour, I stopped at a place called Kittery in the Provence of Main, the River Piscataqua being the boundary between New Hampshire and it. From hence I went by the Old Fort (formerly built while under the English government) on an Island which is at the Entrance of the Harbour and where the Light House stands.[1] As we passed this Fort we were saluted by 13 Guns. Having Lines we proceeded to the Fishing banks a little with out the Harbour and fished for Cod —but it not being a proper time of tide we only caught two—with wch. about 1 Oclock we returned to Town.[2] Dined at Col. Langdons, and drank Tea there with a large Circle of Ladies and retired a little after Seven O'clock. Before dinner I recd. an address from the Town—presented by the Vice-President and returned an answer in the Evening to one I had recd. from Marblehead and an other from the Presbiterian Clergy of the State of Massachusetts & New Hampshire delivered at Newbury Port; both of which I had been unable to answer before.[3]

[1] Fort William and Mary, later called Fort Constitution, was on Newcastle Island in Portsmouth harbor.
[2] According to tradition in Tobias Lear's family, "On the trip down the Piscataqua River, Washington landed for a few minutes on the opposite

bank at Kittery, or rather Kittery Point, Maine, and made a short call on the Reverend Dr. Stevens, the pastor of the old Kittery Church. The President landed on the old stone dock." Rev. Dr. Benjamin Stevens (1720–1791) had been pastor of the First Church in Kittery, Maine, since 1751. His daughter Sally was married to Rev. Joseph Buckminster whose church GW had attended on 1 Nov. GW's first attempt at deep-sea fishing was apparently even less successful than he intimates. One of the two cod "was hooked by a fisherman named Zebulon Willey, who was trying his luck in a neighboring boat. Getting a bite, he handed his line to the President, who landed the fish and rewarded Zebulon with a silver dollar. When returning to town, the President saw an old acquaintance. This was Captain John Blunt, the helmsman of the boat during the famous crossing of the Delaware" (DECATUR, 84; DEXTER, 562).

³ These addresses and replies are in DLC:GW.

Tuesday 3d.    Sat two hours in the forenoon for a Mr. [     ] Painter of Boston, at the Request of Mr. Brick of that place; who wrote Majr. Jackson that it was an earnest desire of many of the Inhabitants of that Town that he might be endulged.¹ After this setting I called upon President Sullivan, and the Mother of Mr. Lear ² and having walked through most parts of the Town, returned by 12 Oclock when I was visited by a Clergyman of the name of Haven,³ who presented me with an Ear, and part of the stalk of the dying Corn, and several small pieces of Cloth which had been died with it, equal to any colours I had ever seen & of various colours. This Corn was blood red & the rind of the stalk deeply tinged of the same colour. About 2 Oclock I recd. an Address from the Executive of the State of New Hampshire; and in half an hour after dined with them and a large Company at their Assembly room which is one of the best I have seen any where in the United States.⁴ At half after Seven I went to the Assembly where there were about 75 well dressed, and many of them very handsome Ladies—among whom (as was also the case at the Salem & Boston Assemblies) were a greater proportion with much blacker hair than are usually seen in the Southern States. About 9 I returned to my Quarters. Portsmouth it is said contains abt. 5000 Inhabitants. There are some good houses (among wch. Colo. Langdons may be esteemed the first) but in general they are indifferent; and almost entirely of wood. On wondering at this, as the Country is full of Stone and good Clay for Bricks I was told that on acct. of the fogs and damps they deemed them wholesomer and for that reason prefered wood buildings. Lumber—Fish and Pot ash with some Provisions compose the principal Articles of Export. Ship building here & at Newbury Port has been carried on to a considerable extent. During & for sometime after the War there was an entire stagnation to it; but it is beginning now to revive again. The number of Ships belonging to the Port are estimated at [      ].⁵

¹ Samuel Breck, a Boston merchant, was interested in various manufacturing concerns in the city including the Boston Duck Manufactory and the Boston Glass House. See also entry for 27 Oct. 1789.

² According to Portsmouth tradition, GW visited Sullivan and the New Hampshire council at the William Pitt Hotel on Pitt Street, kept since 1770 by John Stavers. Mrs. Mary Lear, the widow of Capt. Tobias Lear, lived on Hunking Street in Portsmouth with her daughter and son-in-law Samuel Storer, a Portsmouth merchant.

³ Rev. Dr. Samuel Haven (1727–1806), a native of Framingham, Mass., and a Harvard graduate, had come to Portsmouth in 1752 to become the vigorous and popular pastor of South Congregational Church. During the Revolution he had operated a small saltpeter works in Portsmouth "using earth which he dug from under the meetinghouse," and was noted for the support he extended out of his own meager salary to the victims of the war in the area (SIBLEY, 12:382–92; BREWSTER, 1st ser., 96, 322–26).

⁴ Letter book copies of an address of welcome from the New Hampshire council, signed by John Sullivan on 3 Nov., and GW's reply are in DLC:GW.

⁵ After visiting New Hampshire, GW had apparently originally intended to continue into Vermont and return to New York City by way of Albany. However, on 3 Nov. a heavy fall of snow blanketed Albany and the surrounding area and GW decided to return to the capital by the most direct route (*Gaz. of the U.S.*, 11 Nov. 1789; *Pa. Packet*, 20 Nov. 1789; WEBB [2], 3:144).

**Wednesday 4th.**    About half after seven I left Portsmouth, quietly & without any attendance, having earnestly entreated that all parade & ceremony might be avoided on my return. Before ten I reached Exeter 14 Miles distance. This is considered as the 2d. Town in New-Hampshire and stands at the head of the tide water of Piscataqua River but Ships of 3 or 400 Tonns are built at it. Above (but in the Town) are considerable Falls which supply several Grist Mills – 2 Oyl Mills A Slitting Mill and Snuff Mill. It is a place of some consequence but does not contain more than 1000 Inhabitants. A jealousy subsists between this Town (where the Legislature alternately sits) and Portsmouth, which, had I known it in time, would have made it necessary to have accepted an Invitation to a Public dinner, but my arrangements having been otherwise made I could not. From hence passing through Kingstown (6 Miles from Exeter) I arrived at Haverhill about half past two & stayed all Night. Walked through the Town which stands at the head of the Tide of Merrimack River and in a beautiful part of the Country. The Lands over which I travelled to day are pretty much mixed in places with Stone And the growth with Pines—till I came near to Haverhill where they disappeared, & the land had a more fertile appearance. The whole were pretty well cultivated but used (principally) for Grass and Indian Corn. In Haverhill is a Duck Manufactury upon a small but ingenious scale under the conduct of Colo. [      ].[1] At this Manufactury one small person turns a Wheel which employs 8 Spinners, each acting independently of each other so as to occasion no interruption to the rest if any one of them is stopped—Whereas at the Boston Manufactury of this Article, each Spinner has a small girl to turn the Wheel. The Looms are also somewhat differently constructed from those of the common kind, and upon an improved plan. The Inhabitts. of this small Village were well disposed to welcome me to it by every demonstration which could evince their joy.

[1] The Sailcloth Manufactory at Haverhill, under the supervision of Samuel Blodgett, began operation in 1789. By 1790 flax for sailcloth was being processed by "a multiple spinning-machine, operated by power, containing 4 heads of 8 spindles each." As in the case of other New England duck manufactories, the Haverhill establishment prospered as long as state bounties were available. After their expiration around 1795, production gradually declined (CLARK [4], 1:425, 531).
GW lodged at Harrod's tavern in Haverhill (DIARIES, 4:46, n.1).

Thursday 5th.    About Sun rise I set out, crossing the Merimack River at the Town over to the Township of Bradford and in nine Miles came to Abbots Tavern in Andover where we breakfasted, and met with much attention from Mr. Philips President of the Senate of Massachusetts,[1] who accompanied us thro' Bellarika [Billerica] to Lexington, where I dined, and viewed the Spot on which the first blood was spilt in the dispute with great Britain on the 19th. of April 1775. Here I parted with Mr. Philips, and proceeded on to Watertown, intending (as I was disappointed by the Weather & bad Roads from travvelling through the Interior Country to Charlestown on Connecticut River) to take what is called the Middle Road from Boston. The Country from Haverhill to Andover is good, and well cultivated. In and about the latter (which stands high) it is beautiful. A Mile or two from it you descend into a pine level pretty Sandy, and mixed with Swamps; through which you ride several Miles till you begin to ascend the heights on which the Town of Bellarika stands, which is also pleasantly situated 10 Miles from Andover. From hence to Lexington—8 Miles and thence to Watertown 8 More the Country is very pleasant, and the roads in general good. We lodged in this

A view of the Green in Lexington, a woodcut in the January 1794 *Massachusetts Magazine*. (Library of Congress)

place at the House of a Widow Coolidge near the Bridge, and a very indifferent one it is.[2]

[1] Samuel Phillips (1752–1802), of Andover, Mass., a Harvard graduate, had served intermittently in the Massachusetts legislature since 1775. During the Revolution he had operated a powder mill at Andover, which was still in operation in 1789, and was also involved in the manufacture of paper. In 1778, in cooperation with his uncle John Exeter, he was a founder of what was later to become the Phillips Exeter Academy. He served as president of the Massachusetts Senate 1775–1802 and as lieutenant governor of the state in 1802 (SIBLEY, 17:593–605).

[2] This tavern was kept by the widow of Nathaniel Coolidge (DIARIES, 4:48).

Friday 6th.   A little after Seven oclock, under great appearances of Rain or Snow, we left Watertown, and Passing through Needham (five Miles therefrom) breakfasted at Sherburn which is 14 Miles from the former. Then passing through Holliston 5 Miles, Milford 6 More, Menden 4 More, and Uxbridge 6 More, we lodged at one Tafts 1 Miles further;[1] the whole distance of this days travel being 36 Miles. From Watertown till you get near Needham, the Road is very level—about Needham it is hilly— then level again, and the whole pleasant and well cultivated 'till you pass Sherburn; between this and Holliston is some Hilly & Rocky ground as there is in places, onwards to Uxbridge; some of wch. are very bad; Upon the whole it may be called an indifferent Rd.—deversified by good & bad land—cultivated and in woods—some high and Barren and others low, wet and Piney. Grass and Indian Corn is the chief produce of the Farms. Rye composes a part of the culture of them, but wheat is not grown on Acct. of the blight. The Roads in every part of this State are amazingly crooked, to suit the convenience of every Mans fields; & the directions you receive from the People equally blind & ignorant; for instead of going to Watertown from Lexington, if we had proceeded to Waltham we should in 13 Miles have saved at least Six; the distance from Lexington to Waltham being only 5 Miles and the Road from Watertown to Sherburn going within less than two miles of the latter (i.e. Waltham). The Clouds of the Morning vanished before the Meridian Sun, and the Afternoon was bright and pleasant. The House in Uxbridge had a good external appearance (for a Tavern) but the owner of it being from home, and the wife sick, we could not gain admittance which was the reason of my coming on to Tafts; where, though the people were obliging, the entertainment was not very inviting.

¹ GW apparently found these accommodations adequate. On 8 Nov. he wrote Samuel Taft: "Being informed that you have given my name to one of your Sons, and called another after Mrs. Washington's family. And being moreover very much pleased with the modest and innocent looks of your two daughters Patty and Polly I do, for these reasons, send each of these Girls a piece of chintz. And to Patty, who bears the name of Mrs. Washington, and who waited more upon us than Polly did, I send five guineas, with which she may buy herself any little ornaments she may want, or she may dispose of them in any other manner more agreeable to herself. As I do not give these things with a view to have it talked of, or even to its being known, the less there is said about the matter the better you will please me; but that I may be sure the chintz and money have got safe to hand, let Patty, who I dare say is equal to it, write me a line informing me thereof directed to 'The President of the United States at New York'" (DLC:GW). Patty, whose given name was Mercy rather than Martha, acknowledged the gifts in a letter to GW, 28 Dec. 1789 (DLC:GW).

Saturday 7th.    Left Tafts before Sunrise, and passing through Douglas wood breakfasted at one Jacobs in Thompson 12 Miles' distant—not a good House.¹ Bated the Horses in Pomfret at Colo. Grosveners,² distant 11 Miles from Jacobs and Lodged at Squire Perkins in Ashford³ (called 10 Miles, but must be 12). The first Stage with a small exception is intolerable bad Road, & a poor and uncultivated Country covered chiefly with woods—the largest of Which is called Douglass, at the foot of which on the East side is a large Pond. Jacobs's, is in the State of Connecticut, and here the Lands are better, and more highly improved. From hence to Pomfret there is some woods & indifferent Land, but in General it is tolerably good and the Farms look well. In and abt. Pomfret they are fine, and from thence to Ashford not bad; but very hilly and much mixed with Rock Stone. Knowing that General Putnam lived in the Township of Pomfret, I had hopes of seeing him and it was one of my inducements for coming this Road; but on enquiry in the Town I found that he lived 5 Miles out of my road, and that without deranging my plan & delaying my journey, I could not do it. [4]

[1] This tavern, just off the main road between Hartford and Boston, was kept by John Jacobs (CROFUT, 2:863).

[2] Thomas Grosvenor (1744–1825), a Pomfret, Conn., attorney, had graduated from Yale in 1765 and practiced law until 1775 when he joined the 3d Connecticut Regiment as a second lieutenant. He ended the war as lieutenant colonel commandant of the 1st Connecticut Regiment.

[3] This tavern was kept by Isaac Perkins (CROFUT, 1:65, 2:792).

[4] Israel Putnam (1718–1790), one of the most colorful of Revolutionary War generals, was born in Salem Village (Danvers), Mass., but moved to Brooklyn, Conn., as a young man. Putnam served in the French and Indian War. In 1775 he was appointed major general in the Continental Army where he was an active and popular but controversial soldier, his habit of independent action proving an irritant to GW on more than one occasion. A paralytic stroke in 1779 had forced his retirement to his Connecticut home. Putnam's farm, which he had purchased from Gov. Jonathan Belcher, was about a mile from present-day Pomfret, Conn. In 1767 after his marriage to Deborah Lothrop Avery Gardiner, he moved to her home in present-day Brooklyn where the Putnams operated a tavern which became a favorite meeting place for Patriots. After Putnam moved to Brooklyn, his farm was occupied by Israel Putnam, Jr., but the elder Putnam had purchased the adjoining farm and it is likely he was living here, rather than in his Brooklyn house, when GW visited the area in 1789 (CROFUT, 2:834).

**Sunday 8th.** It being contrary to Law & disagreeable to the People of this State (Connecticut) to travel on the Sabbath day [1] and my horses after passing through such intolerable Roads wanting rest, I stayed at Perkins's Tavern (which by the bye is not a good one) all day—and a meeting House being with in a few rod of the Door, I attended Morning & evening Service, and heard very lame discourses from a Mr. Pond.[2]

[1] GW correctly interpreted New England attitudes toward travel on the Sabbath. The *Pennsylvania Packet,* 3 Nov. 1789, noted with approval that Tristram Dalton and John Adams, on their way to Boston, broke their journey at Springfield in order not to travel on Sunday. "How pleasing the

idea, that the most venerable and respectable characters of our Federal Legislature, pay such strict attention to the Sabbath." See also *Mass. Centinel,* 24 Oct. 1789.

[2] Rev. Enoch Pond (1756–1807) had been ordained only the year before (CROFUT, 2:827).

**Monday 9th.**    Set out about 7 Oclock and for the first 24 Miles had hilly, rocky and disagreeable Roads. The remaining 10 was level and good, but in places Sandy. Arrived at Hartford a little before four. We passed through Mansfield (which is a very hilly Country and the Township in which they make the greatest qty. of Silk of any in the State) and breakfasted at one Brighams in Coventry.[1] Stopped at Woodbridges[2] in Et. Hartford where the level land is entered upon & from whence through East Hartford the Country is pleasant, and the Land in places very good – in others Sandy and Weak. I find by Conversing with the Farmers along this Road that a medium Crop of Wheat to the Acre is about 15 bushels – of Corn 20 – of Oats the same – and in their strong & fresh Lands they get as much Wheat as they can Rye to the Acre – but in worn, or Sandy Land the latter yields most. They go more however upon grasing than either; & consequently Beef Butter & Cheese – with Porke are the articles which they carry to Market.

[1] Presumably Gershom Brigham, who had been licensed in 1778 to keep a tavern in Coventry, Conn. (CROFUT, 2:792).

[2] Deodatus and Esther Woodbridge kept a tavern at present-day Manchester Green in Hartford County (CROFUT, 1:299).

**Tuesday 10th.**    Left Hartford about 7 Oclock & took the Middle Road (instead of the one through Middleton which I went). Breakfasted at Worthington in the Township of Berlin, at the House of one Fuller.[1] Bated at Smiths on the plains of Wallingford 13 Miles from Fullers, which is the distance Fullers is from Hartford – and got into New Haven which is 13 Miles more, about half an hour before Sun-down. At this place I met Mr. Gerry[2] in the Stage from New York who gave me the first certn. acct. of the health of Mrs. Washington.

[1] The Fuller with whom GW breakfasted is probably Ephraim Fuller, listed in the 1790 census as a resident of Berlin (HEADS OF FAMILIES, CONN., 34).

[2] Elbridge Gerry, United States congressman from Massachusetts, was probably on his way to his home, Elmwood, in Cambridge, where he had lived since 1787.

Wednesday 11th.  Set out about Sunrise, and took the upper Road to Milford, it being shorter than the lower one through West haven. Breakfasted at the former—Bated at Fairfield and dined and lodged at a Majr. Marvins 9 Miles further; which is not a good House, though the People of it were disposed to do all they cou'd to accomodate me.[1]

[1] Ozias Marvin's tavern was located "on the Westport-Norwalk road, at the intersection of the King's Highway with the turnpike. Washington is said to have eaten only bread and milk" (CROFUT, 1:162).

Thursday 12th.  A little before Sunrise we left Marvins and breakfasting at Stamford 13 Miles distant, reached the Widow Havilands 12 Miles further; where, on acct. of some lame horses, we remained all Night. The badness of these Rds. having been described as I went, I shall say nothing of them now.

Friday 13th.  Left Mrs. Havilands as soon as we could see the Road and breakfasted at Hoyets Tavern this side Kings-bridge and between two and three Oclock arrived at my House at New York where I found Mrs. Washington and the rest of the family all well. And its being Mrs. Washington's Night to receive visits a pretty large Company of Ladies and Gentlemen were present.

Saturday 14th.  At home all day—except taking a Walk round the Battery in the Afternoon.
    At 4 Oclock received and answered an Address from the President & Corporation of Dartmouth College and about Noon sundry visits.

Sunday 15th.  Went to St. Pauls Chapel in the forenoon and after returning from thence was visited by Majr. Butler Majr. Meridith and Mr. Smith So. Cara.[1] Received an Invitation to attend the Funeral of Mrs. Roosevelt (the wife of a Senator of this State) but declined complying with it—first because the propriety of accepting any invitation of this sort appeared very questionable and secondly (though to do it in this instance might not be improper) because it might be difficult to discriminate in cases wch. might thereafter happen.[2]

[1] Pierce Butler (1744–1822), United States senator from South Carolina, was a native of Ireland and came to America in the early 1770s as a major in the British army. After holding various posts under the state government, he was elected to the Continental Congress in 1787 and represented South

Carolina at the Federal Convention. He was elected to the Senate as a Federalist in 1789 and served until 1796.

Samuel Meredith (1741–1817), of Philadelphia, was an active Patriot before the Revolution and served in the Pennsylvania militia until 1778 when he resigned to resume his career in business and politics. In 1788 he was appointed surveyor of the Port of Philadelphia, and in Mar. 1789, anticipating GW's election, he wrote him requesting an appointment in the "Impost Department" (Meredith to GW, 23 Feb. 1789, DLC:GW). GW replied 5 Mar. stating that if he assumed the presidency, he had resolved "to go into it, perfectly free from all engagements of every nature whatsoever. A conduct, in conformity to this resolution, would enable me in ballancing the various pretentions of different Candidates for appointments, to act with a sole reference to justice and the public good. This is, in substance, the answer that I have given to all applications (and they are not few) which have already been made" (DLC:GW). See also entry for 20 June 1787.

William Loughton Smith (1758–1812), congressman from South Carolina, had studied at the Middle Temple and also at Geneva. Before the Revolution he practiced law in Charleston and was elected to the state legislature. In 1789 he was elected as a Federalist to Congress where he served until 1797, rapidly becoming one of the administration's most reliable supporters, especially in financial matters.

² Isaac Roosevelt's wife was Cornelia Hoffman Roosevelt (1734–1789), daughter of Martinus Hoffman of Dutchess County, N.Y.

**Monday 16th.** The Commissioners, who had returned from the proposed Treaty with the Creek Indians before me, to this City dined with me to day, as did their Secretary Colo. Franks and young Mr. Lincoln who accompanied them.

During the summer of 1789 an increasing stream of reports came from state officials and frontier settlers telling of Indian attacks by war parties from southern tribes, particularly urged on by the Creek chief Alexander McGillivray. The administration in Aug. 1789 appointed Benjamin Lincoln, Cyrus Griffin, and David Humphreys United States commissioners to open negotiations with the southern tribes on behalf of the government and "establish peace between the State of Georgia and the Creeks" (ASP, INDIAN AFF., 1:65–68). The commissioners arrived in Savannah 10 Sept. and conducted negotiations with state officials and Indian leaders over the next three weeks. By 10 Nov. they were back in New York. On 17 and 20 Nov. they reported to Knox that the Creek were determined not to make a treaty; however, as McGillivray and the other Creek chiefs "have given strong assurances in their talks, and by writing, that no further hostilities or depredations shall be committed on the part of their nation; and as the Governor of Georgia . . . will prevent the commission of hostilities and depredations upon the Creek nation, on the part of Georgia, the commissioners, in the best of their judgment, report, that all animosities with the Creek nation should henceforth cease." In obedience to their instructions, however, they included detailed information on the Creek country and plans for "offensive and defensive measures" in case hostilities should break out (ASP, INDIAN AFF., 1:78). The reports and the commissioners' journal containing their correspondence with Creek leaders and Georgia officials are in ASP, INDIAN AFF., 1:68–80.

David Salisbury Franks (c.1740–1793), son of John Franks, a prominent Jewish merchant of Philadelphia, served as aide-de-camp to Benedict Arnold 1778–80, with the rank of major, but was acquitted of complicity in Arnold's treason. In 1781 he was designated an official courier by Robert Morris to carry dispatches to John Jay in Spain and served as vice-consul at Marseilles from 1784 to 1787. In 1789 he asked GW to appoint him to a foreign diplomatic post, preferably that of consul general in France, but instead received the minor appointment of secretary to the commissioners (Franks to GW, 12 May, 11 June 1789, DLC:GW; STRAUS, 101–8). After his return from the mission to the Creek, he served as assistant cashier of the Bank of the United States. He died of yellow fever during the 1793 epidemic in Philadelphia (see also WOLF, 158–64).

Tuesday 17th.    The Visitors at the Levee to day, were numerous.

Wednesday 18th.    Took a walk in the forenoon, & called upon Mr. Jay on business but he was not within. On my return paid Mr. Vaughan Senr. a visit—informal.

Sent a Commission as District Judge of So. Carolina to the Honble. William Drayton of that State.

Samuel Vaughan (1720–1802), formerly a London merchant, had been living in Philadelphia since 1783 where, with his son John, he was conducting the family's mercantile business and was extensively involved in elaborate plans for the planting of trees and shrubs in the city. He was particularly noted for his role in ornamenting the State House Yard. Vaughan had recently corresponded with GW concerning the possibility of a federal appointment for his son Samuel Vaughan, Jr. (GW to Vaughan, 21 Mar. 1789, Vaughan to GW, 28 May 1789, DLC:GW; STETSON [3], 459–74).

Thursday 19th.    The following Company dined here today— viz.—Mrs. Adams (Lady to the Vice President) Colo. Smith & Lady & Miss Smith Mrs. Adams's Niece—Govr. Clinton and Lady & Miss Cornelia Clinton and Majr. Butlar, his Lady and two Daughters.

Gov. George Clinton's wife, whom he had married in 1770, was Cornelia Tappan Clinton, a connection of the prominent Wynkoop family of Ulster County, N.Y.

Pierce Butler's wife was Mary Middleton Butler, daughter of Thomas Middleton of Prince William's Parish, S.C.

Friday 20th.    The Visitors of Gentn. and Ladies to Mrs. Washington this evening were numerous & respectable.

Saturday 21st.    Received in the Afternoon the Report from the Commissioners appointed to Treat with the Southern Indians. Gave it one reading & shall bestow another and more attentive one on it.

See entry for 16 Nov. 1789.

Sunday 22d.    Went to St. Pauls Chappel in the forenoon—heard a charity Sermon for the benefit of the Orphans School of this City.

Had a good deal of conversation in the Evening with the above Commissioners on the more minute part of their transactions at the Treaty with the Creek Indians and their opinion with respect to the real views of Mr. McGillivry—The principles of whose conduct they think is self-Interest, and a dependence for support on Spain. They think also, that having possessed himself of the outlines of the terms he could Treat with the United States upon, he wished to Postpone the Treaty to see if he could not obtain better from Spain. They think that, though he does not want abilities, he has credit to the full extent of them and that he is but a short sighted politicion. He acknowledges however, that an Alliance between the Creek Nation & the United States is the most Natural one, & what they ought to prefer if to be obtained on equal terms. A *Free* port in the latter seems to be a favourite object with him.

This benefit was conducted to aid the Charity School operated by Trinity Church. The school consisted of "eighty-six scholars, viz. fifty-six boys and thirty girls. The children are instructed in the principles of the Christian Religion and in Psalmody; they constantly attend divine service at church on week days as well as on Sundays and the greatest attention is paid to their morals. . . . The school is regularly visited the first Monday in every month, and the children carefully examined by a committee of the Corporation of Trinity Church." The sermon was preached by Rev. Dr. Benjamin Moore, and £80 8s. 10d. was collected for the Charity School (*N.Y. Daily Advertiser,* 16 and 23 Nov. 1789).

Monday 23d.    Rid five or Six miles between Breakfast & dinner. Called upon Mr. Vanberkel & Mrs. Adams.

Franco Petrus Van Berckel had succeeded his father as minister to the United States from the Netherlands in Aug. 1788 and presented his credentials in May 1789 (Van Berckel to Jay, 11 May 1789, letter of credence, 1 Aug. 1788, DNA: PCC, Item 126). He was generally popular in New York, although Sen. William Maclay termed him "gaudy as a peacock" (MACLAY, 41).

Tuesday 24th.    A good deal of Company at the Levee to day. Went to the Play in the Evening. Sent Tickets to the following Ladies and Gentlemn. & invited them to Seats in my Box viz.— Mrs. Adams (Lady of the Vice-President) Genl. Schuyler & Lady, Mr. King & Lady, Majr. Butler and Lady, Colo. Hamilton & Lady Mrs. Green—all of whom accepted and came except Mrs. Butler who was indisposed.

The play GW attended was a performance of a comedy *The Toy; or a Trip to Hampton Court* which, with several shorter pieces, was performed by the Old American Company at the John Street Theatre (FORD [5], 37–38). The *Gazette of the United States* noted that "On the appearance of The President, the audience rose, and received him with the warmest acclamations" (28 Nov. 1789).

Philip Schuyler was now United States senator from New York. In 1755 he had married Catherine Van Rensselaer (1734–1803), daughter of John Van Rensselaer of Claverack. Their second daughter, Elizabeth Schuyler (1757–1854), had married Alexander Hamilton in 1780.

Rufus King (1755–1827) had graduated from Harvard in 1777, studied law with Theophilus Parsons in Newburyport, Mass., and served in the Massachusetts General Court 1783–85. As a delegate to the Constitutional Convention and the Massachusetts Ratifying Convention he provided invaluable support in securing the adoption of the Constitution in Massachusetts. He was elected United States senator to the First Congress. In 1786 King had married Mary Alsop (c.1770–1819), daughter of John Alsop, a prominent New York merchant.

**Wednesday 25th.**  Exercised on Horse-back between Breakfast & dinner—in which returning I called upon Mr. Jay and Genl. Knox on business and made informal visits to the Govr., Mr. Izard, Genl. Schuyler, and Mrs. Dalton. The following Company dined with me. viz.

Doctr. Johnson & Lady and daughter (Mrs. Neely)—Mr. Izard & Lady & Son—Mr. Smith (So. Carolina) & Lady—Mr. Kean & Lady and the Chief Justice Mr. Jay.

After which I went with Mrs. Washington to the Dancing Assembly at which I stayed until 10 Ock.

MRS. NEELY: William Samuel Johnson's eldest daughter Charity Johnson (d. 1810) had married Rev. Ebenezer Kneeland of Stratford, Conn. (GROCE, 39).

In 1767 Sen. Ralph Izard had married Alice DeLancey (1745–1832) of New York. The son who accompanied them today was Henry Izard (1771–1826), George Izard (1776–1828), or, less likely, their youngest son, four-year-old Ralph Izard (1785–1824). Also in the party was the Izard's second daughter Charlotte Izard (1770–1792), who had married Sen. William Loughton Smith in 1786 (ROGERS [1], 404).

John Kean (1756–1795), of South Carolina, had served in the Continental Congress 1785–87, and in Aug. 1789 GW appointed him one of the commissioners for settling accounts between the United States and the individual states (EXECUTIVE JOURNAL, 1:17).

**Thursday 26th.**  Being the day appointed for a thanksgiving I went to St. Pauls Chapel though it was most inclement and stormy —but few people at Church.

On 25 Sept. 1789 the House of Representatives resolved that the president should recommend a day of thanksgiving and prayer to the people of the

United States acknowledging divine favor and especially the "opportunity peaceably to establish a Constitution of government for their safety and happiness." The Senate concurred on 26 Sept. (DE PAUW, 3:226; ANNALS OF CONGRESS, 1:92). The wording of the resolution did not escape comment. Rep. Aedanus Burke of South Carolina objected to the "mimicking of European customs." Thomas Tudor Tucker, of South Carolina, felt that Congress had no right to ask for a day of thanksgiving. Citizens "may not be inclined to return thanks for a Constitution until they have experienced that it promotes their safety and happiness. We do not yet know but they may have reason to be dissatisfied with the effects it has already produced; but whether this be so or not, it is a business with which Congress have nothing to do. . . . If a day of thanksgiving must take place, let it be done by the authority of the several States; they know best what reason their constituents have to be pleased with the establishment of this Constitution" (ANNALS OF CONGRESS, 1:949–50). GW issued the proclamation on 3 Oct., assigning 26 Nov. as the first Thanksgiving Day under the Constitution (DLC:GW). In celebration of the day the president contributed £7 10s. 4d. for "provisions & beer" to prisoners confined for debt in the New York City jail (DECATUR, 91; *N.Y. Journal*, 3 Dec. 1789).

**Friday 27th.** Not many Visitors this evening to Mrs. Washington.

**Saturday 28th.** Exercised on Horseback.

**Sunday 29th.** Went to St. Pauls Chapel in the forenoon.

**Monday 30th.** Went to the Play in the Evening and presented Tickets to the following persons—viz.—Doctr. Johnson and Lady —Mr. Dalton & Lady—The Chief Justice of the United States and Lady—Secretary of War & Lady—Baron de Steuben and Mrs. Green.

On 30 Nov. 1789 the Old American Company gave a benefit performance of *Cymon and Sylvia,* an "Opera or Dramatic Romance," at the John Street Theatre (FORD [5], 40–43). GW noted in his letter of invitation to the Jays that "this is the last night the President proposes visiting the theatre for the season" (NNC: Jay Papers). Sarah Livingston Jay, the lovely and vivacious daughter of Gov. William Livingston of New Jersey, had become one of New York's leading hostesses while her husband was secretary for foreign affairs during the Confederation. Lucy Flucker Knox was the daughter of Thomas Flucker, who had been royal secretary of the Province of Massachusetts Bay. Mrs. Knox's social ambitions were occasionally noted derisively by her contemporaries (see Jefferson's "Anas," BERGH, 1:357). Abigail Adams Smith wrote her mother, 15 June 1788, that Mrs. Knox is "neat in her dress, attentive to her family, and very fond of her children. But her size is enormous; I am frightened when I look at her" (GRISWOLD, 95).

# [December 1789]

Tuesday Decr. 1st.    A pretty full Levee to day—among the Visitors was the Vice President and all the Senators in Town.

Exercised on Horseback betwn. 10 and 12.

Read the Papers relative to our Affairs with the Emperer of Morocco and sent them to Mr. Jay to prepare answers to them.

Presumably GW is referring to papers submitted by Jay 1 Dec. concerning United States relations with the emperor of Morocco (DNA: RG 59, Misc. Letters). In 1788 the emperor had granted special privileges to American vessels, permitting them to pay only a 5 percent duty on the importation of merchandise into Morocco, and from time to time he had used his good offices to aid American shipping in the area. With his letter to GW, Jay submitted letters of 25 April and 18 July 1789 from Giuseppi Chiappe, United States agent at Mogadore, intimating that the emperor felt that his concessions had not received sufficient recognition from the United States (DNA: RG 59, George Washington's Correspondence with the Secretaries of State). Jay also submitted the draft of a letter from GW to the emperor, 1 Dec., expressing the United States's appreciation (owned by *Forbes Magazine*). Also included were drafts of letters dated 1 Dec. from Jay to Giuseppi Chiappe and Francisco Chiappe, United States agent in Morocco, attributing the seeming neglect of the emperor to the exigencies of establishing the new government (DNA: RG 59, George Washington's Correspondence with the Secretaries of State).

Wednesday 2d.    Exercised in the Post Chaise with Mrs. Washington. Visited on our return the Vice-President and family. Afterwards walked to Mr. Kings—Neither he nor his Lady were at home; or to be seen.

John Adams by Charles Willson Peale. (Independence National Historical Park Collection)

Thursday 3d.    The following Gentlemen & Ladies dined here—viz.—Genl. Schuyler, his Lady & daughter (Mrs. Ranselaer) —Mr. Dalton and his Lady, the Secretary of the Treasury & his Lady—Genl. Knox and Lady & Mrs. Green—Baron de Steuben, Colo. Osgood (Postmaster Genl.) & the Treasurer Majr. Meridith.

MRS. RANSELAER: The Schuylers's third daughter, Margaret (Peggy) Schuyler, was born in 1758. In 1783 she had married Stephen Van Rensselaer (1764–1839), eighth patroon of Rensselaerswyck.

Friday 4th.    A great number of Visiters (Gentlemen & Ladies) this evening to Mrs. Washington.
    The Governor of New Jersey and the Speaker of the House of Assembly of that State presented an Address from the Legislature thereof and received an answer to it—after which they dined with me.

The letter of congratulation to GW from the New Jersey legislature was signed, 1 Dec. 1789, by Gov. William Livingston on behalf of the council and, 30 Nov. 1789, by Speaker John Beatty for the assembly (DLC:GW). GW's reply is in MHi: William Livingston Papers.

Saturday 5th.    Exercised on Horseback between 10 and 12 oclock.
    The Vice President & Lady and two Sons—Colo. Smith & Lady & his Sister, & Mrs. Adam's Niece dined here.

The two sons who accompanied the Adamses today were Charles Adams and Thomas Boylston Adams (1772–1832). William Stephens Smith had several sisters. The one who dined with GW today may have been Sarah Smith (1769–1828) who married Charles Adams in Aug. 1795.

Sunday 6th.    Went to St. Pauls Chapel in the Forenoon.

Monday 7th.    Walked round the Battery in the afternoon.

Tuesday 8th.    Finished my Extracts from the Commissioners Report of their proceedings at the Treaty with the Creek Indians and from many other Papers respecting Indian matters and the Western Territory.
    A full Levee today.

GW had received the report of the commissioners appointed to negotiate with the southern Indians on 21 Nov. (see entry for that day). His 18-page extract of material found in the commissioners' reports and journals is in DLC:GW.

Wednesday 9th. Walked round the Battery.

Abigail Adams (Mrs. John Adams), by Gilbert Stuart. (National Gallery of Art, Gift of Mrs. Robert Homans, 1954)

Thursday 10th.    Exercised on Horseback—between 10 and 12 Oclock.

The following Company dined here to day—viz.—Mrs. King and Mrs. Few—Mr. & Mrs. Harrison—Mr. & Mrs. Wolcot—Mr. Duer, his Lady and Miss Brown—Mr. Griffin & Lady and Lady Christiana and her daughter.

Catherine Few was the wife of Sen. William Few of Georgia and the daughter of Comdr. James Nicholson.

HARRISON: probably Richard Harison (1747–1829), a Federalist attorney and Columbia College graduate from New York City whom GW had appointed district attorney for New York in Sept. 1789. His wife was the former Frances Ludlow, daughter of Chief Justice George Duncan Ludlow of New Brunswick.

Elizabeth Stoughton, a daughter of Col. John Stoughton of Windsor, Conn., had married Oliver Wolcott, Jr., in 1785 when he was state comptroller for Connecticut. When GW appointed him auditor of the treasury in Sept. 1789 Wolcott accepted the offer only after repeated urgings from his friends; his reluctance stemmed not only from disappointment at not receiving the post of comptroller of the treasury but also from an apprehension that the salary was not adequate for living expenses in New York City. However, hoping that the "example of the President and his family, will render parade and expense improper and disreputable," he accepted, and the Wolcotts arrived in New York early in November. They were unable to find a house and at this time were lodging at Mrs. Grinnell's, No. 27 Queen Street (Wolcott to Elizabeth Wolcott, 24 Sept. 1789; Wolcott to Oliver Wolcott, Sr., 3 Nov. 1789, GIBBS [2], 1:22–23).

William Stephens Smith, by Mather Brown. (The Adams National Historic Site, National Park Service, Department of the Interior)

Abigail Adams Smith, wife of William Stephens Smith. (The Adams National Historic Site, National Park Service, Department of the Interior)

Mr. Griffin is Samuel Griffin of Williamsburg (see entry for 11 Sept. 1774). Mrs. Samuel Griffin is Betsy Braxton Griffin, daughter of Carter Braxton. Lady Christiana Griffin's daughter was either Mary Griffin (d. 1851), who later married her cousin Maj. Thomas Griffin, or, less likely, her younger sister Louise Griffin (d. 1859), who in 1799 married Col. Hugh Tenant Weeden Mercer (1776–1853) of Fredericksburg, the youngest son of Hugh Mercer.

Friday 11th.  Being Rainy and bad no person except the Vice-President visited Mrs. Washington this evening.

Saturday 12th.  Exercised in the Coach with Mrs. Washington and the two Children (Master & Miss Custis) between Breakfast & Dinner—went the 14 Miles round.

THE 14 MILES ROUND: A favorite excursion for New Yorkers was the ride around a portion of Manhattan Island, covering a distance of approximately 14 miles. Although the route varied somewhat, the path frequently taken led up the Bloomingdale Road along the Hudson River on the west side of Manhattan to the vicinity of present-day 94th Street and then east by a crossroad as far as Kingsbridge. The return journey to the city was south by the Old Boston Post Road (see *Mag. of Am. Hist.*, 19 [1888], 110).

Sunday 13th.    Went to St. Pauls Chapel in the forenoon.

Monday 14th.    Walked round the Battery in the afternoon.

Tuesday 15th.    Exercised on horseback about 10 Oclock. Called on the Secretary for the Department of War and gave him the heads of many Letters to be written to characters in the Western Country relative, chiefly, to Indian Affairs.

Visitors at the Levee today were not very numerous, though respectable.

Wednesday 16th.    Dined with Mrs. Washington and all the family (except the two Children) at Governor Clintons – where also dined the Vice-President, his Lady Colo. & Mrs. Smith – The Mayor (Colo. Varick) and his Lady and old Mr. Van Berkel and his Daughter.

Richard Varick (1753–1831) was born in Hackensack, N.J., and moved to New York City in 1775 to practice law. During the Revolution he was Philip Schuyler's aide-de-camp and in 1780 became aide to Benedict Arnold, a post he was occupying at the time of Arnold's defection to the British. Partly to exhibit confidence in Varick's loyalty GW made him his recording secretary in 1781 and as such he was responsible for the transcription of a large part of GW's military correspondence. In 1784 he was appointed recorder of New York City, was a member of the New York Assembly 1787–88, and attorney general of the state 1788–89. Varick succeeded James Duane as mayor of New York City in 1789 and held the position until 1801. His wife, Maria Roosevelt Varick, was the daughter of Isaac Roosevelt.

OLD MR. VAN BERKEL: Pieter Johan Van Berckel (1725–1800), minister to the United States from the Netherlands 1783–88 and father of Franco Petrus Van Berckel, the current minister. His daughter had arrived in the United States in 1785 and had become an active member of New York society. After his son replaced him Van Berckel remained in the United States (BIOGRAPHISCH WOORDENBOEK, 2:128).

Thursday 17th.    The following Company dined here – viz. – The Chief Justice of the U. States and his Lady; Mr. King, Colo. and Mrs. Lawrence – Mr. Gerry, Mr. Egbert Benson, Bishop Provost and Doctr. Lynn & his Lady.

John Laurance (1750–1810) was United States congressman from New York. A native of England, he had settled in New York City in 1767, studied law, and was admitted to the bar in 1772. During the Revolution he served as aide-de-camp to Brig. Gen. Alexander McDougall and as judge advocate general at the trial of Maj. John André. Laurance served in the Continental Congress 1785–87 and in the state legislature 1788–90. Shortly before the Revolution, he married Elizabeth McDougall (d. 1790), daughter of his wartime commander.

By 1789 Egbert Benson (1746–1833), a New York City attorney, had already had a distinguished political career, serving in the New York legislature 1777–81, 1788, as the state's attorney general 1777–89, and as a delegate to the Continental Congress 1784–88. After his election to the House of Representatives in 1789, he became one of the administration's staunchest supporters in Congress.

Samuel Provoost (1742–1815) a native New Yorker, was the first Protestant Episcopal bishop of New York. Educated at Cambridge, he was ordained by the bishop of London in 1766. Upon his return to America, he served as assistant minister at Trinity Church in New York City, but his Whig sympathies so incensed the Loyalist members of the parish that he was forced to resign in 1771. After the evacuation of New York by the British, the vestry invited him to return as rector. In 1786 he was elected bishop of New York and was consecrated in England in the chapel of Lambeth Palace in Feb. 1787. In addition he still acted as rector of Trinity Church and was chaplain of the Senate.

Rev. Dr. William Linn (1752–1808) was born in Shippensburg, Pa., graduated from Princeton in 1772, and was ordained a minister in the Collegiate Reformed Protestant Dutch Church in 1776. He had become pastor of the Collegiate Church in New York City in 1786 and at this time was also chaplain of the House of Representatives (SMITH [4], 133–34).

**Friday 18th.    Read over, and digested my thoughts upon the subject of a National Militia, from the Plans of the Militia of Europe—those of the Secretary at War & the Baron de Steuben.**

In Aug. 1789 GW had pointed out to both houses of Congress the "national importance and necessity" of a "uniform and effective system for the Militia of the United States. . . . I am particularly anxious it should receive an early attention as circumstances will admit; because it is now in our power to avail ourselves of the military knowledge disseminated throughout the several States by means of the many well instructed Officers and soldiers of the late Army; a resource which is daily diminishing by death and other causes" (GW to Senate and House of Representatives, 7 Aug. 1789, DLC:GW). On 8 Aug. the House of Representatives appointed a committee to bring in a militia bill (ANNALS OF CONGRESS, 1:714). In preparation for his notes on the militia system, GW probably examined his own statements drawn up in 1783 after a committee of the Continental Congress had requested his views on a peace establishment (see Alexander Hamilton to GW, 9 April 1783, and GW to Hamilton, 2 May 1783, DLC:GW). GW's "Sentiments on a Peace Establishment," 1 May 1783, deals with such matters as a militia system, arsenals, military academies, and provisioning of troops (DLC:GW). Knox's plans for the militia are undoubtedly those which had been submitted to Congress on 18 Mar. 1786 and later published by printer John Dunlap as *A Plan for the General Arrangement of the Militia of the United States* (New York, 1786). Baron von Steuben's plan on the militia, *A Letter on the Subject of an Established Militia,* was published in 1784. GW also had access to lengthy statements on a peace establishment prepared by Knox, 17 April 1783, and Steuben, 15, 21 April 1783 (DLC:GW), and sent to the commander-in-chief in preparation for his own report of 1 May 1783 to the military committee of Congress. GW's written comments on the militia and his letter to Knox (see entries for 19 and 21 Dec. 1789) have not been found, but at least some of his suggestions were incorporated by Knox into a Jan. 1790 report to Congress on the militia. On 18 Jan. 1790 Knox wrote GW that "Having submitted to your consideration a plan for the arrangement of the militia of the United States, which I had presented to the late Congress, and you having approved the general principles thereof, with certain exceptions, I now respectfully lay the same before you, modified according to the alterations you were pleased to suggest." GW transmitted Knox's letter and report to Congress, 21 Jan. 1790. Both are in ASP, MILITARY AFF., 1:6–13. "An Act more effectually to provide for the National Defence by establishing an Uniform Militia Throughout the United States" was not finally passed until 8 May 1792 (1 STAT. 271–74).

Saturday 19th.    Committed the above thoughts to writing in order to send them to the Secretary for the Department of War to be worked into the form of a Bill with which to furnish the Committee of Congress which had been appointed to draught one.

Sunday 20th.    Went to St. Pauls Chapel in the forenoon.

Monday 21st.    Framed the above thoughts on the subject of a National Militia into the form of a Letter and sent it to the Secretary for the Department of War.

Sat from ten to one Oclock for a Mr. Savage to draw my Portrait for the University of Cambridge in the State of Massachusetts at the request of the President and Governors of the said University.

The portrait begun today by Edward Savage (1761–1817) was commissioned by the trustees of Harvard to be hung at the college. "It represents Washington in a military coat, with angular opening between coat collar and lapel. On the latter are two large buttons. . . . On the left lapel is the badge of the Order of the Cincinnati." At today's sitting and at those of 28 Dec. and 6 Jan. 1790, Savage may also have made preliminary sketches for his Washington Family Portrait although the latter was interrupted by his sojourn in England 1791–94 and was not finished until 1796 (EISEN, 2:457, 462–63).

Tuesday 22d.    A pretty full & respectable Levee to day—at which several Members of Congress, newly arrived, attended.

Wednesday 23d.    Exercised in the Post-Chaise with Mrs. Washington to day.

Sent the dispatches which came to me from the Assembly of Virginia and from the Representatives of several Counties therein respecting the State of the Frontiers and depredations of the Indians to the Secretary for the Department of War requesting his attendance tomorrow at 9 Oclock that I might converse more fully with him on the subject of these communications.

Henry Knox, secretary of war, by Charles Willson Peale. (Independence National Historical Park Collection)

These dispatches included an undated "Address of the General Assembly of Virginia to the President of the United States," expressing the assembly's concern about Indian depredations in the state's western counties and assuring GW of Virginia's financial support if the administration should find it necessary to mount an expedition against the western tribes. A second letter, 12 Dec. 1789, signed by the representatives of the frontier counties of Ohio, Monongalia, Harrison, and Randolph, warned the president of the vulnerability of the counties to Indian attack (ASP, INDIAN AFF., 1:85–86).

Thursday 24th.    The Secretary at War coming according to appointment, he was instructed, after conversing fully on the matter, what answers to return to the Executive of Virginia and to the Representatives of the Frontier Counties.

Friday 25th.    Christmas day.
    Went to St. Pauls Chapel in the forenoon.
    The Visitors to Mrs. Washington this afternoon were not numerous but respectable.

Saturday 26th.    Exercised on Horseback in the forenoon. Chief Justice Morris and the Mayor (Colo. Varick) and their Ladies, Judge Hobart, Colo. Cole, Majr. Gilman, Mrs. Brown, Secretary Otis, & Mr. Beckley dined here.

Richard Morris (1730–1810) was elected chief justice of the New York Supreme Court in 1779. His wife was Sarah Ludlow Morris.
    John Sloss Hobart (1738–1805) of Fairfield, Conn., was a justice of the New York Supreme Court.

Isaac Coles (1747–1813) had been elected as an Antifederalist to the First Congress from Virginia. Coles was educated at William and Mary, served as a colonel of militia during the Revolution, and was a member of the Virginia Ratifying Convention. His Virginia plantation was at Coles Ferry on the Staunton River, Halifax County, Va.

Samuel Allyne Otis (1740–1814) had been secretary of the United States Senate since April 1789. A native of Barnstable, Mass., he graduated from Harvard in 1759, served in the state legislature 1776, 1784–87, and was a Massachusetts delegate to the Continental Congress 1787–88.

John Beckley (1757–1807), born in England, came to America at the age of 11 and was apprenticed as a scribe to Virginia botanist John Clayton. Under his employer's guidance he quickly became an expert clerk and by 1780 had acted as clerk to at least 12 official bodies in Virginia, including the Virginia Senate and House of Delegates. At the same time he read law and devoted at least a portion of his time to his law practice. In 1783 and again in 1788 Beckley was elected mayor of Richmond and in April 1789 became clerk of the United States House of Representatives.

**Sunday 27th.** At home all day – weather being bad.

**Monday 28th.** Set all the forenoon for Mr. Savage who was taking my Portrt.

**Tuesday 29th.** Being very Snowing not a single person appeared at the Levee.

**Wednesday 30th.** Exercised in a Carriage.

**Thursday 31st.** Bad weather and close House.

The Vice Presidt. & Lady, Colo. Smith & Lady Chanr. Livingston Lady & Sister – Baron Steuben Messrs. White, Gerry Patridge & Tucker of the Ho. of Representatives – dined here today.

Robert R. Livingston (1746–1813) of New York, one of the Clermont branch of the powerful Livingston family, had been among the most active and influential members of the Continental Congress during his service 1775–76, 1779–81, and 1784–85. In Aug. 1781 he was elected secretary for foreign affairs and served until May 1783. From 1777 to 1801 he held the vaguely defined post of chancellor of New York and by virtue of this position administered the oath of office to GW in 1789. At this time he was a Federalist although by 1791 he was openly supporting Republican candidates for office in New York. In 1770 he had married Mary Stevens (1752–1814), daughter of John and Elizabeth Alexander Stevens and sister of inventor and engineer John Stevens (1749–1838). Although it is uncertain which of the chancellor's five living sisters accompanied the family, it was probably Janet Montgomery (1743–1828), widow of Gen. Richard Montgomery, since she wrote the chancellor in the summer of 1789 that "I have been often at the President . . . who each time is more pleased to see me. Mrs. Washington has asked me to

Chancellor Robert R. Livingston (1782), by Charles Willson Peale. (Independence National Historical Park Collection)

visit with her this evening and is to introduce me to Mrs. Adams" (DANGER-FIELD, 243).

Alexander White (1738–1804) of Frederick County, Va., was elected a member of the House of Representatives from Virginia to the First Congress and served until 1793. In 1795 GW appointed him a commissioner for laying out the new federal capital. George Partridge (1740–1828) of Duxbury, Mass., held a number of state offices and served in the Continental Congress 1779–82 and 1783–85. He was elected to Congress in 1789 and served until his resignation 14 Aug. 1790. Thomas Tudor Tucker (1745–1828) of South Carolina, born in Bermuda and a brother of St. George Tucker, had studied medicine at the University of Edinburgh and served during the Revolution as a surgeon in the Continental Army. He was elected as a Federalist to the First and Second Congresses.

Repository Symbols

Bibliography

Index

# Repository Symbols

| | |
|---|---|
| Arch. Aff. Etr. | Archives du Ministère des Affaires Etrangères (photostats and microfilm at Library of Congress) |
| CSmH | Henry E. Huntington Library, San Marino, Calif. |
| DLC | Library of Congress |
| DLC:GW | George Washington Papers, Library of Congress |
| DNA | National Archives |
| ICHi | Chicago Historical Society |
| LNHT | Tulane University, New Orleans |
| MdBJ | Johns Hopkins University, Baltimore |
| MdHi | Maryland Historical Society, Baltimore |
| MH | Harvard University, Cambridge |
| MHi | Massachusetts Historical Society, Boston |
| NBLiHi | Long Island Historical Society, Brooklyn, N.Y. |
| Nc–Ar | North Carolina State Department of Archives and History, Raleigh |
| NHi | New-York Historical Society |
| NHpR | Franklin D. Roosevelt Library, Hyde Park, N.Y. |
| NjP | Princeton University |
| NN | New York Public Library |
| NNC | Columbia University, New York |
| PEL | Lafayette College, Easton, Pa. |
| PHi | Historical Society of Pennsylvania, Philadelphia |
| PPAmP | American Philosophical Society, Philadelphia |
| Vi | Virginia State Library, Richmond |
| ViMtV | Mount Vernon Ladies' Association of the Union |
| ViU | University of Virginia, Charlottesville |

# Bibliography

ABBOTT                  Wilbur Cortez Abbott. "James Blox-
                        ham, Farmer." Massachusetts Histori-
                        cal Society *Proceedings,* 59 (1925–26),
                        177–203.

ADAMS [1]               Lyman Butterfield, ed. *Diary and Au-
                        tobiography of John Adams.* 4 vols.
                        Cambridge, Mass.: Belknap Press,
                        1961–62.

ANDREWS                 Matthew Page Andrews. *The Fountain
                        Inn Diary.* New York: Richard R.
                        Smith, 1948.

ANNALS                  Arthur Young, ed. *Annals of Agricul-
                        ture & Other Useful Arts.* 46 vols. Lon-
                        don: various publishers, 1784–1815.

ANNALS OF CONGRESS      Joseph Gales, ed. *The Annals of Con-
                        gress: The Debates and Proceedings in
                        the Congress of the United States.* 42
                        vols. Washington, D.C.: Gales and Sea-
                        ton, 1834–56.

ASP                     Walter Lowrie et al., eds. *American
                        State Papers: Documents, Legislature
                        and Executive, of the Congress of the
                        United States.* 38 vols. Washington,
                        D.C.: Gales and Seaton, 1832–61.

BACON–FOSTER            Corra Bacon-Foster. *Early Chapters
                        in the Development of the Patomac
                        Route to the West.* Washington, D.C.:
                        Columbia Historical Society, 1912.

BAGNALL                 William R. Bagnall. *The Textile In-
                        dustries of the United States.* Cam-
                        bridge, Mass.: Riverside Press, 1893.

BAKER [2]               William Spohn Baker. *Washington
                        after the Revolution.* Philadelphia:
                        J. B. Lippincott Co., 1898.

BEDINI                  Silvio A. Bedini. *Thinkers and Tink-
                        ers: Early American Men of Science.*
                        New York: Charles Scribner's Sons,
                        1975.

# Bibliography

BENTLEY  The Diary of William Bentley. 4 vols. Salem, Mass.: Essex Institute, 1905–14.

BERGH  Albert Ellery Bergh, ed. The Writings of Thomas Jefferson. Memorial Edition. 20 vols. Washington, D.C.: The Thomas Jefferson Memorial Association, 1903–4.

BETTS [1]  Edwin M. Betts, ed. Thomas Jefferson's Farm Book. Princeton, N.J.: Princeton University Press, for the American Philosophical Society, 1953.

BETTS [2]  Edwin M. Betts, ed. Thomas Jefferson's Garden Book, 1766–1824. Philadelphia: American Philosophical Society, 1944.

BIOGRAFISCH WOORDENBOEK  Nieuw Nederlandsch Biografisch Woordenboek. Ed. P. C. Molhuysen, P. J. Blok, and K. H. Kossman. 10 vols. Leiden, A. W. Sijthoff's Uitgevers-Maatschappij N.V., 1911–37.

BIOG. UNIVERSELLE  Biographie universelle ancienne et moderne . . . . 45 vols. Paris: A. Thoisnier Desplaces, 1843–65.

BLANTON  Wyndham B. Blanton. Medicine in Virginia in the Eighteenth Century. Richmond: Garrett & Massie, 1931.

BOOGHER  William Fletcher Boogher. Miscellaneous Americana: A Collection of History, Biography, and Genealogy. Philadelphia: Dando Printing and Publishing Co., 1893.

BOWEN  Clarence Winthrop Bowen, ed. The History of the Centennial Celebration of the Inauguration of George Washington as First President of the United States. New York: D. Appleton and Co., 1892.

BOWIE  Effie Gwynn Bowie. Across the Years in Prince George's County. Richmond: Garrett & Massie, 1947.

BRANT  Irving Brant. James Madison: Father of the Constitution, 1787–1800. 6 vols. Indianapolis and New York: Bobbs-Merrill Co., 1941–61.

# Bibliography

BREWSTER  Charles W. Brewster. *Rambles about Portsmouth*. 1st ser., 1873. Reprint, Somersworth, N.H.: New Hampshire Publishing Co., 1971.

BRISSOT  Jean Pierre Brissot de Warville. *New Travels in the United States of America, 1788*. Trans. from French by Mara Soceanu Vamos and Durand Echeverria. Ed. Durand Echeverria. Cambridge, Mass.: Belknap Press of Harvard University Press, 1964.

BROCKETT  Franklin Longdon Brockett. *The Lodge of Washington: A History of the Alexandria Washington Lodge, No. 22, A.F. and A.M. of Alexandria, Va.* Alexandria: George E. French, 1876.

BRUMBAUGH  Gaius Marcus Brumbaugh. *Maryland Records: Colonial, Revolutionary, County, and Church from Original Sources*. Vol. 1. Baltimore: Williams & Wilkins Co., 1915.

CARY [2]  Wilson Miles Cary. "The Dandridges of Virginia." *William and Mary Quarterly,* 1st ser., 5 (1896–97), 30–39.

CHAPPELEAR [4]  Curtis Chappelear. "Robert Burwell's Land on the Shenandoah River." *Proceedings of the Clarke County Historical Association,* 5 (1945), 10–17.

CHASTELLUX  François Jean de Beauvoir, Marquis de Chastellux. *Travels in North America in the Years 1780, 1781, and 1782.* 2 vols. Ed. Howard C. Rice, Jr. Chapel Hill: University of North Carolina Press, 1963.

CLARK [4]  Victor S. Clark. *History of Manufactures in the United States.* 3 vols. New York: McGraw-Hill Book Co., for the Carnegie Institution, 1929.

COLLES  Christopher Colles. *A Survey of the Roads of the United States of America, 1789.* Ed. Hugh Edward Egerton. 1915. Reprint, New York: Arno Press, 1969.

CONTENSON  Ludovic de Contenson. *La Société des Cincinnati de France et La Guerre d'Amérique, 1778–1783.* Paris: Editions Auguste Picard, 1934.

COPELAND
Pamela C. Copeland and Richard K. MacMaster. *The Five George Masons: Patriots and Planters of Virginia and Maryland.* Charlottesville: University Press of Virginia for the Regents of Gunston Hall, 1975.

COVEY
Cyclone Covey. "Of Music, and of American Singing." Pp. 490–552 in Max Savelle, *Seeds of Liberty.* New York: Alfred A. Knopf, 1948.

CROFUT
Florence S. Marcy Crofut. *Guide to the History and the Historic Sites of Connecticut.* 2 vols. New Haven: Yale University Press, 1937.

CROZIER [2]
William Armstrong Crozier, ed. *Spotsylvania County Records, 1721–1800.* Baltimore: Southern Book Co., 1955.

CRUMP
W. B. Crump. *The Leeds Woollen Industry, 1780–1820.* Publications of the Thoresby Society for the Year 1929. Vol. 32. Leeds, Eng.: The Thoresby Society, 1931.

CURRIER
John J. Currier. *History of Newburyport, Mass., 1764–1905.* Newburyport: privately printed, 1906.

CUSTIS
George Washington Parke Custis. *Recollections and Private Memoirs of Washington.* New York: Derby & Jackson, 1860.

DANDRIDGE [2]
John Dandridge. "Letters of John Dandridge to John Hopkins." *William and Mary Quarterly,* 1st ser., 20 (1911–12), 149–67.

DANGERFIELD
George Dangerfield. *Chancellor Robert R. Livingston of New York, 1746–1813.* New York: Harcourt, Brace & Co., 1960.

DECATUR
Stephen Decatur, Jr. *Private Affairs of George Washington, from the Records and Accounts of Tobias Lear, Esquire, His Secretary.* Boston: Houghton Mifflin Co., 1933.

# Bibliography

DE PAUW      Linda Grant De Pauw, ed. *Documentary History of the First Federal Congress of the United States of America.* Baltimore: Johns Hopkins University Press, 1972—.

DEXTER      Franklin Bowditch Dexter. *Ezra Stiles, D.D., L.L.D., 1775–1794.* New Haven: Yale University Press, 1916.

DIARIES      John C. Fitzpatrick, ed. *The Diaries of George Washington, 1748–1799.* 4 vols. Boston and New York: Houghton Mifflin Co., 1925.

DICT. BIOG. FRANÇAISE      *Dictionnaire de biographie française.* 14 vols. Paris: Librarie Letouzez et Ané, 1931—.

DOUGHERTY      Daniel J. Dougherty. *History of the Society of the Friendly Sons of St. Patrick.* Philadelphia: published by the Friendly Sons of St. Patrick, 1952.

DUNLAP      William Dunlap. *History of the Rise and Progress of the Arts of Design in the United States.* 3 vols. 1834. Reprint, New York: Benjamin Blom, 1965.

EBERLEIN      Harold Donaldson Eberlein and Courtlandt Van Dyke Hubbard. "Music in the Early Federal Era." *Pennsylvania Magazine of History and Biography,* 69 (1945), 103–27.

EISEN      Gustavus A. Eisen. *Portraits of Washington.* 3 vols. New York: Robert Hamilton & Associates, 1932.

ENYS      Elizabeth Cometti, ed. *The American Journals of Lt. John Enys.* Syracuse, N.Y.: Syracuse University Press, 1976.

EUBANK      H. Ragland Eubank. *Touring Historyland: The Authentic Guide Book of Historic Northern Neck of Virginia, the Land of George Washington and Robert E. Lee.* Colonial Beach, Va.: Northern Neck Association, 1934.

EVANS [2]      Nelson W. Evans. "Colonel John O'Bannon." *Ohio Archaelogical and Historical Publications,* 14 (1905), 319–27.

# Bibliography

EXECUTIVE JOURNAL, 1     *Journal of the Executive Proceedings of the Senate of the United States of America.* Vol. 1. Washington, D.C.: Duff Green, 1828.

FARRAND     Max Farrand, ed. *The Records of the Federal Convention of 1787.* Rev. ed. 4 vols. New Haven and London: Yale University Press, 1966.

FORD [5]     Paul Leicester Ford. *Washington and the Theatre.* New York: The Dunlop Society, 1899.

FREEMAN     Douglas Southall Freeman. *George Washington.* 7 vols. New York: Charles Scribner's Sons, 1949–57.

GAMBRILL     Olive Moor Gambrill. "John Beale Bordley and the Early Years of the Philadelphia Agricultural Society." *Pennsylvania Magazine of History and Biography,* 66 (1942), 410–39.

GARNETT [2]     James Mercer Garnett. *Biographical Sketch of Hon. James Mercer Garnett of Elmwood, Essex County, Virginia, with Mercer-Garnett and Mercer Genealogies.* Richmond: Whittet & Shepperson, Printers, 1910.

GIBBS [2]     George Gibbs. *Memoirs of the Administrations of Washington and John Adams. Ed. from the Papers of Oliver Wolcott, Secretary of Treasury.* 2 vols. New York: privately printed, 1846.

GODFREY     Carlos E. Godfrey. *The Commander-in-Chief's Guard, Revolutionary War.* Washington, D.C.: Stevenson-Smith Co., 1904.

GRAYSON     "The Grayson Family." *Tyler's Quarterly Magazine,* 5 (1923–24), 195–208, 261–68.

GRISWOLD     Rufus Wilmot Griswold. *The Republican Court, or American Society in the Days of Washington.* New York: D. Appleton and Co., 1855.

GROCE     George C. Groce. *William Samuel Johnson.* New York: Columbia University Press, 1937.

GURNEY

C. S. Gurney. *Portsmouth . . . Historic and Picturesque.* Portsmouth, N.H.: C. S. Gurney, 1902.

GW ATLAS

Lawrence Martin, ed. *The George Washington Atlas.* Washington, D.C.: United States George Washington Bicentennial Commission, 1932.

HAMILTON [2]

Harold C. Syrett et al., eds. *The Papers of Alexander Hamilton.* New York: Columbia University Press, 1961—.

HARRISON [1]

Fairfax Harrison. *Landmarks of Old Prince William.* Reprint. Berryville, Va.: Chesapeake Book Co., 1964.

HART

Charles Henry Hart. "Mary White—Mrs. Robert Morris." *Pennsylvania Magazine of History and Biography,* 2 (1878), 157–84.

HAYDEN

Horace Edwin Hayden. *Virginia Genealogies: A Genealogy of the Glassell Family of Scotland and Virginia.* 1891. Reprint, Baltimore: Genealogical Publishing Co., 1973.

HAYS

Minis Hays, ed. *Calendar of the Papers of Benjamin Franklin in the Library of the American Philosophical Society.* 6 vols. Philadelphia: printed for the American Philosophical Society, 1908.

HEADS OF FAMILIES, CONN.

*Heads of Families at the First Census of the United States Taken in the Year 1790: Connecticut.* 1908. Reprint, Spartanburg, S.C.: Reprint Co., 1964.

HEADS OF FAMILIES, MD.

*Heads of Families at the First Census of the United States Taken in the Year 1790: Maryland.* 1907. Reprint, Baltimore: Genealogical Publishing Co., 1965.

HEADS OF FAMILIES, MASS.

*Heads of Families at the First Census of the United States Taken in the Year 1790: Massachusetts.* 1908. Reprint, Spartanburg, S.C.: Reprint Co., 1964.

HEADS OF FAMILIES, PA.

*Heads of Families at the First Census of the United States Taken in the Year 1790: Pennsylvania.* 1908. Reprint, Baltimore: Genealogical Publishing Co., 1970.

HEADS OF FAMILIES, VA.

*Heads of Families at the First Census of the United States Taken in the Year 1790: Virginia.* 1908. Reprint, Baltimore: Genealogical Publishing Co., 1970.

HEDRICK

U. P. Hedrick. *A History of Horticulture in America to 1860.* New York: Oxford University Press, 1950.

HEITMAN [2]

Francis Bernard Heitman. *Historical Register of Officers of the Continental Army during the War of the Revolution, April, 1775, to December, 1783.* Rev. ed. Washington, D.C.: Rare Book Shop Publishing Co., 1914.

HENING

William Waller Hening, ed. *The Statutes at Large: Being a Collection of All the Laws of Virginia from the First Session of the Legislature, in the Year 1619.* 13 vols. New York, Philadelphia, and Richmond: various publishers, 1819–23.

HILTZHEIMER

Jacob Cox Parsons, ed. *Extracts from the Diary of Jacob Hiltzheimer of Philadelphia, 1765–1798.* Philadelphia: Press of William F. Bell & Co., 1893.

HOWARD

James L. Howard. *Seth Harding, Mariner: A Naval Picture of the Revolution.* New Haven: Yale University Press, 1930.

HOYT [1]

William D. Hoyt, Jr. "Self-Portrait: Eliza Parke Custis, 1808." *Virginia Magazine of History and Biography,* 53 (1945), 89–100.

IRVING

Washington Irving. *Life of George Washington.* 5 vols. New York: G. P. Putnam & Co., 1857–59.

JACKSON [2]

Harry F. Jackson. *Scholar in the Wilderness: Francis Adrian Van der Kemp.* Syracuse, N.Y.: Syracuse University Press, 1963.

JACKSON [3]

Joseph Jackson. *America's Most Historic Highway, Market Street, Philadelphia.* New ed. Philadelphia and New York: John Wanamaker, 1926.

JCC · Worthington Chauncey Ford et al., eds. *Journals of the Continental Congress, 1774–1789.* 34 vols. Washington, D.C.: Government Printing Office, 1904–37.

JEFFERSON [1] · Julian P. Boyd, ed. *The Papers of Thomas Jefferson.* Princeton: Princeton University Press, 1950–.

JOHNSTON [5] · Edith Duncan Johnston. *The Houstons of Georgia.* Athens: University of Georgia Press, 1950.

JOHNSTON [6] · Christopher Johnston. "Hall Family of Calvert County." *Maryland Historical Magazine,* 8 (1913), 291–301, 381–82.

KELLAM · Sadie Scott Kellam and V. Hope Kellam. *Old Houses in Princess Anne, Virginia.* Portsmouth, Va.: Printcraft Press, 1931.

KIDD · George Eldridge Kidd. *Early Freemasonry in Williamsburg, Virginia.* Richmond, Va.: Dietz Press, 1957.

KILMER · Kenton Kilmer and Donald Sweig. *The Fairfax Family in Fairfax County: A Brief History.* Fairfax, Va.: The Fairfax County Office of Comprehensive Planning, 1975.

KING [4] · J. Estelle Stewart King, comp. *Abstract of Wills and Inventories, Fairfax County, Virginia, 1742–1801.* Beverly Hills, Calif.: privately printed, 1936.

KOOPMAN · H. L. Koopman. "Kilty's Manuscript Travesty of the *Iliad.*" *Maryland Historical Magazine,* 13 (1918), 103–9.

LA ROCHEFOUCAULD · Duke de La Rochefoucauld Liancourt. *Travels through the United States of North America, the Country of the Iroquois, and Upper Canada, in the Years 1795, 1796, and 1799; with an Authentic Account of Lower Canada.* 2 vols. London: R. Phillips, 1799.

LEDGER A AND B · Manuscript Ledger in George Washington Papers, Library of Congress.

LEDGER C · Manuscript Ledger in Morristown National Historical Park.

LEE [5]  Edmund Jennings Lee. *Lee of Virginia, 1642–1892.* Philadelphia: Edmund Jennings Lee, 1895.

LEE [7]  Ida J. Lee, comp. "The Heth Family." *Virginia Magazine of History and Biography,* 42 (1934), 273–82.

LORD  Priscilla Sawyer Lord. *Marblehead.* Philadelphia: Chilton Book Co., 1971.

LOVELL  Caroline Couper Lovell. *The Golden Isles of Georgia.* Boston: Little, Brown and Co., 1933.

LUDLUM [2]  David M. Ludlum. *Early American Hurricanes, 1492–1870.* Boston: American Meterological Society, 1963.

MCDONALD  Cornelia McDonald. *A Diary with Reminiscences of the War and Refugee Life in the Shenandoah Valley, 1860–1865.* Nashville: Cullom & Ghertner Co., 1935.

MCILHANY  Hugh Milton McIlhany, Jr. *Some Virginia Families.* Staunton, Va.: Stoneburner & Prufer, 1903.

MACLAY  Charles A. Beard, ed. *The Journal of William Maclay: United States Senator from Pennsylvania, 1789–1791.* 1927. Reprint, New York: Frederick Ungar Publishing Co., 1965.

MADISON  William T. Hutchinson et al., eds. *The Papers of James Madison.* Chicago: University of Chicago Press, 1962–1975; Charlottesville: University Press of Virginia, 1977–.

MALONE [2]  Dumas Malone. *Jefferson and His Time.* Boston: Little, Brown and Co., 1948–.

MARSHALL [3]  John Marshall. *The Life of George Washington.* 5 vols. Philadelphia: C. P. Wayne, 1805–7.

MASON [1]  Frances Norton Mason, ed. *John Norton & Sons, Merchants of London and Virginia: Being the Papers from Their Counting House for the Years 1750 to 1795.* New York: Augustus M. Kelley, 1968.

MASON [2]

Robert A. Rutland, ed. *The Papers of George Mason, 1725–1792.* 3 vols. Chapel Hill: University of North Carolina Press, 1970.

MAYO

Abigail De Hart Mayo. *An American Lady in Paris: The Diary of Mrs. John Mayo.* Ed. Mary Mayo Crenshaw. Boston and New York: Houghton Mifflin Co., 1927.

MEADE [1]

William Meade. *Old Churches, Ministers, and Families of Virginia.* 2 vols. Philadelphia: J. B. Lippincott Co., 1910.

MINTZ

Max M. Mintz. *Gouveneur Morris and the American Revolution.* Norman: University of Oklahoma Press, 1970.

MITCHELL

Stewart Mitchell, ed. *New Letters of Abigail Adams, 1788–1801.* New York: Houghton Mifflin Co., 1947.

MOORE [1]

Gay Montague Moore. *Seaport in Virginia: George Washington's Alexandria.* Reprint. Charlottesville: University Press of Virginia, 1972.

MORRIS [2]

Robert Morris. *The Papers of Robert Morris, 1781–1784.* Pittsburgh: University of Pittsburgh Press, 1973–.

MORSE

James King Morse. *Jedidiah Morse: A Champion of New England Orthodoxy.* New York: Columbia University Press, 1939.

NASATIR AND MONELL

Abraham P. Nasatir and Gary Elwyn Monell. *French Consuls in the United States: A Calendar of Their Correspondence in the Archives Nationales.* Washington, D.C.: Government Printing Office, 1967.

NEILL

Edward Duffield Neill. *The Fairfaxes of England and America in the Seventeenth and Eighteenth Centuries, Including Letters from and to Hon. William Fairfax, President of Council of Virginia, and His Sons, Col. George William Fairfax and Rev. Bryan, Eighth Lord Fairfax, the Neighbors*

# Bibliography

|   |   |
|---|---|
| | and Friends of George Washington. Albany: Joel Munsell, 1868. |
| NEWBURYPORT VITAL RECORDS | *Vital Records of Newburyport, Massachusetts, to the End of the Year 1849.* 2 vols. Salem, Mass.: Essex Institute, 1911. |
| NICKLIN [2] | J. B. Calvert Nicklin. "The Calvert Family." *Maryland Historical Magazine,* 16 (1921), 50–59, 189–204, 313–18, 389–94. |
| O'BRIEN | Michael J. O'Brien. *George Washington's Associations with the Irish.* New York: P. J. Kenedy & Sons, 1937. |
| PA. ARCH. | Samuel Hazard et al., eds. *Pennsylvania Archives.* 9 ser., 138 vols. Philadelphia and Harrisburg: various publishers, 1852–1949. |
| PAGE | Richard Channing Moore Page. *Genealogy of the Page Family in Virginia.* New York: Jenkins & Thomas, 1883. |
| PARKINSON | Richard Parkinson. *A Tour in America, in 1798, 1799, and 1800. Exhibiting . . . a Particular Account of the American System of Agriculture, with Its Recent Improvements.* 2 vols. London: T. Davidson, 1805. |
| PLATT | John D. R. Platt. "Jeremiah Wadsworth: Federalist Entrepreneur." Ph.D. dissertation, Columbia University, 1955. |
| PLEASANTS | J. Hall Pleasants. "Jacob Hall, Surgeon and Educator, 1747–1812." *Maryland Historical Magazine,* 8 (1913), 217–35. |
| POWELL [2] | Robert C. Powell. *A Biographical Sketch of Col. Leven Powell.* Alexandria, Va.: G. H. Ramey & Son, 1877. |
| PRICE [2] | Jacob M. Price. *France and the Chesapeake: A History of the French Tobacco Monopoly, 1674–1791, and of Its Relationship to the British and American Tobacco Trades.* 2 vols. Ann Arbor: University of Michigan Press, 1973. |

# Bibliography

RANDALL | E. O. Randall. "Washington's Ohio Lands." *Ohio Archaeological and Historical Publications,* 19 (1910), 303–18.

RICE | Howard C. Rice, Jr., and Anne S. K. Brown, eds. *The American Campaigns of Rochambeau's Army, 1780, 1781, 1782, 1783.* 2 vols. Princeton and Providence: Princeton University Press and Brown University Press, 1972.

RIGHTMYER | Nelson Waite Rightmyer. *Maryland's Established Church.* Baltimore: Church Historical Society for the Diocese of Maryland, 1956.

ROGERS | George C. Rogers, Jr. *Evolution of a Federalist: William Loughton Smith of Charleston, 1758–1812.* Columbia: University of South Carolina Press, 1962.

ROSSMAN | Kenneth R. Rossman. *Thomas Mifflin and the Politics of the American Revolution.* Chapel Hill: University of North Carolina Press, 1952.

RUSH | Benjamin Rush. *Letters of Benjamin Rush.* Ed. L. H. Butterfield. 2 vols. Princeton: Princeton University Press, 1951.

SALLEY [1] | A. S. Salley. *Delegates to the Continental Congress from South Carolina, 1774–1789.* Columbia: The State Co., 1927.

SCHARF [1] | John Thomas Scharf and Thompson Westcott. *History of Philadelphia, 1609–1884.* 3 vols. Philadelphia: Louis H. Everts & Co., 1884.

SCHARF [2] | John Thomas Scharf. *The Chronicles of Baltimore; Being a Complete History of "Baltimore Town" and Baltimore City from the Earliest Period to the Present Time.* Baltimore: Turnbull Brothers, 1874.

SCHARF [4] | John Thomas Scharf. *History of Maryland, from the Earliest Period to the Present Day.* 3 vols. Baltimore: John B. Piet, 1879.

SCHOEPF     Johann David Schoepf. *Travels in the Confederation.* Ed. and trans. Alfred J. Morrison. 2 vols. Philadelphia: William J. Campbell, 1911.

SEILHAMER     George O. Seilhamer. *History of the American Theatre.* 3 vols. Philadelphia: Globe Printing House, 1889.

SELLERS     Charles Coleman Sellers. *Charles Willson Peale.* 2 vols. Philadelphia: The American Philosophical Society, 1947.

SHACKELFORD     George Green Shackelford. "Nanzatico, King George County, Virginia." *Virginia Magazine of History and Biography,* 73 (1965), 387–404.

SHEPPERSON     Archibald Bolling Shepperson. *John Paradise and Lucy Ludwell, of London and Williamsburg.* Richmond: Dietz Press, 1942.

SIBLEY     John Langley Sibley and Clifford K. Shipton. *Sibley's Harvard Graduates: Biographical Sketches of Those Who Attended Harvard College.* Boston and New York: various publishers, 1873–.

SLAUGHTER [2]     Philip Slaughter. *A History of St. Mark's Parish, Culpeper County, Virginia, with Notes of Old Churches and Old Families and Illustrations of the Manners and Customs of the Olden Time.* Baltimore: Innes & Co., 1877.

SMITH [4]     Thomas E. V. Smith. *The City of New York in the Year of Washington's Inauguration, 1789.* Intro. Joseph Veach Noble. Rev. ed. Riverside, Conn.: Chatham Press, 1972.

SNYDER     Martin P. Snyder. *City of Independence.* New York: Praeger Publishers, 1975.

SONNECK     O. G. Sonneck. *Early Concert-Life in America, 1731–1800.* Leipzig, Germany: Breitkopf & Hartel, 1907.

SPARKS     Jared Sparks, ed. *The Writings of George Washington: Being His Correspondence, Addresses, Messages, and Other Papers, Official and Private, Selected and Published from the Original*

# Bibliography

*Manuscripts.* 12 vols. Boston: John B. Russell, 1833–37.

SPROUSE [2]  Edith Moore Sprouse, ed. *A Surname and Subject Index of the Minute and Order Books of the County Court, Fairfax County, Virginia, 1783–1802.* Fairfax, Va.: Fairfax County Historical Commission, 1976.

1 STAT.  Richard Peters, ed. *The Public Statutes at Large of the United States of America.* Vol. 1. Boston: Charles C. Little and James Brown, 1845.

STEADMAN [2]  Melvin Lee Steadman, Jr. *Falls Church by Fence and Fireside.* Falls Church, Va.: Falls Church Public Library, 1964.

STEINER  Bernard C. Steiner. "Maryland's Adoption of the Federal Constitution." *American Historical Review,* 5 (1889–1900), 22–44.

STETSON [1]  Charles W. Stetson. *Four Mile Run Land Grants.* Washington, D.C.: Mimeoform Press, 1935.

STETSON [3]  Sarah P. Stetson. "The Philadelphia Sojourn of Samuel Vaughan." *Pennsylvania Magazine of History and Biography,* 73 (1949), 459–474.

STILES  Franklin Bowditch Dexter, ed. *The Literary Diary of Ezra Stiles.* 3 vols. New York: Charles Scribner's Sons, 1901.

ST. PAUL'S  George H. S. King, comp. *The Register of Saint Paul's Parish, 1715–1798.* Fredericksburg, Va.: George Harrison Sanford King, 1960.

STRAUS  Oscar S. Straus. "New Light on the Career of Colonel David S. Franks." *Publication of the American Jewish Society,* 10 (1902), 101–8.

SWEM AND WILLIAMS  Earl G. Swem and John W. Williams, eds. *A Register of the General Assembly of Virginia, 1776–1918, and of the Constitutional Conventions.* Richmond: Davis Bottom, Superintendent of Public Printing, 1918.

# Bibliography

SWIGGETT

Howard Swiggett. *The Extraordinary Mr. Morris.* Garden City, N.Y.: Doubleday & Co., 1952.

VA. COUNCIL JLS.

H. R. McIlwaine et al., eds. *Journals of the Council of the State of Virginia.* 4 vols. Richmond: Division of Purchase and Printing, Virginia State Library, 1931–67.

VAN DER KEMP

Helen Lincklaen Fairchild, ed. *Francis Adrian Van der Kemp, 1752–1829: An Autobiography Together with Extracts from His Correspondence.* New York: G. P. Putnam's Sons, 1903.

VAN RENSSELAER

Florence Van Rensselaer, comp. *The Livingston Family in America and Its Scottish Origins.* New York and Richmond: William Byrd Press, 1949.

VIRKUS

Frederick Adams Virkus, ed. *The Compendium of American Genealogy: The Standard Genealogical Encyclopedia of the First Families of America.* 7 vols. Chicago: various publishers, 1925–42.

VSP

William P. Palmer et al., eds. *Calendar of Virginia State Papers and Other Manuscripts.* 11 vols. Richmond: various publishers, 1875–93.

WAYLAND [1]

John Walter Wayland. *The Washingtons and Their Homes.* 1944. Reprint, Berryville: Virginia Book Co., 1973.

WEBB [2]

Worthington Chauncey Ford, ed. *Correspondence and Journals of Samuel Blachley Webb.* 3 vols. New York: Wickersham Press, 1893.

WEEMS

Mason L. Weems. *The Life of Washington.* Ed. Marcus Cunliffe. Cambridge, Mass.: Belknap Press of Harvard University Press, 1962.

WMQ

*The William and Mary Quarterly: A Magazine of Early American History.* Williamsburg: published by the Institute of Early American History and Culture.

WOLF

Edwin Wolf 2nd and Maxwell Whiteman. *The History of the Jews of Philadelphia from Colonial Times to the*

*Age of Jackson.* Philadelphia: The Jewish Publication Society of America, 1956.

W.P.A. [2]     W.P.A. Writers' Project. *Maryland: A Guide to the Old Line State.* New York: Oxford University Press, 1940.

WRITINGS     John C. Fitzpatrick, ed. *The Writings of George Washington from the Original Manuscript Sources, 1745–1799.* 39 vols. Washington, D.C.: Government Printing Office, 1931–44.

YOUNG     Arthur Young. *The Farmer's Calendar: Containing the Business Necessary to be Performed on Various Kinds of Farms during Every Month of the Year.* 8th ed. London: printed for Richard Phillips, 1809.

# Index

Individuals and places mentioned for the first time in this volume have been identified in the footnotes; identification notes for those which previously appeared in the first four volumes may be located by consulting the indexes for those volumes. A cumulative index will be included in the last volume of the *Diaries*.

## Index

Simpson, Gilbert, Jr., 28, 102, 112, 199

Simpson, Gilbert, Sr., 102

Sinah (slave, Home House), 355, 356

Singleton, Anthony, 38-39

Sion Hill, 186

Skerrett (tavern keeper), 154, 186, 237, 247

Skerrett's tavern (Cheyns's tavern), 154

Skillin, Simeon, 484

Skinner, Alexander, 432

Smallwood, William (illus., 59), 60, 61

Smith (tavern keeper), 496

Smith (sister of William Stephens Smith), 504

Smith, Abigail Amelia Adams (illus., 506), 456, 457, 459, 499, 502, 507, 511

Smith, Charlotte Izard, 501

Smith, James, 3, 335

Smith, Louisa, 456, 457, 499

Smith, Sarah, 504

Smith, Simon, 91

Smith, Thomas (1745-1809; of Pa.), 28, 74

Smith, William (brother of Abigail Adams), 457

Smith, William Loughton, 497, 498, 501

Smith, William Stephens (illus., 506), 456, 457, 458, 459, 499, 504, 507, 511

Smith's tavern, 496

Snickers, Edward, 50

Snickers, Elizabeth Taliaferro, 50

Snickers, Frances Washington, 50

Snickers, William, 50

Snow, Gideon, 41, 122, 235, 429

Snowden, Thomas, 153, 186, 247, 372

Society of the Friendly Sons of St. Patrick, 170

Solitude, The (John Penn's home), 176

Southwark Theater, 175

Spaight, Richard Dobbs, 353, 354, 410

Speake, Francis, 386

Spence (child of William Spence), 383

Spence, Mrs. William, 383

Spence, William (doctor), 382, 383

Spencer, Mass., 472

Spotswood, Alexander (1751-1818): purchases oats for GW, 112; oats sent to GW, 121, 123, 135, 219, 290, 291, 303, 358, 374, 381; barley sent to GW, 130, 131, 315, 321, 346; corn sent to GW, 337; GW visits, 340

Sprigg (Mount Vernon visitor), 20

Sprigg, Richard, 20, 137, 140, 141

Springett, Gulielma Maria, 172

Springettsbury Manor, 172

Springfield, Mass., 470, 471

Spring Mill, 177

Spurrier (tavern keeper), 186

Spurrier's tavern (Widow Ball's tavern), 186

Square House, 462

Stamford, Conn., 462, 464

Stavers, John, 491

Stead, Benjamin, 63

Stenton, 175

Stephenson, John, 74

Steuben, Friedrich Wilhelm Augustus von, 502, 504, 508, 511

Stevens, Benjamin, 490

Stevens, Elizabeth Alexander, 511

Stevens, John (father of John Stevens, 1749-1838), 511

Stevens, John (1749-1838), 511

Stewart (Stuart), Richardson, 3, 47, 48, 81, 335

Stiles, Ezra (illus., 463), 464, 465

Stirling, William Alexander, Lord, 449

Stith (Mount Vernon visitor), 50

Stith, Ann Walker, 235

Stith, Ann ("Nancy") Washington, 51

Stith, Buckner (d. 1800), 235

Stith, Buckner (captain), 235

Stith, Buckner (1722-1791), 50

Stith, John, 50, 51

Stith, Robert. 51

Stone, Walter, 330

Storer, Samuel, 491

Storer, Mrs. Samuel, 491

Stoughton, John, 505

Stratford, Conn., 463, 464

# Index